The Variorum Edition of the *Poetry of* JOHN DONNE

VOLUME 8

The Variorum Edition of the *Poetry of* JOHN DONNE

VOLUME 8

GENERAL EDITOR

Gary A. Stringer

CHIEF EDITOR OF THE COMMENTARY

John R. Roberts

COMMENTARY

William A. McClung

Volume Commentary Editor

Jeffrey Johnson

Contributing Editor

TEXTS

Ted-Larry Pebworth

Gary A. Stringer

Ernest W. Sullivan, II

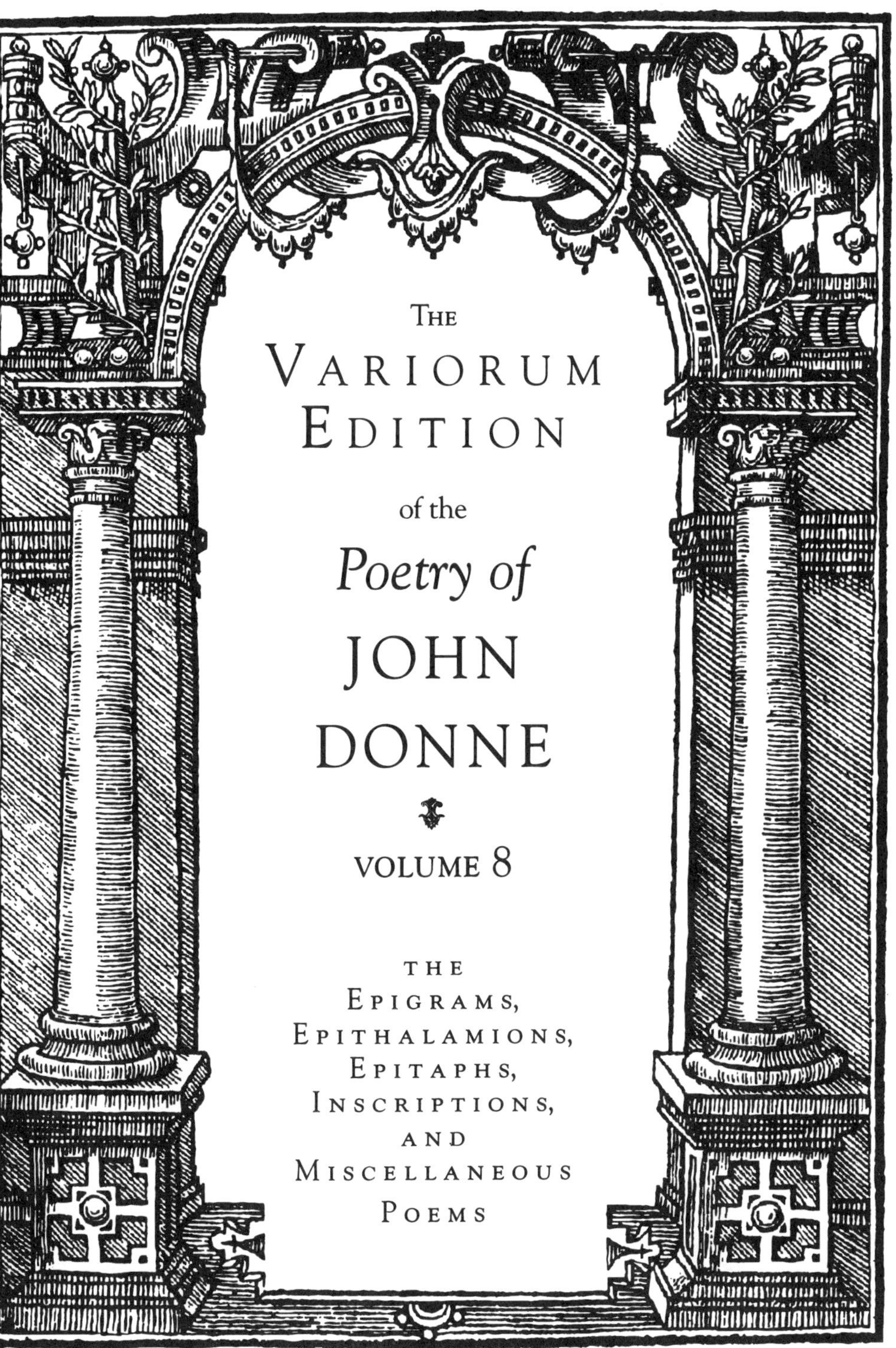

The Variorum Edition of the *Poetry of* John Donne

VOLUME 8

THE EPIGRAMS, EPITHALAMIONS, EPITAPHS, INSCRIPTIONS, AND MISCELLANEOUS POEMS

Gary A. Stringer, *General Editor*

Indiana University Press Bloomington and Indianapolis

The preparation of this volume was made possible in part by grants from the Program for Research Tools of the National Endowment for the Humanities, an independent federal agency. Work on this volume was also supported by funds from the University of Southern Mississippi Foundation.

Printed and bound in the United States of America

This paper meets the requirements of the American National Standard for Information Sciences—Permanence of Paper for Printed Library Materials, ANSI Z39.48–1984.

The Committee's emblem indicates that this volume is based on an examination of all available relevant textual sources, that it is edited according to principles articulated in the volume, that the source texts and the edited text's deviations from them are fully described, that the editorial principles and the text and apparatus have undergone a peer review, that a rigorous schedule of verification and proofreading was followed to insure a high degree of accuracy in the presentation of the edition, and that the text is accompanied by appropriate textual and other historical contextual information.

Library of Congress Cataloging-in-Publication Data

Donne, John, 1572–1631.
[Poems (Bloomington, Ind.)]
The variorum edition of the poetry of John Donne / Gary A. Stringer, general editor
p. cm.
Includes bibliographical references and index.
Contents: —v. 8. The Epigrams, Epithalamions, Epitaphs, Inscriptions, and Miscellaneous Poems
ISBN 0-253-31812-2 (alk. paper : v. 8)
I. Stringer, Gary A. II. Title.
PR2245.A5P37 1995
821′.3—dc20 93-11800

1 2 3 4 5 00 99 98 97 96 95

For

Claude
Eleanor
Jeff
and
Lee

CONTENTS

The Epithalamions

Epitaphs and Inscriptions

Miscellaneous Poems

Acknowledgments

A great many people and institutions have generously supported the Donne Variorum project since its inception in 1981, not only by providing specific services and financial aid, but also by offering encouragement, advice, and other forms of intangible support. We wish to acknowledge here those friends, colleagues, university administrators, library staffs, research assistants, and granting agencies and foundations that have made the work on this volume possible; and we look forward to recording similar debts as successive volumes proceed to publication.

University Administrators and Programs

We are grateful to the following university administrators and programs for providing financial support, adjusted teaching schedules, equipment and supplies, and staff assistance:

The University of Kentucky: The University of Kentucky Research Foundation.

The University of Michigan-Dearborn: Robert L. Simpson, Academic Vice-Chancellor and Provost; John W. Presley, Dean of the College of Arts, Sciences, and Letters; Emily L. Spinelli, Chair of the Department of Humanities; Campus Grants Committee; Office of Sponsored Research and Grant Administration, Drew Buchanan, Director.

Mississippi State University: Lida K. Barrett, former Dean of the College of Arts and Sciences; Joseph E. Milosh, Jr., former Head of the Department of English.

The University of Missouri-Columbia: J. Robert Barth, S. J., former Chair of the Department of English; Jerome Brouder, Provost; Ronald Bunn, former Provost; Larry Clark, Dean of the College of Arts and Sciences; Lois LeFleur, former Provost; Timothy Materer, former Chair of the Department of English; Judson Sheridan, former Dean of the Graduate School and Provost for Research.

Texas Tech University: Wendell Aycock, Chair of the Department of English; Bruce Cammack, Library Special Collections; E. Dale Cluff, Director of Libraries; Faculty Development Leave Program; Friends of the Texas Tech University Library; Kathleen Harris, Office of Research Services; David Murrah, Director of Library Special Collections.

The University of Southern Mississippi: USM Foundation, William H. Pace, Executive Director of Development; Glenn T. Harper, Dean of the College of Liberal Arts; Aubrey K. Lucas, President; Office of Research and Sponsored Programs, Donald R. Cotten, Director; David M. Wheeler, Chair of the Department of English; Karen M. Yarbrough, Vice-President for Research and Planning.

Libraries and Archives

We also wish to thank the administrators and staffs of the following libraries and repositories, who have provided indispensable aid and ready access to materials: Aberdeen University Library; Universiteits-Bibliotheek, Amsterdam; Bedfordshire Record Office; Bodleian Library; Bradford District Archives; British Library; Cambridge University Library; Chetham's Library, Manchester; William Andrews Clark Memorial Library; Cook Memorial Library, University of Southern Mississippi; Derbyshire Record Office; East Sussex Record Office; Edinburgh University Library; Ellis Library, University of Missouri; Emmanuel College Library, Cambridge; Fitzwilliam Museum; Guildhall Library; Harvard University Libraries; Hertfordshire Record Office; University of Illinois Library; University of Kentucky Library; Leeds Archives Department; Leicestershire Record Office; Lincoln's Inn Library; University of London Library; London Public Record Office; University of Michigan Libraries, Ann Arbor and Dearborn; Mitchell Memorial Library, Mississippi State University; National Art Library, Victoria and Albert Museum; National Library of Scotland; National Library of Wales; Library of the University of Newcastle upon Tyne; University of Nottingham Library; University of Pennsylvania Library; Pierpont Morgan Library; Princeton University Library; Rosenbach Museum and Library; Rutgers University Library; John Rylands Library, University of Manchester; St. John's College Library, Cambridge; St. John's College Library, Oxford; St. Paul's Cathedral Library; South African Public Library; University of Texas Library; Texas A&M University Library; Texas Tech University Library; Trinity College Library, Cambridge; Trinity College Library, Dublin; United States Air Force Academy Library; University Research Library, University of California at Los Angeles; Wayne State University Library; Westminster Abbey Library; Library of the University College of North Wales; Yale University Library.

We wish to call special attention to the bibliographical contributions of the following librarians: François Dupuigrenet Desroussilles, chef du service de l'Inventaire général, Bibliothèque Nationale; Clive Hurst, Head of Special Collections, Bodleian Library;

Richard H. Laver, Assistant Librarian, Brasenose College, Oxford; Elisabeth Leedham-Green, Deputy Keeper, Cambridge University Archives; H. J. R. Wing, Assistant Librarian, Christ Church, Oxford; N. Aubertin-Potter, Sub-Librarian, The Codrington Library, All Souls College, Oxford; Chris. Butler, Assistant Archivist, Corpus Christi College, Oxford; Georgianna Ziegler, Reference Librarian, The Folger Shakespeare Library; Thomas V. Lange, Curator of Early Printed Books and Bindings, The Huntington Library; Thomas L. Amos, Assistant Head of Public Services, The Lilly Library, Indiana University; G. F. Holborn, Librarian, Lincoln's Inn Library; Samantha Kahn Herrick, Special Collections, The Newberry Library; Stephen Crook, Executive Secretary, the Berg Collection, The New York Public Library; Helen Powell, Assistant Librarian, The Queen's College, Oxford; J. Joseph Wisdom, Librarian, St. Paul's Cathedral; D. J. McKitterick, Librarian, Trinity College Library, Cambridge; Oliver Pointer, Assistant Librarian, Old Books Collection, Wadham College, Oxford; Joanne H. Parker, Librarian, Worcester College, Oxford.

The Volume Commentary editors would like to pay special thanks to past and present Directors and staff of the Huntington Library, where a fellowship and many subsequent visits made much of the research possible. Their many kindnesses and courtesies can never be sufficiently repaid.

Foundations and Granting Agencies

In addition to support from the National Endowment for the Humanities, we should also like to express our gratitude for agency support as follows: American Council of Learned Societies Grant-in-Aid (1983); American Philosophical Society Grant (1985); William Andrews Clark Memorial Library Mellon Fellowship (1982) and Summer Fellowship (1987); Huntington Library Visiting Fellowship (1985); National Endowment for the Humanities Travel to Collections Grant (1984, 1985, 1988, 1992); South Central Modern Language Association Huntington Library Fellowship (1988); Texas Organized Research Funds: Institute for University Research (1985, 1986, 1988-89).

Research Assistants

Our gratitude also goes to the following research assistants who have aided us over the years: James Denk, Mary Evich, Karen Knippa, John P. Kolinski, Gordon Laatz, Christian Michener, Melissa Poole, Celestin Walby, Willy Wood.

We would like to draw special attention to the contributions made to this volume by Theodore J. Sherman, former research assistant to the General Editor, and by J. Syd Conner, Editorial Assistant to the Donne Variorum project.

Friends and Colleagues

We owe specific debts for bibliographical assistance to D. C. Greetham, Dennis Flynn, Dayton Haskin, Paul A. Parrish, H. W. R. Payling, and Jean-Marc Sens, and we are grateful to Mark Clark, Charles Faulhaber, Giovanni Fontecchio, Traianos Gagos, Ed George, and Sam Slick for assistance with items in foreign languages. We also extend our thanks to Jeffrey S. A. Stringer, who wrote the Donne Variorum Frame File Generator program, and to Mary Ann Stringer, who helped with the proofreading and hosted many a work session with grace and good humor.

The commentary editors wish to thank Rodney Simard and Gregory Bentley for their contributions to this project at earlier stages of its development and George Klawitter, who called attention to several obscure items relevant to their work. Jeffrey Johnson extends special thanks to his wife, Lee Johnson, without whom his work on this project would have been more arduous and his life incomplete. Takashi Tasaka, of the Department of English at Meisei University, Tokyo, graciously provided a translation of an article in Japanese by Mitsutoshi Somura.

Consultants

Three consultants have contributed immeasurably to our work by providing specialized assistance and expertise. We should like to thank Peter Beal, who has provided continuing aid in identifying and facilitating access to manuscripts and other hard-to-locate bibliographical materials; Raoul Jerome, who has maintained The Donne Variorum Textual Collation Program, as well as offering continuing guidance in our use of the computer; and Yoshihisa Aizawa, who has continued in his role as general consultant for items of commentary in Japanese.

Short Forms of Reference for Donne's Works

(In the interests of convenience and economy, we have used the following short forms throughout the Variorum commentary and the textual introductions. These forms are based on traditional headings or numberings except in cases where traditional designations are confusing, imprecise, or nonexistent. Spelling, capitalization, font, and pointing in this list are regularized, and none of these details should be accorded bibliographical or textual significance.)

Poems

Air	Air and Angels ["Twice or thrice had I loved"]
AltVic	A Letter Written by Sir H. G. and J. D. Alternis Vicibus ["Since every tree begins"]
Amic	Amicissimo et Meritissimo Ben Jonson ["Quod arte ausus es hic tua"]
Anniv	The Anniversary ["All kings and all their favorites"]
Annun	Upon the Annunciation and Passion ["Tamely frail body"]
Antiq	Antiquary ["If in his study"]
Apoth	Apotheosis Ignatij Loyolae ["Qui sacer antefuit"]
Appar	The Apparition ["When by thy scorn"]
AutHook	Ad Autorem ["Non eget Hookerus"]
AutJos	Ad Autorem ["Emendare cupis Joseph"]
Bait	The Bait ["Come live with me"]
BB	To Mr. B.B. ["Is not thy sacred hunger"]
BedfCab	Epitaph on Himself: To the Countess of Bedford ["That I might make your cabinet"]
BedfDead	To the Countess of Bedford: Begun in France ["Though I be dead and buried"]
BedfHon	To the Countess of Bedford ["Honor is so sublime"]
BedfReas	To the Countess of Bedford ["Reason is our soul's left hand"]

BedfRef — To the Countess of Bedford ["You have refined me"]
BedfShe — Elegy to the Lady Bedford ["You that are she"]
BedfTwi — To the Countess of Bedford: On New-Year's Day ["This twilight of two years"]
BedfWrit — To the Countess of Bedford ["To have written then"]
Beggar — A Lame Beggar ["I am unable, yonder beggar cries"]
Blos — The Blossom ["Little thinkest thou"]
BoulNar — Elegy upon the Death of Mrs. Boulstrode ["Language thou art too narrow"]
BoulRec — Elegy on Mrs. Boulstrode ["Death, I recant"]
Break — Break of Day ["'Tis true, 'tis day"]
Broken — The Broken Heart ["He is stark mad"]
Cales — Cales and Guiana ["If you from spoil"]
Calm — The Calm ["Our storm is past"]
Canon — The Canonization ["For God's sake hold your tongue"]
Carey — A Letter to the Lady Carey and Mrs. Essex Rich ["Here where by all"]
CB — To Mr. C. B. ["Thy friend whom thy deserts"]
Christ — A Hymn to Christ at the Author's Last Going into Germany ["In what torn ship soever"]
Commun — Community ["Good we must love"]
Compu — The Computation ["For the first twenty years"]
ConfL — Confined Love ["Some man unworthy"]
Corona — La Corona
  Cor1 — "Deign at my hands"
  Cor2 — Annunciation ["Salvation to all that will is nigh"]
  Cor3 — Nativity ["Immensity cloistered in thy dear womb"]
  Cor4 — Temple ["With his kind mother who partakes thy woe"]
  Cor5 — Crucifying ["By miracles exceeding power of man"]
  Cor6 — Resurrection ["Moist with one drop of thy blood"]
  Cor7 — Ascension ["Salute the last and everlasting day"]
Coryat — Upon Mr. Thomas Coryat's Crudities ["Oh to what height"]
Cross — The Cross ["Since Christ embraced"]
Curse — The Curse ["Whoever guesses, thinks, or dreams"]
Damp — The Damp ["When I am dead"]
Disinher — Disinherited ["Thy father all from thee"]
Dissol — The Dissolution ["She is dead"]
Dream — The Dream ["Dear love, for nothing less"]
Eclog — Eclogue at the Marriage of the Earl of Somerset ["Unseasonable man, statue of ice"]
Ecst — The Ecstasy ["Where, like a pillow on a bed"]
ED — To E. of D. with Six Holy Sonnets ["See, Sir, how as the sun's"]
EdHerb — To Sir Edward Herbert ["Man is a lump"]
EG — To Mr. E. G. ["Even as lame things"]
EgDD — Epigraph from *Death's Duel* ["Corporis haec animae"]

Elegies:

ElAnag	The Anagram ["Marry and love thy Flavia"]
ElAut	The Autumnal ["No spring nor summer beauty"]
ElBed	Going to Bed ["Come, Madam, come"]
ElBrac	The Bracelet ["Not that in color it was like thy hair"]
ElChange	Change ["Although thy hand and faith"]
ElComp	The Comparison ["As the sweet sweat of roses in a still"]
ElExpost	The Expostulation ["To make the doubt clear"]
ElFatal	On His Mistress ["By our first strange and fatal interview"]
ElJeal	Jealousy ["Fond woman which would'st have thy husband die"]
ElNat	"Nature's lay idiot"
ElPart	His Parting From Her ["Since she must go"]
ElPerf	The Perfume ["Once and but once found in thy company"]
ElPict	His Picture ["Here take my picture"]
ElProg	Love's Progress ["Whoever loves, if he do not propose"]
ElServe	"Oh, let me not serve so"
ElVar	Variety ["The heavens rejoice in motion"]
ElWar	Love's War ["Till I have peace with thee"]
EpEliz	Epithalamion upon . . . the Lady Elizabeth ["Hail, Bishop Valentine"]
EpLin	Epithalamion Made at Lincoln's Inn ["The sunbeams in the east"]
EtAD	Epitaph for Ann Donne ["Annae / Georgii More de filiae"]
EtED	Epitaph for Elizabeth Drury ["Quo pergas, viator"]
EtRD	Epitaph for Robert and Anne Drury ["Roberti Druri / quo vix alter"]
EtSP	John Donne's Epitaph . . . in St. Paul's Cathedral ["Iohannes Donne / Sac: Theol: Profess:"]
Expir	The Expiration ["So, so, break off"]
Fare	Farewell to Love ["Whilst yet to prove"]
Father	A Hymn to God the Father ["Wilt thou forgive"]
Faust	Faustinus ["Faustinus keeps his sister"]
Fever	A Fever ["Oh do not die"]
FirAn	The First Anniversary. An Anatomy of the World ["When that rich soul"]
Flea	The Flea ["Mark but this flea"]
Fun	The Funeral ["Whoever comes to shroud me"]
FunEl	A Funeral Elegy ["'Tis lost to trust a tomb"]
Gaz	Translated out of Gazaeus ["God grant thee thine own wish"]
GHerb	To Mr. George Herbert with One of My Seals ["Qui prius assuetus serpentum"]
Goodf	Goodfriday, 1613. Riding Westward ["Let man's soul be a sphere"]
GoodM	The Good Morrow ["I wonder by my troth"]
Ham	An Hymn to the Saints and to the Marquis Hamilton ["Whether that soul which now comes"]
Har	Obsequies upon the Lord Harrington ["Fair soul, which wast not only"]

Harb	The Harbinger to the Progress (by Joseph Hall) ["Two souls move here"]
Heart	"When my heart was mine own"
Henry	Elegy on the Untimely Death of . . . Prince Henry ["Look to me, Faith"]
Hero	Hero and Leander ["Both robbed of air"]
HG	To Sr. Henry Goodyere ["Who makes the past a pattern"]

Holy Sonnets:

HSBatter	"Batter my heart"
HSBlack	"O my black soul"
HSDeath	"Death be not proud"
HSDue	"As due by many titles"
HSLittle	"I am a little world"
HSMade	"Thou hast made me"
HSMin	"If poisonous minerals"
HSPart	"Father part of his double interest"
HSRound	"At the round earth's imagined corners"
HSScene	"This is my play's last scene"
HSShe	"Since she whom I loved"
HSShow	"Show me dear Christ"
HSSighs	"O might those sighs"
HSSouls	"If faithful souls"
HSSpit	"Spit in my face"
HSVex	"O to vex me"
HSWhat	"What if this present"
HSWhy	"Why are we by all creatures"
HSWilt	"Wilt thou love God"
HuntMan	To the Countess of Huntingdon ["Man to God's image"]
HuntUn	To the Countess of Huntingdon ["That unripe side of earth"]
HWHiber	H. W. in Hibernia Belligeranti ["Went you to conquer?"]
HWKiss	To Sir Henry Wotton ["Sir, more than kisses"]
HWNews	To Sir Henry Wotton ["Here's no more news"]
HWVenice	To Sir H. W. at His Going Ambassador to Venice ["After those reverend papers"]

Ignatius, verse from:

IgAver	"Aversa facie Janum referre"
IgFeath	"Feathers or straws swim on the water's face"
IgFlow	"As a flower wet with last night's dew"
IgLark	"The lark by busy and laborious ways"
IgNoise	"With so great noise and horror"
IgOper	"Operoso tramite scandent"
IgPiece	"That the least piece which thence doth fall"
IgPlum	"Aut plumam, aut paleam"

IgQual	"Qualis hesterno madefacta rore"
IgResemb	"Resemble Janus with a diverse face"
IgSport	"My little wandering sportful soul"
IgTanto	"Tanto fragore boatuque"
ILBlest	To Mr. I.L. ["Blest are your north parts"]
ILRoll	To Mr. I.L. ["Of that short roll"]
Image	"Image of her whom I love"
InAA	Inscription in the *Album Amicorum* of Michael Corvinus ["In propria venit"]
Ind	The Indifferent ["I can love both fair and brown"]
InLI	Inscription in a Bible Presented to Lincoln's Inn ["In Bibliotheca Hospitii"]
Jet	A Jet Ring Sent ["Thou art not so black"]
Jug	The Juggler ["Thou callest me effeminate"]
Klock	Klockius ["Klockius so deeply hath sworn"]
Lam	The Lamentations of Jeremy ["How sits this city"]
Lect	A Lecture upon the Shadow ["Stand still and I will read"]
Leg	The Legacy ["When I died last"]
Liar	The Liar ["Thou in the fields walkest"]
Libro	De Libro Cum Mutuaretur ["Doctissimo Amicissimoque v. D. D. Andrews"]
Licent	A Licentious Person ["Thy sins and hairs"]
Lit	A Litany ["Father of heaven and him"]
LovAlch	Love's Alchemy ["Some that have deeper digged"]
LovDeity	Love's Deity ["I long to talk with some old"]
LovDiet	Love's Diet ["To what a cumbersome unwieldiness"]
LovExch	Love's Exchange ["Love, any devil else but you"]
LovGrow	Love's Growth ["I scarce believe my love to be so pure"]
LovInf	Lovers' Infiniteness ["If yet I have not all thy love"]
LovUsury	Love's Usury ["For every hour that thou wilt spare me"]
Macaron	In Eundem Macaronicon ["Quot, dos, haec, linguists"]
Mark	Elegy on the Lady Markham ["Man is the world"]
Martial	Raderus ["Why this man gelded Martial"]
Merc	Mercurius Gallo-Belgicus ["Like Aesop's fellow slaves"]
Mess	The Message ["Send home my long strayed eyes"]
Metem	Metempsychosis ["I sing the progress of a deathless soul"]
MHMary	To the Lady Magdalen Herbert, of St. Mary Magdalen ["Her of your name"]
MHPaper	To Mrs. M. H. ["Mad paper stay"]
NegLov	Negative Love ["I never stooped so low"]
Niobe	Niobe ["By children's birth and death"]
Noct	A Nocturnal upon St. Lucy's Day ["'Tis the year's midnight"]
Para	The Paradox ["No lover saith, I love"]
Philo	An Obscure Writer ["Philo with twelve years' study"]
Phrine	Phrine ["Thy flattering picture, Phrine"]

Praise	To the Praise of the Dead and the Anatomy (by Joseph Hall) ["Well died the world"]
Prim	The Primrose ["Upon this primrose hill"]
Prohib	The Prohibition ["Take heed of loving me"]
Pyr	Pyramus and Thisbe ["Two by themselves each other"]
Ralph	Ralphius ["Compassion in the world again is bred"]
Relic	The Relic ["When my grave is broke up again"]
Res	Resurrection Imperfect ["Sleep, sleep, old sun"]
RWEnvy	To Mr. R. W. ["Kindly I envy thy song's"]
RWMind	To Mr. R. W. ["Muse not that by thy mind"]
RWSlumb	To Mr. R. W. ["If as mine is thy life a slumber be"]
RWThird	To Mr. R. W. ["Like one who in her third widowhood"]
RWZeal	To Mr. R. W. ["Zealously my muse"]
Sal	To the Countess of Salisbury ["Fair, great, and good"]
Sappho	Sappho to Philaenis ["Where is that holy fire"]

Satires:

Sat1	"Away thou fondling motley humorist"
Sat2	"Sir, though (I thank God for it) I do hate"
Sat3	"Kind pity chokes my spleen"
Sat4	"Well, I may now receive and die"
Sat5	"Thou shalt not laugh in this leaf, Muse"
SB	To Mr. S. B. ["O thou which to search"]
SecAn	The Second Anniversary. Of the Progress of the Soul ["Nothing could make me sooner"]
SelfAc	A Self Accuser ["Your mistress, that you follow whores"]
SelfL	Self Love ["He that cannot choose but love"]
SGo	Song ["Go, and catch a falling star"]
Sheaf	A Sheaf of Miscellany Epigrams
Sheaf1–61: individual poems within *Sheaf*	
Ship	A Burnt Ship ["Out of a fired ship"]
Sickness	A Hymn to God My God, in My Sickness ["Since I am coming"]
Sidney	Upon the Translation of the Psalms by Sir Philip Sidney ["Eternal God, (for whom who ever dare...)"]
Sorrow	Elegia ["Sorrow, who to this house"]
SSweet	Song ["Sweetest love, I do not go"]
Stat	Stationes from *Devotions* ["Insultus morbi primus"]
Storm	The Storm ["Thou which art I"]
SunRis	The Sun Rising ["Busy old fool, unruly sun"]
Tilman	To Mr. Tilman after He Had Taken Orders ["Thou whose diviner soul"]
Token	Sonnet. The Token ["Send me some token"]
Triple	The Triple Fool ["I am two fools, I know"]
TWHail	To Mr. T. W. ["All hail sweet poet"]
TWHarsh	To Mr. T. W. ["Haste thee harsh verse"]

TWHence	To Mr. T. W. ["At once from hence"]
TWPreg	To Mr. T. W. ["Pregnant again"]
Twick	Twickenham Garden ["Blasted with sighs and surrounded with tears"]
Under	The Undertaking ["I have done one braver thing"]
ValBook	A Valediction of the Book ["I'll tell thee now"]
ValMourn	A Valediction Forbidding Mourning ["As virtuous men pass mildly away"]
ValName	A Valediction of My Name in the Window ["My name engraved herein"]
ValWeep	A Valediction of Weeping ["Let me pour forth"]
Wall	Fall of a Wall ["Under an undermined and shot-bruised wall"]
Will	The Will ["Before I sigh my last gasp"]
Wing	Sir John Wingfield ["Beyond th'old pillars"]
Witch	Witchcraft by a Picture ["I fix mine eye on thine"]
WomCon	Woman's Constancy ["Now thou has loved me one whole day"]

Prose Works

Biathanatos	*Biathanatos*, ed. Ernest W. Sullivan, II. Newark: U of Delaware P, 1984.
Devotions	*Devotions upon Emergent Occasions*, ed. Anthony Raspa. Montreal: McGill-Queen's UP, 1975.
Essays	*Essays in Divinity*, ed. Evelyn M. Simpson. Oxford: Clarendon, 1952.
Ignatius	*Ignatius His Conclave*, ed. T. S. Healy, S.J. Oxford: Clarendon, 1969.
Letters	*Letters to Severall Persons of Honour (1651)*. A Facsimile Reproduction with an Introduction by M. Thomas Hester. Delmar, N. Y.: Scholars' Facsimiles & Reprints, 1977.
Paradoxes	*Paradoxes and Problems*, ed. Helen Peters. Oxford: Clarendon, 1980.
Sermons	*The Sermons of John Donne*, ed. George R. Potter and Evelyn M. Simpson. 10 vols. Berkeley: U of California P, 1953–62.

Abbreviations Used in the Commentary

Eighteenth- and Nineteenth-Century Periodicals

Ac	*Academy*. London, 1869–1916.
AR	*Andover Review*. Boston, 1884–1893
Arc	*Arcturus*. New York, 1840–42.
Arg	*Argosy*. London, 1865–1901.
Art	*Artist and Journal of Home Culture*. London, 1880-1902.
Ath	*Athenaeum*. London, 1828–1921.
BC	*British Critic, and quarterly theological review*. London, 1793–1843.
Bo	*Bookman*. London, 1891–1934.
Ci	*Citizen*. Philadelphia, 1839–41.
EM	*European Magazine and London Review*. London, 1782–1826.
FR	*Fortnightly Review*. London, 1865–1934.
GM	*Gentleman's Magazine*. London, 1731–1907.
Gu	*Guardian*. London, Mar. 12 – Oct. 1, 1713.
HW	*Household Words: A Weekly Journal. Conducted by Charles Dickens*. London, 1850–1859.
LA	*Living Age*. Boston, 1897–1941.
LEM	*Lowe's Edinburgh Magazine*. Edinburgh, 1846–48.
LiA	*Literary Age*. Philadelphia, 1842–43.
LiM	*Literary Magazine, or, Universal Review*. London, 1756–58.
LLA	*Littell's Living Age*. Boston, 1844–96.
LoM	*London Magazine*. London, 1732–85.
MLNo	*Modern Language Notes*. Baltimore, 1886+.
MR	*Monthly Review*. London, 1749–1844.
NBR	*North British Review*. Edinburgh, 1844–1871.
NC	*Nineteenth Century, a monthly review*. London, 1877–1900.
NewR	*New Review*. London, 1889–1897.
NMag	*National Magazine*. Boston, 1894–1933.
NQR	*Notes and Queries for readers and writers, collectors and librarians*. London, 1849–1924.

NR	*National Review*. London, 1855–64.
PM	*Pall Mall Magazine*. London, 1893–1914.
QR	*Quarterly Review*. London, 1809–1967.
RR	*Retrospective Review*. London, 1820–28, 1852–54.
SN	*Studies and Notes in Philology and Literature*. Cambridge, MA, 1892–1907.
TB	*Temple Bar*. London, 1860–1906.
US	*Universal Spectator, and Weekly Journal*. London, 1728–46.

Modern Journals

AION-SG	*Annali Istituto Universitario Orientale, Napoli, Sezione Germanica*
ANQ	*ANQ: A Quarterly Journal of Short Articles, Notes, and Reviews;* formerly *American Notes and Queries*
ATR	*Anglican Theological Review*
BJRL	*Bulletin of the John Rylands University Library of Manchester*
BSEAA	*Bulletin de la Société d'Etudes Anglo-Américaines des XVII*[e] et *XVIII*[e] *Siècles*
BSUF	*Ball State University Forum*
BuR	*Bucknell Review*
ChauR	*The Chaucer Review: A Journal of Medieval Studies and Literary Criticism*
CLAJ	*College Language Association Journal*
CML	*Classical and Modern Literature: A Quarterly*
CP	*Concerning Poetry*
CR	*Critical Review*
CritQ	*Critical Quarterly*
DHLR	*D. H. Lawrence Review*
DUJ	*Durham University Journal*
EA	*Etudes Anglaises: Grande-Bretagne, Etats-Unis*
E&S	*Essays and Studies* (London, England)
EIC	*Essays in Criticism: A Quarterly Journal of Literary Criticism*
ELH	[formerly *Journal of English Literary History*]
ELN	*English Language Notes*
ELR	*English Literary Renaissance*
ES	*English Studies: A Journal of English Language and Literature*
ESA	*English Studies in Africa: A Journal of the Humanities*
Expl	*Explicator*
HLQ	*Huntington Library Quarterly: A Journal for the History and Interpretation of English and American Civilization*
ISJR	*Iowa State Journal of Research*
JAAC	*Journal of Aesthetics and Art Criticism*
JDJ	*John Donne Journal: Studies in the Age of Donne*
JEGP	*Journal of English and Germanic Philology*

JHI	*Journal of the History of Ideas*
JRMMRA	*Journal of the Rocky Mountain Medieval and Renaissance Association*
JRUL	*Journal of the Rutgers University Libraries*
KR	*Kenyon Review*
LangQ	*The USF Language Quarterly*
Library	*The Library: A Quarterly Journal of Bibliography*
LIT	*Lit: Literature Interpretation Theory*
LQR	*London Quarterly Review*
MLN	[formerly *Modern Language Notes*]
MLQ	*Modern Language Quarterly*
MLR	*The Modern Language Review*
MP	*Modern Philology: A Journal Devoted to Research in Medieval and Modern Literature*
Names	*Names: Journal of the American Name Society*
Neophil	*Neophilologus*
NewQ	*New Quarterly*
NM	*Neuphilologische Mitteilungen: Bulletin de la Société Néophilologique/ Bulletin of the Modern Language Society*
NQ	*Notes and Queries*
PCP	*Pacific Coast Philology*
Person	*The Personalist*
PLL	*Papers on Language and Literature: A Journal for Scholars and Critics of Language and Literature*
PMLA	*PMLA: Publications of the Modern Language Association of America*
PQ	*Philological Quarterly* (Iowa City, IA)
PSt	*Prose Studies*
QJS	*The Quarterly Journal of Speech*
Ren&R	*Renaissance and Reformation / Renaissance et Réforme*
RES	*Review of English Studies: A Quarterly Journal of English Literature and the English Language*
RLMC	*Rivista di Letterature Moderne e Comparate* (Pisa, Italy)
RLV	*Revue des Langues Vivantes* (Brussels, Belgium)
SB	*Studies in Bibliography: Papers of the Bibliographical Society of the University of Virginia*
SCRev	*South Central Review: The Journal of the South Central Modern Language Association*
SEL	*Studies in English Literature, 1500–1900*
SELit	*Studies in English Literature (Tokyo, Japan)*
SoAR	*South Atlantic Review*
SoQ	*The Southern Quarterly: A Journal of the Arts in the South* (Hattiesburg, MS)
SP	*Studies in Philology*
SR	*Sewanee Review*
StTCL	*Studies in Twentieth Century Literature*
Style	*Style* (DeKalb, IL)

TCA	*Twentieth Century: An Australian Review*
TLS	[London] *Times Literary Supplement*
TSLL	*Texas Studies in Literature and Language*
UTQ	*University of Toronto Quarterly: A Canadian Journal of the Humanities*
WSUB	*Wichita State University Bulletin*

Hebrew Bible

Gen.	Genesis
Exod.	Exodus
Num.	Numbers
Deut.	Deuteronomy
Josh.	Joshua
Judg.	Judges
1 Sam.	1 Samuel
2 Sam.	2 Samuel
1 Chron.	1 Chronicles
Esth.	Esther
Ps.	Psalms
Prov.	Proverbs
Eccles.	Ecclesiastes
Cant.	Canticles (Song of Solomon)
Isa.	Isaiah
Jer.	Jeremiah
Ezek.	Ezekiel
Dan.	Daniel
Mal.	Malachi
Zech.	Zechariah

Apocryphal Works

2 Esd.	2 Esdras
Jth.	Judith

New Testament

Matt.	Matthew
Rom.	Romans
1 Cor.	1 Corinthians
2 Cor.	2 Corinthians

Col.	Colossians
Heb.	Hebrews
1 Pet.	1 Peter
2 Pet.	2 Peter
Rev.	Revelation (Apocalypse)

Shakespeare's Works

AWW	*All's Well That Ends Well*
AYL	*As You Like It*
Cor.	*Coriolanus*
Cym.	*Cymbeline*
Ham.	*Hamlet*
1H4	*Henry IV, Part 1*
2H4	*Henry IV, Part 2*
JC	*Julius Caesar*
Jn.	*King John*
LLL	*Love's Labour's Lost*
Lr.	*King Lear*
Mac.	*Macbeth*
MM	*Measure for Measure*
MND	*A Midsummer Night's Dream*
Oth.	*Othello*
PhT	*The Phoenix and the Turtle*
Rom.	*Romeo and Juliet*
Tmp.	*The Tempest*
TN	*Twelfth Night*
Tro.	*Troilus and Cressida*
WT	*The Winter's Tale*

Other Works

AV	Authorized Version
CYT	The Canon's Yeoman's Tale (*The Canterbury Tales*)
DNB	*Dictionary of National Biography*
OED	*Oxford English Dictionary*
P.G.	*Patrologia Graeca*, ed. J. P. Migne
P.L.	*Patrologia Latina*, ed. J. P. Migne
Summa	*Summa Theologica* (St. Thomas Aquinas)

Sigla for Textual Sources

Manuscript Sources

(Entries listed as "Beal, *Index*" refer to citations in Peter Beal, comp., *Index of English Literary Manuscripts*.)

AF United States Air Force Academy, Colorado

AF1 H. Mapletoft volume (ms. emendations and transcriptions in a copy of A)

AU Aberdeen University Library

AU1 Aberdeen ms. 29

B British Library

B1 Add. 5956; B2 Add. 10309; B3 Add. 10337 (Elizabeth Rogers's Virginal Book); B4 Add. 15226; B5 Add. 15227; B6 Add. 18044; B7 Add. 18647 (Denbigh ms.); B8 Add. 19268; B9 Add. 21433; B10 Add. 22118; B11 Add. 23229 (Conway Papers); B12 Add. 25303; B13 Add. 25707 (Skipwith ms.); B14 Add. 27407; B15 Add. 28000; B16 Add. 30982 (Leare ms.); B17 Add. 32463; B18 Add. 34324 (Sir Julius Caesar's Papers); B19 Add. 34744 (West Papers XVIII); B20 Add. 44963; B21 Egerton 923; B22 Egerton 2013; B23 Egerton 2230 (Glover ms.); B24 Egerton 2421; B25 Egerton 2725; B26 Harley 3511 (Capell ms.); B27 Harley 3910; B28 Harley 3991 (Rawlinson ms.); B29 Harley 3998; B30 Harley 4064 (Harley Noel ms.); B31 Harley 4888; B32 Harley 4955 (Newcastle ms.); B33 Harley 5110; B34 Harley 5353; B35 Harley 6057; B36 Harley 6383; B37 Harley 6396; B38 Harley 6918; B39 Harley 6931; B40 Lansdowne 740; B41 Lansdowne 878; B42 Lansdowne 984; B43 Sloane 542; B44 Sloane 1792; B45 Sloane 1867; B46 Stowe 961; B47 Stowe 962; B48 *entry canceled*; B49 *entry canceled*; B50 Harley 791

BD Bradford District Archives

BD1 Hopkinson's M.S.S., Vol. 17; BD2 Hopkinson's M.S.S., Vol. 34; BD3 Spencer-Stanhope Calendar No. 2795 (Bundle 10, No. 34)

BR Bedfordshire Record Office
BR1 J1583 (St. John ms.)

C Cambridge University Library
C1 Add. ms. 29 (Edward Smyth ms.); C2 Add. ms. 5778(c) (Cambridge Balam ms.); C3 Add. ms. 8460 (Mary Browne Commonplace Book); C4 Add. ms. 8470 (Edward Hyde ms.); C5 Ee. 4. 14 (Moore ms.); C6 Ee. 5. 23; C7 Iosephi Scaligeri [Joseph Scaliger], *OPVS NOVVM DE EMENDATIONE TEMPORVM* (1583), holograph epigram; C8 Add. ms. 8467 (Leconfield ms.); C9 Add. ms. 8468 (Narcissus Luttrell ms.); C10 Giles Oldisworth volume (ms. emendations in a copy of C); C11 Add. ms. 8466, Michael Corvinus, "Album Amicorum," holograph inscription; C12 Add. ms. 9221

CE Cambridge University, Emmanuel College Library
CE1 I.3.16 (James 68)

CJ Cambridge University, St. John's College Library
CJ1 S.32 (James 423); CJ2 U.26 (James 548)

CT Cambridge University, Trinity College Library
CT1 R.3.12 (James 592; Puckering ms.)

DR Derbyshire Record Office
DR1 D258/28/5i; DR2 D258/31/16; DR3 D258/60/26a

DT Trinity College Library, Dublin
DT1 877 (formerly G.2.21); DT2 877 (formerly G.2.21, second collection)

ES East Sussex Record Office
ES1 RAF/F/13/1

EU Edinburgh University Library
EU1 D.c.1.69; EU2 Laing III.436; EU3 Laing III.493; EU4 ms. 401 (Halliwell-Phillips Collection)

F Folger Shakespeare Library
F1 L.b.541 (Loseley); F2 V.a.96; F3 V.a.97; F4 V.a.103 (Thomas Smyth ms.); F5 V.a.124; F6 V.a.125; F7 V.a.162 (Welden ms.); F8 V.a.169; F9 V.a.170; F10 V.a.241 (Gosse ms.); F11 V.a.245; F12 V.a.262; F13 V.a.276; F14 V.a.319; F15 V.a.322; F16 V.a.339; F17 V.a.345 (Curteis ms.); F18 V.b.43; F19 V.b.110; F20 W.a.118

FM Fitzwilliam Museum, Cambridge
FM1 Fitzwilliam Virginal Book

H Harvard University Library

H1 ms. Eng. 626; H2 ms. Eng. 686; H3 ms. Eng. 966.1 (Norton ms. 4502, Carnaby ms.); H4 ms. Eng. 966.3 (Norton ms. 4503); H5 ms. Eng. 966.4 (Norton ms. 4506, Dobell ms.); H6 ms. Eng. 966.5 (Norton ms. 4504, O'Flahertie ms.); H7 ms. Eng. 966.6 (Norton ms. 4500, Stephens ms.); H8 ms. Eng. 966.7 (Norton ms. 4620, Utterson ms.); H9 ms. Eng. 1107(15) (Gell Commonplace Book); H10 William Covell, *A IUST AND TEMPERATE DEFENCE OF THE FIVE BOOKS OF ECCLESIASTICALL POLICIE . . .* (1603), holograph epigram

HH Henry E. Huntington Library

HH1 EL 6893 (Bridgewater ms.); HH2 HM 116; HH3 HM 172; HH4 HM 198 (Book I, Haslewood-Kingsborough ms.); HH5 HM 198 (Book II, Haslewood-Kingsborough ms.); HH6 HM 41536; HH7 HM 46323

HR Hertfordshire Record Office

HR1 ms. 19061

IU University of Illinois Library

IU1 William Leigh Commonplace Book; IU2 ms. 821.08/c737/17 (Joseph Butler Commonplace Book)

LA Leeds Archives Department

LA1 MX237

LL Lincoln's Inn Library, London

LL1 Douai Bible, Vol. 1, holograph inscription

LP London Public Record Office

LP1 State Papers Miscellaneous S.P. 9/51

LR Leicestershire Record Office

LR1 DG7/Lit.2 (Burley ms.); LR2 DG9/2796

LU University of London Library

LU1 Cornelius Schrevelius, M. *VALERII MARTIALIS EPIGRAMMATA . . .* (1661), Sir James Astry copy, ms. transcription

MC Chetham's Library, Manchester

MC1 Farmer-Chetham ms. 8012, A.4.15

NP University of Nottingham Library

NP1 Portland ms. PwV 37 (Welbeck ms.); NP2 Portland ms. PwV 191

NT University of Newcastle upon Tyne Library

NT1 Bell/White 25

NY New York Public Library
NY1 Arents Collection, Cat. No. S191 (John Cave ms.); NY2 Arents Collection, Cat. No. S288 (Hugh Barrow ms.); NY3 Berg Collection, Westmoreland ms.

O Bodleian Library, Oxford
O1 Add. B.97; O2 Ashmole 36, 37; O3 Ashmole 38; O4 Ashmole 47; O5 Ashmole 51; O6 Aubrey 6; O7 Aubrey 8; O8 Don.b.9; O9 Don.c.54; O10 Don.d.58; O11 Douce f.5; O12 Eng. poet. c.9; O13 Eng. poet. c.50; O14 Eng. poet. c.53; O15 Eng. poet. d.197; O16 Eng. poet. e.14 (Lawson ms.); O17 Eng. poet. e.37; O18 Eng. poet. e.40; O19 Eng. poet. e.97; O20 Eng. poet. e.99 (Dowden ms.); O21 Eng. poet. f.9 (Phillipps ms.); O22 Eng. poet. f.25; O23 Eng. poet. f.27; O24 Malone 16; O25 Malone 19; O26 Malone 23; O27 Music d.238; O28 Music f.575; O29 Rawlinson poet. 26; O30 Rawlinson poet. 31; O31 Rawlinson poet. 84; O32 Rawlinson poet. 90; O33 Rawlinson poet. 116; O34 Rawlinson poet. 117 (Wase ms.); O35 Rawlinson poet. 142; O36 Rawlinson poet. 160; O37 Rawlinson poet. 172; O38 Rawlinson poet. 199; O39 Rawlinson poet. 212; O40 Rawlinson poet. 214; O41 Sancroft 53; O42 Tanner 465; O43 Tanner 466; O44 Tanner 876 (ms. emendations in a copy of c); O45 ms. 1018 (St. Michael's College Library, Tenbury Wells); O46 ms. 1019 (St. Michael's College Library, Tenbury Wells)

OC Oxford University, Corpus Christi College Library
OC1 ms. 327; OC2 ms. 328

OJ Oxford University, St. John's College Library
OJ1 Nathaniel Crynes volume (ms. emendations in a copy of A)

OQ Oxford University, Queen's College Library
OQ1 ms. 216

OX Oxford University, Christ Church Library
OX1 ms. Music 350; OX2 mss. 736–738; OX3 ms. Evelyn 254

P Private hands
P1 ms. Bedford 26 (Woburn ms. HMC. No. 26), Bedford Estates, London; P2 Beal, *Index*, DnJ 1430; P3 Heneage ms.; P4 Frendraught ms. (Thomas Fraser Duff ms.); P5 Abel Berland volume (ms. emendations in a copy of A, plus ms.)

PM Pierpont Morgan Library, New York
PM1 MA1057 (Holgate ms.)

PT Princeton University Library, Robert H. Taylor Collection
PT1 ms. transcriptions in a copy of 22c; PT2 Beal, Index, DnJ 1431

R Rosenbach Museum and Library, Philadelphia

R1 239/16; R2 239/18; R3 239/22; R4 239/23; R5 239/27; R6 240/2; R7 243/4; R8 1083/15; R9 1083/16 (Bishop ms.); R10 1083/17

RU Rutgers University Library

RU1 FPR 2247, E37

SA South African Public Library, Capetown

SA1 Grey 7 a 29 (formerly 2.a.II)

SN National Library of Scotland

SN1 Advocates' ms. 19.3.4; SN2 2060 (Hawthornden ms. VIII); SN3 2067 (Hawthornden ms. XV); SN4 6504 (Wedderburn ms.); SN5 Advocates' ms. 33.3.19

SP St. Paul's Cathedral Library

SP1 49.B.43; SP2 52.D.14

TA Texas A&M University Library

TA1 Henry White/Alan Haughton volume (ms. emendations in a copy of A)

TM Meisei University, Tokyo

TM1 Crewe ms. (formerly Monckton Milnes ms.)

TT Texas Tech University Library

TT1 PR 1171 D14 (Dalhousie I); TT2 PR 1171 S4 (Dalhousie II); TT3 St. John Brodrick volume (ms. emendations in a copy of A)

VA Victoria and Albert Museum, Dyce Collection

VA1 Cat. No. 17, ms. 25.F.16 (Neve ms.); VA2 Cat. No. 18, ms. 25.F.17 (Nedham ms.); VA3 Cat. No. 44, ms. 25.F.39 (Todd ms.)

WA Westminster Abbey Library

WA1 ms. 41 (Morley ms.)

WB Library of the University College of North Wales

WB1 ms. 422 (Bangor ms.)

WC William Andrews Clark Memorial Library, Los Angeles

WC1 S4975M1

WN National Library of Wales

WN1 Dolau Cothi ms. 6748; WN2 Peniarth 500B; WN3 NLW ms. 5308E (Herbert ms.); WN4 NLW ms. 5390D; WN5 NLW ms. 12443A, Part ii; WN6 NLW ms. 16852D

Y Yale University Library, James Osborn Collection

Y1 b62; Y2 b114 (Raphael King ms.); Y3 b148 (Osborn ms.); Y4 b150; Y5 b197; Y6 b200; Y7 b205; Y8 f b66; Y9 f b88

Printed Sources

(Citations in parentheses following seventeenth-century publications below are *STC* numbers from A. W. Pollard and G. R. Redgrave, eds., *Short-Title Catalogue of Books Printed in England . . . 1475–1640*, and from Donald Wing et al., eds., *Short-Title Catalogue of Books Printed in England . . . 1641–1700*. Items listed ambiguously in the *STC* are further identified by location and shelfmark. Locations of printed sources are as follows:

AUB	Universiteits-Bibliotheek, Amsterdam
C	Cambridge University Library, Cambridge
CLU–C	William Andrews Clark Memorial Library, Los Angeles, CA
CSmH	Huntington Library, San Marino, CA
CT	Trinity College, Cambridge
CtY	Yale University Library, New Haven, CT
DFo	Folger Shakespeare Library, Washington, DC
ICN	Newberry Library, Chicago, IL
InU	University of Indiana Library, Bloomington, IN
IU	University of Illinois Library, Urbana, IL
KyU	University of Kentucky Library, Lexington, KY
L	British Library, London
LG	Guildhall Library, London
LU	London University Library
M	John Rylands Library, University of Manchester
MC	Chetham's Library, Manchester
MH	Harvard University Library, Boston, MA
MiU	University of Michigan Library, Ann Arbor, MI
NjP	Princeton University Library, Princeton, NJ
O	Bodleian Library, Oxford
OCh	Christ Church, Oxford
OWa	Wadham College Library, Oxford
TxLT	Texas Tech University Library, Lubbock, TX
TxU	University of Texas Library, Austin, TX.)

Seventeenth-Century Collected Editions/Issues:

A	1633	*POEMS* (*STC* 7045)
B	1635	*POEMS* (*STC* 7046)
C	1639	*POEMS* (*STC* 7047)
D	1649	*POEMS* (*STC* D1868)
E	1650	*POEMS* (*STC* D1869)
F	1654	*POEMS* (*STC* D1870)
G	1669	*POEMS* (*STC* D1871)

Selected Modern Editions:

H	1719	John Donne, *Poems on Several Occasions* [Tonson edition]
I	1779	John Bell, ed., *The Poetical Works of Dr. John Donne*. Vols. 23–25 of *Bell's Edition: The Poets of Great Britain Complete from Chaucer to Churchill*
J	1793	Robert Anderson, ed., *The Poetical Works of Dr. John Donne*. In vol. 4 of *A Complete Edition of the Poets of Great Britain*
K	1810	Alexander Chalmers, ed., *The Poems of John Donne, D. D.* Vol. 5 of *The Works of the English Poets, from Chaucer to Cowper*
L	1839	Henry Alford, ed., *The Works of John Donne, D. D.*, vol. 6
M	1855	[James Russell Lowell, ed.?], *The Poetical Works of Dr. John Donne*
N	1872–73	Alexander B. Grosart, ed., *The Complete Poems of John Donne*, 2 vols.
O	1895	James Russell Lowell, ed., rev. with notes by Charles Eliot Norton, *The Poems of John Donne*, 2 vols.
P	1896	E. K. Chambers, ed., *The Poems of John Donne*, 2 vols.
Q	1912	H. J. C. Grierson, ed., *The Poems of John Donne*, 2 vols.
R	1923	John Sparrow, ed., with bibliographical note by Geoffrey Keynes, *Devotions upon Emergent Occasions by John Donne*
S	1929	John Hayward, ed., *John Donne, Dean of St. Paul's: Complete Poetry and Selected Prose*
T	1942	Roger Bennett, ed., *The Complete Poems of John Donne*
U	1952	Helen Gardner, ed., *John Donne: The Divine Poems*
V	1956	Theodore Redpath, ed., *The Songs and Sonets of John Donne*
W	1963	Frank Manley, ed., *John Donne: The Anniversaries*
X	1965	Helen Gardner, ed., *John Donne: The Elegies and The Songs and Sonnets*
Y	1967	Wesley Milgate, ed., *John Donne: The Satires, Epigrams, and Verse Letters*
Z	1967	John T. Shawcross, ed., *The Complete Poetry of John Donne*
AA	1971	A. J. Smith, ed., *John Donne: The Complete English Poems*
BB	1978	Wesley Milgate, ed., *John Donne: The Epithalamions, Anniversaries, and Epicedes*
CC	1983	Theodore Redpath, ed., *The Songs and Sonets of John Donne*, 2nd ed.
DD	1985	C. A. Patrides, ed., *The Complete English Poems of John Donne*

Other Seventeenth-Century Sources and Locations:

1	1607	Thomas Dekker, *A KNIGHTS Coniuring* (*STC* 6508)
2	1607	Thomas Deloney, *Strange Histories* (*STC* 6567)
3	1607	Ben Jonson, *BEN: IONSON his VOLPONE Or THE FOXE* (*STC* 14783)
4	1609	Alfonso Ferrabosco, *AYRES* (*STC* 10827)
5	1609	Joseph Wybarne, *THE NEW AGE OF OLD NAMES* (*STC* 26055)
6	1611	Thomas Coryat, *Coryats Crudities* (*STC* 5808)
7	1611	Thomas Coryat, *THE ODCOMBIAN BANQVET* (*STC* 5810)

8a 1611 John Donne, *Conclaue Ignati* (*STC* 7026); b 1611, Continental ed. (*L* C.110.f.46.); c 1681, in Thomas Barlow, *PAPISMUS* (*STC* B836); d 1682, in *PAPISMUS* (*STC* B837)

9a 1611 John Donne, *Ignatius his Conclaue* (*STC* 7027); b 1626 (*STC* 7028); c 1634 (*STC* 7029); d 1635 (*STC* 7030); e 1652, in *PARADOXES, PROBLEMS, ESSAYES, CHARACTERS* (*STC* D1866); f 1652, in *PARADOXES, PROBLEMES, ESSAYES, CHARACTERS* (*STC* D1867)

10 1611 John Donne, Elizabeth Drury Inscription (Hawstead)

11 1612 William Corkine, *THE SECOND BOOKE OF AYRES* (*STC* 5769)

12a 1613 Josuah Sylvester, *Lachrymæ Lachrymarū* (*STC* 23578; *LU* [D.–L.L.] (XVII) Bc [Sylvester] S.R.); b 1613 (*STC* 23578; *DFo* STC 23578.2); c 1613 (*STC* 23578; *ICN* CASE Y 185. S 9993); d 1613 (*STC* 23577.5; *CtY* Ig Sy57 612Ld); e 1613 (*STC* 23577.5; MC J.1.39); f 1613 (*STC* 23578; *CtY* Ig Sy57 612Lc); g 1613 (*STC* 7 23578; *DFo* STC 23578 copy 4); h 1613 (*STC* 23578; *DFo* STC 23578 copy 1); i 1613 (*STC* 23577.5; *MH* STC 21652 [14455.3517*]); j 1613 (*STC* 23577.5; M R37802)

13a 1614 Michael Scott, *THE PHILOSOPHERS BANQVET* (*STC* 22062); b 1633 (*STC* 22063)

14a 1616 Ben Jonson, *THE WORKES OF Beniamin Jonson* (*STC* 14751; *CSmH* 62101); b 1616 (*STC* 14751; *CSmH* 62104); c 1616 (*STC* 14751; *TxU* Ah J738 +B616a); d 1616 (*STC* 14752); e 1640 (*STC* 14753); f 1640 (*STC* 14754); g 1692 (*STC* J1006)

15 1617 John Donne, Robert Drury Inscription (Hawstead)

16 1617 Henry Fitzgeffrey, *SATYRES: AND SATYRICALL EPIGRAM'S* (*STC* 10945)

17a 1618 Henry Fitzgeffrey, *CERTAIN ELEGIES, DONE BY SVNDRIE Excellent Wits* (*STC* 10945.3); b 1620 (*STC* 10945.6)

18a 1619 William Basse, A HELPE TO DISCOVRSE (*STC* 1547); b 1620 (*STC* 1548); c 1621 (*STC* 1549); d 1623 (*STC* 1549.5); e 1627 (*STC* 1550); f 1628 (*STC* 1551); g 1629 (*STC* 1551.3); h 1630 (*STC* 1551.5); i 1631 (*STC* 1551.7); j 1635 (*STC* 1552); k 1636 (*STC* 1553); l 1638 (*STC* 1554); m 1640 (*STC* 1554.5); n 1648 (*STC* E23); o 1654 (*STC* E24); p 1663 (*STC* E25); q 1667 (*STC* E25A); r 1682 (*STC* E25B)

19a 1621 William Basse, *A HELPE TO MEMORIE AND DISCOVRSE* (*STC* 13051); b 1630 (*STC* 13051.3)

20a 1624 John Donne, *DEVOTIONS VPON Emergent Occasions* (*STC* 7033a); b 1624 (*STC* 7033); c 1624 (*STC* 7034); d 1626 (*STC* 7035); e 1627 (*STC* 7035a); f 1634 (*STC* 7036); g 1638 (*STC* 7037)

21 1631 John Donne, Epitaph (St. Paul's Cathedral)

22a 1632 John Donne, *DEATHS DVELL* (*STC* 7031); b 1633 (*STC* 7032); c 1633 (*STC* 7032a; *C* Keynes B.5.24); d 1633 (*STC* 7032a; *C* Keynes B.5.29)

23a 1633 Henry Holland, *ECCLESIA SANCTI PAVLI ILLVSTRATA* (*STC* 13584; *L* 577.c.4.[2].); b 1633 (*STC* 13584; *LG* A.7.6. no. 2 in 32); c 1634 (*STC* 13585)

24a 1633 John Stow, *THE SURVEY OF LONDON* (*STC* 23345); b 1640 [or later] (*STC* 23345.5) 25a 1635 John Swan, *SPECVLVM MUNDI* (*STC* 23516); b 1643 (*STC* S6238); c 1643 (*STC* S6238A); d 1665 (*STC* S6239); e 1670 (*STC* S6240); f 1698 (*STC* S6240A)

26 1635 Katherine Thimelby, *TIXALL LETTERS*, ed. Arthur Clifford [prints from lost seventeenth-century ms. dated 1635 by Keynes]

27 1640 [John Mennes?], *Wits RECREATIONS* (*STC* 25870)

28a 1640 Izaak Walton, *THE LIFE AND DEATH OF Dr DONNE*, in John Donne, *LXXX SERMONS* (*STC* 7038); b 1658 (*STC* W668)

29a 1645 John Gough, *THE ACADEMY OF Complements* (*STC* G1401A); b 1646 (*STC* G1401B); c 1650 (*STC* G1401C); d 1650 (*STC* G1402); e 1654 (*STC* G1403); f 1658 (*STC* G1404); g 1663 (*STC* G1405); h 1670, *THE Academy OF COMPLEMENTS Newly Refin'd* (*STC* G1405B); i 1684 (*STC* 1406; *IU* Hill 31 Mr.43 Gen. res.); j 1684 (*STC* 1406; *O* Vet. A3 f. 313)

30 1650 *THE MIRROUR OF Complements* (*STC* M2223)

31a 1651 Lucius Cary [Viscount of Falkland], *Discourse of INFALLIBILITY* (*STC* F317); b 1660 (*STC* F318)

32a 1653 Francis Beaumont, *POEMS* (*STC* B1602); b 1653 (*STC* B1603); c 1660, Francis Beaumont and John Fletcher, *POEMS* (*STC* B1604)

33a 1653 Samuel Sheppard, *MERLINVS ANONYMVS* (*STC* A1588; *DFo* A1588); b 1653 (*STC* A1588; *L* E.1348.[1.]); c 1654 (*STC* A1589)

34a 1653 Izaak Walton, *The Compleat Angler* (*STC* W661); b 1655 (*STC* W662); c 1661 (*STC* W663); d 1664 (*STC* W664); e 1668 (*STC* W665); f 1676 (*STC* W666); g 1676, Izaak Walton, Charles Cotton, and Robert Venables, *THE UNIVERSAL ANGLER* (*STC* W674; *L* C.31.a.7); h 1676, Izaak Walton, Charles Cotton, and Robert Venables, *THE UNIVERSAL ANGLER* (*STC* W674; *CSmH* 138284)

35 1654 [Robert Chamberlain?], *THE HARMONY OF THE MUSES* (*STC* C105)

36a 1654 Edmund Gayton, *PLEASANT NOTES UPON Don Quixot* (*STC* G415; *CSmH* 148580); b 1654 (*STC* G415; *CSmH* 148581)

37a 1654 Izaak Walton, *THE LIFE OF Sir Henry Wotton, in Henry Wotton, Reliquiæ Wottonianæ* (*STC* W3649); b 1672 (*STC* W3650); c 1685 (*STC* W3651)

38 1654 Richard Whitlock, *ZΩOTOMIA* (*STC* W2030)

39a 1655 John Cotgrave, *WITS INTERPRETER* (*STC* C6370); b 1662 (*STC* C6371); c 1671 (*STC* C6372)

40 1655 Johann Grindal, *Aendachtige BEDENCKINGEN* (*AUB* 2328 F28)

41 1655 Samuel Sheppard, *THE MARROVV OF COMPLEMENTS* (*STC* M719)

42a 1656 John Mennes, *WIT AND DROLLERY* (*STC* W3131); b 1661 (*STC* W3132)

43 1656 Abraham Wright, *Parnassus Biceps* (*STC* W3686)

44a 1657 Joshua Poole, *The English PARNASSUS* (*STC* P2814; *ICN* CASE X 997.69); b 1657 (*STC* P2814; *CSmH* 12886); c 1677 (*STC* P2815); d 1678 (*STC* P2816)

45 1658 William Dugdale, *THE HISTORY OF St. PAULS CATHEDRAL IN LONDON* (*STC* D2482)

46 1658 Henry Stubbs, *DELICIÆ Poetarum* ANGLICANORUM *IN GRÆCVM VERSÆ* (*STC* S6040)

47 1659 John Suckling, *THE LAST REMAINS OF Sr JOHN SVCKLING* (*STC* S6130)

48a 1660 William Winstanley, *England's WORTHIES* (*STC* W3058); b 1684 (*STC* W3059)

49 1661 Thomas Forde, *A THEATRE OF WITS* (*STC* F1548A)

50a 1661 Thomas Forde, *Virtus Rediviva* (*STC* F1550); b 1661 (*STC* F1550A)

51 1662 Margaret Cavendish [Duchess of Newcastle], *PLAYES* (*STC* N868)

52a 1670 Izaak Walton, *THE LIFE OF Mr. GEORGE HERBERT* (*STC* W669); b 1674, in George Herbert, *The Temple* (*STC* H1521); c 1678, in *The Temple* (*STC* H1522); d 1679, in *The Temple* (*STC* H1523); e 1695, in *The Temple* (*STC* H1524)

53a 1670 Izaak Walton, *THE LIVES Of Dr. John Donne, Sir Henry Wotton, Mr. Richard Hooker, Mr. George Herbert* (*STC* W671); b 1675 (*STC* W672)

54a 1673 Andrew Marvell, *THE REHEARSALL TRANSPROS'D: The SECOND PART* (*STC* M882); b 1673 (*STC* M882A); c 1674 (*STC* M883)

55 1677 William Winstanley, *Poor ROBIN'S VISIONS* (*STC* H1598)

56a 1678 S. N., *THE LOYAL GARLAND* (O Douce H. 80 [2].); b 1686 (O Douce S 23)

57a 1680 Nathaniel Lee, *THEODOSIUS* (*STC* L877); b 1684 (*STC* L878); c 1692 (*STC* L879); d 1697 (*STC* L880)

58 1681 *A PARADOX Against LIFE* (*STC* P331)

59 1683 John Shirley, *The Compleat Courtier* (*STC* S3503)

60a 1684 Payne Fisher, *THE Tombes, Monuments, And Sepulchral Inscriptions, Lately Visible in St. Pauls Cathedral* (*STC* F1041); b 1684 (*STC* F1042)

61	1687	William Winstanley, *THE LIVES Of the most Famous English Poets* (*STC* W3065)
62	1688	Jane Barker, *POETICAL RECREATIONS* (*STC* B770)
63	1688	Henry Playford, ed., *Harmonia Sacra* (*STC* P2436)
64a	1691	John Dryden, *Eleonora*, in *THE WORKS* (*STC* D2207); b 1692 *Eleonora* (*STC* D2270); c 1693, in *THE WORKS* (*STC* D2208); d 1694, in *THE WORKS* (*STC* D2209); e 1695, in *THE WORKS* (*STC* D2210)
65	1696	Mary de la Rivière Manley, *LETTERS* (*STC* M434)

Modern First Printings:

66	1784	Sir John Cullum, *The History and Antiquities of Hawstead, in the County of Suffolk.*
67	1802	F. G. Waldron, *A Collection of Miscellaneous Poetry*
68	1802	F. G. Waldron, *The Shakespearean Miscellany*
69	1852	T. E. Tomlins, *The Life of John Donne, D. D. Late Dean of St. Paul's Church, London. By Izaak Walton. With Some Original Notes, By An Antiquary.*
70	1856	John Simeon, *MISCELLANIES OF THE Philobiblon Society*
71	1894	Sir Edmund Gosse, *The Jacobean Poets*
72	1899	Sir Edmund Gosse, *The Life and Letters of John Donne*
73	1958	Sir Geoffrey Keynes, "Dr. Donne and Scaliger," *TLS*, 21 February: 93, 108.
74	1967	John T. Shawcross, "John Donne and Drummond's Manuscripts," *American Notes & Queries* 5:104–105.

Symbols and Abbreviations Used in the Textual Apparatus

(used singly or in combination)

~	base word
∧	punctuation mark omitted
→	changed to: A → B = A changed to B
*	obscured letter (the number of asterisks approximating the number of letters obscured)
/	line break (used in instances of ambiguous hyphenation)
|	scribal mark indicating the end of a sentence or section
›. . .‹	alteration/insertion in the scribal hand
». . .«	alteration/insertion in a second hand
cor	corrected state of a press variant
del	deleted
err	reading from errata list
ind	indented, indentation
Keynes	Geoffrey Keynes, *A Bibliography of . . . Donne*, 4th ed.
M	margin, marginal
missing	missing because of damage to the artifact
om	omitted
SS	subscription
st, sts	stanza, stanzas
unc	uncorrected state of a press variant
var	variant reading(s)

General Introduction

Origin and Plan of the Edition

Modern interest in Donne's poetry is amply demonstrated by the appearance of some fourteen major editions of the whole or of parts of the canon in the twentieth century and by the flood of critical and scholarly commentary catalogued in various periodic checklists (including the annual bibliographies published by the Modern Language Association of America, *Studies in Philology*, and the Modern Humanities Research Association) and in a number of specialized reference works. Among these are the four editions of Geoffrey Keynes, *Bibliography of the Works of Dr. John Donne*; Theodore Spencer and Mark Van Doren, *Studies in Metaphysical Poetry: Two Essays and a Bibliography*; Lloyd E. Berry, *A Bibliography of Studies in Metaphysical Poetry, 1939–60*; John R. Roberts, *John Donne: An Annotated Bibliography of Modern Criticism, 1912–67*; A. J. Smith, *John Donne: the Critical Heritage*; and John R. Roberts, *John Donne: An Annotated Bibliography of Modern Criticism, 1968–1978*. In response to the accumulated bulk and the continuing vitality of the critical activity reflected in these works and to a growing conviction within the community of Donne scholars that Donne's text needed to be reedited—a conviction strongly buttressed by the publication in 1980 of Peter Beal's *Index of English Literary Manuscripts*, which identified important manuscript material that none of Donne's editors had ever incorporated—the project to produce this variorum edition was conceived.

After considerable prior discussion about the feasibility and usefulness of such a work, the effort was formally organized in the fall of 1981 when a group of scholars was invited to meet on the Gulf Park campus of the University of Southern Mississippi to define the nature of the task and outline procedures for carrying it out. At that meeting Gary A. Stringer of the University of Southern Mississippi was designated General Editor, and an advisory board comprising the following members was established: William B. Hunter, Jr., University of Houston (Emeritus); Albert C. Labriola, Duquesne University; Paul A. Parrish, Texas A&M University; Ted-Larry Pebworth, University of Michigan-Dearborn; John R. Roberts, University of Missouri; John T. Shawcross, University of Kentucky; and Ernest W. Sullivan, II, Texas Tech University. Later this group was expanded to include M. Thomas Hester, North Carolina State University, and C. A. Patrides, University of Michigan, who sat on the Advisory Board until his death in 1986. In response to evolving organizational and individual purposes, the make-up of the Advisory Board has inevitably changed over the years, but it has been an abiding principle that members would not only help to steer the project, but also actively engage in the editorial work; and the respective contributions of Advisory Board members are noted in the various volumes of the edition, along with those of the other scholars who have participated in various ways. The project has also received widespread support from other individuals and institutions throughout the academic community and from a number of foundations and granting agencies. The contributions of all these supporters are gratefully and specifically acknowledged in the pages of the various volumes.

In accordance with the traditional ways of grouping Donne's works, the edition is organized into volumes, some of multiple parts, as follows:

Volume 1: General Commentary: the Historical Reception of Donne's Poetry from the Beginnings to the Present
General Textual Introduction and Appendices
Volume 2: Elegies
Volume 3: Satyres, Metempsychosis
Volume 4: Songs and Sonets
Volume 5: Verse Letters
Volume 6: Anniversaries, Epicedes and Obsequies
Volume 7: Divine Poems
Volume 8: Epigrams, Epithalamions, Epitaphs, Inscriptions, Miscellaneous Poems

As this outline indicates, all volumes except the first contain texts and commentary for a set of generically or thematically related poems, and the volumes are numbered in a rough approximation of the order in which the poems were composed. Although this system of numbering may entail a certain amount of bibliographical confusion while the edition is in progress, we trust that upon completion of the entire project this method of ordering the parts will appear rational to bibliographers and critics alike.

The Commentary

Purpose and Scope

Although the material here presented will undoubtedly lend itself to other uses as well, our fundamental motive in compiling this variorum commentary is to facilitate further understanding of Donne's poems by situating them squarely within the tradition of critical and scholarly discussion that has grown up around them from the poet's own time to the present. This purpose, in turn, has required that we identify and examine all items that properly belong within that tradition. As existing bibliographical aids indicate, the body of commentary on Donne is not only vast, but widely scattered. In his 458-page synopsis of comments on Donne in the Critical Heritage series, for instance, A. J. Smith locates and excerpts 222 items published between 1598 and 1889; and John R. Roberts, in his bibliographies of twentieth-century criticism, lists and annotates well over 2,400 items written on Donne between 1912 and

1978, the second of these registering a trend that now sees the publication of approximately 100 books, articles, and notes on Donne every year. In addition to sheer bulk, as suggested above, the corpus of Donne commentary exhibits two further features that make it difficult to master: much of the material, both that identified in existing bibliographies and that which we have discovered, is dispersed throughout the pages of obscure or inaccessible editions and periodicals, and a good bit of it is written in foreign languages. The result of these circumstances is that scholarly or critical works of our own time frequently fail to align themselves distinctly within the critical tradition, and the continuing interpretive enterprise is marked by repetition and fragmentation.

There has been no previous attempt of this kind. None of the existing editions marshalls more than a minute part of the available material, and the bibliographical volumes produced by Smith and Roberts have neither the scope nor the design of a variorum commentary, in addition to leaving entirely uncovered the periods 1890–1911 and 1979–present. This variorum commentary, therefore, will fill a conspicuous gap in the field of Donne studies. In the effort to meet this need, we have defined our task in the broadest chronological and geographical terms. Although bibliographical considerations have dictated that we attempt coverage in each volume only to within three years of the completion of the typescript, we have otherwise sought to bring together and synthesize all relevant items from the seventeenth through the twentieth centuries, and we have included material written not only in English, but also in French, German, Dutch, Italian, Spanish, Portuguese, Polish, Czech, and Japanese. Displaying the poems against this evolving, variegated background of critical discourse will, we believe, not only enable a better appreciation of individual works and of Donne's overall poetic achievement, but also provide materials toward an enhanced understanding of the aesthetic and intellectual history of the modern period. In short, the material here gathered will point the way to further research in a number of areas and facilitate the ongoing critical dialogue.

An undertaking like this, of course, is by its very nature conservative, bespeaking respect not only for what Donne has left us, but also for the contributions of those prior critics who have made possible our present understanding. Like those of contemporary critics, of course, the judgments of previous commentators are inevitably conditioned by cultural and personal assumptions about what poetry is (or should be), about how it functions in the world, and about the nature of criticism itself; and the validity of such assumptions tends to appear self-evident to those who hold them, with the frequent result that they are never explicitly stated. While the clarification of such preconceptions is itself a legitimate scholarly aim, we have not attempted in these pages to interpret the criticism nor to examine the various epistemological constructs that have shaped it, but have chosen rather to let each item of commentary speak for itself as best it can in the reduced form that it must necessarily take in these volumes. We recognize, of course, that no summary, however carefully prepared, can fully replace the original upon which it is based; indeed, the longer and more complex a given argument is, the less satisfactorily it submits to condensation. The compilation of commentary here offered is thus intended as a guide to, not as a substitute for, the primary works of scholarship that make up the tradition.

Editorial Stance

In attempting this consolidation of the critical heritage we have striven for both completeness and objectivity. Within the historical and linguistic limits noted above, we have sought to gather all published items of commentary and to represent each as accurately and extensively as our format permits. We have, furthermore, presented all these materials without interjecting editorial opinion on their validity or ultimate significance, though we have reduced redundancy in the presentation by fully reporting ideas only upon their first appearance, in some cases briefly tracing the progress of a given observation or line of argument by means of a system of internal cross-referencing. We have added neither glosses nor more general interpretations of our own, and have restricted instances of editorial intrusion (denoted by the abbreviation *ed.* in the text) to the correction of obvious factual error.

Organization of the Material within Volumes

As is customary in a variorum commentary, all material included here is organized chronologically and, when necessary within a given year, alphabetically by author's surname; and each item is aligned as precisely as possible with whichever aspects of the poetry it bears on. Thus, as noted above, Volume 1 traces in general terms the reception of Donne's poetry over the centuries, while the remaining volumes focus on individual genres and groups of poems. We have arranged the commentary in each genre-based volume along a continuum of particularity, beginning with the most general and proceeding to commentary on sub-sets of poems (where appropriate), commentary on particular poems, and line-by-line notes and glosses.[1] The material at all levels except glosses, moreover, is further organized into topical sub-units whenever a common theme or critical concern runs through a number of items. In cases where an individual item of commentary depends specifically upon a previous version of Donne's text, we have included the relevant readings from that version.

Style of Presentation

We have attempted to present the commentary as efficiently and readably as possible. At all levels of organization above Notes and Glosses, the material is invariably summarized in narrative form, as the user is guided through the content by the editor's controlling voice, and the normal conventions of interpreting prose summary apply. In Notes and Glosses, however, which derive variously both from specific observations abstracted from longer discursive comments and from the brief, telegraphic annotations often employed by editors, we have alternated between the narrative and the dramatic styles as necessary in an attempt to present each bit of material as economically as possible (though we have not intermixed the two modes within the entry for a single author). Following any lemma in the Notes and Glosses, therefore,

[1]In glosses keyed to specific lines or words, of course, commentators frequently annotate items in surrounding lines as well, and it is not always possible to subdivide such manifold glosses into their component elements without destroying the author's sense. Especially in Notes and Glosses sections of the commentary, therefore, users are advised to examine each entry in the context of those that come before and after in order to ensure full coverage of what has been reported about a particular point.

one commentator's remarks may be rendered dramatically, as though the original author were speaking in his or her own voice, while those of the next may be paraphrased in the editor's voice. The dramatic mode, whether or not any words or phrases in the entry appear in quotation marks, is signaled mechanically by a colon after the bibliographical citation in parentheses, the narrative mode by the absence of a colon. Editorial insertions thus appear in brackets in the dramatic mode and in parentheses in the narrative mode.

Bibliographical Conventions in the Commentary

Works mentioned in the Commentary are cited parenthetically by author and date, and these citations are keyed to a master list of Works Cited in each olume. Since the commentary throughout the Variorum is ordered according to a multi-leveled taxonomic system, the author index included in each volume, used in conjunction with the master list of works cited, will provide the further information needed to index the content of the volume. We have used standard nonverbal symbols and short forms of reference insofar as possible, and have derived common scholarly abbreviations, including those for such items as the titles of Shakespeare's plays and books of the Bible, from the current *MLA Style Manual*. For titles of current journals we have used the abbreviations given in the *MLA International Bibliography*, and for early books we have appropriated the short forms of reference standardized by Pollard and Redgrave and by Wing in the *STC*. Lists of abbreviated references to all works cited in the commentary and to Donne's poems and prose works are provided in each volume, and we have standardized all citations of Donne's prose works in the commentary in accordance with the editions specified in the list of Short Forms. Unless otherwise indicated, cross-references pertain to the section of commentary within which they appear.

The Text

Materials and Theory

Ideally stated, the goal of our work on the text is to recover and present exactly what Donne wrote. It is important, however, that we be clear about certain practical and theoretical limits that are imposed upon this goal by the available materials. Apart from about forty prose letters and certain occasional jottings, four inscriptions in the books of friends or acquaintances, and an epitaph on his wife, only a single poem—a verse epistle addressed to the Lady Carey and Mrs. Essex Riche—is known to survive in Donne's hand. Of the relatively few poems published before his death in 1631, only for the Anniversaries, in the edition of 1612, and in the first Latin and English editions of *Ignatius* is there any evidence to suggest that the author may have proofread and corrected copy. The remainder of the poems survive only in nonauthorial copies (which amount to well over 5,000 separate transcriptions of individual poems), at indeterminate degrees of remove from holograph and therefore of indeterminate authority. During and immediately following Donne's lifetime these poems, circulating individually or in groups of various sizes and composition, were copied into diaries, commonplace books, miscellanies, and poetic collections that form several distinct strands of scribal transmission; and these strands, in ways impossible to determine exactly, lie behind the print tradition that begins for most of the poems with the publication in 1633 of *Poems, by J. D. with Elegies on the Authors Death* and continues in six additional seventeenth-century collected editions and issues.

The almost total absence of holograph materials or of authorially approved printings renders impossible any attempt to locate textual authority in the author's intentions, as that concept is generally applied in scholarly editing. Indeed, the only "intention" Donne seems to have had for most of his poems in this regard was that they *not be printed at all.* Commenting on the publication of the Anniversaries in a letter to George Garrard from Paris on April 14, 1612, Donne wrote, "I . . . do not pardon my self" for having "descended to print any thing in verse" (*Letters* 238), and when in 1614 he thought himself "brought to a necessity of printing" (*Letters* 196) the poems as a "valediction to the world" before taking holy orders (a necessity he apparently escaped), he sought to borrow from his friend Henry Goodyer an "old book" (*Letters* 197) containing copies of them, thus suggesting that—at least for some of the poems—he had failed even to retain manuscript copies for his own use or reference.

If virtually none of them bears the author's imprimatur, the surviving materials for constructing a text of Donne's poems are nonetheless numerous and diverse. In addition to the seven collected printings issued between 1633 and 1669, they include 239 manuscript sources (nearly 100 of which have been unknown to any of Donne's previous editors); 3 inscriptions on monuments; over 200 seventeenth-century books that collectively contain over 700 copies of individual Donne poems or excerpts (approximately 500 of which have been unknown to Donne's previous editors); and over 20 historically significant editions of all or of parts of the canon from the eighteenth century to the present. No one would argue, of course, that all of this material is equally valuable for establishing the text, but all of it, including both corrected and uncorrected states of the seventeenth-century editions (among which we have identified many previously unrecorded press variants), is part of the bibliographical tradition that provides what we currently know of Donne's poems and their textual history. A full description of these textual artifacts and the relations among them is provided in volume 1 of the edition.

The nature of the material described above severely complicates the question of textual authority—not only with respect to the presentation of the individual poems, but also in the matters of how to order the poems within an edition and, to a lesser extent, what works to admit to the canon. No scribal artifact and no pre-twentieth-century edition includes the full complement of what are now generally recognized as authentic poems. While it preserves a general continuity in the texts of individual poems, the tradition represented by the seventeenth-century collected editions shows a gradual expansion and, especially in 1635, rearrangement of the canon, as printers sought to publish increasingly comprehensive and generically rationalized editions; and not until Grosart's edition of 1872–73 do we find a modern editor basing his work extensively on manuscript sources rather than on the print tradition. From Grierson (1912) onward, most of Donne's twentieth-century editors have adopted as copy-text for each poem an early seventeenth-century printing, sometimes emending its details (especially verbal variants) toward manuscript readings, and virtually all modern editions order their contents according to the broad generic divisions introduced in the edition of 1635.

As noted above, we also have adopted the traditional generic divisions as an ordering principle. We have not, however, necessarily followed the majority practice of locating primary textual authority for each poem in an early printing, and we have not practiced the eclecticism that has frequently accompanied such a choice. In accordance with the considerations outlined below, we have selected copy-texts variously from among all the available artifacts, and we have presented them with a minimum of editorial intervention. Both practices require explanation.

We have chosen manuscript copy-texts for many of the poems simply because they seem in fact and in theory more likely to represent the lost originals accurately than do the early printings. As noted above, the exact textual genesis of the early collected editions cannot be ascertained. Although individual poems in some of these editions *may* have been set from holograph, it is extremely unlikely that even the printer in 1633 possessed authorial copies of more than a few of the poems—and perhaps of none at all. Given the occasional composition, the piecemeal distribution, and the wide circulation of the poems in manuscript—and especially the author's apparent failure to maintain a comprehensive personal archive—it is very hard to imagine that an extensive holograph collection of Donne's poems ever existed, even in the seventeenth century. Indeed, the phrasing of Donne's request for Goodyer's "old book" may suggest that the author himself expected to retrieve transcriptions rather than original copies. Most probable is that the original holographs gradually dropped out of circulation as the poems made the rounds of transmission, and there is thus the virtual certainty that even the earliest editions were set from derivative manuscript collections very much like those that survive.

Whatever their origins, moreover, comparison of the early printings with the surviving scribal manuscripts—or even with the extant holograph verse letter—shows clearly that as texts underwent translation from manuscript to print in the publishing house, they not only suffered some measure of verbal corruption, but also were subjected to institutional conventions of punctuation, spelling, capitalization, and so forth—even in instances when the printer may have been setting from holographs. In thus reflecting the intersection of private scribal or authorial practices with the social norms of commercial printing, the printed text inevitably became a collaborative product that differed in a number of important ways from what Donne had originally set down.[2]

The data clearly show, of course, that the poems were similarly vulnerable to change in the course of scribal transmission. Undoubtedly, many scribes automatically restyledthe poems to accord with their own habits of formatting, spelling, capitalization, and punctuation; and some no doubt made conscious verbal "improvements." As they transcribed poems into private collections for their own use or that of pa-

[2]Between the holograph of the 63-line verse letter and the text printed in 1633, for instance, there are 56 differences in punctuation, 63 differences in capitalization, 120 differences in spelling, and 3 differences in wording.

trons, however, the early copyists did not necessarily share the printer's programmatic determination to groom the text into a publicly negotiable, regularized form; and most of the substantive changes they introduced into the text are more likely attributable to carelessness, ignorance, and the general entropy of the transmissional system.

Most of the manuscripts antedate the printed editions, of course, and thus are chronologically closer to the hand of the author. A number of factors, however, seriously restrict any attempt to determine their dates of compilation and thus to construct a comprehensive genealogy of manuscripts. For one thing, many of the manuscripts cannot be dated except in very approximate terms; moreover, an indeterminate number of manuscripts are evidently missing. The greatest limitation on developing a reliable stemma of manuscripts, however, is that virtually all the major manuscript collections, like the printed editions, are composite artifacts containing texts of individual poems drawn from multiple sources, and a given manuscript may thus preserve an early state of one text and a late state of another side by side. In some cases, of course, particular features of content, format, and scribal style point to family relationships among manuscripts and sometimes even reveal direct lines of descent within families. Generally speaking, however, the effort to locate textual authority in a genealogy of manuscripts is doomed to fail.

Given the situation described above, the only remaining alternative is to approach Donne's text on a poem-by-poem basis, examining all copies of each poem and determining insofar as possible its individual history of transmission. As with whole manuscripts, the possibility of missing copies and the intractability of the surviving evidence also make it impossible to construct a complete genealogy for many of the poems. With varying degrees of precision, however, it is possible to identify patterns of variation that lead back to the least corrupted surviving version(s) of a poem and to chart the transmission of its text in a schema of textual relations. As this procedure implies, of course, the effort to recover Donne's poems necessarily rests partly in the editor's evaluation of the relative semiological integrity of the surviving copies of individual poems. Once this determination has been made, the question then becomes one of how those individual copies shall be edited.

As noted above, most of Donne's twentieth-century editors have created synthetic or eclectic texts, adopting a seventeenth-century printing of each poem as copy-text and generally following that printing's accidentals, while sometimes emending its substantives toward manuscript readings. There are, however, a number of problems with this approach. A major one, in our view, as Charles Moorman has argued in discussing a similar case, is that the practice involves the highly questionable assumption that any modern editor—even one very sensitive, learned, and wise—can reach back over hundreds of years and somehow ascertain what must have been in Donne's mind, root out instances of corruption, and synthetically reconstruct a text reflecting what he actually wrote. Indeed, as Fredson Bowers has pointed out, Greg's rationale of copy-text, the classic formulation of the synthetic principle, was intended to apply in cases in which the variant forms of a work could be assumed to form a single ancestral sequence reaching back to the author's holographs. Clearly, in the case of Donne, whose poems survive in many genealogical strands of indeterminate proximity to each other and to the manuscript originals, an eclectic approach that privileges the early printings offers only a qualified hope of recovering the author's exact words—and even less of recovering his accidentals. Additionally, of course, in cases where an author has revised a work (as Donne did in some instances), an eclectic approach entails the risk of conflating earlier and later states of the text.

Any editor of Donne must, of course, exercise judgment; but there are legitimate differences of opinion about where, how often, and especially at what stage of the editorial process that judgment can most defensibly be exercised. In light of the circumstances described above, we have attempted to identify—by combining bibliographical analysis with such logical criteria as completeness and general semantic coherence—the earliest, least corrupted state of each poem from among the surviving seventeenth-century artifacts or, in the case of poems surviving in multiple authorial versions, the least corrupted state of each version; and once that judgment has been reached, we have edited the text in the conservative manner explained below. The theory underlying our work is thus fundamentally historicist, but balanced by a respect for what we have called the semiological integrity of the individual poem as preserved in an early artifact. We recognize that, except by extreme good fortune, we are not likely to present any nonholographic poem exactly as Donne wrote it, but this approach does allow us to present a text of every poem essentially free of conjecture and anachronistic intervention.

This, then, is the sense in which we mean that we have sought to recover and present exactly what Donne wrote. Our text is a representation of the poem that stands in a metonymic relationship to the lost original, different both in that it may not have the exact wording and pointing of that original and—for texts based on manuscript originals—in that it will be a print exemplum of the copy from which it derives. It is, however, a text that somebody in Donne's own time—the one who had the copy closest to his hand and transcribed it most accurately, if we are lucky—set down as what the author had written. Because it provides an illuminating background for our work and because it is a legitimate scholarly concern in its own right, we have further undertaken to outline the textual history of each poem as fully and as accurately as possible.

Procedures for Choosing and Emending Copy-text

To the ends specified above we have adopted the following procedures for choosing and emending copy-texts and constructing the textual apparatus. First, since most of the texts survive only in nonauthorial copies, we have necessarily examined every surviving seventeenth-century manuscript and multiple copies of seventeenth-century printings.[3] In order to do this, we have entered the texts of all manuscript and early print copies of the poems into computer files and compared the files for each

[3]When a seventeenth-century printing is used as copy-text, we have collated at least five copies (or all copies, if fewer than five copies survive); when the copy-text is a manuscript, we have collated at least three copies of all seventeenth-century printings of the poems, except that we have generally collated only one copy if a print source contains only an excerpt from a poem.

poem by means of the Donne Variorum Collation Program.[4] On the basis of these collations, we have constructed for each poem a schema of textual relationships that accounts, insofar as the evidence permits, for all permutations of the texts in the early artifacts. In order to corroborate the evidence of this analysis, as suggested above, wehave independently assessed the evidentiary value of each artifact by determining insofar as possible its date, provenance, and process of compilation and by evaluating all this bibliographical detail in the context of what is known about manuscript transcription and practices of typesetting in the late sixteenth and earlier seventeenth centuries. The copy-text finally chosen is what seems to be the earliest, least-corrupted state of the text as preserved in the best witness among the artifacts in which it appears. Having made this identification, we have corrected obvious errors in the copy-text, emended punctuation when absolutely necessary to prevent misreading, and applied certain print conventions to manuscript copy-texts, but we have not conflated readings from multiple sources. In cases where one or more artifacts preserve a poem in a state so extensively revised or changed as to constitute a new version, we present the successive versions in full and, whenever it seems useful to do so, provide a separate historical collation for each.

In accordance with our determination to represent the copy-text authentically and accurately, we have retained in the Variorum texts a number of seventeenth-century orthographical and typographical features and, except for the silent changes specified below, have noted in the apparatus accompanying each poem all emendations to the copy-text. The Variorum texts preserve the distinct forms of "i" and "j" and "u" and "v," the ligatured vowels "æ" and "œ," and the fonts of words as they appear in the copy-text. We have, however, expanded brevigraphs, regularized "VV" to "W" and "ff" to "F," and imposed on manuscript copy-texts such print conventions as the consistent capitalization of the first word of each line of poetry. All such emendations, as well as the few editorial corrections deemed necessary, are noted in the lists of emendations. Our only silent emendations of the copy-text are typographical and affect neither spelling nor meaning: we have reduced the long "ſ" to "s," separated such ornamental ligatured consonants as "ſt" and "ct," and regularized inconsistencies of font and the spacing of punctuation.

Because Donne's syntax is often knotty, punctuation itself is frequently interpretive. Recognizing this, we have emended the punctuation of the copy-text very conservatively, and this principle has resulted in an actual, though not a theoretical, inconsistency. Since printers of the earlier seventeenth century tended to punctuate heavily and grammatically, while many scribes of that period punctuated lightly and rhetorically (sometimes even to the point of regarding the line end as sufficient punctuation in itself), the Variorum texts based on printed copy-texts and those based on

[4]We have verified all data files used in the preparation of these texts against original sources, and have compared multiple copies of printed artifacts not only by sight, but also, when it has been possible to bring the requisite materials together, by means of the Lindstrand Comparator or the Hinman Collator. At all stages of transcription and data entry, at least three editors have proofread the work independently, resolving any problems or differences of interpretation in conference. At each stage of production we have taken similar care to verify the accuracy of both text and apparatus.

manuscript copy-texts show markedly different degrees of punctuation. But we think it better to present texts that, in each case, accurately reflect a bibliographically defensible choice of copy-text than to impose consistency of punctuation and with it the possibility of editorial interpretation. Variant seventeenth-century pointing that may affect the sense of a given passage is recorded in the historical collation.

Introductions and Apparatuses

Each poem is provided with a brief textual introduction, and groups of related poems are introduced collectively when it is useful to do so. The introduction to each poem briefly locates the poem in the context of Donne's life or poetic development (when possible) and outlines the seventeenth-century textual history of the poem by grouping the artifacts into families and describing insofar as possible the relationships of those families, as well as noting readings of particular bibliographical or critical interest. It then sketches the treatment of the poem by modern editors and briefly discusses the choice and emendation of the copy-text.

For complete textual information on any poem, of course, readers must consult both the textual introductions and the various parts of the textual apparatus. As suggested above, the textual apparatus may include data drawn from five different classes of material: (1) manuscripts, (2) independent seventeenth-century editions of Donne's poetical works (including seventeenth-century editions of the Anniversaries and collected editions or issues), (3) uncollected seventeenth-century printings of individual poems and excerpts of two or more lines, (4) modern first printings of individual poems, and (5) selected modern editions of Donne's poetical works. In general, the apparatus lists the sigla of source materials in the demonstrable or probable order of the transmission of the text, ordering items within classes alphabetically or numerically as appropriate.

The following categories of information are included in the textual apparatus for each poem, except that in cases where there is nothing to report, the category is omitted:

1. Copy-text and Sources Collated. Lists by sigla the copy-text and the copies and excerpts collated, specifying the folio or page numbers on which the poem or excerpt appears in each artifact, and, in the case of deliberate excerpts, which lines are excerpted.
2. Emendations of the Copy-text. Specifies differences between the copy-text and the Variorum text.
3. Historical Collation.
   a. Format. Details noteworthy features of the artifacts or transcriptions, including typefonts, paragraphing, patterns of indentation (though not occasional deviations) in stanzaic verse, scribal eccentricities, lines missing in damaged artifacts, and other information affecting text or indicating authorship or provenance.
   b. Headings. Lists variant headings (not called "titles," since their authority is uncertain) in seventeenth-century artifacts.
   c. Line-by-line collation. Lists all substantive and selected semisubstantive variants (specified below) in seventeenth-century sources, as well as any omissions of words or lines in copies intended to be complete.
   d. Subscriptions. Lists all subscriptions in seventeenth-century artifacts.

4. Verbal Variants in Selected Modern Editions. Lists verbal variants in twenty-three historically or bibliographically significant editions from the eighteenth century to the present.
5. Schema of Textual Relationships. Charts in schematic form the genealogy of each poem and the relationships of the textual artifacts, denoting definite lines of transmission with arrows, definite associations and family linkages with solid lines, and conjectural lines of relationship with dotted lines.
6. Analyses of Early Printed Copies. Lists copies collated, describes the physical make-up of each, and details press variants.

Reportage of Variants

We have tried to make the list of variants useful to many kinds of readers, from textual scholars and literary historians to critics and metricians. In order to do so, we have reported the following kinds of substantive and semisubstantive variants:

1. All verbal variants in seventeenth-century artifacts, including variant spellings that may be read as different words in context.
2. All nonverbal substantive variants from all seventeenth-century sources, including differences in punctuation that materially affect meaning.[5]
3. All semisubstantive variants from all seventeenth-century sources that may affect either meaning or meter. Included in this category are the capitalization of such words as "Fate," "Nature," and "Heaven"; elided and nonelided vowels and marks of syncope that may affect the number of syllables in a line and therefore meter; and variants of spelling that, in context, may suggest different words or orthographic puns.
4. Variants that illuminate a poem's textual history. This is the broadest and most discretionary category, but an important one nonetheless in that the details it includes clarify the transmission and history of the text. Under this heading are reported verbal variants in modern editions, which are listed separately at the end of the historical collation for each poem.

In reporting the kinds of variants here specified, we intend to provide users with the data necessary to reconstruct in all essential respects any version of the text of any poem.[6]

[5]Lists in the historical collations do not record inconsequential variants of punctuation—such as commas separating items in simple compound constructions; neither do they record the absence of nonsubtantive punctuation in corollary copies in cases where the copy-text contains the punctuation necessary for understanding.

[6]It should be noted that obvious errors in printed editions, such as "effential" for "essential" and "Beddded" for "Bedded," are not reported in the historical collations except when they result in verbal variants, such as the erroneous "patts" for "parts" (1621 ed. of *SecAn* 233) and the erroneous "close-weaning" for "close-weauing" (1611–25 eds. of *FirAn* 153) or later become the source of error, such as the misprint "*ealth*" for *health*" (1625 ed. of *FirAn* 91M), which leads to the mistaken emendation "*earth*" in the subsequent edition of 1633. It should further be noted that in the case of severely damaged or mutilated manuscripts (always so designated in the Format section of the Historical Collation), only fully discernible variants and features that aid in the filiation of manuscripts are reported; no attempt is made to itemize each missing word or feature.

Bibliographical Conventions in the Apparatus

The format for entries in the historical collation generally follows standard practices of bibliographical notation. Each word or item in the Variorum text for which variant readings are reported is presented as a lemma to the left of a right bracket (lemma]) and followed by the variant and a list of sigla for the sources in which the variant appears. Multiple variants and sigla for a given item are presented seriatim and separated by semicolons. When the lemma is a single word, a swung dash (~) is used after the bracket to stand for the word in the lemma. When the lemma consists of multiple words, whether substantive or accidental variants are at issue, verbal variants are written out in full. A caret (‸) preceeding or following a word or swung dash to the right of the bracket indicates omitted punctuation.

It should be noted that the swung dash does not imply exact identity of spelling, capitalization, or font between the word it represents and the corresponding word in the lemma, but only that the two are variant forms of the same word. For example, the final word of line 8 in "*ELEGIE* on the untimely Death of the *incomparable Prince*, HENRY" reads as follows in the artifacts: "*Circumference:*" in 12a–j; "Circumference." in B14, C9, H3, and H6; "Circumference" in DT1; "Cyrcumference" in H4; "circumference." in O29, WN1, and A; and "circumference:" in B through G. Since differences of spelling, font, and capitalization are not substantive in this case and are thus not reported, these variants are collapsed into the following synthetic entry in the historical collation:

Circumference:] ~. B14 C9 H3 H6 O29 WN1 A; ~‸ DT1 H4.

When the artifacts generally agree in a lengthy variation, but contain minor differences that need to be reported, we have minimized clutter in the apparatus by recording such subvariations parenthetically immediately after the siglum of the source from which they derive. For example, 13a and 13b preserve the variant readings "Wheres now the" and "Where's now the" in the first half of *FirAn* 127. These variant readings, which differ only in the use of the apostrophe, are reported in the historical collation as follows:

Where is this] Wheres now the 13a 13b(Where's).

In cases where a reading right of the bracket expresses as a single, synthetic entry variations of spelling, font, or capitalization that do not affect meaning or meter (and thus are not reported explicitly), the accidentals of any word that may appear in the entry are those of the artifact reported first in the sequence unless otherwise indicated.

As noted above, the Schema of Textual Relationships accompanying each poem is designed to outline in broad terms what can be determined of the poem's genealogy. Each schema presents, within the context of full lines, the variants that permit separation of the artifacts into family groups. Accidentals in lines selected for the Schema are those of a representative member of the family, and the defining variants are shown in boldface type. Significant intra-family variations are reported parenthetically at the end of each line. Detail reported in the schema is necessarily limited; information enabling the establishment of further genealogical links among copies of the text can be derived from the Historical Collation.

The Editors

Introduction to Volume 8

This volume, the second in the series to be published, represents a departure from the mainstream of Donne editing in two different but complementary ways, both of which tend to the expansion of Donne's canon and enable appreciation of a poetic talent that exercised itself more widely, diversely, and self-consciously than has hitherto been recognized. First, we have included a number of items that, if most of them have been printed by one or another of Donne's previous editors, have not generally found their way into the collected editions and cannot be said to have gained unquestioned acceptance among Donne's poetic works. With the controverted *Sheaf of Miscellany Epigrams* (Appendix 1), moreover, we present a collection of poems that has never before been published in an edition of the poetry. Perhaps of even greater significance than these small additions to the canon, however, is the evidence here adduced to illustrate Donne's revisions of a number of these poems over the course of time. This evidence is discussed and laid out schematically in the case of the two later epithalamions (*EpEliz* and *Eclog*), but it assumes a more radical form in the presentation of the English epigrams, where readers will encounter three distinct sequences of poems, each of which differs significantly from the others at both the macro and the micro levels. We are not the first editors ever to suggest that Donne may have revised a poem or altered a sequence, but we are the first whose editorial practice has been significantly influenced by that recognition. The presentation of distinct versions of the epigrams, each with its own clear reading text, is the signal feature of this volume, and seems destined not only to illuminate a previously unappreciated aspect of Donne's poetic practice, but also to set a precedent for the treatment of Donne's texts in other genres.

The Critical Tradition

The poems collected in this volume vary about as widely as possible in form, ranging from the long, elaborate eclogue with epithalamion on the marriage of the Earl of Somerset and Lady Frances Howard, erstwhile Countess of Essex, to one mere line of Latin (with Greek admixture), the epigraph to the sermon *Deaths Duell*. Perhaps what they have in common is their relative neglect, at least (in the case of the epithalamions and a few of the epigrams) until about 1970. These are poems, for the most part, not honored by the critical canonization of "metaphysical poetry" in the first half of the twentieth century, although much of the attention paid to them during that time, such as it was, was undoubtedly indebted to Donne's revived status. Among the volumes in the present Variorum series, this one may plausibly claim to present both those poems that have been most disparaged or neglected and those that recent criticism has most strenuously sought to revaluate.

It would be unfortunate if the only works of Donne to survive some bibliographic disaster were these; yet they would tell us more about him than might be supposed. For one thing, they appear to embrace virtually his entire literary career, possibly—for both the dating of some of the poems and Donne's involvement in the external events to which they refer are conjectural, and are debated within these pages—from some time prior to the Cadiz expedition of the mid-1590s to nearly the hour of his death, memorialized in the epitaph that he is recorded as having written for himself. The epigrams purportedly translated from Latin by Jasper Mayne and here printed in Appendix 1, if they be admitted as genuine, may push the dates of authorial activity covered in this volume back into the 1580s and so represent Donne's earliest extant works.

Dating Donne's poems is, as is well known, a difficult business, made easy only in the cases of those printed in his lifetime or produced for documented occasions. Two of the epithalamions fall into the latter category, both written for great weddings of 1613; the third has generally, though not universally, gained recognition as a product of the author's years as a law student at Lincoln's Inn. The four epitaphs have been, unsurprisingly, easy to date, having not printed but chiseled or inscribed histories: two mark the closings of Donne's important connection with the Drury family, and the others the deaths successively of his wife and himself. The last of these has received by far the most attention, glossed first by Izaak Walton in his dramatic account of Donne's last days and subsequently by critics attracted to the idea that even in death the poet practiced a self-fashioning.

However problematic their connection to datable events, Donne's epigrams are an attractive point of departure for understanding his life and work, if only because Ben Jonson praised them in an epigram of his own while apparently declaring to William Drummond both that Donne was a master in this genre and that Donne had composed his best works before the age of twenty-five. It is not unreasonable to conflate these remarks to mean that Donne's epigrams launched his poetic career. Other occasional poems, like Donne's commendatory poem to Ben Jonson on the publication of *Volpone*, may be seen not only as extensions of a literary dialogue, but also as markers in Donne's long public life, as opposed to the private life more often examined in studies of the erotic and devotional verse. The public poems remind us not only of his duties, but also of the ceremonies attendant on their performance: the inscription in a Bible presented to Lincoln's Inn, for example, records the transition from his position as preacher there to loftier responsibilities as Dean of St. Paul's. *AutJos* and *AutHook*, epigrams inscribed in Donne's hand in learned books of science and theology, afford glimpses of Donne's intellectual preoccupations. The publication of apparently private anguish in the *Stationes* (the poetic headnotes to the famous *Meditations*) and the calculated abuse of St. Ignatius Loyola (in both the verses from *Ignatius His*

Conclave and the dubious "Apotheosis") remind us of the complex interplay between Donne's religion and politics on the one hand and the states of his body and mind on the other.

That interplay is perhaps most clearly dramatized in the longest, most elaborate, and most formal of these poems. Products, or very nearly so, of the same year, 1613, and similar in that both were written for court weddings, *EpEliz* and *Eclog* have until recent decades, nevertheless, enjoyed nearly opposite reputations, the former being frequently praised, especially for its lyrical opening stanza, and the latter as often attacked, primarily on biographical grounds. To a remarkable degree, critical commentary on *Eclog* has been either hostile or defensive, either imputing corrupt motivations to Donne or rationalizing his act, whether by situating it within the exigencies of the patronage system or by discovering the poet's *apologia* within the text itself. It is perhaps noteworthy that *EpEliz*, a poem equally at home within the context of court power and mythology, has stimulated far less analysis on those grounds.

Whereas criticism of the two poems of 1613 rarely strays far from the personalities and politics of the two Court weddings, commentary on *EpLin* has persistently raised questions about those very circumstances, especially the date and nature of the occasion celebrated. Printed last in the order of the epithalamions in the edition of 1633, *EpLin* remains the odd poem within its group, usually, though not invariably, assigned to Donne's student days. If *EpEliz* seems to invite few questions, and *Eclog* subtle ones, about Donne's attitude towards his subjects, *EpLin* by contrast has provoked extended controversy over such issues as its relationship to Spenser's prior effort in the genre, its stance towards its aristocratic and bourgeois participants, and even the gender of the bride.

The institution of marriage, so apparently central to the form, has received special attention in recent studies not only of *EpEliz* and *Eclog*, but also of *EpLin*, even when the latter is read as a parody of the wedding ceremony. An interest that has arisen in recent decades in the political and social context of literature, however, is reflected in a substantial increase of attention to *Eclog*, a poem implicated in the high drama of the Somerset-Essex affairs that extended actually from the King's first notice of Robert Carr to the final disgrace and rustication of Carr and Frances Howard. With few exceptions, however, this critical interest might be seen as an extension and development rather than a repudiation of previous treatments of the poem.

EpLin, like *Eclog*, has been assailed, though on grounds of indecency rather than opportunism, and, also like *Eclog*, has in recent decades both enjoyed a defensive rehabilitation and been subjected to a revival of old objections on such newer grounds as feminist theory. All three epithalamions have been studied as exemplars, modifications, or deformations of generic conventions, with many questions raised about the poet's (or "speaker's") role as observer, participant, celebrant, critic, or mocker. All three wedding-poems have been disputed in arguments over Donne's presumed points of view insofar as his attitude towards his subjects—variously understood as affirming, questioning, subversive, or cynical—has appeared to ratify, modify, or upset existing notions of his evolution as a careerist and a poet.

Despite Jonson's and Drummond's early praise, no other poems by Donne have suffered so great a decline in critical esteem as have the epigrams. Evidence of their popularity in the seventeenth and eighteenth centuries includes a wide variety of manuscript copies and numerous imitations and translations, some of which are printed below in Appendix 2. Yet their reception by Victorian and early twentieth-century critics was generally hostile or disparaging; more recent criticism has variously sought to justify their earlier popularity or to praise them on new grounds.

The appended series of epigrams by Jasper Mayne purporting to translate lost originals by Donne might serve as an introduction to some of the major issues in the criticism surrounding the canonical epigrams, in part because they raise intriguing biographical questions, in part because they were both attacked and justified by Victorian editors. The disagreements of these editors usefully sum up both the canons of taste and judgment on the question of Donne's "indecency" in the mid-to-late nineteenth century and the defensive strategies used to shield the poet from attack; they point also to the continuing interest in revising Donne's biography, an interest marked in this case by learned speculation on his primarily youthful and military activities and elsewhere in this volume by analysis and evaluation of his status within the system of court and aristocratic patronage.

A word should be said about the Latin poetry in this volume, Donne's relatively slender contribution to the vast Renaissance enterprise of literature in "dead" languages. With respect to Donne few dimensions of cultural and intellectual history are so neglected as this. That a strong defense of, and wide claims for, the significance of Donne's Latin verse (Vizioli 1967) should appear in the Sunday supplement of a great Brazilian newspaper is evidence that canons of judgment and taste are made to be broken and reformed and that Donne's poetry is, happily, not the exclusive property of academic scholarship and study.

The Order and Arrangement of the Poems in this Volume

The poems are ordered in this volume in accordance with both generic and chronological considerations. As is explained below in the General Textual Introduction to the Epigrams, epigrams are among the earliest of Donne's poems; and though the Latin originals putatively lying behind the *Sheaf of Miscellany Epigrams* may antedate them, the earliest of the undeniably canonical works presented here are those first English epigrams that formed the basis of Donne's evolving collection. Indeed, with the likely exception of *EpLin*, all the English epigrams were written prior to the other poems in this volume. It is clear that at some fairly early point in their history, if not from the very beginning, Donne conceived of the epigrams as a distinct (though malleable) poetic work and began to circulate the collection independently. Once the sequence began to percolate through the culture and to appear in various permutations in manuscript miscellanies and collections, of course, the epigrams were necessarily positioned amongst other poems, but there is great variety in their placement within the artifacts and no clear evidence that any of these contextual associations reflects authorial purpose. In H5, H8, and HH1—the manuscripts containing the early sequence of epigrams—the poems appear, variously, early (H8) and late (H5 and HH1) in the artifact, amidst love lyrics, elegies, and verse letters. In the expanded intermediate sequences in LR1 and NY3, moreover, they appear respectively as almost the only Donne poems in the artifact (LR1) and—following a collection of prose paradoxes—as the very last entry (save a single love lyric) in the manuscript (NY3). They also appear as the final poems in H6, where they precede a collection of Donne's prose paradoxes; and in the small collection of mixed genre in SN3, they follow the noncanonical "Absence, heare thou my protestation," constituting the last Donne poems entered in the artifact. In B7, CT1, DT1, H4—the four manuscripts containing the truncated late sequence—the epigrams appear after a large, variegated collection of elegies, verse letters, epicedes, and love lyrics and immediately precede the two epithalamions *EpLin* and *Eclog*, which are in turn followed in DT1 and H4 by epicedes and then in all four artifacts by Divine Poems and prose paradoxes. WN1, the sole manuscript to contain the sixteen-poem late sequence in full, exhibits slightly more integrity of genre within its various sections than does the B7–H4 group, but it orders its generic groupings differently: WN1 opens with *Corona* and eight Holy Sonnets, then follows with two verse letters, thirteen love elegies, *Storm*, *Calm*, the sixteen epigrams (*Hero* through *Martial*), fifty love lyrics in a row, *EpLin*, four epicedes, and a succeeding assortment of Divine Poems and verse letters.

Thus, whatever significance may inhere in the association of one epigram with another in the sequence, the evidence suggests that Donne circulated the group as an independent unit and that the early collectors of his poetry saw no necessary connection between it and other particular poems. The same may be said of the compilers of the seventeenth-century printed editions. It is true that the epigrams are kept together as a unit in all these issues, but their position relative to other poems varies: the compiler of A opens the 1633 edition with *Corona* and then continues with twelve Holy Sonnets, the epigrams, and a group of Ovidian elegies and poems of assorted genre; in the generic organization introduced in B in 1635 (and maintained in C–G), the epigrams are given the collective heading "EPIGRAMS," but are moved to follow *Metem* and the collection of fifty-four "SONGS AND SONETS" with which the volume opens. As in A, the epigrams are followed by love elegies in B–G.

It is doubtful that Donne ever thought of his three epithalamions as a group, partly because as occasional poems they derive from widely different periods in his career: *EpLin* was very probably written in the 1590s, while the last two (*EpEliz* and *Eclog*) date from nearly two decades later. Reflecting the cumulative manner in which the large manuscript collections of Donne's poems grew as various poems entered the stream of transmission, moreover, relatively few artifacts contain all three epithalamions. NY3, for instance, which generally contains earlier poems, has only the early *EpLin*, lacking *EpEliz* and *Eclog*. All of the members of the traditional B30–B32–C2–C8–O20–SP1 family (Grierson's Group I manuscripts) lack *EpLin*, and B30 contains none of the three poems. Of the Group II manuscripts (B7, B40, CT1, DT1, H4, TT1, TT2, WN1), only DT1 and H4 have all three epithalamions: B7 and CT1 lack *EpEliz*; WN1 lacks both *EpEliz* and *Eclog*, although they may have originally appeared on the now missing pages following *EpLin* in that manuscript; and B40, TT1, and TT2 contain none of the three. Of Grierson's large and somewhat amorphous family "associated with Group III" (B13, H3, H7, HH1, HH4, HH5, NY1, O21, VA2, Y2, Y3—see Beal 252), only HH1 contains all three, and in this case *EpLin* is absent from the original collection and has been entered in a later hand. B13, HH5, NY1, and VA2 lack *EpLin* and *Eclog*; HH4 lacks *EpLin* and *EpEliz*; O21 and the cognate Y3 lack *Eclog*; and none of the three epithalamions appears in H3, H7, and Y2. The only family all of whose members contain all three poems is that consisting of B46, C9, H5, and H6—Grierson's Group III family.

Of the six manuscripts that contain all three epithalamions in the primary scribal hand, two fail to group them all together, and none presents them in chronological order of composition. DT1 and the related H4 place *EpEliz* among the love lyrics (where it is preceded by *Fun* and followed by *ElProg*) and then group *EpLin* and *Eclog* (in that order) between the epigrams and two funeral poems (*Henry* and *Har*). B46 presents the three epithalamions as a unit, but without a generic heading, in the order *Eclog*, *EpEliz*, and *EpLin*, within a group of elegies. H5 also groups the three poems together, without a generic heading, within a group of elegies, but in the order *EpEliz*, *Eclog*, *EpLin*. The cognate manuscripts C9 and H6, the latter bearing a completion date of 1632 on its title page and apparently intended as the basis of an edition of Donne's poetry (see Beal 252), present the three as an autonomous unit headed "Epithalamions" in the order *EpEliz*, *EpLin*, *Eclog*. In the case of C9 the section is placed between the verse letters and the divine poems, while in H6 it appears between a group of noncanonical poems and the epigrams that constitute the last poetry in the artifact. All of the seventeenth-century editions of Donne's poems (A–G) group the three epithalamions together in the same order as is found in H5—*EpEliz*, *Eclog*, *EpLin*. A places them, without a generic heading, after a group of verse letters and before *Har*; B adds the section heading "EPITHALAMIONS, OR, MARRIAGE SONGS" and places them between the elegies and the satires. C–G retain B's generic section heading, order, and placement.

Except for the epitaph on his wife (*EtAD*), which survives in Donne's holograph and five scribal copies, each of the epitaphs and inscriptions in this volume exists in a single primary copy or (in the case of *EgDD*) edition; and none of these verses derives major significance from its artifactual association with other Donne poems. Essentially the same may be said of the miscellaneous poems that round out the volume—*Amic*, the verse from *Ignatius*, *Gaz*, *Stat*, and the dubious *Apoth*. None of these has a history of manuscript circulation (*Apoth* exists in two known copies), and only *Amic* and *Gaz* appear in the seventeenth-century collected editions, both having been introduced into the print tradition by Donne's son in E (1650), where they appear toward the end of the volume after the section of Divine Poems. The composition of all these poems, moreover—epitaphs, inscriptions, and miscellaneous poems alike—can be dated with considerable precision; we have thus grouped them here generically and, within generic groups, chronologically. As noted above, we have also followed this principle in the overall organization of the volume.

William A. McClung is the Commentary Editor for this volume as a whole, and was responsible primarily for the collection of commentary from materials before 1912, for all materials in languages other than English, for all editions of Donne's poetry, and for materials for the years 1979–88. Jeffrey Johnson, the Contributing Editor, was primarily responsible for commentary in the years 1912–78 and 1989–90, and exclusively for that on the *Stationes*, the verses from *Ignatius His Conclave*, and the epigraph to *Deaths Duell*.

Though the texts and apparatuses prepared for this volume are finally the product of collaborative analysis and effort, the editors carried out the primary work according to the following division of labor: Gary A. Stringer, beginning with a set of transcriptions from microfilm prepared by John T. Shawcross, was responsible for the epigrams, Ted-Larry Pebworth for the epithalamions, and Ernest W. Sullivan, II, for the epitaphs, inscriptions, and miscellaneous poems.

William A. McClung
Volume Commentary Editor

Ted-Larry Pebworth
Gary A. Stringer
Ernest W. Sullivan, II
Textual Editors

Effigy of Donne in his shroud in St. Paul's Cathedral. Photograph by the Courtauld Institute of Art. Printed by permission of the Dean and Chapter of St. Paul's Cathedral.

Texts and Apparatuses

THE
Epigrams

Early Sequence

Epigrams.

1.

If, in his study, Hamon hath such care,
To hang all old things, let his wife beware.

2.

Thy father all from thee, by his last will,
Gave to the poore, thou hast good title still.

3.

Thou in the feilds walk'st out thy supping houres
And yet thou sayst thou hast sup'd like a king
Like Nebuchadnezar, perchaunce, with grasse and floures
A sallade worse than Spanish dyeting.

4.

Mercurius Gallobelgicus. Græcus.

Like Æsops fellowe slaves, (O Mercury!)
Which could doe allthings, thy fayth is, and I,
Like Æsops selfe, which nothing: I confesse
I should have had more fayth, if thou hadst lesse
Thy credit lost thy credit; 'tis sinne to doe
In this case as thou wouldst be done unto,
To beleive all: chaunge thy name, thou arte like
Mercury in stealing, and ly'st like a Greeke.

5.

Thy flattering picture, Phrine, is lyke thee,
Only in this, that you both painted bee.

6.

Phylo with 12 yeares study hath beene greiv'd
To be understoode, when will he bee beleiv'd?

7.

Klockius so deeply hath vow'd ne're to come
In bawdy-house that he dares not goe home.

8.

Compassion in the world againe is bred
Ralphius is sicke, the broker keeps his bed.

9.

Under an undermin'de and shot-bruisd wall
The too-bold captaine perish'd by the fall
Whose brave misfortune happyest men envye'd
That had a towne for tombe his cor'ps to hyde.

Intermediate Sequence

Hero and Leander.

Both robd of ayre, we both ly in one ground,
Both whom one fyer had burn'd, one water dround.

Pyramus and Thisbe.

Two, by themselues, each other, Love and Feare
Slayne, cruell frinds, by parting haue ioynd here.

Niobe.

By chilldrens birth, and death I ame become
So dry, that I am now made myne owne tombe.

Nave arsa.

Out of a fyred Ship, which by no way
But drowning could be rescued from the flame,
Some men leap'd forthe, and ever as they came
Nere the foes Ships, did by ther Shott decay.
So all were lost, which in the Ship were found:
They in the Sea beeing burn't, they in the burnt ship drownd.

Caso d'vn muro.

Vnder an vnder-min'd, and shott brusd wall
A too bold Captaine perish'd by the fall;
Whose braue Misfortune happiest men envyde
That had a towne for tombe his corps to hyde.

Zoppo.

I ame vnable (yonder begger cryes)
To stand or move; yf he say trew, he lyes.

Calez and Guyana.

If you from spoyle of th'old worlds fardest end
To the new world your kindled valors bend
What brave Examples then do prove it trew
That one things end doth still begine a new.

Il Caualliere Gio: Wingefield.

Beyond th'old Pillers many'haue trauailed
Towards the Suns cradle, and his throne, and bed.
A fitter Piller our Earle did bestow
In that late Iland; for he well did know
Farther then Wingefield no man dares to go.

A selfe accuser.

Your Mistres, that you follow whores, still taxeth you,
Tis strange, she should confes it, though'it be true.

A licentious person.

Thy Sins and haires may no man equall call
For as thy Sins increase, thy haires do fall.

Antiquary.

If in his study Hammon hath such care
To'hang all old strange things, let his wife beware.

The Iughler.

Thou call'st me effeminat, for I love womens ioyes
I call not thee manly, though thou follow boyes.

Disinherited.

Thy father all from thee by his last will
Gaue to the poore; thou hast good title still.

The Lier.

Thou in the fields walkst out thy supping howres
And yet thou swearst thou hast supd like a king;
Like Nabuchadnezar perchance with gras and flowres
A Sallet, worse then Spanish dyeting.

Mercurius Gallobelgicus.

Like Æsops fellow slaues, O Mercury
Which could do all things, thy fayth is, and I
Like Æsops selfe, which nothing; I confes
I should haue had more fayth if thou hadst les.
Thy credit lost thy credit: tis Sinne to doo
In this case as thou wouldst be done vntoo,
To beleeue all. Change thy Name; thou art like
Mercury in stealing, and lyest like a Greeke.

Phrine.

Thy flattering picture Phrine, is like thee
Only in this that you both painted bee.

An obscure writer.

Philo, with 12 yeares study hath beene griev'd
To be'vnderstood, when will he be beleevd?

Klockius.

Klockius so deeply'hath vowd nere more to come
In bawdy house, that he dares not go home.

Martial: castratus.

Why this Man gelded Martial I muse;
Except himselfe alone his tricks would vse
As Katherine for the Coarts sake put downe Stews.

Ralphius.

Compassion in the World agayne is bredd
Ralphius is sick, the Broker keepes his bedd.

Late Sequence

Hero and Leander.

Both robd of aire wee both lie in one grownd,
Both whome one fire had burnd, one water drownd.

Piramis and Thisbe.

Two by them selues, each other, loue, and feare
Slaine, cruell frends by parting, haue ioynd here.

Niobe.

By childrens birth, and death, I am become
Soe dry, that I am now myne owne tombe.

A Burnt Ship.

Out of a fired Ship, which by noe waie
But drowning, could bee rescued from the flame,
Some men leapt forth, and euer as they came
Neer the foes ships did by their shott decaie.
Soe all were lost, which in the Ship were founde
They in the Sea being burnt, they in the burnt ship drownd.

Fall of a Wall.

Vnder an vndermind, and shott bruisd wall
A too bold Captaine perished by the fall;
Whose braue misfortune happiest men enuied,
That had a Towne for tomb, his bones to hide.

A Lame Begger.

I am vnable, yonder begger cryes
To stand, or moue, if hee say true hee lies.

A Selfe Accuser.

Your Mistrisse that yow follow whores still taxeth yow
Tis strange that shee should thus confess it though itt bee true.

A Licentious Person.

Thy sinns, and haires may no man equall call
For as thy sins increase, thy haires doe fall.

Antiquarye.

If in his studdie hee haue soe much care
To hang all, old strange thinges let his wife beware.

Disinherited.

Thy father all from thee by his last will
Gaue to the poore thou hast good title still.

Mercurius. Gallo-Belgicus.

Like Esops fellowe-slaues O Mercury,
Which could doe all things thi fayth is and I
Like Esops selfe, which nothinge: I confesse
I should haue had more fayth if thou hadst lesse.
Thy creditt, lost thy creditt: tis sin to doe
In this case, as thou woldst bee donne vnto,
To beleeue all. Change thy name: Thou art like
Mercury in stealing, but liest like a Greeke.

Phrine.

Thy flattering picture Phrine, is like thee
Only in this that yow both painted bee.

An Obscure Writer.

Philo with twelue yeares studie hath been griued
To bee vnderstood. When will hee bee beleeud?

Klockius.

Klockius so deeply hath sworne, nere more to come
In bawdy howse, that hee dares not goe home.

Raderus.

Why this Man gelded Martiall I mvse
Except him selfe alone his tricks would vse
As Katherin for the courts sake put downe stues.

Ralphius.

Compassion in the world againe is bred,
Ralphius is sicke, the Broker keeps his bed.

Additional Epigrams

Faustinus.

Faustinus keepes his Sister, and a Whore,
Faustinus keepes his Sister, and noe more.

Ad Autorem.

Emendare cupis Ioseph qui tempora; Leges
praemia, Supplicium, Religiosa cohors
Quod iam conantur frustra, Conabere frustra;
Si per te non sunt deteriora sat est.

Ad Autorem.

Non eget Hookerus tanto tutamine; Tanto
Tutus qui impugnat sed foret Auxilio.

Variant Versions of *Beggar*

Version 2

On a Begger.

I cannot goe, nor sitt, nor stand, the beggar cryes;
Yf that be true the beggar sayes, he lyes.

Version 3

On a criple.

I cannot goe, nor stand the cripple cryes.
What doth hee then? If he say true hee lyes.

Version 4

A beggar.

I cannot stand, nor sitt, this begger cries
How can this bee, if he say true, he lies.

Version 5

Of a beggar that lay on the ground.

He can not goe nor sitt nor stand the beggar cryes.
Then though he speake the truthe yet still he Lyes.

Version 6

On a Cripple.

I can nor go, nor stand, the cripple cries,
Nor yet can sitt; if he sayes true, he lies.

Version 7

A Lame Beggar.

Lord helpe lorde helpe the beggar cries
I can neyther goe sit nor stand.
If he say true he lies.

General Textual Introduction to the Epigrams

The epigrams are among Donne's earliest poems. Indeed, R. C. Bald has suggested that *Wall* was inspired by an event that took place at Corunna in 1589 and that Donne may have witnessed the event personally and have written the poem soon thereafter (see the Commentary on *Wall*). Further, in H5 and HH1, the manuscripts preserving the earliest text of the poem and the earliest grouping of epigrams, *Wall* is preceded by eight other epigrams, a placement implying that Donne was already an active practitioner of the genre before the occurrence at Corunna evoked his response. Without further evidence, unfortunately, the dating of these earliest epigrams and the order of their composition cannot be determined exactly; a number of others, however, may be dated with a fair degree of precision, for they are clearly based on Donne's experiences at Cadiz in 1596 and must have been written very close to that time. *Martial*, on the other hand, another poem traceable to a specific historical event, cannot have been written before 1602, when Matthew Rader's expurgated edition of Martial's epigrams first appeared. Donne's active period as a writer of epigrams, therefore, would appear to have spanned, roughly, the last decade of the sixteenth century; and, as the following discussion will show, various groups of them began to circulate in manuscript almost immediately after their composition. For further information on the subject matter and occasions of the epigrams, including evidence for dating the various poems, see the Commentary.

As Figure 1 shows, the epigrams circulated widely in the seventeenth century. The manuscripts preserve nearly 300 separate copies of these 21 poems, and some of the individual epigrams were highly popular—*Beggar* survives in 53 manuscript transcriptions, for instance, and *Licent* in 28. A group of 16 epigrams was included in the seventeenth-century collected editions of 1633–1669 (A–G), and several appeared in print elsewhere in anthologies and poetical miscellanies. Because their brevity and point made them easy to remember, moreover, some of the epigrams were apparently passed about by word of mouth, outside the more stable medium of written communication, and this oral proliferation is evident in the variety of the forms in which some of the poems survive. There is also compelling evidence that Donne revised the texts of individual poems over the course of time and that the sequences in which the epigrams are arranged in various major artifacts reflect the author's controlling hand as well. Indeed, although minor differences in the contents of the artifacts make it impossible to describe each stage with absolute precision, a comprehensive examination of the seventeenth-century data shows that Donne worked on his epigrams in at

Figure 1:
Copies of Epigrams in Seventeenth-Century Artifacts

Source	Hero	Pyr	Niobe	Ship	Wall	Beggar	Cales	Wing	SelfAc	Licent	Antiq	Jug	Disinher	Liar	Merc	Phrine	Philo	Klock	Martial	Ralph	Faust
B5						3															
B7	1	1	2	1	3	1				1	3				2	1	1	3	1		
B20						6															
B23	1,1									1											
B24						3															
B26						3															
B28	1	1		1		1			3	1	3		1			1	1	3		1	
B34						5															1
B37						3															
B45						1			3	1						1					
B46											1										
B47	1	1	1	1	3	1					3				2	1			1		
BD1						3															
C5						4															
C10			3																		
C12						2															
CJ1						1			X	1											
CT1	1	1	2	1	3	1				1	3				2	1	1	3	1		
DR2						3															
DT1	1	1	2	1	3	1				1	3				2	1	1	3	1		
F3						3				1											
F7						2				1	1			1							
F12						3															
F17						3,3															
H3		1									2		1	1							
H4	1	1	2	1	3	1				1	3				2	1	1	3	1		
H5					1	2			1	1	1		1	1	1	1	1	1		1	
H6	1	1	1	1	2	1	1	1	1	1	1		1	1	1	1	1	1	1	1	
H7															1						
H8											1		1	1	1	1	1	2			
HH1					1				1		1		1	1	1	1	1	1		1	
HH2						3															
HH4															2						
LA1										1											
LR1	1	1	1	1	2	1			2	1	2	1	1	2	1	1	1	2			
LR2						1,3															
LU1																			1		
NY3	1	1	1	1	2	1	1	1	2	1	2	1	1	2	1	1	1	2	1	1	
O1										1											
O3										1											
O4						1															
O10						3				1											
O11						3															
O16						3															
O18											3										
O21		1				1					2		1	1							
O23						3															
O25		1									1		1	1							
O30										1											
O36													1								
O41						1			X	1			1					X			
O42						3															
OC2						3				1						1					
R3						1				1											
R8						2															
R9						3									1						
SA1	1	1		1	3	1				1	3					1	1				
SN3	1	1	1		2	4			2	1	1	1	1	2		1		X		1	1
SN4						4															1
TM1						1															
TT1																					1
VA3	1					1,7				1			1					2			
WN1	1	1	2	1	3	1			3	1	3		1		2	1	1	3	1	1	
Y1						3				1											
Y2															2						
Y3		1				1					2		1	1							
Y5						3															
Y6										1											
Y7	1					1															
A-G	1	1	3	1	3	1			3	1	3		1		2	1	1	3	1	1	
16										1											
17A										1											
17B										1											
30					3	1							1			1		3			
46	1									1											

Arabic numeral = version of poem x = version indeterminate

least three major phases over the years. Initially he circulated a group of some eight to ten poems, and these were subsequently subsumed into a reorganized and expanded sequence comprising, in the fullest collection, twenty epigrams. In the last phase he circulated the slightly reduced sequence of sixteen poems that found its way into print in the 1633 edition. What points to the author's controlling hand in this development is not only the continuity in the ordering of poems observable at the points of major expansion or contraction of the work, but also the existence of distinct forms of individual poems at the three separate stages through which the larger whole evolved. Evidence of the author's shaping of The Epigrams at the macro level is thus supported by evidence of his alteration at the micro level of the texts of individual epigrams.

In order to facilitate critical appreciation of the epigrams as an evolving work constituted by distinct versions, therefore, we have presented them here in multiple sequences—sequences that not only represent the various arrangements within which the poems occur in the seventeenth-century artifacts, but also preserve within their contents the alternate versions of individual epigrams. For the fullest sequence (that found in NY3) we have provided a textual apparatus that contains a collation of all existent copies of each poem and represents schematically the significant variant forms of particular poems. Additionally, for *Beggar*, the variant versions of which cannot all be adequately represented in a single apparatus, we have printed each version separately and provided each with its own historical collation. In Figure 2, moreover, we have charted the appearance and ordering of epigrams in all manuscripts that contain at least four poems and in the collected editions. Looking at these arrangements in conjunction with the details of the texts they contain provides the following general picture of the seventeenth-century textual history of the epigrams.

The earliest group of epigrams in circulation seems to be that preserved (with some variation) in H5, H8, HH1, and the first part of the sequence in H6.[1] These manuscripts present a core of seven poems—*Antiq*, *Disinher*, *Liar*, *Merc*, *Phrine*, *Philo*, *Klock*—though H5 has *Liar* and *Merc* out of sequence and H8 gives the intermediate text of *Klock*, suggesting that it (or its source) may originally have contained only six poems. Following *Klock* in H5, H6, and HH1 is *Ralph*; and *Wall* follows immediately in HH1 and closely in H5 (indeed, H5's copy of *Beggar*, which intervenes between *Ralph* and *Wall*, is a variant version, probably reconstructed from memory, and it is followed by the noncanonical "Two fallinge out" [see Appendix 2], facts suggesting that these poems were interpolated into the received sequence either by the scribe of H5 or at some earlier stage of the transmission of the group). Both H5 and HH1 preserve a similar (and early) form of the text of *Wall*, and H6 shares their distinctive reading in line 2—"The" (for "A") "too bold Captayne"—but H6's heading ("Cæso d'un muro"), as well as its position in its sequence, suggests that the H6 scribe acquired his copy of

[1]In referring variously to "early," "intermediate," or "late" forms of texts in this discussion, we necessarily associate these forms with specific manuscripts and printed books. Readers should bear in mind, however, a distinction between the date or relative evolutionary position of the text as linguistic structure and the actual chronological relationships of various acts of inscription or of the physical artifacts within which the poems appear: a manuscript compiled in 163[illegible], for instance, may preserve a text in an earlier form than an artifact assembled in 1620.

Figure 2: Sequences of Epigrams in Seventeenth-Century Artifacts

(Listed are all collections of four or more of the poems.)

Poem	Early Sequence/ Texts			Intermediate Sequence/ Texts		Collections of Mixed Origins		Minor Collections of Indeterminate or Mixed Origins								Late Sequence/Texts							Texts Derived From Print		
	H5	H8	HH1	LR1	NY3	H6	SN3	B47	F7	H3	O25	O21	Y3	O41	VA3	B7	CT1	DT1	H4	SA1	WN1	A-G	B28	B45	30
Hero				1	1	**17**	**3**	2							1	1	1	1	1	8	1	1	1		
Pyr				2	2	**12**	**4**	4		4	4	1	1			2	2	2	2	9	2	2	2		
Niobe				3	3	**14**	**5**	1								3^2	3^2	3^2	3^2		3^2	3^3			
Ship				4	4	**15**		6								4	4	4	4	**6**	4	4	3		
Wall	9		9	5^2	5^2	**18^2**	**6^2**	7^3								5^3	5^3	5^3	5^3	**7^3**	5^3	5^3			1^3
Beggar	8^2			6	6	**16**	2^4	5	**2^2**			5	5	**5**	2;6^7	6	6	6	6	1	6	6	4	1	2
Cales					7	**11**																			
Wing					8	**10**																			
SelfAc	2		**10**	7^2	9^2	**19***	**7^2**							1							7^3	7^3	5^3	2^3	
Licent	12			8	10	**13***	**8**		**4**					**4**	3	7	7	7	7	2	8	8	6	3	
Antiq	1	1	1	10^2	11^2	2	**9**	8^3	1	1^2	3	**2^2**	**2^2**			8^3	8^3	8^3	8^3	3^3	9^3	9^3	7^3		
Jug				9	12		**12**																		
Disinher	3	2	2	11	13	**3**	**13**			2	2	**3**	**3**	**2**	4						10	10	8		3
Liar	10	3	3	12^2	14^2	**4**	**15^2**		3	3	1	**4**	**4**												
Merc	11	**4**	**4**	16	15	**5**		10^2								9^2	9^2	9^2	9^2		11^2	15^2			
Phrine	4	5	5	13	16	**6**	**14**	**3**								10	10	10	10	4	12	11	9	4	4
Philo	5	6	6	14	17	**7**										11	11	11	11	5	13	12	10		
Klock	6	7^2	7	15^2	18^2	**8**	**11**							**3**	5^2	12^3	12^3	12^3	12^3		14^3	13^3	11^3		5^3
Martial					19	1*		9								13	13	13	13		15	14			
Ralph	7		8		20	**9**	**10**														16	16	12		
Faust							1																		

Arabic numerals = ordinal position of poem among epigrams in ms.
* = poem squeezed in after others were entered.

Normal/boldface changes = breaks in sequence.
Superscripts = numbered variant version of the poem.

Wall at a somewhat later stage of that poem's evolution ("Cæso"—for "Caso"—is in fact an orthographic anomaly and may point to an oral link somewhere in the chain of transmission). *SelfAc* also appears in a related—and early—text (though not in the same place in the sequence) in H5, H6, and HH1. Both H5 and H6, moreover, include the text of *Licent* in an early form, the copy in H6 definitely being a late addition to the artifact and that in H5, which appears at the bottom of a page, perhaps being such.

Though some refinement of the account here given may be possible (see the discussion of O21 and Y3 below), the next major stage in the transmissional history of the epigrams appears to involve Donne's revision of certain details in these early texts and his integration of the revised poems into the enlarged arrangement represented in LR1. In every case of notable variation between the H5–HH1 texts and those of LR1 (i.e., in *Antiq* 2, *Liar* 2, *Klock* 1, *Wall* 2, and *SelfAc* 1), LR1 has the later version; and in addition to incorporating these revisions of individual texts, the lost holograph from which LR1 ultimately derives added *Hero*, *Pyr*, *Niobe*, *Ship*, *Beggar*, and *Jug* to the eleven early epigrams in the H5–HH1 group, Donne having forgotten to include the previously circulated *Ralph* in this expanded sequence or the LR1 scribe having failed to copy it for some reason. The appearance of *Ship* and *Beggar* in LR1, epigrams apparently inspired by Donne's military experiences in 1596–97, and the absence of *Martial* place the compilation of this arrangement between June of 1596 and 1602, the earliest date by which the latter poem could have been composed.

Unique readings in LR1's texts of *Antiq* 1 ("take" for "hath"), *Liar* 3 ("hearbes" for "gras"), *Phrine* 1 ("Latrine" for "Phrine"), *Klock* 1 ("Rawlings" for "Klockius"), and *Jug* 2 ("thee not" for "not thee") differentiate LR1's texts from those of NY3, which represents not only the subsequent stage of textual transmission for the epigrams mentioned above, but also the author's further expansion of the sequence to include *Cales*, *Wing*, and *Martial*, as well as the reintroduction of the omitted *Ralph*. It will be noted, of course, that the two manuscripts order their sixteen shared poems in exactly the same way, except that LR1 reverses the order of *Antiq* and *Jug* and places *Merc* at the end of the group rather than after *Liar*, the latter change almost certainly owing to the scribe's having lacked sufficient space in which to enter the eight-line *Merc* after *Liar* at the bottom of folio 279v in the manuscript. The presence of *Martial* necessitates a post-1602 date for the formation of the NY3 sequence, and most noteworthy in light of this fact is Donne's inclusion of *Cales* and *Wing*, two poems that he must have had in hand since his days as a soldier in 1596–97. These two epigrams, as Figure 1 shows, appear only in NY3 and H6 among seventeenth-century artifacts, and variants in the H6 texts—especially that of the corrupt *Wing*—suggest that the scribe may have been transcribing from memory rather than actually copying from another manuscript. If this is so, then NY3's copies of *Cales* and *Wing* may represent the sole instance of the written dissemination of these texts. Whether Donne regarded these epigrams as politically incendiary or in some other way indecorous, it is clear that he carefully restricted their circulation, and it is probably only because the scribe of NY3 was his friend Rowland Woodward that he allowed those copies to be taken. *Cales* and *Wing* did not appear again for almost three centuries.

Though H6 and SN3, the latter a manuscript written in the hand of the Scottish poet William Drummond, contain relatively large collections of epigrams, neither stands in the mainstream of transmission for these poems. Both, however, are highly important to an understanding of the textual history of the epigrams, providing perspective on specific details within other collections, witnessing to the dispersal of the texts throughout the culture, and, more broadly, illuminating the means by which manuscript collections came into being in the earlier seventeenth century. As suggested above, the texts of a number of the poems in H6 are very early. Generally speaking, however, for those in the latter half of its sequence—*Pyr*, *Niobe*, *Beggar*, *Hero*, and *Wall*, as for *Cales* and *Wing*—its texts are later, appearing to descend in some unspecifiable way from NY3 or its prototype (H6's copy of *Martial*, squeezed in on the bottom of page 336 after the main body of epigrams had been entered, is headed "Raderus," thus reading with even later manuscripts). In addition to entitling *Wall* "Cæso d'un muro," H6 follows NY3 in providing foreign-language headings for *Ship*, *Beggar*, and *Wing*, and its texts for these later epigrams generally read with NY3 and, in those many instances where the two agree, with NY3's immediate predecessor LR1 (that H6 gives the foreign title for *Wall* while LR1 does not suggests that its texts for this second group of poems derive from the tradition somewhat later than those of LR1). We have noted above the possibility that H6's texts of *Cales* and *Wing* were reconstructed from memory, and its unique reading "doth taxe" in line 1 of *SelfAc*, a poem the scribe apparently acquired at the very end of his collecting, suggests that this text may also have been entered from memory. As will be noted below, H6 has three epigrams—two of which are related to Donne's youthful military adventures and the other of which contains a derisive reference to Spain—that never appear in the seventeenth-century printed editions (A–G). Since other evidence suggests that in 1635 the printer of B used H6 (or a manuscript very like it) to correct and supplement A (see Beal 252), it seems likely that the printer of B regarded these "Spanish" epigrams as untimely, politically inappropriate, or pointless in some way and passed up the opportunity to interpolate them into his augmented edition.

The genealogy of the epigrams in SN3 is somewhat muddled, no doubt partly because the scribe, William Drummond the poet, made conscious alterations in accordance with his own aesthetic lights (some of the variations Drummond records can hardly be accounted for otherwise) and partly because Drummond was a careless copyist. It is even arguable that in some cases Drummond did not transcribe from a manuscript at all, but entered from memory something he had picked up in conversation or read at an earlier time (see the Commentary on *Phrine* for Drummond's reminiscence of Ben Jonson's quoting an epigram from memory). Whatever mental and physical conditions affected their inscription, the appearance of epigrams in two separate places within the manuscript and the ordering of the major group suggest that SN3 does not derive from a single ancestral source. For most of the poems that exhibit enough variation to enable the drawing of family distinctions, however, Drummond's texts are related to the LR1–NY3 secondary stage of evolution, reading "now made my" in *Niobe* 2, "Caso di muro" in the (grammatically incomplete) heading of *Wall*, "still taxeth" in *SelfAc* 1, and "swearst" in *Liar* 2. His text of *Antiq*, on the other hand, which omits "strange" in line 2, reads with the earliest H5–HH1 group, and his version of *Beggar* is considerably removed from the primary version. Several of Drummond's unique readings—"paine ion'd heere" in *Pyr* 2, "Klockius hath sworne so deep neuer" in *Klock* 1, and "that I loue woemens toyes" in *Jug* 1, for instance—reflect either a conscious attempt at improvement, carelessness, or possibly (especially in the case of the extremely rare *Jug*) a failure of memory. Cavalier as Drummond was in the handling of these texts, SN3 is an important witness to the breadth of their circulation, and its copies of both *Jug* and *Faust* constitute a third of the total contemporary evidence that these epigrams ever existed. Possibly, though not certainly, the absence of *Martial* provides a *terminus ad quem* for the assembly of Drummond's collection, since we might expect one poet to be interested enough to record another's epigrammatic attack on an edition of a third if he knew that attack existed.

As with H6 and SN3, the texts of the epigrams in the group of eight artifacts listed to the immediate right of SN3 in Figure 2 stand outside the mainstream of transmission, assuming their major importance as indices of the way in which the poems circulated through the culture in poetical miscellanies and commonplace books. Though O25 and H3 are cognate, as are O21 and Y3, no further relationships among these eight artifacts are apparent, and they are grouped in Figure 2 and here discussed together for the sake of convenience.

(1) B47 derives its first three poems (*Niobe*, *Hero*, and *Phrine*) from the stage of transmission represented in NY3 (reading "now, made mine" in *Niobe* 2, for instance), but its texts of *Pyr* through *Merc* (numbered 4–10 on the chart), which include the second version of *Antiq*, are late, related to those that eventually appear in the printed editions.

(2) F7's copies of *Antiq* and *Liar* reflect the earliest textual tradition for those poems (reading "all old thinges" in *Antiq* 2 and "sayst" in *Liar* 2), and its texts of both *Beggar* and *Licent* stand at some distance from the standard version, suggesting that they may derive from a tradition of oral transmission.

(3) O25 and H3 contain the same group of four poems in virtually the same order, and are further linked by their subscriptions for each poem (H3 attributes all four to "J. D.," while O25 subscribes two "J. D." and two "J. Deane," a discrepancy suggesting either their descent from a common source or the priority of O25) and by the reading "perhaps" in *Liar* 3. The first three epigrams in O25 and H3—*Antiq*, *Disinher*, and *Liar*—are, of course, among the earliest epigrams Donne circulated, while *Pyr* enters the tradition at the subsequent stage of development; and the traditions reflected in the texts of these poems are correspondingly varied: in *Antiq*, *Disinher*, and *Pyr* the pair read with the middle texts LR1 and NY3, while their text of *Liar* stems from the earlier H5–HH1 tradition.

(4) O21 and Y3—though they have four poems in common with O25 and H3—are not closely related to the latter pair. The family relationship of O21 and Y3, however, also observable in their texts of Donne poems in other genres, is manifest here not only in their presenting the same five poems analogously dispersed amongst the rest of their respective contents, but, especially, in their running together as a single poem *Antiq*, *Disinher*, and *Liar* above the identical subscription "ffinis." Their texts of these three epigrams are genealogically mixed: with LR1 and NY3 they read "Hamon" and "all old strange things" in *Antiq*, yet in *Liar* 2 they read "saist" with the earlier H5–HH1 group (as opposed to the "swearst" found in LR1 and NY3). Taken together, these readings suggest that this cluster of poems derives from the stream of transmis-

sion at some point of transition between the earliest and the secondary stage of evolution—somewhere between the H5–HH1 compilation and that found in LR1. Separated from the other epigrams and from each other, the texts of *Pyr* and *Beggar* in these two artifacts are necessarily middle to late, in each case showing the effects of distance from the mainstream. They share the illiteracy "Slain'd" in *Pyr* 2, and while they record the primary version of *Beggar*, they read "stand or goe" rather than the normative "stand or move," O21 reversing the two words through carelessness.

(5) O41 is a manuscript book of jests compiled by Archbishop William Sancroft in the mid- to late-seventeenth century (see Beal 327). None of its five Donne epigrams is attributed, however, and they do not follow the sequence found in A–G; they thus do not seem to derive directly from the printed tradition, though such would have been historically possible. In ways either slight (*Beggar* 2 reads "To go, or move: if he sth true...") or major (*Klock* begins "So deeply N. hath vow'd," e.g.), each of Sancroft's texts is variant, and it is not clear whether he or some earlier transmitter of the poems is responsible for the differences. If somewhat outside the mainstream of transmission, Sancroft's updated versions nonetheless provide interesting testimony of the way in which epigrams could be adapted to serve in a time far removed from their original moment of piquancy.

(6) The five epigrams initially entered into VA3 (*Hero*, *Beggar* [authorial version], *Licent*, *Disinher*, and *Klock*) are collectively subscribed "J. D." and must have come into the copyist's hands as a previously circulating collection. The order in which they occur, as well as the form of their individual texts, furthermore, indicates that they derive from the tradition at some point after the establishment of the major sequence represented in LR1 and NY3 (the second copy of *Beggar* is a unique, highly unmetrical version entered below the initial group and the subscription). The lack of a heading on any of the poems except *Hero* suggests that the original of the group was assembled at a stage after the Italian headings found in LR1 and NY3 had disappeared and before the later addition of a title for *Disinher*; and the reading "no man may" (for "may no man") in *Licent* 1 similarly suggests some distance between these copies and Donne's holograph, yet enough proximity that the phrase had not metamorphosed to the "no man can" found in more derivative manuscripts.

In the final stage of transmission prior to their publication in 1633, the epigrams appear in the five major manuscripts shown next in Figure 2—B7, CT1, DT1, H4, and WN1 (the texts in SA1 derive from a subfamily comprising B7 and CT1, and their particular features are discussed in the introductions to individual poems). These sources confirm certain aspects of the previously existing tradition, while introducing a number of changes that surely reflect authorial intention. Of major significance is the fact that, *mutatis mutandis*, these manuscripts recapitulate the sequence of epigrams found in LR1 and NY3, thus confirming Donne's continued endorsement of it. They also evince his modification of the thematic content of the collection, omitting in particular the "Spanish" poems *Cales*, *Wing*, and *Liar*. The first two of these, as noted above, Donne seems never to have felt comfortable in circulating, and the last, with its explicit derogation of "Spanish dyeting," might have seemed politically tactless or even inflammatory (under a generic title, of course, he was able to salvage "Zoppo" for inclusion in the revamped sequence). Also missing from all these artifacts is the extremely rare *Jug*, and the cognate manuscripts B7, CT1, DT1, and H4 lack *SelfAc*, *Disinher*, and *Ralph* as well. The scarcity of *Jug* may always have been due to its indelicate subject matter (indeed, the poem never saw print until the edition of Bennett in 1942, though editors had known of its existence since at least the 1890s, when Edmund Gosse owned NY3), but whether these three latter omissions and the shorter sequence thus produced reflect a distinct stage of authorial intention is unclear. The theme of *SelfAc* might have rendered it undesirable for circulation over the name of a man who wished to polish his image as a trustworthy citizen and husband, but it is hard to see how this objection would account for his withholding *Disinher* and *Ralph* from the B7–H4 sequence. If this smaller grouping is authorial and does not merely represent an accident or a scribal mishandling of the sixteen-poem sequence from which WN1 ultimately stems, its reduced size is more likely traceable to carelessness or forgetfulness than to conscious purpose on Donne's part (we might recall that he had apparently forgotten *Ralph* when compiling the LR1 sequence). In any case, the texts of the individual epigrams shared by the B7–H4 group and by WN1 are identical in all important respects (differences are discussed in the introductions to individual poems); and the sixteen-poem sequence preserved in WN1, except for one bibliographically explainable alteration of its order, is that which appears not only in the seventeenth-century collected editions, but also in all subsequent editions prior to the twentieth century. This sixteen-poem sequence is essentially that which Donne had constituted sometime between 1596 and 1601 when inscribing the prototype for LR1 and had reconfirmed, with certain additions appropriate for an intimate friend, in the papers upon which NY3 is based. When it appeared in print in 1633, it thus bore an accumulated authorial endorsement of over thirty years' standing.

In this last major stage, the texts of a number of the epigrams undergo a final evolution, and the alternative to ascribing the majority of these changes ultimately to Donne is to imagine a massive editorial revision at the hands of an enormously presumptuous scribe. The "now made myne owne" of *Niobe* 2 is changed to "now myne owne" in these latest manuscripts, thus resolving a semantic contradiction between "made" and "become" in the previous line (though not without a loss in metrical regularity); and the reading "A too bold" in *Wall* 2, which had already been changed from "The too bold" as the poem moved from the H5–HH1 group to the LR1–NY3 stage, is retained in the B7–WN1 group and joined by the alteration of the phrase "corps to hyde" to "Bones to hide" in line 4, a revision reflecting the even further recession into the past of the inspiring event at Corunna. Like *Wall*, the previously revised *SelfAc* here shows a third stage of evolution (the poem appears in only WN1 of these latest manuscripts), changing the "strange, she should confes it" reading of LR1–NY3 to "strange that shee should thus confess it" and presenting a couplet in alexandrines rather than one of mixed hexameter and pentameter meters. In *Antiq*, as with "Zoppo"/"A Lame Beggar," Donne apparently saw the opportunity to salvage an epigram that had become either obscure or, in altered political circumstances, awkward: in any case, he revises the specific "Hammon" of the earlier version to the categorical "hee haue," creating what we have presented in this edition as a third distinct version of the poem. The text of *Merc* likewise manifests a significant change, the reading "and lyest" in line 6 moving to "but lyest" in this later stage. And Donne here makes a final adjustment to *Klock*. The earliest H5–HH1 texts read "vow'd ne're to come" in *Klock* 1; this wording gives way to "vowd nere more to come" at the intermediate stage of LR1–NY3, and is here replaced with "sworne nere more to come," thus evincing a three-step evolution over the years similar to that noted above in *Antiq*, *Wall*, and *SelfAc*.

In addition to the previously noted alterations within the lines of the epigrams, headings for several of them are either changed or, in half a dozen cases, added for the first time; and in light of Donne's efforts in revising the texts of the poems, it seems likely that he effected these revisions of the headings as well. Generally speaking, the headings on the epigrams in B7–WN1 and, later, A–G reflect the increasing distance of the poems from the occasions that originally inspired them and bespeak an effort to give them currency in a different, more public arena. Several of the earliest poems—*SelfAc*, *Licent*, *Disinher*, *Phrine*, and *Philo*—receive their first titles ever at this third stage of their evolution, as does the revised version of *Antiq*; and those that had born Italian or Latin titles in LR1–NY3—*Ship*, *Wall*, *Beggar*, and *Martial*—are refitted with more accessible English equivalents. In accordance with Drummond's personal habits of inscription, *Klock* and *Ralph* are given formal headings in SN3, but they remain untitled in these late—and, indeed, in all other authoritative—manuscripts (for headings given these poems in B28, see the respective historical collations). Whether, when preparing his final collection (or collections) of epigrams, Donne consciously declined to title these two poems or whether the headings he assigned them were lost, they were apparently judged intelligible without titles by the compiler of the 1633 edition and his seventeenth-century successors, for they remain untitled in A–G.

Among the seventeenth-century printed editions, A's text of the epigrams derives directly from WN1 or a lost cognate manuscript, as is shown both in the verbal detail of individual poems and in the arrangement of the sequence. As M. Thomas Hester (1990) has pointed out, A's headings for the poems are identical to those in WN1; and, with minor exceptions, A reads with WN1 in its texts of the poems—indeed, in the reading "hairs" (rather than "hair") in *Licent* 1, A aligns itself with WN1 against all other major manuscripts that preserve late texts of the poems (i.e., B7, CT1, DT1, and H4). In some few cases, it should be noted, A diverges from WN1 in ways that either point to compositorial intervention or suggest that the setting text of A was a lost manuscript differing slightly from WN1. A prints "Phryne" for WN1's "Phrine," for example, and changes WN1's "haue" to "hath" in *Antiq* 1; and A corrects WN1's erroneous "with" to "which" in *Merc* 3 and its similarly mistaken "as" in *Wall* 1 to "an"—all alterations of which a reasonably alert compositor might be capable. A's most noticeable alteration of WN1's wording, however—almost certainly representing an attempt at compositorial sophistication—occurs in the text of *Niobe*, where the "birth" of line 1 is pluralized to "births" and the meter of line 2 is regularized by the interjection of "sad" between "owne" and "tombe." As Figure 2 shows, A also in one instance changes the order of the epigrams found in WN1, moving *Merc* from its place after *Disinher* to a later point in the sequence. As in its placement in LR1, the repositioning of *Merc* in A can be accounted for bibliographically: at ten lines (including title, blank line, and text), the epigram could not have been set between *Disinher* and *Phrine* on page 42 in A without disrupting the pattern of the page layout;

it appears, therefore, that the compositor extracted *Merc* from its place in the sequence, moved the remaining poems forward in the queue, and reinserted *Merc* on the following page, where he had more room to maneuver (see Shawcross, 1986a, 123). B–G derive successively from A, retaining A's alterations of WN1 and, at two different points, independently introducing an additional verbal change that carries forward in the train of transmission: B, on no manuscript authority, alters "towne" in *Wall* 4 to "towre"; and D, in an apparent attempt at metrical repair of *Phrine* 1, inserts "to" after "like" at the end of the line. B28, B45, and 30, listed to the right of A–G in Figure 2, take their texts from one of the printed editions—apparently A, B, or C, since none contains the "like to" reading of D–G in *Phrine* 1.

The modern editions of Tonson (H), Bell (I), Anderson (J), Chalmers (K), and Lowell? (M) derive successively from the printed tradition in G, presenting sixteen epigrams in G's sequence and printing its readings "towre" for "towne" in *Wall* 4 and "like to" in *Phrine* 1, as well as repeating G's error "I amuse" (for "I muse") in *Martial* 1. Grosart (N) also follows the print tradition embodied in D–G, giving sixteen epigrams in the standard order and reproducing the distinctive readings of D–G in *Wall* 4 and *Phrine* 1; in addition, however, Grosart appends *Liar* from Simeon (70), correcting its orthography against H8. Lowell (O) uses A as copy-text, following it in both sequence and wording, as does Chambers (P), although Chambers, like Grosart before him, adds *Liar* (from Simeon) at the end of the group. Grierson (Q) follows the order and text of A, except that he appropriates *Cales*, *Wing*, and *Liar* from NY3, interpolating the first two between *Lame* and *SelfAc* and adding *Liar* at the end. Hayward (S) imitates Grierson's procedure exactly, as does Bennett (T), except that Bennett also appropriates *Jug* from NY3, printing it for the first time and inserting it (under the coined heading "Manliness") between *Antiq* and *Disinher*—the position it occupies in NY3. Milgate (Y), while denoting A as his copy-text for the sixteen poems it contains, actually presents an eclectic text that includes all twenty of NY3's epigrams in NY3's order and frequently diverges from A toward NY3 in its texts of individual poems. Shawcross (Z) also uses A as copy-text for the text of its sixteen poems, adding *Cales*, *Wing*, and *Jug* from NY3 and *Faust* from SN3; Shawcross arranges the poems in an editorially constructed sequence that follows A's order for the first eight epigrams (*Hero* through *Licent*) and then interpolates *Cales* and *Wing* before continuing with *Antiq*, *Disinher*, *Liar*, *Merc*, *Phrine*, *Philo*, *Klock*, *Ralph*, *Jug*, *Faust*, and *Martial*. Declining to declare a copy-text for the epigrams, Smith (AA) generally follows A in the major verbal variants of individual poems (his readings of *Niobe* 2 and *SelfAc* 2 diverge from this rule), and his ordering of the poems resembles that of the seventeenth-century editions except that he inserts *Cales* and *Wing* after *Beggar* and attaches *Liar* and *Jug* (entitled "Manliness," as in T) at the end. Patrides (DD) generally follows A in both verbal structure and sequence, appending *Liar*, *Cales*, *Wing*, and *Jug* in eclectically constructed texts that seem to show the influence of both NY3 and, to a lesser extent, SN3.

For each of the three sequences of epigrams here presented we have used a single copy-text, chosen with respect both to the integrity of the texts of its individual poems and to the overall contents and ordering of the poems within the group. The early sequence is derived from HH1, a manuscript containing some 122 Donne poems, entered in two hands and, before its subsumption into the library of her husband in the mid-seventeenth century, probably owned by Frances Egerton, first Countess of Bridgewater, whose initials ("F B") are stamped in gold on both covers and whom Donne may have known since her birth in the 1580s (see Flynn, 1989a, 129). The epigrams were entered in the hand of the second scribe, at some time after April 1631, when the manuscript was apparently expanded, reorganized, and rebound. Among the artifacts containing the early sequence (H5, H6, H8, and HH1), HH1 preserves the group in the least corrupted state: H5, though generally containing early texts, must be rejected because it does not present the poems in the standard order; H6 presents early texts only through *Ralph*, and its omission of "perchaunce" in *Liar* 3 and its reading "That" (for "Which") in *Merc* 2 represent serious corruptions of the text; and H8, in addition to containing only seven epigrams in all, gives the intermediate text of *Klock* and exhibits such corruptions as "feild" (for "feilds") in *Liar* 1 and "Like Æsops selfe wch nothing I confesse" in *Merc* 3, the absence of punctuation in the latter instance rendering the line nonsensical. By contrast, HH1 preserves an intact sequence and is devoid of textual corruptions. Beyond the conventional expansion of abbreviations and brevigraphs, the raising of a few lower-case letters at the beginnings of lines to capitals, and the adaptation of the numerical headings to a standard format, HH1 requires only six emendations—all involving terminal punctuation at the end of a poem.

The choice of NY3 as copy-text for the intermediate sequence is inevitable. Not only does this manuscript preserve the greatest number of epigrams among seventeenth-century artifacts, but its provenance lends high authority both to its overall sequence and to its texts of individual epigrams. Once owned by Francis Fane, first Earl of Westmoreland, NY3 contains seventy-nine poems by Donne and is, as noted above, written in the hand of Donne's friend and Fane's quondam secretary Rowland Woodward. Its copies of the extremely scarce *Cales* and *Wing* may be the only ones that Donne ever consciously allowed to be taken, and its copy of *Jug* is one of only three that survive from the seventeenth century; moreover, its texts of all the epigrams are extremely clean. Apart from expanding abbreviations and supplying headings to several of the poems, in accordance with the conventions of print, almost no emendation of NY3 is required—we have had only to separate the "Iame" of *Niobe* 1 into "I ame" and supply a final period in *Ship*.

For the late sequence we have necessarily chosen WN1 as copy-text, since among the manuscripts that preserve late texts of the poems it alone contains the full complement of sixteen poems and since compositorial interference with the text and sequence of A renders it an unacceptable candidate. Once owned by the Lloyd family of Cynwyl Gaeo, Dyfed (formerly Carmarthenshire), WN1 is a compilation dating from *circa* 1622–33 of 129 poems by Donne, all entered in a single hand (Beal 251). In addition to the various adjustments necessary to prepare a scribal document for printing—expanding brevigraphs, providing italicized and punctuated headings, capitalizing the first letters in lines in a couple of instances, and regularizing the end-punctuation of lines in a few cases—the text requires two verbal emendations—of "as" to "an" in *Wall* 1 and of "with" to "which" in *Merc* 3. The text of *Merc* in particular is problematic, and providing a readable text has required not only the verbal emendation previously noted, but also major adjustment of the punctuation in lines 3, 4, and 7.

Copy-texts for the Three Sequences and List of Emendations

Early Sequence

Copy-text: HH1. **Emendations of the copy-text:** General Heading: *italics supplied* *Epigrams.*] Epigrams‸ **Antiq:** Heading: 1.] ~‸ 2 To] to beware.] ~‸ **Disinher:** Heading: 2.] ~‸ 2 Gave] gave the] y^{e} **Liar:** Heading: 3.] ~‸ 2 And] & 3 Like] like perchaunce] ꝑchaunce with] wth and] & 4 A] a dyeting.] ~‸ **Merc:** Heading: *italics supplied* 4.] ~‸ *Græcus*.] Græcus‸ 2 Which] wch and] & 3 Like] like which] wch 6 In] in 8 and] & Greeke.] ~‸ **Phrine:** Heading: 5.] ~‸ 2 Only] only that] y^{t} **Philo:** Heading: 6.] ~‸ 1 with] wth 2 To] to beleiv'd?] ~‸ **Klock:** Heading: 7.] ~‸ 2 In] in bawdy-house] bawdy=house that] y^{t} **Ralph:** Heading: 8.] ~‸ 1 the] y^{e} 2 the] y^{e} bed.] ~‸ **Wall:** Heading: 9.] ~‸ 1 and] & shot-bruisd] shot=bruisd 2 The] y^{e} too-bold] too=bold perish'd] ꝑish'd the] y^{e} 3 Whose] whose 4 That] y^{t} hyde.] ~‸

Intermediate Sequence

Copy-text: NY3. **Emendations of the copy-text:** **Hero:** Heading: *italics supplied* *and*] & **Pyr:** Heading: *italics supplied* *Pyramus*] Pyramꝰ *and*] & **Niobe:** Heading: *italics supplied* 1 and] & I ame] Iame 2 that] y^{t} **Ship:** Heading: *italics supplied* 1 which] wch 2 But] but 4 the] ye 5 which] wch 6 drownd.] drownd‸ **Wall:** Heading: *italics supplied* 1 and] & **Beggar:** Heading: *italics supplied* **Cales:** Heading: *italics supplied* *and*] & 1 from] frō 2 your] yor **Wing:** Heading: *italics supplied* *Wingefield.*] Wingef: 2 and] & and] & 3 our] o^{r} **SelfAc:** Heading: *supplied from* A 1 that] y^{t} **Licent:** Heading: *supplied from* A 1 and] & 2 For] for **Antiq:** Heading: *italics supplied* 1 Hammon] Ham̃on **Jug:** Heading: *supplied from* SN3, *italics supplied* **Disinher:** Heading: *supplied from* A 1 from] frō **Liar:** Heading: *supplied from* SN3 *and regularized, italics supplied* 3 with] w^{t} and] & **Merc:** Heading: *Mercurius Gallobelgicus*] Mercuriꝰ Gallobelgicꝰ 2 Which] W^{ch} and] & 3 which] wch 7 Change] change 8 and] & **Phrine:** Heading: *supplied from* SN3, *italics supplied* 2 that] y^{t} **Philo:** Heading: *supplied from* A 1 with] w^{t} **Klock:** Heading: *supplied from* SN3, *italics supplied* 2 that] y^{t} **Martial:** Heading: *italics supplied* *castratus*] castratꝰ 3 Katherine] katherine **Ralph:** Heading: *supplied from* SN3, *italics supplied* 1 the] ye 2 the] y^{e}

Late Sequence

Copy-text: WN1. **Emendations of the copy-text:** **Hero:** Heading: *italics supplied* 2 drownd.] ~ | **Pyr:** Heading: *italics supplied* *and*] And 2 here.] ~. | **Niobe:** Heading: *italics supplied* 2 tombe.] ~. | **Ship:** Heading: *italics supplied* *Ship.*] Ship$_{\wedge}$ 6 drownd.] ~. | **Wall:** Heading: *italics supplied* *Wall.*] Wall$_{\wedge}$ 1 an] as 4 hide.] ~ | **Beggar:** Heading: *italics supplied* *Begger.*] Begger. | 2 lies.] ~ | **SelfAc:** Heading: *italics supplied* *Accuser.*] Accuser. | 2 true.] ~$_{\wedge}$ **Licent:** Heading: *italics supplied* 2 fall.] ~$_{\wedge}$ **Antiq:** Heading: *italics supplied* *Antiquarye.*] Antiquarye$_{\wedge}$ 2 beware.] ~$_{\wedge}$ **Disinher:** Heading: *italics supplied* *Disinherited.*] Disinherited$_{\wedge}$ **Merc:** Heading: *Gallo-Belgicus.*] Gallo-Belgicus$_{\wedge}$ 1 fellowe-slaues] fellowe=slaues 3 which] with nothinge:] ~, confesse] ~. 4 lesse.] ~$_{\wedge}$ 7 all.] ~$_{\wedge}$ Change] change 8 Greeke.] ~ | **Phrine:** Heading: *italics supplied* *Phrine.*] Phrine$_{\wedge}$ 2 bee.] ~. | **Philo:** Heading: *italics supplied* *Writer.*] Writer$_{\wedge}$ 2 When] when beleeud?] ~$_{\wedge}$ **Klock:** Heading: *heading supplied* 1 Klockius] ~. 2 home.] ~. | **Martial:** Heading: *italics supplied* 3 stues.] ~ | **Ralph:** Heading: *heading supplied* 2 bed.] ~. |

Textual Introductions and Apparatuses for Individual Epigrams

(The Textual Introductions and Apparatuses presented here are arranged alphabetically by Donne Variorum short forms.)

Antiq

Textual Introduction

As is suggested in the General Textual Introduction to the Epigrams, *Antiq* is one of the first epigrams Donne composed—perhaps even *the* first—and it appears in each of the sequences printed above, occupying the initial position in the first sequence and a medial position in the intermediate and late arrangements. Further, the poem exhibits distinct early, intermediate, and late forms corresponding to the succession of the sequences, thus supporting at the micro level the evidence that the sequences themselves are ultimately authorial. The early and intermediate forms of the text, both of which read "Hammon" (variously spelled) in line 1, are distinguished by the change of "old things" to "old strange things" in line 2, and this alteration carries over into the late form of the text, which further changes line 1's "Hammon" to "he hath" and "such" to "soe much" (see the Schema of Textual Relationships). For discussion of the possible topical reasons for this change in the poem, see the Commentary.

The third version of *Antiq*, with the manuscripts' "haue" in line 1 altered to "hath," is that which appears in all seventeenth-century collected editions/issues and in all modern editions except Milgate (Y). The poem is positioned ninth, after *Licent*, in A–G and all modern editions up to Grierson (Q), who begins the twentieth-century practice of integrating various epigrams from NY3 into the traditional sequence. See the General Textual Introduction to the Epigrams for the placement of the poem in twentieth-century editions.

Textual Apparatus

Copy-text: NY3. **Texts collated:** B7 (f. 58v); B28 (f. 113v); B46 (f. 77v); B47 (f. 155v); CT1 (p. 126); DT1 (f. 92v); F7 (f. 33); H3 (p. 48); H4 (p. 148); H5 (p. 435); H6 (p. 337); H8 (f. 24); HH1 (f. 107); LR1 (f. 279v); NY3 (f. [46v]); O18 (f. 46); O21 (p. 36); O25 (p. 79); SA1 (p. 60); SN3 (f. 36v); WN1 (p. 44); Y3 (p. 56); A (p. 42); B (p. 69); C (p. 69); D (p. 66); E (p. 66); F (p. 66); G (p. 63).

Emendations of the copy-text: Heading: *italics supplied* 1 Hammon] Hām̄on

Historical Collation

Format:

Imperfections: *trimming affects possible period after l. 2* HH1.

Miscellaneous: 69 *in* M B28; 10 *penciled in* M *in later hand* LR1; *heading in left* M *beside l. 2*, | p. *in left* M *in second hand* NY3; 111 *above heading* O18; *Disinher and Liar appended as ll. 3–4 and 5–8, respectively* O21 Y3.

Headings: Antiquarie B7 B28 B47 CT1 DT1 H4 NY3 O21 SA1 WN1 Y3 A–G. Epigram: B46. 1 HH1. the Antiquary O18. Hammon SN3. *om* F7 H3 H5 H6 H8 LR1 O25.

1 If] ~, HH1. in his study Hammon] in his Study he B7 B28 B47 CT1 DT1 H4 O18 SA1 WN1 A–G; Hammon in his study F7 O25; in his study, Hamon HH1. hath] haue B7 CT1 DT1 H4 O21 SA1 SN3 WN1 Y3; take LR1. such] so much B7 B28 B47 CT1 DT1 H4 O18 SA1 WN1 A–G. care] ~, HH1 O25.

2 To'hang all old strange] to hang all Old Strange B28 B47 DT1 H3 H4 O18 O21 Y3; To hange old B46; To hange vpp all old F7; to hange all old H5 H6 H8 HH1 SN3; To hang'old straunge LR1; To hang vp all old filthy O25; To hang all, old strange WN1. things,] ~$_\wedge$ B28 WN1; things, then B46; ~; O21 O25. let his] let'his DT1 LR1; let's F7(lets') H3 O18 O21 O25 SA1 Y3. beware.] ~$_\wedge$ B7 B28 CT1 F7 H4 H6 O18 O21 SA1 WN1 Y3; ~. | DT1 H3; ~[*missing*] HH1; be Ware. SN3.

Subscriptions: J.D. H3. J. Deane O25. *om* B7 B28 B46 B47 CT1 DT1 F7 H4 H5 H6 H8 HH1 LR1 NY3 O18 O21 SA1 SN3 WN1 Y3 A–G.

Verbal Variants in Selected Modern Editions

Editions collated: H I J K M N O P Q S T Y Z AA DD.

Headings: *Antiquary.* H–K M O–Q S T Y–AA DD. IX. ANTIQUARY. N.

1 Hammon] he H–K M–Q S T Z AA DD. such] so much H–K M–Q S T Z AA DD.

2 all] *om* J.

Schema of Textual Relationships

Version 1

B46 F7 H5 H6 H8 HH1 O25 SN3

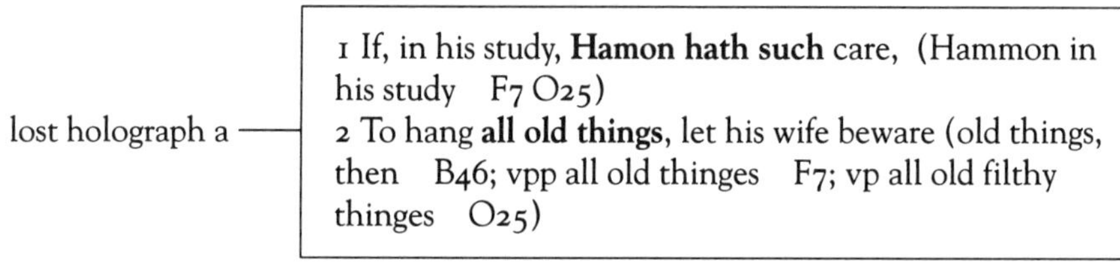

lost holograph a

1 If, in his study, **Hamon hath such** care, (Hammon in his study F7 O25)
2 To hang **all old things**, let his wife beware (old things, then B46; vpp all old thinges F7; vp all old filthy thinges O25)

Version 2

H3 LR1 NY3 O21 Y3

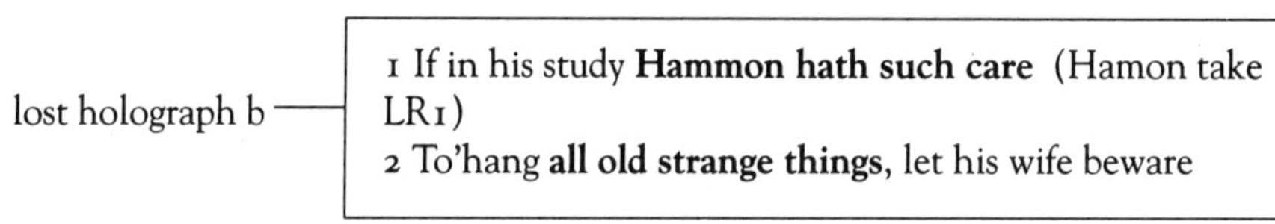

lost holograph b

1 If in his study **Hammon hath such care** (Hamon take LR1)
2 To'hang **all old strange things**, let his wife beware

Version 3

B7 B28 B47 CT1 DT1 H4 O18 SA1 WN1 A–G

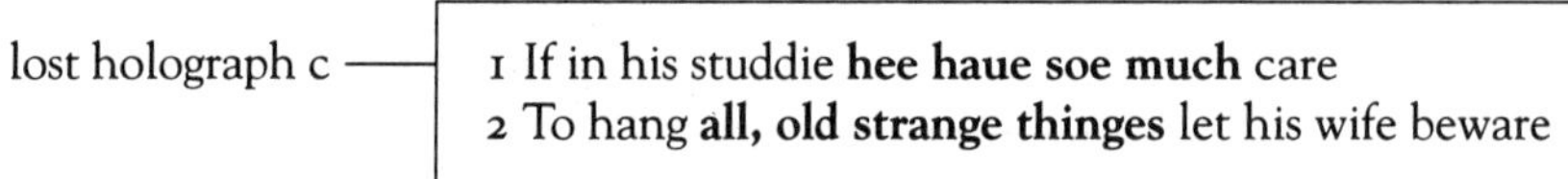

lost holograph c

1 If in his studdie **hee haue soe much** care
2 To hang **all, old strange thinges** let his wife beware

AutHook

Textual Introduction

Inscribed in the flyleaf of H10, *AutHook* is one of a handful of poetical writings surviving in Donne's hand. No additional seventeenth-century copies of the epigram are known to exist. For discussion of the occasion and motive behind this inscription, as well as of how it should be translated, see the Commentary.

Bibliographically, the most interesting features of the inscription are Donne's mistake and correction—he initially left out the "u" in "Auxilio" and had to go back and insert it over a caret, an error that may have distracted him to the point of omitting the final period—and his distinctive autograph subscription. The epigram was first printed by Gosse (siglum 72) in 1899 and has appeared subsequently in every edition of the complete poems except Grierson (Q)—i.e., in Hayward (S), Bennett (T), Milgate (Y), and Shawcross (Z).

Textual Apparatus

Copy-text: H10. **Texts collated:** H10 (sig. A1v); 72 (1:270).
Emendations of the copy-text: Heading: *italics supplied* 2 Auxilio.] A›u‹xilio$_{\wedge}$

Historical Collation

Format:
Indentations: *l. 2 ind* H10 72.
Headings: Ad Autorem. H10. AD AUTHOREM. 72.

2 Auxilio.] ~$_{\wedge}$ H10.

Subscriptions: I: Donne. H10 72(J.).

Verbal Variants in Selected Modern Editions

Editions collated: S T Y Z.
Format:
Font: *heading in italics* Y Z.
Headings: AD AUTOREM S T Y Z.
Subscriptions: J. Donne. S Y. *om* T Z.

AutJos

Textual Introduction

Inscribed in the flyleaf of C7, *AutJos* is one of a handful of poetical writings surviving in Donne's hand. No additional seventeenth-century copies of the epigram are known to exist. For discussion of the occasion and motive behind this inscription, as well as of how it should be translated, see the Commentary.

Textually, the inscription presents one difficult reading—in the "conantur" of line 3 (see Notes and Glosses to *AutJos*)—a problem first recognized by Keynes (siglum 73), who discovered and published the poem in 1958. The epigram has subsequently appeared in Milgate (Y) and Shawcross (Z).

Textual Apparatus

Copy-text: C7. **Texts collated:** C7 (flyleaf); 73 (p. 108).
Emendations of the copy-text: Heading: *italics supplied* 3 conantur] conāt^{r}

Historical Collation

Format:
Indentations: *ll. 2 and 4 ind* C7.
Headings: Ad Autorem. C7 73.

1 tempora;] ~, 73.

Subscriptions: I: Donne. C7 73(J.).

Verbal Variants in Selected Modern Editions

Editions collated: Y Z.
Format:
Font: *all except subscription in italics* Y; *heading only in italics* Z.
Headings: *Ad Autorem* Y Z.
Subscriptions: J. Donne. Y. *om* Z.

Beggar

Textual Introduction

Beggar is the most widely dispersed of all Donne's epigrams, appearing in some 53 copies among the seventeenth-century manuscripts. Under the Italian title "Zoppo," it first shows up among the "Spanish" poems added to the epigrams at the LR1–NY3 phase of expansion and retains the place it there occupies (immediately after *Wall*) in the late sequence that appeared in B7–WN1 and the seventeenth-century printed editions. The heading of the poem is changed from "Zoppo" to "A Lame Begger" as the epigram is refurbished for inclusion in the late sequence, perhaps in an effort to remove all traces of foreignness. The text is not otherwise altered in the move from intermediate- to late-stage manuscripts, however, and this uniformity suggests that Donne himself was responsible for but one essential form of the poem. The contemporary popularity of the epigram, however, which undoubtedly circulated by both written and oral means, spawned a plethora of distinct forms, as well as of copies; and we have attempted to introduce order into this bewildering proliferation by presenting a number of different versions of the epigram.

The primary, authorial version is distinguished by the reading "I am unable" in line 1 and by the compound adverbial infinitive "To stand or move" at the beginning of line 2; the minor variants "not able" and "stand or goe" (or the reversed "go, or stand") preserved in half a dozen manuscripts probably spring from lapses of memory and represent instances of oral transmission within the principal family of texts. Version two, distinguished by the reading "Yf that be true" (or a similar subjunctive formulation) at the beginning of the second line, appears in only four manuscripts; and the variation among their texts suggests that all are independent memorial reconstructions at some remove from the primary stream of transmission. Version three is distinguished by a distinctive form of line 2, which opens with the question "What doth hee then?" and concludes with the answer, "If he say true hee lyes." A highly similar form of this line appears in all twenty-one copies except that of the extremely corrupt LR2, which omits the opening question. This verbal consistency is hardly matched in the form assumed by line 1 in these manuscripts, however. Remarkably, the initial line does show all but three of these scribes referring to a "cripple" (as opposed to version one's "beggar"), but the number and kinds of actions of which the cripple claims to be incapable vary widely within the group. Although this version must have originated in one or more faulty transcriptions or memorial reconstructions of the primary version and although it undoubtedly continued to proliferate by these same means, textual similarity within such copies as those in BD1, DR2, F17, and O10, for instance—which share the line 1 reading "I can neither goe nor stand"—suggests that certain distinct sub-forms of version three may have circulated in writing among poetical miscellanies and commonplace books. The question "How can/may this bee" at the beginning of line 2 is the distinctive feature of version four. Referring to "this" (rather than "the") "begger" and linked by their subscriptions, the copies in SN3 (Drummond's notebook) and SN4 are closely related, probably deriving from a common source ultimately based on someone's memory of the poem. That the copy in C5 shares the version's defining feature—the question in line 2—may be more accidental than genealogical, since it otherwise differs considerably from the SN3–SN4 text. Versions five (from Manningham's diary), six, and seven all exist in single copies, and all are apparently memorial reconstructions. These versions have in common that the subject—either a "beggar" (B34 and VA3) or a "cripple" (B20)—cannot "goe," "sit," nor "stand," though they disperse these verbs variously across the lines. Among all the tinkering with the primary version evident in versions two through seven, the efforts of the B20 scribe (version six) stand out as particularly artful, as he confects a metrically smooth revision the verbal economy and rhetorical point of which compare favorably with Donne's in the original.

First printed in A, version one is that which has been included in all subsequent editions, and its placement as the sixth poem in the sequence never varies. For instances of the epigram's popularity in eighteenth- and nineteenth-century anthologies and miscellanies, see the Commentary.

Textual Apparatus

Version 1

Copy-text: NY3. **Texts collated:** B7 (f. 58v); B28 (f. 113v); B45 (f. 33); B47 (f. 155); CJ1 (f. 29v); CT1 (p. 126); DT1 (f. 92); H4 (p. 148); H6 (p. 339); LR1 (f. 279v); LR2 (p. 35); NY3 (f. [46]); O4 (f. 97v); O21 (p. 47); O41 (p. 58); R3 (f. 7v); SA1 (p. 60); TM1 (p. 2); VA3 (f. 78v); WN1 (p. 43); Y3 (p. 68); Y7 (f. 103v rev.); A (p. 41); B (p. 69); C (p. 69); D (p. 66); E (p. 66); F (p. 66); G (p. 63); 30 (p. 143).

Emendations of the copy-text: Heading: *italics supplied*

Historical Collation

Format:

Miscellaneous: 69 *in* M B28; 6 *penciled in* M *in later hand* LR1; *poem written perpendicularly across end of page* LR2; *heading beside l. 2 in left* M, | p. *in left* M *in second hand* NY3; *numbered* 155 *in a second hand in red ink* O4; *section headed* Epigrams. SA1; *couplet united by left brace* Y3; 7 *left of heading in modern hand* Y7.

Headings: A Lame Beggar B7 B28 B47 CT1 DT1 H4 WN1 A–G. On a lame beggar: B45 30. On a Beggar CJ1 LR2. Zoppo H6 LR1 NY3. On a cripple O4. In Claudum Y7. *om* O21 O41 R3 SA1 TM1 VA3 Y3.

1 vnable] ~, H4 WN1 A–F; not able LR2 TM1. (yonder] ^~ B7 B28 B45 B47 CJ1 CT1 DT1 H4 H6 LR2 O4 O21 R3 SA1 TM1 VA3 WN1 Y3 Y7 A–G 30. beggar] bagger CJ1. cryes)] ~^ B7 B28 B47 CJ1 CT1 DT1 H4 H6 O4 O21 R3 SA1 TM1 VA3 WN1 Y3 Y7 30; ~, B45 LR2 A–G.

2 stand] ~, B7 B45 CT1 DT1 H4 LR2 WN1 Y7 A–G; go; O21; go, O41. move;] ~, B7 B45 B47 CJ1 CT1 DT1 H4 H6 SA1 WN1 Y7 30; ~. B28; ~: LR1 VA3; goe, LR2 O4 TM1; stand; O21; stand: O41; ~^ R3; goe^ Y3. say] sayes B45 CJ1 30; s[th] O41. trew,] ~^ B7 B28 CT1 H6 LR1 LR2 O4 R3 SA1 TM1 VA3 WN1 Y3 Y7 30; ~,: O21. lyes.] ~^ B7 B28 B45 CT1 H6 O4 O21 R3 SA1 TM1; ~. | CJ1 LR1 LR2; ~ | WN1; ~: Y3 30.

Subscriptions: Jo. D CJ1. | finis. | O21. ffinis Y3. *om* B7 B28 B45 B47 CT1 DT1 H4 H6 LR1 LR2 NY3 O4 O41 R3 SA1 TM1 VA3 WN1 Y7 A–G 30.

Verbal Variants in Selected Modern Editions

Editions collated: H I J K M N O P Q S T Y Z AA DD.
Headings: A *lame Begger.* H–K M O–Q S T Y–AA DD. VI. A LAME BEGGAR. N.

2 say] says I J.

Version 2

Copy-text: H5. **Texts collated:** C12 (f. [84]) F7 (f. 37); H5 (p. 435); R8 (p. 139).
Emendations of the copy-text: Heading: *supplied from* C12, *italics supplied*
2 Yf] yf

Historical Collation

Headings: On a Begger. C12 F7. *om* H5 R8.

1 I] The begger F7. cannot goe,] cannot goe^ C12; can neither → >nowte< stand, R8. nor sitt,] *om* C12 F7. stand,] ~^ C12 F7; goe, R8. the beggar] hee F7. cryes;] ~^ C12 F7; ~: R8.

2 Yf] But if C12. that] *om* C12; it F7 R8. be true] *om* C12; be so, R8. the beggar sayes,] the Begger then sayes True, C12; & he sayes true, R8. he] the begg[r] R8.

Subscriptions: *none.*

Version 3

Copy-text: O23. **Texts collated:** B5 (f. 2v); B24 (f. 46v rev.); B26 (f. 73); B37 (f. 19v); BD1 (f. 15v); DR2 (p. 10); F3 (p. 151); F12 (p. 83); F17 (*first appearance*, p. 6); F17 (*second appearance*, p. 25); HH2 (p. 50); LR2 (p. 35); O10 (p. 74); O11 (f. 5); O16 (f. 85v rev.); O23 (p. 123); O42 (f. 95); OC2 (f. 26v); R9 (p. 117); Y1 (p. [3]); Y5 (p. 103).

Emendations of the copy-text: Heading: *italics supplied* *criple.*] criple‸

Historical Collation

Format:

Miscellaneous: 113 *in* M O16; 13 *in* M O42; X *left of heading* Y1.

Headings: In Claudum Epig: B5. On a cripple B24 B37 BD1 DR2 F17(*first appearance*, Vppon) HH2 O16 O23 O42(Vpon) OC2 Y1. A Criple B26 F17(*second appearance*). The Cripple F3. Of a Cripple. | F12. Of a Beggar. LR2. In Claudipedem. O10. On a beggar & cripple O11. The Beggar R9. *om* Y5.

1 I cannot goe,] Nor stand, no sit, B26; I cannot goe‸ B37 HH2 Y1; I can neither goe‸ BD1 DR2 F17(*both appearances*) O10; I can, nor sitt, LR2; Nor goe nor sit, O11; The criple nether sitts‸ O16; I cannot stand‸ R9. nor stand] ›---‹ nor stand, B5; stand, sitte, B24; nor goe B26; sit, stand F3; nor stand, F12 LR2 O10 Y5; nor stands O16; sitt, stand, O42 OC2; nor moue →›goe‹ R9. the cripple] this cripple B24; ye beggar LR2 R9; hee O16; yon beggar Y5. cryes.] ~, B5 B37 F12 F17(*first appearance*) R9; ~: B24; ~‸ B26 BD1 DR2 F3 F17(*second appearance*) HH2 LR2 O10 O11 O16 OC2 Y1 Y5.

2 What doth hee then?] What doth he then, B37 F17(*second appearance*) R9; What doth he then‸ DR2 HH2 O16; What does hee then? F12 Y5; What doth he then?, F17(*first appearance*); *om* LR2; What sayes he then‸ O11; what dos he then! Y1. he] *om* O16. say] speakes B5; saith B26 F17(*first appearance*); tell DR2; says HH2 O11 O42 Y1. true] truth, B5 F12; ~, B24 F3 F17(*first appearance*) LR2 O11 O42 Y1 Y5; trueth DR2; truth? R9. lyes.] ~, B5; ~‸ DR2 F17(*both appearances*) HH2 O16 Y1; ~. | F12 O10 O11; ~.- | LR2; ~: R9.

Subscriptions: Dr Donne. B24. Donne. Y5. *om* B5 B26 B37 BD1 DR2 F3 F12 F17(*both appearances*) HH2 LR2 O10 O11 O16 O23 O42 OC2 R9 Y1.

Version 4

Copy-text: SN3. **Texts collated:** C5 (f. 62v); SN3 (f. 32v); SN4 (f. 48).
Emendations of the copy-text: Heading: *italics supplied*

Historical Collation

Format:
Miscellaneous: *couplet united by end-of-line brackets* C5.
Headings: A beggar. SN3. *om* C5 SN4.

1 cannot stand,] Cannot goe, C5; can nor stand, SN4. nor sitt,] sitt, stande, C5. this] Yonder C5. cries] ~. C5; ~, SN4.

2 can] may C5. bee,] ~$_\wedge$ C5. true,] ~$_\wedge$ C5. lies.] ~. | SN4.

Subscriptions: ID. SN3. J D. SN4. *om* C5.

Version 5

Copy-text: B34. **Text collated:** B34 (f. 118).
Emendations of the copy-text: Heading: *italics supplied* *ground.*] ground$_\wedge$

Historical Collation

Format:
Miscellaneous: (Dun) *in right* M *beside heading, entry of poem dated* 31 (*left* M) Marche 1603 (*top of page*) B34.
Headings: Of a beggar that lay on the ground B34.
Subscriptions: *none.*

Version 6

Copy-text: B20. **Text collated:** B20 (f. 38).
Emendations of the copy-text: Heading: *italics supplied* 1 the] y[e]

Historical Collation

Heading: On a Cripple. B20.
Subscriptions: *none.*

Version 7

Copy-text: VA3. **Text collated:** VA3 (f. 78v).
Emendations of the copy-text: Heading: *heading supplied* 1 the] y[e]
2 stand.] ~$_{\wedge}$

Historical Collation

Headings: *none.*
Subscriptions: *none.*

Schema of Textual Relationships, Version 1

Earlier text

H6 LR1 NY3

lost holograph a —— | HE *Zoppo.* |

Later text

B7 B28 B45 B47 CT1 DT1 H4 SA1 WN1 A–G

lost holograph b —— | HE A *Lame Begger.* (On a lame beggar: B45) |

Unaffiliated: CJ1 LR2 O4 O21 O41 R3 TM1 VA3 Y3 Y7

Cales

Textual Introduction

As noted in the General Textual Introduction to the Epigrams, *Cales* (like *Wing* certainly, and *Ship* and *Beggar* probably) derives from Donne's military experiences in the mid-1590s, and Donne seems carefully to have restricted the circulation of the poem: among contemporary textual artifacts the epigram appears only in the intermediate-stage manuscript NY3 and the corresponding part of H6, following *Beggar* immediately in both sources. The relationship between the two extant manuscript copies is indeterminate. Since NY3 is written in the hand of Donne's friend Rowland Woodward, its copy undoubtedly stands very close to the author's own papers, and H6's may in some manner have derived from it (see the Textual Introduction to *Wing* for further discussion of the relationship of these texts that are unique to NY3 and H6). For suggestions on the events that inspired the poem and the precise date of its composition, see the Commentary.

Since Donne withheld the poem from the late sequence, it did not appear in the seventeenth-century printed editions; indeed, it was not printed until 1899, when Edmund Gosse owned NY3 and printed the poem in *The Life and Letters* (72) from that manuscript. In a text ultimately based on NY3, *Cales* has subsequently appeared in all twentieth-century collected editions from Grierson (Q) onward. For information on where various editors position it relative to the other poems, see the General Textual Introduction to the Epigrams.

Textual Apparatus

Copy-text: NY3. **Texts collated:** H6 (p. 338); NY3 (f. [46]); 72 (1:47).
Emendations of the copy-text: Heading: *italics supplied* and] & 1 from] frõ 2 your] yor

Historical Collation

Format:
Miscellaneous: *heading in left* M NY3.
Headings: Calez & Guyana. H6(Cales) NY3. Cales [*i. e.* Cadiz] and Guyana. 72.

1 the'old] the old 72. fardest] farthest H6 72.

2 bend] ~, 72.

4 new.] ~! H6 72.

Subscriptions: *none.*

Verbal Variants in Selected Modern Editions

Editions collated: Q S T Y Z AA DD.
Headings: *Cales* and *Guyana.* Q S Y–AA DD. CADIZ AND GUIANA T.

Disinher

Textual Introduction

Disinher is included in all three sequences of the epigrams—early, intermediate, and late. It appears as the second poem in the early sequence, following *Antiq* and preceding *Liar*, and essentially remains in this context in the intermediate and late sequences, though Donne moves the first sequence *in toto* to the end of the expanded group comprised in the middle and late arrangements (see Figure 2 in the General Textual Introduction to the Epigrams). Except for the copy in Sancroft's manuscript (O41), which exchanges the positions of "all" (l. 1) and "Gave" (l. 2), the poem is substantively free of textual variation, first acquiring an authoritative title in WN1 (it does not appear in B7–H4, and the heading in SN3 is probably of Drummond's manufacture). The epigram was included in the seventeenth-century editions A–G, which reproduce the late manuscript sequence, and has appeared, similarly placed, in all subsequent collected editions (see the General Textual Introduction to the Epigrams for the exact ordering of the epigrams by twentieth-century editors).

Textual Apparatus

Copy-text: NY3. **Texts collated:** B28 (f. 113v); H3 (p. 48); H5 (p. 435); H6 (p. 337); H8 (f. 24); HH1 (f. 107); LR1 (f. 279v); NY3 (f. [46v]); O21 (p. 36); O25 (p. 79); O36 (f. 163v); O41 (p. 58); SN3 (f. 36v); VA3 (f. 78v); WN1 (p. 44); Y3 (p. 56); A (p. 42); B (p. 69); C (p. 69); D (p. 66); E (p. 66); F (p. 66); G (p. 63); 30 (p. 143).

Emendations of the copy-text: Heading: *supplied from* A 1 from] frō

Historical Collation

Format:

Miscellaneous: 69 *in* M B28; 11 *penciled in M in later hand* LR1; | p. *beside l. 1 in left* M *in second hand* NY3; *written as lines 3 and 4 of Antiq* O21 Y3.

Headings: Disinherited B28 WN1 A–G(*Disinherited.*). 2 HH1. one disherited. SN3. *On a yong man disinherited.* 30. *om* H3 H5 H6 H8 LR1 NY3 O21 O25 O36 O41 VA3 Y3.

1 Thy] ye O21. father] Father H3 H5 O25 O41 30. all] gave O41. from] ›~‹ H6. thee] ~, H5 HH1 O25 O36 A–G; thee both → ›thee‹ H6. will] ~, HH1; Will O36 O41 SN3 A–G 30.

2 Gaue] All O41. poore;] ~‸ B28 O21 O36 WN1 Y3; ~, H3 H6 H8 HH1 SN3 VA3 30; ~: LR1 O41. thou] Thou H6 O41 A–G. title] Title H3 H8 O41. still.] ~. | H3 LR1; ~‸ H6 VA3 Y3.

Subscriptions: J.D. H3 O25. *om* B28 II5 H6 H8 HH1 LR1 NY3 O21 O36 O41 SN3 VA3 WN1 Y3 A–G 30.

Verbal Variants in Selected Modern Editions

Editions collated: H I J K M N O P Q S T Y Z AA DD.
Headings: *Disinherited.* H–K M O–Q S T Y–AA DD. X. DISINHERITED. N.

Schema of Textual Relationships

Early and intermediate texts

H3 H5 H6 H8 HH1 LR1 NY3 O21 O25 O36 O41 SN3 VA3 Y3

lost holographs a & b —— HE *om* (one disherited. SN3)

Late text

B28 WN1 A–G

lost holograph c —— HE *Disinherited.*

Faust

Textual Introduction

At four manuscript copies *Faust* is among the rarest of Donne's epigrams, and it alone, of all the twenty-one English poems presented as Donne's epigrams in this edition, fails to appear in NY3. The three main copies of the poem all appear in manuscripts of Scottish provenance (SN3, SN4, and TT1), and the fourth—a memorial reconstruction substituting "Latus" for "Faustus/Faustinus" and "doth keepe" for "keepes"—is included with other information that John Manningham entered in his diary (siglum B34) on 15 June 1602. It seems likely that Manningham heard his version on the street, and the physical grouping of the epigram with the same derivative version of *Beggar* in both SN3 and SN4 further suggests a history of oral circulation for the poem, as does its appearance alone among non-Donne poems in TT1. As suggested above in the General Textual Introduction to the Epigrams, the scarcity of this epigram within the written record may reflect Donne's reluctance to distribute a work on a morally volatile theme, though it would appear to be no more objectionable on this score than such widely dispersed epigrams as *Klock* and *SelfAc*. It is tempting to suspect that this poem bears an encrypted topical allusion or some other personal dimension that caused Donne to restrict its circulation.

Within the primary family, both SN4 and TT1 give the subject's name as "Faustinus," producing a couplet of regular decasyllables, whereas Drummond (in SN3) reduces the name to "Faustus" and each line to nine syllables. Since SN4 and TT1 concur in giving the name with three syllables, since the dropping of one syllable by one scribe seems more plausible than the insertion of a syllable by two scribes working independently, and since Drummond's texts of the other epigrams are of limited reliability, it seems likely that "Faustinus" is the correct reading.

The epigram was first printed in 1967 by Shawcross (siglum 74), whose arguments for believing the poem Donne's are summarized in the Commentary. Shawcross includes *Faust* among the epigrams in his *Complete Poems* (Z), and it is quoted among "Poems attributed to Donne" in Patrides (DD).

Textual Apparatus

Copy-text: SN4. **Texts collated:** B34 (f. 26v); SN3 (f. 32v); SN4 (f. 48); TT1 (f. 57); 74 (p. 105).

Emendations of the copy-text: Heading: *heading and italics supplied*

2 more.] ~. |

Historical Collation

Headings: *om* B34 SN3 SN4 TT1 74.
Format:
Miscellaneous: *entry dated* 15 (M) June 1602 (*top of page*) B34.

1 *Faustinus*] Latus B34; Faustus SN3 74. keepes] doth keepe B34. Sister,] ~‸ B34 SN3 TT1 74. a] his B34. Whore,] ~. B34; ~‸ TT1.

2 *Faustinus*] Latus B34; Faust[us] SN3 74. keepes] doth keepe B34. Sister,] ~‸ B34 SN3 TT1 74. more.] ~, SN3 74; ~. | SN4; ~ | TT1.

Subscriptions: »G M« B34. ID SN3. J D | SN4 74. *om* TT1.

Verbal Variants in Selected Modern Editions

Editions collated: Z DD.
Headings: *Faustus.* Z. *om* DD.

1 *Faustinus*] Faustus Z DD.

2 *Faustinus*] Faustus Z DD.

Hero

Textual Introduction

Hero first appears among the epigrams in the intermediate sequence, where it occupies the first position in the expanded arrangement. It retains this placement in all the major manuscript collections of epigrams, moreover, including those containing the late sequence printed in A and the subsequent editions, except for the groups assembled piecemeal in H6, B47, and SA1; indeed, it is even the initial poem in Drummond's primary sequence in SN3 (see Figure 2 in the General Textual Introduction to the Epigrams). Except for the two copies in B23, furthermore, the poem invariably bears the heading "Hero and Leander" in the manuscripts and in all the printed editions from 1633 (A) through Patrides's (DD). The variant reading "on the [for 'in one'] grownd" found in B7 and CT1 distinguishes these texts from those in DT1 and H4, the other manuscripts containing the thirteen-poem version of the late sequence; and SA1's inclusion of this error shows its derivation from the B7–CT1 subgroup. Further, B7's reading "hath" (for "had") in line 2 is unique among this subgroup, suggesting that both it and SA1 derive independently from CT1, a conclusion corroborated by B7's unique reading "neare to" in *Ship* 4. If, as prior commentators have suggested, the same scribe produced both CT1 and DT1 (see Beal 251), this "on the"/"in one" variant may indicate that he copied CT1 first and somehow discovered his error or had it brought to his attention before transcribing DT1.

The poem appears, without verbal variation, as the first epigram in all collected editions of Donne's poetry from A through DD. Since the text of the poem is essentially identical in the intermediate and late sequences, we have not included a Schema of Textual Relationships in the Textual Apparatus.

Textual Apparatus

Copy-text: NY3. **Texts collated:** B7 (f. 58); B23 (*first appearance*, f. 33); B23 (*second appearance*, f. 48); B28 (f. 113); B47 (f. 131v); CT1 (p. 125); DT1 (f. 92); H4 (p. 147); H6 (p. 339); LR1 (f. 279v); NY3 (f. [46]); SA1 (p. 64); SN3 (f. 36); VA3 (f. 78v); WN1 (p. 43); Y7 (f. [103]v rev.); A (p. 40); B (p. 68); C (p. 68); D (p. 65); E (p. 65); F (p. 65); G (p. 62); 46 (p. 38).
Emendations of the copy-text: Heading: *italics supplied* *and*] &

Historical Collation

Format:

Font: *text in italics* 46.

Miscellaneous: *general heading* Epigrammes. *precedes this poem* B7 CT1 DT1 H4 SN3 WN1; 68 *in* M B28; *heading in left* M *beside l.* 1 B47; 1 *penciled in* M *in later hand* LR1; *heading in left* M, | p. *in left* M *in second hand* NY3; 6 *left of heading in modern hand* Y7.

Headings: *Hero and Leander* B7 B28 CT1 DT1 H4 H6 LR1 NY3 SA1 SN3 VA3 WN1 Y7 A–G 46. Hero. & Leader. B47. *om* B23(*both appearances*).

1 robd] robb'd B7 CT1 DT1 H6. ayre,] ~: B23(*both appearances*); One Ayre‸ B28; ~‸ B47 H4 H6 LR1 VA3 WN1 Y7. ly] liue B28. in one] on the B7 CT1 SA1. ground,] ~‸ B7 B23(*both appearances*) B28 B47 CT1 DT1 H4 H6 LR1 SA1 VA3 Y7.

2 whom] wee whome B23(*both appearances*). had] hath B7 B28; *om* B23(*both appearances*). burn'd,] ~‸ B23(*first appearance*) B28 B47 VA3; burn't, H6 LR1 SA1 A–G 46; burnt‸ SN3 Y7. one] on SN3. dround.] ~‸ B7 B28 CT1 H4 H6 Y7; ~. | LR1; ~ |. WN1.

Subscriptions: J.D. SA1. *om* B7 B23(*both appearances*) B28 B47 CT1 DT1 H4 H6 LR1 NY3 SN3 VA3 WN1 Y7 A–G 46.

Verbal Variants in Selected Modern Editions

Editions collated: H I J K M N O P Q S T Y Z AA DD.

Headings: *Hero* and *Leander*. H–K M O–Q S T Y–AA DD. I. HERO AND LEANDER N.

Jug

Textual Introduction

Appearing in only LR1, NY3, and SN3 among seventeenth-century artifacts, *Jug* is among the rarest of Donne's epigrams. Although it does not occur in any manuscript containing the early sequence, it is inserted near the beginning of the group of early epigrams that was subsequently incorporated into the intermediate sequence (see Figure 2 in the General Textual Introduction to the Epigrams). This pattern of placement and distribution suggests that if *Jug* was not among the very earliest epigrams Donne wrote, he saw it as the same kind of poem as *Antiq*, *Disinher*, and *Liar* and either wrote it soon after the early sequence began to circulate or added it to the expanded intermediate sequence to round out the collection. Perhaps because of its controversial subject matter, *Jug* was not included in the manuscripts containing the late sequence nor, consequently, in the seventeenth-century printed editions.

In LR1 and NY3, where it appears without a heading, *Jug* exhibits no significant variation; indeed, the occurrence of a scribally cancelled redundant "not" in line 2 of LR1 suggests that LR1's reversal of NY3's "not thee" to "thee not" in that line is a blunder that the scribe decided against correcting and that the original in both cases read "not thee." Suffering from either a lapse of memory or a desire to improve the poem, however, Drummond (in SN3) writes "that" (for "for") and "toyes (for "ioyes") in line 1. Whether scribally supplied or derived from the source-text, SN3 also registers the only contemporary title for the poem.

Under the invented title "Manliness," Bennett (T) first published the poem in 1942, using NY3 as copy-text. Under this title it was subsequently included in Milgate (Y) and Smith (AA), Shawcross (Z) and Patrides (DD) after him printing it as "The Jughler." For information on where these editors position the poem relative to the other epigrams, see the General Textual Introduction to the Epigrams.

Textual Apparatus

Copy-text: NY3. **Texts collated:** LR1 (f. 279v); NY3 (f. [46v]); SN3 (f. 36v); T (p. 112).
Emendations of the copy-text: Heading: *supplied from* SN3, *italics supplied*

Historical Collation

Format:
Miscellaneous: 9 *penciled in* M *in later hand* LR1.
Headings: The Iughler. SN3. MANLINESS T. *om* LR1 NY3.

1 me effeminat,] m'effeminate$_{\wedge}$ LR1; mee effeminate$_{\wedge}$ SN3. for] that SN3. ioyes] toyes, SN3; ~; T.

2 not thee] thee not LR1. manly,] ~$_{\wedge}$ LR1 SN3.

Subscriptions: *none.*

Verbal Variants in Selected Modern Editions

Editions collated: Y Z AA DD.
Headings: Manliness Y AA. *The Jughler.* Z DD.

Klock

Textual Introduction

As indicated in the General Textual Introduction to the Epigrams, *Klock* is among the first epigrams Donne circulated, and it appears in each of the sequences printed above, occupying the seventh position in the early sequence and, accordingly, a position near the end of the expanded intermediate and late arrangements. Further, the poem exhibits distinct early, intermediate, and late forms corresponding to the succession of the sequences, thus supporting at the micro level the evidence that the sequences themselves are ultimately authorial. The early form of the text reads line 1 as "vow'd ne're to come"; the intermediate text inserts "more" after "ne're," in an apparent effort to regularize the iambic meter of the second half of the line; and the late text retains "more," while altering the "vow'd" of the previous sequences to "sworne" (see Schema of Textual Relationships). Drummond's transcription of the poem in SN3, impossible to affiliate precisely, is either an edited or a remembered rendition, reading "hath sworne so deep" (for "so deeply hath sworne/vowd") and "neuer" (for "ne're/nere more") in line 1 and showing further deviation in line 2. Drummond's, however, is the only pre-1633 copy that bears a title, and we have adopted that title in this edition. In two manuscripts, both of which preserve the intermediate text, the addressee of the poem is given an alternate name, H8 calling him "Rockius" and LR1 naming him "Rawlings." The H8 reading is surely a scribal blunder of some sort, and that in LR1 may also be a scribal alteration, although "Rawlings" is sufficiently different from "Klockius" to raise the possibility that this reading derives from the authorial prototype upon which LR1 is ultimately based. (A similar alteration occurs in LR1's copy of *Phrine*, which reads the subject's name as "Latrine.") Adapting the poem for use in a time and context considerably removed from those in which it originated, O41 substitutes a generic name ("N.") for "Klockius" and further revises line 1 to accommodate this change metrically. For critical opinion on the significance of some of these variants in the name, see the Commentary.

In its late form, positioned between *Philo* and *Martial* and untitled, *Klock* appears in the seventeenth-century editions A–G and in the earlier modern editions H–K and M. Although they title it variously (see the Textual Apparatus below), the subsequent modern editions all likewise present the late form of the text, Hayward (S) and Milgate (Y) explicitly mentioning SN3 as their source for the title.

Textual Apparatus

Copy-text: NY3. **Texts collated:** B7 (f. 59); B28 (f. 114); CT1 (p. 127); DT1 (f. 92v); H4 (p. 149); H5 (p. 435); H6 (p. 338); H8 (f. 24v); HH1 (f. 107v);

LR1 (f. 280); NY3 (f. [46v]); O41 (p. 58); SN3 (f. 36v); VA3 (f. 78v); WN1 (p. 44); A (p. 42); B (p. 70); C (p. 70); D (p. 67); E (p. 67); F (p. 67); G (p. 64); 30 (p. 143).

Emendations of the copy-text: Heading: *supplied from* SN3, *italics supplied*

2 that] y[t]

Historical Collation

Format:

Miscellaneous: 70 *in* M B28; 15 *penciled in* M *in later hand* LR1; | p. *beside l.* *1 in left* M *in second hand* NY3.

Headings: Sharpe Equiuoq: B28. 7 HH1. Klookius → ›Klockius.‹ SN3. *On* Cutbeard *the Barber*. 30. *om* B7 CT1 DT1 H4 H5 H6 H8 LR1 NY3 O41 VA3 WN1 A–G.

1 Klockius] Rockius H8; Rawlings LR1; *om* O41; Clockius VA3; ~. WN1; CUTBERT 30. so] So O41; hath SN3. deeply'hath] deeply hath B7 B28 CT1 H4 H5 H6 H8 HH1 LR1 WN1 A–G 30; deeply N. hath O41; sworne so SN3; deeplye VA3. vowd] sworne B7 B28 CT1 DT1 H4 30; vowed LR1; ~, O41; deep SN3; sworne, WN1 A–G. nere] neuer SN3. more] *om* B7 B28 H5 H6 HH1 SN3.

2 bawdy house,] Baudy house‸ B7 B28 H6; a Bawdy House, H4 SN3; Bawdy-house, H5 30; bawdy=house‸ HH1. dares] dare SN3. home.] ~‸ B7 B28 H6; ~. | DT1 LR1 WN1.

Subscriptions: J:D. VA3. *om* B7 B28 CT1 DT1 H4 H5 H6 H8 HH1 LR1 NY3 O41 SN3 WN1 A–G 30.

Verbal Variants in Selected Modern Editions

Editions collated: H I J K M N O P Q S T Y Z AA DD.

Format:

Miscellaneous: *untitled, follows Philo immediately after a one-line break* K M.

Headings: XIII. THE CUCKOLD. N. [A DILEMMA.] O. [KLOCKIUS.] P. *Klockius*. Q S T Y–AA DD. *om* H–K M.

1 vowd] sworn H–K M–Q S T Z AA DD.

Schema of Textual Relationships

Version 1

H5 H6 HH1

lost holograph a —— | 1 Klockius so deeply hath **vow'd ne're** to come |

Version 2

H8 LR1 NY3 VA3

lost holograph b —— | 1 Klockius so deeply'hath **vowd nere more** to come (Rockius H8; Rawlings LR1) |

Version 3

B7 B28 CT1 DT1 H4 WN1 A–G

lost holograph c —— | 1 Klockius so deeply hath **sworne, nere more** to come |

Unaffiliated: O41 SN3

Liar

Textual Introduction

Exhibiting two corresponding textual forms, *Liar* appears in both the early and the intermediate sequences of epigrams, in both of which it follows *Disinher* immediately. With *Cales* and *Wing*, however, it is absent from the late sequence, failing to appear in either B7–H4, WN1, or A–G. The reading that distinguishes the two distinct forms of the poem occurs in line 2, the early text reading "sayst" where the later form reads "swearst" (see the Schema of Textual Relationships). Among the three manuscripts preserving the later form of the text, LR1 also uniquely reads "hearbes" (for the "gras" found in NY3 and SN3), possibly a scribal sophistication, but also possibly a second-stage authorial sophistication that Donne momentarily adopted before reverting in NY3 to the superior accuracy of allusion provided by "gras." SN3's introduction of an extra "and" into line 2, which technically renders the line hypermetric, may represent a conscious scribal alteration of the rhythm, although the irregular order to the poems in this part of the SN3 arrangement raises the possibility that Drummond is here transcribing from memory. SN3's title, unique among seventeenth-century artifacts, is likely of Drummond's making. Like SN3's superfluous "and" in line 2, H6's omission of "perchance" in line 3 probably also represents a scribal regularization of meter.

As suggested in the General Textual Introduction to the Epigrams, the poem's absence from the late sequence may be a deliberate exclusion, reflecting Donne's unwillingness to circulate any poem possibly offensive to the Spanish. In any case, the poem remained virtually unknown until 1856, when Simeon (70) published it, without a title, from H8. Grosart (N) then picked it up from 70 (correcting Simeon's "orthography" against H8) and headed it "SUPPING HOURS," a title also adopted by the poem's next editor, Chambers (P), who derives the text from Simeon. All twentieth-century editors of collected editions from Grierson (Q) to Patrides (DD) print the poem from NY3, but adopt Drummond's title from SN3. For information on where these editors position the poem relative to the other epigrams, see the General Textual Introduction to the Epigrams.

Textual Apparatus

Copy-text: NY3. **Texts collated:** F7 (f. 79v); H3 (p. 48); H5 (p. 436); H6 (p. 337); H8 (f. 24); HH1 (f. 107); LR1 (f. 279v); NY3 (f. [46v]); O21 (p. 36); O25 (p. 79); SN3 (f. 37); Y3 (p. 56); 70 (3:31).

Emendations of the copy-text: Heading: *supplied from* SN3 *and regularized, italics supplied* 3 with] w[t] and] &

Historical Collation

Format:

Indentations: *ll. 2 and 4 ind* H6 70.

Miscellaneous: 12 *penciled in M in later hand* LR1; *written as ll. 5–8 of Antiq* O21 Y3.

Headings: 3 HH1. the Lier. SN3. *om* F7 H3 H5 H6 H8 LR1 NY3 O21 O25 Y3 70.

1 fields] feild H8 O21 SN3 70; ~, O25. walkst] walks LR1; walkest O21. supping] supper F7. howres] ~, F7 H5 O25 70; houeres SN3.

2 swearst] sayst F7 H3 H6 H8 HH1 O21 Y3 70; sayest H5 O25. thou] y° LR1. supd] supped LR1 70. like] and like SN3. king;] ~: F7; ~‸ H3 H6 HH1 LR1 O21 Y3; ~, H5 H8 SN3; ~. O25 70.

3 Like] Nabuchadner F7. Nabuchadnezar] like F7; ~, H3 HH1 SN3 Y3. perchance] perhapps F7 H3; *om* H6; ~, HH1; perhapps, O25. gras] hearbes LR1; ~, O25. flowres] floores H3; ~, H5 O25 70; floweres SN3.

4 Sallet,] ~‸ F7 H3 H6 H8 LR1 O25 Y3 70; sallade‸ HH1 O21 SN3. then] than H3 HH1 SN3 70. dyeting.] ~‸ H6 HH1 O21 Y3; ~. | LR1.

Subscriptions: J.D. H3. ffinis | O21 Y3. J. Deane O25. *om* F7 H5 H6 H8 HH1 LR1 NY3 SN3 70.

Verbal Variants in Selected Modern Editions

Editions collated: N P Q S T Y Z AA DD.

Format:

Indentations: *ll. 2 and 4 ind* N S AA DD; *l. 4 ind* Q.

Headings: XVIII. SUPPING HOURS. N. SUPPING HOURS. P. *The Lier.* Q S T Y–AA DD.

1 fields] field N.

2 swearst] say'st N P.

4 Sallet] salad P T AA. then] than N P S T AA.

Schema of Textual Relationships

Version 1

F7 H3 H5 H6 H8 HH1 O21 O25 Y3

lost holograph a —— 2 And yet thou **sayst** thou hast sup'd like a king

Version 2

LR1 NY3 SN3

lost holograph b —— 2 And yet thou **swearst** thou hast supd like a king (supd and like SN3)

Licent

Textual Introduction

Next to *Beggar*, *Licent* is the most widely dispersed of the epigrams in the seventeenth century, surviving in 28 different manuscripts and appearing in A–G, as well as in several later seventeenth-century books. Apparently composed after the early sequence had already begun to circulate, the epigram is absent from two of the manuscripts containing the early sequence (H8 and HH1) and occurs as the last of twelve epigrams in the atypical arrangement preserved in H5. In the intermediate and late sequences the poem appears, in a single basic text, between *SelfAc* and *Antiq*, the only significant change being its acquisition of the heading "A Licentious Person" in the late arrangement. Predictably for a poem so frequently transcribed, the various copies exhibit some variation, yet not so much as we might expect within a body of text that must have been created to a significant degree by oral means. All the major manuscripts give what is surely the authorial reading "may no man" in line 1, while the peripheral copies that show up principally in commonplace books read either "no man may" or "no man can" (see the Historical Collation). Essentially these same divisions hold with respect to the titles: the major intermediate- and late-stage manuscripts record either no title or the standard "A Licentious Person," while a hodgepodge of headings, including several Latin variants, appear on the copies in the commonplace books. No artifact, it might be noted, gives the heading "Whore" as recorded by Grierson and Smith.

The general relationships among the texts of the epigrams in B7, CT1, DT1, H4, SA1, and WN1 are partly clarified in line 2 of this poem, where B7 uniquely reads "skinns" for "sins" and the B7–H4 group reads "hayre" for the plural "haires" found in WN1, SA1, and the print tradition. (For evidence on the links between B7, CT1, and SA1 see the Textual Introduction to *Hero*.) B7's misreading "skinns" indicates its descent from CT1 (rather than vice versa), and SA1's correct reading "sins" shows it to be the sibling rather than the child of B7. WN1's divergence from B7–H4 in the "hayre/haires" variant suggests its independent derivation from a sixteen-poem prototype that differed in this reading from a cognate thirteen-poem source lying behind B7–H4, thus supporting the notion that the third major phase of Donne's work on the epigrams comprised two stages. SA1 apparently pluralizes "hayre" independently.

In the late text of WN1 and positioned as in that manuscript (immediately after *SelfAc*), *Licent* appears in A, and all subsequent seventeenth-century and modern collected editions derive their texts of the poem successively from that source. For the exact positioning of the poem in twentieth-century editions, see the General Textual Introduction to the Epigrams. For some adaptations and "answer" poems, see Appendix 2.

Textual Apparatus

Copy-text: NY3. **Texts collated:** B7 (f. 58v); B23 (f. 35); B28 (f. 113v); B45 (f. 34); CJ1 (f. 30v); CT1 (p. 126); DT1 (f. 92v); F3 (p. 63); F7 (f. 83); H4 (p. 148); H5 (p. 436); H6 (p. 338); LA1 (f. 24r); LR1 (f. 279v); NY3 (f. [46]); O1 (f. 39v); O3 (p. 156); O10 (p. 74); O30 (f. 22); O41 (p. 58); OC2 (f. 47v); R3 (f. 8); SA1 (p. 60); SN3 (f. 36); VA3 (f. 78v); WN1 (p. 44); Y1 (p. [95]); Y6 (p. 409); A (p. 42); B (p. 69); C (p. 69); D (p. 66); E (p. 66); F (p. 66); G (p. 63); 16 (sig. D7v); 17a (sig. D7v); 17b (sig. D7v); 46 (p. 40).

Emendations of the copy-text: Heading: *supplied from* A 1 and] & 2 For] for

Historical Collation

Format:

Indentations: *l. 2 ind* 17a–b 46.

Font: *text in italics* 46.

Miscellaneous: *poem inscribed as the second couplet of a four-line poem (see Appendix 2)* B23; 69 *in* M B28; *added after other epigrams were transcribed* H6; 8 *penciled in* M *in later hand* LR1; | p. *beside l. 1 in* M *in second hand* NY3; *numbered* 239 *in red ink in later hand* O3; *poem followed by* "An Answer to the same./ Epig. 52." *(see Appendix 2)* 16 17a–b.

Headings: A Licentious person B7 B28 B45 CT1 DT1 H4 SA1 WN1 46. On a Whoremaster CJ1 LA1(To). Of a bald man F3. De Caluo F7. In quendã Libidinosũ. O1. Epigram on a whore m[r] O3. In meretricem. O10. Of an ould vitious man O30. On a licentious person OC2. a Whorer. SN3. One a whore master Y1. In Calvum: Y6. *A licentious person.* A–F G(A). *Incerti Authoris / Of a Bald-man.* Epig. 51. 16 17a–b. *om* B23 H5 H6 LR1 NY3 O41 R3 VA3.

1 Thy] His O30. Sins] skinns, B7; ~, CT1 DT1 O3 O41 WN1 Y6; haires F3; hayres, O30 16 17a–b. haires] hayre B7 B23 CT1 DT1 H4; sinnes F3; heyres LR1; ~, O3; synns, O30 16 17a–b. may no man] no man can B23 F3 F7 LA1 O3 O30 O41 OC2 Y1 Y6; noe man may CJ1 O1 O10 R3 VA3 16 7a–b. call] ~, B45 H4 OC2 SA1 Y6 A–G 16 17a–b 46; ~; H5 O30; ~: O41.

2 For] ~, A–G 46. as] all B23. thy] his O30. increase,] ~$_{\wedge}$ B7 B28 B45 CT1 F3 F7 H6 LA1 O1 O10 R3 SA1 SN3 Y1 16 17a–b; ~,(*var:* ›do rise,‹) O41. thy] his O30. haires] heyres LR1; hayre O3. fall.] ~$_{\wedge}$ B7 B28 CT1 F3 F7 H6 LA1 O3 O10 R3 WN1; ~. | CJ1 DT1 LR1 O1; ~: O30; ~ | Y1; ~! Y6.

Subscriptions: finis LA1. *om* B7 B23 B28 B45 CJ1 CT1 DT1 F3 F7 H4 H5 H6 LR1 NY3 O1 O3 O10 O30 O41 OC2 R3 SA1 SN3 VA3 WN1 Y1 Y6 A–G 16 17a–b 46.

Verbal Variants in Selected Modern Editions

Editions collated: H I J K M N O P Q S T Y Z AA DD.
Headings: A *licentious person.* H–K M O–Q S T Y–AA DD. VIII. A LICENTIOUS PERSON N.

Schema of Textual Relationships

Early and intermediate texts

B23 H5 H6 LR1 NY3 O41 R3 VA3

lost holograph a —— HE *om*

Late text

B7 CT1 DT1 H4 SA1 WN1 A–G

lost holograph b —— HE A *Licentious Person.*

Unaffiliated: F3 F7 O1 O3 O10 O30 SN3 Y1 Y6

Martial

Textual Introduction

Composed in response to the publication of Matthew Rader's publication of an expurgated edition of Martial in 1602, *Martial* may be the last epigram Donne wrote. The poem first appears in NY3, where it bears the Latin heading "Martial: castratus"; and under an English title designed to render the poem intelligible at a somewhat later time, it is subsequently included in the late sequence, appearing in B7–H4 as well as in WN1. In both sequences it stands next-to-last in the arrangement, a position perhaps in keeping with its place in the order of composition. As suggested in the General Textual Introduction to the Epigrams, the datability of Rader's edition and this epigram's absence from the intermediate-stage manuscripts LR1 and SN3 indicates both a *terminus a quo* for the assembly of the NY3 sequence and, possibly, a *terminus ad quem* for compilation of the groups in LR1 and SN3. The copy in H6, squeezed in after the scribe had entered his initial body of epigrams, derives from the later text of the poem headed "Raderus." *Martial* does not seem to have enjoyed much of an independent contemporary circulation; apart from its inclusion in the major manuscripts here discussed, the only other manuscript copy, which may well derive from a printed edition, is that entered on the flyleaf of LU1, a copy of a 1661 edition of Martial's epigrams.

The general relationships among the texts of the epigrams in B7, CT1, DT1, and H4 are partly clarified in the headings given this poem, where B7 and CT1 read "Randerus" while DT1 and H4 read "Raderus." If, as prior commentators have suggested, the same scribe produced both CT1 and DT1 (see Beal 251), this "Randerus/Raderus" variant may indicate that he copied CT1 first and somehow discovered his error or had it brought to his attention before transcribing DT1. For further information on these relationships, see the Textual Introductions to *Hero* and *Licent*.

Martial appears in A among the other epigrams of the late sequence, and the subsequent seventeenth-century editions (B–G) derive their texts successively from A. G, however, independently introduces the reading "amuse" (for "muse") in line 1, and the modern editions H–M follow G in this error. Grosart (N), who generally follows D–G for his copy-text, corrects the mistake by returning to the reading of A, as do all later modern editors. In the modern editions the poem is generally positioned after *Klock* (as in WN1), its placement in Z being the exception (see General Textual Introduction to the Epigrams above). On the identity of "Katherine" and other topical references in the poem, see the Commentary.

Textual Apparatus

Copy-text: NY3. **Texts collated:** B7 (f. 59); B47 (f. 155v); CT1 (p. 127); DT1

(f. 92v); H4 (p. 149); H6 (p. 336); LU1 (flyleaf); NY3 (f. [46v]); WN1 (p. 45); A (p. 43); B (p. 70); C (p. 70); D (p. 67); E (p. 67); F (p. 67); G (p. 64).

Emendations of the copy-text: Heading: *italics supplied* *castratus.*] castrat9.
3 Katherine] katherine

Historical Collation

Format:
Miscellaneous: *heading in left* M, | p. *in left* M *in second hand* NY3.

Headings: Randerus B7 CT1. Raderus. B47 DT1 H4 H6 WN1 A–G. Dr Donn sen. on Raderus LU1. Martial: castrat9. NY3.

1 Martial] ~, DT1 G. muse;] ~‸ B7 B47 CT1 DT1 H4 H6 WN1; ~, LU1 A–F; amuse, G.

2 himselfe] ~' B47; him selfe WN1. tricks] tricke B47. vse] ~, LU1 A–G.

3 As] ~' DT1. Katherine] Katterine B47; ~, A–G. Coarts] Courts B7 B47 CT1 DT1 H6 LU1 WN1 A–G; Court H4. sake] ~, LU1 A–G. put] but B. Stews.] ~‸ B7 CT1 H4; ~. | DT1; ~ | WN1.

Subscriptions: *none.*

Verbal Variants in Selected Modern Editions

Editions collated: H I J K M N O P Q S T Y Z AA DD.

Headings: *Raderus.* H–K M O–Q S T Y–AA DD. XIV. RADERUS. N.

1 Man gelded] man-gelded M. muse] amuse H–K M.

Schema of Textual Relationships

Earlier text

NY3

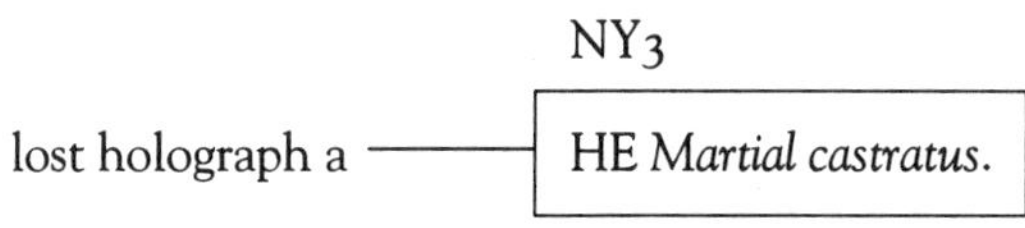

Later text

B7 B47 CT1 DT1 H4 H6 WN1 A–G

lost holographs b & c — HE *Raderus.* (Randerus B7 CT1)

Merc

Textual Introduction

Merc is among the first epigrams Donne circulated, and it appears in each of the sequences printed above, following *Liar* immediately in the three manuscripts containing the early sequence and in the authoritative intermediate-stage NY3; and it occupies this relative position in the late-sequence manuscripts, though neither the B7–H4 group nor WN1 contains *Liar* (see Figure 2 in the General Textual Introduction to the Epigrams). Indeed, as suggested in the General Textual Introduction to the Epigrams above, *Merc* almost certainly should have retained this placement in LR1 and A, in each of which its length seems to have dictated that it be repositioned in the artifact. Corresponding to the succession of the sequences, the poem exhibits two distinct forms, distinguished by a variant in line 8. Reading "and ly'st like a Greeke," the earlier of these texts appears in the manuscripts that preserve the early and intermediate sequences, while the revised reading "but liest" appears in the manuscripts containing the late sequence (see Schema of Textual Relationships).

Perhaps because of the poem's length or density of meaning, the scribes of several manuscripts—including some of those containing the late sequence—had trouble with this text. Of the B7–WN1 group, for instance, all except H4 (which apparently corrects the error on its own) misread the "which" in line 3 as "with," and WN1 further obfuscates the line by including only a comma after "nothing" and placing a full stop after "confesse" at the end. The problematic nature of line 3 is further reflected in the reading "which nothing I confess" in H7, H8, R9, and Y2—a reading, incidentally, picked up much later by Grosart (N) from H8, though without explicit acknowledgment. Additionally, WN1 corrupts the text in line 7, where it fails to give any punctuation whatsoever after "all." H6's use of parentheses in the reading "(ô Mercury)" in line 1, as well as its substitution of "That" for "Which" at the beginning of line 2, is perhaps due to conscious scribal tinkering, as may be its spelling "donne" in line 6—a visual pun also present in WN1. A contemporary penchant for visual wit is also manifest in H7's spelling of "like" as "Lyeke" in both lines 7 and 8, where it makes a sight rhyme with "Greeke."

With the troublesome "which" in line 3 spelled correctly, *Merc* appears in A as the fifteenth of sixteen epigrams, an apparent compositorial rearrangement discussed above. Whether "which" is a compositor's correction of "with" or whether the actual setting text of A was a clone of WN1 that read "which" is indeterminate (see the General Textual Introduction to the Epigrams for fuller discussion of the relationship between WN1 and A). Whatever the case, B–G take their texts successively from A, and follow A's arrangement. The modern editions H–M derive specifically from G. With the above-noted exception in Grosart, who generally follows D–G as his copy-text, all subsequent modern editors use A as copy-text and, with the exception of Milgate

(Y) and Shawcross (Z), place the poem after *Martial* as does A (for the arrangement of the poems in the modern editions, see the General Textual Introduction to the Epigrams above).

Textual Apparatus

Copy-text: NY3. **Texts collated:** B7 (f. 58v); B47 (f. 156); CT1 (p. 126); DT1 (f. 92v); H4 (p. 148); H5 (p. 436); H6 (p. 337); H7 (p. 318); H8 (f. 24v); HH1 (f. 107); HH4 (p. 89); LR1 (f. 280); NY3 (f. [46v]); R9 (p. 303); WN1 (p. 44); Y2 (f. 68v); A (p. 43); B (p. 70); C (p. 70); D (p. 67); E (p. 67); F (p. 67); G (p. 64).

Emendations of the copy-text: Heading: *Mercurius Gallobelgicus*] Mercuri^{9} Gallobelgic^{9} 2 Which] W^{ch} and] & 3 which] wch 7 Change] change 8 and] &

Historical Collation

Format:

Indentations: *ll. 7–8 ind* H5 H6.

Miscellaneous: LC. *in left M beside heading in scribal hand* HH4; 16 *penciled in M in later hand* LR1; *heading in left M beside l. 2*, | p. *in left M in second hand* NY3.

Headings: Mercurius Gallo Belgicus B7. Mercurius Gallo-Belgicus. B47 CT1 DT1 H4 H5 H6 R9 WN1 A–G. *Vppon Mercurius Gallo-Belgicus.* H7. *Mercurius Gallobelgicus.* H8 LR1 NY3. 4 / Mercurius Gallobelgicus. Græcus HH1. Vpon Mercurius Gallobelgicus HH4. Vpon Mercurius Gallo belgicus. Y2.

1 Æsops] Esope HH4. fellow slaues,] fellowe-slaues, DT1 H5 A–C; fellow slaves$_\wedge$ H4 H6; fellow-slave, H7; fellow-slaues$_\wedge$ H8 R9 WN1; fellow slaue, HH4; fellow slaue$_\wedge$ LR1; fellowe slaue: Y2. O] (ô H6 HH1; and R9. Mercury] ~) H6; ~!) HH1; ~, WN1 A–G.

2 Which] That H6. could] wold H7. all things,] all thinges$_\wedge$ H4 H6 H7 H8 LR1 WN1; allthings, HH1 HH4. is,] ~$_\wedge$ H4 WN1; ~; LR1 A–G. I] ~, HH1.

3 selfe,] ~$_\wedge$ B7 B47 CT1 DT1 H4 H6 H8 R9 D–G. which] wth B7 CT1 DT1 R9 WN1. nothing;] ~: B7 B47 CT1 DT1 H4 H5 HH1 LR1; ~. H6; ~$_\wedge$ H7 H8 R9 Y2; ~, HH4 WN1. confes] ~, H8 R9; ~. WN1.

4 should] would H4. fayth] ~, B7 CT1 DT1 H5 H7 HH1 Y2 A–G. thou] y^{o} LR1; you R9. hadst] hadt LR1; had R9; hads Y2. les.] ~$_\wedge$ B7 B47 CT1 DT1 H4 HH1 HH4 LR1 WN1 Y2; ~: H5 H8 R9; ~; A–G.

5 credit] ~, WN1. credit:] ~. DT1; ~, H4 H8 HH4 R9 Y2; ~; H6 HH1. tis] is itt HH4. doo] ~, H6 A–G.

6 In] (~ HH4. case] ~, B47 H5 H6 WN1 A–C; ~) HH4. done] donne H6 WN1. vntoo,] ~‸ B7 DT1 H4 H5 H6 H7 HH4 LR1 Y2; ~. B47 CT1 H8.

7 all.] ~, B7 B47 CT1 DT1 H4; ~: H5 H8 HH1 LR1 R9 A–G; ~; H6 Y2; ~‸ WN1. name;] ~, B7 CT1 DT1 H5 H6 HH1 R9; ~. B47; ~: H4 WN1 A–G; ~‸ H7 H8 HH4 LR1 Y2. thou] y^{w} H7. like] Lyeke H7; leike HH4.

8 in] is B7. stealing,] ~‸ H6 LR1. and] but B7 B47 CT1 DT1 H4 H5(M *var:* ›and‹) HH4 WN1 Y2 A–G. lyest] lye'st DT1 H5 H6 HH1 G. like] lyeke H7. a] *om* B7. Greeke.] ~‸ B7 CT1 H6 HH1 HH4; ~. | DT1 LR1; ~: H4; ~, R9; ~ | WN1.

Subscriptions: *none.*

Verbal Variants in Selected Modern Editions

Editions collated: H I J K M N O P Q S T Y Z AA DD.
Format:
Miscellaneous: *Ralphius appended as ll. 9–10 and ind 2 spaces* I J; *Ralphius, untitled, follows after a one-line break* K M.
Headings: *Mercurius Gallo-Belgicus.* H–K M O–Q S T Y–AA DD.
XV. MERCURIUS GALLO-BELGICUS. N.

8 and] but H–K M–Q S T Y–AA DD.

Schema of Textual Relationships

Version 1

H5 H6 H7 H8 HH1 LR1 NY3 R9

lost holographs a & b — 8 Mercury in stealing **and** ly'st like a Greeke

Version 2

B7 B47 CT1 DT1 H4 HH4 WN1 Y2 A–G

lost holograph c — 8 Mercury in stealinge, **but** liest like a Greeke.

Niobe

Textual Introduction

Niobe first appears among the epigrams in the intermediate sequence, where it occupies the third position, following *Pyr* in the expanded arrangement. Except for the groups of epigrams assembled piecemeal in H6 and B47, moreover, it generally retains this placement in all the major manuscript collections, including those containing the late sequence that made its way into the printed editions; indeed, it is even the third poem in Drummond's primary sequence in SN3 (see Figure 2 in the General Textual Introduction to the Epigrams). Further, the poem exhibits two possibly authorial forms in the manuscripts, corresponding to the succession of the sequences; and a third, apparently compositorial revision is printed in A. These three forms are distinguished by points of variation in each of the poem's two lines: in line 1, A alters the "birth" found in both the earlier and later manuscript texts to the plural "births," and line 2 is rendered differently in each of the three successive forms of the text. The earlier manuscript text, found in the artifacts containing the intermediate sequence, presents "made myne owne tombe"; the later manuscript text (in B7–WN1) then resolves the contradiction between "become" and "made" by omitting "made," but leaves a catalectic line; and, finally, A repairs the meter of the later manuscript text by inserting "sad" after "owne" (see Schema of Textual Relationships).

The texts of B–G derive successively from A, and all modern editions except those of Milgate (Y) and Shawcross (Z), which give the earlier manuscript reading "made mine own," follow suit in reproducing the compositorial "mine own sad" in line 2. Y and Z also return to the singular "birth" of the manuscripts in line 1, as do Chalmers (K) and Smith (AA), which retain A's reading of line 2. All collected editions from A onward print *Niobe* as the third epigram in the sequence.

Textual Apparatus

Copy-text: NY3. **Texts collated:** B7 (f. 48); B47 (f. 131v); C10 (p. 68); CT1 (p. 125); DT1 (f. 92); H4 (p. 148); H6 (p. 339); LR1 (f. 279v); NY3 (f. [46]); SN3 (f. 36); WN1 (p. 43); A (p. 40); B (p. 68); C (p. 68); D (p. 65); E (p. 65); F (p. 65); G (p. 62).

Emendations of the copy-text: Heading: *italics supplied* 1 and] & I ame] Iame 2 that] y[t]

Historical Collation

Format:

Miscellaneous: *heading beside l. 1 in left M* B47; 3 *penciled in M in later hand*

LR1; *heading beside l. 2 in left* M, | p. *in left* M *in second hand* NY3.
Headings: Niobe B7 B47 CT1 DT1 H4 H6 LR1 NY3 SN3 WN1 A–G.

1 birth,] ~‸ B47 H6 LR1 SN3; births, A–G. death] Death CT1 DT1; Death, SN3; ~, WN1 A–G. I ame] Iame NY3.

2 now] ~, B47. made] *om* B7 CT1 DT1 H4 WN1 A–G. myne] my LR1 SN3. tombe.] ~‸ B7 B47 CT1 DT1 H6; wet tombe. C10; »sad« Tombe. H4; ~. | WN1; sad tombe. A–G.

Subscriptions: *none.*

Verbal Variants in Selected Modern Editions

Editions collated: H I J K M N O P Q S T Y Z AA DD.
Headings: *Niobe.* H–K M O–Q S T Y–AA DD. III. NIOBE. N.

1 birth] births H–J M–Q S T DD.

2 made myne owne] mine own sad H–K M–Q S T AA DD.

Schema of Textual Relationships

Version 1

B47 H6 LR1 NY3 SN3

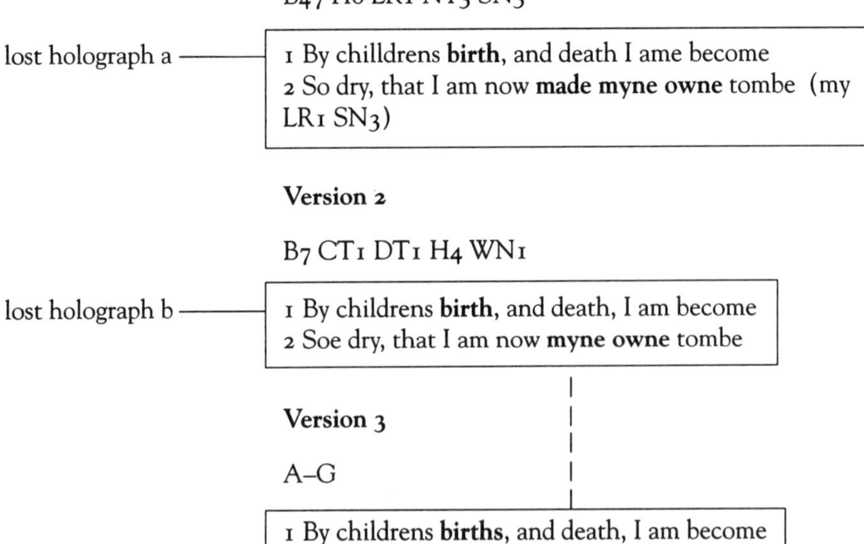

Philo

Textual Introduction

Philo is included in all three sequences of the epigrams—early, intermediate, and late. It appears as the sixth poem in the early sequence, placed between *Phrine* and *Klock*, and remains in this context in the intermediate and late sequences, even though Donne moves the first sequence *in toto* to the end of the expanded group comprised in the middle and late arrangements (see Figure 2 in the General Textual Introduction to the Epigrams). The poem is substantively free of textual variation, first acquiring a title in the manuscripts containing the late sequence. The epigram was included in the seventeenth-century editions A–G, which reproduce the late manuscript sequence, and has appeared, similarly placed, in all subsequent collected editions. For its exact position in twentieth-century editions, see the General Textual Introduction to the Epigrams above.

Textual Apparatus

Copy-text: NY3. **Texts collated:** B7 (f. 58); B28 (f. 113v); CT1 (p. 126); DT1 (f. 92v); H4 (p. 149); H5 (p. 435); H6 (p. 338); H8 (f. 24v); HH1 (f. 107v); LR1 (f. 280); NY3 (f. [46v]); SA1 (p. 61); WN1 (p. 44); A (p. 42); B (p. 70); C (p. 70); D (p. 67); E (p. 67); F (p. 67); G (p. 64).
Emendations of the copy-text: Heading: *supplied from* A   1 with] w[t]

Historical Collation

Format:
Miscellaneous: 70 *in* M B28; 13 *penciled in* M *in later hand (should be* 14*)* LR1; | p. *beside l.* 1 *in left* M *in second hand* NY3.
Headings: An obscure writer B7 B28 CT1 DT1 H4 WN1 A–G. 6 HH1. *om* H5 H6 H8 LR1 NY3 SA1.

1 Philo,] ~‸ B7 B28 CT1 DT1 H4 H5 H6 H8 HH1 LR1 SA1 WN1. 12] twelve B7 CT1 DT1 H4 H5 H8 SA1 WN1 A–G. yeares] yeare B7. study] ~, A. griev'd] grieued B28 H8 WN1; ~, A–G.

2 To be'vnderstood,] To be vnderstood, B7 CT1 H4 H6 H8 HH1; to be understood‸ B28; to b'vnderstood; H5; To bee vnderstood: LR1; To bee

vnderstood. WN1; To'be understood, A–G. beleevd?] ~^ B7 H6 HH1 WN1; beleiued? B28 H8; ~.| SA1; ~. A B.

Subscriptions: *none.*

Verbal Variants in Selected Modern Editions

Editions collated: H I J K M N O P Q S T Y Z AA DD.
Format:
Miscellaneous: *Klockius, untitled, follows after a one-line break* K M.
Headings: *An obscure Writer.* H–K M O–Q S T Y–AA DD. XII. AN OBSCURE WRITER. N.

Schema of Textual Relationships

Early and intermediate text

H5 H6 H8 HH1 LR1 NY3

lost holographs a & b — HE *om* (6 HH1)

Late text

B7 B28 CT1 DT1 H4 SA1 WN1 A–G

lost holograph c — HE *An Obscure Writer.* (*om* SA1)

Phrine

Textual Introduction

Phrine is included in all three sequences of the epigrams—early, intermediate, and late. It appears as the fifth poem in the manuscripts containing the early sequence (the irregularly ordered H5 excepted), placed between *Merc* and *Philo*, and—with two bibliographically explainable exceptions—retains this position when the entire first sequence is moved to the end of the expanded group comprised in the middle and late manuscripts and the printed editions (see Figure 2 in the General Textual Introduction to the Epigrams). As explained in the General Textual Introduction to the Epigrams, the eight-line length of *Merc* very likely caused both the scribe of LR1 and the compositor of A to move it to the end of their collections. Except for the acquisition of a title in the late sequence, the text of *Phrine* is essentially invariant, though both B47 and LR1 rename the addressee of the epigram, B47 calling her "Phriscus" and LR1 calling her "Latrine." B47's alteration here is very likely scribal, and that in LR1 may be as well, though LR1's inclusion of a further variant—the reversal of "you both" to "both you" in line 2—suggests that throughout the whole poem the scribe may have been faithfully copying his source as he found it. If, as has been suggested (see Beal 251), H4 is a copy of DT1, its correction of DT1's erroneous "wee" to "ye" in line 2 shows that its scribe was capable of exercising independent judgment to restore sense to a corrupted passage.

The text of A is that given in the B7–WN1 group, although A spells the poem's title with a "y" in both the heading and line 1. B and C derive successively from A. D, on no manuscript authority, introduces the word "to" before "thee" in line 1, an alteration retained in the seventeenth-century editions E–G and the modern editions H–K M N. G also misspells the subject's name "Phyrne," but the corrected spelling is immediately restored to the tradition in H. Beginning with Lowell (O) in 1895, all subsequent collected editions have reverted to the text as found in A and, except for Y, have positioned the epigram as in A.

Textual Apparatus

Copy-text: NY3. **Texts collated:** B7 (f. 58v); B28 (f. 113v); B45 (f. 34v); B47 (f. 131v); CT1 (p. 126); DT1 (f. 92v); H4 (p. 149); H5 (p. 435); H6 (p. 337); H8 (f. 24v); HH1 (f. 107); LR1 (f. 280); NY3 (f. [46v]); OC2 (f. 47v); SA1 (p. 61); SN3 (f. 36v); WN1 (p. 44); A (p. 42); B (p. 70); C (p. 70); D (p. 67); E (p. 67); F (p. 67); G (p. 64); 30 (p. 143).

Emendations of the copy-text: Heading: *supplied from* SN3, *italics supplied*
2 that] y[t]

Historical Collation

Format:
Miscellaneous: 70 *in* M B28; 13 *penciled in* M *in later hand* LR1; | p. *beside l.* 1 *in left* M *in second hand* NY3.
Headings: Phrine B7 CT1 DT1 H4 SN3 WN1. A Coquette B28. Phryne B45 SA1 A–F. 5 HH1. On Phryne OC2. *Phyrne.* G. On Ledaes *Picture.* 30. *om* B47 H5 H6 H8 LR1 NY3.

1 flattering] flattring B28 H6. picture] ~, B7 B45 CT1 DT1 H5 HH1 OC2 SN3 A–G. Phrine,] Phryne‸ B28 H6 SA1 C; Phryne, B45 H5 OC2 A–B D–F; ~‸ H4 H8; Phriscus‸ B47; Latrine‸ LR1; *Phyrne,* G; only‸ 30. thee] ~, B45 HH1 OC2 A–C 30; to thee, D–G.

2 Only] LEDA 30. this] ~, B45 DT1 H4 H5 H8 HH1 OC2 SA1 SN3 A–G 30. you both] wee both DT1; ye both H4; both y° LR1. bee.] ~ | B7; ~‸ B28 CT1 DT1 H6 SA1; ~. | OC2 WN1.

Subscriptions: *none.*

Verbal Variants in Selected Modern Editions

Editions collated: H I J K M N O P Q S T Y Z AA DD.
Headings: *Phryne.* H–K M O–Q S T Y–AA DD. XI. PHRYNE. N.

1 thee] to thee H–K M N.

Schema of Textual Relationships

Early and intermediate text

H5 H6 H8 HH1 LR1 NY3

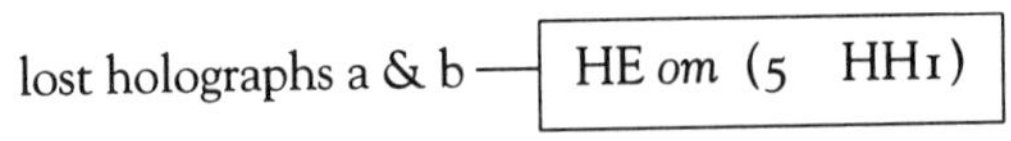

Late text

B7 B47 CT1 DT1 H4 SA1 SN3 WN1 A–G

lost holograph c — HE *Phrine.* (*om* B47)

Pyr

Textual Introduction

Pyr first appears among the epigrams in the intermediate sequence, where it occupies the second position, following *Hero*, in the new, expanded arrangement. It retains this placement in all the major manuscript collections of epigrams, moreover, including those containing the late sequence printed in A and the subsequent editions, except for the groups assembled piecemeal in H6, B47, and SA1; indeed, it is even the second poem in Drummond's primary sequence in SN3 (see Figure 2 in the General Textual Introduction to the Epigrams). The poem invariably bears the heading "Pyramus and Thisbe" in the manuscripts and in all the printed editions from 1633 (A) through Patrides's (DD). It is impossible to say with certainty whether the variants in the SN3 copy—"others" (for "other") in line 1 and "paine" for "haue" in line 2—represent an attempt to improve the poem or a mere failure of memory, but they must surely be scribal in origin, as must the solecism "slain'd" in the cognate manuscripts O21 and Y3. Since the text of the poem is essentially identical in the intermediate and late sequences, we have not included a Schema of Textual Relationships in the Textual Apparatus.

The poem appears as the second epigram in all collected editions of Donne's poetry from A through DD, exhibiting no verbal variation except for Grosart's independent emendation (in N) of "other" to "other's" in line 1.

Textual Apparatus

Copy-text: NY3. **Texts collated:** B7 (f. 58); B28 (f. 113); B47 (f. 155); CT1 (p. 125); DT1 (f. 92); H3 (p. 48); H4 (p. 148); H6 (p. 338); LR1 (f. 279v); NY3 (f. [46]); O21 (p. 26); O25 (p. 80); SA1 (p. 64); SN3 (f. 36); WN1 (p. 43); Y3 (p. 23); A (p. 40); B (p. 68); C (p. 68); D (p. 65); E (p. 65); F (p. 65); G (p. 62).
Emendations of the copy-text: Heading: *italics supplied* *Pyramus*] Pyram^9 *and*] &

Historical Collation

Format:

Miscellaneous: 68 *in* M B28; 2 *penciled in* M *in later hand* LR1; *heading in left* M *beside line* 2, | p. *in left* M *in second hand* NY3.

Headings: Piramis and Thisby B7 CT1 DT1 H4 O21 SA1 WN1 Y3. Pyramus & Thisbe B28 B47 H3 H6 LR1 NY3 O25 A–G. Pyramus and Tisbe. SN3.

1 Two,] ~‸ B7 B28 B47 CT1 DT1 H3 H4 H6 LR1 O21 O25 SA1 WN1 Y3. themselues,] ~‸ B28 B47 CT1 DT1 H3 H4 H6 LR1 O21 O25 SN3 Y3. other,] ~‸ B28 H4 H6 LR1 O21 Y3 B–G; others‸ SN3. Love] loue B28 B47 LR1 SN3 Y3 A–G; ~, DT1; loue, H3 H4 O25 SA1 WN1. Feare] feare B7 B28 CT1 H3 H4 H6 LR1 O21 WN1 Y3 A–G; feare, B47 O25 SA1 SN3.

2 Slayne,] ~‸ B28 LR1 O25; ~. H3; Slain'd‸ O21 Y3. frinds,] ~‸ B28 LR1 O21 O25 WN1 Y3; Friends, DT1 H4. parting] ~, WN1. haue] paine SN3. ioynd] ioyned B47. here.] ~‸ B7 B28 B47 CT1 DT1 H4 H6 O21 Y3; ~.| LR1 WN1.

Subscriptions: J.D. H3 O25 SA1. J D ffinis O21 Y3(J:). *om* B7 B28 B47 CT1 DT1 H4 H6 LR1 NY3 SN3 WN1 A–G.

Verbal Variants in Selected Modern Editions

Editions collated: H I J K M N O P Q S T Y Z AA DD.
Headings: *Pyramus* and *Thisbe*. H–K M O–Q S T Y–AA DD. II. PYRAMUS AND THISBE. N.

1 other] other's N.

Ralph

Textual Introduction

Ralph is included in all three sequences of the epigrams—early, intermediate, and late. It appears near the end of the group in the manuscripts containing the early sequence, following *Klock* immediately in H5, HH1, and H6 (which recapitulates the early sequence in this part of its arrangement). The poem is missing from LR1, because either of a slip of Donne's memory in preparing the prototype upon which LR1 is based or of a scribal oversight, but reappears as the last epigram in NY3, the most important middle-stage manuscript, where it follows *Martial*. It precedes *Klock* in the jumbled order of SN3. The poem is also missing (or excluded) from the late-stage manuscripts B7–H4, but reemerges in WN1, where it again follows *Martial* and assumes the final position in the sequence. The poem retains this final position in the printed editions, but is placed after *Merc*, in accordance with the compositor's rearrangement of the sequence in A (see the Textual Introduction to *Merc*).

Except for the headings "Ralphius" in SN3 and "Witty Epigram" in B28, both scribal in origin, the poem is untitled in the manuscripts, in the seventeenth-century printed editions, and in all modern editions up through M. The lack of demarcation arising from this absence of a title, in fact, is undoubtedly that which leads to the poem's being printed as lines 9–10 of *Merc* in I and J, a situation only slightly remedied in K and M, which set the poem off from the preceding *Merc* with a mere one-line break and include no title. Both Grosart (N) and Lowell (O) invent titles for the poem (see the Textual Apparatus), however, and from Chambers (P) onward the poem has appeared under the heading "Ralphius." In all modern editions except Y and Z *Ralph* follows *Merc*, its traditional position from 1633 onward. Since the text of the poem is essentially identical in the early, middle, and late sequences, we have not included a Schema of Textual Relationships in the Textual Apparatus.

Textual Apparatus

Copy-text: NY3. **Texts collated:** B28 (f. 114); H5 (p. 435); H6 (p. 338); HH1 (f. 107v); NY3 (f. [46v]); SN3 (f. 36v); WN1 (p. 45); A (p. 43); B (p. 70); C (p. 70); D (p. 67); E (p. 67); F (p. 67); G (p. 64).

Emendations of the copy-text: Heading: *supplied from* SN3, *italics supplied*

1 the] ye 2 the] y^e

Historical Collation

Format:

Miscellaneous: 70 *in* M B28; | p. *beside l.* 1 *in left* M NY3.

Headings: Witty Epigram B28. 8 HH1. Ralphius. SN3. *om* H5 H6 NY3 WN1 A–G.

1 bredd] ~, H5 SN3 WN1; ~: A–G.

2 sick,] ~‸ B28 H6. bedd.] ~‸ B28 H6 HH1; ~.| WN1.

Subscriptions: *none.*

Verbal Variants in Selected Modern Editions

Editions collated: H I J K M N O P Q S T Y Z AA DD.
Format:
Indentations: *l.* 2 *ind* AA.
Miscellaneous: *printed as ll.* 9–10 *of Merc* I J.
Headings: XVI. THE SICK BROKER. N. A WONDER. O. [RALPHIUS.] P. *Ralphius.* Q S T Y–AA DD. *om* H–K M.

SelfAc

Textual Introduction

SelfAc appears in manuscripts that contain, respectively, the early, middle, and late sequences of the epigrams, and its text exhibits corresponding early, middle, and late forms. In the early manuscript collections, the poem's position relative to the other epigrams varies—it appears second in H5, not at all in H8, and tenth in HH1, where it is separated from HH1's other nine epigrams by several manuscript pages. This bibliographical evidence suggests that the poem entered the stream of transmission at some point after Donne had already begun to circulate the early sequence, though perhaps quite soon after; and for this purely bibliographical reason we have not presented *SelfAc* as part of the early sequence, even though it is thematically similar to such early epigrams as *Antiq* and *Disinher* that treat of character types. Once the poem is authorially integrated into the sequence, however, in the intermediate-stage manuscripts LR1 and NY3, it becomes the first of the "character" epigrams that follow the military epigrams *Ship*, *Wall*, *Beggar*, and—in NY3—*Cales* and *Wing*. It retains this position in WN1, the only late-stage manuscript to include it (see Figure 2 in the General Textual Introduction to the Epigrams).

Separate variants in each of the poem's two lines divide the text into distinct early, intermediate, and late forms. In line 1 the early text reads "oft taxeth" for the "still taxeth" found in the intermediate and late forms; and line 2 reads differently in each of the three forms: the early text gives "shee should confesse though it"; the intermediate text inserts a second "it" after "confes"; and the late text expands the line to thirteen syllables, retaining the second "it" and adding "that" and "thus" to give "that shee should thus confess it" (see the Schema of Textual Relations). The poem thus metamorphoses from a couplet of mixed hexameter and pentameter meters to one composed of matching alexandrines. Filiating the texts in both H6 and SN3 is slightly problematical: the copy in H6, inserted after the scribe had already entered his primary collection and possibly written down from memory, uniquely reads "doth taxe" in line 1, but has the early form of line 2; we have thus sorted it with the early texts in H5 and HH1. SN3 records the early form of line 2, but in line 1 gives the distinctive "still taxeth" reading of the intermediate text. That Drummond would independently regularize meter seems more likely than that he would alter "oft" to "still," so we have linked SN3 with LR1 and NY3 in the Schema of Textual Relationships. Characteristically, Drummond also gives the poem a title ("A mistrisse"), but it otherwise remains untitled until the compilation of the final sequence, where it is headed "A Selfe Accuser." The highly variant texts in CJ1 and O41 are almost certainly memorial reconstructions.

The late text of the poem found in WN1 is printed in the seventeenth-century editions (A–G), and this text subsequently appears in all modern editions except Y and AA, which give the intermediate form. As in WN1 and A–G, it is invariably positioned after *Beggar* until the rediscovery of *Cales* and *Wing* in the late nineteenth century, after which it is sometimes shoved down in the order to make room for these beside the other military epigrams. For its exact position in modern editions, see the General Textual Introduction to the Epigrams.

Textual Apparatus

Copy-text: NY3. **Texts collated:** B28 (f. 113v); B45 (f. 34); CJ1 (f. 32v); H5 (p. 435); H6 (p. 339); HH1 (f. 114v); LR1 (f. 279v); NY3 (f. [46]); O41 (p. 52); SN3 (f. 36); WN1 (p. 43); A (p. 41); B (p. 69); C (p. 69); D (p. 66); E (p. 66); F (p. 66); G (p. 63).

Emendations of the copy-text: Heading: *supplied from* A 1 that] y^{t}

Historical Collation

Format:

Miscellaneous: 69 *in* M B28; *poem squeezed in after other epigrams were transcribed* H6; 7 *penciled in* M *in later hand* LR1; | p. *beside l.* 1 *in* M *in second hand* NY3.

Headings: A Selfe accuser B28 B45 WN1 A–G. on a M^{rs}. CJ1. 10th Epigram HH1. A mistrisse SN3. *om* H5 H6 LR1 NY3 O41.

1 Your Mistres,] y^{r} Mistris$_{\wedge}$ B28 B45 H6 HH1 LR1 WN1; That you$_{\wedge}$ CJ1; You follow$_{\wedge}$ O41. that you follow whores,] y^{t} you follow whores$_{\wedge}$ B28 B45 H6 HH1 LR1 WN1 B–G; haunt whores yor M$^{rs}_{\wedge}$ CJ1; Whores; (yor Mistress$_{\wedge}$ O41. still] oft H5 HH1; *om* CJ1 H6 O41. taxeth] taxes H5; doth taxe H6. you,] ~$_{\wedge}$ B28 CJ1 H5 H6 HH1 LR1 WN1; ~:) O41; ~: A; ~; D–G.

2 strange,] Strange$_{\wedge}$ B28; ~$_{\wedge}$ B45 CJ1 H5 H6 HH1 LR1 WN1 A–G. she] y^{t} Shee B28 B45 WN1 A–G. should] should thus B28 B45 WN1 A–G; would CJ1. confes] ~, H5 SN3. it,] ~$_{\wedge}$ B45 CJ1 WN1; ~; O41; *om* H5 H6 HH1 SN3. though'it] though it B28 B45 H5 H6 HH1 SN3 WN1; thought LR1; though 'tis O41. be] *om* O41. true.] ~$_{\wedge}$ B28 B45 CJ1 H5 HH1 WN1.

Subscriptions: *none.*

Verbal Variants in Selected Modern Editions

Editions collated: H I J K M N O P Q S T Y Z AA DD.

Headings: A *Self-accuser.* H–K M O–Q S T Y–AA DD. VII. A SELFE-ACCUSER. N.

2 she should] that she should thus H–K M–Q S T Z DD.

Schema of Textual Relationships

Version 1

H5 H6 HH1

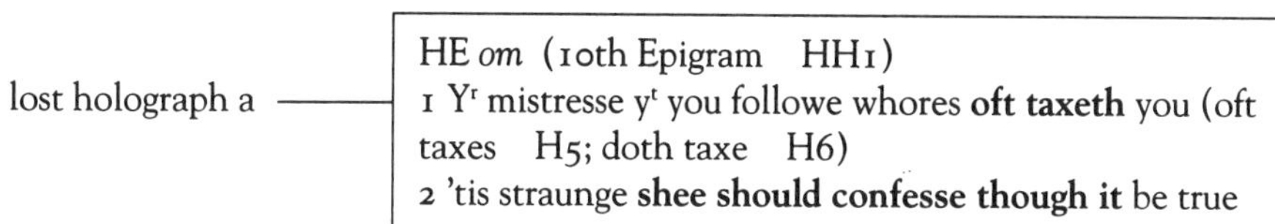

Version 2

LR1 NY3 SN3

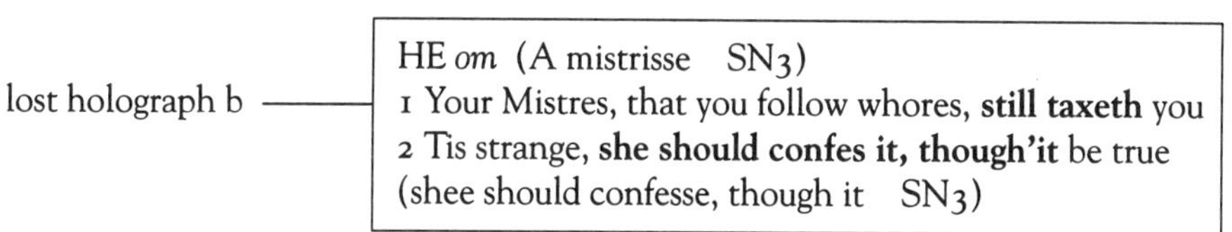

Version 3

B28 B45 WN1 A–G

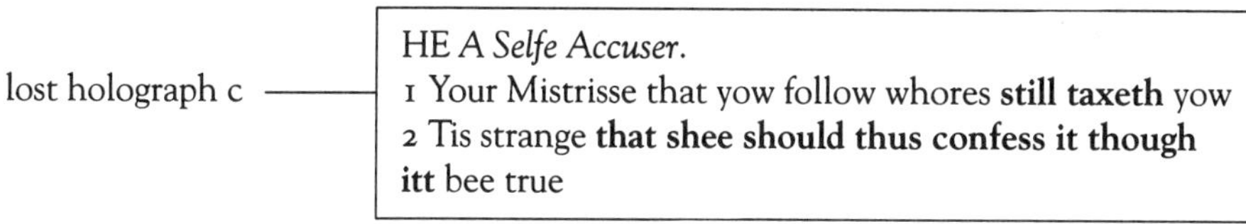

Unaffiliated: CJ1 O41

Ship

Textual Introduction

Apparently inspired by an event that Donne witnessed at Cadiz in 1595, *Ship* initially appears as the first of the "Spanish" epigrams introduced into the intermediate sequence in LR1 and NY3, and continues in this position (immediately after *Niobe*) in the manuscripts containing the late sequence (see the Commentary for alternate accounts of the poem's inspiration). Although some textual variation occurs in the course of transmission, the only change likely to be authorial in origin is the alteration of the Italian title "Nave arsa" found in LR1 and NY3 to the English "A Burnt Ship" in the late manuscripts—a revision, like the change of "Zoppo" to "A Lame Begger," perhaps politically motivated. The non-English heading on H6's copy of the poem, as well as their mutual inclusion of the otherwise unrecorded *Cales* and *Wing*, suggests a link between NY3 and this part of the H6 sequence, but the nature of that link is indeterminate. Questions remain not only about H6's positioning of this poem, but also about its inept attempt to latinize the Italian title (it reads "De Naue arsa") and its reduction of the last line from an alexandrine to pentameter by the omission of "being" and the elision of "in the" to one syllable. These are undoubtedly scribal alterations, but whether they represent conscious editorializing on the part of the H6 scribe, corruption in the source from which he copied, or possibly even imperfect efforts at memorial reconstruction is not clear. Similarly perplexing are the three instances in LR1 where the scribe writes "y^r^" instead of the normative "y^e^": if not impossible, these readings seem highly unlikely, yet the repetition of this mistake three times in an otherwise sound transcription suggests that the LR1 scribe may in these instances have copied what he saw in his source. B47's omission of "could" in line 2 and its pluralization of "shott" in line 4 are undoubtedly scribal blunders, as is B7's expansion of "Nere" to "Neere to" in line 4, the latter error further confirming B7's derivation from CT1 as well as the similar descent of SA1 (see the Textual Introduction to *Hero*).

In the late manuscript text of WN1 and positioned as in WN1—as the fourth epigram, appearing immediately after *Niobe*—*Ship* enters the print tradition in A and continues in this text and placement in B–G and, successively, in all modern editions.

Textual Apparatus

Copy-text: NY3. **Texts collated:** B7 (f. 58); B28 (f. 113v); B47 (f. 155v); CT1 (p. 125); DT1 (f. 92); H4 (p. 148); H6 (p. 339); LR1 (f. 279v); NY3 (f. [46]); SA1 (p. 63); WN1 (p. 43); A (p. 41); B (p. 68); C (p. 68); D (p. 65); E (p. 65); F (p. 65); G (p. 62).

Emendations of the copy-text: Heading: *italics supplied* 1 which] w[ch] 2 But] but 4 the] y[e] 5 which] w[ch] 6 drownd.] drow[nd]‸

Historical Collation

Format:

Imperfections: *part of last word in l. 6 lost in trimming* B7.

Indentations: *ll.* 5–6 *ind* B7 B47 CT1 DT1 H4 SA1; *l.* 6 *ind* A–G.

Miscellaneous: 68 *in* M B28; 4 *penciled in* M *in later hand* LR1; *heading beside l.* 2 *in left* M, | p. *in left* M *in second hand* NY3.

Headings: A Burnt Ship B7(burunt) B28 B47 CT1 DT1 H4 WN1 A–G. De Naue arsa H6. Nave arsa. LR1 NY3. Epigrams. A burnt ship. SA1.

1 ship,] ~‸ B7 B28 B47 DT1 LR1. which] ~, A.

2 drowning] droning → ›drowning‹ B28; drowing LR1; ~, WN1 A–G. could] *om* B47. rescued] rescu'ed B47 H6. flame,] ~‸ B7 B28 B47 CT1 DT1 H4 H6 LR1.

3 leap'd] leapt H4 SA1 WN1; lept LR1. forthe,] ~‸ B28 LR1. ever] ~, H6.

4 Nere] Neere to B7. ships,] ~‸ B28 CT1 H6 LR1 WN1. ther] their B7 B28 B47 CT1 DT1 H4 H6 SA1 WN1 A–G; there LR1. shott] shotts B47. decay.] ~‸ B7 B28 B47 CT1 DT1 H4 H6 LR1; ~; SA1 A–C; ~: D–G.

5 lost,] ~‸ B7 B28 B47 DT1 H4 H6 LR1. the] y[r] LR1. found:] ~‸ B7 B28 B47 CT1 DT1 H4 H6 LR1 SA1 WN1 B C; ~, A D–G.

6 the] y[r] LR1. Sea] ~, H6. beeing] *om* H6. burn't,] ~‸ B28 SA1. they] the B7. in the] it'h H6; in y[r] LR1. ship] ~, B7. drownd.] drow[*missing*] B7; ~‸ B28 CT1 DT1 H6 NY3; ~. | LR1 WN1; dround. A(*unc*).

Subscriptions: J: D. SA1. *om* B7 B28 B47 CT1 DT1 H4 H6 LR1 NY3 WN1 A–G.

Verbal Variants in Selected Modern Editions

Editions collated: H I J K M N O P Q S T Y Z AA DD.

Headings: A *burnt Ship*. H–K M O–Q S T Y–AA DD. IV. A BURNT SHIP. N.

Format:

Indentations: *l.* 6 *ind* O–Q S Z AA DD; *ll.* 2 *and* 4 *ind* T.

Schema of Textual Relationships

Earlier text

H6 LR1 NY3

lost holograph a —— | HE *Nave arsa.* (De Naue arsa H6) |

Later text

B7 B28 B47 CT1 DT1 H4 SA1 WN1 A–G

lost holograph b —— | HE A *Burnt Ship.* |

Wall

Textual Introduction

Apparently inspired by an event at Corunna in 1589 (see the Commentary for alternative explanations), *Wall* is one of Donne's earliest epigrams, and it appears in each of the sequences printed above, occupying the ninth position in the first sequence and a medial position—among the "Spanish" epigrams—in the intermediate and late arrangements. Further, the poem exhibits distinct early, intermediate, and late forms corresponding to the succession of the sequences, thus supporting at the micro level the evidence that the sequences themselves are ultimately authorial. The early and intermediate forms of the text, both of which read "corps" in line 4, are distinguished by the change of "The" to "A" in line 2; and this alteration carries over into the late form of the text, which further changes "corps" to "bones"—thus completing a pattern of revision, as suggested above in the General Textual Introduction to the Epigrams, that reflects the poem's increasing remoteness from the event that inspired it. Though it is present in the LR1 sequence and is there positioned fifth, as in NY3, *Wall* first acquires a title in the latter manuscript, a fact suggesting that when assembling the LR1 sequence Donne had not yet conceived of the Italian title as a means for recycling this used battle poem into the expanded arrangement that he put together after his experiences at Cadiz. Under the heading "Caso d'vn muro" in NY3, however, the poem seems of a piece with "Nave arsa," "Zoppo," "Calez and Guyana," and "Il Caualliere Gio: Wingefield." With the early texts in H5 and HH1, H6 reads "The" (for "A") in line 2; its partially latinized title ("Cæso d'un muro" for "Caso d'vn muro"), however, which shows no signs of being a late addition to the transcription, links its copy of the poem with that in NY3. As explained in the Textual Introduction to *Ship* (q.v.), such anomalies raise unanswerable questions about where the H6 scribe obtained his copies of the poems. Like that in H6, the copy of *Wall* in SN3 bears Donne's Italian heading in a mangled form ("Caso di muro") and reads with the intermediate version of the text in lines 2 and 4, in the latter instance uniquely recording "corse" for "corpse."

In its late revision, with an English heading designed to dissociate the poem from any specific foreign campaign and with the "corpse" of line 4 turned to "bones," *Wall* appears in B7–H4, SA1, and WN1 (this is also the text given in B47). As in the intermediate sequence, it remains in the fifth position, following immediately after *Ship*. The scribe of WN1 flagrantly (and uniquely) blunders in writing "as" for "an" in line 1, and SA1 inadvertently flip-flops the order of "towne" and "tombe" in line 3, further confirming its descent from CT1 (see the Textual Introduction to *Hero*); but there is otherwise no substantive variation among these late copies.

In this late form, the poem makes its way into the print tradition in A, but B independently introduces the variant "towre" (for "towne") in line 4; and this error persists in C–G, which derive successively from B, and in the modern editions H–K M N. It is also repeated in the corrupt rendition printed in the 1650 *Mirrour of Complements* (siglum 30). With Lowell (O), however, the modern editors return to "towne," and this reading from A continues in all subsequent editions. The poem retains its position as the fifth epigram in all collected editions from A onward.

Textual Apparatus

Copy-text: NY3. **Texts collated:** B7 (f. 58); B47 (f. 155v); CT1 (p. 125); DT1 (f. 92); H4 (p. 148); H5 (p. 436); H6 (p. 339); HH1 (f. 107v); LR1 (f. 279v); NY3 (f. [46]); SA1 (p. 63); SN3 (f. 36); WN1 (p. 43); A (p. 41); B (p. 69); C (p. 69); D (p. 66); E (p. 66); F (p. 66); G (p. 63); 30 (p. 142).
Emendations of the copy-text: Heading: *italics supplied* 1 and] &

Historical Collation

Format:

Miscellaneous: 5 *penciled in M in later hand* LR1; *heading beside l. 2 in left M*, | p. *in left M in second hand* NY3.

Headings: ffall of a walle B7 B47 CT1 DT1 H4 SA1 WN1 A–G. Caso d'vn muro. H6(Cæso) NY3 SN3(di). 9 HH1. *On a Captaine killed by the fall of a Wall.* 30. *om* H5 LR1.

1 an] as WN1. vnder-min'd,] ~$_\wedge$ B47 H5 H6 HH1 LR1 SA1 SN3 30. shott brusd] shott bruized B7 B47; shott-bruiz'd CT1 DT1 H4 H5 H6 HH1 SN3 A–G 30. wall] ~, SN3 30.

2 A] the H5 H6 HH1. too bold] too=bold HH1 SN3 A–G. perish'd] perished B47(pished) LR1(pished) SN3 WN1 30. fall;] ~$_\wedge$ B7 B47 CT1 DT1 H4 H6 HH1; ~, H5 SA1 SN3 A–G; ~. LR1.

3 Whose] When 30. braue] bare 30. Misfortune] ~, H4 A. happiest] happy'st H5. envyde] enuyed CT1 LR1 SN3; enuied, WN1; ~, A–G.

4 towne] tombe SA1; towre B–G 30. tombe] ~, B7 H4 H5 WN1 A–G; towne SA1. corps] Bones B7 B47 CT1 DT1 H4 SA1 WN1 A–G 30; corse SN3. hyde.] ~$_\wedge$ B7 CT1 H4 H6 HH1; ~. | LR1; ~ | . WN1.

Subscriptions: J. D. SA1. *om* B7 B47 CT1 DT1 H4 H5 H6 HH1 LR1 NY3 SN3 WN1 A–G 30.

Verbal Variants in Selected Modern Editions

Editions collated: H I J K M N O P Q S T Y Z AA DD.
Headings: *Fall of a Wall.* H–K M O–Q S T Y–AA DD. V. FALL OF A WALL. N.

4 towne] tower H–K M N. corps] bones H–K M–Q S T Z AA DD.

Schema of Textual Relationships

Version 1

H5 HH1

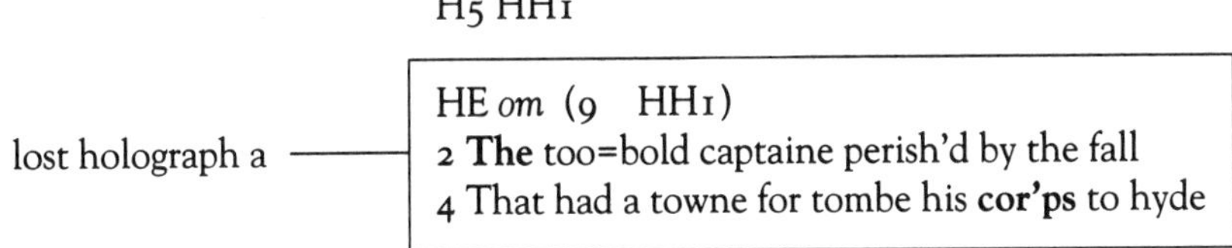

Version 2

H6 LR1 NY3 SN3

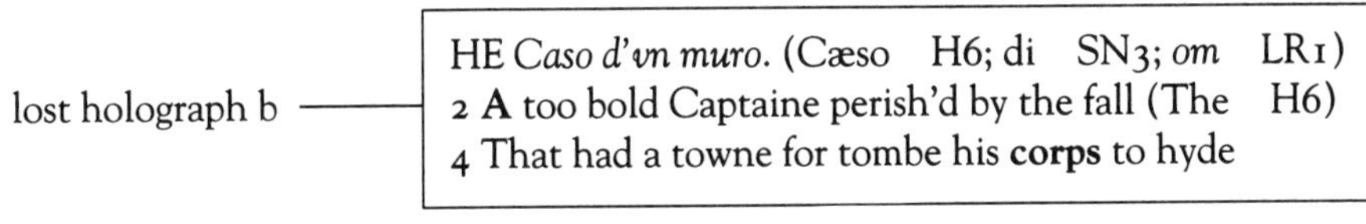

Version 3

B7 B47 CT1 DT1 H4 SA1 WN1 A–G

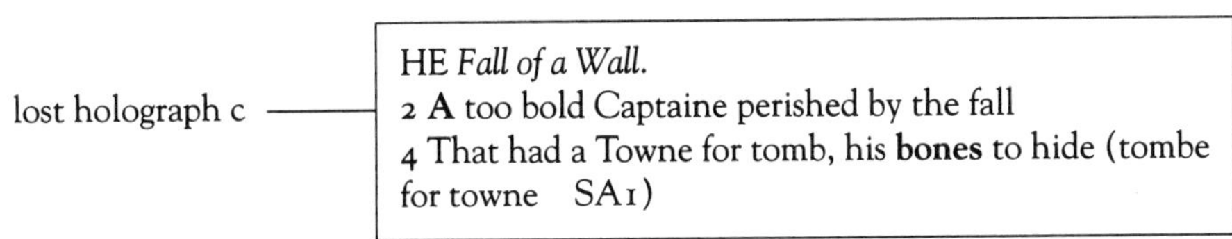

Wing

Textual Introduction

As noted in the General Textual Introduction to the Epigrams, *Wing* (like *Cales* certainly, and *Ship* and *Beggar* probably) derives from Donne's military experiences in the mid-1590s, and Donne seems carefully to have restricted the circulation of the poem: among contemporary textual artifacts the epigram appears only in the intermediate-stage manuscript NY3 and the corresponding part of H6. Since NY3 is written in the hand of Donne's friend Rowland Woodward, its copy undoubtedly stands very close to the author's own papers, and H6's may in some manner have derived from it. A number of factors, however, render the relationship between the two extant manuscript copies indeterminate. In NY3, for example, *Wing* immediately follows *Cales*, whereas it precedes *Cales* in H6; and in NY3 the pair of poems follow *Beggar*, becoming the last of the series of "Spanish" epigrams that follow the opening three on classical subjects, whereas in H6 they precede the "classical" poems. And there is H6's curious transformation of the title from the correct Italian "Il Caualliere Gio: Winge:" to the macaronic "On Cauallero Wingfeild," which mixes English and Spanish. H6, moreover, seriously corrupts the text of the epigram, reading "Cradle . . . graue . . . bedd" in line 2 for NY3's "cradle . . . throne . . . bed" and "Lady" for "late" in line 4. As noted in the analogous instance of *Ship* (see the Textual Introduction to that poem), these are undoubtedly scribal alterations, but whether they represent conscious editorializing on the part of the H6 scribe, corruption in the source from which he copied, or possibly even imperfect efforts at memorial reconstruction is not clear. For discussion of the events that inspired the poem and the precise date of its composition, see the Commentary.

Since Donne withheld the poem from the late sequence, it did not appear in the seventeenth-century printed editions; indeed, it was not printed until 1899, when Edmund Gosse owned NY3 and printed the poem in *The Life and Letters* (siglum 72) from that manuscript. In a text ultimately based on NY3, *Wing* has subsequently appeared in all twentieth-century collected editions from Grierson (Q) onward. For information on where various editors position it relative to the other poems, see the General Textual Introduction to the Epigrams.

Textual Apparatus

Copy-text: NY3. **Texts collated:** H6 (p. 338); NY3 (f. [46]); 72 (1:51).
Emendations of the copy-text: Heading: *italics supplied* *Wingefield.*] Wingef:
2 and] & and] & 3 our] o[r]

Historical Collation

Format:
Miscellaneous: *heading in left* M NY3.
Headings: On Cauallero Wingfeild H6. Il Caualliere Gio: Wingef: NY3. IL CAVALIERE GIO: WINGFIELD. 72.

1 many'haue] many haue H6 72. trauailed] trauelled H6; travellèd 72.

2 cradle,] ~$_{\wedge}$ H6. throne,] graue$_{\wedge}$ H6. bed.] ~$_{\wedge}$ H6.

4 late] Lady H6; base 72. Iland;] ~, H6.

5 then] than 72. go.] ~$_{\wedge}$ H6.

Subscriptions: *none.*

Verbal Variants in Selected Modern Editions

Editions collated: Q S T Y Z AA DD.
Headings: *Sir Iohn Wingefield.* Q S Y–AA DD. IL CAVALLIERE GIO. WINGFIELD T.

1 trauailed] traveled T AA.

5 then] than S T AA.

Analyses of Early Printed Copies

(Since the same sixteen epigrams appear in the same order in all seventeenth-century editions and issues, the Epigrams are treated in this analysis as a single bibliographical unit.)

Poems, by J. D., 4to, 1633 (siglum A)

Copies collated: *CtY*, *DFo*, *L* (G.11415), M, *MH*, *MiU*, *OWa*.
Relevant section: F4v–G2; pp. 40–43.
Press variants:

Sheet F, outer forme

	Uncorrected (*OWa*):	Corrected (*CtY*, *DFo*, *L*, M, *MH*, *MiU*):
F4v (p. 40):		
Hero, l. 2	dround.	drownd.

Miscatchings: *none.*

§

Poems, by J. D., 8vo, 1635 (siglum B)

Copies collated: *CtY, MH, MiU.*
Relevant section: E8v–F1 v; pp. 68–70.
Press variants: *none.*
Miscatchings: *none.*

§

Poems, by J. D., 8vo, 1639 (siglum C)

Copies collated: *CtY, MH, MiU.*
Relevant section: E6v–E7v; pp. 68–70.
Press variants: *none.*
Miscatchings: *none.*

§

Poems, by J. D., 8vo, 1649, 1650, 1654 (sigla D, E, F)

Copies collated: 1649: *CtY, MH* 1650: *CtY, MH* 1654: *CSmH, CtY.*
Relevant section: F1–F2; pp. 65–67.
Press variants: *none.*
Miscatching:

	Catchword:	Initial Word:	Affects:
F1v	*Phryne*	*Phryne.*	*Phrine*, heading

Note: Examination of multiple copies on the Lindstrand Comparator shows that the sections of 1649, 1650, and 1654 containing the epigrams are printed from a single typesetting, 1650 and 1654 being reissues of the sheets of 1649.

§

Poems, by J. D., 8vo, 1669 (siglum G)

Copies collated: *CtY, L, TxLT.*
Relevant section: E7v–E8v; pp. 62–64.
Press variants: *none.*
Miscatching:

	Catchword:	Initial Word:	Affects:
E8	*Phŕyne.*	*Phyrne.*	*Phrine*, heading

THE EPITHALAMIONS

Epithalamium.

.1.   The Sun-beames in the East are spred
Leaue leaue fayr bride your solitary bed.
No more shall you returne to it alone.
It nourseth sadnes and your bodyes print
Like to a graue the yielding Downe doth dint.
You and your other you meete ther anone.
Put forth, put forth that warme balme-breathing thigh
Which when next time you in these Sheetes will smother
Ther it must meet an other
Which neuer was, but must be ofte more nigh;
Come glad from thence, go gladder then you came
To day put on perfection and a womans name.

.2.   Daughters of London, you which bee
Our golden Mines and furnish'd Treasuree;
You which are Angels, yet still bring with you
Thousands of Angels on your mariage dayes,
Helpe with your presence and deuise to prayse
These rites which allso vnto you grow due.
Conceitedly dres her, and be assignd
By you fitt place for euery flower and Iewell
Make her for love fitt fuell,
As gay as Flora, and as rich as Inde,
So may she fayre, rich, glad, and in nothing lame
To day put on perfection and a womans name.

.3.   And you frolique Patricians
Sonnes of these Senators, wealths deepe Oceans
Yee painted Courtiers, Barrells of others witts
Yee Cuntrymen, who but your Beasts, love none
Yee of those fellowships wherof he'is one
Of study and play made strange Hermaphroditts
Here shine: This bridegroome to the Temple bring.
Lo, in yon path which store of strawd flowers graceth

The sober Virgin paceth
Except my sight fayle: t'is no other thing.
Weepe not, nor blush; here is no griefe nor shame
To day put on perfection and a womans name.

.4. Thy too-leaud gates fayre Temple vnfold
And these two in thy sacred bosome hold
Till mistically ioynd but one they bee:
Then may thy leane and hunger sterved wombe
Long time expect their bodyes and ther tombe
Long after ther owne Parents fatten thee.
All elder claymes and all cold barrennes
All yielding to new loves, be farr for euer
Which might these two disseuer.
All wayes, all th'other may each one possesse
For the best bride, best worthy of prayer and fame
To day puts on perfection and a Womans name.

.5. O, Winter dayes bring much delight
Not for themselues, but for they soone bring night.
Other sweetes waight thee, then these diuers meates,
Other disports then dauncing iolityes,
Other Love-tricks then glauncing with the eyes
But that the Sun still in our halfe spheare sweates.
He flyes in Winter, but now he stands still.
Yet shadows turne: Noone point he hath attained
His steedes nill be restrained
But gallop liuely downe the Westerne hill
Thou shalt when he hath run the Worlds halfe frame
To night put on perfection and a Womans name.

.6. The amorous euening Star is rose
Why should not then our amorous Star enclose
Herselfe in her wish'd bed: release your Strings
Musitians; and Dauncers take some truce
With these your pleasing Labors; for great vse
As much wearines as perfection brings.
You, and not only you, but all toyld beasts
Rest duly: at night, all ther toyles are dispenced,
But in ther beds commenced
Are other Labors and more dainty feasts.
Shee goes a Mayd, who least She turne the same
To night puts on perfection and a Womans name.

·7· Thy Virgins girdle now vnty
And in thy nuptiall bed, Loves Altar, ly
A pleasing Sacrifice: Now disposses
Thee of these chaines and robes, which were put on
To'adorne the day not thee; for thou alone
Like Vertu and Truthe art best in nakednes.
This bed is only to Virginitee
A graue, but to a better state a Cradle
Till now thou wast but able
To bee, what now thou art: then that by thee
No more be sayd, I may be, but I ame
To night put on perfection and a Womans name.

.8. Euen like a faythfull Man content
That this life for a better should be spent
So She a Mothers riche Stile doth prefer.
And at the bridegroomes wish'd approch doth ly
Like an appointed Lambe, when tenderly
The Priest comes on his knees to'embowell her.
Now sleepe or watche with more ioye: and O Light
Of heauen, to morrow rise thou hott and early:
This Sun will love so dearly
Her rest, that long, long, we shall want her sight;
Wonders are wrought, for She which had no maime
To night puts on perfection and a Womans name.

Textual Introduction

For the debate over the occasion, date, and nature of this epithalamion (*EpLin*), see the Commentary.

The poem survives in sixteen seventeenth-century manuscripts, and its transmission history is marked by a progressive deterioration of the text. Distinctive readings in the heading and in lines 10, 12, 23, 24, 26, 32, 35, 46, 47, 51, 57, 59, and 95 show that these manuscript copies of *EpLin* form five families and subfamilies of textual transmission (see Schema of Textual Relationships).

Standing alone in its text of *EpLin* is NY3, which gives evidence of being the least corrupted copy of the poem now extant. Headed simply "Epithalamiū," it has the readings "must be ofte" in line 10, "To day" in line 12, "fayre, rich, glad, & in" in line 23, "To day put on" in line 24, "Sonnes of these" and "Oceans" in line 26, "Lo" and "of strawd flowers" in line 32, "shame" in line 35, "All wayes, all th'other" and "each" in line 46, "prayer" in line 47, "these diuers" in line 51, "nill" in line 57, "run y[e] Worlds" in line 59, and "maime"in line 95.

Representing a separate strand of transmission from the lost holograph are the B19 family and its C9/H6 subfamily. Both (with the exception of HH1) expand the heading to "Epithalamion on a Citizen" and read "oft must bee" for "must be ofte" in line 10, "To night" for "To day" in line 12, "fayre, and rich, in" (or variants of the same in B19 and B46) for "fayre, rich, glad, & in" in line 23, "Sonnes of those" (or B19's "some of yo[w]") for "Sonnes of these" in line 26, "So" for "Lo" in line 32, "Alwayes th'each other may th'each" (or variants of the same) for "All wayes, all th'other may each" in line 46, "prayse" for "prayer" in line 47, "those diuers" (or "diuerse") for "these diuers" in line 51, "will" for "nill" in line 57, and "name" for "maime" in line 95; and both omit "To day" in line 24 and "strawd" in line 32. In addition, both the C9/H6 subfamily and B46 in the B19 family read "Ocean" for "Oceans" in line 26. The C9/H6 subfamily differs from the B19 family in two instances, reading "shame" for "blame" in line 35 and "runne the heauens" for "runne the worlds" in line 59.

Representing a third strand of transmission from the lost holograph is the B7 family. It introduces the heading "Epithalamion made at Lincolnes Inn" and is characterized by the readings "Some of those" for "Sonnes of these" in line 26, "Alwayes" for "All wayes" in line 46, "prayers" for "prayer" in line 47, and "Come" for "run" in line 59, and by the omission of "diuers" in line 51. In this last instance, all of the scribes of the B7 family recognized that a word was missing in the line and left a blank space to accommodate its later insertion. In the cases of DT1 and H4 only, second hands have inserted "diuerse" in the blank spaces.

The C4/O21/Y3 family is an anomaly. In some of its readings, it may be seen as a subfamily of the B19 family, but it does not make as many changes as the B19 family does, and in one line it reads with the B7 family. With the B19 family, it shares the variants "to night" (excepting C4) for "To day" in line 12 and "praise" for "prayer" in line 47 and the omission of "glad" in line 23. With the B7 family, it shares the variant "Some" for "Sonnes" in line 26. In addition, two of its members, O21 and Y3, wrongly assign the poem to the marriage of Princess Elizabeth and the Count Palatine (see *EpEliz*), and C4 misleadingly heads it "Epitaphium."

The copy in the first seventeenth-century edition (A) matches none of the manuscript families exactly. It seems to have been set from a manuscript similar to those in the B7 family with some readings taken from a manuscript resembling the B19 family. With the B7 family it shares the readings "Some" for "Sonnes" in line 26 and "come" for "run" in line 59; with the B19 family, it shares "praise" for "prayer" in line 47, it omits "glad" in line 23, and it restores "diverse" in line 51. A does, however, differ from both the B7 and the B19 families in reading "maime" at the end of line 95. The compiler/editor of the second edition (B) must have referred to a manuscript similar to C9 or H6 in revising A's text of *EpLin*, altering "these" to "those" in line 26, "come the worlds" to "runne the Heavens" in line 59, and "maime" to "name" in line 95. The subsequent editions and issues through that of 1654 (F) follow the verbals of B, each being set from the preceding edition. The compiler/editor of the final seventeenth-century edition (G), which was set from a copy of D, E, or F, also referred to a manuscript similar to C9 or H6 and replaced "Some" with "Sons" in line 26.

The modern editions of Tonson (H), Bell (I), Anderson (J), Chalmers (K), Lowell? (M), and Grosart (N) present texts of *EpLin* ultimately deriving from G. Lowell (O), Grierson (Q), Hayward (S), Bennett (T), Shawcross (Z), Smith (AA), Milgate (BB), and Patrides (DD) use A as their copy-texts, though most selectively emend its verbals on the authority of manuscript readings. Chambers (P) creates a modernized, eclectic text drawing from A, B, E, and G.

The copy-text, NY3, is written in the hand of Donne's close friend Sir Rowland Woodward (1573–1636/7) and was once owned by Francis Fane, the first Earl of Westmoreland (1582/3–1628), to whom Woodward was secretary. This manuscript contains seventy-nine Donne poems, perhaps transcribed from two sources around 1620 (Beal, 252). Its completeness, superiority of readings at points of textual crux, and intelligent punctuation suggest that it preserves the least corrupted extant version of *EpLin*. Its reading "Sonnes of these Senators" in line 26 is clearly superior to "Some of those [or these] Senators" in the B7 and C4 families as it preserves the parallel with the "Daughters of London" (l. 13) in the previous stanza: the "frolique Patricians" who are the groomsmen are the dandified sons of wealthy and politically powerful fathers just as the bridesmaids are the daughters of the rich London merchants. Likewise, NY3's description of the bride as "best worthy of prayer and fame" (l. 47) is more apt than the reading "best worthy of praise & fame" found in the C9/H6, B19, and C4 families, since the stanza in which the line occurs is addressing the church and its participation in the marriage. In addition, in line 59, it is the "Worlds halfe frame" of NY3 that the sun must run to bring on night, not simply the "heauens halfe frame," as in the C9/H6 family; and "come" in that same line in the B7 family is obviously a misreading of the stronger, and therefore more likely authorial, verb "runne," an especially easy error to make when reading "runne" as written in the secretary hand. And finally, its reading "maime" at the end of line 95—where all other seventeenth-century sources except A read "name"—is unique among the surviving manuscripts and is surely the authorial reading.

Aside from the expansion of scribal brevigraphs and the addition of a period at the end of line 5 and a comma at the end of line 16, NY3's text of *EpLin* requires only one further emendation, the change of "put" to "puts" in line 72. One textual crux does deserve comment, however—the reading "nill" in line 57 of NY3, where all other surviving early artifacts of the poem read "will." Some have found the first two letters ("ni") in the word ambiguous and have regarded the "n" as a malformed "w"; but a close comparison of the first two letters of the word with numerous other instances of "wi" and "ni" in the manuscript indicates that Woodward did indeed write "nill." In addition to having a Spenserian association, the archaic "nill" seems to fit the sense of the passage better than does "will," since the contrastive phrase "But gallop liuely down the Westerne hill" in line 58 implies a previous negative construction (see the Commentary on line 57 for other views of this issue). One early scribe recognized the problem with the commonly received text. After copying out the line with the reading "will," the conscientious scribe who augmented and corrected HH1 obviously noticed the interpretive difficulty with "will be restrain'd" and inserted "not" between "will" and "be" (see the Historical Collation).

Textual Apparatus

Copy-text: NY3. **Texts collated:** B7 (ff. 59–60v); B19 (ff. 47–48); B46 (ff. 46–47v); C4 (ff. 31–32v); C9 (ff. 84–85v); C10 (pp. 119–23); CT1 (pp. 127–30); DT1 (ff. 93–94); H4 (ff. 75–76); H5 (ff. 158v–60); H6 (pp. 321–25); HH1 (ff. 107v–09v); NY3 (ff. [22–23]); O21 (pp. 26–29); SA1 (pp. 108–10); WN1 (pp. 106–09); Y3 (pp. 24–26); 33a (*ll.* 49–50 *only*, sig. B7v); 33b (*same lines*, sig. B7v); A (pp. 135–38); B (pp. 119–23); C (pp. 119–23); D (pp. 114–17); E (pp. 114–17); F (pp. 114–17); G (pp. 114–17).

Emendations of the copy-text: Heading: *Epithalamium.*] Epithalamiū. | Line 1 the] y^{e} 4 and] & 5 the] y^{e} dint.] ~$_{\wedge}$ 6 and] & 7 that] y^{t} 8 Which] W^{ch} 10 Which] W^{ch} 11 from] frō 13 which] wch 14 Our] O^{r} and] & 15 which] wch with] w^{t} 16 dayes,] ~$_{\wedge}$ 17 with] w^{t} and] & 18 which] wch 19 and] & 20 and] & 23 and] & 24 and] & 30 and] & 31 the] y^{e} 32 which] wch 36 and] & 40 and] & 41 and] & 43 and] & 45 Which] W^{ch} 47 and] & 48 and] & 53 with] wth 54 that] y^{t} the] y^{e} our] o^{r} 58 the] y^{e} 59 the] y^{e} 60 and] & 62 our] o^{r} 65 With] Wth 67 and] & 69 commenced] cōmenced 70 and] & 71 the] ye 72 puts] put and] & 76 and] & which] wch 78 and] & 82 that] y^{t} 84 and] & 88 the] ye 91 with] w^{t} and] & 92 and] & 94 that] y^{t} 95 which] wch 96 and] &

Historical Collation

Format:

Imperfections: *leaf containing ll.* 73–96 *missing* WN1.

Font: *l.* 12 *of each st in italics* A–G.

Indentations: *ll.* 4, 5, *and* 9 *of each st ind* B7 DT1 WN1; *ll.* 3, 6, 7, *and* 10 *of each st medium ind, ll.* 9, 11, *and* 12 *long ind* B19; *ll.* 3, 6, 7, *and* 10 *of each st short ind, l.* 9 *medium ind* B46 C9 H5; *ll.* 1 *and* 9 *of each st medium ind, l.* 12 *extended into left M* C4; *ll.* 4 *and* 5 *of each st short ind, l.* 9 *medium ind, l.* 12 *extended into left M* CT1; *ll.* 4 *and* 5 *of each st short ind, l.* 9 *medium ind* H4 SA1; *ll.* 3, 6, *and* 10 *of each st short ind, l.* 7 *medium ind, l.* 9 *long ind* H6; *ll.* 3, 6, *and* 8 *of each st short ind, l.* 9 *long ind* HH1; *l.* 1 *of each st ind, l.* 12 *extended into left M* NY3; *l.* 1 *of each st ind* O21 Y3; *ll.* 3, 6, 7, *and* 9 *of each st short ind, l.* 10 *medium ind* A–G.

Miscellaneous: *sts numbered in arabic* B19 C9 H5 H6(sts 2–8) HH1(sts 2–8) NY3(in left M) O21 Y3; *heading in left M* NY3; *sts not numbered* B7 B46 C4 CT1 DT1 H4 SA1 WN1 A–G.

Headings: Epithalamion made at Lincolnes Inn | B7 CT1 DT1 H4(Epithalamium) SA1(An Epithalamion) WN1(Epithalamie) A–G. Epithalamion on a Cittisen B19(one a) B46 C9 H5(Epithalumiū) H6 HH1. Epitaphium. C4. Epithalamiū. | NY3. Epithal: of ye La: Eli: O21. Epithalamiū: One ye Marriage of ye La: Elizabeth Y3.

1 spred] ~, B46 C4 H5 WN1 A–G.

2 Leaue] ~, B7 B46 C4 C9 CT1 DT1 H4 H5 H6 HH1 SA1 A–G. leaue] ~, B7 C4 C9 H5 H6 HH1 SA1 A–G; *om* O21. fayr] (~ O21 Y3. bride] Bride, B7 B46 CT1 H5 H6 A–G; ~, C4 HH1; Bride C9 DT1 H4 WN1; ~) O21; Bride) Y3. bed.] ~‸ B7 B19 C9 CT1 DT1 H4 H6 HH1 O21 Y3; ~; B46 WN1; ~: C4; ~, H5 SA1 A–G.

3 *om* O21. No] ~, WN1. it] ~, C4. alone.] ~‸ B7 B19 B46 C9 CT1 DT1 H4 H6 SA1 Y3; ~, C4 H5 A–G; ~; WN1.

4 nourseth] nourisheth B7. sadnes] ~, B7 B46 C4 C9 CT1 DT1 H4 H5 H6 HH1 SA1 WN1 A; ~; B–G. bodyes] body A(*unc*). print] ~, C4 C9 H6 WN1 A–C G; ~. H5 D–F; ~: O21.

5 Like] (~ O21 Y3. a] the B7; *om* CT1. graue] ~, H6 WN1 A–G; ~) O21 Y3. the] that H4. Downe] ground O21. dint.] ~‸ B7 B19 CT1 DT1 H4 HH1 NY3 O21 Y3; ~, C4 SA1 WN1; ~; A–G.

6 You] ~, B7 C4 C9 DT1 H6 HH1 WN1. other] ~, C4; ~: WN1. you] ~, B46 C9 H6 HH1. anone.] ~‸ B7 B19 B46 C9 CT1 DT1 H4 H5 H6 O21 Y3; ~, SA1 WN1 B–G; ~; A.

7 forth,] ~‸ B19 H6 SA1 Y3; ~; H5. forth] ~, WN1 C–G. balme-breathing] Balme breathinge B7 B19 B46 C4 CT1 SA1 WN1 Y3. thigh] ~, C4 H5 A–G.

8 Which] ~, C4 C9 H6. when] ~, HH1. time] ~, HH1. these] those B46 C9 H5 H6 HH1; the C4. will] would C9. smother] ~. B46; ~, C4 C9 H6 D–G.

9 it] you SA1. an other] another B19 C9 CT1 DT1 H4 H5 H6 HH1 O21 SA1 WN1 Y3; another. B46; another: C4; another, A–G.

10 was,] ~, B19 C9 H6 O21 SA1 Y3. must be ofte] ofte must be B19 B46

C9 H5 H6 HH1; must be, oft,   A–G.   nigh;] ~‸   B7 B19 C9 CT1 DT1 H6 HH1 O21 WN1 Y3; ~.   B46 H5; ~:   C4; ~,   H4 SA1.

11 thence,] ~‸   B19 O21; ~;   CT1.   then] than   HH1 C–G.   came] ~,   C4 A–G.

12 day] night   B19 B46 C9 H5 HH1 O21 Y3; night → >~<   H6.   perfection] ~,   B7 B46 C4 CT1 H4 SA1 WN1 A–G.   name.] ~‸   B7 B19 C4 CT1 H6 HH1 O21; ~. | C9.

13 London,] ~‸   B19 B46 H4 O21 Y3; ~!   HH1.   which] y^{t} C4.

14 Our] Of   WN1.   Mines] ~,   B7 C4 CT1 DT1 H4 H5 SA1 WN1 A–G.   Treasuree;] ~‸   B7 B19 B46 C9 CT1 DT1 H4 H5 H6 O21 Y3; ~,   C4 SA1 A–F; ~!   HH1; ~.   G.

15 You] ~,   B7 C4 DT1.   Angels,] ~‸   B19 H4 Y3; angells,   C4; angels‸   O21.

16 Thousands] Thousand   B19.   Angels] angels   O21.   your] the   C4.   dayes,] ~‸   B7 B19 B46 CT1 DT1 H4 HH1 NY3 O21 WN1 Y3.

17 your] you   C4.   presence] ~,   B7 C4 CT1 DT1 H4 SA1 WN1 A–G; ~;   Y3.   deuise] deuice   DT1 H4.

18 rites] rights,   C4; ~,   DT1 HH1 A–G; rights   O21 Y3.   due.] ~‸   B7 B19 B46 CT1 DT1 H4 HH1 WN1 Y3; ~:   C4; ~,   C9 H6; ~;   SA1 A–G.

19 her,] ~:   HH1; ~;   O21; ~‸   WN1; ~.   Y3.   assignd] ~,   A–C.

20 you] ~,   A.   Iewell] ~,   C4 SA1 A–G.

21 Make her] Make'her   CT1.   love] Loue   B46 CT1.   fuell,] ~‸   B7 B19 C9 CT1 DT1 H6 WN1 Y3 A–G; ~.   B46 O21; iewell: C4.

22 gay] gray   C4 WN1.   Flora,] ~‸   C9 H4 O21 SA1.   Inde,] ~‸   B7 B19 B46 C9 CT1 DT1 H4 H5 HH1 WN1 Y3; ~:   C4; ~.   H6; ~;   A–F; *Indie*;   G.

23 she] ~,   H6.   fayre, rich, glad, and] faire & rich &   B19; faire, rich, and   B46 C4 O21 Y3; faire & rich   C9 HH1; faire and rich,   H5 A–G; fayre, and rich,   H6; fayre rich glad &   SA1.   lame] ~.   H6; ~,   SA1 A–G.

24 To day] *om*   B19 B46 H5 H6(>To day<) HH1.   perfection] ~,   B7 C4 CT1 DT1 SA1 A C–G.   name.] ~‸   B7 B19 C9 CT1 DT1 H4 H6 HH1 Y3.

25 Patricians] Puritans B7; ~, C4 SA1 B–G; ~; WN1.

26 Sonnes of] Some of B7 B19 C4 CT1 DT1 H4 SA1 WN1 A; Sum̄ō O21; some Y3. these] those B7 B46 C9 CT1 DT1 H4 H5 H6 HH1 SA1 B–G; yo^{w} B19; the O21. Senators,] ~‸ B7 B46 CT1 DT1 H4 O21 SA1 WN1 Y3 A. wealths] welth's B19; wealths' H5. Oceans] Ocean B46; ~, C4 SA1 A–G; Ocean, C9 H6; ~; H5; ~: HH1.

27 Yee] yea B7 CT1 DT1 WN1; ye C9 H5 A–G; You → >~< NY3. Courtiers,] ~‸ B46 O21 Y3. witts] ~, B7 C4 C9 CT1 DT1 H5 H6 SA1 A–G; ~: HH1; ~. WN1.

28 Yee] yea B7 CT1 WN1; You C4 O21; ye SA1 G. Cuntrymen,] Countrymen, B7 C9 CT1 DT1 H5 SA1; Cuntymen‸ B19; Country men‸ B46 Y3; country men, C4 H6 HH1 WN1 A–G; Conntrymen‸ H4; ~‸ O21. who] wch B19 B46 C9 H5 H6 WN1; w^{ch}, HH1. but] by C4. Beasts,] ~‸ B7 B19 B46 CT1 DT1 H4 H5 HH1 O21 SA1 Y3 A–G. none] ~, C4 WN1 A–G; ~. H6 O21; ~; HH1.

29 Yee] yea B7 CT1 WN1; ~, HH1; ye SA1 G. those] that B46. fellowships] ~, B7 C4 CT1 DT1 H5 HH1 WN1 B–G; fellowship B46. he'is] he is B7 CT1 DT1 H4 O21 SA1 WN1 Y3; his is B19; he's B46 C4 C9 H5 H6 HH1 A–G. one] none B7; ~, C4 H5 A–G.

30 play] place WN1. Hermaphroditts] ~, C4 C9 H6 A–G; ~. WN1.

31 Here] Heare B7 B19 CT1 SA1. shine:] thine;: B7; ~‸ B19 B46 Y3; ~, C4 C9 H5 H6 O21; thine: CT1; ~; HH1 A–G; all; SA1. bring.] ~‸ B7 B19 B46 C9 CT1 DT1 H4 H6 O21 SA1 WN1 Y3 A–C; ~: C4; ~, D–G.

32 Lo,] ~‸ B7 CT1 DT1 H4 O21 SA1 WN1 Y3; So‸ B19 C9 H5 H6(M *var:* >~<); See, B46; so! HH1. yon] yo^{w} B7; you^{r} B19 C4. path] ~, B7 C4 CT1 DT1 H4 O21 WN1. strawd] strawed B7; *om* B19 B46 C9 H5 H6 HH1; strew'd DT1 H4 O21 SA1 Y3; strow'd G. graceth] ~, C4 A–G; ~. WN1.

33 Virgin] virgin B7 B19 B46 C4 H4 H6 HH1 NY3 O21 WN1 Y3 A–G. paceth] ~, C4 H5 HH1 SA1; ~; A–G.

34 fayle:] ~‸ B7 B19 B46 CT1 H4 WN1; ~, C4 C9 DT1 H5 H6 HH1 SA1 Y3 A–G; fayle me‸ O21. thing.] ~‸ B7 B19 B46 C9 CT1 DT1 H4 H5 H6 O21 Y3; ~, C4; ~; SA1 A; ~: WN1.

35 blush;] ~‸ B7 B19 B46 CT1 Y3; ~, C4 C9 DT1 H4 H5 H6 HH1 SA1 WN1

A–G. shame] blame B19 B46 H5 HH1; ~, C4 A–G; ~. O21.

36 To day] To'day DT1. on] on. ec. C4. perfection] ~, B7 B46 CT1 H4 WN1 A–G; *om* C4. and a womans] *om* C4. name.] ~‸ B7 B46 CT1 H6 Y3; ~ | B19; *om* C4.

37 too-leaud] two=leau'd B7 CT1 DT1 HH1 A–C G; two leau'd B19 B46 C4 H4 H5 H6 O21 SA1 WN1 Y3 D–F; twoleav'd C9. gates] ~, C9 H6; gate HH1 O21 Y3. fayre] *om* C4. Temple] Ianus C4. vnfold] ~, C4 H5 A–G; now ~ → ›~‹ H6; now ~. O21.

38 these] those B19 B46 H5 HH1. hold] ~, C4 H5 SA1 A–G; ~. O21.

39 Till] ~, A–F. mistically] mistually B7 CT1 DT1 WN1; mutually SA1. ioynd] ~, B7 CT1 DT1 WN1 Y3 A; ioined O21. but] both in B19 C9 H5 H6(→ ›~‹) HH1; in B46; both C4 O21 Y3. bee:] ~‸ B7 B19 C9 CT1 DT1 H4 H6 HH1 Y3; ~. B46 O21; ~, C4 SA1; ~; WN1 A–G.

40 Then] ~, C9 H6. hunger sterved] hungerstarved B7 B46 O21; hunger staru'd B19; hunger=sterued C9 DT1 H5 HH1 A–G. wombe] ~, C4.

41 their] there Y3. bodyes] ~, B7 B19 C4 CT1 DT1 SA1 WN1 B–G; ~; O21. ther] their B7 B19 B46 C4 C9 CT1 DT1 H4 H5 H6 HH1 O21 SA1 WN1 A–G; there Y3. tombe] ~. B46 H4 H6 O21; ~, C4 H5 SA1 A–G.

42 *om* O21 Y3. ther] their B7 B19 B46 C4 C9 CT1 DT1 H4 H5 H6 HH1 SA1 WN1 A–G. fatten] satten B7 CT1 DT1 H4 WN1. thee.] there‸ B7 CT1 DT1 H4(→ »~‸«); ~‸ B19 B46 C9 H6; ~: C4; ~, H5; ~; SA1 A; these‸ WN1.

43 claymes] ~, B7 B46 C4 C9 CT1 DT1 H4 H5 H6 HH1 SA1 WN1 A–G. cold] old B19 B46 C9 H5 HH1. barrennes] ~, C4 H5 HH1 A–G; ~. O21 WN1.

44 farr] ~, B46 HH1. for euer] foreuer B46; for euer, C4 HH1 SA1 A–G; foreuer. O21.

45 Which] Never B7 CT1 DT1 H4 SA1 WN1. might] night B7. disseuer.] ~‸ B7 B19 B46 C9 CT1 DT1 H4 H5 H6 O21 SA1 WN1 Y3; ~: C4; ~, A–G.

46 All wayes,] Alwayes‸ B7 B19 B46 C9 CT1 H5 H6 HH1 SA1; All wayse‸ C4 Y3; Allwayes, DT1 H4 O21 WN1 A–G. all th'other] the each other B19

HH1; theach other B46; th'each other C9 H5 H6(*var*: ›all th' other‹); al the other O21 WN1 Y3. each] the each B19 B46; th'each C9 H5 H6(→ ›~‹) HH1. possesse] ~, C4; ~. O21; ~; SA1 A–G.

47 For] ~, A–G. bride,] Bride, B7 CT1 DT1 H4 H5 A–G; Bride‸ B46 WN1; ~‸ C9 O21 SA1. of] *om* C4. prayer] prayres, B7 CT1; praise B19 B46 C9 H5 H6 HH1 O21 Y3 A–G; prayse, C4; ~, DT1; ~; H4; prayers SA1 WN1. fame] ~, B7 C4 A–G; ~. WN1.

48 puts] put B7 B46 C4 HH1. on] ~. ect. C4. perfection] *om* C4; ~, CT1 DT1 H4 H6 SA1 WN1 A–G. and a Womans] *om* C4. name.] ~ | B7; ~‸ B19 CT1 HH1 Y3; *om* C4.

49 O,] *om* B7 CT1 DT1 H4 SA1 WN1 A–G; ~‸ B19 C9 H6 O21 Y3; ~. B46; Our‸ H5 HH1; The‸ 33a–b. Winter] winters C9 H6 HH1. bring] do ~ 33a–b. much] the most 33a–b. delight] ~, C4 33a–b A–G; ~: O21.

50 Not] Nor C4 G. *second* for] cause C4 33a–b. night.] ~‸ B7 B19 B46 C9 CT1 DT1 H4 H6 HH1 WN1 Y3; ~, C4 SA1; ~: O21 33a–b; ~; A–G.

51 waight] waite B7 B19 B46 C4 C9 CT1 DT1 H4 H5 H6 HH1 O21 SA1 Y3 A–G; waigst WN1. thee,] ~‸ B7 B19 C9 CT1 DT1 H4 H6 HH1 A–G; ~; O21. then] than HH1. these] those B19 B46 C9 H5 H6 HH1. diuers] *om* B7 CT1 DT1(»diuerse«) H4(»diverse«) SA1 WN1; diuerse B46 C4 HH1 O21 A–G. meates,] ~‸ B7 B19 B46 C9 CT1 DT1 H4 H5 H6 HH1 SA1 WN1 Y3; ~. O21.

52 disports] ~, C4 WN1 Y3. then] than HH1. iolityes,] ~‸ B7 B19 B46 C9 CT1 DT1 H4 H6 HH1 O21 SA1 WN1 Y3.

53 then] than HH1. glauncing] dancinge B46(→ ›~‹) SA1. eyes] ~, B46 B–G; ~. C4 H6 O21 WN1; ~; A.

54 that] if B19 B46 C9 H5 H6(*var*: ›~‹) HH1 O21 Y3. sweates.] ~‸ B7 B19 B46 C9 CT1 DT1 H4 H5 H6 O21 Y3; ~, C4 SA1; ~? HH1; ~; A–G.

55 now he] he now B7 CT1 DT1 H4 SA1 WN1 A–G. still.] ~‸ B7 B19 C9 CT1 DT1 H4 H6 O21 SA1 WN1 Y3; ~, C4 H5 A–G; ~! HH1.

56 turne:] ~; B7 H4 A–G; ~, B19 B46 C4 C9 H5 H6 HH1 SA1; turn'd‸ O21; ~. WN1; turn'd, Y3. Noone] noons B19. attained] attain'd B7 B19 B46 C9 CT1 DT1 H4 H5 H6 HH1 SA1 WN1 Y3; attaind, C4 A–G; obtain'd O21.

57 nill] will B7 B19 B46 C4 C9 CT1 DT1 H4 H5 H6 O21 SA1 WN1 Y3 A–G; will → will ›not‹ HH1. restrained] restrain'd B7 B19 B46 C9 CT1 DT1 H4 H5 H6 HH1 O21 WN1 Y3; restraind, C4 SA1 A–G; refrain'd C10.

58 Westerne] Easterne C9 H6. hill] ~, C4 H5 D–G; ~. HH1; ~; A–C.

59 shalt] ~, B46 C4 H6 A–G. run] come B7 CT1 DT1 H4 SA1 WN1 A. Worlds] world B7 CT1 DT1 H4; heauens C9 H6 B–G. frame] ~, C4 H5 A–G.

60 To night] *om* B19 B46 C9 H5 H6(›To night‹) HH1. put] but A. on] on. ect. C4. perfection] ~, B7 B46 CT1 DT1 H4 WN1 A–G; *om* C4. and a Womans] *om* C4. name.] ~ | B7; *om* C4; ~. | DT1; ~‸ H6 HH1 Y3; ~,. SA1.

61 euening] Eveing B19. Star] Starrie H4. is] *om* → »~« H4. rose] ~: C4; ~, H5 SA1 A–G.

62 should not then] should not thou B7 CT1 SA1(should'st); then should not A–G. amorous] evening SA1.

63 wish'd] wished B19. bed:] ~, B19 H5 O21; ~? B46 C4 C9 H6 HH1 SA1 WN1 A–G. your] the B19 B46 H5 H6 HH1. Strings] ~, C4.

64 Musitians;] ~‸ B7 CT1 Y3 B C; ~, B19 B46 C4 C9 DT1 H4 H5 H6 O21 SA1 WN1 A D–G. Dauncers] ~, B46 C4 C9 H6 O21.

65 these] those B19 B46 C9 H5 H6 HH1 SA1. Labors;] ~, B7 B19 C4 C9 CT1 DT1 H5 H6 SA1 WN1 A–G; ~. B46; ~‸ H4; ~: Y3.

66 brings.] ~‸ B7 B19 B46 CT1 DT1 H4 O21 SA1 WN1 Y3; ~: C4 H5; ~; A.

67 You,] ~‸ B19 O21 WN1 Y3. not only] not'only B46. you,] ~‸ B7 B19 B46 CT1 H4 H6 Y3.

68 duly:] ~‸ B7 B19 B46 C4(dewely) C9 CT1 DT1 H4 H5 H6 HH1 SA1; dayly; O21; ~, WN1; dayly, Y3; ~; A–G. night,] ~‸ B19 H4 O21 Y3 A–G; ~; H5. all] and WN1. dispenced,] ~‸ B7 CT1 DT1 H4; dispens'd‸ B19 B46 C9 H5 H6 O21 SA1 Y3; dispencd, C4; dispenc'd. HH1; ~: WN1; ~; A–G.

69 beds] bed O21. commenced] Comenc'd B19 C9 H5 H6 HH1 O21 SA1 Y3; Commenc't B46; commencd, C4.

70 other] others SA1. Labors] ~, B7 B19 C4 CT1 DT1 H4 H5 H6 SA1

Y3 A–G; ~; O21. feasts.] ~‸ B7 B19 B46 CT1 DT1 H4 H5 O21 WN1 Y3; ~, C4; ~; SA1 A.

71 who] but B46; ~, H6 A–G. least] lest B46 D–G. same] ~, C4 C9 H6 A–G; ~. WN1.

72 puts] put B7 NY3 O21. on] ~. ect. C4. perfection] ~, B46 CT1 DT1 WN1 A–G; *om* C4. and a Womans] *om* C4. name.] ~ | B7; *om* C4; ~‸ C9 CT1 H6 HH1 Y3.

73 Thy] The B7 B46 C9 CT1 H6 HH1 SA1. Virgins] virgin B19 B46 C4 C9 H5 H6 HH1 O21 Y3. vnty] ~, C4 SA1 A–G.

74 bed,] ~‸ B7 B19 B46 C4 CT1 O21 Y3 A–G. Loves] (~ B19 C4 Y3; [~ A–G. Altar,] ~‸ B7 B46 CT1 DT1 H4 O21; ~) B19 C4 Y3; ~] A–G. ly] ~, C4 H6.

75 Sacrifice:] ~, B7 B19 B46 C4 C9 CT1 H5 H6 SA1; ~; DT1 A–G; ~‸ O21 Y3.

76 these] those B7 B19 B46 C4 C9 CT1 DT1 H4 H5 H6 HH1 O21 SA1 Y3. were] wee A(*unc*).

77 To'adorne] T'adorne B7 B19 C9 CT1 DT1 H4 H5 H6 HH1 SA1 A–G; To adorne C4 O21 Y3. day] ~, B7 B19 B46 C4 CT1 DT1 H5 HH1 SA1 A–G. thee;] ~, B7 B19 B46 C4 C9 CT1 H5 H6 HH1 O21 SA1; ~‸ Y3. thou] ~, A–G. alone] ~, H6 O21 A–G.

78 Vertu and] vertue, and B7 C4 CT1 SA1 D–G; vertue & B19 B46 C9 H4 H5 O21 Y3; Virtue, & DT1; vertue'and A–C. Truthe] truth B7 B19 CT1 H4 H5 HH1 O21 SA1 Y3; truthe, B46 C4 C9 H6 A–G; ~, DT1. art] are B7 B46 O21 G. nakednes.] ~‸ B7 B19 B46 C4 CT1 DT1 H4 H5 H6 O21 Y3; ~, SA1; ~; A–G.

79 bed] graue C4.

80 graue,] ~; DT1. but] ~, A B. state] ~, H5 A–G. Cradle] ~, C4 SA1; ~. H4 B–G; ~; A.

81 now] ~, C4 G.

82 bee,] ~‸ B7 B19 B46 C4 C9 CT1 DT1 H4 H5 H6 HH1 O21 SA1 A–G. art:] ~, B7 B19 C4 C9 CT1 DT1 H5 H6 O21 SA1; ~; B46 A–G; ~‸ H4; ~. Y3. then] ~, B19. thee] shee B7 CT1 DT1 H4 SA1.

83 sayd,] ~‸ B19 CT1 DT1 H4 HH1 SA1; ~; O21. I may be,] I should bee, DT1 H4; I may, be, H5; [I may be] HH1; I may bee: O21; I may bee‸ Y3; *I may bee,* A–G. but] ~, B46 A. I ame] I am: B19; [I am] HH1; I am, SA1; *I am,* A–G.

84 put] puts SA1. on] ~. ec. C4. perfection] ~, B46 DT1 A–G; *om* C4. and a Womans] *om* C4. name.] ~‸ B7 B19 H4 H6 HH1 O21 Y3; *om* C4; ~. | DT1.

85 Euen] Ee'ne, HH1. like] as SA1. faythfull] *om* O21 Y3. Man] ~, C4 C9 H6 HH1. content] ~, C4 A–G.

86 this] his Y3. life] ~, HH1. better] ~, HH1. spent] ~: C4 B–G; ~. HH1 O21; ~; A.

87 So] ~, A. prefer.] ~‸ B7 B19 B46 C9 CT1 DT1 H4 H6 HH1 O21 Y3; ~, C4 H5 SA1 A–G.

88 bridegroomes] Bridgroomes B7 B46 CT1 DT1 H4 H5 H6 A–G. wish'd] wished B19. ly] ~, C4 A–G.

89 Lambe,] ~‸ B7 B19 CT1; ~; O21; ~: Y3. tenderly] ~, C4.

90 knees] ~, B–G. to'embowell] t'embowell B7 B46 C9 CT1 DT1 H4 H5 H6 HH1 SA1 A D–G; to embowell B19 C4 O21 Y3. her.] ~‸ B7 B19 B46 CT1 DT1 H4 H5 O21 Y3; ~, H6 SA1; ~; A.

91 sleepe] ~, B7 C4 CT1 DT1 H4 HH1. watche] ~, B46 C4 HH1 O21. ioye:] ~, B19 B46 C4 H5 O21; ~‸ C9 Y3; ~; H6 SA1 A–G. and] or B46; ~, C4 HH1. O] *om* B46; a C9 O21 Y3.

92 Of] *om* SA1. heauen] Heau'n B7 CT1 SA1. morrow] ~, C9 H6; ~; O21. thou] then B19. early:] ~‸ B7 B19 B46 C9 CT1 DT1 H4 H5 H6 O21 Y3; ~, C4 SA1 C–G; ~; A; ~. B.

93 This] Thy C9. will] well H4.

94 sight;] ~‸ B7 B19 B46 CT1 H4 H6 O21 SA1 Y3; ~, C4 H5; ~. C9 DT1 HH1 B–G.

95 She] ~, DT1. maime] name B7 B19 B46 C9 CT1 DT1 H4(M *var:* »~«) H6(→ ›~‹) HH1 O21 SA1 Y3; name, C4 H5 B–G; ~, A(*cor*).

96 night] day SA1. puts] put B7. on] ~. ect. | C4. perfection] ~, B46 CT1 DT1 H4 H5 H6 SA1 A–G; *om* C4; ꝑfections HH1. and a Womans] *om* C4. name.] ~ | B7 H4; ~. | B19 DT1; *om* C4; ~‸ H6 HH1; ~: Y3.

Subscriptions: finis B46 O21 Y3. I.D. C4. finis. I.D. SA1. *The end of the Epithalamions or Marriage Songs.* B–G. *om* B7 B19 C9 CT1 DT1 H4 H5 H6 HH1 NY3 A.

Verbal Variants in Selected Modern Editions

Editions collated: H I J K M N O P Q S T Z AA BB DD.

Format:

Font: *l. 12 of each st in italics* H M–O Q S T Z–BB DD.

Indentations: *ll. 6 and 7 of each st short ind, l. 10 long ind* H; *no ind* I J; *ll. 3, 6, and 9 of each st short ind, l. 10 long ind* K P; *ll. 6 and 9 of each st short ind, l. 10 long ind* M O; *ll. 3, 6, 7, and 10 of each st ind equally* N; *l. 3 of each st short ind* Q S DD; *ll. 3, 6, 7, and 10 of each st short ind, l. 9 long ind* T; *ll. 3 and 6 of each st short ind* Z; *ll. 3 and 6 of each st short ind, ll. 7 and 10 long ind* AA; *ll. 6, 7, and 10 of each st short ind, l. 9 long ind, l. 12 extended into left M* BB.

Miscellaneous: *sts not numbered* H K M O P Q S Z–BB DD; *sts numbered in roman* I J N; *sts numbered in arabic* T.

Headings: *Epithalamion made at* Lincoln's Inn. H–J K(*EPITHALAMIUM*) M–Q S T Z–BB DD.

17 deuise] device T AA.

23 fayre, rich, glad, and] fair and rich H–K M–P Z AA DD.

26 Sonnes] Some O. these] those H–K M N P T.

32 strawd] strow'd H–K; strewed M N P T AA.

46 All wayes] Always H–K M–Q Z–BB DD.

47 prayer] praise H–K M–Q S T Z–BB DD.

48 puts] put K.

49 O] *om* H–K M–P DD.

50 Not] Nor H I; None J.

55 now he] he now H–K M–Q S T Z AA DD.

57 nill] will H–K M–P Z BB DD.

59 run] come O. Worlds] Heav'ns H–K M N P.

62 should not then] then should not H–K M–Q S T AA DD.

67 beasts] beast H–K.

76 were] we O.

95 maime] name H–K M N.

Subscriptions: *none*.

Schema of Textual Relationships

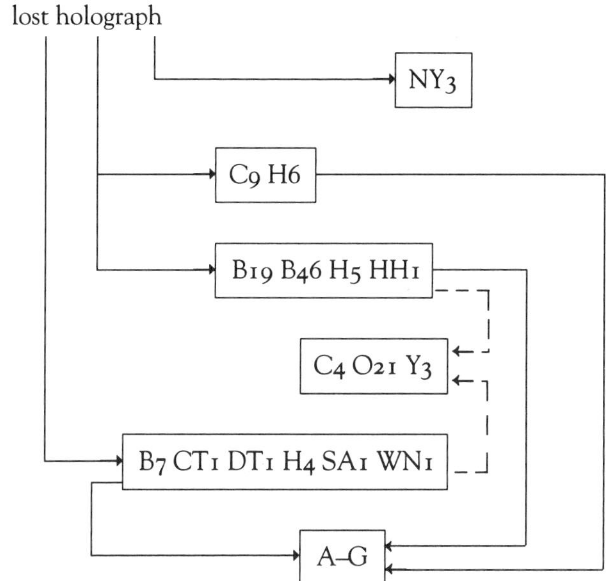

NY3

HE **Epithalamiū.** |
10 Wch neuer was, **but must be ofte** more nigh;
12 **To day** put on perfection and a womans name.
23 So may she **fayre, rich, glad, & in** nothing lame
24 **To day put on** perfection & a womans name.
26 **Sonnes of these** Senators, wealths deepe **Oceans**
32 **Lo**, in yon path wch store **of strawd flowers** graceth
35 **Weepe not**, nor blush; here is no griefe nor **shame**
46 **All wayes, all th'other** may **each** one possesse
47 For the best bride, best worthy of **prayer** & fame
51 Other sweetes waight thee, then **these diuers** meates,
57 His steedes **nill** be restrained
59 Thou shalt when he hath **run ye Worlds** halfe frame
95 Wonders are wrought, for She wch had no **maime**

C9 H6

HE **Epithalamion on·a Citizen**
10 Wch never was but **oft must bee** more nigh
12 **To night** put on Perfection and a womans name

23 So may shee, **fayre, and rich, in** nothing lame.
24 **Put on** Perfection and a womans name
26 **Sonnes of those** Senato^{rs}, wealths deepe **Ocean,**
32 **So** in yon path wch. store **of flowers** graceth
35 **Weepe not,** nor blush, heere is no greefe nor **shame**
46 **Alwayes th'each other** may **th'each** one possesse
47 ffor the best bride, best worthy of **prayse** and fame
51 Other sweetes wayte thee then **those diuers** meats
57 His steedes **will** bee restraynd
59 Thou shalt, when hee hath **runne the heauens** halfe frame
95 wonders ar wrought, for shee wch. had no **name**

B19 B46 H5 HH1

HE **Epithalamiū on a Citizen.**
(Epithalamion HH1)
10 wch neuer was, but **oft must be** more nigh.
12 **to night** put on perfection and a womans name.
23 so may she **faire and rich, in** nothinge lame
(faire & rich & in B19; faire, rich, and in B46)
24 **put on** perfection and a womans name.
26 **Sonnes of those** Senators, wealths' deepe **Oceans;**
(some of yo^{w} B19; Ocean B46)
32 **So** in yon path wch store **of flowers** graceth
(you^{r} path B19; See, in B46)
35 **weepe not**, nor blush, heere is no greife nor **blame**
46 **allwayes th'each other** may **th'each** one possesse
(the each other B19 HH1; the each one B19 B46)
47 for the best Bride, best worthy of **prayse** and fame
51 other sweets waite thee, then **those diuers** meats
(diuerse B46 HH1)
57 his steeds **will** bee restrained
(wilbe B46 H5; will ›not‹ be HH1)
59 Thou shalt when he hath **runne the worlds** halfe frame,
95 Wonders are wrought, for shee wch had no **name,**

C4 O21 Y3

HE **Epithalamiū: One ye Marriage of ye La: Elizabeth**
(Epitaphium. C4; Epithal: of ye La: Eli: O21)
10 wch neu^{r} was butt **must bee oft** more nigh
12 **to night** put on perfection & a womans name
(To day C4)
23 soe may shee **faire, rich, & in** nothinge lame

24 **to day put on** perfectiō & a womans name.
26 **Some of these** senatours, wealths deepe **Oceans,**
(Sum̄ō the Senat^{rs} O21; some these senato^{r}s Y3)
32 **loe** in yon pathe wch store **of strew'd flowers** graceth
(your path C4; strawd C4)
35 **weepe nott** nor blush here is noe greife nor **shame**
46 **all wayes all the other** may **each** one possesse
(Alwayes, O21; th'other C4)
47 for the best bride, best worthy of **praise** & fame
(of *om* C4)
51 other sweets waite thee, then **these diuers** meates
57 His steedes **will** bee restraind,
(wilbee O21)
59 thou shalt when hee hath **runne ye worlds** halfe frame
95 Wonders are wrought, for shee wch had noe **name,**

B7 CT1 DT1 H4 SA1 WN1

HE **Epithalamion made at Lincolnes Inn.**
10 W^{ch} neuer was, but **must bee ofte** more nigh
12 **To day** putt on perfection, and a womans name
23 So may shee **faire, Rich, Glad, & in** nothing lame
24 **To day put on** perfection, & a womans name
26 **Some of those** Senatours wealthes Deepe **Oceans**
32 **Loe** in yon path, wch store **of straw'd** flowers graceth
(yo^{w} path B7; strew'd DT1 H4 SA1)
35 **Weep not**, nor blush here is no griefe nor **shame**
46 **Alwayes all th'other** may **each** one possesse
(the other WN1)
47 ffor ye beste Bride, best worthy of **prayers**, & fame
(Prayer DT1 H4)
51 Other sweets wait thee then **these [blank space]** meates
57 His Steeds **will** bee restrain'd
(wilbee DT1)
59 Thou shalt when hee hath **Come ye world** half frame
(worlds SA1 WN1)
95 Wonders are wrought, for shee wch had noe **name**

A–G

HE ***Epithalamion made at Lincolnes Inne***.
10 Which never was, but **must be, oft,** more nigh;
12 ***To day*** *put on perfection, and a womans name.*
23 So may shee **faire and rich, in** nothing lame,

24 ***To day put on*** *perfection, and a womans name.*
26 **Some of these** Senators wealths deep **oceans,**
(Sons of G; those Senatours B–G)
32 **Loe,** in yon path which store **of straw'd flowers** graceth,
(strow'd G)
35 **Weep not** nor blush, here is no griefe nor **shame,**
46 **Alwaies, all th'other** may **each** one possesse;
47 For, the best Bride, best worthy of **praise** and fame,
51 Other sweets wait thee then **these diverse** meats,
57 His steeds **will** bee restrain'd,
59 Thou shalt, when he hath **come the worlds** half frame,
(hath runne the Heavens half B–G)
95 Wonders are wrought, for shee which had no **maime,**
(no name, B–G)

Analyses of Early Printed Copies

Poems, by J.D., 4to, 1633 (siglum A)

Copies collated: *CtY*, *DFo*, *L* (G.11415), M, *MH*, *MiU*.
Relevant section: sigs. S4–T1v; pp. 135–38.
Press variants:

	Sheet S, inner forme	
	Uncorrected (*L*):	Corrected (*CtY*, *DFo*, M, *MH*, *MiU*):
S4r (p. 135):		
l. 4	body	bodies

	Sheet T, inner forme	
	Uncorrected (*L*):	Corrected (*CtY*, *DFo*, M, *MH*, *MiU*):
T1v (p. 138):		
l. 95	maime‸	maime,

	Sheet T, outer forme	
	Uncorrected (*CtY*, *L*):	Corrected (*DFo*, M, *MH*, *MiU*):
T1r (p. 137):		
l. 76	wee	were

Miscatchings: *none.*

Note: Milgate erroneously designates "wee" as the reading of the corrected state in *EpLin* 76.

§

Poems, by J.D., 8vo, 1635 (siglum B)

Copies collated: *CtY, MH, MiU.*
Relevant section: sigs. I2–I4; pp. 119–23.
Press variants: *none.*
Miscatchings: *none.*

§

Poems, by J.D., 8vo, 1639 (siglum C)

Copies collated: *CtY, MH, MiU.*
Relevant section: sigs. H8–I2; pp. 119–23.
Press variants: *see note 2 below.*
Miscatchings: *none.*

Notes: 1) In the section containing *EpLin*, this edition is a page-for-page resetting of B.

2) The period at the end of *EpLin* 66 does not print in the *CtY* and *MiU* copies; either it was inked poorly in those copies, or it was lost during the course of the press run.

§

Poems by J.D., 8vo, 1649, 1650, 1654 (sigla D, E, F)

Copies collated: 1649: *CtY, MH.* 1650: *CtY, MH.* 1654: *CSmH, CtY.*
Relevant section: sigs. I1v–I3; pp. 114–17.
Press variants: *see note 2 below.*
Miscatchings: *none.*

Notes: 1) Examination of multiple copies on the Lindstrand Comparator shows that the sections of 1649, 1650, and 1654 containing *EpLin* are printed from a single typesetting, 1650 and 1654 being reissues of the sheets of 1649.

2) The top half of the semicolon following "joy" in *EpLin* 91 does not print clearly in most of the copies collated; it prints very clearly, however, in the *CtY* copy of 1650.

§

Poems, &c. by John Donne, 8vo, 1669 (siglum G)

Copies collated: *CtY, L, TxLT.*
Relevant section: sigs. I1v–I3; pp. 114–17.
Press variants: *see note below.*
Miscatchings: *none.*

Note: The period at the end of *EpLin* 94 does not print in the *L* copy; it prints clearly in the *CtY* and *TxLT* copies.

Epithalamion *Vpon* Frederick *Count Palatine* *and the Lady* Elizabeth *marryed on St.* *Valentines day.*

Hayle Bishop Valentine whose day this is
All the Ayre is thy Diocesse
And all the chirping Queristers
And other birds ar thy parishioners.
Thou marryest every yeare
The Lyrick Larke and the graue whispering Doue
The Sparrow that neglects his life for loue
The houshold bird with the redd stomacher.
Thou makst the Blackbird speede as soone
As doth the Goldfinch or the Halcyon,
The Husband Cock lookes out and soone is spedd
And meetes his wife which brings her feather bedd.
This day more cheerefully then ever shine
This day which might inflame thy selfe old Valentine.

Till now thou warmdst with multiplying loues
Two Larkes, two Sparrows, or two Doues,
All that is nothing vnto this
For thou this day couplest two Phænixes.
Thou makst a Taper see
What the Sunne never sawe, and what the Arke
(Which was of fowles and beasts the cage and parke)
Did not contayne, one bedd contaynes through thee,
Two Phænixes whose ioyned brests
Are vnto one another mutuall nests
Whose motion kindles such fires as shall giue
Young Phænixes and yet the old shall liue
Where Love and Courage never shall decline
But make the whole yeare through thy day ô Valentine.

Vp then fayre Phænix-Bride, frustrate the Sunne.
Thy selfe from thine Affection
Tak'st warmth enough, and from thine eye
All lesser birds will take theyr Iollity.
Vp vp, fayre bird, and call
Thy Starrs from out theyr severall boxes, Take
Thy Rubyes Pearles and Dyamonds forth and make
Thyselfe a Constellacion of them all
And by theyr blazing signify
That a Greate Princesse falls but doth not dye.
Bee thou a new Starre that to vs pretends
Ends of much wonder, And bee thou those ends.
Since thou dost this day in new glory shine
May all men date Records from this thy Valentine.

Come forth, come forth, And as one glorious flame
Meeting another, growes the same
So meete thy Frederick, and so
To an vnseperable vnion growe.
Since separation
Falls not on such things as ar infinite
Nor things which are but one can disunite
You are twice vnseperable, Greate, and one.
Goe then Two where the Bishop stayes
To make you one, his way, which diuers wayes
Must bee effected, and when All is past
And that you ar one by harts and hands made fast
You two haue one way left your selues to entwyne
Besides this Bishops knott or Bishop Valentine.

But oh what ayles the Sunne that heere hee stayes
Longer to day then other dayes?
Stayes hee new light from these to get
And finding heere such starrs, is loth to sett?
And why doe you two walke
So slowly pac'd in this Procession?
Is all your care but to bee lookd vpon
And bee to others Spectacle and talke?
The feast with gluttonous delayes
Is eaten, and too long theyr meate they prayse.
The Maskers come late, and, I thinke, will stay
Like Fayrys, till the Cock crow them away.
Alas; did not Antiquity assigne
A night as well as day to thee ô Valentine?

They did, and night is come, and yet wee see
Formalitys retarding thee.
What meane these Ladyes, which, as though
They were to take a Clock in peeces, goe
So nicely about the Bride?
A Bride, before a Good night could bee say'd,
Should vanish from her clothes into her bedd
As Soules from bodyes steale, and are not spy'd.
But now Shee's layd; What though Shee bee?
Yet there are more delayes, for, where is hee?
Hee comes, and passes through Spheare after Spheare
First her Sheetes, then her Armes, then any where.
Oh let not this day but this night bee thine.
Thy day was but the Eue to this ô Valentine.

Heere lyes a Shee-Sunne, and a Hee-moone there
Shee giues the best light to his Spheare
Or each is both, and all, and so
They vnto one another nothing owe.
And yet they doe; but are
So iust and rich in that coyne which they pay
That neyther would nor needs forbeare or stay
Neyther desires to bee spar'd, nor to spare.
They quickly pay theyr debt, and then
Take no Acquittances, but pay agen.
They pay, they giue, they lend, and so let fall
No such ocasion to bee liberall.
More Truth, more Courage, in these two doe shine
Then all thy Turtles haue, and Sparrows Valentine.

Now by this Act of these two Phænixes
Nature agayne restored is
For since these two are two no more
Theres but one Phænix still as was before.
Rest now at last, and wee
As Satyres watch the Sunns vp-rise, will stay
Wayting when your eyes opened let out day
Onely desird because your face wee see.
Others, neere you, shall whispring speake
And wagers lay at which side day will breake
And winn by obseruing whose hand it is
That opens first a Curtayne, Hers, or His.
This will bee try'd to morrow after Nyne
Till which hower wee thy day enlarge ô Valentine.

Textual Introduction

This epithalamion (*EpEliz*) was written to celebrate the marriage of Princess Elizabeth, daughter of King James I, to Frederick, the Elector Palatine, which occurred on 14 February 1613.

The poem survives in 28 seventeenth-century manuscripts. Milgate alleges that since *EpEliz* and *Eclog* "were composed for patrons, it would have been discourteous for Donne to have reissued them in a revised form, even if he desired to improve them" (1978, liv–lv). The artifactual evidence, however, shows that the transmissional history of each of these two epithalamions is marked by two successive revisions of the text; and the nature of these changes—at each stage multiple verbal alterations that cannot plausibly be explained as corruptions, sophistications, or necessary repairs of obviously defective language and that carry forward in the stream of transmission once they have entered—suggests that the revisions are authorial. Charting the transmissional history of *EpEliz* reveals that the extant manuscripts fall into five discrete families (see Schema of Textual Relationships).

The C9/H6 family preserves what is no doubt the earliest version of the poem. It is marked by the readings "soone" in line 11, "Where" in line 27, "bird" in line 33, "vnseperable" in line 50, "starrs" in line 60, "there" at the end of line 85, "Now" in line 99, and "win by obseruing" in line 109.

The first revision, represented by a single surviving manuscript, B46, changes "Where" to "Whose" in line 27, "bird" to "Bride" in line 33, and "starrs" to "store" in line 60; and it adds "then" to "win by obseruing" in line 109.

The second revision, from which all the other surviving manuscript copies ultimately derive, preserves the four changes of the first revision and makes four additional alterations, changing "soone" to "straight" in line 11, "vnseperable" to "inseparable" in line 50, "there" to "here" in line 85, and "Now" to "And" in line 99. Two families derive directly from this second revision, the large B13 family and the smaller B32 family.

The B13 family is not homogenous; some of its members reflect one or more of the original readings in the C9/H6 family, notably H8, which reads "Where" in line 27 and "starrs" in line 60. Such anomalies may reflect contaminations in the textual tradition: some scribes may have had before them exempla from more than one family and combined readings from multiple sources in their own recensions.

The DT1/H4 family derives from an uncontaminated member of the B13 family. Its distinctive readings—notably "out" for "forth" in line 35 and "lend they giue" for "giue, they lend" in line 95—are obviously scribal blunders.

The B32 family, which derives from the second revision of the poem independently of the B13 family, is marked by the scribal insertion of "too" before "late" in line 67. As originally written ("The Maskers come late, and, I thinke, will stay") the line is in regular iambic pentameter (though it has a trochaic substitution in the third foot), and the insertion of "too" makes it necessary to elide "and I" if the meter is to be preserved. Such elision is not unknown in Donne, of course, but it seems likely that the extraneous "too" here reflects the contamination of line 67 by the phrase "too long" in line 66 immediately above. A subfamily of B32, consisting of C2 and C8, corrupts line 109, reading "then observinge wiselye" and "wiselie obseruing then," respectively, for "win by Obseruing then."

The text of *EpEliz* in the first of the seventeenth-century editions (A) was obviously set from a manuscript in the B32 family that closely resembled O20 and SP1. It avoids B32's error of "send" for "lend" in line 95 and the corruptions of line 109 in C2 and C8. The compiler/editor of the second edition (B) must have consulted a manuscript resembling C9 and H6 in revising A's text of *EpEliz*, since that second printing restores "starres" in line 60 and omits the intrusive "too" in line 67. The third edition (C) was then set from the second without verbal alteration. The compiler/editor of the fourth edition (D), which was set from C, may also have consulted a manuscript in either the C9/H6 or the B46 tradition, since that printing in all three of its issues (including E and F) restores "there" at the end of line 85. This revision might possibly have been made solely on aesthetic grounds, however, as an attempt to avoid the repetition of "here" in the line and to distinguish clearly between the bride "here" and the groom "there." The final seventeenth-century edition (G) was set from a copy of D, E, or F.

The modern editions of Tonson (H), Bell (I), Anderson (J), Chalmers (K), Lowell? (M), and Grosart (N) present texts of *EpEliz* ultimately deriving from G. Alford (L), Lowell (O), Grierson (Q), Hayward (S), Bennett (T), Shawcross (Z), Smith (AA), Milgate (BB), and Patrides (DD) use A as their copy-texts, though most selectively emend its verbals on the authority of manuscript readings. Chambers (P) creates a modernized, eclectic text drawing from A, B, E, and G.

H6, the copy-text for *EpEliz*, with its 169 Donne poems is the largest extant manuscript collection of Donne's poems and may have been prepared for an edition: its title page reads "The Poems of D. I. Donne not yet imprinted . . . Finishd this 12 of October 1632." The compiler of Harvard MS Eng 966.2 (transcribed from H6 in the eighteenth century) notes that H6 belonged "to D[r] Parnel, Arch Deacon of Clogher, and after his decease to M[r]. Tho[s]: Burton of Dublin." Now at Harvard, H6 was most recently owned by the Rev. T. R. O'Flahertie of Capel, near Dorking, Surrey (Beal 252). Its cognate, C9, derives either from H6 or from a common progenitor, with the latter being most likely.

The text of *EpEliz* preserved in H6 is the least corrupted copy of the poem in its original version. Its readings are internally consistent and it is intelligently punctuated. Moreover, H6's unusual reading of "Two" in line 51 ("Goe then Two where the Bishop stayes") may well preserve an authorial orthographic pun, suggesting both the expected "to" and the "two" persons whom the Bishop "stayes / to make . . . one" at the altar.

It should be noted that after it was inscribed, H6 was contaminated by its original scribe with variant readings from A, notably in lines 25, 33, and 109 (see the Historical Collation). All of these contaminations have been rejected in the reading text.

H6 generally provides a clean, legible text (though with *s*'s and *l*'s it is frequently impossible to be certain whether the scribe intended a capital or a miniscule letter). Aside from the expansion of brevigraphs and the alteration of initial *ff*'s to *F*'s, the only emendations of the copy-text have been a minor adjustment of the wording in the heading, the imposition of italics in the heading to conform to ordinary seventeenth-century printing practices, and the addition of a few punctuation marks throughout the text where needed to prevent misreading. It should be noted that H6's inscription of "Phoenix" as "Phænix" throughout the poem is a common variant spelling in the seventeenth century; and we should call attention to the reading "pretends" in line 39, where a modern reader would expect "portends"—the reading recorded in most of the witnesses. We have expanded H6's "p^{r}" to "pre" in accordance with the common understanding of Renaissance brevigraphs, and this interpretation is supported by the appearance of a fully spelled-out "pre" in H6's cognate manuscript, C9. It is thus virtually certain that both the H6 and the C9 scribes were looking at "pretends" as they copied, and this may have been Donne's earliest spelling of the word. The *OED* (v. 10) records "portend, presage, foreshow" as a meaning of "pretend" in the seventeenth century.

Textual Apparatus

Copy-text: H6. **Copies collated:** B13 (ff. 35–36); B26 (ff. 20v–22v); B32 (ff. 128v–30); B46 (ff. 43v–45v); BR1 (ff. 2–3v); C1 (*ll. 1, 15–28 only*, f. 17v); C2 (ff. 71v–73); C8 (ff. 104–06v); C9 (ff. 82–83v); DT1 (ff. 53–54v); H4 (ff. 40–41v); H5 (ff. 152–53v); H6 (pp. 317–21); H8 (ff. 10–12); HH1 (ff. 45v–47v); HH5 (ff. 120v–21v); NY1 (pp. 67–71); O17 (*ll. 1–70, 85–112 only*, pp. 63–66); O20 (ff. 130v–33); O21 (pp. 128–32); O34 (ff. 216v–15 rev.); O35 (*ll. 1–4, 11–29, 34–38, 51, 67–70, 72, 74–82, 85–86, 97–102, and 110–12 only*, f. 23r–v); O36 (ff. 29v–30v); SP1 (ff. 108–10v); VA2 (ff. 37v–39); WA1 (ff. 70v–72v); Y3 (pp. 122–25); Y5 (pp. 27–30); A (pp. 118–22); B (pp. 103–07); C (pp. 103–07); D (pp. 99–103); E (pp. 99–103); F (pp. 99–103); G (pp. 100–04).

Emendations of the copy-text: Heading: *italics supplied* Epithalamion] »P.« Epithalamions [*as section heading*] Frederick] ffrederick *day*.] day$_\wedge$ Line 4 parishioners.] ~$_\wedge$ 8 stomacher.] ~$_\wedge$ 10 Halcyon,] ~$_\wedge$ 12 which] wch. 14 which] wch. 16 Doues,] ~$_\wedge$ 18 For] ffor Phænixes.] ~$_\wedge$ 21 Which] W^{ch} 22 thee,] ~$_\wedge$ 25 Whose] Wh<u>ose</u>(*var*: Wh›ere‹) 28 Valentine.] ~$_\wedge$ 29 Sunne.]~$_\wedge$ 33 bird] <u>bird</u>(M *var*: ›Bride‹) 36 Constellacion] Constellacon̄ 37 theyr] this → ›~‹ 38 dye.] ~.. 39 pretends] p^{r}tends 42 Valentine.] ~$_\wedge$ 46 growe.] ~$_\wedge$ 48 Falls] ffalls 49 which] wch. 50 You] Yo^{u} one.] ~$_\wedge$ 51 Two] <u>Two</u>(*var*: ›to‹) 52 you] yo^{u} which] wch. 54 you] yo^{u} 55 You] Yo^{u} your] yor 56 Valentine.] ~$_\wedge$ 60 starrs] stares → ›~‹ 61 you] yo^{u} 63 your] yor 68 Fayrys] ffayrys 72 Formalitys] fformalitys 73 which] wch 82 First] ffirst 84 Valentine.] ~$_\wedge$ 90 which] wch. 98 Valentine.] ~$_\wedge$ 101 *ind supplied* For] ffor 102 before.] ~$_\wedge$ 105 your] yor 106 your] yor 107 you] yo^{u} 108 which] wch. 109 obseruing whose] obseruing ›then‹ whose 110 His.] ~$_\wedge$ 112 which] wch. Valentine.] ~$_\wedge$

Historical Collation

Format:

Imperfections: *damage causing the loss of the heading and ll. 7, 9–20, 33, and 46–60 entirely and the partial loss of text in other lines* BR1; *possibly some punctuation lost to trimming in ll. 9–22* H8.

Indentations: *ll. 2, 3, 5, and 9 of each st ind* B13 B26 B32 B46 C2 C8 C9 DT1 H4 H5 H6 H8 HH1 HH5 NY1 O20 O34 SP1 VA2 Y3 Y5 A–G; *ll. 2, 5, and 9 of each st ind* BR1; *ll. 16, 17, 19, 20, 22, 23, and 26 ind* C1; *ind irregular* O17 WA1; *ll. 2, 3, 5, and 9–14 of each st ind* O21; *no ind* O35; *ll. 2, 3, 5, 9, 13, and 14 of each st ind* O36.

Miscellaneous: *sts not numbered* B13 B46 BR1 C1 C9 DT1 H4 H6 H8 O17 O21 O34 Y3; *sts numbered in arabic* B26 B32 C2 C8 H5 HH1 HH5 NY1 O20 O36 SP1 VA2 WA1 Y5; *l. 54 initially om and inserted in M in scribal hand* H6; *not divided into sts* O35; *sts numbered in roman* A–G.

Headings: Epithalamion at the Mariage of the Princess Elyzabeth, and the Palzgaue celebrated on S^{t}. Valentines Daye. B13 C1(Palsgraue). Epithalamion on the Lady Elizabeth & Count palatine married on St Valantine's day. B26. A Epithalamion or Marriage song, on the Lady Elisabeth, and Fredericke Covnt Palatine, beeing St Valentines Day. | B32. An Epithelamion or mariadge Songe, on the Ladie Elisabeth and Fredericke Count Palat: being maried on St Valentines Day: B46 C2(Fredericke *om*) C8(Fredericke *om*) O20 SP1(on mariage) A–F(Fredericke *om*). Epithalamions.[*section heading*] / vpon ffrederick Count Palatine & the Lady Elizabeth marryed on S^{t} valentines day. C9 H6(»P.« Epithalamions). Epithalamium. | DT1 H4 O34(*adds* by D. Donne. »pag. 103.«). Vpon the marriage of the Prince Palatine and the Lady Elizabeth on St Valentines day. H5. S$^{t.}$ Valentine. H8. Vppon the mariage of the Prynce Palatyne & the Princes on St Valentynes Daye | HH1 O21 Y3. Epithalamion | HH5. An Epithalamion. On the Ladye Elizab. & Count Palat. NY1 VA2 WA1. Epithalamiū at the mariage of y^{e} Palsgrave & Lady Elizab: on St: Valentines day. | O17. Fredirick Elizabeth on Valenti day. O35. AN EPITHALAMIE Or Nuptiall hymne vpon the Marriage of the Paltsgraue & the Ladye, Elizabeth O36 Y5(Epithalamium; *second* the *om*). *An Epithalamion on* Frederick *Count Palatine of the* Rhene, *and the Lady* Elizabeth, *being married on St*. Valentines *day*. G.

1 Valentine] ~, B32 B46 C2 C8 DT1 H4 H5 HH1 O20 VA2 A–G; ~: NY1 WA1; ~; O34. whose] whole O34. this] is O34. is] ~, B26 B32 C2 C8 DT1 H5 HH1 O20 A–G; this O34.

2 the] th' O17. Diocesse] ~, B13 C2 C8 HH1 O20 A–G; ~; B26; Dyocye, B32; ~. O17.

3 Queristers] ~, B13 B32; Choirsters, B26; ~. C8; Choristers H5 O35 A; choristers, HH1 B–G.

4 parishioners.] Parish'oners$_{\wedge}$ B13; ~, B26 B32 C2 A–G; ~$_{\wedge}$ B46 H4 H6 HH5 NY1 O17 O20 O34 O35 O36 SP1 VA2 WA1 Y3; ~: H8; ~; HH1.

5 *om* O36. marryest] mary'est, B13; marryes O34. yeare] ~, B13 B26 HH5 O17 O20 SP1; ~. C8 H8 WA1.

6 Lyrick] lirque C8; lyriquicke H5. Larke] ~, B13 B26 B46 C2 C8 DT1 H5 H8 HH1 HH5 O20 SP1 VA2 Y5 A–G; lanke, B32; ~; O34. the] *om* B46. graue whispering] grave whispring B26 O36; graue whisp'ing O21; graue-whispering VA2. Doue] ~, B13 B26 B32 C2 C8 DT1 H5 H8 HH1 O20 SP1 A–G; ~: NY1; ~. O34.

7 Sparrow] ~, B26 DT1 HH1 HH5. loue] ~, B13 B26 B32 C2 C8 H5 HH1 O20 SP1 A–G; ~; H8; ~: NY1; ~. O34 VA2.

8 bird] ~, B13 B32 C2 C8 DT1 HH5 O20 A–G; birds, HH1. With] & HH1 HH5 Y3. stomacher.] ~, B13 B26 B32 C2 C8 H5 HH1 O20 SP1 A–F; ~; DT1 H8 G; ~‸ H4 H6 HH5 O17 O21 O36 VA2 WA1 Y3 Y5; ~: NY1.

9 makst] makes C2; madst H5; makest VA2 Y3 Y5. soone] ~, B13 B26 B32 C2 O20 SP1 A–G; ~. O21 O34.

10 doth] *om* H8. Goldfinch] ~, B13 B26 B32 C2 C8 DT1 H4 H5 H8 HH5 O20 SP1 A–G; blackbird O21. Halcyon,] ~; B26 H5 A–G; ~‸ B46 H4 H6 HH5 O17 O34 O36 VA2 WA1 Y3 Y5; ~: DT1 NY1; ~. H8.

11 Husband Cock] howsecocke O34. lookes] chucks HH1. out] ~, B13 B32 C2 C8 DT1 H4 H5 H8 HH1 O20 SP1 VA2 A–G; but forth O34. soone] straight B13 B26 B32 C2 C8 DT1 H4 H8 HH5 NY1 O17 O20 O21 O35 O36 SP1 VA2 WA1 Y5 A–G. spedd] ~, B13 B32 DT1 HH1 O17 O20 SP1 A–G; ~; B26; ~. C8 O21.

12 wife] ~, B13 B26 B32 C2 C8 DT1 H5 HH1 HH5 O20 O34 SP1 A–G. which] y^t O17; who O21 O35. her] his HH5 O17 O36 Y5. bedd.] ~‸ B13 C9 H4 HH1 HH5 NY1 O17 O21 O34 O35 O36 SP1 VA2 WA1 Y3; ~, B26; ~; H5; bedd[*trimmed*] H8.

13 This] Thy H5. then] than B26 C–G. ever] others O17. shine] ~, B26 C2 C9 H5 O20 SP1 Y5; ~; B32; ~: DT1; ~. A–G.

14 day] ~, B32 C2 DT1 H5 HH1 O20 A–G; night O34. which] y^t B13 O17 O21; *om* O34. might] *om* O34. thy selfe] thy selfe, B26 B32 B46 C2 C8 DT1 H5 O20 SP1 Y3 A(*cor*)–G; thy selfe: HH1; thy selfe; Y5; the self, A(*unc*). old] (~ NY1 VA2 WA1. Valentine.] ~‸ B13 DT1 H4 HH5 O17 O35 O36 Y3; ~! B26; ~. | B32 SP1; Valentine[*trimmed*] H8; ~!) NY1 VA2; Valentine[*lost to sewing*] WA1.

15 Till] Tell B26. now] ~, B32 B46 C2 C8 DT1 O20 SP1 A–G. warmdst] warm'st B32 C2 C8 DT1 H4 NY1 O20 O21 O34 O36 SP1 VA2 WA1 Y3. loues] ~, B26 DT1.

16 or] & HH1 HH5 NY1 O34 VA2 WA1 Y3. Doues,] ~‸ B13 B26 C1 C9 H4 H6 HH5 NY1 O21 O34 O35 O36 WA1 Y3 Y5; ~. C8 VA2; ~; DT1; ~: H8; dowes‸ O17.

17 that] ~, DT1. is] was O21. nothing] Nothing B32 O20. this] ~, B32 C2 DT1 H5 HH1 O17 SP1 A–G; vs O21 Y3.

18 couplest] coupest H4; ~, HH5; couples O34. Phænixes,] ~‸ B13 B26 B46 C1 C9 DT1 H4 H6 HH5 NY1 O17 O21 O34 O35 O36 VA2 WA1 Y3 Y5; ~; H5 H8; ~. B–G.

19 makst] makest B32 C8 O20 VA2 Y3; makes WA1. a Taper] Taper a A(*unc*). see] ~, B13 B32 C2 O20 SP1 Y5.

20 never] nuer H4; nere NY1 O21 VA2 WA1 Y5. sawe,] ~‸ B26 B46 C1 NY1 O35 WA1 Y3; ~; B32 H5 O20 O21 SP1; ~. O17. Arke] ~, H5; ~. O34; ~; Y5.

21 (Which] ‸~ B26 C1 HH1 O21 O34 O35 WA1 Y3 Y5. was] ~ not O17. fowles] fowle B26(foule) O35 B–G; beastes O34. beasts] fowles O34; beast O35 Y3. parke)] ~‸ B26 C1 HH1 O21 O34 O35 WA1 Y3; ~,) B32 C2 H4 H5 O36 A–G; ~, Y5.

22 contayne,] ~‸ B46 C1 O21 O35 WA1; ~; DT1 H4 H8 HH1 NY1; ~? O34; ~: Y3. contaynes] ~, B46 C8 A–G; ~. O17. through] by O35; though Y5. thee,] ~‸ B13 B26 B46 C1 C8 C9 DT1 H4 H5 H6 HH1 HH5 NY1 O17 O21 O36 VA2 WA1 Y3 Y5; the[*trimmed*] H8; ~. O34 O35; ~: B C.

23 Phænixes] ~, B32 B46 C2 C8 H5 O20 A–G; ~; DT1 H4 HH1; ~: O34. brests] ~, B13 BR1; beasts, B32; brest O35.

24 *om; inserted in a second hand* O21. Are] And H4. another] an others Y5. nests] ~, B13 B32 C2 C8 H5 HH5 O34 A–C; ~; BR1 H8 HH1; ~. DT1 VA2 D–G; nest O35.

25 Whose] Where B13 B26 B32 C1 C2 C8 C9 DT1 H4 H6(*as var*) H8 NY1 O17 O34 O35 SP1 VA2 WA1 A–G; When O20. motion] motions H5 HH1 O21 Y3. kindles] kindle H5 HH1 O21. such] *om* Y5. fires] ~, B32 BR1 C2 C8 DT1 H4 A–G; fire, H5 Y5; fyre HH1 HH5 O21 O36 Y3. as] *om* O17.

26 Young] Two O34. Phænixes] ~; B13 B46; ~, B26 B32 C1 C2 C8 DT1 H5 H8 HH1 HH5 O17 O20 O34 SP1 VA2 WA1 Y5 A–G. yet] that H8. liue] ~, B32 C2 Y5; ~: BR1; ~. C8 DT1 O20 SP1 WA1 A–G; ~; H5.

27 Where] Whose B13 B26 B32 B46 C1 C2 C8 DT1 H4 H5 HH1 HH5 NY1 O17 O20 O21 O34 O35 O36 SP1 VA2 WA1 Y3 Y5 A–G. decline] ~, B32 BR1 C2 C8 H5 O20 SP1 A–G; ~; O34.

28 make] *om* HH1. through] ~, B26 B46 H5 HH1 A–G; ~; SP1. thy] *om* B26 O17. day] *om* B26 O17; ~, B32 B46 BR1 C2 C8 DT1 H5 O20 SP1 A–G. ô] ~, B46; *om* H8; (~ NY1 VA2 WA1. Valentine.] ~‸ B13 B26 C8 H4 H6 O17 O34 O35 O36 Y3; ~: BR1; ~ &c‸ C1; ~? HH1; ~ | HH5; ~!) NY1; ~. | SP1; ~.) VA2; Valentin[*lost to sewing*] WA1.

29 Phænix-Bride,] ~‸ B13 B46 H4 HH5 O36; Phenix Birde‸ B26 O21 Y3 Y5; ~; BR1 H5; Phænix bird, HH1 O34; Phœnix bird; NY1 VA2 WA1; ~: O35. Sunne.] ~, B13 B32 BR1 C2 H5 O20 SP1 VA2 A; ~‸ B26 B46 C8 C9 H4 H6 H8 HH5 NY1 O17 O21 O35 O36 WA1 Y3 Y5; ~; DT1 B–G; sonne. O34.

30 selfe] ~, B13 B46 HH1 NY1. thine] thy B46 H8 HH1.

31 Tak'st] Takes H8; Takest O20 O36 Y5 A. enough,] ~; B32 O20 O21 SP1; ~: B46; ~‸ HH5 O17 O36 Y3 Y5. and] *om* O36. eye] ~, BR1 DT1; ~. C8.

32 lesser] lessers D–G. will] do HH1 O21 Y3. theyr] there HH5 Y3 Y5. Iollity.] ~‸ B26 C9 H4 HH5 NY1 O17 O21 O34 O36 VA2 Y3 Y5; ~, B32 C2 C8 O20 SP1 WA1; ~; H8 HH1.

33 Vp vp,] Vp, vp‸ B13 C8 C9 DT1 H4 H5 HH1 NY1 O20; Up up‸ B26 B46 H8 HH5 O34 O36 SP1 WA1; Vp, vp, B32 C2 Y5 A–G; Vp‸ O17 O21 Y3. bird] bride B13 B32 B46 C2 C8 DT1 H4 H5 H6(*as var*) H8 HH1 O17 O20 O21 O34 O36 SP1 Y3 A–G; birds Y5. call] ~, C2 O36 A; ~. HH5 Y5.

34 Thy] The NY1 O21 VA2 WA1 Y3; Call O35. Starrs] ~, B26 B32 C2 C8 O20 SP1 A–C; up O35. from] *om* O21; thy O35. out] stars. O35. theyr] thy C9 H8 HH5; & O35. severall] frō thy O35. boxes, Take] boxes take B13 B26 HH5 O17 O34 O35 O36 VA2 Y3; boxes; Take B32 DT1 H4 H5 O20 SP1; boxes,'Take C8; boxes: Take H8.

35 Rubyes] ~, B13 B32 B46 C2 C8 DT1 H4 H5 H8 HH1 HH5 O17 O20 O21 O34 SP1 VA2 Y5 A–G. Pearles] ~, B13 B32 B46 C2 C8 DT1 H4 H5 H8 HH5 NY1 O20 O34 SP1 VA2 Y5 A–G. Dyamonds] dymonds Y3. forth] ~, B32 B46 C2 C8 H5 H8 O17 O20 O35 SP1 WA1 Y5 A–G; ~ | BR1; out, DT1 H4; ~; O21; ~? O34.

36 them] all them SP1. all] ~, B13 B26 B32 C2 C8 H5 H8 HH1 O20 A–C; ~ B46 DT1 O34 WA1 D–G; ~; BR1

37 theyr] this B13 B32 DT1 H4 H5 H8 HH1 HH5 NY1 O17 O21 O34 O36 VA2 WA1 Y3 Y5; this → ›theyr‹ H6; there O35. blazing] ~, B46 C2 C8 A; flaringe HH5. signify] ~, BR1 C2 DT1 H5 VA2 A–G; ~. HH5.

38 a] *om* Y5. Princesse] Princes B13 C2 HH1 O35 O36 Y5; Prince NY1 VA2 WA1. falls] ~, B13 B32 B46 C8 DT1 H4 H5 H8 HH1 HH5 O20 O34 SP1 Y5 A–G; fall B26; fall, C2. but] yet B46 O36 Y5; and HH5 NY1 VA2 WA1. doth] do BR1; does HH5 O34. dye.] ~, B13 H4; ~‸ B26 HH1 HH5 NY1 O17 O36 Y3; ~; B32 BR1 C2 C8 O20 SP1 A–G; ~.. H6; ~: H8.

39 Starre] ~, B13 B26 B32 B46 C2 C8 DT1 H5 HH1 HH5 O20 O34 SP1 A–F. pretends] ~, B13; portends B26 B46 C8 DT1 H4 H5 H8 HH1 HH5 NY1 O17 O20 O21 O34 O36 SP1 VA2 WA1 Y5 A–G; portends, B32 BR1 C2; p^{r}tends H6 Y3.

40 much] such O34. wonder,] ~; B13 B32 C2 C8 O20 SP1 A–G; ~‸ HH5 NY1 O17 O21 VA2 WA1 Y3. those] the BR1 H8 O34; these H4 VA2; o^{r}. HH5; their O36; there Y5. ends.] ~, B13 B32 C2 C8 H4 H8 HH1 O20 SP1 A; ~‸ B26 B46 HH5 O17 O21 O34 O36 VA2 WA1 Y3; ~; BR1 H5.

41 dost] doest, VA2. day] ~, B46 C2 C8 HH1 SP1 A(*unc*). shine] ~, B32 BR1 C2 DT1 H5 O20 SP1 A–G; ~. O34.

42 May all] may'all O21. Records] ~, B32 C2 C8 DT1 H5 HH5 O20 O34 SP1 A–F; recorde H8 HH1. this] thy WA1. thy] daye B13 NY1 O17 VA2 WA1 G. Valentine.] ~‸ B13 B46 DT1 H4 H6 HH1 HH5 O17 O21 O34 O36 Y3; ~.| B32 SP1; ~: H8; (~!) NY1; (~.) VA2; (Valentin[*trimmed*] WA1.

43 forth,] ~; H5; ~‸ HH5 O17 O21 O36 WA1 Y3. forth,] ~‸ B26 HH5 NY1 O17 O21 O36 VA2 WA1 Y3; ~; B32 C2 H5 O20. flame] ~, B32 SP1; ~. C8.

44 Meeting] ~. O20. another,] ~‸ B26 B32 C8 DT1 H4 H8 HH5 NY1 O17 O21 O34 O36 SP1 VA2 WA1 Y3 Y5. growes] growe B13 O17; maks O21; greets O36. same] ~, B13 B32 C2 C8 H5 H8 O20 SP1 A; ~; BR1; ~: DT1 B–G; ~. VA2.

45 thy] *om* O17. Frederick,] ~‸ NY1 O21 O36 WA1 Y3 Y5; ~; O17.

46 To] Into O21. an vnseperable] an inseperable B13 DT1 H4 H8 HH1 HH5 O17 O34 O36 Y3; anseperable B26; an vnspeakable NY1 VA2 WA1. growe.] ~, B13 H5; goe‸ B26 C2; ~‸ B46 C9 H4 H6 HH5 NY1 O17 O21 O34 O36 WA1 Y3 Y5; goe, C8 A–G; ~: H8.

47 separation] ~, B32 HH1 SP1; ~. O34.

48 things] ~, B32 C2 C8 O20 SP1. infinite] ~, B13 B32 C2 C8 DT1 H5 H8 HH1 O20 SP1 VA2 Y5 A D–G; ~. O34; ~; B C.

49 Nor] Not B46; Now WA1. things] ~, C8; those O21. which] that B13 O17 O21 O34 O36 Y3. are] anye, O34. one] ~, B32 B46 C2 C8 H5 HH1 HH5 O20 O34 SP1 A–G; ~; O36; on → on»e« WA1. disunite] ~; B32 O20 SP1; ~, C2 C8 H5; ~. DT1 H8 HH1 Y5 A–G; disioynte O34.

50 You are] Y'art VA2; You'are A–F. twice] '~ B C G. vnseperable,] inseperable, B13 B32 C2 C8 DT1 H5 H8 HH5 NY1 O20 O21 O36 SP1 A–G; vnseparably‸ B26; inseperable; H4; inseperable‸ HH1 O17 O34 VA2 WA1 Y3. Greate,] ~‸ B26 C9 H5 H8 HH5 NY1 O17 O21 O34 O36 VA2 WA1 Y3 Y5; ~; SP1. one.] ~‸ B13 B26 B46 H4 H6 HH5 NY1 O17 O21 O34 O36 WA1 Y3 Y5; ~, B32 C2; ~; C8 H8 HH1 O20 SP1 A; ~: H5.

51 Goe] *om* B46; to make you one, goe O34; The O35. then] *om* B46; ~; H5; ~, HH1 O34; Bp O35. Two] to B13 B26 B32 C2 C8 DT1 H4 H6(*as var*) HH5 NY1 O17 O20 O21 O34 SP1 VA2 WA1 Y3 A–G; Loe B46; Loe, H5; toe → ›loe‹ HH1; is O35. where] while B26; here O35. the] you^{r} HH1; at O35. Bishop] ye Period O35. stayes] ~, B32 C2 C8 A–G; of ye cherre O35.

52 *om; inserted in a second hand* HH1. To make you] *om* O34. one,] ~‸ B13 B46 C2 H8 HH1 O17 O36 SP1 WA1 Y3; ~; DT1; on‸ HH5 O21 VA2 Y5; *om* O34. way,] ~‸ H4 HH1 NY1 O34 WA1 Y3; ~; H5; wayes, O21. diuers] diuerse NY1 O21 O34 VA2 WA1 Y3 Y5.

53 bee] *om* (M: »be«) WA1. effected,] ~‸ B26 O17 O36 Y3; ~; B32 C2 C8 DT1 NY1 O20 O21 SP1 VA2 A–G; ~. B46 WA1; ~: H8; affected; Y5. all is] all s B13. past] ~, B13 B32 C2 C8 DT1 H5 O20 O21 SP1 A–G; ~; HH1.

54 that] when NY1 VA2 WA1; *om* O34. you ar] y'are B13 B46 VA2 D–G; you'are DT1 H4 A–C; you're O17; yow O36. one] ~, B13 B32 C2 C8 O20 O34 SP1 A–G; all one B26. harts] hands B46 HH5; hart H5 O21 Y3; hearts → ›heart‹ HH1. hands] harts B46 HH5; hand O21 Y3. fast] ~, B32 C2 C8 DT1 O20 SP1 A–G; ~; H5.

55 two] *om* HH1 O21 Y3. left] ~, B13 B26 B32 B46 C2 C8 H5 HH1 O20 SP1 A–G; less → »~« HH5; *om* O34; more, DT1; more H4. to entwyne] t'entwine B13 B46 DT1 H4 H8 NY1 O36 VA2 WA1; to intwine. B26 O34; to entwine, B32 C2 O20 SP1; t^{o} vntwine H5; to'entwine, A–C; t'entwine, D–G

56 Besides] After H8 O34 O36 Y5. this] thy H5; thy → »~« HH1; the Y5. Bishops] Bishop B13 B26 NY1 VA2. knott] ~, B13 B32 B46 C2 C8 DT1 H4 H5 H8 HH1 HH5 NY1 O17 O20 O21 O36 SP1 WA1 A–F; Knockt B26; ~: Y5. or] o B26 A–F; »of« H4(*as var*); o^{r} NY1 O17 O21 VA2 WA1 Y3; of O34 G. Valentine.] ~.| B13 B32 SP1; ~$_{\wedge}$ B46 H4 H6 O17 O21 O36 WA1 Y3; ~| HH5.

57 oh] ~, B32 B46 C2 C8 C9 DT1 H4 HH1 O20 SP1 VA2 A–G; ~! H5 O36; ~. O17. Sunne] ~, B32 C2 DT1 H4 H5 HH1 O20 SP1 Y5 A–G; ~? O17; sonne, O34. that heere] *om* B13 O17. stayes] ~. C8; ~, A–G.

58 then] than B26 O20 B–G. dayes?] ~$_{\wedge}$ B13 B46 C9 NY1 O17 O21 VA2 WA1 Y3; ~, C2 C8 HH1 HH5; ~?. H8.

59 hee] *om* O36 Y5. new light] from thee H5 HH1 O21 Y3; from thie HH5. from these] from hence B26; from thee DT1 H4; newe light H5 HH1 HH5 O21 Y3; from them H8 O34 O36 Y5. get] ~? B26 B32 C2 C8 DT1 H4 O20 SP1 Y5 A–G; ~, H5 HH1 NY1; ~; H8.

60 And] or O21. heere] *om* HH1; there O36. starrs] store B13 B32 B46 C2 C8 DT1 H4 H5 HH5 NY1 O17 O20 O21 O34 O36 SP1 VA2 WA1 Y3 Y5 A; storie faire → »store here« HH1. sett?] ~$_{\wedge}$ B13 HH5 O21 VA2 WA1 Y3; ~. B46 NY1; ~,? C2; ~: C8; ~; HH1 O36; ~, O34.

61 doe you two] you two doe Y5. walke] ~? B13 C8; ~, B32 C2 A–G; ~? → ›~‹ H6.

62 pac'd] placed HH5; paced O34. in] to O34. this] his Y5. Procession?] ~$_{\wedge}$ B13 HH5 O34; ~; BR1; p̱gression$_{\wedge}$ O21 Y3.

63 care] ~, B32 O20 SP1. lookd] looked HH1. vpon] ~, B26 B32 O20 SP1 A–G; ~. BR1; ~? C8 DT1 H4 H5 H8 NY1 VA2 Y5; on, HH1.

64 bee to] to be B46 DT1 H4 H5 O36 Y5; to be to HH5. Spectacle] spectacles BR1 H8. talke?] ~$_{\wedge}$ B46 HH5 O17 O21 O34 O36 WA1 Y3; ~. BR1; ~,? C2; ~, HH1.

65 feast] feasts O36 WA1. with] wch O34. gluttonous] glorious H5 HH1 HH5 NY1 O21 VA2 WA1 Y3; gluttons O34. delayes] ~, B32 C2 A–C; ~. HH5; (~) O34.

66 eaten,] ~$_{\wedge}$ C9 HH5 NY1 O17 O21 O36 WA1 Y3; ~? Y5. theyr] there HH5 O17 Y3 Y5; the O21. they] thy B13; the BR1. prayse.] ~, B13 B32 C2 C8 O20 A–F; ~$_{\wedge}$ B26 B46 C9 DT1 HH5 NY1 O17 O21 O34 O36 SP1 VA2 WA1 Y3; ~; BR1 H4 H5 H8.

67 Maskers] Masques H5 HH1; mask's O21; maskes Y3. come] came O34. late,] too late, B32(to) B46 C2 C8(to) O20(to) SP1(to) VA2 A; ~; BR1; last, HH5; too late$_{\wedge}$ NY1 WA1; ~$_{\wedge}$ O17 O34 O36 Y3 Y5. and, I] & I B13 B26 B32 BR1 C2 C8 DT1 H4 H8 HH1 HH5 NY1 O17 O20 O21 O35 O36 SP1 VA2 WA1 Y3 Y5 B–F; I B46; and (I O34; and'I A. thinke,] ~$_{\wedge}$ B13 B26 B32 B46 C8 H8 HH1 HH5 NY1 O17 O20 O21 O35 O36 SP1 VA2 WA1 Y3 Y5 G; thinge$_{\wedge}$ BR1; feare$_{\wedge}$ DT1 H4; ~) O34. stay] ~, B32 C2 C8 H4 A–G.

68 till] tell O34. Cock] cockes H5 HH1. crow] call O34; crows O35. them] then HH5. away.] ~$_{\wedge}$ B13 B26 B46 H4 HH5 NY1 O17 O21 O34 O35 O36 WA1 Y3; ~; B32 H5 O20; ~, HH1 SP1; ~: Y5.

69 Alas;] ~$_{\wedge}$ B13 B26 BR1 DT1 H4 HH5 NY1 O17 O21 O34 VA2 WA1 Y3 D–G; ~, B32 C2 C8 HH1 O20 SP1 A–C; ~! B46 C9 H5 H8 O36 Y5; Alass why O35. Antiquity] Antiquities HH5.

70 night] ~, B32 B46 C2 C8 H5 HH1 O20 SP1 A. *first* as] soe HH5. day] ~, B13 B32 C2 C8 DT1 O20 SP1 A–G; a day Y3; ~; Y5. to] *om* O34. thee] ~, B32 C2 H5 HH1 O20 SP1 A–G; ~. B46; *om* O34. ô] (~ NY1 VA2 WA1; ~, O21; old G. Valentine?] ~. | B13 O36 SP1; ~. B32 B46 C2 HH1 O20 O34 Y5; ~:? H4; ~ | HH5; ~!) NY1 VA2; ~$_{\wedge}$ O17 O21 O35 WA1 Y3.

71 They] It NY1 VA2 WA1; Shee O21. did,] ~; DT1 H8 NY1 VA2; ~$_{\wedge}$ HH5 O21 O34 O36 Y3 Y5; ~:, WA1. come,] ~; B32 C8 NY1 O20 SP1 A–C; ~$_{\wedge}$ O21 O36 Y3; ~: WA1 D–G. yet] it WA1. wee] I B13. see] ~, B26 B32 BR1.

72 Formalitys] formallitie HH1 O21 Y3; But wt ~ O35. retarding] disturbinge HH5; retard? O35. thee.] ~$_{\wedge}$ B13 B26 B46 H4 HH5 O21 O36 SP1 VA2 WA1 Y3 Y5; ~, B32 C2 C8 HH1 O34; ~; DT1 H5; *om* O35.

73 meane] means BR1; ment O21 Y3. these] those H8 O21 O36 Y3 Y5. which] w[t] O21. as] (~ BR1 H8 A–G.

74 were] went O35 O36 Y5. in] a DT1. peeces,] ~) BR1 H8 D–G; ~$_{\wedge}$ HH5 O21 O34 O35 WA1 Y3 Y5; ~; O36; ~,) A–C.

75 about] 'bout B13 O35. Bride?] ~, B13 O34; ~. | B32; ~$_{\wedge}$ B46 O21 O35 SP1 WA1 Y3; ~: BR1; ~; C2 C8 A; B**d* → »~«. HH5; ~. O20.

76 a] *om* H8. good night] God night C2 C8; (good night) VA2. could] well H8; should HH1; can O35.

77 Should] would O34. into] in to C9 H4. her] y^{e} Y3 Y5. bedd] ~, B32 C2 C8 H5 H8 O20 SP1 A–G; ~. B46 C9 O21 Y5; ~; DT1.

78 steale,] ~; B32; ~‸ B46 C9 H5 H8 HH5 NY1 O21 O34 O35 O36 VA2 WA1 Y3 Y5; steales, DT1 H4. spy'd.] ~‸ B13 B26 B46 HH1 HH5 O21 O36 WA1 Y3 Y5; spyed. B32 C2 DT1 O20 O35 SP1 VA2; spied‸ H4 O34.

79 now] *om* O34. Shee's] shee ys B32 C2 C8 HH5 O20 O34 A–G; she'is O35. layd;] layed, B13; ~‸ B46 O34 O35 Y3 Y5; ~. C9; ~, H4 HH1 HH5 O21; ~: H5 H8 D–G; ~! O36. bee?] ~‸ B26 B46 HH5 O21 O34 WA1 Y3; ~,? C2; ~, HH1.

80 there are] are there B13. delayes,] ~‸ B46 O21 WA1 Y3; ~; H5 HH5 Y5 D–G; ~,; HH1; ~: O35.

81 comes, and] cometh VA2. passes] passeth H8 NY1 WA1 D–G; passing VA2. through] ~, DT1 H4; thorough HH1. Spheare] sheer O34. after] of her B26; & HH5; aft O21; *om* O35. Spheare] ~: B32 O20 SP1 B–G; ~, DT1 H4 H5 H8; sheer O34; *om* O35; sph/ea[*trimmed*] WA1; ~. A.

82 her] *om* O35. Sheetes,] ~‸ B26 HH5 NY1 O36 WA1 Y3; ~; O21. her] *om* O35. then] than WA1. any] euery HH5 O21. where.] ~‸ B13 B26 B46 H4 HH1 HH5 O21 O35 O36 SP1 WA1 Y3; ~, B32 C2 C8 C9 A–C; ~; BR1 DT1; ~: H8.

83 Oh] *om* B13 B26 B32 BR1 C2 C8 DT1 H4 H5 H8 HH1 HH5 NY1 O20 O21 O34 O36 SP1 VA2 WA1 Y3 Y5 A–G. not] ~ then B13 B32 BR1 C2 C8 DT1 H4 H8 HH5 NY1 O20 O21 O36 SP1 VA2 WA1 Y3 Y5. day] ~, B13 B32 B46 C2 C8 DT1 O20 O21 SP1 Y5; ~ then B26 H4; ~ then, H5; ~, then, HH1 A–G. night] ~ too B13. thine.] ~‸ B13 B26 B46 C8 C9 DT1 H4 HH1 HH5 NY1 O21 O36 VA2 WA1 Y3 Y5; ~; B32; ~, C2 H8 O20 SP1 A–G.

84 Thy] The B26 NY1 O21 O34 VA2 WA1; This B46 HH1 Y3. was] *om* HH1. the] thy B32 C2 C8 DT1 H4(M *var:* »~«) NY1 O20 SP1 WA1; *om* H8; the → »th'« HH1. this] ~, B32 C2 C8 DT1 H5 O20 SP1 Y5 A–G; thee; HH1. ô] (~ NY1 VA2 WA1. Valentine.] ~‸ B26 B46 H4 H6 HH1 O21 O36 WA1 Y3; ~. | B32 SP1; ~ | HH5; ~!) NY1 VA2; ~, B.

85 Shee-Sunne,] shee Suñ, B13 B32 C2 C8 H4 H8 HH1 O17 O20 O34 SP1 Y5 A–G; she sun‸ B26 NY1 O21 VA2 WA1 Y3; she sun. O35; ~‸ O36. a] an B46; *om* O35. Hee-moone] hee Moone B13 B26 B32 C2 C8 H4 H8 HH1 HH5 NY1 O17 O21 O34 O35 SP1 VA2 WA1 Y3 Y5 A–G; Hee Maine O20; He moone: O35. there] heere B13 B26 H4 H5 H8 HH1 HH5 NY1 O35 O36 VA2 WA1 Y3 Y5; here, B32 C2 DT1 O20 SP1 A–C; heere. C8; *om* O34; ~, D–G.

86 Spheare] ~, B13 B32 C2 C8 DT1 H8 A–G; ~; H5; ~. O34.

87 Or] And O34. *first* and] or B26 HH1. so] ~, B32 C2 C8 O20 SP1.

88 one] *om* HH1(»~«) O34. another] other BR1. owe.] ~‸ B13 B26 B46 C9 H4 HH5 NY1 O17 O21 O34 O36 VA2 WA1 Y3; ~, B32 C2 H5 O20 SP1 A–G; ~; H8 Y5; ~: HH1.

89 doe;] ~, B13 B26 B32 B46 BR1 C2 C8 C9 DT1 H5 HH1 HH5 O17 O20 O34 SP1 WA1 Y5 A–G; ~‸ O36 Y3.

90 that] their B13 O17. coyne] ~, B13 C2 C8 DT1 H4 O20 SP1. pay] ~, B13 B32 C2 C8 DT1 HH1 O20 SP1 A–G.

91 would] ~, B13 B32 BR1 C2 C8 DT1 H4 H5 HH1 O17 O20 O34 SP1 A–G; needs B46; ~; O21. nor] or B46 HH1. needs] woulde, B46. or] nor B26 B32 BR1 C2 C8 DT1 H4 HH5 O20 O36 SP1 Y5 A–G; of WA1. stay] ~, B26 B32 C2 C8 H5 H8 O20 O34 SP1 A–G; ~: DT1; sta[*trimmed*] WA1; ~. Y5.

92 desires] deserves B32 O20 SP1; desire BR1. to] for to HH5. bee] *om* H8. spar'd] spared BR1 DT1 H4 Y5. nor] or Y3. to] *om* O21. spare.] ~‸ B13 B26 B46 C9 H4 H5 HH5 NY1 O17 O21 O34 O36 VA2 WA1 Y3; ~; B32 BR1 O20 SP1; ~, C2 C8 DT1 H8 HH1 Y5 A–F.

93 quickly] quick → ~»ly« HH5. theyr] the NY1 VA2 WA1. debt,] ~‸ B26 HH5 NY1 O17 O36 VA2 WA1 Y3 Y5; ~; O21; debtes‸ O34. then] ~, B32 O20 SP1.

94 Acquittances] acquittance B13 B32 B46 C2 C8 HH1 HH5 O17 O20 SP1 A. but] then B13; & then O17. pay] pay quicke B46. agen.] ~, B13 B32 C2 C8 H8 O20; ~‸ B26 B46 HH5 NY1 O21 O34 O36 SP1 WA1 Y3; ~: BR1; ~; H4 H5 A–G.

95 They] The BR1; thy H5. pay,] ~‸ B26 HH5 O17 O36 WA1 Y3; ~; O21. they] the BR1; & O17. giue,] ~‸ B26 O17 O36 WA1 Y3; lend‸ DT1; lend, H4; ~; O21. they] thy B32; the BR1. lend,] ~‸ B26 C9 O17 O36 VA2 WA1; send, B32; giue, DT1 H4; send; O21; send‸ Y3. so] be O17. fall] ~, B32 BR1 C2 O20 SP1 A(*unc*).

96 such] *om* G. liberall.] ~, B13 C2 C8 O34; ~: BR1 HH1; deliberall. DT1; deliberall → ›~‹‸ H4; ~‸ HH5 NY1 O17 O21 O36 WA1 Y3 Y5.

97 more] & B13 DT1 H4 O17. these] those Y5. doe] doth BR1 H5

HH1 HH5 O36 Y5. shine] ~, B32 BR1 C2 DT1 O20 A–G; ~. O34.

98 Then] Than G. thy] they C8 H8. Turtles] Sparrowes O21 Y3. Sparrows] ~, B26 C2 DT1 H5 HH1 Y5 A–G; Turtles O21 Y3. Valentine.] ~$_{\wedge}$ B13 H4 H6 HH1 O17 O21 O34 O36 Y3; ~. | B32 SP1; ~ | HH5; (~!) NY1; (~.) VA2; (~$_{\wedge}$ WA1; ~, B.

99 Now] And B13 B26 B32 BR1 C2 C8 DT1 H4 H5 H8 HH1 HH5 NY1 O17 O20 O21 O34 O35 O36 SP1 VA2 WA1 Y3 Y5 A–G. this] the B13 HH5; thy H5. Act] art O36 Y5. these two] the two B13; both theis HH5. Phænixes] ~, B13 B26 B32 BR1 DT1; ~. C8.

100 restored] restore'd B32. is] ~, B13 B32 C2 C8 H5 H8 NY1 O20 SP1 VA2 A–G; ~. DT1.

101 these] they HH5. two] ~, B32 BR1 C2 DT1 H4 H5 HH1 HH5 O20 O34 SP1 Y5. are] ~, B13. two] ~, B46. no] or O36. more] ~, B26 B46 BR1 C2 C8 H5 O20 A–G; ~; B32.

102 Theres] There ys B32 B46 BR1 C2 C8 H8 NY1 O20 O34 SP1 WA1. still] ~, B26 B32 C2 C8 DT1 H5 HH1 HH5 O20 SP1 A–G; *om* B46. was] *om* B46. before.] ~, B13; ~$_{\wedge}$ B26 B46 C9 H4 H6 HH1 HH5 NY1 O17 O21 O34 O35 O36 WA1 Y3 Y5; ~; B32 C2 C8 O20 SP1

103 last,] ~$_{\wedge}$ C9 H8 O17 O21 O36 SP1 Y3; ~. NY1 VA2 WA1; ~: Y5. and] ~, B46. wee] ~, B13 B32; ~. O34.

104 As] (~ C8 H5 HH5 O17 D–G; A H8. watch] ~, HH1; ~; O21. the] & HH1. vp-rise,] ~$_{\wedge}$ B26 B46 H4 H8 HH1 O21 O34 Y3 Y5; ~,) C8; ~) H5 HH5 O17 D–G; ~; NY1. will] *om* Y5. stay] ~, B32 C2 DT1 H5 O20; *om* Y5.

105 Wayting] Watchinge B13 BR1 H8 O17; ~, C2 A B. your] still our B26. opened] (open'd) B13; ~, B32 C2 C8 DT1 H4 O20 O34 SP1 WA1 A–G; open, to BR1; openinge, H5; opening HH1 O21 Y3; open'd, HH5; ~) O17; op'ned VA2. day] ~, B32 BR1 B–G; ~. C2 C8 DT1 O21 A; ~; H8 O20 SP1.

106 Onely] Onlye' O34. desird] ~, B32 C2 C8 H5 O20 A; desired, BR1 DT1 SP1; desired H4 O34 WA1 Y3 Y5; desireinge → »desired« HH5. your] our B26; y^{t} WA1. wee] wee'd BR1; weele O21. see.] ~$_{\wedge}$ B13 B26 C9 H4 HH1 HH5 O17 O34 O36 Y3 Y5; ~, B32 C8 DT1; ~: BR1 H5 H8; ~; C2 O20 SP1 A–G.

107 Others,] ~$_{\wedge}$ B13 B26 B32 B46 BR1 C2 C8 DT1 H4 H5 H8 HH1 HH5 NY1

O17 O20 O21 O34 O36 SP1 VA2 WA1 Y3 Y5 A–G. neere] nearer BR1 O21 Y3; (~ H8; ~, O36. you,] ~‸ B13 B26 BR1 DT1 H4 H5 HH1 HH5 NY1 O17 O21 O34 VA2 Y3 Y5 A–G; ~) H8; ~; O36. whispring] whispering B32 BR1 C2 C8 DT1 H4 H5 H8 HH1 HH5 NY1 O17 O20 O21 O34 O36 SP1 VA2 WA1 Y3 Y5 A–G. speake] ~, B13 B32 C2 H5 O20 SP1 WA1 A–G.

108 lay] ~, B13 C2 C8 DT1 H4 H5 H8 HH1 HH5 O20 SP1 WA1 A–G; ~; B32. which] whose O17. breake] ~, B13 BR1 C2 C8 H5 H8 O20 SP1 A–G; ~. B32 NY1 VA2 Y5; ~; DT1.

109 winn] *om* C2 C8. by obseruing] b' observinge, then B13; by observing, then B26 O21; by Obseruing then, B32 B46 BR1 H5 O20 O34 SP1; then observeinge wiselye, C2; wiselie obseruing then, C8; by obseruing; then DT1; by obseruing then H4 HH1 HH5 NY1 O17 O36 VA2 WA1 Y3 Y5; by obseruing ›then‹ H6; by'observing, then, A–F; by observing, then, G. it] I** → »~« HH5. is] ~, B13 B32 C8 O20 SP1.

110 That] But O35; And SP1. opens] oftens → »~« HH5; open'de O21 Y3; see O35. first] then BR1; who O35. a] *om* O17; first O35. Curtayne,] ~‸ B26 H8 HH5 NY1 O21 VA2 WA1 Y3; *om* O17; salutes, O35. Hers,] ~‸ C8 HH5 NY1 O17 O21 O34 O36 VA2 WA1 Y3 Y5 A–G; y^{e}‸ O35. or] Infant O35. His.] ~‸ B13 C9 H4 H6 HH1 HH5 O21 O34 O36 WA1 Y3 Y5; ~, B26 B46 C2 C8; ~: BR1 H8; ~; H5 O20 SP1 A–G; shine‸ O35.

111 try'd] tryed B32 BR1 C2 C8 DT1 HH5 O20 O34 O35 SP1 A–G. Nyne] ~, B32 BR1 C2 C8 DT1 H5 HH5 O20 A–G; ~. O35.

112 Till] to HH1. hower] ~, B32 C2 C8 DT1 H5 HH1 O20 SP1 A–G; *om* O34. wee] all B46 H5 HH1 O21 Y3; neare, BR1; ne're H8; *om* O34. enlarge] ~, B32 C8 DT1 H5 HH1 O20 SP1 A–G; ~. C2 Y5; ~ not O34. ô] (~ NY1 VA2 WA1. Valentine.] ~. | B13 B32 DT1 O17 SP1; ~‸ C9 H4 H6 HH1 O21 O34 O36 Y3; ~ | HH5; Bishop ~!) NY1; ~: O35; Bishop ~.) VA2; Bishop ~‸ WA1.

Subscriptions: I D B13 BR1 C1 O17. Finis B46 DT1 H4. Finis The Epithalamion | | Io. Donn. | . | NY1. I:D: ffinis O21 Y3. . | .ffinis. | . I:Dunne. | . O36. I. Donn. VA2. *om* B26 B32 C2 C8 C9 H5 H6 H8 HH1 HH5 O20 O34 O35 SP1 WA1 Y5 A–G.

Verbal Variants in Selected Modern Editions

Editions collated: H I J K L M N O P Q S T Z AA BB DD.
Format:

Indentations: *irregular ind* H, *no ind* I J; *ll. 2 and 3 of each st short ind* K; *l. 2 of each st short ind, ll.* 5 *and* 9 *long ind* L; *ll.* 2, 3, 5, *and* 9 *of each st ind equally* M O P Z AA DD; *ll.* 2, 5, *and* 9 *of each st ind equally* N; *l.* 2 *of each st short ind* Q S; *ll.* 2, 3, 5, *and* 9 *of each st ind equally, l.* 14 *extended into left* M T; *l.* 5 *of each st long ind, l.* 14 *extended into left* M BB.

Miscellaneous: *sts numbered in roman* H–J M–Q S Z BB DD; *sts not numbered* K AA; *sts numbered in arabic* L T.

Headings: *An Epithalamion on* Frederick *Count Palatine of the* Rhyne, *and the Lady* Elizabeth, *being married on St.* Valentine's *Day.* H I J(*and* LADY) K M N. AN EPITHALAMION, OR MARRIAGE SONG, ON THE LADY ELIZABETH AND COUNT PALATINE, BEING MARRIED ON ST. VALENTINE'S DAY. L O–Q S T Z–BB DD.

8 the] *om* J.

11 soone] strait H–Q S T Z–BB DD.

13 then] than H–K M–P S T AA DD.

21 fowles] fowl H–K M N.

37 theyr] this BB.

39 pretends] portends H–Q S T Z–BB DD.

42 thy] day H–K M N P.

46 growe] go H–P.

49 one] once H–K. can] an H–J; and K.

50 vnseperable] inseparable H–Q S T Z–BB DD.

51 Two] to H–Q S T Z–BB DD.

56 or] of H–K N P; O L M O.

57 here] hence I J.

58 then] than H–P S T AA.

60 Starrs] store L O Q S T Z–BB DD; stores M N.

63 your] you L.

67 late] too late L N O Q S Z BB DD.

70 ô] old H–K N P.

81 passes] passeth H–J.

83 Oh] *om* H–Q S T Z–BB DD. day] day then H–Q S T Z AA DD.

85 a Hee-moone] he a moon J. there] here L O Q S T Z–BB DD.

91 or] nor H–Q S T Z–BB DD.

94 Acquittances] acquittance O.

96 such] *om* H–K.

98 Then] Than H J–P S T AA.

99 Now] And H–Q S T Z–BB DD.

109 obseruing] ~ then H–Q S T Z–BB DD.

Subscriptions: *none.*

Schema of Textual Relationships

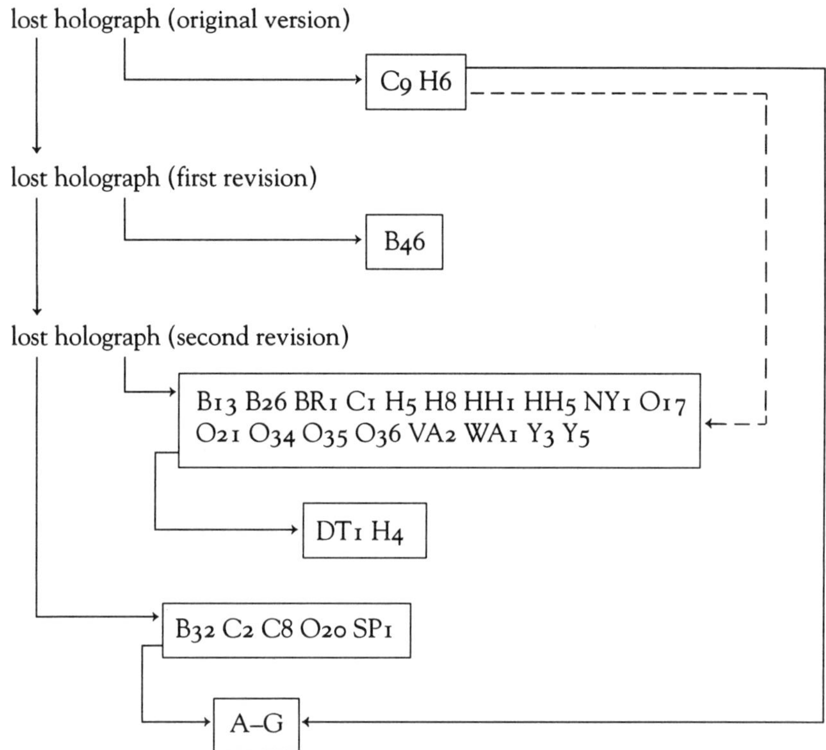

C9 H6

11 The Husband Cock lookes out and **soone** is spedd
27 **Where** Love and Courage never shall decline
33 Vp vp, fayre **bird**, and call
35 Thy Rubyes Pearles and Dyamonds **forth** and make
50 Yo^{u} are twice **vnseperable**, Greate, and one
55 Yo^{u} two haue one way **left** yor selues to entwyne
60 And finding heere such **starrs**, is loth to sett?
64 And **bee** to others Spectacle and talke!

67 The Maskers come **late**, and, I thinke, will stay
85 Heere lyes a Shee-Sunne, and a Hee-moone **there**
95 They pay, they **giue, they lend**, and so let fall
99 **Now** by this Act of these two Phænixes
109 And **winn by obseruing** whose hand it is

B46

11 The husband Cocke lookes out and **sone** is Sped
27 **Whose** Loue and Courage, neuer shall decline
33 Vp vp faire **Bride**, and call
35 Thy Rubies, Pearles, and Diamonds **forth**, and make
50 You are twise **Vnseparable**, Great, an One
55 You two haue one way left, **your** Selues t'intwine
60 And findinge here such **store** is loath to Sett.
64 And **to be** others Spectacle, and talke
67 The Masquers come **too late**, I thincke will stay
85 Here lies a shee-Sun, and an hee-moone **there**
95 They pay, they **giue, they lend**, and so let fall
99 **Now** by this Act of these two Phœnixes
109 And **win, by obseruinge then**, whose hand it is

B13 B26 BR1 C1 H5 H8 HH1 HH5 NY1 O17 O21 O34 O35 O36 VA2 WA1 Y3 Y5

11 The husband Cock lookes out, & **straight** is sped, (and soone H5 HH1 O34 Y3)
27 **Whose** loue, and courage neu^{r} shall decline (where loue H8)
33 Vp, vp faire **bride** & call (faire birde B26 HH5 NY1 VA2 WA1; faire birds Y5)
35 Thy Rubies, Pearles, & Diamonds **forth** & make
50 You are twice **inseperable**, greate, & one (vnseparably B26)
55 You two haue one waye **left**, your selves t'entwine (vntwine H5; two *om* HH1 O21 Y3)
60 And findinge heere such **store**, is loath to sett (starres B26 H8)
64 And **bee to** others spectacle, and talke? (and to be H5 O36 Y5; & to be to HH5)
67 The maskers come **late**, & I thinke will staye (Masques H5 HH1 O21 Y3; come too late NY1 VA2 WA1; come last HH5; came O34)
85 Heere lyes a shee Sun̄, & a hee Moone **heere** (hee moone there O17 O21)
95 They paye, they **give, they lend**, & soe let fall (they send; & O21 Y3)
99 **And** by this act of these two Phenixes, (the act B13 HH5; thy act H5; this art O21 O36 Y5; of the two B13; of both theis HH5)
109 and **winne by observinge then**, whose hand it is

DT1 H4

11 The Husband-Cock looks out, and **straight** is sped,
27 **Whose** loue, and courage neuer shall decline
33 Vpp, vp faire **Bride**, and call
35 Thy Rubies, Pearles, & Diamonds **out**, and make
50 You are twice **in seperable**, Great, and one. (inseperable H4)
55 You twoe have one way **more**, yor selues t'entwine
60 And finding here such **store**, is loath to sett?
64 And **to bee** others spectacle, and talk?
67 The Maskers come **late**, & I **f'eare** will staye (fear H4)
85 Here lyes a shee-Sun, and a Hee-Moone **here**,
95 They pay, they **lend they giue**, & soe lett fall
99 **And** by the acte of these twoe Phœnixes,
109 And **winn by obseruing; then** whose had it is

B32 C2 C8 O20 SP1

11 The husband Cocke lookes out, and **streight** ys sped
27 **Whose** loue and Courage never shall declyne,
33 Vp, Vp, Fayre **Bride**, and Call,
35 Thy Rubyes, Pearles, & Diamonds **forth**, & make
50 Yo^{w} are twice **inseperable**, Great, & one,
55 Yo^{w} two haue one way **left**, yor Selves to entwine,
60 And findinge here such **store**, ys loth to sett,?
64 And **be to** others Spectacle, and Talke,?
67 The Masquers come **too** Late, & I thinke, will stay,
85 Here lyes a shee Sunne, & a hee Moone **here**,
95 They pay, they **giue, they lend**, & soe lett fall, (thy send B32)
99 **And** by thys Act of these Two Phenixes
109 And **win by Obseruing then**, whose hand it is, (And then observeinge wiselye C2; And wiselie obseruing then C8)

A–G

11 The husband cocke lookes out, and **straight** is sped,
27 **Whose** love and courage never shall decline,
33 Up, up, faire **Bride**, and call,
35 Thy Rubies, Pearles, and Diamonds **forth**, and make
50 You'are twice **inseparable**, great, and one;
55 You two have one way **left**, your selves to'entwine,
60 And finding here such **store**, is loth to set? (starres B–G)
64 And **be to** others spectacle, and talke?

67 The masquers come **too late**, and'I thinke, will stay, (too *om* B–G)
85 Here lyes a shee Sunne, and a hee Moone **here**, (Moone there D–G)
95 They pay, they **give, they lend,** and so let fall
99 **And** by this act of these two Phenixes
109 And **win by'observing, then,** whose hand it is

Analyses of Early Printed Copies

Poems, by J.D., 4to, 1633 (siglum A)

Copies collated: *CtY, DFo, L* (G.11415), M, *MH, MiU.*
Relevant section: sigs. Q3v–R1v; pp. 118–22.
Press variants:

Sheet Q, inner forme

		Uncorrected (*CtY*):	Corrected (*DFo, L,* M, *MH, MiU*):
Q3v (p. 118):			
	l. 14	the	thy
Q4r (p. 119):			
	l. 15	warm'dst	warmd'st
	l. 19	Taper a	a Taper
	l. 41	day,	day‸

Sheet R, inner forme

		Uncorrected (*MH*):	Corrected (*CtY, DFo, L,* M, *MiU*):
R1v (p. 122):			
	l. 91	forbeare‸	forbeare,
	l. 95	fall,	fall‸

Miscatchings: *none.*

§

Poems, by J.D., 8vo, 1635 (siglum B)

Copies collated: *CtY, MH, MiU.*
Relevant section: sigs. H2–H4; pp. 103–07.
Press variants: *none.*
Miscatchings: *none.*

§

Poems, by J.D., 8vo, 1639 (siglum C)

Copies collated: *CtY, MH, MiU.*
Relevant section: sigs. G8–H2; pp. 103–07.

Press variants: *see note 2 below.*
Miscatchings: *none.*

Notes: 1) In the section containing *EpEliz*, this edition is a page-for-page resetting of B.

2) In *EpEliz* 19, the apostrophe in "mak'st" does not print in the *CtY* copy.

§

Poems by J.D., 8vo, 1649, 1650, 1654 (sigla D, E, F)

Copies collated: 1649: *CtY, MH.* 1650: *CtY, MH.* 1654: *CSmH, CtY.*
Relevant section: sigs. H2–H4; pp. 99–103.
Press variants: *none.*
Miscatchings: *none.*

Note: Examination of multiple copies on the Lindstrand Comparator shows that the sections of 1649, 1650, and 1654 containing *EpEliz* are printed from a single typesetting, 1650 and 1654 being reissues of the sheets of 1649.

§

Poems, &c. by John Donne, 8vo, 1669 (siglum G)

Copies collated: *CtY, L, TxLT.*
Relevant section: sigs. H2v–H4v; pp. 100–04.
Press variants: *none.*
Miscatchings: *none.*

Eclogue. 1613. *December* 26.

Allophanes *finding* Idios *in the Country in the Christmas, reprehends his Absence from Court at the Marriage of the Earle of Somerset.* Idios *giues an account of his purpose therein, and of his Actions there.*

Allophanes.
Vnseasonable man, statue of Ice
   What could to Countryes Solitude entice
Thee in this yeares cold and decrepit Time?
   Natures Instinct drawes to the warmer clime
Even small birds, who by that Courage dare
   In numerous fleets sayle through theyr Sea the Ayre.
What delicacy can in fields appeere
   Whilst Flora her selfe doth a buff Ierkin weare
Whilst winds doe all the Trees and hedges stripp
   Of Leaues, to furnish rodds enough to whipp
Thy madnesse from thee, And all springs by frost
   Haue taken cold and theyr sweete murmure lost?
If thou thy faults or fortunes wouldst lament
   With iust solemnety, doe it in Lent.
At Court the Spring already aduanced is
   The Sunne stayes longer vp, And yet not his
The Glory is. Far other, other fires
   First Zeale to Prince and State, then Loues desires
Burne in one brest, And like heauens two great lights
   The first doth gouerne dayes, the other nights.
And then that early light (which did appeere
   Before the Sunn and Moone created were)
The Princes fauour, is diffusd o're all
   From which all fortunes names and natures fall.
Then from those wombes of Stars the Brides bright eyes
   At every Glaunce a Constellation flyes
And sowes the Court with Stars, and doth prevent
   In light and power the all-eyd firmament.
First her eyes kindle other Ladyes eyes
   Then from theyr beames theyr Iewells lusters rise

And from theyr Iewells torches do take fire
   And all is warmth and light, and good desire.
Most other Courts, alas, ar like to Hell,
   Where, in darke plotts, fire without light doth dwell
Or but like stooves (for lust and envy get
   Continewall (but artificiall) heate.)
Heere Zeale and Loue growne one all clouds digest
   And make our Court an everlasting East
And canst thou bee from thence?

Idios. No I am there:
   As Heauen to men disposd is every where:
So are those Courts whose Princes animate
   Not onely all theyr house but all theyr state.
Let no man thinke because hee's full hee hath all.
   Kings (as theyr patterne God) are liberall
Not onely in fulnesse but Capacity
   Enlarging narrow men to feele and see
And comprehend the blessings they bestow:
   So reclus'd Hermits often times doe knowe
More of heauens Glory then a worldling can.
   As man is of the world: the hart of man
Is an Epitome of Gods greate booke
   Of Creatures, and Man neede no farther looke:
So is the Country of Courts, where sweete peace doth,
   As theyr owne common Soule, giue life to both
And am I then from Court?

Alloph. Dreamer thou art.
   Thinkst thou, fantastique, that thou hast a part
In the East India fleete, because thou hast
   A little Spice or Amber in thy tast?
Because thou art not frozen, art thou warme?
   Seest thou all good because thou seest no harme?
The Earth doth in her inward Bowells hold
   Stuff well disposd, and which would fayne bee gold
But never shall, except it chance to lye
   So vpward that heauen guild it with his eye.
As for diuine things fayth comes from aboue
   So for best ciuill vse all tinctures moue
From higher powers. From God Religion springs,
   Wisedome and honour from the vse of kings.
Then vnbeguile thy selfe, And knowe with mee
   That Angels, though on earth employd they bee
Are still in heauen; so is hee still at home

That doth abrode to honest Actions come.
Chide thy selfe then (ô foole) which yesterday
Mightst haue read more then all thy bookes bewray.
Hast thou a History which doth present
A Court, where all Affections doe assent
Vnto the Kings, and that the Kings are iust?
And where it is no Leuity to trust
Where there is no Ambition but to obay
Where Men neede whisper Nothing, and yet may
Where the Kings fauours are so plac'd, that all
Find that the King therein is liberall
To them in him, because his fauours bend
To Vertue vnto which they all pretend?
Thou hast no Such: yet heere was this and more
An earnest Louer, wise, then, and before.
Our little Cupid hath su'd Lyvery
And is no more in his Minority
Hee is admitted now into that brest
Where the Kings Counsells and his Secrets rest.
What hast thou lost, ô Ignorant man?

Idios. —I Knewe
All this, and onely therefore I withdrew.
To knowe and feele all this, and not to haue
Words to expresse it, makes a man a graue
Of his owne thoughts. I would not therefore stay
At a greate feast, hauing no grace to say
And yet I scap't not heere, for beeing come
Full of the common Ioye I vtterd some.
Reade then this Nuptiall song, which was not made
Eyther the Court or mens harts to inuade
But since I am dead and buryed, I could frame
No Epitaph which might aduance my fame
So much as this poore song, which testifies
I did vnto that day some sacrifice.

Epithalamion.

1. *The Time of the Marriage.*

Thou art repriu'd Old yeare, thou shalt not dye
Though thou vpon thy deathbed lye
And shouldst within fiue dayes expire
Yet thou art rescewd by a mightier fire
Then thy old Soule the Sunn

When hee doth in his largest Circle runn.
The passage of the West or East would thaw
And open wide theyr easy liquid Iaw
To all our Ships, could a Promethean Art
Eyther vnto the Northerne Pole impart
The fire of these inflaming eyes, or of this louing hart.

2. *Equality of Persons.*

But vndiscerning Muse, which hart, which eyes
In this new couple dost thou prise?
When his eye as enflaming is
As hers, and her heart loues as well as his.
Bee tryd by beauty and than
The Bridegrome is a Mayd and not a man.
If by that manly Courage they bee tryd
Which scornes vniust opinion, then the Bride
Becomes a man; Should chance or enuyes Art
Diuide these two whome Nature scarse did part
Since both haue both th'enflaming eyes, and both the Loving hart.

3. *Raysing the Bridegrome.*

Though it bee some diuorce to thinke on you
Singly (so much one are you two)
Yet let mee heere contemplate thee
First, cheerefull Bridegrome, And first let mee see
How thou prevent'st the Sunne
And his redd foming horses dost outrunn
How (hauing layd downe in thy Soueraignes brest
All businesses, from thence to reinvest
Them, when these Triumphs cease,) thou forward art
To shewe to her who doth the like empart
The fire of thy enflaming eyes and of thy louing hart.

4. *Raysing of the Bride.*

But now to thee (fayre Bride) it is some wrong
To thinke thou wert in bedd so long.
Since, soone, thou ly'st downe first, tis fitt
Thou in first rising shouldst allow for it.
Powder thy radiant hayre
Which if without such Ashes thou shouldst weare

Thou, which to all that come to looke vpon
Wert ment for Phæbus, wouldst bee Phaeton.
For our ease giue thine eyes th'vnusuall part
Of ioye, a Teare, So quenchd thou mayst empart
To vs that come thy enflaming eyes, to him thy louing hart.

5. *Her Apparrelling.*

Thus thou discendst to our Infirmity,
Who can the sunn in water see;
So dost thou when in Silke, and Gold
Thou cladst thy selfe; since wee which do behold
Ar dust and wormes, tis iust
Our obiects bee the fruites of wormes and dust.
Let every Iewell bee a glorious starre
Yet Starrs ar not so pure as theyr Spheares ar
And though thou stoope to appeere to vs in part,
Still in that picture, thou entirely art
Which thy enflaming eyes haue made within his louing hart.

6. *Going to Chappell.*

Now from your Easts you issue forth; and wee
(As men which through a Cypresse see
The rising sunne, do thinke it two)
So as you goe to church doe thinke of you.
But that vayle beeing gon
By the Church rites, you are from thenceforth one.
The Church Triumphant made this Match before
And now the Militant doth striue no more.
Thou Reverend Priest who Gods Recorder art
Doe from his Dictates to these two impart
All blessings which ar seene or thought by Angels eye or heart.

7. *The Benediction.*

Blest payre of Swanns, Oh may you enter-bring
Dayly new ioyes, and never sing.
Liue till all grounds of wishes fayle
Till honour, yea till wisedome growe so stale
That new greate heights to trye
It must serue your Ambition to dye.
Rayse heyres, and may heere to the worlds end liue

Heyres, for this King, to take thankes, yours, to giue.
Nature and grace doe all, and nothing Art.
May never Age or errour ouerthwart
With any West these radiant eyes, with any North this hart.

8. *Feasts and Revells.*

But you are overblest, plenty this day
  Iniures; It causes time to stay.
  The Tables grone, as though this feast
Would, as the floud, destroy all fowle and beast
    And, were the doctrine new
That the earth mou'd, this day would make it true
For every part to dance and revells goes
They tread the Ayre and fall not where they rose.
Though sixe howers since the Sun to bedd did part
The Masques and Banquets will not yet impart
A Sun-set to those weary eyes, a Center to this hart.

9. *The Brides Going to Bedd.*

What mean'st thou, Bride, this company to keepe
  To sitt vp till thou fayne wouldst sleepe?
  Thou mayst not, when th'art layd, doe so.
Thy selfe must to him a new banquet growe
    And you must entertayne
And doe all this dayes dances or'e agayne.
Knowe that if Sunn and Moone together doe
Rise in one point, they doe not sett so too
Therefore thou mayst to Bedd, fayre Bride, depart
Th'art not gon beeing gon, where e're thou art
Thou leau'st in him thy watchfull eyes in him thy louing hart.

10. *The Bridegroomes Comming.*

As hee that sees a Starr fall, runns apace
  And finds a gelly in the place
  So doth the Bridegroome hast as much
Beeing told this Starre is fall'ne and finds her such.
    And as frinds may looke strange
By a new fashion or apparrells change
Theyr Soules, though long acquaynted they had beene,
These Clothes, the bodyes never yet had seene.

Therefore at first shee modestly might start
But must forthwith surrender every part
Freely as each to each before gaue eyther eye or hart.

11. *The Goodnight.*

Now as in Tullias Tombe one Lamp burnt cleere
  Vnchangd for fifteene hundred yeere
  May these loue lamps wee heere enshryne,
In warmth, light, lasting æquall the diuine.
    Fyre ever doth aspire
And makes all like it selfe, turnes all to fyre
But ends in ashes, which these cannot doe
For none of them is fewell but fyre too.
This is Ioyes bonfire, then, where Loues strong Arts
Made of so noble Indiuiduall parts
One fire of 4 enflaming eyes, and of 2 louing harts.

Idios.
As I haue brought this Song, that I may doe
  A perfect Sacrifice, Ile burne it too.

Alloph.
No Sir, this paper I haue iustly got
  For in burnt Incense the perfume is not
His onely that presents it, but of all.
  Whatever celebrates this Nuptiall
Is common, since the Ioye thereof is so
  Nor may your selfe bee Priest; But let mee goe
Back to the Court, and I will lay it on
  Such Altars as prize your deuotion.

Textual Introduction

This epithalamion with its framing eclogue (*Eclog*) was written to commemorate the marriage of Robert Ker (or Carr), Earl of Somerset, and Frances Howard, which occurred on 26 December 1613.

The poem survives in 22 seventeenth-century manuscripts. Milgate alleges that since *EpEliz* and *Eclog* "were composed for patrons, it would have been discourteous for Donne to have reissued them in a revised form, even if he desired to improve them" (1978, liv–lv). The artifactual evidence, however, shows that the transmissional history of each of these two epithalamions is marked by two successive revisions of the text; and the nature of these changes—at each stage multiple verbal alterations that cannot plausibly be explained as corruptions, sophistications, or necessary repairs of obviously defective language and that carry forward in the stream of transmission once they have entered—suggests that the revisions are authorial. Charting the transmissional history reveals that the extant manuscripts fall into six discrete families and subfamilies (see Schema of Textual Relationships).

The C9/H6 family preserves what is no doubt the earliest version of the poem. It is marked by the readings "buff" in line 8, "And am I" in line 55, "India" in line 57, "that the Kings" in line 77, "vnto" in line 84, "Yet let" in line 129, "Wert" in line 145, "cladst" in line 152, "Thou Reverend Priest who" in line 168, "for this King" and "yours, to giue" in line 178, "to Bedd, fayre Bride" in line 201, "ffreely" in line 214, and "Nuptiall" in line 231.

The first revision, represented by a single surviving manuscript (B46), changes "buff" to "freese" in line 8, "And am I" to "I am not" in line 55, "India" to "Indian" in line 57, "Yet let" to "Let" in line 129, "Wert" to "Art" in line 145, "cladst" to "clothe'st" in line 152, "to Bedd, ffayre Bride" to "Faire Bride to bed" in line 201, and "ffreely" to "As freely" in line 214.

The second revision, from which all the other surviving manuscript copies ultimately derive, preserves seven of the eight changes of the first revision and makes six additional alterations, changing "that the kings" to "that that Kings" in line 77, "vnto" to "to the" in line 84, "Raysing the Bridegrome" to "Raysinge of the Bridegroome" in the heading to stanza 3 of the Epithalamion, "clothe'st" to "cloud'st" in line 152, "Thou Reverend Priest who" to "Then Reuerend Preist, who" in line 168, "for this King" to "from this kinge" in line 178, and "Nuptiall" to "festivall" in line 231. Two families derive directly from this second revision, the large B11 family and the smaller B32 family.

The B11 family is not homogenous. While its members generally reflect the distinctive readings of the second revision, some of these manuscripts preserve one or more of the original readings from the C9/H6 family—notably H5 in line 77 ("that the Kings"), H8 in line 168 ("Thou Reuerend Priest"), and B11 in line 129 ("yet lett")—and such anomalies cannot readily be explained. Some may reflect the conflation of readings from more than one textual tradition in a single manuscript; some may represent independent alteration at the hands of a careless or officious scribe. The surviving data are simply insufficient to allow a full description of the textual history of this manuscript family.

The B7 family derives from an uncontaminated member of the B11 family. Its distinctive readings—notably "kisse" for "his" in line 16, "when" for "where" in lines 76 and 78, "lenity" for "levity" in line 78, "those" for "thou" in line 157, "you to giue" for "yours, to giue" in line 178, and "these" for "them" in line 222—are obviously scribal blunders.

The B32 family, which derives from the second revision of the poem independently of the B11 family, is distinguished by the readings "Are" for "Art" in line 145 in two of its three members and "yo^{w}, to give" for "yours, to giue" in line 178. The C2/C8 family is actually a subfamily of the B32 family that makes an additional change in the text, reading "places" for "plotts" in line 34.

The text of *Eclog* in the first of the seventeenth-century editions (A) was obviously set from a manuscript closely resembling the C2/C8 subfamily of the B32 family, as it reads "places" for "plotts" in line 34 as well as "Are" for "Art" in line 145 and "you, to give" for "yours, to giue" in line 178. The compiler/editor of the second edition (B) must have consulted a manuscript resembling C9 and H6 in revising A's text of *Eclog*, since that second printing restores "And am I" in line 55 and "Wert" in line 145. The third edition (C) was then set from the second without verbal alteration. The compiler/editor of the fourth edition (D), which was set from C, may also have consulted a manuscript from a family other than C2/C8, since that printing in all three of its issues (including E and F) restores "plots" in line 34. Moreover, apparently on no manuscript authority, D also substitutes "hand" for "eye" in line 214. The final seventeenth-century edition (G) was set from a copy of D, E, or F.

The modern editions of Tonson (H), Bell (I), Anderson (J), Chalmers (K), Lowell? (M), and Grosart (N) present texts of *Eclog* ultimately deriving from G. Alford (L), Lowell (O), Grierson (Q), Hayward (S), Bennett (T), Shawcross (Z), Smith (AA), Milgate (BB), and Patrides (DD) use A as their copy-texts, though most selectively emend its verbals on the authority of manuscript readings. Chambers (P) creates a modernized, eclectic text drawing from A, B, E, and G.

H6, the copy-text for *Eclog*, with its 169 Donne poems is the largest extant manuscript collection of Donne's poems and may have been prepared for an edition: its title page reads "The Poems of D. I. Donne not yet imprinted . . . Finishd this 12 of October 1632." The compiler of Harvard MS Eng 966.2 (transcribed from H6 in the eighteenth century) notes that H6 belonged "to Dr Parnel, Arch Deacon of Clogher, and after his decease to M^{r}. Thos: Burton of Dublin." Now at Harvard, H6 was most recently owned by the Rev. T. R. O'Flahertie of Capel, near Dorking, Surrey (Beal 252). Its cognate, C9, derives either from H6 or from a common progenitor, the latter being more likely.

The text of *Eclog* preserved in H6 is the least corrupted copy of the poem in its original version. Its readings are internally consistent, and it is intelligently punctuated. It should be noted that after it was inscribed, H6 was contaminated by its original scribe with variant readings from A, notably in lines 8, 126, and 178 (see the Historical Collation). All of these contaminations have been rejected in the reading text.

Aside from the expansion of scribal brevigraphs and the alteration of initial *ff*'s to *F*'s, the only emendations made in the copy-text have been the imposition of italics in the heading and induction and the moving of speech prefixes to the left margins in lines 39, 55, and 92 (both changes made to conform to ordinary seventeenth-century printing practice) and the addition of a few punctuation marks throughout the text where needed to prevent misreading.

Textual Apparatus

Copy-text: H6. **Texts collated:** B7 (ff. 61–65v); B11 (ff. 10–14v); B32 (ff. 132–35); B46 (ff. 38–43); C2 (ff. 73–77); C8 (ff. 106v–13); C9 (ff. 86–89v); CT1 (pp. 131–40); DR1 (*ll. 1–104 only*, ff. [1–2]); DT1 (ff. 94v–98); EU2 (*ll. 193–203 only*, p. 6); H4 (ff. 76v–80); H5 (*ll. 1–225 only*, ff. 154–58); H6 (pp. 325–35); H8 (*ll. 1–170 only*, ff. 49–52v); HH1 (*ll. 1–225 only*, ff. 49–53); HH4 (*ll. 1–170 only*, pp. 93–96); O20 (ff. 133–38v); R9 (*ll. 1–4, 7–14, 115b–25; 171–74, 180–81b, 184–92 only*, pp. 304–09 [*pp. 305–08 now missing*]); SA1 (pp. 102–08); SP1 (ff. 110v–16v); Y7 (*ll. 182–209, 211–14 only*, ff. 25–26); A (pp. 123–35); B (pp. 108–19); C (pp. 108–19); D (pp. 104–14); E (pp. 104–14); F (pp. 104–14); G (pp. 105–14).

Emendations of the copy-text: *italics supplied; speech prefixes in ll. 39, 55, and 92 moved from center of line to left M.* Heading: *Eclogue*] »P.« Eclogue *December*] Decemb^{r}. Induction: *reprehends*] rep^{r}hends *Court*] Co^{r}t *Somerset.*] Somerset$_{\wedge}$ *Actions*] Absence → ›~‹ Speech Prefix: *Allophanes.*] Allophanes$_{\wedge}$ 2 *ind supplied* 6 the] y^{e} Ayre.] ~$_{\wedge}$ 8 Flora] fflora buff] ~ → ›freeze‹ 18 First] ffirst 21 which] wch 23 fauour] fauo^{r} 24 which] wch. 29 First] ffirst 32 desire.] ~$_{\wedge}$ 42 state.] ~$_{\wedge}$ 47 comprehend] comp^{r}hend 54 common] com̄on 55 *Alloph.*] Alloph: art.] ~$_{\wedge}$ 62 which] wch. 67 From] ffrom From] ffrom 68 honour] hono^{r} 73 which] wch. 74 bewray.] ~$_{\wedge}$ 75 thou] | ~ | which] wch. 82 Find] ffind 84 which] wch. 86 before.] ~$_{\wedge}$ 90 rest.] ~$_{\wedge}$ 91 *Idios.*] Idios$_{\wedge}$ 92 withdrew.] ~$_{\wedge}$ 98 Full] ffull common] com̄on some.] ~$_{\wedge}$ 99 which] wch. 102 which] wch. 103 which] wch. 104 sacrifice.] ~$_{\wedge}$ Section Heading: *Epithalamion.*] »P.« Epithalamion$_{\wedge}$ St Heading: 1.] ~$_{\wedge}$ *Marriage.*] Marriage$_{\wedge}$ St Heading: 2.] ~$_{\wedge}$ *Persons.*] Persons$_{\wedge}$ 116 which] wch. which] wch. 121 man.] ~$_{\wedge}$ 123 Which] W^{ch}. 126 eyes] ~ → ›eye‹ hart.] ~$_{\wedge}$ St Heading: 3.] ~$_{\wedge}$ *Bridegrome.*] Bridegrome$_{\wedge}$ 127 you] yo^{u} 128 you] yo^{u} 130 First] ffirst 137 hart.] ~$_{\wedge}$ St Heading: 4.] ~$_{\wedge}$ *Bride.*] Bride$_{\wedge}$ 143 Which] W^{ch}. 144 which] wch 146 For] ffor 148 hart.] ~$_{\wedge}$ St Heading: 5.] ~$_{\wedge}$ *Apparrelling.*] apparrelling$_{\wedge}$ 152 which] wch. 159 hart.] ~$_{\wedge}$ 160 your] yor you] yo^{u} 161 which] wch. 162 two)] ~$_{\wedge}$ 163 So] ~) you] yo^{u}. you.] yo^{u}$_{\wedge}$ 165 you] yo^{u} 170 which] wch heart.] ~$_{\wedge}$ St Heading: 7.] ~$_{\wedge}$

Benediction.] Benediction$_{\wedge}$ 171 you] yo^{u} 174 honour] hono^{r}
176 your] yor dye.] ~$_{\wedge}$ 178 for] ~ → ›from‹   yours] yo^{rs} → ›yo^{w}‹
179 Art.] ~$_{\wedge}$ 181 hart.] ~$_{\wedge}$ St Heading: 8.] ~$_{\wedge}$ *Revells*.] Revells$_{\wedge}$
182 you] yo^{u} 188 For] ffor   189 rose.] ~$_{\wedge}$ 192 hart.] ~$_{\wedge}$
St Heading: 9.] ~$_{\wedge}$ *Going*] going   *Bedd*.] bedd$_{\wedge}$ 197 you] yo^{u}
203 hart.] ~$_{\wedge}$ St Heading: 10.] ~$_{\wedge}$ *Comming*.] Com̄ing$_{\wedge}$ 214 Freely] ffreely   hart.] ~$_{\wedge}$ St Heading: 11.] ~$_{\wedge}$ *Goodnight*.] Goodnight$_{\wedge}$
219 Fyre] ffyre   221 which] w^{ch}.   222 For] ffor   too.] ~$_{\wedge}$
225 harts.] ~$_{\wedge}$ 226 *Idios*.] Idios$_{\wedge}$ 227 *ind supplied*   too.] ~$_{\wedge}$
228 Sir] S^{r}.   229 For] ffor   232 common] com̄on   233 your] yor
235 your] yor

Historical Collation

Format:

Imperfections: *damage causing the loss of ll.* 51 *and* 149 *entirely and the loss of text in other lines*   B11; *damage causing the loss of ll.* 81–82 *entirely and the loss of text in other lines*   DR1.

Indentations: *ll.* 1–104, 226–35 *alternate lines ind, ll.* 2 *and* 3 *of each st of Epithalamion short ind, l.* 5 *long ind*   B7 B11 B32 C8 CT1 DT1 H4 H6 O20 SP1 A; *ll.* 1–104, 226–35 *alternate lines ind, ll.* 2, 3, *and* 5 *of each st of Epithalamion ind equally*   B46 C2 C9; *no ind*   DR1; *l.* 197 *ind*   EU2; *ll.* 1–104 *alternate lines ind, ll.* 2, 3, *and* 5 *of each st of Epithalamion ind equally*   H5; *ll.* 1–104 *no ind, ll.* 2, 3, *and* 5 *of each st of Epithalamion ind equally*   H8; *ll.* 1–104 *no ind, ll.* 2, 3, *and* 5 *of each st of Epithalamion ind equally*   HH1; *ll.* 1–104 *alternate lines ind, ll.* 2, 3, *and* 5–10 *of each st of Epithalamion ind equally*   HH4; *ll.* 117, 118, 120, 172, 181, *and* 186 *ind equally*   R9; *ll.* 1–104, 226–35 *no ind, ll.* 2 *and* 3 *of each st of Epithalamion short ind, l.* 5 *long ind*   SA1; *ll.* 186, 197, 205, 206, *and* 208 *ind equally*   Y7; *ll.* 1–104, 226–35 *no ind, ll.* 2, 3, *and* 5 *of each st of Epithalamion ind equally*   B–G.

Miscellaneous: *sts of Epithalamion numbered in arabic*   B7 B32 C2 C8 C9 CT1 DT1 H4 H6 H8 HH1 (*except st* 1) O20 SA1 SP1; *sts of Epithalamion not numbered*   B11 B46 H5 HH4; *some use of shorthand*   Y7; *sts of Epithalamion numbered in roman*   A–G.

Headings: Eclogue Inducinge an Epithalamion at the Marriage of the: E: of S: B7 CT1 DT1 H4 SA1 (Earle).   *om*   B11 EU2 HH4 Y7.   Eclogue: 1613 Decemb: 26.   B32 C2 C8 C9 H6 (»P.« Eclogue) O20 SP1 A–G.   Eclogue 1613. December. 16.   B46.   *missing*   DR1.   Eclogue.   H5 HH1.   ECLOGVE. I. D.   H8.   To her ffrend   R9.

Induction: Allophanes findinge Idios in the Conntry that Chrismas, reprehends his absence from Court at that marriage: Idios giues an accompt of his purpose therein, and of his actions there | B7 CT1 DT1 H4 SA1 (an account). [*missing*] this Christmas [*missing*] this mariadge [*missing*]pose there in and [*missing*]ctio[*missing*] B11. Alloph: Allophanes finding Idios in the Country thys Christmas, reprehends his Absence from the Court, at thys Maryage of the Earle of Sommersett; Idios giues an account of his Purpose therin, And of his Actions there. | B32 H5(Alloph: *om*; frō Court; y[e] Marriage; purpose herein; and his actions here.) H8(Alloph: *om*; from Court; of the Earle of Sommersett *om*) HH1(Alloph: *om*; from Court; the mariage; a acompt; & his) HH4(Alloph: *om*; from Court; y[e] mariage; giues account). Allophanes findinge Idios in the Country in the Christmas, reprehends his absence from the Court; at the mariage of the Earle of Summersett. Idios giues an account of his purpose therein and of his absence then. B46 C9(from Court; his Actions there) H6(from Co[r]t; his Absence → ›Actions‹ there) O20(and Account; Absence there) SP1(an accompt; absence there). Allophanes findinge Idios in the Countrye in Christmas Tyme, reprehends his absence from Court, at the mariadge of The Earle of Sommersett, Idios giues an Account, of his purpose therein, and of hys Absence thence. C2 C8 A B–G(his Actions there). [*missing*]s in the cuntrie [*missing*] this [*missing*]equireth his absence [*missing*] court at this marriage. Ideos giues an [*missing*] of his purpose therein, and of his actions there DR1. *om* EU2 R9 Y7.

1 man,] ~‸ B7 DR1 HH4; ~! R9. Ice] ~, B32 C2 C8 O20 SA1 A–G; ~! H5.

2 could] cold H5 O20. to] the → »~« HH1; the HH4. Countryes] Conntry B7 CT1 DT1 H4 HH1 SA1. entice] ~, C2 C8.

3 Thee] ~, B7 B32 B46 C2 C8 CT1 DT1 H4 H5 HH1 O20 SA1 SP1 A–G. Time?] ~, HH1; ~‸ HH4.

4 warmer] warme DR1 HH4. clime] ~. B32 HH1 O20 SP1; ~, C2 C8 R9; ~: D–G.

5 *om* B46. small] smaller B–G. birds,] ~‸ H8. who] w[ch] B11 HH1. that] their HH4. dare] ~, B32 C2 C8 HH1 O20 A–G.

6 *om* B46. fleets] Fleete, B7 B32; ~, C2 CT1 DT1 H4 HH1 HH4 O20 SP1 A–G. theyr] the B7 CT1 HH4 SA1; y[t] H8. Sea] ~, B32 C2 C8 C9 CT1 DR1 DT1 H4 H5 HH1 HH4 O20 SP1 A–G. the] and SA1. Ayre.] ~‸ B7 DR1 H4 H6 HH1; ~: DT1; ~; H8 SA1; ~, HH4.

7 fields] the ~ B7. appeere] ~, B32 C2 C8 H5 HH1 O20 SP1 A–G; ~? B46; ~., H8.

8 Whilst] While B7; Whyles C2 C8; Whilest SP1. Flora her selfe] Flora'herselfe, B32; Flora's Selfe B46 SA1; Flora' her selfe H5; Flora herselfe, O20 SP1; Flora'herselfe A–C. buff Ierkin] Freeze Ierkin B7 B32 B46 C2 C8

CT1 DT1 H4 H5 HH1 HH4 O20 R9 SA1(Ierking) SP1 A–G; freeze=jerkin B11 DR1 H8; buff → ›freeze‹ Ierkin H6. weare] ~. B11 B46; ~? B32 C2 C8 DT1 H4 H5 HH1 O20 R9 SA1 SP1 A–G.

9 Whilst] Whilsts DR1; Whyst O20. doe] doth DR1. stripp] ~, HH1.

10 Leaues,] leafes, B32 C2 O20 A; ~‸ C8 DR1 H4 H8 HH4. to] (~ HH4. enough] enow B11; inowe, B32 O20; ~, C2 C8 H5 HH1. whipp] ~. C8.

11 Thy] Thee B46. madnesse] *om* B46; ~, DT1. thee,] ~: B7 B32 CT1 DT1 H4 H5 O20; ~; B11 C2 C8 DR1 H8 HH1 A; this madnes. B46; ~) HH4; ~? R9 SA1; ~,: SP1. springs] Springe B7 H4; ~, H5 HH4. by] hye B11. frost] ~, B32.

12 Haue] Having B–G. cold] ~, B7 B11 B32 B46 C2 C8 CT1 DT1 H4 H5 H8 HH1 O20 R9 SA1 SP1 A–G. murmure] Murmures C2 C8 DR1 H8 A–G. lost?] ~‸ B7 CT1 DR1 H4 HH4; ~. | B11; ~. B32 B46 DT1 H5 H8 HH1 O20 SP1; ~; C2 C8 A; ~: R9.

13 or] and DR1 H8. Fortunes] ~, C8. wouldst] woulds DR1; would HH1. lament] ~, C2 C8 HH1.

14 solemnety,] ~‸ B11 B46 C2 DR1; ~; H5 HH4; solemnities, R9. it] *om* SP1. Lent.] ~‸ B7 CT1 H4 HH4; ~. | B11; ~; C2 C8 A–C; the ~: R9; ~, SA1; ~: D–G.

15 Court] ~, B32 B46 C8 H5. the] alreadie, y[e] HH1; allready th' SA1. Spring] ~, C2 C8 O20 SP1. already aduanced] already advaunc'd B7; allread' aduanced B46; already'aduanced CT1 DT1 O20; advanced HH1 SA1. is] ~, B11 C2 C8 H5 HH1 SP1 A–G; ~; B32 O20.

16 vp,] ~; B7 B11 B32 C2 C8 CT1 HH1 O20 A–G; ~. B46 H8; ~‸ HH4. yet] ~, O20. his] kis B7 CT1 DT1 H4(M *var:* »~«); kisse,. SA1.

17 is.] ~‸ B7 CT1 DR1 DT1 H4 H8 HH4 SA1; ~: B32 H5 O20 SP1; ~, C2 A–G; ~; C8 HH1. Far] for DR1 H8. other,] ~; H8. fires] ~, B32 C8 HH1; ~. C2 A; ~; H5; ~: B–G.

18 First] ~, B32 C2 O20 SP1 A–G; (~ DR1 H8. Zeale] ~, C2. State,] ~; C2 C8 O20 SP1 A–G. Loues desires] loue desires B7 DT1 H4; Loves desires, B11 B32 C2 O20 SP1; loue=desires B46; loue desires, C8; loues desires) DR1 H8.

19 brest,] ~‸ D–G. heauens] Heau'ns B32 CT1 DT1 H5 O20. lights] ~, B32 C2 C8 H5 O20 SP1 A–G.

20 dayes,] ~‸ DR1; ~; DT1; Day, HH4. the other] and th'other B7 CT1; the other, B–G. nights.] ~‸ B7 CT1 DR1 H4 HH1; ~; B32 O20 SP1; ~: H5; ~, HH4 SA1.

21 then] *om* HH1; thow HH4. that] *om* C8. light] ~, B32 C2 DR1 DT1 H5 O20 SP1 A. (which] ‸~ B7 B32 B46 C2 C8 CT1 DT1 H4 H5 HH1 HH4 O20 SA1 SP1 A–G.

22 were)] ~‸ B7 CT1 DR1 DT1 H4 HH1 HH4 SP1; ~, B32 C8 H5 O20 SA1; ~. B46 C2; ~; A–C; ~: D–G.

23 fauour,] favours, B7 CT1 SA1; ~‸ B32 B46 C2 C9 H8 HH1 HH4 O20 SP1 A–G; ~) DR1; fauours‸ DT1 H4. is] *om* B7 CT1 DT1 H4 HH4 SA1. diffusd] diffused HH4 SP1. o're] on C8; to DR1 H8; ouer HH4 SA1. all] ~, B32 C2 H5 H8 O20 A–G.

24 which] ~, C8. fortunes] ~, B7 B32 B46 C8 CT1 DR1 H4 H5 H8 HH1 HH4 O20 SA1 SP1 B–G; Fortunes, C2 DT1 A. names] Names, B32 C8 HH4 O20 SP1 A–G; ~, B46 C2 CT1 DR1 DT1 H4 H5 H8 SA1. natures] Natures B32 C2 C8 HH4 O20 A–C; naturall DR1. fall.] ~‸ B7 C9 CT1 HH1; ~, C2 HH4 SA1; ~: DR1; ~; A–G.

25 those] these SA1. wombes] numbers B7. of] as DR1 H8. Stars] ~, B7 B11 B32 B46 C2 C8 CT1 DT1 HH1 HH4 O20 SA1 SP1 A–G; ~; H5. Brides bright] bright birds HH4. eyes] ~, B32 C2 C8 O20 SP1 A–G.

26 every] eurey B46. Glaunce] ~, B32 B46 C2 C8 O20 SP1 A–G. a] and B7. flyes] ~, B7 B11 B32 C2 C8 H5 H8 O20 SP1 A–G.

27 sowes] lowes B7 CT1 DT1(*var*: lo»th«es) H4(*var*: »^{s}«owes) SA1. Stars,] ~‸ C9 DR1 HH1; ~; H4. prevent] ~, C8.

28 power] ~, B7 B32 C2 C8 CT1 HH1 O20 SA1 SP1 A–G. the all-eyd] the all eyed B7 CT1 DR1 H4 HH1; ye all ey'd B11 B32 HH4 SA1; the all-eyed DT1; th'all-ey'd H5. firmament.] ~‸ B7 CT1 DR1 HH4; ~, SA1; ~; A–G.

29 First] ~, DT1 H5 HH1. eyes] ~, B32 C2 O20 SP1. kindle] kindled B46; kindles C2 SP1 A; kindles, C8; ~, HH1. eyes] ~, B11 C2 C8 DR1 H5 SA1 A–G; ~; B32 H8 O20 SP1; ~. B46.

30 Then] ~, H5 HH1. theyr] those SA1. beames] ~, B7 C2 C8 CT1 DT1 H5 O20 SP1. theyr] the B11. lusters] luster DR1 H8 HH1 HH4. rise] ~, B11 C2 H5 H8 SA1 A–G; ~. B32 C8 O20 SP1.

31 from] form H4. Iewells] ~, B7 B11 B32 B46 C2 C8 H5 HH1 O20 SP1. fire] ~, B11 B32 C2 C8 H5 O20 SA1 SP1 A–G; ~. B46.

32 *om* DR1. warmth] ~, B7 B32 B46 C2 CT1 DT1 H4 H5 H8 O20 SP1 A–G; light B11. light] warmth B11. desire.] ~‸ B7 B46 CT1 DT1 H4 H6 HH4; ~; C2 HH1 A; ~, SA1.

33 Courts,] ~‸ B46 DR1 DT1 H4 H8 HH4 SA1. alas,] ~‸ B46 DR1 H8; (~) HH4. Hell,] ~‸ B7 B11 CT1 DR1 DT1 H4 H8 HH1 HH4; ~. B46 C8.

34 Where, in] Wherein B7 CT1 DR1 DT1 H4 H8 SA1; Where in B11 B32 C2 C9 HH1 HH4 O20 SP1 A–G. plotts,] ~‸ B11 DR1; places, C2 C8 A; ~. H8. fire] *om* DR1. dwell] ~, B11 H4 SA1; ~. B32 B46 C2 C8 H8 O20 SP1; ~: H5 A–G.

35 stooves] ~; B11 B32 B46 C2 C8 O20 SP1; ~, DR1 H8 SA1 A–G; stowes; H5; stones → ›~‹; HH1; stones, HH4. (for] ‸~ B7 B11 B32 B46 C2 C8 CT1 DR1 DT1 H4 H5 H8 HH1 HH4 O20 SA1 SP1 A–G.

36 Continewall] ~, B11 B32 B46 C2 C8 DT1 H4 H5 HH1 HH4 O20 SP1 A–G. (but] ‸~ B7 B11 B32 B46 C2 C8 CT1 DR1 DT1 H4 H5 H8 HH1 HH4 O20 SA1 SP1 A–G. artificiall)] ~‸ B7 B11 B32 B46 C2 C8 C9 CT1 DR1 DT1 H4 H5 H8 HH1 HH4 O20 SA1 SP1 A–G. heate.)] ~‸‸ B7 CT1 DR1 DT1 HH1 HH4; ~.‸ B11 B32 B46 H4 H5 H8 O20 SP1; ~;‸ C2 C8 SA1 A–G; ~‸) C9.

37 Heere] ~, B32 H5 O20 SP1. Zeale] loue C8 HH4. Loue] zeale C8 HH4. growne] growen B32 C9 O20 SP1; growe HH1(→ »~«) SA1. one] ~, B7 B11 B32 B46 C2 CT1 DT1 H4 H5 O20 SA1 SP1 A–G; ~; C8. digest] disgest B7(→ ›~‹) DR1 H8; disgest, B32 C2 H5 A–C; ~, C8 O20 SP1 D–G.

38 make] made B7 CT1 DT1 H4. our] one B46 C2 C8 O20 SP1; a DR1 H8. Court] ~, B32 C2 C8 H4 O20 SP1. an] but DR1. East] ~. B11 B32 B46 C2 C8 H4 H5 O20 SP1 A–G; rest C9; *om* DR1; ~, DT1; ~; H8; ~: SA1.

39 thence?] ~‸ B7; ~.| B32; ~?| C2; hence? C9; ~. DR1; ~?— DT1; hence‸ HH4; ~.|? SP1. *Idios*.] ~‸ B7 B46 H5 HH1; ~: B32; *om* DR1; (Idus: HH4. No] —~ B7 CT1 DT1; ~: B32 HH1 O20; ~, B46 C8 A–G; *om* DR1; :~ H4; ~; H5. I am] *om* DR1. there:] ~‸ B7 C9 CT1 DT1 H4 H5 HH1 SA1 SP1 A–C; ~.| B32; ~. B46 C2 O20; ~, C8 H8 D–G; *om* DR1; heer‸ HH4.

40 Heauen] heau'n B7 CT1 DT1 H4 H5; ~, B32 C2 SP1 A–G; Heaun, O20.

disposd] ~, B32 C2 C8 H5 O20 SA1 SP1 A–G. every] ev'ry B32 O20. where:] ~‸ B7 C9 HH1 HH4 SP1; ~. B32 B46 O20; ~, C2 C8 CT1 DT1 H4 SA1 A; ~; H8.

41 are] in HH4. those] these H8. Courts] ~, B32 C2 C8 H4 H5 O20 SA1 SP1 A–G. animate] annimates B7 CT1 DT1 H4; ~, A–G.

42 house] ~, B7 B11 B32 B46 C2 C8 CT1 DT1 H4 H5 HH4 O20 SA1 SP1 A–G. state.] ~‸ B7 C9 CT1 DR1 DT1 H6 HH1 HH4; ~, B32 C2 C8 A; ~: H8; ~; SA1.

43 no] not → »~« DT1. thinke] ~, B32 C2 C8 H4 H5 HH1 O20 SP1 A–G. because] cause HH4. hee's] he is B32 C2 C8 DR1 HH4 O20 SP1 A–G. full] ~, B32 B46 C2 C8 C9 H4 H5 H8 HH4 O20 SP1 A–G. hee hath] h'hath B46 SA1; hee'hath DT1. all.] ~‸ B7 C9 CT1 DR1 DT1 H4 HH1 HH4; ~, B32 C2 C8 H5 O20 SP1 A B D–G; ~; H8 SA1.

44 Kings] ~, DT1 HH1. (as] ‸~ DR1 H8. theyr] they → »~« HH1. patterne] ~, B46 C9 H5 A–G. God)] ~,) C9; ~‸ DR1 H8; ~;) H4. liberall] ~. B46; ~, DT1 H4.

45 in] ~ their B11. fulnesse] ~, B7 B32 B46 C2 C8 CT1 DT1 H4 H5 O20 SA1 SP1 A–G. but] ~ in H5. Capacity] ~ | B7; ~, B32 C2 C8 H5 O20 SA1 A–G.

46 men] ~, B32 C2 CT1 O20 SP1 A. feele] foole DR1. see] ~. | B7; ~, B32 C2 H5 O20 SP1 A–G; ~; SA1.

47 blessings] blessinge B7 DR1 H8 HH4. bestow:] ~‸ B7 B11 B46 CT1 DR1 DT1 H4 HH1 HH4 SP1; ~. B32 C9 O20 A–G; ~, C2 C8 SA1; ~; H8.

48 So] ~, B32 B46 C2 HH1 O20 A–C; The DR1. reclus'd] reclused B7 CT1. often] oft DR1.

49 of] *om* C2 C8. heauens] Heau'ns B7 CT1 DT1 H5; Heauen HH4. Glory] ~, B11 B32 B46 C2 C8 H5 O20 SA1 SP1 A–G. then] than B–F. worldling] wordlinge B7 B32 DR1 H5 O20. can.] ~‸ B7 B32 CT1 DR1 DT1 H4 HH1 HH4; ~, C2 C8; ~: H8; ~; SA1.

50 As] A B11; That DR1. world:] ~‸ B7 D–F; ~, B32 B46 C2 C8 CT1 DR1 DT1 H4 H8 HH1 HH4 O20 SA1 SP1 A–C G; ~; C9 H5. hart] part DR1. man] ~; C2; ~, A–G.

52 Man] men B32. neede] needs DR1 H8. farther] further B7 C8

CT1 DR1 H4 H5 SA1. looke:] ~‸ B7 B11 B46 C9 CT1 DR1 DT1 H4 HH1 HH4; ~. B32 C2 O20 SP1; ~, C8 SA1; ~; H8 A–G.

53 Country] Cuntry B32 DR1. Courts,] ~‸ DR1 H8 HH1 HH4; ~; H5. where] ~, B7; when DR1 H8 HH4. doth,] ~‸ B7 B11 B32 B46 C2 C8 C9 CT1 DR1 DT1 H4 H5 H8 HH1 HH4 O20 SA1 SP1 B–G.

54 owne] One B32 O20 SP1 A. Soule,] ~‸ B7 CT1 DR1 H4 H8 HH1 SA1. both] ~. B11 B32 B46 C2 C8 H5 O20 SP1 B–G; ~, C9 H8 A; ~; SA1.

55 And am I] I am not B7 B32 B46 C2 C8 CT1 DR1 DT1 H4 H5 H8 HH1 HH4 O20 SA1 SP1 A; I [*missing*] B11. from] at B7. Court?] ~‸ B7 B32 DR1 HH1; ~. B46 C8 H4 H5 H8 O20 SA1 A; ~. | C2 SP1; ~— CT1 DT1; ~: HH4. *Alloph.*] ~: B7 B32 C9 CT1 DT1 H5 H6 H8 O20 SA1 SP1; Allophenes. B11 C2 C8 A–G; *om* B32; Allop: B46 HH1; Al.) DR1; Allopho: H4; | Aloph |: HH4. Dreamer] ~, B46 H5 O20 A. art.] ~‸ B7 C9 CT1 DR1 DT1 H4 H6 H8 HH1 HH4 SA1 SP1; ~, B11 A–C; ~: B32 O20; ~; C8.

56 Thinkst] Thinckest DR1. thou,] ~‸ B7 B11 B46 C2 C8 CT1 DR1 DT1 H4 H8 HH1 HH4 SA1 A D–G. fantastique,] ~‸ B11 CT1 DR1 H8 HH1 SA1 A; (Fantastique) B46; Fantastique, C2 DT1 H5 O20; ffantastique‸ H4; (~) HH4. hast] has B32. a part] Part B32; apart DR1.

57 the] he H5. East India] East Indian B7 B11 B46(east) C2 C8(Idian) CT1 DR1(east) DT1 H8 HH1 HH4 SA1 SP1(indian); East-Indyan B32 H5 O20; Indian A–G.

58 or] and SA1. tast?] ~‸ HH4.

59 warme?] ~‸ B7 HH4; ~, CT1 DT1.

60 good] ~, B32 B46 C2 C8 H4 H5 HH4 O20 SP1. seest] hast B11; feelst HH4. harme?] ~‸ B7 HH4.

61 doth] doe H4. her] his H4. inward] inner A–G.

62 well disposd] well disposed CT1 DT1; well-disposd' H5. which] what HH4. gold] ~, B32 C2 C8 H5 O20 SP1 A; ~. B46 H4; ~: B–G.

63 shall] is B11. except] vnles B46 DR1 H8. it] by B11. to] it B11. lye] ~, B32 C2 O20 SP1 A–G.

64 vpward] ~, B11 B32 B46 C2 C8 DT1 H5 O20 SA1 SP1 A–G. heauen]

heau'n B7 B11 C8 CT1 DT1 H5 O20. guild] guilds HH4. his eye.] her eye$_\wedge$ B7 CT1 SA1(eye,); his Eye; B32 C2 C8 O20 SP1 A–G; his'eye. B46; his eye$_\wedge$ DR1 HH1 HH4.

65 As] ~, A–G. things] ~, B7 CT1 DT1 H5 HH1 HH4 SA1 A–G; ~; B32 C2 H4 O20 SP1; ~: B46 C8. aboue] ~, B32 C2 C8 H8 O20 SP1 A–G; ~; H5.

66 So] ~, B7 B32 B46 CT1 DT1 H4 O20 SP1 A–G. vse] ~, B7 B32 B46 C2 C8 CT1 DT1 H4 H5 HH4 O20 SA1 SP1 A–G. tinctures] tincture H5.

67 powers.] ~, B7 C2 DR1 H4 SA1; ~; B11 B46 H8 HH1 A–G; ~: B32 C8 H5 O20 SP1; points; HH4. springs,] ~$_\wedge$ B7 B46 C8 CT1 DR1 DT1 H4 H8 HH4; ~. C; ~; D–G.

68 kings.] ~$_\wedge$ B7 B46 CT1 DT1 HH4; ~., | B11; ~, SA1; ~; B–G.

69 thy selfe,] thy selfe; B32 B46 C2 C8 HH1 O20 SP1; thy selfe$_\wedge$ SA1. mee] ~, B32 C2 C8 H5 A–G.

70 Angels,] ~$_\wedge$ B7 B11 B46 CT1 DR1 H4 H8; ~; HH4. though] (~ C8; thou H4(*var*: thou»gh«). on] the B7. employd] employed B7 CT1 SP1. they] *om* B7; the DR1. bee] ~, B11 B32 C2 H5 O20 SA1 SP1 A–G; ~) C8.

71 heauen:] ~$_\wedge$ B7; heav'n, B11 C8 A–F; heaun: B32 O20; ~; B46 DT1 H4 H8; ~, C2 DR1 HH1 SA1 G; heau'n$_\wedge$ CT1. home] ~, B32 C2 C8 H5 HH1 O20.

72 doth] ~, A–G. abrode] ~, C8 HH1 A–G. come.] ~$_\wedge$ B7 DR1 HH4; ~. | B11; ~, SA1; ~: B–G.

73 Chide] ~, C8; O hide DR1. thy selfe then] thy selfe then, B32 H5 HH1 O20 SP1 A–G; thy self, then C8; then thy selfe DR1 H8(then,). (ô] $_\wedge$~ B32 C2 C8 DR1 H5 H8 HH1 O20 SP1 A–G. foole)] ~, B32 C2 C8 H5 O20 SP1 A–G; ~$_\wedge$ DR1 H8 HH1.

74 Mightst] Might DR1 HH4; Mightest O20. more] ~, B11 B32 B46 C2 H5 O20 SP1. then] than B–G. bewray.] ~, B7 SA1; ~$_\wedge$ B11 C9 CT1 DR1 H4 H6 HH4; ~; C2 C8 A–C; ~: D–G.

75 Hast] Hadst B32. thou] | ~ | C9 H6. a] an H8. History] ~, B32 C2 C8 DT1 O20 SP1 A–G. present] represent B7 CT1 DT1 H4 SA1.

76 where] when B7 CT1 DT1 H4(*var*: whe»re«) SA1. doe] doth B7. assent] ~.? B46; ~. C8; ~? → »~$_\wedge$« H4.

77 Kings,] ~,? B46; ~; C8 SP1; ~? H8; king‸ HH4. that] ~, C2 C8 CT1 DT1 H4 A–G. the] that B11 B32 C2 C8 DR1 DT1 H4 H8 O20 SP1 A–G; *om* HH4. iust?] ~‸ B11 B46 DR1 HH1 HH4; ~. C2 C8; ~, H5; ~: H8.

78 where] when B7 CT1 DT1 H4(*var*: whe»re«) SA1. Leuity] lenity B7 CT1 DT1 H4 SA1. trust] ~? B7 B32 B46 CT1 DT1 H4 HH1 O20 SA1 SP1; ~. B11 C2 C8 A–C; ~; H5 H8; ~, D–G.

79 Where] And ~ H8. there] *om* H8. Ambition] ~, B32 C2 C8 DT1 H4 H5 HH1 O20 SP1 A–C. to obay] t'obaye B7 B46 H4 H5 HH1; to obaye, B32 C2 C8 O20 SP1; t'obay, CT1 DT1 H8 SA1 B–G; to'obey, A.

80 Men] none H5 HH4; *om* (»~«) HH1. Nothing] anny thing HH4. and] *om* HH4. may] ~., B11; ~. B46 DR1 DT1 HH1 O20 SP1; ~, C2 C8 CT1 SA1; ~; H5 H8 A–G.

81 the] y^{t} DT1 H4. plac'd,] ~‸ B7 CT1 H8 HH1 HH4; ~; SA1.

82 King] kings H5. therein] *om* (»~«) HH1. liberall] ~. B46 H4; ~, C2 C8 CT1 DT1 H8 SA1.

83 To] *om* (»~«) HH1. them] ~, B32 B46 C2 C8 H5 O20 SP1 A–G; *om* (»~«) HH1. him,] ~‸ B7 CT1 SA1; ~; C8.

84 Vertue] ~, B7 B11 B32 B46 C2 C8 CT1 DT1 H4 H5 HH1 HH4 O20 SA1 SP1 A–G. vnto] to the B7 B32 C2 C8 CT1 DT1 H4 H5 HH1 HH4 O20 SA1 SP1 A–G; to [*missing*] B11. pretend?] ~‸ B7 CT1 HH4; pre[*missing*]. | B11; ~. B32 B46 C2 C8 DT1 H4 HH1 O20 SP1 A–G; p[*missing*]d‸ DR1; ~, SA1.

85 Such:] ~, B7 CT1 DR1 DT1 H4 SA1 SP1; ~; B46 C2 C8 H8 HH1 HH4 A–G. heere] there DR1; this H8. this] here H8. more] ~; B32 O20 SP1; ~, C2 C8 HH1 A; ~. B–G.

86 An] A HH4. Louer,] ~‸ B7 B11 C8 CT1 H8 HH4 SA1. wise,] ~‸ B7 B11 B32 B46 C2 C8 CT1 DR1 DT1 H4 H5 H8 HH1 HH4 O20 SA1 SP1 A–G. then,] ~‸ DR1 HH1. before.] ~‸ B7 C9 DR1 H4 H6 H8 HH1 HH4; ~. | B11; ~; B32 O20 SP1; ~, C2 C8 SA1 A(*unc*).

87 Our] One H8. su'd] sued B7 B32 B46 C2 C8 CT1 DR1 DT1 H4 H8 HH1 HH4 O20 SP1 A–G; su[*missing*]d B11. Lyvery] ~, B11 B32 C2 C8 H5 H8 O20 SP1 A–G.

88 more] man B7 CT1 SA1. Minority] ~, B11 C2 C8 SA1 A–G; ~. B32 B46 DT1 O20 SP1; ~: H5; ~; H8.

89 now] new H8. into] within HH4. brest] ~, B11 B32 C8 O20.

90 Counsells] Councell B7 HH4 SA1; counsayles B11 B32 C2 H5 HH1 O20; Councells C8 DR1 G; Counsaile CT1 DT1 SP1; counsell H4. rest.] ~‸ B7 C9 CT1 DR1 DT1 H4 H6 HH1 HH4; ~, B11 SP1; ~; C8 SA1; ~: H8.

91 hast] has H8. lost,] ~‸ B7 B11 B46 CT1 HH1 SA1; left‸ → ›~‸‹ DR1; left H8. ô] thou B7 CT1 SA1; (~ HH1. man?] ~: B32 HH4; ~. B46; ~?| C2; ~‸ DR1; ~) HH1. *Idios*.] ~— B7 CT1 SA1; ~: B32; ~‸ B46 H5 H6 HH1 SP1; ~, C2; ~| DR1; ~.— DT1; Ieos: H4; Id: HH4. —I] ‸~ B11 B32 B46 C2 C8 DR1 DT1 H4 H5 H8 HH1 HH4 O20 SA1 SP1 A–G. Knewe] know— B7; ~. B46; ~, C2 C8 A(*unc*); know C9 DR1 SA1.

92 onely therefore] therefore only B7 B46 CT1 DT1 H4 HH4; therefore C2 SA1. withdrew.] ~‸ B7 B11 C2 C9 CT1 DR1 DT1 H4 H6 H8 HH1 HH4 SA1 A; ~, C8.

94 *second* a] *om* DR1. graue] ~. B11; ~, B32 C2 C8 H4.

95 thoughts.] ~; B7 B32 B46 C2 CT1 DR1 DT1 H8 HH4 O20 SP1 A–G; ~: B11 C8 H4 H5; ~, HH1 SA1. stay] ~, B32 C2 C8.

96 feast,] ~‸ B7 B11 CT1 H8 HH1; ~; DR1; ~:, H4. grace] Grace B7 B32 B46 C9 CT1 DT1 O20 A(*cor*)–F. say] ~, B11 C2 C8 SA1 A; ~; B32 H8 O20 SP1; ~. C9 H4 B–G; ~: H5.

97 scap't] scaped B7. heere,] ~; B32 C2 C8 O20 SP1 A–F; ~‸ G. come] ~, C8.

98 Ioye] ~, B7 B11 B32 B46 C9 CT1 DR1 DT1 H4 H5 HH4 O20 SP1; ~; C2 C8 A–G. vtterd] vttered B7 B11 CT1 DR1 H5 HH1 HH4. some.] ~‸ B7 B11 CT1 DR1 DT1 H6 HH1 HH4; ~, C2 C8 SA1 A; ~; H5.

99 Reade then] Then reade SA1.

100 inuade] ~: B32; ~, C2 C8 SA1 A–G; ~. H5; ~; H8 HH1 O20 SP1.

101 I am] I'ame B32 O20 SA1 A; I'me B46 B–G.

102 *om* DR1. Epitaph] ~, B32 C2 H5 O20 SP1 A–G; Epithath → »~« HH1. might] could HH1. fame] ~, C2 C8 HH1 A(*unc*); name H4.

103 song,] ~‸ B7 B46 C9 CT1 DT1 H4 SA1; ~: DR1. testifies] ~, B32 C8 O20 SP1.

104 day] ~, B32 C8 HH1 O20. sacrifice.] ~ | B7; ~. | C2 C9 SP1; ~‸ CT1 DT1 H4 H6 HH4; ~. | | | | DR1; ~:—. SA1.

Section Heading *Epithalamion.*] *om* B7 CT1 DT1 H4 SA1 A–G; ~: B32; Epithalamium. H5; »P.« ~‸ H6; ~‸ HH1; EPithalamium: HH4.

St Heading *the*] *om* B46. *Marriage.*] ~‸ B7 B32 B46 CT1 DT1 H6 HH1 SA1; ~: HH4; ~. | SP1.

105 repriu'd] ~, B32 H5 HH4 O20 SP1. yeare,] yeares‸ B7; ~; B32 C8 HH1 O20; ~. B46; ~: C2; ~‸ CT1. dye] ~, B32 C2 C8 HH1 O20 A–G.

106 lye] ~, B32 C2 C8 H8 HH1 O20 SA1 SP1 A–G; ~. B46 H5.

107 shouldst] ~ thou B7 CT1 SA1. within] wth H4(*var*: w$^{th»in«}$). fiue] few → »~« HH1. expire] ~, B32 C8 H5 HH1 O20 SA1 D–G.

108 thou art] art thou B11; thou SP1. rescewd] rescued B7 B32 B46 CT1 DT1 H4 H5 HH1 O20 SA1 SP1; reuiu'd HH4. by] from B–G. fire] ~, C2 C8 A–G.

109 Then] Than G. Soule] ~, B32 C9 CT1 H5 O20 SP1 A–G; ~. HH1. Sunn] ~, B32 C2 C8 H4 H5 O20 SA1 SP1 A–G.

110 doth] hath B7 CT1 SA1. Circle] Christe B7. runn.] ~‸ B7 B11 B46 CT1 DT1 HH4 SA1; ~; B32 O20 SP1; ~, C2 H4 HH1.

111 West] East B7 B11 B46 CT1 H5 HH1 HH4 SA1. or] and B7 CT1 H8 SA1. East] West B7 B11 B46 CT1 H5 HH1 HH4 SA1. thaw] ~, B32 C2 HH1 O20 A–G.

112 wide] ~, B32 C2 C8 O20 SP1. easy liquid] liquid easy B11.

113 Ships,] ~‸ C9; ~; H5 HH1.

115 hart.] ~‸ B7 B11 DT1 HH4; ~. | B32 C2; heart[*trimmed*] H8.

St Heading *of*] of the B7 CT1 DT1 H4 H8 SA1; in R9. *Persons.*] ~‸ B7 H6 HH1 HH4; ~. | B32 SP1; ~: H4; Both: R9.

116 vndiscerning] vndiscoveringe B7 CT1 SA1; undeseruing HH4. which] what HH4. which] wth B7 CT1; or B11; what HH4. eyes] ~, B11 C2 C8 HH1 A–G; Eye, B32.

117 couple] ~, O20 SP1 A–G. dost] canst B11; doest HH1 HH4. prise?] ~‸ B11 HH4 O20 SP1; ~.? B46; ~, C2 C8 A–G.

118 When] Where C2 C8 R9. eye] eyes R9. is] ~, B32 C8.

119 hers,] ~‸ B11 R9; here, B32. as] all H4. his.] ~‸ B7 B11 B46 CT1 DT1 H4 HH1; hye; B32; ~; H5; ~, R9 SA1; ~? HH4 A–G.

120 Bee tryd] Betrid B7 DT1; bee tryed B11 B32 C2 C8 O20 SP1 A–G; Betried CT1. beauty] ~, B7 B32 B46 C2 C8 CT1 DT1 H4 H5 H8 O20 SA1 A–G; ~; HH4. than] Then C2 R9 SA1.

121 Mayd] ~, B7 B32 B46 C2 C8 CT1 DT1 H4 H5 H8 HH1 O20 SA1 SP1 A–G. man.] ~‸ B7 B11 CT1 DT1 H4 H6 HH1 HH4; ~, C2 C8 R9 A–C; ~: C9 H5; ~; H8 SA1 D–G.

122 by that] that by B7; by'that R9. they] the B7. tryd] tryed B7 B11 CT1; tryed. B32; tryed, C2 C8 O20 SP1 A–G.

123 opinion,] ~; B7 C2 C8 H5 A–G; ~‸ B11 B46. then] loe then H8.

124 man;] ~, B7 B46 C2 C8 H4 HH4 O20 SP1; ~. C9 A–G; ~: H5 H8 HH1. chance] chang HH4. or] our G.

125 these] those H4. two] ~, B7 B32 B46 C2 C8 DT1 H4 H5 H8 O20 R9 SA1 A–G. Nature] nature B11 C8 C9 HH1 SP1 A–G. part] ~? B32 C2 C8 H5 H8 O20 SP1 A; ~: | R9; ~, B–G.

126 haue] hath SP1. both] *om* C2 C8 A–G. th'enflaming] the inflaming C8 HH4 B–G. eyes,] ~‸ B46; eye, C2 C8 A–G; ~, → »eie,« H4; ~, → ›eye,‹ H6. and both] *om* HH4. the] a H8; the^{r} SA1. hart.] ~‸ B7 DT1 H4 H6 HH1 HH4 SA1; ~. | C2; ~? B–F.

St Heading *the*] of ~ B7 B32 C2 C8 CT1 DT1 H4 H8 HH1 HH4 O20 SA1 SP1 A–G; of H5. *Bridegrome.*] ~‸ B7 C8 CT1 DT1 H6 HH1 SP1; ~. | C9; ~ | HH4.

127 on] of B7 B32 B46 C2 C8 CT1 DT1 H4 H5 H8 HH1 O20 SA1 SP1 A–G.

128 Singly] ~, B7 B32 B46 CT1 DT1 H4 H5 H8 HH1 HH4 O20 SA1 SP1; Single, C2 C8 A–G. (so] ‸~ B7 B11 B32 B46 C2 C8 CT1 DT1 H4 H5 H8 HH1 HH4 O20 SA1 SP1 A–G. two)] ~‸ B7 CT1 DT1 H4 H8 HH4; ~, B32 C2 C8 O20 SA1 SP1 A–C; ~. B46 D–G; ~; H5 HH1.

129 Yet] *om* B7 B32 B46 C2 C8 CT1 DT1 H4 H5 H8 HH1 HH4 O20 SA1 SP1 A–G. thee] ~, B32 C2 O20 SP1 A–G.

130 First,] ~‸ B7 B11 B32 B46 C2 C8 CT1 DT1 H4 H5 H8 HH4 O20 SA1 SP1.

cheerefull] (~ HH4. Bridegrome,] ~; B46 H5 HH1; ~,) HH4. see] ~, B32 C2 C8 O20 SP1 A–G.

131 Sunne] ~. B11; ~, B32 C8 H4 O20 SA1 SP1 A–G; ~; H8; sonne, HH1.

132 redd foming] redd-flaming H8. dost] doest C8 HH1. outrunn] ~. B32 C2 DT1 H5 O20 SP1; '~, C8; ~, H4 HH1 SA1 A–G; ~; H8.

133 How] ~, B46 HH1 HH4 A–G. (hauing] ‸~ B7 B11 B32 B46 C2 C8 CT1 DT1 H4 H5 H8 HH1 HH4 O20 SA1 SP1 A–G. Soueraignes] Soveraigne B32 DT1 H4 HH1.

134 All] ~ his HH4. businesses,] ~‸ B7 CT1 DT1 H4; busyness, HH1 SA1. reinvest] ~, C8.

135 these] the HH4. cease,)] ~‸‸ B7 CT1 DT1 H4 HH1 SA1; ~,‸ B11 B32 B46 C2 C8 H5 H8 HH4 O20 SP1 A–G.

136 shewe] show B11 B32. her] ~, B11 B32 B46 C2 C8 H8 HH1 O20 SA1 SP1 A–G. empart] ~, SA1 A–G.

137 thy enflaming] th' inflaminge B7 CT1 SA1. eyes] ~, B7 B32 C2 C8 CT1 DT1 H4 H5 H8 HH1 HH4 O20 SA1 SP1 A–G. hart.] ~‸ B7 B11 C9 CT1 H6 HH1; ~. | B32 C2 O20; ~ | DT1; ~: SP1.

St Heading *Raysing*] Rising HH1. *of*] *om* HH4. *Bride*.] ~‸ B7 B32 C2 CT1 DT1 H6 HH1 HH4 SA1; ~. | C9.

138 now] ~, B32 C2 C8 O20 SP1 A. thee] ~, B32 B46 C2 H4 H5 O20 SP1 A–G; the HH4. (fayre] ‸~ B7 B11 B32 B46 C2 C8 CT1 DT1 H4 H5 H8 HH1 O20 SA1 SP1 A–G. Bride)] ~, B7 B32 C2 C8 CT1 DT1 H4 H5 O20 SA1 SP1 A–G; ~‸ B11 B46 H8 HH1. is] were B11 B46. wrong] ~, B32 O20 SP1 A–G.

139 wert] art H8; wast SA1. long.] ~‸ B7 B11 B32 B46 CT1 DT1 H4 HH1 HH4 SP1; ~, C2 C8 H8 O20 SA1 A–G; ~; H5.

140 ly'st] lyest B7 B11 B32 B46 C2 CT1 H8 HH1 HH4 O20 SP1 A–G; laiest C8. first] the ~ B7. tis fitt] *om* B7 CT1 DT1 H4(M *var*: »'t is fit«).

141 shouldst] should G. it.] ~‸ B7 B11 B46 CT1 H4; ~, C2 HH4 SA1 A; ~; C8 H8.

142 hayre] ~, B32 C2 C8 H5 A–G

143 such] much DT1(→ »sutch«) H4; *om* HH1. Ashes] *om* C2 C8. shouldst] would'st B7 B32 B46 C2 C8 CT1 DT1 H4 H5 HH4 O20 SA1 A–G; wouldest HH1. weare] ~, B32 C2 H5 H8 O20 SA1 SP1 A–G.

144 Thou,] ~‸ B11 B46 H4 H5 B–G. which] ~, B32 C2 C8 H8 A–G. all] ~, B46 H5. that] wch B7 B32 B46 C2 C8 CT1 DT1 H4 H8 HH1 HH4 O20 SA1 SP1 A–G. come] comes B7 CT1 DT1 H4; ~, B46; comes, SA1. vpon] ~, B32 C2 C8 H5 O20 SP1 A–G.

145 Wert] Art B7 B11 B46 CT1 H5 H8 HH1 HH4 SA1 SP1 A; Are B32 C2 C8 DT1 H4 O20 A. for] ~, A. Phæbus,] ~; B7. wouldst] would SA1. bee] proue H8. Phaeton.] ~, B7 C2 SA1 A; ~‸ B46 DT1 H4 HH4; ~; C8.

146 ease] ~, B32 B46 C2 C8 H5 HH1 HH4 SP1 A–G. thine] your SP1. eyes] eye, B11; ~, C2 C8 SP1 A. th'vnusuall] th'vniuersall B46 SA1; the vnvsuall HH1 B–G. part] ~, B32.

147 ioye,] ~‸ B11 H8 HH4; ~; B46. Teare,] ~; B7 B11 B32 B46 C2 C8 CT1 DT1 H4 HH1 A–G; ~: H5 O20 SP1; ~. H8. quenchd] quenched B7; ~, B32 C2 C8 H5 SA1 A–G; ~; HH1. mayst] mayest HH1. empart] ~, C2 SP1 A–G.

148 vs] ~, B32 O20 SP1. come] ~, B32 C2 C8 H4 HH1 O20 SP1 A–G. thy enflaming] th' inflaming B11 B46 H5 SA1; thy'inflameing DT1 H4. eyes,] ~; C2 B–G. to] & → »~« HH1. him] ~, B32 C2 O20 SP1 A–G; of → »~« HH1; us HH4. hart.] ~‸ B7 B46 C9 H6 HH1 HH4 SP1; ~. | C2 DT1; heart[*trimmed*] H8.

St Heading *Apparrelling.*] ~‸ B7 CT1 DT1 H4 H6 HH1; ~. | C9; ~ | HH4.

149 discendst] descendest B32. Infirmity,] ~‸ B7 B32 B46 C8 C9 CT1 DT1 H4 H5 H8 HH4; ~: HH1.

150 water] winter B7; waters HH4. see;] ~‸ B7 B11 B32 C9 CT1 DT1 H4 HH4; ~. B46 C8 HH1 O20 SP1 A–G; ~, C2 H8; ~: H5; ~? SA1.

151 dost] doest C8 HH1 HH4. thou] ~, B32 B46 C2 C8 HH1 O20 SP1 A–G. Gold] ~, C2 C8 A–G.

152 cladst] cloud'st B7 B32 C2 C8 CT1 DT1 H4 H5 H8 HH1 O20 SA1 A–G; clothe'st B46 HH4; shouldst SP1. thy selfe;] thy selfe, B7 B46 C2 C8 C9 CT1 DT1 HH1 SA1; thy selfe‸ H4 HH4. which] that HH4. do] did SP1. behold] ~, C2 A.

153 wormes,] ~‸ H4 HH4; ~; HH1.

154 fruites] fruite H8 SP1. dust.] ~‸ B7 B11 B46 CT1 DT1 H4 HH4; ~, C2 SA1; ~; A.

155 starre] ~, B32 C2 C8 H5 H8 O20 SA1 SP1 A–G; ~; HH1.

156 pure] ~, B11 B32 B46 C2 C8 O20 SP1 A–G. theyr] the B7; our DT1(→ »~«) H4(*var:* »~«). ar] ~, B32 C8 H8 HH1 O20 SP1; ~. C2 A–G; ~; H5 SA1.

157 And] So H8. thou] those B7 CT1 DT1 H4(*var:* »~«); these SA1. stoope] ~, B32 C2 O20 SP1 A–G. to appeere] t' appeare B7 B11 B46 C2 CT1 DT1 H4 H5 H8 HH1 SA1; to'appeare O20 A–C. vs] ~, B32 B46 C2 O20 SP1 A–C. part,] ~‸ B7 B11 B46 C2 C8 C9 DT1 H4 H8 HH4 O20 SP1.

158 that] the SA1. picture,] ~‸ B7 B11 CT1 DT1 H4 H5 H8 HH1 HH4 SA1 A–G. art] ~, B32 C2 C8 H5 A–G; ~. SP1.

159 enflaming] in faming HH4. made] ~, B32 C2 HH1 O20 SP1. hart.] ~‸ B7 B11 CT1 H6 HH1 HH4; ~. | C2 C8 DT1; ~: H4; heart[*trimmed*] H8.

St Heading *Going*] | ~ HH4. *to*] ~ the C2 C8 DT1 H4 H5 HH4 O20 SP1 A–G. *Chappell.*] ~:— B7; ~‸ B32 CT1 DT1 HH1; Bed. B46; ~: | C8; ~. | C9; ~: H4; ~ | HH4.

160 Easts] Easte B7 HH1; ease HH4. forth;] ~, B7 B32 B46 C2 C8 C9 CT1 DT1 H5 H8 HH1 O20 SA1 A–G; ~‸ B11 H4 HH4 SP1. wee] ~, C2 HH1 A–G.

161 (As] ‸~ B7 B11 B32 C2 C8 CT1 DT1 H4 H5 HH1 HH4 O20 SA1 SP1 A–G. men] ~, B32 C8 O20 SP1. a] *om* HH4. Cypresse] Cip** → »~« HH1; ~ tree SP1. see] ~, C2 C8.

162 rising] ~ of the H5. sunne,] ~‸ B11 H4 HH4. two)] ~‸ B7 B11 B32 C2 C9 CT1 DT1 H4 H6 HH4; ~, C8 H5 SA1 A B; ~; HH1 O20 SP1 C–G.

163 So] ~) C9 H6; ~, H8 O20 SP1 A–G. church] ~, B11 B32 C2 C8 DT1 H5 H8 HH1 O20 SP1 A–G. of] on HH4. you.] ~‸ B11 CT1 DT1 HH4; ~, B32 C2 C8 SA1 A; ~; H8 HH1 B C; ~: D–G.

164 gon] ~, B32 C8 O20 SP1 A–G.

165 rites,] ~‸ B7 B11 CT1 H8 SA1 A–G; rights‸ HH4. thenceforth] hence forth B11 HH4 SA1. one.] ~‸ B7 B11 B46 CT1 DT1 H4 HH4; ~; B32 O20; ~, SP1.

166 Triumphant] ~, B32 C8 O20; Trium'phant HH1. Match] Church (*var:* »~«) H4. before] ~, B32 C2 C8 H5 HH1 A–G.

167 more.] ~‸ B7 B11 C9 HH4; ~, B32 C2 C8 CT1 H4 O20 SA1 SP1 A.

168 Thou] Then B7 B11 B32 C2 C8 CT1 DT1 H5 HH1 HH4 O20 SA1 SP1 G; Then, A–F. Reverend] revered G. Priest] ~, B11 B32 B46 C2 C8 CT1 DT1 H4 H5 H8 HH1 HH4 O20 SA1 SP1 A–G. who] whose B7 CT1 DT1; wch B11. art] ~, B32 C2 C8 H5 O20 SP1 A–G.

169 Doe] ~, B32 B46 C2 C8 HH1 O20 SP1 A–G. Dictates] ~, B32 B46 C2 C8 O20 SP1 A–G; Dictate HH4. to] vnto H8.

170 blessings] ~, B32 C2 C8 H5 O20 SP1 A. ar] were euer H8. seene] ~, B7 B32 B46 C2 CT1 H5 HH1 O20 SA1 SP1 A–G. thought] ~, B32 C2 C8 H5 HH1 HH4 O20 SP1 A–G. heart.] ~‸ B7 B46 CT1 H4 H6 HH4; ~; | C2; ~ | DT1.

St Heading *The*] *om* SP1. *Benediction*.] ~‸ B7 C2 CT1 H4 H6 HH1 SA1; ~. | C9.

171 Swanns,] ~; B32 HH1. enter-bring] inter-bringe B7 B32 B46 C8 CT1 DT1 H4 H5 HH1 O20 R9 SA1 SP1 A; interbringe, C2 B–G.

172 Dayly] ~, B–F. new] newly SA1. sing.] ~‸ B7 B46 C9 CT1 DT1 H4; singes. B32; ~, C2 C8 HH1 R9 SA1 A; ~: B–G.

173 Liue] ~, B32 B46 H5 O20 SP1 A–G. fayle] ~, B32 C2 C8 H5 O20 R9 SA1 SP1 A–G.

174 till] all HH1. so] to R9. stale] ~, B32 C2 C8 H5 A–G; ~. SP1.

175 trye] ~, B32 C2 C8 HH1 O20 SP1 A–G.

176 It] I B7 CT1 DT1 H4(*var:* »~«) SA1. Ambition] ~, A–G. dye.] ~‸ B7 B11 B46 C9 CT1 DT1 H4 H6 HH1; ~, C2 SA1; ~; A–G.

177 heyres,] ~., B11; ~; B32 H5 O20 SP1. heere] ~, B32 H5 A–G; they B46; hence, C8. to] the B7; *om* CT1 DT1 H4(*var:* »~«) SA1; from HH1. worlds] world SA1. end] ~, B7 CT1 DT1 H5 SA1 A–G. liue] ~, B32 C2 O20 SP1.

178 Heyres,] ~‸ B7 B11 B32 C2 CT1 DT1 H4 H5 HH1 O20 SA1 SP1 A–G. for] from B7 B11 CT1 DT1 H4 H5 HH1 SA1 A–G; ~ → ›from‹ H6. this] ~, B32; the B46. King,] ~‸ B7 B11 B46 C8 CT1 DT1 H4 H5 SA1; Ring, C9.

thankes,] ~‸ B11. yours,] yo^{w}‸ B7 C2 C8 CT1 DT1 H4 SA1; you, B32 O20 SP1 A–G; ~‸ B46 C9 HH1; yo^{rs}, → ›yo^{w},‹ H6. giue.] ~‸ B7 B11 B46 CT1 H4 HH1; ~, C2 A; ~; SA1.

179 grace] Grace B32 B46 C2 C8 CT1 DT1 O20. all,] ~‸ B11 C9 SA1; ~; B46. Art.] ~‸ B7 B11 B46 C9 CT1 H5 H6; ~, C2 C8 DT1 HH1 A–G; ~; SA1.

180 Age] ~, B7 B32 C2 C8 CT1 H4 O20 SP1 A–F; ~; DT1. or] nor B7 B11 CT1 SA1. ouerthwart] ~, B32 C8 O20 SP1; ~; HH1.

181 West] ~, C2 C8 HH1 R9 A–G. North] ~, B32 C2 C8 H5 HH1 O20 A–G. hart.] ~‸ B7 B11 CT1 H6 HH1 C; ~.| C2 C9 DT1; ~: H4 R9.

St Heading *Feasts*] ffeast H5; A feast: R9. *and*] *om* R9. *Revells*.] ~‸ B7 CT1 DT1 H6 HH1 Y7; ~.| B32 C8 C9; ~: B46 H4; *om* R9.

182 overblest,] ~: B7 B32 CT1 DT1 H4 H5 O20 SP1; ~. C2 C8 Y7 A–G. plenty] ~, B32 O20 SP1.

183 Iniures;] Iniuries, B7; ~, B11 C2 C8 C9 CT1 DT1 H4 SA1 SP1; inures; H5; Invites, Y7. causes] causeth Y7 A–G. stay.] ~, B7 B32 C2 C8 CT1 DT1 O20 SA1 SP1; ~‸ B11 B46 H4 Y7; ~; HH1 A–G.

184 grone,] growe‸ B11 H4(M *var:* »~‸«); grow, CT1 DT1 SA1; ~‸ R9. as] a B32. though] if B11 R9. this] ye C2 C8.

185 Would,] ~‸ B7 B11 B46 C2 C8 CT1 DT1 H4 HH1 O20 R9 SA1 SP1 Y7. floud,] ~‸ B7 B11 B46 CT1 DT1 H4 R9 SA1 Y7. fowle] soules Y7. beast] ~. B32 C8 C9 H5 HH1 O20 SP1 A–G; ~, C2 SA1.

186 new] ~, B7 B32 CT1 SA1.

187 true] ~. B32 C9 H5 HH1 O20 Y7; ~, C2 C8 SA1 SP1; ~; A–G.

188 every] ev'ry B32 O20. revells] Revell B7 B32 B46 C2 C8 CT1 DT1 H4 H5 HH1 O20 R9 SA1 SP1 Y7 A–G. goes] ~; B32; ~, C2 SA1 B–G; ~. C8 A; ~: O20 SP1.

189 the] ~' C2. Ayre] ~, B7 B32 B46 C2 C8 CT1 DT1 H4 H5 HH1 O20 SA1 SP1 A–G. not] ~, B46; no C8. where] when B7 CT1 DT1 H4 SA1; ~, C8. rose.] ~‸ B7 B46 C8 CT1 DT1 H4 H5 H6 R9 Y7; ~; B32 O20 SP1; ~, C2 SA1.

190 since] ~, B7 B32 B46 C2 C8 CT1 DT1 HH1 O20 SP1 A–G. to bedd] *om* SA1. part] ~, C2 C8 O20 SA1 SP1 A–G.

191 Masques] Maske C2 C8. Banquets] re[*missing*] B11. not] *om* C8.

192 those] these B7 B32 B46 C2 C8 CT1 DT1 H4 H5 HH1 O20 R9 SA1 SP1 A–G. eyes,] ~; C8; ~‸ Y7; ~. G. Center] centry Y7. this] thie Y7. hart.] ~‸ B7 CT1 H6 HH1 Y7; ~. | B32 C2 C9 DT1; ~: H4 R9.

St Heading *The*] *om* EU2. *Bedd.*] ~‸ B7 B11 C8 CT1 H6 HH1 SA1 Y7; ~. | B32 C9 DT1; ~: H4.

193 means't] meanest EU2; meantst H4. keepe] ~? B7 B32 C2 C8 CT1 DT1 H5 O20 SA1 SP1 A–G.

194 vp] ~, B32 B46 C2 H5 O20 SP1 A–G. wouldst] would C2 EU2 G. sleepe?] ~‸ B7 B11 CT1 DT1 EU2 H4 Y7; ~, HH1.

195 mayst] mayest EU2 HH1. not,] ~‸ B7 B46 CT1 DT1 H4 H5 HH1 SA1. th'art] thou art B7 B32 C2 C8 CT1 EU2 H4 HH1 O20 SP1 Y7 A–G; thou'art DT1. layd,] ~‸ B7 B11 B46 C8 CT1 DT1 H4 H5 HH1 SA1 Y7; Layed downe EU2. doe] so B11. so.] ~‸ B7 B46 C9 DT1 EU2 H4 SA1 Y7; doe‸ B11; ~, C8 CT1 HH1.

196 him] ~, B32 B46 C2 C8 EU2 O20 SP1. new] better Y7. growe] ~; B32 C9; ~, C2 C8 H5 HH1 O20 SA1 SP1 A–G.

197 you] *om* Y7. entertayne] ~, B32 C9 O20 SP1.

198 agayne.] ~‸ B7 B11 B46 CT1 DT1 EU2 H4 SA1 Y7; ~; B32 HH1 O20 SP1.

199 that if] if y^{t} B11. Sunn] ~, B7 B11 B32 CT1 H4.

200 not] *om* Y7. sett] *om* EU2. too] ~ | B7; ~. B32 B46 C2 C8 C9 H4 H5 O20 SP1 A–G; ~; HH1; ~, SA1.

201 mayst] ~, B32 C2 C8 H5 O20 SP1 A–G; mayest, EU2 HH1. to Bedd,] faire Bride‸ B7 B11 B46 CT1 DT1 EU2 H4 HH1 SA1 Y7 G; fayre Bride, B32 C2 C8 H5 O20 SP1 A–F. fayre Bride] to bed B7 B11 B32 B46 C2 C8 CT1 DT1 EU2 H4 H5 HH1 O20 SA1 SP1 Y7 A–G. depart] ~, C2 H5 O20 A–G.

202 Th'art] Thou art B7 B11 B32 B46 C2 C8 CT1 DT1 EU2 H4 H5 HH1 O20 SA1 SP1 Y7 A–G. not] *om* Y7. gon] ~, B7 B32 B46 C2 C8 CT1 DT1 EU2 H4 H5 HH1 O20 SA1 SP1 Y7 A–G. gon,] ~‸ EU2 H4 Y7 D–G. art] ~, B32 C2 H5 A–G.

203 leau'st] leauest EU2 Y7. eyes] ~, B7 B32 B46 C2 C8 C9 CT1 DT1 H4 H5 HH1 O20 SA1 SP1 A–G. in him] *om* Y7. hart.] ~‸ B7 B11 B32 CT1 EU2 H4 H6 HH1; ~.| C2 C9 DT1.

St Heading *Comming*.] ~‸ B7 B11 B46 CT1 DT1 H4 H6 HH1 Y7; ~.| C8.

204 As] And (M *var*: »~«) H4. fall] falls SA1. apace] a pace B46 HH1 SA1; a Pace, C2; ~, O20 SP1 A–G.

205 gelly] peece of jelly B11. place] ~, B32 C2 C8 SA1 A–G; ~: H5; ~. HH1.

206 So] Lo HH1; she SA1. doth] *om* Y7. hast] bost → »~« HH1; hasts Y7. much] ~; B32; ~, C2 C8 HH1 O20 SP1 A–G.

207 told] ~, C2 C8. this] his HH1. fall'ne] ~, B7 B11 B32 B46 C2 C8 CT1 DT1 H4 H5 HH1 O20 SA1 A–G; fallen, SP1; fallen Y7. such.] ~‸ B7 B11 CT1 DT1 H4 HH1 SP1 Y7; ~, C2 C8 SA1 A; ~: H5.

208 strange] ~, C2 A–G.

209 fashion] ~, B32 B46 C2 C8 C9 DT1 H4 HH1 O20 SA1 SP1 A–G. or] as B11. apparrells] ~ → »apparrell« HH1. change] ~, B32 C2 C8 H5 O20 SP1 A; ~; HH1; ~: B–G.

210 Soules,] ~‸ B7 B32 C2 CT1 DT1 H4 O20 SA1 SP1. acquaynted] ~, B32 C2 C8 O20 SP1. they] there B7 CT1 DT1 H4 SA1. beene,] ~‸ B7 B11 B32 B46 CT1 DT1 H4 SA1.

211 These] those Y7. Clothes,] ~‸ B7 CT1 DT1 H4 SA1 SP1 Y7 B C G; cloths‸ D–F. the] their B7 B32 B46 C2 C8 CT1 DT1 H4 H5 HH1 O20 SA1 SP1 Y7 A–G. bodyes] ~, B7 B32 C2 C8 H5 O20 A. seene.] ~‸ B7 B11 B32 B46 CT1 DT1 H4 Y7; ~, SA1.

212 shee] this → »~« HH1. modestly] modestie → »~« HH1. start] ~, B32 C2 C8 H5 HH1 O20 A–G.

213 forthwith] forew[th] B32 C2 O20 SP1. part] ~. B32; ~, C2 C8 O20 SP1 A–G.

214 Freely] As ~, B7 CT1 H5 O20 SA1 SP1 A–G; As ~ B32 B46 C2 C8 DT1 H4 HH1 Y7. each] ~, B7; *om* H5. to each] to each, B7 CT1 SA1; t'each H5. before] *om* B7 CT1 HH1(»~«) SA1; ~, B32 B46 C2 C8 DT1 H4 O20 A–G. eye] hand D–G. hart.] ~, B7; ~‸ B11 CT1 H4 H6 HH1 Y7; ~.| C2.

St Heading *Goodnight.*] ~‸ B7 CT1 DT1 H6 HH1 O20 SA1; ~: B46; ~.| C8 SP1.

215 Now] ~, B32 DT1 O20 SP1 A–G. Tombe] ~, B32 B46 C2 C8 DT1 H4 O20 SP1 A–G. one] a H5. burnt cleere] did burne B7 CT1 SA1(→ ›burnt cleare‹); burn't cleare, B32 C2 C8 O20 SP1 A–F; burn clear, G.

216 yeere] ~| B7; ~, B32 C2 C8 H5 O20 SP1 A–G.

217 loue] loues SA1. enshryne,] ~‸ B7 B11 B46 C9 CT1 DT1 H4 H5 HH1 SA1.

218 warmth,] ~', HH1. light,] ~‸ B7 C2 C8 CT1 H4 HH1 SA1. lasting] ~, B32 C2 C8 H4 HH1 O20 SP1 A–G. diuine.] ~‸ B7 B11 B46 CT1 DT1; ~.| B32; ~, C2 SA1; ~; A.

219 aspire] ~, B32 C2 C8 H5 HH1 O20 SP1 A–G.

220 like] ~ to B46. it selfe,] it selfe‸ B11 SA1; it self; HH1 O20. fyre] ~, B32 C2 C8 H5 O20 SP1 A–G; ~; HH1.

221 ashes,] ~‸ B11 C8 H4; ~: H5. doe] ~; B32 O20 SP1; ~, C2 H5 A–G.

222 them] these B7 CT1 DT1 H4 SA1 A–G. fewell] ~, B7 B32 C2 C8 CT1 DT1 H5 HH1 O20 SP1 A; ~; B–G. too.] ~‸ B7 B11 CT1 DT1 H4 H5 H6; ~, C2 C8 SA1.

223 bonfire,] Bonefire, B7 B46 CT1 DT1; bonefire‸ B11 C2 H5; ~‸ B32 C8 HH1 O20 SP1; banefire‸ SA1. then,] ~‸ B7 B46 CT1 DT1 H4; ~; B32; that‸ SA1. where] who B7; were B46; when CT1 DT1 H4 H5 HH1 SA1.

224 Made] Make B7 B11 B32 C2 C8 CT1 DT1 H4 H5 HH1 O20 SA1 SP1 A–G.

225 of] in H5 HH1. 4] theire H5; your HH1. of] *om* CT1; in H5 HH1. 2] theire H5; your HH1. harts.] ~‸ B7 B11 CT1 H6 HH1; ~.| C2 C8 O20 SP1; ~: H4.

226 *Idios.*] ~‸ B7 B11 B32 B46 C8 H6 SP1; ~.| DT1; ~: H4. Song,] ~‸ B11; ~; B32 O20.

227 too.] ~|. B7; ~.| C2; ~‸ CT1 H6 SA1; ~: H4.

228 *Alloph.*] ~‸ B7; Allophanes. B11 C2 C8 A–G; ~: B32 C9 CT1 DT1 H4 O20 SA1 SP1; Allop: B46. Sir,] ~‸ B7 B11 C8 CT1 DT1 H4 O20 SA1 SP1

A; ~. B C. paper] ~, B32 O20 SP1. got] ~, B32 C2 O20 SA1 SP1 A–G; ~. C8.

229 Incense] ~, B32 B46 C8 O20 SP1 A. not] ~, B32 O20 SP1; ~. C8.

230 onely] ~, B46 C8. presents] ~, B32. all.] ~‸ B7 B11 B46 CT1 DT1 H4 SA1; ~, C2 C8 A; ~; B–G.

231 Nuptiall] Festivall B7 C2 C8 CT1 DT1 H4 O20 SA1 SP1 A–G; festivall, B32; ~, B46.

232 the Ioye thereof] thereof the joy SP1. so] ~. B32 O20 SP1 A–G; ~, C2 C8 C9.

233 Priest;] ~: B7 B46 CT1 DT1 SA1 A–G; ~, C8 H4 SP1. goe] ~, B32 C2 C8 A; ~; B.

234 Court,] ~‸ B11 C9. lay it] lay't B7 CT1 B–G; lay'it DT1 H4 A; light SA1. on] vppon B7 B32 C2 C8 CT1 DT1 O20 SA1 SP1 A–G; ~ → ›vp‹on H4.

235 Altars] ~, B32 B46 C2 C8 DT1 H4 O20 SP1 A–G. deuotion.] ~‸ B7; ~. | B32 C2 C8 C9 SP1; ~: H4.

Subscriptions: Finis / AP B46. ffinis | DT1 H4(~‸) H6. finis. I. D. SA1. *om* B7 B11 B32 C2 C8 C9 CT1 DR1 EU2 H5 H8 HH1 HH4 O20 SP1 Y7 A–G.

Verbal Variants in Selected Modern Editions

Editions collated: H I J K M N O P Q S T Z AA BB DD.

Format:

Indentations: *ll. 1–104, 226–35 no ind, ll. 2, 3, and 5 of each st of Epithalamion ind equally* H K P; *no ind* I J; *ll. 1–104, 226–35 no ind, ll. 3 and 5 of each st of Epithalamion ind equally* M–O; *irregular ind* Q S DD; *ll. 1–104, 226–35 no ind, ll. 2 and 3 of each st of Epithalamion short ind, l. 5 long ind, l. 11 extended into left M* T BB; *ll. 1–104, 226–35 alternate lines ind, ll. 2, 3, and 5 of each st of Epithalamion ind equally* Z; *ll. 1–104, 226–35 alternate lines ind, ll. 3 and 5 of each st of Epithalamion ind equally* AA.

Miscellaneous: *sts of Epithalamion numbered in roman* H–K M–Q S Z BB DD; *sts of Epithalamion numbered in arabic* T; *sts of Epithalamion not numbered* AA.

Headings: E C L O G U E, *December*. 26, 1613. H–K M–O. ECLOGUE. 1613, DECEMBER 26. P Q S Z AA DD. EPITHALAMION FOR THE EARL OF SOMERSET DECEMBER 26, 1613 ECLOGUE T. Epithalamion at the Marriage of the Earl of Somerset *Ecclogue* 1613. December 26. BB.

Induction: Allophanes *finding* Idios *in the Country in* Christmas *time, reprehends his absence from Court, at the marriage of the Earl of* Somerset; Idios *gives an account of his purpose therein, and of his actions there.* H–K M N(that Christmas time; that Marriage) O(his absence thence) P Q(his absence thence) S(his absence thence) T(Country this Christmas, reprehends) Z(his absence thence) AA(his absence thence) BB(his absence thence) DD(his absence thence).

5 small] smaller H–K M N.

8 buff] Frize H–K M–Q S T Z–BB DD.

12 Haue] Having J K. murmure] murmurs H–K M–O.

34 plotts] places O P.

37 digest] disgest N O T.

52 farther] further M.

54 owne] one O Q S T Z–BB DD.

55 And am I] I am not O Q S T Z–BB DD.

57 East India] Indian H–K M–P; East-Indian Q S T Z–BB DD.

61 inward] inner H–K M–P.

77 *second* the] that H I K M–Q S T Z–BB DD; *om* J.

80 Men] none N. Nothing] anything N. and] *om* N.

84 vnto] to the H–K M–Q S T Z–BB DD.

Section Heading *Epithalamion.*] *om* H–K M–P.

108 by] from H–K M N.

124 or] on K.

126 *second* both] om H–K M–P. eyes] eye H–K M–O.

St Heading *the*] of the H–K M–Q S T Z–BB DD.

127 on] of H–K M–Q S T Z–BB DD.

128 Singly] Single H–K M–P.

129 Yet] *om* H–K M–P DD.

141 shouldst] should J M N.

143 shouldst] would'st H–K M–Q S T Z–BB DD.

144 which] who H–K M N. that] which H–K M–Q S T Z–BB DD.

145 Wert] Art O Q S T Z–BB DD.

150 water] Winter N.

152 cladst] cloud'st H–K M–Q S T Z–BB DD.

St Heading *to*] to the H–K M–Q S T Z–BB DD.

160 Easts] East H–K M.

168 Thou] Then H–K M–Q S T Z–BB DD.

171 enter-bring] interbring H–K M–Q S T Z–BB DD.

178 for] from H–K M–Q S T Z–BB DD. yours] you H–K M–Q S Z BB DD.

188 revells] revel H–K M–Q S T Z–BB DD.

192 A] As DD. Sun-set] *om* DD. those] these H–K M–Q S T Z–BB DD.

201 to Bedd, fayre Bride] fair bride, to bed H–K M–Q S T Z–BB DD.

211 the] their H–K M–Q S T Z–BB DD.

214 Freely] As freely H–K M–Q S T Z–BB DD. eye] hand H–K M N.

222 them] these H–K M–Q S T Z AA DD.

224 Made] Make H–K M–O S T Z–BB DD.

231 Nuptiall] Festival H–K M–Q S T Z–BB DD.

234 on] upon H–K M–Q S T Z–BB DD.

Subscriptions: *none.*

Schema of Textual Relationships

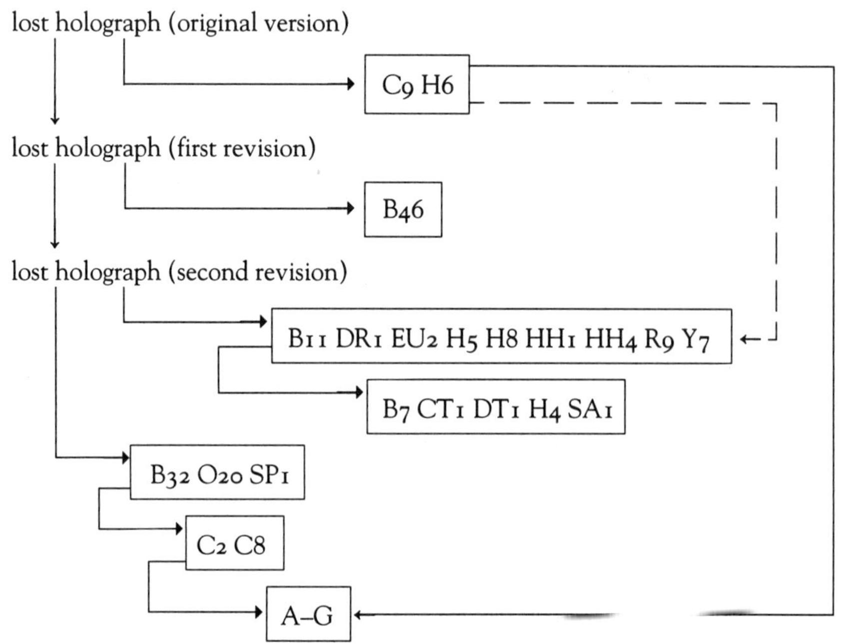

C9 H6

8 Whilst fflora her selfe doth a **buff** Ierkin weare
16 The Sunne stayes longer vp, And yet not **his**
34 **Where, in** darke **plotts**, fire without light doth dwell
55 **And am I** then from Court?
57 In the **East India** fleete, because thou hast
76 A Court, **where** all Affections doe assent
77 Vnto the Kings, and that **the** Kings are iust?
78 And **where** it is no **Leuity** to trust
84 To Vertue **vnto** wch. they all pretend?
92 All this, and **onely therefore** I withdrew
St heading 3 Raysing **the** Bridegrome
129 **Yet let** mee heere contemplate thee
145 **Wert** ment for Phæbus, wouldst bee Phaeton.
152 Thou **cladst** thy selfe; since wee wch. do behold
157 And though **thou** stoope to appeere to vs in part,
168 **Thou** Reverend Priest **who** Gods Recorder art
178 Heyres, **for** this King, to take thankes, **yours**, to giue.
201 Therefore thou mayst **to Bedd, fayre Bride**, depart
214 **ffreely** as each to each before gaue eyther eye or hart
222 ffor none of **them** is fewell but fyre too
231 Whatever celebrates this **Nuptiall**

B46

8 Whilst Flora's Selfe doth a **freese** ierkin weare.
16 The Sun stayes longer vp. And yet not **his**
34 **Where, in** darke **plots**, fire without light doth dwell.
55 **I am not** then from Court.
57 In the **east Indian** Fleete, because thou hast
76 A Court, **where** all Affections doe assent.?
77 Vnto the Kings,? and that **the** Kings are Iuste
78 And **where** it is no **leuity** to trust?
84 To virtue, **vnto** which they all pretend.
92 All this, and **therefore onlie** I withdrewe.
St heading Raisinge **the** Bridegroome.
129 **Let** me here contemplate thee
145 **Art** meant for Phæbus, wouldst be Phaeton
152 Thou **clothe'st** thy selfe, since we which do behould
157 And though **thou** stoope t'appeare to us, inpart
168 **Thou** reuerend Preest, **who** Gods Recorder art
178 Heyres, **for** the Kinge to take thanckes, **yours** to giue
201 Therefore thou maist **Faire Bride to bed** depart

214 **As freely** as each to each before, gaue either eye, or Hart.
222 For none of **them** is Fuell but fire too.
231 What euer celebrates this **Nuptiall,**

B11 DR1 EU2 H5 H8 HH1 HH4 R9 Y7

8 Whilst Flora' her selfe doth a **freeze** Ierkin weare?
16 the Sunne stayes longer vp, and yet not **his**
34 **where, in** darke **plotts**, fire without light doth dwell: (Wherein DR1; fire *om* DR1)
55 **I am not** then from Court.
57 in the **East-Indian** fleete, because thou hast (in he H5)
76 a Court, **where** all affections doe assent
77 Vnto the Kings? & that **that** Kings are iust: (that the Kings H5; and that kings HH4)
78 and **where** it is no **leuity** to trust; (not levitie HH1)
84 to Vertue, **to the** wch they all pretend? (vnto which H8)
92 All this, and **only therefore** I withdrewe. (therfore only HH4)
St heading 3. *Raisinge* ***of the*** *Bridegroome*. (the *om* H5)
129 **let** me heere contemplate thee (yet lett B11)
145 **art** meant for phæbus, wouldst be Phaeton. (proue Phaeton H8)
152 thou **cloud'st** thy selfe; since we wch doe behold (cloth'st HH4)
157 and though **thou** stoope t'appeare to vs in part, (So though H8)
168 **Then** Reuerend Preist, **who** Gods Recorder art, (Thou H8; wch Gods B11)
178 Heires **from** this kinge to take thankes, **yours,** to giue.
201 therefore thou mayst, **faire Bride, to bed** depart,
214 **as** freely, as each t'each before gaue eyther eye, or Hart. (before *om* HH1)
222 for none of **them** is Fewell, but fire too
231 *Line om or missing*

B7 CT1 DT1 H4 SA1

8 Whil'st fflora herself doth a **freeze** Ierckin weare? (While B7; fflora's selfe SA1)
16 The Sun stayes longer vpp, and yet not **kisse**
34 **Wherein** darck **Plotts,** fire w^{th}out light doth dwell
55 **I am not** then from Court—
57 In the **East Indian** ffleet, because thou hast
76 A Court, **when** all Affections doe assent (doth assent B7)
77 Vnto the Kings, & that, **that** Kings are iust? (that the B7 CT1 SA1)
78 And **when** it is noe **lenity** to truste?
84 to virtue, **to the** wch they all pretend.
92 All this, and **therefore only** I withdrewe (only *om* SA1)

St heading 3. *Raiseing* ***of the*** *Bridegroome*
129 **Let** mee here contemplate thee
145 **Are** meant for Phœbus, would'st bee Phaëton (Art B7 CT1 SA1; would SA1)
152 Thou **clowd'st** thy self, since wee wch doe behold
157 And though **those** stoop t'appeare to vs in part (these SA1)
168 **Then** Reuerend Priest, **whose** Gods Recorder art (who H4 SA1)
178 Heires **from** this King to take thankes, **you** to giue.
201 Therefore thou maist **faire Bride to Bed** depart
214 **As** freely as each to each before, gaue either eye, or heart. (before *om* B7 CT1 SA1)
222 ffor none of **these** is fuell, but fire too
231 what euer Celebrates this **ffestiuall**

B32 O20 SP1

8 Whilst Flora'herselfe, doth a **freeze** ierkin weare?
16 The sunne stayes longer vp; And yett not **his**
34 Where in darke **Plotts**, fire wth out light doth dwell.
55 **I ame not** then from Court
57 In the **East-Indyan** fleete, because thou hast
76 A Court, **where** all affections, doe assent
77 Vnto the Kinges, and that **that** Kinges are iust?
78 And **wheare** it is no **levitye** to trust?
84 To vertue, **to the** wch they all pretend.
92 All this, and **only therfore** I wth drewe.
St heading 3. Raysing **of the** Bridegroome. (3. *om* B32)
129 **Lett** mee here contemplate Thee,
145 **Are** ment for Phebus, would'st bee Phaeton. (Art SP1)
152 Thou **clowdst** thy selfe; Since wee wch doe beholde (Thou shouldst SP1; did behold SP1)
157 And though **thou** stoope, to appeare to vs, in Part,
168 **Then** Reverend Priest, **who** Gods Recorder art,
178 Heires **for** this kinge, to take thanks, **yo^{w}**, to give.
201 Therefore thou mayst, **fayre Bride, to bed** depart
214 **As freely**, as Each to Each before, gaue eyther Eye or Hart.
222 For none of **them** is Fuell, but Fire too.
231 Whatever celebrates thys **festivall**,

C2 C8

8 Whyles Flora herselfe doth a **Freeze** Ierkin weare?
16 The Sunne stayes longer Vp; & yett not **hys**

34 Where in darke **places**, fyre wthout light doth dwell.
55 **I am not** then from Court. |
57 In the **East Indian** Fleete, because Thou hast,
76 A Court, **where** all Affections, doe assent
77 Vnto the Kings, and that, **that** Kings are Iust.
78 And **where** yt ys noe **levitye** to Trust.
84 To Vertue, to the wch they all pretend.
92 All this, and **onlie therfore** I withdrewe, (onlie *om* C2)
St heading 3. Rayseinge **of y^{e}** Bridegroome.
129 **Let** me here Contemplate Thee,
145 **Are** ment for Phœbus, wouldst be Phaeton,
152 Thou **Cloudst** thy selfe, since wee wch doe behold,
157 And though **Thou** stoope, t'appeare to vs, in part
168 **Then** Reverend Priest, **Who** God's recorder art,
178 Heyres **for** thys Kinge, to take Thanks, **Yo^{w}** to giue,
201 There fore Thou mayst, **Fayre Bryde, to bed** depart,
214 **As freely** as each to each before, gaue eyther eye or Hart. |
222 For none of **them** ys Fuell, but fyre too,
231 What ever Celebrates thys **Festivall**

A–G

8 Whil'st Flora'herselfe doth a **freeze** jerkin weare?
16 The Sunne stayes longer up; and yet not **his**
34 Where in darke **places**, fire without light doth dwell: (plots D–G)
55 **I am not** then from Court. (And am I B–G)
57 In the **Indian** fleet, because thou hast
76 A Court, **where** all affections do assent
77 Unto the Kings, and that, **that** Kings are just?
78 And **where** it is no **levity** to trust.
84 To vertue, **to the** which they all pretend.
92 All this, and **onely therefore** I withdrew
St heading III. *Raysing* ***of the*** *Bridegroome.*
129 **Let** me here contemplate thee,
145 **Are** meant for, Phœbus, would'st be Phaëton, (Wert B–G)
152 Thou **cloudst** thy selfe; since wee which doe behold,
157 And though **thou** stoope, to'appeare to us, in part,
168 **Then**, reverend Priest, **who** Gods Recorder art,
178 Heires **from** this King, to take thankes, **you**, to give,
201 Therefore thou maist, **faire Bride, to bed** depart,
214 **As freely**, as each to each before, gave either eye or heart. (hand or D–G)
222 For none of **these** is fuell, but fire too.
231 What ever celebrates this **Festivall**

Analyses of Early Printed Copies

Poems, by J.D., 4to, 1633 (siglum A)

Copies collated: *CtY*, *DFo*, *L* (G.11415), M, *MH*, *MiU*.
Relevant section: sigs. R2–S4; pp. 123–35.
Press variants:

Sheet R, inner forme

	Uncorrected (*MH*):	Corrected (*CtY*, *DFo*, *L*, M, *MiU*):
R2r (p. 123):		
Heading	ECCLOGUE	ECCLOGVE
R3v (p. 126):		
l. 86	before,	before.
l. 91	knew,	knew‸
l. 96	grace	Grace
R4r (p. 127):		
l. 101	buried‸	buried,
l. 102	fame,	fame‸

Miscatching:

	Catchword:		Initial word:	Affects:
S1v	Then	S2	Then,	l. 168

§

Poems, by J.D., 8vo, 1635 (siglum B)

Copies collated: *CtY*, *MH*, *MiU*.
Relevant section: sigs. H4v–I2; pp. 108–19.
Press variants: *none*.
Miscatching:

	Catchword:		Initial word:	Affects:
H7	*Raising*.	H7v	*Raising*	heading of st 4

§

Poems, by J.D., 8vo, 1639 (siglum C)

Copies collated: *CtY*, *MH*, *MiU*.
Relevant section: sigs. H2v–H8, pp. 108–19.
Press variants: *none*.
Miscatchings: *none*.

Note: In the section containing *Eclog*, this edition is a page-for-page resetting of B.

§

Poems, by J.D., 8vo, 1649, 1650, 1654 (sigla D, E, F)

Copies collated: 1649: *CtY*, *MH*. 1650: *CtY*, *MH*. 1654: *CSmH*, *CtY*.
Relevant section: sigs. H4v–I1v; pp. 104–14.
Press variants: *see note 2 below.*
Miscatchings: *none.*

Notes: 1) Examination of multiple copies on the Lindstrand Comparator shows that the sections of 1649, 1650 and 1654 containing *Eclog* are printed from a single typesetting, 1650 and 1654 being reissues of the sheets of 1649.

2) In *Eclog* 130, the comma after "Bridegroome" does not print in the *CtY* copy of 1649.

§

Poems, &c. by John Donne, 8vo, 1669 (siglum G)

Copies collated: *CtY*, *L*, *TxLT*.
Relevant section: sigs. H5–I1v; pp. 105–14.
Press variants: *none.*
Miscatchings: *none.*

Epitaphs and Inscriptions

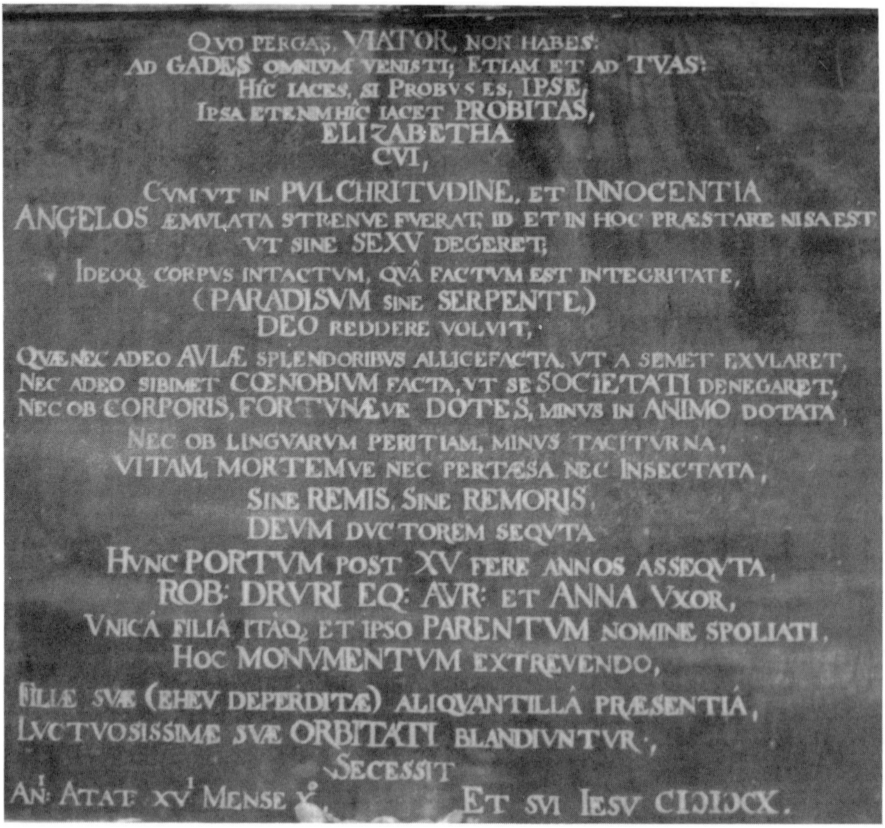

QVO PERGAS, VIATOR, NON HABES:
AD GADES OMNIVM VENISTI; ETIAM ET AD TVAS:
HIC IACES, SI PROBVS ES, IPSE,
IPSA ETENIM HIC IACET PROBITAS,
ELIZABETHA
CVI,
CVM VT IN PVLCHRITVDINE, ET INNOCENTIA
ANGELOS ÆMVLATA STRENVE FVERAT; ID ET IN HOC PRÆSTARE NISA EST
VT SINE SEXV DEGERET;
IDEOQ CORPVS INTACTVM, QVÂ FACTVM EST INTEGRITATE,
(PARADISVM SINE SERPENTE,)
DEO REDDERE VOLVIT;
QVÆ NEC ADEO AVLÆ SPLENDORIBVS ALLICEFACTA, VT A SEMET EXVLARET,
NEC ADEO SIBIMET CŒNOBIVM FACTA, VT SE SOCIETATI DENEGARET,
NEC OB CORPORIS, FORTVNÆVE DOTES, MINVS IN ANIMO DOTATA,
NEC OB LINGVARVM PERITIAM, MINVS TACITVRNA,
VITAM, MORTEMVE NEC PERTÆSA NEC INSECTATA,
SINE REMIS, SINE REMORIS,
DEVM DVCTOREM SEQVTA
HVNC PORTVM POST XV FERE ANNOS ASSEQVTA,
ROB: DRVRI EQ: AVR: ET ANNA VXOR,
VNICÂ FILIÂ ITAQ, ET IPSO PARENTVM NOMINE SPOLIATI,
HOC MONVMENTVM EXTRVENDO,
FILIÆ SVÆ (EHEV DEPERDITÆ) ALIQVANTILLÂ PRÆSENTIÂ,
LVCTVOSISSIMÆ SVÆ ORBITATI BLANDIVNTVR,
SECESSIT
AN: ÆTAT: XV MENSE X. ET SVI IESV CIƆIƆCX.

Donne's epitaph for Elizabeth Drury in All Saints Church, Hawstead. Photograph by Paul A. Parrish, A. A. G. G., B. B. Printed by permission of the Reverend K. A. Fennimore, Rector of Hawstead.

Epitaph for Elizabeth Drury.

QVO PERGAS, VIATOR, NON HABES:
AD GADES OMNIVM VENISTI; ETIAM ET AD TVAS:
HîC IACES, SI PROBVS ES, IPSE;
IPSA ETENIM HîC IACET PROBITAS,
ELIZABETHA:
CVI,
CVM, VT IN PVLCHRITVDINE, ET INNOCENTIA
ANGELOS ÆMVLATA STRENVE FVERAT, ID ET IN HOC PRÆSTARE NISA EST,
VT SINE SEXV DEGERET;
IDEOQVE CORPVS INTACTVM, QVÂ FACTVM EST INTEGRITATE,
(PARADISVM SINE SERPENTE,)
DEO REDDERE VOLVIT,
QVÆ NEC ADEO AVLÆ SPLENDORIBVS ALLICEFACTA, VT A SEMET EXVLARET,
NEC ADEO SIBIMET CŒNOBIVM FACTA, VT SE SOCIETATI DENEGARET,
NEC OB CORPORIS, FORTVNÆVE DOTES, MINVS IN ANIMO DOTATA,
NEC OB LINGVARVM PERITIAM, MINVS TACITVRNA,
VITAM, MORTEMVE NEC PERTÆSA, NEC INSECTATA,
SINE REMIS, SINE REMORIS,
DEVM DVCTOREM SEQVTA
HVNC PORTVM POST XV FERE ANNOS ASSEQVTA,
ROB: DRVRI EQ: AVR: ET ANNA VXOR,
VNICÂ FILIÂ, ITÂQVE ET IPSO PARENTVM NOMINE SPOLIATI,
HOC MONVMENTVM EXTRVENDO,
FILIÆ SVÆ (EHEV, DEPERDITÆ) ALIQVANTILLÂ PRÆSENTIÂ,
LVCTVOSISSIMÆ SVÆ ORBITATI BLANDIVNTVR;
SECESSIT
AN^{I}: ÆTAT: XV^{I} MENSE X$^{\circ}$, ET SVI IESV CIϽIϽCX.

Textual Introduction

EtED was written on the occasion of the death of Elizabeth Drury prior to 13 December 1610. She was buried in the church at Hawstead on 17 December 1610.

The copy-text for *EtED* followed here is the inscription on the monument of Elizabeth Drury on the south wall of the chancel in the parish church at Hawstead, Suffolk (see photographs, pages 174 and 179). Carved into a black stone tablet and painted in with gilt, the text on the monument is the only surviving seventeenth-century text of the epitaph. The earliest printing of the epitaph appears in Cullum (1784 [siglum 66]), with a second expanded and corrected edition in 1813 (for Cullum's description of the monument, see the Commentary). Because Cullum saw the text in a possibly less deteriorated state, variants in his text are reported in the Historical Collation. Other early reprintings of the epitaph are found in Nichols (1790), which reproduces a slightly reduced facsimile of Cullum, and Ford (1818), which derives its text from 66.

Since Milgate (BB), the only modern editor to include *EtED*, has an important part in the early textual transmission of *EtED*, variants in his text are reported at the level of those in primary texts.

We have followed 66 and BB in correcting "EXTREVENDO" (l. 23) to "EXTRVENDO" and "ATAT" (l. 27) to "ÆTAT."

Textual Apparatus

Copy-text: 10. **Texts collated:** 10; 66 (pp. 53–54).
Emendations of the copy-text: *heading supplied* Line 10 IDEOQVE] IDEOQ; 22 ITÂQVE] ITÂQ; 23 EXTRVENDO] EXTREVENDO 27 ÆTAT] ATAT

HISTORICAL COLLATION

Format:

Font: *text in all capital letters of equal size* 66.

Indentations: *text not centered, ll.* 8, 13–15, 24–25, *and* 27 *not ind* 10; *text centered, ll.* 8, 13, *and* 14 *overhang* 66.

Miscellaneous: *the superscript* I *in l.* 27 *is directly over the* N 10; QUAE *conjectured as emendation for* CVI *in l.* 6 66.

Headings: *none.*

1 HABES:] ~. 66.

2 VENISTI;] ~, 66.

3 IPSE;] ~, 66.

5 ELIZABETHA:] ~, 66.

7 CVM,] ~‸ 66. VT] ~, 66. PVLCHRITVDINE,] ~‸ 66.

9 DEGERET;] ~: 66.

10 IDEOQVE] IDEOQ; 10; IDEOQ. 66. INTEGRITATE,] ~‸ 66.

11 SERPENTE,] ~‸ 66.

12 VOLVIT,] ~. 66.

14 DENEGARET,] ~: 66.

15 CORPORIS,] ~‸ 66. DOTES,] ~‸ 66. DOTATA,] ~; 66.

16 PERITIAM,] ~‸ 66. TACITVRNA,] ~. 66.

17 VITAM,] ~‸ 66.

19 SEQVTA] ~, 66.

20 ASSEQVTA] ~. 66.

21 ROB:] ~. 66. EQ:] ~. 66. AVR:] ~. 66.

23 EXTRVENDO] EXTREVENDO 10.

24 EHEV,] ~$_{\wedge}$ 66. PRÆSENTIA,] ~$_{\wedge}$ 66.

25 BLANDIVNTVR;] ~. 66.

27 AN^{l}:] ANNI 66. ÆTAT:] ATAT: 10; ÆTAT. 66. XV^{l}] XV 66. X^{o}] X 66.

Subscriptions: *none.*

Variants in Selected Modern Edition

Edition collated: BB.
Format:
Font: *reduces most small capitals to lower case* BB.
Indentations: *lines centered* BB.
Miscellaneous: *orthography modernized* BB.
Heading: *Epitaph for Elizabeth Drury* BB.

1 HABES:] ~. BB.

2 VENISTI;] ~, BB.

5 ELIZABETHA:] ~, BB.

7 VT] ~, BB.

8 EST,] ~$_{\wedge}$ BB.

21 ROB:] ~. BB. EQ:] ~. BB.

24 EHEV,] ~$_{\wedge}$ BB.

27 AN^{l}:] Anni BB. X^{o}] X BB.

Subscription: *none.*

The tomb of Elizabeth Drury in All Saints Church, Hawstead. Photograph by Paul A. Parrish, A. A. G. G., B. B. Printed by permission of the Reverend K. A. Fennimore, Rector of Hawstead.

The tomb of Robert Drury in All Saints Church, Hawstead. Photograph by Paul A. Parrish, A. A. G. G., B. B. Printed by permission of the Reverend K. A. Fennimore, Rector of Hawstead.

Epitaph for Robert *and* Anne Drury.

Roberti Drvri

Qvo vix alter eivs Ordinis Maioribvs Maioribvs ortvs
Cvm nec Ephæbos excesserat,
Nec vestem de paterna morte lvgvbrem exverat,
EQVIT: AVR: honore, (nec id Domi,
Sed obsidione RHOTOMAGENSI) A^{o} 1591 Insigniti,
QVEM
Et Bellicæ Expeditiones
Et Exteræ Peregrinationes
Et Avlicæ Occvpationes,
Satis, (Ipsâ Invidiâ, Qvâ sæpe tactvs, fractvs nvmqvam, teste) Instrvxerant
Tam ad Exercitvs dvcendos
Qvam ad Legationes peragendas
Avt Res Civiles pertractandas,
Iam A^{o} svo 40: Et svi IESV 1615
Animâ, svmmâ Constantiâ, Eâqve CHRISTIANÂ, DEO traditâ
BONORVM bona parte PAVPERIBVS
V, ante FEBREM, qva correptvs annis (idqve perenniter) erogata
CORPVS, olim SPIRITVS S^{ti} TEMPLVM,
ANIMÆ POSTLIMINIO reddendvm
TERRÆ POSTLIMINIO reddi
Hoc loco Cvravit

Anna Vxor

Nec infæcvnda nec Mater tamen
DOROTHEÆ. et ELIZABETHÆ, filiarvm, orba
Illvstri familia BACON orivnda,
Cvi vnice, hoc dedit DEVS stirpi,
vt pater et filivs, eodem Mvnere, eoqve svmmo, fvngerentvr
NICOLAO patre SIGILLI CVSTODE
FRANCISCO filio CANCELLARIO
Etiam
Officio, erga defvnctvm pie, pie fvncta,
Hoc qvod restat, Saxi spativm
qvæ de Ipsâ dicenda ervnt, inserendis,
(Ita velit DEVS, Ita velint Illi,)
POSTERIS reliqvit.

Textual Introduction

EtRD was occasioned by the death of Sir Robert Drury on 2 April 1615 (see Bald 1959, 135), who was buried in the church at Hawstead on 1 June 1615.

The copy-text for *EtRD* is the inscription on Nicholas Stone's monument (erected 1617) for Sir Robert Drury on the north side of the chancel of the church at Hawstead, Suffolk, the only surviving seventeenth-century text of the epitaph (see photograph, page 162). Since *EtRD* refers to Francis Bacon as Lord Chancellor, it must have been inscribed after his appointment to that position in January of 1618. The text was carved into the black stone of two tombstone-shaped compartments above the sarcophagus of Robert Drury, with the incisions gilded. The text in the compartment to the viewer's left (ll. 1–22) begins "Roberti Drvri"; that on the right (ll. 23–36) "Anna Vxor." The earliest printing of the epitaph appears in Cullum (1784 [siglum 66]), of which a second expanded and corrected edition appeared in 1813. Because Cullum saw the text in a possibly less deteriorated state, variants in his text are reported in the Historical Collation. Nichols (1790) reproduces a slightly reduced facsimile of 66 in his *Bibliotheca Topographica Britannica.*

Milgate (BB), the only modern editor to include *EtRD*, emends the location of the closing parenthesis in "(nec id Domi) / Sed obsidione RHOTOMAGENSI," to "(nec id domi, / sed obsidione Rhotomagensi)" (ll. 5–6), an emendation first suggested by Sparrow (1949; see the Commentary). But Milgate obscures the linear formatting of the epitaph on the monument, leaving no blank line after the opening Roberti Drvri and failing to separate spatially the inscription in the second compartment from that in the first. He thus gives the impression that the epitaph is incised as a continuous, top-to-bottom sequence of lines, broken only by a blank left after line 23 (for explanations of this gap, see the Commentary on lines 23–24). Since Milgate's text has an important part in the textual transmission of *EtRD*, variants in his text are reported at the level of those in the primary texts.

By printing the two parts of the epitaph on separate pages, we have preserved the basic physical design of the epitaph on the monument. We have also followed Sparrow and Milgate in emending the closing parenthesis in "Domi)" to a comma—printing "Domi," in line 5—and we have altered the comma after "RHOTOMAGENSI," to a closing parenthesis—printing "RHOTOMAGENSI)"—because the punctuation in the original text obscures the sense of the passage. It is impossible to determine how this error in punctuation came about. It may have existed in the transcription from which the stone mason worked, or he may have mistaken a comma in his copy-text for a closing parenthesis at the end of line five, thus incising the incorrect "Domi)." If so, when he then arrived at the closing parenthesis after "RHOTOMAGENSI," having already closed the parenthetical insertion, he was forced to substitute a comma for the closing parenthesis in his copy-text.

Textual Apparatus

Copy-text: 15. **Texts collated:** 15; 66 (pp. 55–56).
Emendations of the copy-text: *heading supplied* Line 4 LVGVBREM] LVGVBR$^{E}_{\wedge}$M 5 DOMI,] ~) 6 RHOTOMAGENSI)] ~, 16 EÂQVE] EÂQ$_{3}$ 18 IDQVE] IDQ$_{3}$ 28 EOQVE] EOQ$_{3}$ 32 PIE FVNCTA] PIEFVNCTA

Historical Collation

Format:

Font: *text in all capital letters of equal size* 66.

Indentations: *l. 11 not ind, ll. 8–10 and 12–14 aligned at their left* M *rather than centered, ll. 34 and 35 also aligned at their left* M 15; *each l. centered* 66.

Miscellaneous: *text inscribed in two black stone compartments above the sarcophagus of Sir Robert Drury in letters of various sizes, small and large capitals are distinguished by letter size within the line* 15; *ll. 11, 18, and 28 overhang, no indication that l. 23 begins a second compartment,* Et jam *offered as a conjectural emendation for* ETIAM *in l. 31* 66.

Headings: *none.*

1 DRVRI] ~, 66.

2 ORTVS] ~, 66.

5 HONORE,] ~$_{\wedge}$ 66. DOMI,] ~) 15 66.

6 RHOTOMAGENSI)] ~, 15; ~$_{\wedge}$ 66. A°] ANNO 66.

8 EXPEDITIONES] ~, 66.

9 PEREGRINATIONES] ~, 66.

11 SATIS,] ~$_{\wedge}$ 66. NVMQVAM] NUNQUAM 66. INSTRVXERANT] ~, 66.

12 DVCENDOS] ~, 66.

13 PERAGENDAS] ~, 66.

15 A°] ANNO 66. 40 ⁝] ~, 66. 1615] ~, 66.

16 ANIMÂ,] ~$_{\wedge}$ 66. TRADITÂ] ~, 66.

17 PAVPERIBVS] ~, 66.

18 V,] ~. 66. FEBREM,] ~$_{\wedge}$ 66. CORREPTVS] ~, 66. EROGATA] ~, 66.

19 CORPVS,] ~$_{\wedge}$ 66. S^{TI}] SANCTI 66.

20 REDDENDVM] ~, 66.

21 REDDI] ~, 66.

23 VXOR] ~, 66.

24 INFÆCVNDA] ~, 66. TAMEN] ~, 66.

25 DOROTHEÆ.] ~‸ 66. ELIZABETHÆ,] ~‸ 66. FILIARVM,] ~‸ 66. ORBA] ~, 66.

27 VNICE,] ~‸ 66.

28 FILIVS,] ~‸ 66. SVMMO,] ~‸ 66. FVNGERENTVR] ~, 66.

29 CVSTODE] ~, 66.

30 CANCELLARIO] ~. 66.

32 OFFICIO,] ~‸ 66. PIE FVNCTA] PIEFVNCTA 15.

33 RESTAT,] ~‸ 66. SPATIVM] ~, 66.

34 ERVNT,] ~‸ 66.

35 ILLI,] ~‸ 66.

Subscriptions: *none.*

Variants in Selected Modern Edition

Edition collated: BB.
Format:
Font: *most small capitals reduced to lower case* BB.
Indentations: *ll. centered, l. 11 printed as two centered ll., poem divided into ll. 1–23 and 24–36* BB.
Miscellaneous: *orthography modernized* BB.
Heading: *Epitaph for Sir Robert Drury* BB.

5 HONORE,] ~‸ BB.

6 A^{o}] Anno BB.

11 NVMQVAM] nunquam BB.

12 DVCENDOS] ~, BB.

15 A^{o}] ANNO BB. 40 ⁝] ~: BB.

16 ANIMÂ,] ~‸ BB. TRADITÂ] ~, BB.

18 V,] ~. BB.

19 S^{TI}] Sancti BB.

21 REDDI] ~, BB.

25 DOROTHEÆ.] ~‸ BB. ELIZABETHÆ,] ~‸ BB. FILIARVM,] ~‸ BB.

Subscriptions: *none.*

Annæ

Georgij Roberti Willelmj Christophorj	More de Lothesley Equit: Aurat:	Filiæ Soror: Nept: Pronept:

Fœminæ Lectissimæ, dilectissimæq;
Coniugi charissimæ castissimæq;
Matrj piissimæ, Indulgentissimæq;
XV annis in coniugio transactis,
vii post xii^m partum (quorum vii superstant) dies
Immani febre correpta,
(Quod hoc saxum farj iussit
Ipse, præ dolore Infans)
Maritus (miserrimum dictu) olim charæ charus
Cineribus cineres spondet suos
Nouo matrimonio (annuat Deus) hoc loco sociandos
Iohannes Donne
Sacr: Theolog: profess:
Secessit
A° xxxiii° Ætat: suæ et sui Jesu
CIↃ DC xvii° 231
Aug: xv.

Donne's holograph epitaph for Ann Donne. Printed by permission of the Folger Shakespeare Library.

Epitaph for Ann Donne.

Annæ

Georgij	More de	Filiæ
Roberti	Lothesley	Soror:
Willelmj	Equit:	Nept:
Christophorj	Aurat:	Pronept:

Fæminæ lectissimæ, dilectissimæque;
Coniugi charissimæ, castissimæque;
Matrj piissimæ, Indulgentissimæque;
Xv annis in coniugio transactis,
Vii post xii^{m} partum (quorum vii superstant) dies
Immani febre correptæ,
(Quod hoc saxum farj iussit
Ipse, præ dolore Infans)
Maritus (miserrimum dictu) olim charæ charus
Cineribus cineres spondet suos
Nouo matrimonio (annuat Deus) hoc loco sociandos
Iohannes Donne
Sacr: Theolog: Profess:
Secessit
A^{o} xxxiii^{o} Ætat: suæ et sui Iesu
CIƆ D C xvii^{o}
Aug: xv.

Textual Introduction

EtAD was occasioned by the death of Ann Donne, Donne's wife, on 15 August 1617.

The early manuscript copies of this epitaph form four families of textual transmission. The copy-text, F1, stands alone as one family (see photograph, page 186). C9 and H6, which exhibit related texts of other poems, form another family; both omit line 8, and both have the identical note immediately below the text of the epitaph: "In the chancell of S[t] Clement Danes church without Temple Barre: made by J: D: himselfe, who was afterwards notwithstanding buried in Paules whereof he dyed Deane: A: D: i63i." Both, furthermore, position the epitaph similarly with respect to other poems, placing it after a series of epicedes (the last of which is *Henry)* and prior to a section of Verse Letters. The leaf on which *EtAD* appears in C9 (f. 57) has been inserted into the manuscript, though the fact that this manuscript has been rebound at least once (and the leaves perhaps reordered) makes this positioning difficult to interpret. 24a, 24b, and B41 form another family, the text in 24a likely deriving from the monument of Ann Donne originally carved by Nicolas Stone and lost in the rebuilding of St. Clement Danes in 1680–82 (the monument is described in 24a; see also the Commentary). The text of *EtAD* in 24b is in the same typesetting as that in 24a. B41 shares with 24a and 24b the line-ending commas in lines 15, 16, 17, and 19 plus the mistaken "XXIII" in line 20; its lineation, moreover, closely resembles that of 24a and 24b—details suggesting either that the texts in both B41 and in 24a–b derive independently from the original monument and that the monument had the erroneous "XXIII" in line 20 or that B41 derives from 24a or 24b. Dates in other inscriptions preserved in B41 indicate that it was completed sometime after 1678. B27 is unique in omitting "vii" in line 10, and B42 alone reads "Septem" for "Vii" in line 10. In the margin beside the text of *EtSP* in B42 (f. 102) appears the scribal note "Hist of S[t] Pauls Cathedral—p. 63," an apparent reference to William Dugdale's *The History of S[t.] Pauls Cathedral* (siglum 45) that establishes a post-1658 date for the inscription of *EtAD* and other items in B42.

The only modern printing, BB, derives from F1.

The copy-text is Donne's holograph on the single leaf of Folger Shakespeare Library ms. Loseley L.b.541. The verso, numbered "129," reads "Epitaph on Ann dau: of S[r] Geo. More / wife of D[r] John Donne / She died 15 Augt 1617 aged 33 / had been married 15 years / 1602."

Textual Apparatus

Copy–text: F1. **Texts collated:** B27 (f. 51); B41 (f. 68v); B42 (ff. 102v–03); C9 (f. 57); F1 (*single leaf*); H6 (p. 187); 24a–b (p. 889).

Emendations of the copy-text: *heading supplied* Line 6 dilectissimæque] dilectissimæq; 7 castissimæque] castissimæq; 8 Indulgentissimæque] Indulgentissimæq; 9 Xv] xv 10 Vii] vii

Historical Collation

Format:

Font: Annæ *(l. 1)*, More *(l. 2)*, *and* Donne *(l. 17) in italics and boldface* B27; *text in italics* 24a–b.

Indentations: *all ll. centered* B27 B41 B42 F1 24a–b; *ll. all centered except that ll. 17–19 appear at far right* C9 H6; *ll. 2–5, 6–8 in centered columns* B27; *ll. 2–5 in centered columns* B41 B42 C9 F1 H6 24a–b.

Miscellaneous: *space between ll. 5–6, 8–9* B27; *space between ll. 5–6* B41 B42 C9 F1 H6 24a–b; *l. 22 part of l. 21* B27 C9 H6; *right brace encloses col. 1, left and right braces enclose col. 2, and left brace encloses col. 3* B41; *wavy ll. separate the three columns and* Aurat. *written beside* Equ. *in l. 4* B42; *left and right braces enclose col. 1, left brace encloses col. 3* C9 H6; *first two columns have braces to their right* F1; *braces between the three columns* 24a–b; *l. 10 written as ll. 10–11, l. 14 as ll. 15–16, l. 16 as ll. 18–19* B41 24a–b; *introduced as* His Wifes Epitaph. B42.

Headings: *none.*

1 Annæ] *Aunæ* 24a(*unc*); *om* B27.

2 Georgij] *Georgi* 24a(*unc*). Filiæ] ~. B41 24a–b.

3 Lothesley] Lothesly C9 H6. Soror:] ~‸ B27 H6; Sorori‸ B42.

4 Willelmj] Willielmi B27; Gulielmi C9 H6. Equit:] ~. B27; Equ. Aurat. B42; ~‸ H6. Nept:] ~. B27 H6; Nepti‸ B42.

5 Christophorj] Christopheri B41 B42 C9 H6 24a–b. Aurat:] Aurati‸ B27; *om* B42; Aurati. C9 H6. Pronept:] ~‸ B27; Pronep: B41 24a–b; Pronepti‸ B42; ~:. C9; ~. H6.

6 Fæminæ] ~, B27; Fœminæ B41 B42 24a–b. lectissimæ,] ~‸ B42 C9 H6. dilectissimæque;] ~‸ B27 B42 C9 H6; ~, B41 24a–b.

7 Coniugi] ~, B27. charissimæ,] ~‸ B41 B42 C9 H6 24a–b. castissimæque;] ~‸ B27 B42 C9; ~, B41 24a–b; ~. H6.

8 *om* C9 H6. Matrj] ~, B27. piissimæ,] ~‸ B41 B42 24a–b. Indulgentissimæque;] ~‸ B27 B42; ~, B41 24a–b.

9 transactis,] ~‸ B27 B42 C9 H6.

10 Vii] ~. B41 24a–b; Septem B42. xii^{m}] XII. B41 24a–b; xii^{ū} B42; duodecimū C9 H6. (quorum] ‸~ B27. vii] *om* B27; ~. B41 24a–b. superstant)] ~‸ B27; suꝑsunt‸ C9 H6. dies] ~. B41; ~) C9 H6.

11 correptæ,] ~‸ B27 B41 B42 C9 H6 24a–b.

12 (Quod] ‸~ C9 H6. iussit] ~, B41 24a–b.

13 Ipse,] ~‸ B41 B42 C9 H6 24a–b. dolore] ~, B27. Infans)] ~.) B42; ~‸ C9 H6.

14 dictu)] ~‸ B27. olim] ~, C9 H6.

15 suos] ~, B41 24a–b.

16 sociandos] ~, B41 24a–b; ~. H6.

17 Donne] ~, B41 24a–b.

18 Sacr:] ~. B27 B42 24a–b. Theolog:] Theologiæ‸ B27; Theol. B42; ~. 24a–b. Profess:] ~. B27 24a–b; Professor‸ B42; ~; H6.

19 Secessit] ~, B41 24a–b.

20 A^{o}] Anno B41 B42 24a–b; ~. C9 H6. xxxiii^{o}] XXIII. B41 24a–b; XXXIII C9 H6. Ætat:] ~. B27 C9 H6 24a–b; Ætatis‸ B41; ~‸ B42. suæ] ~; C9 H6.

21 CIƆ D C xvii^{o}] CIƆ D C XVII B27 C9 H6; CIƆ. DC. XVII. B41 24a–b; MDCXVII. B42.

22 Aug:] ~‸ B27; ~. B42 24a–b. xv] xv^{o} B27 C9 H6.

Subscriptions: *none.*

Grierson (Q) includes *EtSP* in the notes to *Sickness*, but Milgate (BB) is the first modern editor to print the epitaph among the poems, using 21 as copy-text. Both Grierson and Milgate format the poem idiosyncratically. Grierson prints a text of fourteen centered lines, while Milgate prints a seventeen-line text that forms the shape of an urn on the page, asserting that "the mason made no attempt at an intelligent distribution of the words (breaking 'moni/tu', 'Iac/obi', and 'amplex/us' at the ends of lines)" (p. 218).

The copy-text followed here is that inscribed on the monument in St. Paul's (21), a text surely derived from Donne's holograph. Thus, with the minor exception noted below, we have not emended the format, text, or punctuation, though all three are problematic. Indeed, the handling of the epitaph in the early sources shows that uncertainty has always surrounded these issues: for example, the various seventeenth-century manuscript and print exempla differ radically in formatting the epitaph as verse, as prose, or as some combination of the two; several center each line; and B42, 23a–b, 24a–b, 28a–b, 45, and 53a–b all present "CVIVS NOMEN EST ORIENS" as a single line. The ease with which the mason could have avoided the syllabic breaks that troubled Milgate suggests that the text on 21 may follow Donne's holograph exactly; and in order to enable critical appreciation of *EtSP* in the form closest to that produced by Donne's own hand, we have retained here the exact wording, lineation, and graphic form of the poem as they appear on the monument, emending only to reposition a misplaced tittle in line 6.

The text contains an error of fact. As the Dean's Registers for 1536–1642 in Guildhall, London, prove, James I ordered the election of Donne as Dean of St. Paul's in a letter to Thomas White on 19 November 1621; and Donne was so elected on 22 November 1621 (ms. 25,630–7), rather than on 27 November, the date given in the epitaph. The source of this error is uncertain: in composing the epitaph, Donne might have misremembered the date, or the mason might have misread "27" for "22" or even "xxvii" for "xxii."

Textual Apparatus

Copy-text: 21 (Donne's monument in St. Paul's). **Texts collated:** B42 (f. 102r–v); 21; 23a–c (sigs. E2v–3); 24a–b (p. 776); 28a (sig. C1v); 28b (pp. 113–14); 45 (*first appearance*, p. 62; *second appearance*, p. 63); 53a (p. 76); 53b (p. 73); 60a–b (p. 56).
Emendations of the copy-text: *heading supplied* Line 6 SC̃TI] SCT~I

Historical Collation

Format:

Font: *ll. 14–16 in italics* 23a–c; *all ll. in italics* 24a–b 28b 45(*second appearance*) 53a–b; *ll. 2–16 in italics* 60a–b.

Indentations: *all ll. centered* B42 24a–b 28a–b 45(*first appearance*) 53a–b 60a–b; *ll. 1–2 centered* 21; *ll. 14–16 centered* 23a–c; *ll. 1–2, 12–16 centered* 45(*second appearance*).

Miscellaneous: *text inscribed in white marble entablature above Donne's effigy in St. Paul's Cathedral* 21; *ll. 1–13 printed as prose* 23a–c; *second half of l. 15 printed with l. 16* 23a–c 24a–b 28a–b 45a–b 53a–b; *line of space left between ll. 2 and 3* 28b 45(*second appearance*); *text within illustration of Donne's monument in St. Paul's* 45(*first appearance*); *ll. 3–11 printed as prose* 45(*second appearance*).

Headings: *none*.

1 IOHANNES] IOHANNI B42 45(*first appearance*); Ioannes 23a–c 24a–b 45(*second appearance*). DONNE] ~. 45(*first appearance*).

2 SAC:] ~. B42 24a–b 28b 45(*second appearance*) 53a–b; *S. S.* 60a–b. THEOL:] ~. B42 24a–b 28b 45(*second appearance*) 53a–b; *Theologiæ* 60a–b. PROFESS] ~. B42 24a–b 45(*second appearance*) 53b; ~: 23a–c 45(*first appearance*); PROFESSOR, 28a; *Professor* 28b 53a; *Professor;* 60a–b.

3 POST] ~, 45(*first appearance*). STVDIA] ~, 23a–c 24a–b 28a 45(*second appearance*) 60a–b. QVIBVS] ~, 60a–b.

4 TENERRIMIS] teneribus B42 45(*first appearance*); ~, 23a–c. FIDELITER] ~, 24a–b 28a–b 45(*both appearances*) 53a–b; *Fidelitèr,* 60a–b.

5 INFELICITER] in fæliciter B42; infæliciter, 23a–c; *infæliciter* 24a–b 45(*both appearances*); ~, 28a; *infelicitèr* 60a–b. INCVBVIT] ~, 23a–c 24a–b 28a 45(*second appearance*); ~; 28b 53a–b 60a–b. INSTINCTV] ~, 24a–b 45(*first appearance*) 60a–b.

6 SPIR:] ~. B42 24a–b; *Sp.* 28b 53a–b; *Spiritus*‸ 45(*second appearance*); *Sancti*‸ 60a–b. SC̃TI] Scti. B42; SCT˜I 21; S^{ti} 23a–c; *Sancti,* 24a–b 28b 45(*second appearance*) 53a–b; *S^{ti}:* 28a; SCTI: 45(*first appearance*); *Spiritûs,* 60a–b.

6–7 MONI-/-TV] ~, 24a–b 60a–b.

7–8 IAC-/-OBI] ~, 23a–c 28a–b 45(*second appearance*) 53a–b 60a–b; ~. 24a–b.

8 ORDINES SACROS] *om* 24a–b 45(*second appearance*) 60a–b.

8–9 AMPLEX-/-VS] ~, 23a–c; *om* 24a–b 45(*second appearance*) 60a–b.

9 ANNO] A^{o}: 28a. SVI] *om* 60a–b. IESV] ~, 24a–b 28b 53a–b. 1614] ~. B42 23a–c 24a–b 28a–b 45(*second appearance*) 53a–b; MDCXIV, 60a–b.

10 ET] *om* 60a–b. SVÆ] SVE 45(*first appearance*); *ætatis* 60a–b. ÆTAT] ~. B42 24a–b; ætatis 23a–c 28a–b 45(*second appearance*) 53a–b; ~: 45(*first appearance*); *suæ* 60a–b. 42] ~. B42 23a–c 24a–b 28a–b 45(*both appearances*) 53a–b 60a–b. DECANATV] Decenatu 23a–c; DECANATVS 45(*first appearance*).

11 ECCLES^{Æ}] Ecclesiæ B42 28a–b 45(*second appearance*) 53a–b 60a–b; Eccles: 23a–c 45(*first appearance*); *Eccles.* 24a–b. 27°] 27. B42 23a–c 24a–b 28b 45(*second appearance*) 53a–b; XXVII. 28a; *est Vicess. Septimo* 60a–b.

12 NOVEMB:] ~. B42 24a–b; Novembris 23a–c 28a–b 53a–b 60a–b; *Nov.* 45(*second appearance*). 1621] ~. 23a–c 24a–b 28a–b 45(*both appearances*) 53a–b; MDCXX. 60a–b. EXVTVS] *Et tandem exutus est,* 60a–b. MORTE] ~, 60a–b.

13 VLTIMO] vlt^{o}. 23a–c. MARTII] ~. 24a–b 28a. A^{o}] *om* 23a–c 28a–b 53a–b 60a–b; *An.* 24a–b; ~. 45(*first appearance*); *Anno* 45(*second appearance*). 1631] MDCXXXV 60a–b.

14 LICET] jacet B42 45(*first appearance*); *licèt* 60a–b. CINERE] ~, 24a–b.

15 EVM] ~, 23a–c. NOMEN] ~, 24a–b.

16 ORIENS] ~. B42 23a–c 24a–b 28a–b 45(*both appearances*) 53a–b 60a–b.

Subscriptions: *none.*

Verbal Variants in Selected Modern Editions

Editions collated: Q BB.
Format:
Indentations: *all lines centered* Q BB.
Headings: *Epitaph for Himself* BB. *om* Q.

1 IOHANNES] Ioannes BB.
6 SPIR:] SP. Q; Spiritus BB. SC̃TI] Sancti Q BB.
9 1614] MDCXIV Q.
10 ÆTAT] ÆTATIS Q. 42] XLII Q.
11 ECCLES^{Æ}] ECCLESIÆ Q; Ecclesiae BB. 27°] XXVII Q.
12 NOVEMB:] NOVEMBRIS Q. 1621] MDCXXI Q.
13 A^{o}] *om* Q; Anno BB. 1631] MDCXXXI Q.
Subscriptions: *none.*

Schema of Textual Relationships

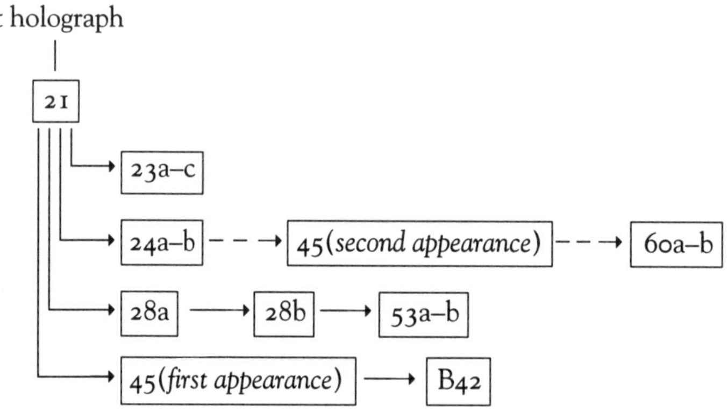

Analyses of Early Printed Copies

Henry Holland, *ECCLESIA SANCTI PAVLI ILLVSTRATA*, 4to, 1633
(sigla 23a, 23b, 23c)

Copies collated: *L*, *LG*, O.
Relevant section: sigs. E2v–E3.
Press variants: *none.*

Miscatching:

	Catchword:		Initial word:	Affects:
E2v	canatu	E3	cenatu	*EtSP* 10

Note: 23a, 23b, and 23c print *EtSP* from the same typesetting.

§

John Stow, *THE SURVEY OF LONDON*, fol., 1633 (sigla 24a, 24b)

Copies collated: *HD*, L^{1} (576.m.14), L^{2} (576.m.19), L^{3} (579.k.23), LG^{1} (A.4.5. no. 16), LG^{2} (AN.5.4.11), O^{1} (Douce S.653), O^{2} (Gough London 134), O^{3} (L.3.7.Art).
Relevant section: sig. 3V2v; p. 776.
Press variants: *none*.
Miscatchings: *none*.

Note: 24a and 24b print *EtSP* from the same typesetting. Copies L^{3}, LG^{2}, and $O^{1,3}$ repeat the pagination for pages 776 and 777; *EtSP* appears on the first occurence of page 776.

§

Izaak Walton, *THE LIFE AND DEATH OF Dr DONNE*, fol., 1640 (siglum 28a)

Copies collated: C^{1} (Keynes B.7.31), C^{2} (4.8.26), C^{3} (Peterborough B.9.3), *CSmH*, TCC^{1} (C.3.64¹), TCC^{2} (C.3.64²).
Relevant section: sig. C1v.
Press variants: *none*.
Miscatchings: *none*.

§

Izaak Walton, *THE LIFE OF JOHN DONNE*, 12mo, 1658 (siglum 28b)

Copies collated: *CSmH*, *L*, *TCC*.
Relevant section: sig. F7r–v; pp. 113–14.
Press variants: *none*.
Miscatchings: *none*.

§

William Dugdale, *THE HISTORY OF S^t. PAULS CATHEDRAL IN LONDON*, fol., 1658 (siglum 45)

Copy collated: *L*.
Relevant sections: (*first appearance*) sig. R1v; p. 62 and (*second appearance*) sig. R2; p. 63.
Press variants: *none*.
Miscatchings: *none*.

§

Izaak Walton, *THE LIVES Of Dr. John Donne, Sir Henry Wotton, Mr. Richard Hooker, Mr. George Herbert*, 8vo, 1670 (siglum 53a)

Copies collated: L^1 (C.45.b.8), L^2 (615.b.1).
Relevant section: sig. F6v; p. 76.
Press variants: *none*.
Miscatchings: *none*.

§

Izaak Walton, *THE LIVES Of Dr. John Donne, Sir Henry Wotton, Mr. Richard Hooker, Mr. George Herbert*, 8vo, 1675 (siglum 53b)

Copies collated: *L*, *TCC*.
Relevant section: p. 73.
Press variants: *none*.
Miscatchings: *none*.

§

Payne Fisher, *THE Tombes, Monuments, And Sepulchral Inscriptions, Lately Visible in St. Pauls Cathedral*, 4to, 1684 (sigla 60a, 60b)

Copies collated: L^1 (131.b.21), L^2 (577.c.6), L^3 (G.1410), O^1 (B.16.12.Linc), O^2 (Gough Lond. 244 4°), O^3 (Wood 534[7]).
Relevant section: sig. G4v; p. 56.
Press variants: *none*.
Miscatchings: *none*.

Note: 60a and 60b print *EtSP* from the same typesetting.

Epigraph in DEATHS DVELL.

Corporis hæc Animæ sit Syndon, Syndon Iesu
Amen.

Textual Introduction

Donne composed *EgDD* shortly before his death on 31 March 1631 (see the Commentary) and preached the sermon *Deaths Dvell*, for which Martin Droeshout produced the frontispiece on which *EgDD* appears, before King Charles I at St. Paul's Cathedral in London on 25 February 1631.

Helen Gardner first recognized the epigraph as verse, printing it in her edition of the Divine Poems (see U, pp. 112–13; see also p. 205 below and the Commentary).

The leaf containing the frontispiece (sig. A2) has been removed from all known copies of 22b, including the two listed in *Keynes* (p. 54): *L* (693.f.11.[11]) and *LP* (actually a copy of 22c: present shelfmark, 40 D; formerly 47^{A} G: 2:). The frontispieces in all collated copies of both issues of the second edition of *Death's Dvell* (22c and 22d) are identical to that in 22a. Keynes (*Keynes*, p. 56) accepts the argument of George R. Potter and Evelyn Simpson (*Sermons* 1: 23) for the priority of 22c (*Keynes*, item 26a) over 22d (*Keynes*, item 26).

The only modern editions to include *EgDD*, Gardner (U) and Shawcross (Z), use the frontispiece as copy-text.

The earliest artifact containing *EgDD*, 22a, provides the copy-text followed here, which requires no emendation.

Textual Apparatus

Copy-text: 22a. **Texts collated:** 22a (sig. A2v); 22c (sig. A2); 22d (sig. A2).
Emendations of the copy-text: *heading supplied*

Historical Collation

Format:
Indentations: Amen. *in l.2 centered under l.1* 22a 22c–d.
Miscellaneous: *text in script below a portrait of Donne in his shroud* 22a 22c–d.
Headings: *none.*
Line-by-line variants: *none.*
Subscriptions: *none.*

Verbal Variants in Selected Modern Editions

Editions collated: U Z.
Format:
Font: *text in roman* U Z.
Indentations: Amen. *(l. 2) justified to right* M U Z.
Miscellaneous: *epigraph printed without portrait* U Z.
Headings: Epigraph to the Portrait of Donne in his Shroud, prefixed to *Deaths Duell* (1632) U. (Epigraph beneath portrait in his shroud, *Deaths Duell*, 1632). Z.
Line-by-line variants: *none.*
Subscriptions: *none.*

Analyses of Early Printed Copies

DEATHS DVELL, 4to, 1632 (siglum 22a)

Copies collated: *CLU-C* (*PR2247 D31), *L* (C.53.k.19), O (Antiq. e.E.1632.11).
Relevant section: sig. A2v.
Press variants: *none.*
Miscatchings: *none.*

Note: An earlier state of 22a without the portrait may exist: in the C copy (Keynes B.5.25) sig. A2r–v is blank, and the portrait has been laid in.

§

DEATHS DVELL, 4to, 1633 (siglum 22b)

Note: No known copies have the leaf containing the portrait.

§

DEATHS DVELL, 4to, 1633 (sigla 22c, 22d)

Copies collated: Issue a: C (Keynes B.5.24); Issue b: C (Keynes B.5.29²), *CSmH* (60135), *L* (Ashley 654).
Relevant sections: sig. A2.
Press variants: *none*.
Miscatchings: *none*.

Engraving of Donne in his shroud, frontispiece in *Deaths Duell.*

In Bibliotheca Hospitij Lincoln: London:
Celeberrimi, in Vrbe, in Orbe
Juris municipalis professorū, Collegij,
Reponi voluit, (petijt potius)

Hæc Sex, in vniuersas Scripturas, Volumina,
Sacræ Theologiæ professor
Serenissmo Munificentissmo

REGI IACOBO
A Sacris
IOANNES DONNE.

Qui huc, in prima iuuentute, ad pdiscendas leges, missu
Ad alia, tam studia, quā negotia, et peregrinatiões deflec
Inter quæ tamen nunqm studia Theologica intermiser
Post multos annos, Agente spiritu Sto, suadente Reg
Ad Ordines Sacros euectus,

Munere suo, frequenter et strenue hoc loco concionan
Per quinque annos functus,

Noui Sacelli primis Saxis sua manu positis
& ultimis fere paratis,

Ad Decanatum Ecclesiæ Cathedr: S: Pauli, London:
A Rege (cui benedicat Domin9)
migrare iussus est

Aº Lº Ætat: suæ, & sui IESV
CIƆIƆCXXI.

Donne's holograph inscription in a Bible presented to Lincoln's Inn. Printed by permission of the Treasurer and Masters of the Bench of the Honourable Society of Lincoln's Inn.

Inscription in a Bible Presented to Lincoln's Inn.

In Bibliotheca Hospitj Lincoln: London:
Celeberrimi, in Vrbe, in Orbe
Iuris Municipalis Professorum, Collegj,
Reponi voluit, (petjt potius)

Hæc Sex, in vniuersas Scripturas, Volumina,
Sacræ Theologiæ Professor
Sereniss^{mo} Munificentiss:^{mo}

REGI IACOBO
A Sacris

IOANNES DONNE.

Qui huc, in prima iuuentute, ad perdiscendas leges, missus
Ad alia, tam studia, quam negotia, et peregrinationes deflectens,
Inter quæ tamen nunq^{m} studia Theologica intermiserat,
Post multos annos, Agente spiritu S^{to}, suadente Rege
Ad Ordines Sacros euectus,

Munere suo, frequenter et strenue hoc loco concionandi
Per quinque annos functus,

Noui Sacelli primis Saxis sua manu positis
Et ultimis fere paratis,

Ad Decanatum Ecclesiæ Cathedr: S: Pauli, London:
A Rege (cui benedicat Dominus)
Migrare iussus est

A^{o} L^{o} Ætat: Suæ, et sui IESV
CIƆIƆCXXI.

Textual Introduction

The occasion for *InLI* was Donne's resignation as Reader at Lincoln's Inn on 11 February 1622 (see the Commentary). Donne entered the inscription on what is now the verso of a 415 x 262 mm. leaf (f. 4v) pasted on a guard following the first three leaves: a blank modern end leaf, a blank contemporary leaf, and the leaf with the half title on its recto (the verso being blank). The inscription thus now faces the very elaborate title page of the first volume of a six-volume Bible that Donne presented to the Lincoln's Inn Society, *BIBLIA SACRA CVM GLOSSA ORDINARIA Primum quidem a* STRABO FVLDENSI . . . Et POSTILLA NICOLAI LYRANI Franciscani, nec non additionibus PAVLI BVRGENSIS . . . et MATTHIÆ THORINGI . . . DVACI Excudebat BALTAZAR BELLERVS suis et IOANNIS KEERBERGII Antuerpiensis sumptibus. Anno cIↃ. IↃ. XVII. The facts that the inscription (now on f. 4v) blotted onto the verso of the second leaf and that folds in the paper indicate that the half-title leaf (now f. 3) and the inscribed leaf (now f. 4) once formed a single sheet mean that originally the inscription must have been on the recto of a leaf preceding the half-title and that the original folio sheet has since been cut in two and the leaf containing the inscription inserted so that it faces the title page. Prior to the repositioning, when the inscription still appeared on a recto, fraying at the right margin (now the gutter) caused some loss of text in lines 12 and 13.

The earliest printing of *InLI* is in T. E. Tomlins (1852; siglum 69), which uses the holograph as copy-text. Two additional early printings derive directly from the holograph: that in the Lincoln's Inn *Black Books* (1898; siglum *LIBB*) and that in Gosse (1899; siglum 72). Since 69, 72, and *LIBB* likely present texts predating the loss of text in lines 12 and 13, variants in these texts are reported in the Historical Collation.

The only modern editor to print *InLI* is Milgate (in BB), who uses the holograph for copy-text. Milgate mentions no damage to the leaf, and his readings at the ends of lines 12 and 13 match those in *LIBB*. Because Milgate may have seen the text prior to its loss of text and because BB has an important part in the early textual transmission of *InLI*, variants in his text are reported below at the level of those in primary texts.

The copy-text for *InLI* followed here is LL1, Donne's holograph inscription, to which material presently lost at the ends of lines 12 and 13 ("deflecte" to "deflectens," and "intermisera" to "intermiserat,") has been restored on the basis of the earlier transcriptions appearing in 69, 72, and *LIBB*. LL1 also requires a correction in line 7: "Munifientiss:^{mo}" to "Munificentiss:^{mo}." Since Donne's practice was allowable in Renaissance Latin, we have not followed Tomlins, Gosse, and Milgate in doubling the terminal "i" in "Hospitj" (l. 1) and "Collegj" (l. 3).

Textual Apparatus

Copy-text: LL1. **Texts collated:** LL1 (f. 4v), 69 (p. 80), 72 (2: 114), *LIBB* (p. 445).

Emendations of the copy-text: *heading supplied* Line 3 Professorum] Professorū 7 Munificentiss:^{mo}] Munifientiss:^{mo} 11 perdiscendas] ꝑdiscendas 12 quam] quā peregrinationes] peregrinatiōes deflectens,] deflecte[*missing*] 13 intermiserat,] intermisera[*missing*] 19 Et] & 21 Dominus] Domin⁹ 23 et] &

Historical Collation

Format:

Indentations: *all ll. centered* 69 72 *LIBB*.

Imperfections: *loss of text at right margin in ll.* 12, 13 LL1.

Miscellaneous: *vertical space left between ll.* 4 *and* 5, 7 *and* 8, 9 *and* 10, 10 *and* 11, 15 *and* 16, 17 *and* 18, 19 *and* 20, *and* 22 *and* 23 LL1; *no vertical spacing* 69; *vertical space left between ll.* 10 *and* 11 72 *LIBB*.

Headings: NOTE VII. Inscription in the Bible given by Dr. Donne, 1622. *LIBB*; *om* LL1 69 72.

1 Hospitj] Hospitii 69 72.

2 Celeberrimi,] ~$_\wedge$ 69 72 *LIBB*. Vrbe] Urbo 72. Orbe] ~, 69 72.

3 Professorum,] ~$_\wedge$ 69 72 *LIBB*. Collegj] Collegii 69 72.

4 voluit,] ~$_\wedge$ 69 72.

5 Hæc] Hæ *LIBB*. Sex,] ~$_\wedge$ 69 72. Scripturas,] ~$_\wedge$ 69 72.

7 Munificentiss:^{mo}] Munifientiss:^{mo} LL1.

8 Iacobo] JOCOBO 69.

10 Ioannes] JOHANNES 69 72. Donne.] ~, 69 72.

11 perdiscendas] perdiscondas 72. leges,] ~$_\wedge$ *LIBB*. missus] ~, *LIBB*.

12 deflectens,] deflecte[*missing*] LL1; deflecteus, 69.

13 tamen] tamon 72. nunq^{m}] nunquam 69 72. intermiserat,] intermisera[*missing*] LL1.

14 Agente] agente 69 72 *LIBB*. spiritu] Spiritu 69 72 *LIBB*. S^{to},] ~; *LIBB*. Rege] ~, 69 72 *LIBB*.

16 suo,] ~$_{\wedge}$ 69 72.

17 quinque] quinqe *LIBB*.

19 fere] fero 72. paratis,] ~$_{\wedge}$ 69 72.

22 est] ~. *LIBB*.

24 CIƆIƆCXXI] MDCXXI *LIBB*.

Subscriptions: *centered triangle-shaped scribal device composed of three triangular dots* LL1; *om* 69 72 *LIBB*.

Variants in Selected Modern Edition

Edition collated: BB.
Format:
Indentations: *all lines centered* BB.
Miscellaneous: *no spaces between lines* BB.
Heading: *Inscription in a Bible presented to Lincoln's Inn* BB.

1 Hospitj] Hospit<i>j BB.

2 Orbe] ~, BB.

3 Collegj] Colleg<i>j BB.

7 Sereniss^{mo}] Serenissimo BB. Munificentiss:^{mo}] Munificentissimo BB.

10 Donne.] ~, BB.

11 missus] ~, BB.

13 nunq^{m}] nunquam BB.

14 Agente] agente BB. spiritu] Spiritu BB. S^{to}] Sancto BB. Rege] ~, BB.

23 A^{o}] Anno BB.

Subscription: *none.*

Inscription in the Album Amicorum *of* Michael Corvinus.

In propria venit, nec sui eum receperunt. Jo: i. ii.
qd enim de Christo dictum, de omni Christiano
dicere licet;
Omnia enim uestra sunt. 1. Cor: 3. 22.

Annuat Deus Opt: Max: ut apud omnes, hanc inveniat
Communionem Sanctorum, vir iste Ornatiss: Doctiss:que
Michael Corvinus Hungar^{is}: quam ei in ædibus
Paulinis, suisque, London: offert spondetque
Ioannes Donne: ibidem Decanus.
Sept: 17. 1623.

Textual Introduction

InAA was written for Michael Corvinus on the occasion of his visit to St. Paul's Cathedral on 17 September 1623 (see the Commentary).

The inscription survives only in Donne's holograph in the *Album Amicorum* of Michael Corvinus, now in the Geoffrey Keynes collection at Cambridge University Library. The manuscript shelfmark "Add. ms. 8466" refers to a box of items that includes not only two manuscripts associated with Corvinus, but also correspondence between Keynes and others regarding the two manuscripts. Measuring 110 mm. x 161 mm., the leaf Donne inscribed with *InAA* has been tipped into a modern folio sheet the leaves of which measure 146 mm. x 180 mm. In addition to the inscription in Donne's hand, the number "59" (evidently an early page number) is written in pencil in the upper right corner of the leaf, and "Chenke p. 926" is written in modern pencil just below Donne's signature. The verso is blank. The second manuscript in the box, a single loose leaf measuring 110 mm. x 169 mm., bears the penciled number "62" in the upper right corner of one side and a similarly inscribed "63" in the upper left corner of the other. Page 62 of this manuscript contains a Latin note (ascribed in modern pencil to "John Donne, jun, Dean of Sion College?") signed "Iohannes Donne" and dated "5. octob: Ao 1633"; page 63 has a note in Latin and Greek dated "14. May Anno Christi 1624." Both this manuscript and that containing *InAA* are of the same paper, and their horizontal chain lines are 27 mm. apart. The second manuscript has a partial watermark (the upper right hand corner of an elaborate shield) in the upper left corner of page 62.

The only modern editor to print *InAA* is Milgate (in BB), who uses the holograph as copy-text. Since Milgate's text has an important part in the textual transmission of *InAA*, variants in his text (the principal one being his misreading of "17" in line 10 as "27") are reported at the level of those in primary texts.

The copy-text followed here is the holograph, which requires no emendation except for expansion of standard manuscript abbreviations.

Textual Apparatus

Copy-text: C11. **Text collated:** C11 (p. 59).
Emendations of the copy-text: *heading supplied* Line 6 Doctiss:que]Doctiss:qꝫ
8 suisque] suisqꝫ offert] ~~of~~ offert spondetque] spondetqꝫ
9 ibidem] ibide˜

Historical Collation

Format:
Indentations: *ll.* 1, 2, 3, 4, 9, 10 *ind* C11.
Miscellaneous: *space between ll.* 4 *and* 5 C11.
Heading: *none.*
Subscription: *none.*

Verbal Variants in Selected Modern Edition

Edition collated: BB.
Format:
Indentations: *ll.* 2–10 *ind variously* BB.
Miscellaneous: *no vertical space between ll.* 4 *and* 5 BB.
Heading: *Inscription in the 'Album Amicorum' of Michael Corvinus* BB.

1 ii.] ~‸ BB.

2 qd] quod BB.

6 Ornatiss:] Ornatissimus BB. Doctiss:que] Doctissimusque BB.

7 Hungar^{is}:] ~, BB.

10 17] 27 BB.

Subscription: *none.*

Miscellaneous Poems

Amicissimo, et meritissimo BEN: IONSON.

Qvod arte ausus es hic tuâ, POETA,
Si auderent hominum Deiq́ue iuris
Consulti, veteres sequi æmularierque,
O omnes saperemus ad salutem.
His sed sunt veteres araneosi;
Tam nemo veterum est sequutor, vt tu
Illos quòd sequeris nouator audis.
Fac tamen quod agis; tuíque primâ
Libri canitie induantur horâ:
Nam cartis pueritia est neganda,
Nascantúrque senes, oportet, illi
Libri, queis dare vis perennitatem.
Priscis, ingenium facit, labórque
Te parem; hos superes, vt et futuros,
Ex nostrâ vitiositate sumas,
Quâ priscos superamus, et futuros.

I. D.

Textual Introduction

Amic first appeared in the 1607 quarto first edition of Ben Jonson's *Volpone* (siglum 3) and must have been written after the play's initial production in 1606 at the Globe Theatre.

Amic survives only in print. After initially appearing in 3, it was subsequently reprinted in the two states of the first issue of the first edition of volume I of Jonson's *WORKES* (14a–b), the second and third issues of the first edition of volume I (14c–d), the second edition of volume I (14e), and the third edition of the *WORKS* (14g). In 14a and 14b *Amic* appears on sig. ¶6 between two other commendatory poems—H. Holland's "*To his worthy friend, the Author*" (at the top of the page) and E. Bolton's "AD VTRAMQVE ACADEMIAM, / De Beniamin Ionsonio" (at the bottom). Specific reference to any Jonson work is absent from the headings of all three of these poems, and sig. ¶6 in 14a contains no marginalia. Examination of the *CSmH* copy (shelfmark: 62104) of 14b, however, shows that the type-case was loosened during printing to allow the insertion of "*Vpon Seiannus.*," "*In Vulponem.*," and "*In Vulponem.*" in the right margin beside the Holland, Donne, and Bolton poems, respectively. "*In Vulponem*" is thus not properly part of the heading of *Amic*. Examined copies of 14a (*CSmH*, shelfmark: 62101), 14c (*TxU*, shelfmark: Ah J738 +B616a), and 14d (*TxU*, shelfmark: Ah J738 +B616ab and *CSmH*, shelfmark: 62100) lack the marginalia on sig. ¶6; therefore, it seems likely that the text in 14e, which incorporates "In Vulponem." into its heading for the poem, derives from a copy of 14b. The text of *Amic* in 14g likely derives from that in 14e (14f, the first edition of volumes 2 and 3 of Jonson's *Workes*, does not contain the poem). The other seventeenth-century strand of print transmission, which began with E (the first collected edition known to reflect the involvement of the younger John Donne), has the superfluous "In Vulponem." in the heading and therefore likely derives from 14e, though it could derive from a copy of 14b. F is a reissue of the sheets of E; a copy of E or F served as copy-text for G.

The paucity of variants makes determining the copy-texts used by modern editors difficult. The modern editions of Bell (I), Anderson (J), Lowell? (M), Grosart (N), Lowell (O), Chambers (P), Grierson (Q), Hayward (S), Bennett (T), Milgate (Y), and Shawcross (Z) all include some variant of "In Vulponem" in the heading of *Amic*, suggesting at least that these editors are aware of post-14b editions; their texts, however, suggest that most editors have examined 3 or followed a text based on 3. With 3, all modern editions read "Nascantúrque" in line 11 (as opposed to the "Nascuntúrque" found in later editions); and the fact that in line 10 I, J, M–O, S, and T read "chartis" (from post-3 editions) for "cartis" (found in 3) must ultimately stem from an effort to improve the Latin.

The copy-text followed here is 3, the earliest printing, and it requires no emendations other than the expansion of traditional abbreviations. The only points of textual controversy occur in lines 2 ("*Deiq́ꝫ*" vs. "*Deiqꝫ*"), 3 ("*æmularierque*" vs. "*æmulariérque*"), 8 ("*tuíque*" vs. "*tuique*"), 10 ("*cartis*" vs. "*chartis*"), and 11 ("*Nascantúrque*" vs. "*Nascuntúrque*"). As these variants involve matters of convention rather than differences of meaning and may well represent Jonson's revisions of the text in 3, we have retained the copy-text readings.

Textual Apparatus

Copy-text: 3. **Texts collated:** 3 (sig. A1); 14a–d (sig. ¶6); 14e (sig. A5v); 14g (sig. A4v); E (pp. 370–71); F (pp. 370–71); G (pp. 396–97).
Emendations **of the copy-text:** Heading: *et*] & Line 1 *Qvod*] QVod 2 *Deique*] *Deiq́ʒ* 3 *æmularierque*] *æmularierqʒ* 14 *et*] & 16 *et*] &

Historical Collation

Format:
Miscellaneous: *heading(s) centered* 3 14a–e 14g E–G; *text in two columns of eight lines* 14a–e; In Vulponem. *in right* M 14b.
Headings: *Amicissimo, & meritissimo* BEN: IONSON. 3 14a–d. Amicissimo, & meritissimo BEN. JONSON. In Vulponem. 14e 14g E–G.

10 *cartis*] *chartis* 14a–e 14g E–G.

11 *Nascantúrque*] *Nascuntúrqʒ* 14a–e 14g E–G.

13 *facit,*] ~. G.

Subscriptions: I. D. 3 14a–e 14g E–G.

Verbal Variants in Selected Modern Editions

Editions collated: I J M N O P Q S T Y Z.
Format:
Font: *text in roman* I J M–P S T Z; *text in italic* Q Y.
Headings: *Amicissimo et meritissimo* BENJ. JOHNSON. IN VULPONEM. I J M N. AMICISSIMO ET MERITISSIMO BEN. JONSON. IN VULPONEM. O P(Volponem) Q S T Y Z.

3 *veteres*] *om* Y.

5 *His*] His (M *note*: Hi?) N.

6 *sequutor*] secutor P.
7 *quòd*] qui N; *quos* Y. *audis*] audes N.
10 *cartis*] chartis I J M–Q S T.
12 *queis*] quîs P.

Subscriptions: I.D. O. J.D. P T. *om* I J M N Q S Y Z.

Schema of Textual Relationships

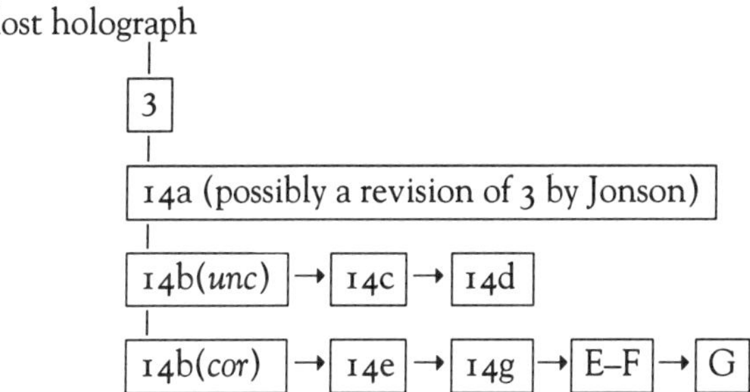

Analyses of Early Printed Copies

BEN: IONSON his VOLPONE Or THE FOXE, 4to, 1607 (siglum 3)

Copies collated: *CSmH*, *L*^{1} (C.12.e.17), *L*^{2} (C.34.d.2.), O^{1} (Mal. 225[4]), O^{2} (Mal. 809).
Relevant section: sig. A1.
Press variants: *none*.
Miscatchings: *none*.

§

THE WORKES OF Beniamin Jonson, fol. (vol. 1), 1616 (sigla 14a, 14b, 14c, 14d)

Copies collated: *CSmH*^{1} (62101), *CSmH*^{2} (62104), *L* (G.11630), *TxU*^{1} (Ah J738 +B616a), *TxU*^{2} (Ah J738 +B616ab).
Relevant section: sig. ¶6.
Press variants: *none*.
Miscatchings: *none*.

§

THE WORKES OF Benjamin Jonson, fol. (vol. 1), 1640 (siglum 14e)

Copies collated: C (Syn.2.64.1), O^1 (G.2.5. Art. Seld), O^2 (Don. d. 65).
Relevant section: sig. A5v.
Press variants: *none.*
Miscatchings: *none.*

§

THE WORKS OF BEN JONSON, fol., 1692 (siglum 14g)

Copies collated: *CLU-C, CSmH, TxU.*
Relevant section: sig. A4v.
Press variants: *none.*
Miscatchings: *none.*

§

Poems, by J. D., 8vo, 1650, 1654 (sigla E, F)

Copies collated: 1650: *CtY*, *L^1* (011641.de.102), *L^2* (1076.f.9). 1654: C^1 (Keynes B.4.12), C^2 (Y.6.10), *CtY*.
Relevant section: sigs. (aa1v)–(aa2); pp. 370–71.
Press variants: *none.*
Miscatchings: *none.*

Note: Examination of multiple copies on a Hinman collator shows that the sections of E and F containing *Amic* are printed from a single typesetting, F being a reissue of the sheets of E.

§

Poems, &c. by John Donne, 8vo, 1669 (siglum G)

Copies collated: *L* (11626.b.16), *CtY*, O (12 Θ 1240).
Relevant section: sigs. Cc6v–7; pp. 396–97.
Press variants: *none.*
Miscatchings: *none.*

Verse from *Conclaue Ignati* and *Ignatius his Conclaue*.

[*IgAver*]

Auersâ facie Ianum referre,

[*IgResemb*]

Resemble Ianus *with a diuerse face,*

•••

[Latin quoted by Donne from Emperor Hadrian]
Animula, vagula, blandula,
Comes hospesque corporis,

[*IgSport*]

My little wandring sportful Soule,
Ghest, and Companion of my body

•••

[*IgOper*]

operoso tramite scandent
Aethereum montem, tangens vicinia solis,
Hymnos ad Phœbi plectrum modulatur Alauda:
Compressis velis, tandem vt remearet, alarum,
Tam subitò recidit, vt saxum segnius ijsset.

[IgLark]

The Larke by busie and laborious wayes,
Hauing climb'd vp th'etheriall hill, doth raise
His Hymnes to Phœbus *Harpe, and striking then*
His sailes, his wings, doth fall downe backe agen
So suddenly, that one may safely say
A stone came lazily, that came that way,

•••

[IgTanto]

Tanto fragore boatuque,
Vt nec sulphureus puluis, quo tota Britanna
Insula, per nimbos Lunam volitasset ad imam,
Si cum substratus Cameræ, conceperat ignem,
Æquando fremeret nostro fragore boatuque.

[IgNoise]

With so great noise and horror,
That had that powder taken fire, by which
All the Isle of Britaine had flowne to the Moone,
It had not equalled this noise and horror.

•••

[Latin quoted by Donne from S. Quaranta, *Summa Bullarii* (1609)]

Parsque minor tantum tota valet integra quantum.

[IgPiece]

That the least peece which thence doth fall,
Will doe one as much good as all.

•••

[IgPlum]

Aut plumam, aut paleam, quæ fluminis innatat ori,
Cùm ventum ad pontem fuerit, qua fornice transit
Angusto flumen, reijci tumide querepelli;
Duxerat at postquam choreas, atque orbibus vndæ
Luserat, à liquidis laqueis, et faucibus hausta,
Fluminis in gremium tandem cedit, reditumque
Desperat spectator scænæ;

[IgFeath]

Feathers or strawes swimme on the waters face,
Brought to the bridge, where through a narrow place
The water passes, throwne backe, and delai'd;
And hauing daunc'd a while, and nimbly plai'd
Vpon the watry circles, Then haue bin
By the streames liquid snares, and iawes, suck'd in
And suncke into the wombe of that swolne bourne,
Leaue the beholder desperate of returne:

•••

[IgQual]

Qualis hesterno madefacta rore,
Et nouo tandem tepefacta sole,
Excutit somnum, Tremulam Coronam
Erigit Herba,
Quæ prius languens, recidens, recurua,
Osculum terræ dederat, Iubarque
Denegatum tamdiu, nunc refulgens
Solis anhelat.

[IgFlow]

As a flower wet with last nights dew, and then
Warm'd with the new Sunne, doth shake of agen
All drowsinesse, and raise his trembling Crowne,
Which crookedly did languish, and stoope downe
To kisse the earth, and panted now to finde
Those beames return'd, which had not long time shin'd,

Textual Introduction

Donne initially published seven Latin verses in the first edition of *Conclaue Ignati* (8a) in 1611. Two of these verses are not original with Donne: he quotes "*Animula, vagula, blandula, / Comes hospesque corporis*" (p. 1) from the apocrypha of the Emperor Hadrian and "*Parsque minor tantum tota valet / integra quantum*" (p. 30) from Stephanus Quaranta, *Summa Bullarii* (Venice, 1609, p. 6). A third verse, *IgQual*, is an original translation into Latin by Donne of lines 127–30 of Dante's *Inferno*, canto 2 (for further information on these derivations, see the Commentary). All five of the verses original with Donne scan: *IgAver* is hendecasyllabic; *IgOper*, *IgTanto*, and *IgPlum* are in dactylic hexameter; and *IgQual* is made up of two Sapphic strophes. The seven English translations, all original with Donne, are printed in verse format in the various issues of *Ignatius*—all are set off from the prose context by space and italics, and the lines begin with upper case letters—and they variously exhibit rhyme, meter, and other technical features of poetry.

Written shortly after or concurrently with *Pseudomartyr* (which was entered in the Stationers' Register on 2 December 1609 and dated 1610), *Conclaue Ignati* must have been completed in late 1610 or very early 1611: it was entered in the Stationers' Register on 24 January 1610/11, and the Earl of Northumberland purchased a copy before 2 February 1611 (see Shapiro, 1953, 96). Also in 1611, Thomas de Villiers published an edition of *Conclaue Ignati* (8b) at Hanau (see Sellin, 1988, 22). Neither Sellin nor Healy (*Ignatius*) dates 8b, though Healy argues (pp. xliii–xlv) for the priority of 8a, and the format of and errors in the errata list in 8b suggest that it was indeed set from a copy of 8a. Finally in 1611 Donne published *Ignatius his Conclaue* (9a), which included seven original English verse translations of his five Latin originals and the two borrowed Latin verses that had appeared in 8a. This work, entered in the Stationers' Register on 18 May 1611, would seem to postdate 8a.

If, as seems almost certain, 8b derives from 8a, then the early printing history of *Conclaue Ignati* is straightforward: Thomas Barlow's 1681 *Papismus* (8c) contains a text of *Conclaue Ignati* (with a title page dated 1680) that must derive from 8b because they agree against 8a in *IgOper* 1 ("*operosa*"); *IgPlum* 2 ("Cum"), 3 ("*tumidéque repelli*"), and 5 ("*hausta*"); and *IgQual* 4 ("*Herba.*"). 8d is a reissue of the sheets of 8c with a collective title page, and its texts of the verses are in the same typesetting.

The first English edition of *Ignatius his Conclaue* (9a) appeared in 1611 and is based on 8a or on an intermediary manuscript. A line-for-line resetting of 9a, the 1626 second edition (9b) makes the corrections called for by 9a's errata list. The 1634 (9c) and 1635 (9d) editions derive from 9b (see variants for *IgResemb* 1, *IgLark* 3, *Iglark* 4, and *IgLark* 5). 9c and 9d present the verses in the same typesetting, though the editions differ at least in the dates on their title pages and in the addition of "*N. Crynes*" at the bottom of page 135 in 9d. Finally, the first and second issues of Donne's *Paradoxes, Problems, Essayes, Characters* (1652; siglum 9e) derive from a copy of 9c or 9d (see variants for *IgSport* 2, *IgLark* 6, and *IgFeath* 6).

Chambers (P), the first modern editor to print these verses, pairs modernized Latin and English versions of each item in an appendix. He follows 8a as copy-text for the Latin, adopting both corrections called for by its errata list in *IgOper* 3; and he uses 9a as copy-text for the English verse, as is evident from his printing the erroneous "eternal" (for the corrected "etheriall") in *IgLark* 2. The subsequent modern editors Hayward (S) and Healy (*Ignatius*) use 9a and its errata list as copy-texts for their English editions, and Healy uses 8a and its errata list as copy-text for his Latin text.

The copy-texts followed here are 8a and 9a and their respective errata lists. All readings in the errata lists for the verses have been accepted; additional emendations include only the expansion of traditional abbreviations. In the original editions the Latin and English verses occur in prose contexts, but are set off from those contexts by space and are printed in italic font; we have left their font and punctuation as they were originally rather than emending them for presentation as autonomous units. The emendation of "*And*" to "*and*" in *IgLark* 3, however, points to an alteration that we have thought it desirable to make in the format of most of this verse. Both 8a and 9a are volumes in duodecimo, a feature dictating that most of the lines, both Latin and English, be broken and printed as runovers; we have followed our modern predecessors in restoring all lines to their original, unbroken form.

Textual Apparatus

Copy-texts: 8a + *its errata list*, 9a + *its errata list*. **Texts collated:** 8a (pp. 1, 2–3, 27, 60, 94); 8b (pp. 5, 5, 13, 23, 34); 8c (pp. 1, 2–3, 22, 48, 75–76); 8d (pp. 1–2, 2–3, 22, 48, 75–76); 9a (pp. 1, 2, 3–4, 40–41, 46, 91, 142); 9b (pp. 1, 2, 3–4, 40–41, 46, 91, 142); 9c (pp. 1, 2, 3, 38, 44, 86–87, 135); 9d (pp. 1, 2, 3, 38, 44, 86–87, 135); 9e (pp. 107, 108, 109, 137–38, 142, 176–77, 215–16); 9f (pp. 107, 108, 109, 137–38, 142, 176–77, 215–16).

Emendations of the copy-text: *headings supplied* **IgOper** Line 3 *Hymnos*] 8a(*err*); *Hymnus* 8a. *Alauda*] 8a(*err*); *Alanda* 8a. **IgLark** Line 2 *th'etheriall*] 9a(*err*); *th'eternall* 9a. 3 *and*] *And* **IgPiece** Line 1 *thence*] *thēce* **IgPlum** Line 5 *et*] *&* **IgQual** Line 3 *somnum*] *somnū* 5 *languens*] *languēs*

Historical Collation

Format:

Font: *text in italics* 8a–d; 9a–f.

Indentations: *IgAver centered on l.* 8a–d; *IgOper l.* 1, *IgTanto l.* 1, *IgQual ll.* 4, *8 ind* 8a–d; *all ll. in IgOper, IgTanto, and IgPlum overhang* 8a–d; *IgResemb centered on l.* 9a–f; *IgNoise l. 1 ind* 9a–f; *all ll. in IgLark, IgNoise, IgPiece, IgFeath, and IgFlow overhang* 9a–f.

Miscellaneous: *all verses set off by space from prose context* 8a–d 9a–f.

Headings: *none.*

IgAver: *no variants.*

IgResemb 1 *face,*] ~; 9b–f.

IgSport 2 *body*] ~, 9c–f.

IgOper 1 *operoso*] *operosa* 8b–d. 2 *montem,*] ~$_{\wedge}$ 8b–d. 3 *Hymnos*] *Hymnus* 8a(*err*: *Hymnos*) 8b(*err*: Hymnos). *Alauda:*] *Alanda:* 8a(*err*: *Alauda:*) 8b(*err*: Alauda:); ~. 8c–d.

IgLark 2 *th'etheriall*] *th'eternall* 9a(*err*: th'etheriall). 3 *Harpe,*] ~: 9b–f. 4 *agen*] ~, 9b–f. 5 *say*] ~, 9b–f. 6 *lazily,*] ~$_{\wedge}$ 9c–f.

IgTanto 2 *sulphureus puluis*] *sulphureuspulvis* 8c–d.

IgNoise: *no variants.*

IgPiece: no variants.

IgPlum 2 *Cùm*] *Cum* 8b–d. 3 *tumide querepelli*] *tumidéque repelli* 8b–d. 4 *vndæ*] *vnda* 8c–d. 5 *hausta,*] ~$_\wedge$ 8b–d.

IgFeath 4 *a while*] *awhile* 9e–f. 6 *iawes,*] ~$_\wedge$ 9e–f. *in*] ~, 9c–f.

IgQual 4 *Herba,*] ~. 8b–d. 8 *anhelat.*] ~, 8c–d.

IgFlow 2 *of*] *off* 9b–f. 6 *shin'd,*] ~. 9e–f.

Subscriptions: *none.*

Verbal Variants in Selected Modern Editions

Editions collated: P S *Ignatius*
Format:
Font: *all ll. in roman* P; *all ll. in italics* S *Ignatius.*
Indentations: *IgOper* 1, *IgTanto* 1, *IgNoise* 1, *IgQual* 4, 8 *ind* P; *IgOper* 1, *IgTanto* 1, *IgQual* 4, 8 *ind* *Ignatius.*
Miscellaneous: *Latin and English versions presented in numbered pairs and printed seriatim in Appendix E* P; *all verses spatially set off from prose context* S; *all verses except IgAver spatially set off from prose context* *Ignatius.*
Headings: *none.*

IgOper 1 *scandent*] *scandens* *Ignatius.*

IgLark 2 *th'etheriall*] th'eternal P.

IgPlum 3 *tumide querepelli*] tumideque repelli P *Ignatius.* 4 *vndæ*] unda P.

IgQual 7 *tamdiu*] tam diu P.

IgFlow 2 *of*] off P S. 6 *Those*] These P.

Subscriptions: *none.*

Schema of Textual Relationships: *Conclaue Ignati*

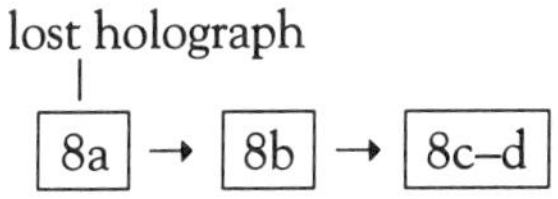

lost holograph
|
[8a] → [8b] → [8c–d]

Schema of Textual Relationships: *Ignatius his Conclaue*

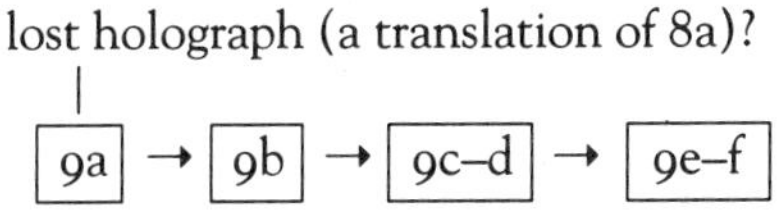

lost holograph (a translation of 8a)?
|
[9a] → [9b] → [9c–d] → [9e–f]

Analyses of Early Printed Copies: *Conclaue Ignati*

Conclaue Ignati, 12mo, 1611 (siglum 8a)

Copies collated: C^{1} (Keynes B.4.22^{1}), C^{2} (Syn.8.60.115), *CT* (C.11.161), *L* (864.b.11.[2]), O (Lister I 90 [1]), *OCh* (f.7.44).
Relevant sections: sig. A4, p. 1; sig. A4v–5, pp. 2–3; sig. B5, p. 27; sig. C9v, p. 60; sig. E2v, p. 94; sig. E5v.
Press variants: *none*.
Miscatchings: *none*.

Note: An errata list is printed on sig. E5v.

§

CONCLAVE IGNATI, 4to, 1611 (siglum 8b)

Copies collated: C^{1} (Acton.c.34.113^{4}), C^{2} (Acton.d.54.3^{3}), *L* (C.110.f.46).
Relevant sections: sig. A3, p. 5; sig. A3, p. 5; sig. B3, p. 13; sig. C4, p. 23; sig. E1v, p. 34; sig. E2, p. 35.
Press variants: *none*.
Miscatchings: *none*.

Note: An errata list is printed on sig. E2.

§

PAPISMUS Regiæ Potestatis Eversor, 8vo, 1681, 1682 (sigla 8c–d)

Copies collated: C (Keynes B.5.20), *DFo* (B837), *L* (1025.a.28), O (8° A.1.Linc.).
Relevant sections: sig. I8, p. 1; sig. I8v–K, pp. 2–3; sig. L2v, p. 22; sig. M7v, p. 48; sig. O5r–v, pp. 75–76.
Press variants: *none*.
Miscatchings: *none*.

Note: The texts of the verses in 8d are in the same typesetting as those in 8c.

Analyses of Early Printed Copies: *Ignatius his Conclaue*

Ignatius his Conclaue, 12mo, 1611 (siglum 9a)

Copies collated: C (Syn.8.61.170), *CSmH* (60176), *L* (C.111.a.12)
Relevant sections: sig. A6, p. 1; sig. A6v, p. 2; sig. A7r–v, pp. 3–4; sigs. C1v–2, pp. 40–41; sig. C4v, p. 46; sig. E3, p. 91; sig. G4v, p. 142.
Press variants: *none*.
Miscatchings: *none*.

Note: An errata list is printed on sig. G8.

§

Ignatius his Conclave, 12mo, 1626 (siglum 9b)

Copies collated: C (Syn.8.62.65), *L* (864.b.11[3]).
Relevant sections: sig. A7, p. 1; sig. A7v, p. 2; sig. A8r–v, pp. 3–4; sigs. C2v–3, pp. 40–41; sig. C5v, p. 46; sig. E5, p. 91; sig. G5v, p. 142.
Press variants: *none*.
Miscatchings: *none*.

Note: The text of 9b is a line-for-line resetting of that in 9a.

§

Ignatius his Conclave, 12mo, 1634, 1635 (Sigla 9c–d)

Copies collated: C^1 (Peterborough E.2.30a), C^2 (Syn.8.63.42), *CSmH*, L^1 (4092.a.9), L^2 (C.122.a.2b), O (Ashmole 950).
Relevant sections: sig. A4, p. 1; sig. A4v, p. 2; sig. A5, p. 5; sig. B10v, p. 38; sig. C1v, p. 44; sigs. D10v–11, pp. 86–87; sig. F11, p. 135.
Press variants: *none*.
Miscatchings: *none*.

Note: 9c and 9d are different editions, but the sheets containing the verses in both were printed from the same typesetting.

§

PARADOXES, PROBLEMS, ESSAYES, CHARACTERS, 12mo, 1652 (sigla 9e–f)

Copies collated: C^1 (Keynes B.5.4), C^2 (Syn 8.65.79), *L* (G.19723 [1.]), O (Douce D.40).
Relevant sections: sig. F6, p. 107; sig. F6v, p. 108; sig. F7, p. 109; sig. G9r–v, pp. 137–38; sig. G11v, p. 142; sig. I4v–5, pp. 176–77; sig. K12r–v, pp. 215–16.
Press variants: *none*.
Miscatchings: *none*.

Note: 9f is a reissue of the sheets of 9e with a new title page reading "*PROBLEMES*" for 9e's "*PROBLEMS*."

Translated out of *Gazæus, Vota Amico facta. fol.* 160.

GOD grant thee thine own wish, and grant thee mine,
Thou, who dost, best friend, in best things outshine;
May thy soul, ever chearfull, nere know cares,
Nor thy life, ever lively, know gray haires.
Nor thy hand, ever open, know base holds,
Nor thy purse, ever plump, know pleits, or folds.
Nor thy tongue, ever true, know a false thing,
Nor thy word, ever mild, know quarrelling.
Nor thy works, ever equall, know disguise,
Nor thy fame, ever pure, know contumelies.
Nor thy prayers, know low objects, still Divine;
God grant thee thine own wish, and grant thee mine.

Textual Introduction

Of the seven editions published during Donne's lifetime of the *Pia Hilaria Variaqve Carmina* by the Belgian Jesuit Angelin Gazet (1568–1653), the Latin original of Donne's "Translated out of *Gazæus, Vota Amico facta. fol.* 160" (*Gaz*) appears on page 160 only in the 1619 edition.

Gaz is among the material first added in E by Donne's son, John Donne the younger; the translation was subsequently issued in the same typesetting in F. A copy of either E or F served as copy-text for the setting in G.

The modern editions of Tonson (H), Bell (I), Anderson (J), Alford (L), Lowell? (M), and Grosart (N) all read the plural "words" in line 8 where E–G have the singular "word." It is likely that editorial trivialization or a typesetting error accounts for the introduction of this variant in H and that I, J, L, and M repeat it successively from that first occurrence (it also seems probable that Grosart derives the plural reading ultimately from H, though he explicitly cites G as his copy-text). All seven editions of Gazaeus available to Donne give the plural construction "verba . . . nesciant" in line 8, however, and it is possible that the plural "words" in the eighteenth- and nineteenth-century editions derives from an awareness of this fact (indeed, whether the singular "word" in E–G shows Donne choosing grammatical parallelism over accuracy of translation or merely reflects a typesetting error is indeterminate). Lowell (O), Chambers (P), Grierson (Q), Hayward (S), Bennett (T), Milgate (Y), Shawcross (Z), and Patrides (DD) all read "word" in line 8 and list E as their copy-text.

E, the earliest artifact in which the poem appears, provides the copy-text, and the only emendation required is the expansion of one abbreviation. How closely the text of E represents what Donne wrote is problematic: elsewhere the younger Donne has not provided accurate texts; and the punctuation in E certainly does not reflect that in any of the Latin originals, all of which treat the verse as a single sentence.

Textual Apparatus

Copy-text: E. **Texts collated:** E (p. 385); F (p. 385); G (p. 409).
Emendations of the copy-text: Line 12 &] and

Historical Collation:

Format: *nothing to report.*
Headings: Translated out of *Gazæus, Vota Amico facta. fol.* 160. E–G.
Line-by-line variants: *none.*
Subscriptions: *none.*

Verbal Variants in Selected Modern Editions

Editions collated: H I J L M N O P Q S T Y Z DD.
Format: *nothing to report.*
Headings: *Translated out of Gazæus, Vota Amico facta. fol.* 160. H I J L–N P Q S Y Z. VOTA AMICO FACTA. TRANSLATED OUT OF GAZÆUS, *fol.* 160. O T. Translated out of Gazæus DD.

8 word] words H I J L–N.

Subscriptions: *none.*

Analyses of Early Printed Copies

Poems, by J. D., 8vo, 1650, 1654 (sigla E, F)

Copies collated: 1650: *CtY*, *MH*, *L*[1] (011641 de 102), *L*[2] (1076 f. 9), O (Antiq. f. E. 1650.2). 1654: C[1] (Keynes B.4.12), C[2] (Y.6.10), *CSmH*, *CtY*.
Relevant section: sig. (bb), p. 385.
Press variants: *none.*
Miscatchings: *none.*

Note: Examination of multiple copies on a Hinman collator shows that the pages of E and F containing *Gaz* are printed from a single typesetting, F being a reissue of the sheets of E.

§

Poems, &c. by John Donne, 8vo, 1669 (siglum G)

Copies collated: *CtY*, *L* (11626 b.16), O (12 Θ 1240).
Relevant section: sig. Dd5, p. 409.
Press variants: *none*.
Miscatchings: *none relevant*.

Stationes, siue Periodi in Morbo, ad quas referuntur Meditationes sequentes.

1 Insultus *Morbi primus;* 2 *Post,* Actio læsa;
3 Decubitus *sequitur tandem;* 4 Medicusque *vocatur;*
5 Solus *adest;* 6 Metuit; 7 Socios *sibi iungier instat;*
8 *Et* Rex *ipse suum mittit;* 9 Medicamina scribunt;
10 Lentè *et Serpenti satagunt occurrere Morbo.*
11 *Nobilibusque trahunt, a cincto corde, venenum,*
Succis, *et* Gemmis; *et quæ* Generosa, *ministrant*
Ars, *et* Natura, *instillant;* 12 *Spirante* Columbâ,
Suppositâ pedibus, reuocantur ad ima vapores;
13 *Atque* Malum Genium, *numeroso* stigmate, *fassus,*
Pellitur ad pectus, Morbique Suburbia, Morbus:
14 *Idque notant* Criticis, Medici, *euenisse* diebus.
15 *Interea* insomnes *Noctes ego duco, Diesque:*
16 *Et properare* meum, *clamant, e turre propinqua*
Obstreperæ Campanæ, aliorum *in funere, funus.*
17 *Nunc* lento sonitu *dicunt,* Morieris; 18 *At inde,*
Mortuus *es, sonitu* celeri, pulsuque agitato.
19 Oceano *tandem emenso, aspicienda resurgit*
Terra; *vident, iustis,* Medici, *iam* cocta *mederi*
Se posse, indicijs; 20 Id agunt; 21 *Atque annuit* Ille,
Qui per eos clamat, linquas iam Lazare *lectum;*
22 *Sit* Morbi Fomes *tibi* Cura; 23 Metusque Relabi.

Traditional Format

Stationes, *siue* Periodi *in* Morbo, *ad quas referuntur* Meditationes sequentes.

1 Insultus *Morbi primus;*
2 *Post,* Actio læsa;
3 Decubitus *sequitur tandem;*
4 Medicusque *vocatur;*
5 Solus *adest;* 6 Metuit;
7 Socios *sibi iungier instat;*
8 *Et* Rex *ipse suum mittit;*
9 Medicamina scribunt;
10 Lentè *et Serpenti satagunt occurrere* Morbo.
11 *Nobilibusque trahunt, a cincto corde, venenum,*
Succis, *et* Gemmis; *et quæ* Generosa, *ministrant*
Ars, *et* Natura, *instillant;*
12 *Spirante* Columbâ,
Suppositâ pedibus, reuocantur ad ima vapores;
13 *Atque* Malum Genium, *numeroso* stigmate, *fassus,*
Pellitur ad pectus, Morbique Suburbia, Morbus:
14 *Idque notant* Criticis, *Medici, euenisse* diebus.
15 *Interea* insomnes *Noctes ego duco, Diesque:*

16 *Et properare* meum, *cla-*
mant, e turre propinqua
Obstreperæ Campanæ, alio-
rum *in funere, funus.*
17 *Nunc* lento sonitu *dicunt,*
Morieris; 18 At *inde,*
Mortuus *es, sonitu* celeri,
pulsuque agitato.
19 Oceano *tandem emenso,*
aspicienda resurgit
Terra; *vident, iustis,* Medici,
iam cocta *mederi*
Se posse, indicijs; 20 Id agunt;
21 *Atque annuit* Ille,
Qui per eos *clamat, linquas*
iam Lazare *lectum;*
22 *Sit* Morbi Fomes *tibi*
Cura; 23 Metusque Relabi.

Meditation Headings in *DEVOTIONS VPON Emergent Occasions.*

1.
Insultus Morbi primus;

The first alteration, The first grudging of the sicknesse.

2. Actio Læsa.

The strength, and the fun= ctiõ of the Senses, & other faculties change and faile.

3. Decubitus sequitur tandem.

The Patient takes his bed.

4. Medicusque vocatur.

The Phisician is sent for.

5. Solus adest.

The Phisician comes.

6. Metuit.

The Phisician is afraid.

7. Socios sibi iungier
instat.

*The Phisician desires to
haue others ioyned with
him.*

8. Et Rex ipse suum
mittit.

*The King sends his owne
Phisician.*

9. Medicamina scribunt.

*Vpon their Consultation,
they prescribe.*

10. Lentè et Serpenti sata-
gunt occurrere Morbo.

*They find the Disease to steale
on insensibly, and endeauour
to meet with it so.*

11. Nobilibusque trahunt, a
cincto Corde, venenum,
Succis et Gemmis, et quæ
generosa, Ministrant
Ars, et Natura, instillant.

*They vse Cordials, to keep
the venim and Malig=
nitie of the disease from
the Heart.*

12.—Spirante Columbâ
Suppositâ pedibus, Reuo-
cantur ad ima vapores.

*They apply Pidgeons, to
draw the vapors from
the Head.*

13. Ingeniumque malum, nu-
meroso stigmate, fassus

Pellitur ad pectus, Morbique Suburbia, Morbus.

The Sicknes declares the infe-ction and malignity thereof by spots.

14. Idque notant Criticis, Medici euenisse Diebus.

The Phisicians obserue these accidents to haue fallen vpon the criticall dayes.

15. Intereà insomnes noctes Ego duco, Diesque.

I sleepe not day nor night.

16. Et properare meum clamant, è Turre pro-pinqua, Obstreperæ Campanæ aliorum in funere, funus.

From the bels of the church adioyning, I am daily remembred of my buri-all in the funeralls of others.

17. Nunc lento sonitu dicunt, Morieris.

Now, this Bell tolling soft-ly for another, saies to me, Thou must die.

18. —At inde Mortuus es, Sonitu cele-ri, pulsuque agitato.

The bell rings out, and tells me in him, that I am dead.

19. Oceano tandem e-menso, aspicienda re-surgit Terra; vident,

iustis, medici, iam
cocta mederi se posse,
indicijs.

At last, the Physitians, after a long and stormie voyage, see land; They haue so good signes of the concoction of the disease, as that they may safely proceed to purge.

20. Id agunt.

Vpon these indications of digested matter, they proceed to purge.

21. —Atque annuit Ille,
Qui, per eos, clamat,
Linquas iam, Lazare,
lectum.

God prospers their practise, and he, by them, calls Lazarus *out of his tombe, mee out of my bed.*

22. Sit morbi fomes
tibi cura;

The Physitians consider the root and occasion, the embers, and coales, and fuell of the disease, and seeke to purge or correct that.

23.—Metusque, Relabi.

They warne mee of the fearefull danger of relapsing.

Textual Introduction

(In its block form, as various commentators have noted, *Stat* is made up of 22 hexameter lines, and we have so presented it in the first version printed above. The volumes in which the poem appeared in the seventeenth century, however, were all of either 12mo or 24mo format, and this fact undoubtedly influenced the physical shape that the poem assumed in those printings. Since much of the commentary responds to the shape as well as to the content of the poem, we have also printed it in its traditional format and have keyed the following introductory remarks, the Textual Apparatus, and the Commentary to this second, traditional version.)

Stat first appeared in the 1624 (siglum 20a) first issue of the first edition of Donne's *Devotions vpon Emergent Occasions* and must have been written during or shortly after a serious illness in late November and early December of 1623.

Surviving in print only, *Stat* appears in two forms: as a continuous block of verse composed of twenty-three numbered segments preceding the prose text of the *Devotions* and as that same body of verse divided into twenty-three separate segments, each of which is accompanied by a loose English translation and printed at the head of one of the twenty-three "Meditations" in the *Devotions*. *Stat* initially appeared in identical typesettings in 20a and 20b (the first and second issues of the first edition), and the text in 20c (the second edition of 1624) derives from that in 20a/20b. 20c supplies the "15." obviously omitted from line 15.1 in the meditation headings in 20a/20b, and in line 20 introduces the erroneous "stignate" (for "stigmate") into the line of transmission. (More specifically, Raspa—in *Devotions*, liii—argues that 20c derives from a copy of 20a/20b that has the corrected state of a note on page 340.) The third edition, which appears in first and second issues dated respectively 1626 (20d) and 1627 (20e), is a line-for-line, error-filled resetting of 20c. The genealogy of the text of the 1634 fourth edition (20f) is not entirely clear: Raspa, citing the text of the prose *Devotions* as well as that of *Stat*, asserts that 20f "was set from a copy" of 20c, "with limited reference, if any" to 20d/20e (liii-liv). 20f in fact lacks a number of the errors found in 20d/20e—correctly reading "INsultus" in line 1 for the erroneous "INcubitus," "*jungier*" in line 6 for the erroneous "*iungitur*," "*Obstreperæ*" in line 29 for the erroneous "*Obstrepera*," "*sonitu*" in line 33 for the erroneous "*sonita*," and "properare" in line 16.1 for the erroneous "properate," for instance—and these readings suggest that the influence of 20d/20e on 20f was indeed "limited . . . , if any." In addition, 20f also avoids errors that 20d and 20e share with 20c, restoring the erroneous "stignate" of line 20 to "stigmate" (the uncorrected state of 20f reads "stignate," as in copy C, shelfmark Keynes B.4.32), the erroneous "11" in line 32 to "18," the erroneous "celari" in lines 18.2–3 to "celeri," and the erroneous "aspicianda" in line 19.2 to "aspicienda"; and these corrections suggest either that the compositor of 20f was a good enough Latinist to institute these changes on his own or, perhaps more likely, that he consulted a copy of the first edition (20a/20b) in setting his text of *Stat*. The text of *Stat* in the 1638 fifth edition (20g) almost certainly derives from that in 20f, as is evident from their many instances of identical line formatting, punctuation, choice of font, and syllabication of run-over words. 20g also appears to show the influence of 20d/20e, as it reverts to the erroneous "*jungitur*" in line 6 (an error it uniquely carries over to line 7.1), the erroneous "stignate" in line 20 (though it could have gotten this reading from an uncorrected copy of 20f), and the erroneous "*sonita*" in line 33. A translation of the *Devotions vpon Emergent Occasions* into Dutch that retains *Stat* in Latin, John Grindal's 1655 *Aendachtige Bedenckingen* (siglum 40) most likely derives its text from 20f rather than from 20g (Grindal reads "jungier" where 20g has "jungitur" in lines 6 and 7.1, "sonitu" where 20g has "sonita" in line 33, and "interea" where 20g has "interia" in line 15.1). The only important instance in which Grindal reads with 20g against 20f occurs in line 42, where 20f has the obviously incorrect "Lazere," which 20g—perhaps influenced by 20d/20e—had corrected to "Lazare." Grindal likely made this correction independently.

Modern editions of the *Devotions vpon Emergent Occasions* have been issued by Alford (L), Pickering (1840; *Keynes*, item 41), D. A. Talboys (1841), Chambers (P), Sparrow (R), William H. Draper (1925; *Keynes*, item 42*b*), Hayward (S), Anonymous (1959; *Keynes*, item 42*h*), Savage (1975; see the Commentary), and Raspa (*Devotions*). Chambers prints in his Appendix F both the block Latin form of *Stat* and "an English version of the Latin" (2:315), written in what Alexander B. Grosart thought was Donne's hand on blank leaves preceding the title-page of Grosart's copy of 20e (see the Commentary). Since Chambers does not reproduce such of 20e's errors as "INcubitus" (l. 1), "stignate" (l. 20), and "sonita" (l. 33), however, it seems likely that he consulted an edition other than 20e in establishing his text—perhaps the first (20a/20b), since he mentions it in introducing the two poems. In the standard modern edition (*Devotions*), Raspa follows 20a/20b as copy-text.

Since 20a/20b has the only text of *Stat* in either its block or segmented form that could possibly derive from an authoritative manuscript, 20a is used here as the copy-text for both forms of *Stat*. Although the block and segmented texts are very similar, they differ verbally in segments two and thirteen and throughout in their accidentals; thus, we have treated the segmented form as a different version of the block *Stat*. In our text of the segmented form, we also provide transcriptions of the English phrases that follow the Latin verse of each segment. The only emendations of the copy-texts are the addition of "15." in line 15.1, the regularization of letter size and font throughout, and the expansion of standard contractions. The only point of textual controversy occurs in line four of the eleventh section of the segmented version: examined copies C^2 and C^4 of 20b (which have the verse in the same typesetting as that of 20a) have a comma following "Ministrant." Since the equivalent reading in the block version (l. 14) lacks the comma, since the only complete copy of 20a examined (*CSmH*^{2})

lacks the comma (C[1], the other examined copy, lacks sheet M on which the verse occurs), and since the corrected and uncorrected readings cannot be distinguished with certainty (though the sense of the passage would suggest that the reading with the comma is the corrected reading), we have retained "Ministrat" without a comma rather than emending.

Textual Apparatus: *Stat*

Copy-text: 20a. **Texts collated:** 20a (sigs. A5–6); 20b (sigs. A5–6); 20c (sig. A5r–v); 20d (sig. A5r–v); 20e (sig. A5r–v); 20f (sig. A4r–v); 20g (sig. A3r–v), 40 (sig. 4r–v).

Emendations of the copy-text: Heading: Me-ditationes] Me=ditationes Line 1 Insultus] INsultus 3 *tandem*] *tandē* 4 Medicusque] Medicusq; 9 *et*] *&* 11 *Nobilibusque*] *Nobilibusq;* 13 *et*] *&* *et*] *&* 15 *et*] *&* 19 *Atque*] *Atq;* 21 *Morbique*] *Morbiq;* 23 *Idque*] *Idq;* *Diesque*] *Diesq;* 34 pulsuque] pulsuq; 40 *Atque*] *Atq;* 44 23] 23 Metusque] Metusq;

Historical Collation: *Stat*

Format:

Font: *text alternates between roman and italics* 20a–g; *text in italics* 40.

Indentations: *even lines ind* 20a–g; *text printed in block of twenty-three segments with second and all following lines ind* 40.

Miscellaneous: *lacks pagination* 20f–g.

Headings: *Stationes, siue Pe- / riodi in Morbo, ad / quas referuntur* Me- / *ditationes se- / quentes.* 20a–g 40.

1 Insultus] INcubitus 20d–e.

6 *iungier*] *iungitur* 20d–e 20g.

14 *ministrant*] ~. 20d–e 20g 40.

16 Columbâ] Columba 20c–g 40.

17 *Suppositâ*] *Supposita* 20c–g 40.

20 stigmate] stignate 20c–f(*unc*) 20g 40. *fassus,*] ~. 20d–e.

24 *Medici,*] ~‸ 20c–g 40.

26 *Diesque:*] ~‸ 20c–f; ~, 20g 40.

27–28 *cla-mant,*] ~‸ 20c–g 40. *e*] *è* 20f–g 40.

29 *Obstreperæ*] *Obstrepera* 20d–e.

32 18] 11 20c–e.

33 *es*,] ~; 20f–g 40. *sonitu*] *sonita* 20d–e 20g.

37 *vident*,] ~‸ 40.

39 agunt;] ~‸ 20c–g 40.

42 *iam*] ~, 40. Lazare] Lazere 20f; ~, 40.

Subscriptions: *none*.

Textual Apparatus: Meditation Headings

Copy-text: 20a. **Texts collated:** 20a (pp. 1, 21, 40, 64, 92, 115, 145, 175, 201, 226, 252, 284, 312, 331, 365, 388, 410, 436, 469, 509, 537, 569, 596); 20b (pp. 1, 21, 40, 64, 92, 115, 145, 175, 201, 226, 252, 284, 312, 331, 365, 388, 410, 436, 469, 509, 537, 569, 596); 20c (pp. 1, 20, 38, 60, 87, 109, 137, 166, 166[190], 215, 239, 269, 295, 314, 346, 368, 389, 389[413], 443, 480, 505, 534, 558); 20d (pp. 1, 20, 38, 61[60], 87, 109, 137, 166, 190, 215, 239, 269, 295, 14, 346, 368, 389, 413, 443, 480, 505, 534, 558); 20e (pp. 1, 20, 38, 61[60], 87, 09, 137, 166, 190, 215, 239, 269, 295, 314, 346, 368, 389, 413, 443, 480, 505, 534, 558); 20f (sigs. A5, B1, B8, C5, D4v, E2, F2, G2, G12v, H11v, I10, K10v, L9, M5, N6v, O4, O12v, P10v, Q12, S4, T3, V4v, X6); 20g (sigs. A4, A11, B5v, C1v, C11v, D8, E7, F5v, G3, G12v, H10, I9, K6v, L1v, M2, M10, N6, O3v, 3v, Q5v, R3, S1v, S10v); 40 (pp. 1, 9, 15, 24, 34, 43, 54, 65, 75, 85, 94, 105, 115, 122, 135, 143, 151, 161, 173, 188, 197, 209, 219).

Emendations of the copy-text: Line 4.1 Medicusque] Medicusq; 9.1 scribunt] scribūt 10.1 et] & 11.1 Nobilibusque] Nobilibusq; 11.3 et] & et] & 13.1 13] 13 Ingeniumque] Ingeniumq; 13.3 Morbique] Morbiq; 14.1 Idque] Idq; 15.1 15.] *om* 21.1 21.] ~$_{\wedge}$

Historical Collation: Meditation Headings

Format:

Imperfections: *sheet* M *missing* 20a(C[1]); *sheet* E *missing* 40(*AUB*).

Indentations: *headings generally centered* 20a–g 40.

Font: *text in roman* 20a–g; *text in italics* 40.

Miscellaneous: *ms. correction* in-/dicis → in-/diciis (*l.* 19.6) 20d(*IU*); *ms. correction* stignate → stigmate (*l.* 13.2) 20g(C).

Headings: *none.*

1.2 primus;] ~. 40.

2.1 Læsa.] ~; 20g.

3.2 tandem.] ~; 20g.

7.1 iungier] jungitur 20g.

11.1 trahunt,] ~‸ 40. a] à 40.
11.2 Corde,] ~‸ 40. venenum,] ~‸ 40.
11.4 generosa,] ~‸ 40. Ministrant] ~, 20b(*cor?*).
11.5 Ars] *ars* 40.
12.1 Columbâ] *Columba* 40. 13.1 malum,] ~‸ 40.
13.2 stigmate,] ~‸ 40. fassus] ~, 20f–g 40.
13.4 Suburbia] Suburdia 20c.
15.1 15.] *om* 20a–b. Intereậ] Interiâ 20g; *Interea* 40.
15.2 duco,] ~‸ 40.
16.1 properare] properate 20d–e. meum] ~, 20f–g 40.
16.2–3 pro-pinqua,] ~‸ 20f–g 40.
18.2–3 cele-ri] celari 20c–e.
19.1 tandem] tandum 40.
19.2 aspicienda] aspicianda 20c–e.
19.3 Terra;] ~, 40. vident,] ~‸ 40.
19.4 medici] Medici 20f–g 40.
19.5 posse,] ~‸ 20f–g 40.
19.6 indicijs] indicis 20d–e.
21.2 eos,] ~‸ 40.
21.3 iam,] ~‸ 20f–g. Lazare] *Lasare* 40.
22.2 cura;] ~. 20f–g 40.
23.1 Metusque,] Metusqȝ‸ 20f–g; ~‸ 40.

Subscriptions: *none.*

Verbal Variants in Selected Modern Editions

Editions collated: P *Devotions.*
Format:
Font: *text in roman* P; *text balanced between roman and italic in Stat,* Meditation *Headings in boldfaced roman* Devotions.
Indentations: *even ll. ind* P; *ll. 2, 4, 6, 8, 16, 22, 29, 40 ind,* Meditation *Headings centered but not printed as verse* Devotions.
Miscellaneous: *does not print* Meditation *Headings separately* P; *runs together ll. 9–10, 11–12, 13–14, 17–18, 19–20, 23–24, 25–26, 27–28, 29–30, 31–32, 32–34, 35–36, 37–38, and 41–42, printing Stat in 34 ll.* Devotions.

Headings: STATIONES SINE PERIODI IN MORBO, AD QUAS REFERUNTUR MEDITATIONES SEQUENTES. P *Devotions(sive)*.

6 *iungier*] iungitur P.

39 *indicijs*] iudiciis P.

Subscriptions: *none*.

Schema of Textual Relationships

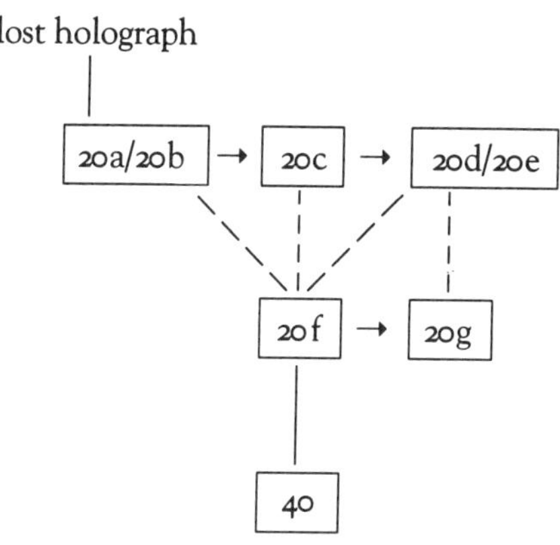

Analyses of Early Printed Copies

DEVOTIONS VPON Emergent Occasions, 12mo, 1624 (sigla 20a, 20b)

Copies collated: C[1] (Keynes B.4.26), C[2] (Keynes B.4.27), C[3] (Peterborough H.2.41[3]), C[4] (Syn.8.62.69), *CSmH*[1] (53917), *CSmH*[2] (53918), *TCC* (C.34.32).
Relevant sections: sigs. A5–6; sig. B1, p. 1; sig. B11, p. 21; sig. C8v, p. 40; sig. D8v, p. 64; sig. E10v, p. 92; sig. F10, p. 115; sig. H1, p. 145; sig. I4, p. 175; sig. K5, p. 201; sig. L5v, p. 226; sig. M6v, p. 252; sig. N10v, p. 284; sig. O12v, p. 312; sig. P10, p. 331; sig. R3, p. 365; sig. S2v, p. 388; sig. T1v, p. 410; sig. V2v, p. 436; sig. X7, p. 469; sig. Z3, p. 509; sig. 2A5, p. 537; sig. 2B9, p. 569.
Press variants:

Sheet M, outer forme

	Uncorrected? (C[1,3], *CSmH*[1–2], *TCC*)	Corrected? (C[2,4])
M6v (p. 252):		
l. 11.4	Ministrant	Ministrant,

Miscatchings: *none*.

Note: The texts of *Stat* and the Meditation Headings in all examined copies of 20b are in the same typesetting as those in 20a.

§

DEVOTIONS VPON Emergent Occasions, 12mo, 1624 (siglum 20c)

Copies collated: C, *CSmH*.
Relevant sections: sig. A5r–v; sig. A6, p. 1; sig. B3v, p. 20; sig. B12v, p. 38; sig. C11v, p. 60; sig. E1, p. 87; sig. E12, p. 109; sig. G2, p. 137; sig. H4v, p. 166; sig. I4v, p. 166[190]; sig. K5, p. 215; sig. L5, p. 239; sig. M8, p. 269; sig. N9, p. 295; sig. O6v, p. 314; sig. P10v, p. 346; sig. Q9v, p. 368; sig. R8, p. 389; sig. S8, p. 389[413]; sig. T11, p. 443; sig. X5v, p. 480; sig. Y6, p. 505; sig. Z8v, p. 534; sig. 2A8v, p. 558.
Press variants: *none*.
Miscatchings: *none*.

§

DEVOTIONS VPON Emergent Occasions, 12mo, 1626/1627 (sigla 20d, 20e)

Copies collated: C[1] (Keynes B.4.29), C[2] (Keynes B.4.31), *IU*, *L* (853.b.5), O.
Relevant sections: sig. A5r–v; sig. A6, p. 1; sig. B3v, p. 20; sig. B12v, p. 20; sig. C11v, p. 61[60]; sig. E1, p. 87; sig. E12, p. 109; sig. G2, p. 137; sig. H4v, p. 166; sig. I4v, p. 190; sig. K5, p. 215; sig. L5, p. 239; sig. M8, p. 269; sig. N9, p. 295; sig. O6v, p. 314; sig. P10v, p. 346; sig. Q9v, p. 368; sig. R8, p. 389; sig. S8, p. 413; sig. T11, p. 443; sig. X5v, p. 480; sig. Y6, p. 505; sig. Z8v, p. 534; sig. A8v, p. 558.
Press variants: *none*.
Miscatchings: *none*.

Note: The texts of *Stat* and the Meditation Headings in all examined copies of 20e are in the same typesetting as those in 20d.

§

DEVOTIONS VPON Emergent occasions, 24mo in 12's, 1634 (siglum 20f)

Copies collated: C (Keynes B.4.32), *MH*.
Relevant sections: sig. A4r–v; sigs. A5, B1, B8, C5, D4v, E2, F2, G2, G12v, H11v, I10, K10v, L9, M5, N6v, O4, O12v, P10v, Q12, S4, T3, V4v, X6.
Press variants:

Sheet A, outer forme

	Uncorrected (C)	Corrected (*MH*)
A4v:		
l. 20	stignate	stigmate

Miscatchings: *none*.

§

DEVOTIONS VPON Emergent occasions, 24mo in 12's, 1638 (siglum 20g)

Copies collated: *C* (Keynes B.4.33), *L*.
Relevant sections: sig. A3r–v; sigs. A4, A11, B5v, C1v, C11v, D8, E7, F5v, G3, G12v, H10, I9, K6v, L1v, M2, M10, N6, O3v, P3v, Q5v, R3, S1v, S10v.
Press variants: *none*.
Miscatchings: *none*.

§

Aendachtige BEDENCKINGEN, 12mo, 1655 (siglum 40)

Copies collated: *AUB* (2328 F 28), W. van Ghent (private copy).
Relevant sections: 4r–v; sig. A1, p. 1; sig. A5, p. 9; sig. A8, p. 15; sig. A12v, p. 24; sig. B5v, p. 34; sig. B10, p. 43; C3v, p. 54; C9, p. 65; sig. D2, p. 75; sig. D7, p. 85; sig. D11v, p. 94; sig. E5, p. 105; sig. E10, p. 115; sig. F1v, p. 122; sig. F8, p. 135; sig. F12, p. 143; sig. G4, p. 151; sig. G9, p. 161; sig. H3, p. 173; sig. H10v, p. 188; sig. I3, p. 197; sig. I9, p. 209; sig. K2, p. 219.
Press variants: *none*.
Miscatchings: *none*.

Dubium

Paul G. Stanwood (1967) first argued for Donne's authorship of "The Apotheosis of Ignatius of Loyola" found in volume 27 of the Hunter manuscript collection owned by the Dean and Chapter of Durham and in the Cathedral Library. For subsequent discussion, see the Commentary. Stanwood's transcription is presented here.

Ignatij Loyolae ἀποθέωσις.

Qui sacer ante fuit, sanctus nunc incipit esse
  Loyola & in divis annumeratus ovat.

Sed queritur plenis a tergo & margine fastis
  in minio, quo stet non superesse locum.

Repperit: expuncto multum Librarius audax
  Germano, haud veritu'st substituisse nothum.

Lis hinc orta ferox, neque enim novus hospes abire,
  cedere nec primus, nec simul esse volunt.

Quid pater hic sanctus? qui vincit et omnia solvit,
  Solvit et hunc nodum dexteritate novâ,

State simul dixit, stabuloque quiescite vestro,
  Ut Simon & Judas, quos tenet una dies;

Sin minus expectet quartani Ignatius anni
  Februa, conflatum possideatque diem.

Dr Dun. Deane of Paules.

Appendix 1

The following group of epigrams first appears in the 1652 issue of *Paradoxes, Problems, Essayes, Characters* (Wing D1866; *Keynes*, item 45), where the title page describes them as "a Book of Epigrams: Written in Latin by the same Author [Donne]; translated into English by *J: Maine*, D. D." For the history of controversy over the status of these poems and their possible relationship to lost Latin originals by Donne, see the Commentary. The poems are here transcribed from a copy of the *Paradoxes* in the British Library, Shelfmark: G. 19723 (1.).

A sheaf of Miscellany

EPIGRAMS.

Written in *Latin* by *J. D.*

Translated by J. Main *D.D.*

1.

Upon one who for his wives fault took it ill to be called Cuckold.

RUde scoffer! why dost cal me Cuckold? No
Loose fires of Love did in my bosome grow.
No wedlock-knot by me unti'd hath bin;
Nor am I guilty of anothers sin.
Thy wife being not her own with thy limbs she,
Fool'd Cuckold, doth commit Adulterie.
Being, then, one flesh, and thou her Head, tis fit
The Horns, in Justice, on thy Brow should sit.

2.

Upon One Roger *a Rich* Niggard, *familiarly unacquainted with the Author.*

BOttomless pit of gold! slave to thy Chest!
Poor in the midst of Riches not possest!
Self *Tantalus*! To thine own wealth a Thief!
Affording scarce thy half-starv'd Womb relief.
Cheating thy limbs with cloths transparent worn;
Plague to thy self! To all men else a scorn!
Who madly dost mens silver shapes adore;
And thence getst Cheeks pale as the silver Ore.
Feare not I'le beg; my mind's above thy pelf;
Good Thrifty *Hodge*, give something to thy self.

3.

Upon a Whore barren and not barren.

THy oft repeated is no Childless sin;
When thou art lain with stil thy purs lies in.

4.

On the same.

Thy dowbak'd Lusts, and Tail which vainly wags,
Are recompenc'd by thy still teeming bags.

5.

On an old Bawd.

Loe, I an old Whore have to young resign'd;
Yet in my old flesh dwels a young whores mind.

6.

On the same.

Though ramage grown, Th'art still for carting fit;
Thy will with others bodies doth commit.

7.

On the same.

She, whose scarce yet quencht lust to freeze begins,
Liv'd by her own once, now by others sins.

8.

On a Bawdy-house.

Here *Mal*, providing for Threescore,
Sets up the Trade she learn'd before,
VVith watchings many, sweatings more.

9.

Upon an old rich scolding Woman who being married to a poor young man upbraided him daily with the smallness of his Fortune.

The Husbands complaint.

VVhat wife like mine hath any Husband known?
By day she is all *Noyse*, by night all *stone*.

10.

Another.

Shut thy purse-mouth, Old Trot, And let's appeal;
VVho'd without sauce taste so deform'd a Meal?

11.

On her unpleasing Kisses.

They can't be Kisses call'd but toothless Nips,
VVhich, *Beldam*, come from thy faint trembling lips.

12.

Another.

When thy dry grissels with my soft lips close,
I give thee kisses, thou return'st me blows.

13.

Another.

Thy senses faile thee, And pray God they may,
To me thy Cofers will their loss defray.

14.

On the same old Wife.

Thou art no Woman, nor no womans part,
Infant, or Girl; say, who the Devil art.

15.

To the same.

Be not seen, Thou, whom I distracted love,
Least my prodigious dotage scandal prove.
For being a meer Image, 'twil be spread,
That I no wife did, but an Idol wed.

16.

Upon one who saw the Picture of his scolding wife in a Painters shop. Dialog.

Painter, whose face is that I see?
Thy wives. Alas! I fear tis she.
Just so her scolding eyes do burn;
And Brow doth into wrincles turn.
I tremble at her sharp nose; so
Her frighting chin doth pointed grow.
All parts are so drawn to the life,
Methinks the picture, like my wife,
Begins to brawl, and kindle strife.

17.

Another.

Say Painter, who's this whom thy hand hath made,
Thy wife who dost enquire, at least her shade.
'Tis so; yet Painter, I had cause to doubt,
Seeing her Tongue, her most known part left out.

18.

Another.

Who's this, Painter? Thy wife, O
That she were in earnest so.

19.

Another.

Venus, when *Pygmalion* praid;
Chang'd a Statue to a Maid;
Whose cold Marble drunk warm bloud.

If at my request she would
My wife into Marble turn,
I would white *Doves* to her burn.

20.

Upon a Pipe of Tobacco mis-taken by the Author for the Tooth-ach.

Outlandish Weed! whilst I thy vertues tell,
Assist me *Bedlam*, Muses come from Hell.

21.

Another.

An Hearb thou art, but useless; for made fire,
From hot mouths puft, thou dost in fumes expire.

22.

Another.

A cloud *Ixion* for a Goddess kist;
So thou thy Lovers cosen'st with a mist.

23.

To the Tobacco-seller.

Merchant of Smoke, when next thou mak'st a feast
Invite some starv'd *Chamelion* to be guest.

24.

Another.

Lothings, stincks, thirst, rhumes, aches, and catarrh,
Base weed, thy vertues, that's, thy poysons are.

25.

Another.

I love thee not, nor thou me having tri'd
How thy scorcht Takers are but Takers fry'd.

26.

Another.

Niggards till dead are Niggards; so vile weed,
Thy bounty from thy ashes doth proceed.

27.

Upon a Town built in the place where a wood grew;
From whence 'tis called Dukes-Wood, *or the* Burse

A Wood into fair buildings chang'd we see;
And th' Oke stands City where 'twas fel'd a tree.

28.

Another.

Falne Okes the Axe doth into Timber hew;
And a Town stands where Trees demolisht grew.

29.

Another.

From a Woods ruines did these Buildings rise,
And it stood Grove where now it Rafters lies.

30.

Another.

This naked Beam which beares up Roofes from ground,
Was once with *branches* & fair *green top*, crown'd.

31.

Another.

Wood yeelds to *stone*, boughs are made joyces here,
And where a *Cops* stood now fair streets appeare.

32,

Upon a navigable River cut through a Town built out of a Wood.

Horsmen turn sailers, *waves* roll where grew *woods*
And against *Nature* Art make ways through *floods*.

33.

Another.

The drownd land here a Crystall garment wears,
And her own trees, made Barges, once more bears.

34.

Another.

The tree her womb bred on the back now floats
Of this o're-flown field, now in wandring Boats.

35.

Another.

The ground whose head was once enricht with Okes,
Her Temples now steept in sea-water sokes.

36.

Another.

The place where once grew Ash for warlike spears
The *Maze* makes *drunk* now with his brinish tears

37.

Upon the Medows *over-flown there.*

The *Medows* which their perfum'd *locks* did boast
Ore-flown with waters have their perfumes lost.

38.

Another.

The hungry Cow here lately did mistake;
And seeking grasse was cosen'd with a lake.

39.

Another.

Here Fishes dwell, till now not us'd to fields;
And Pasture ground here sportful *Gudgeons* yeelds.

40.

Another.

Mere pleasant fields drownd by the wandring *Maze*,
See scaly flocks swim where once sheep did graze.

41.

Another.

Dukes-wood where once thick bushes did appear,
Like a new Iland now stands in a meer.

42.

Upon a piece of ground ore-flown, where once a Leaguer quartered.

Here where Tents stood, *Mars* now to *Neptune* yeelds,
And *Sea-nymphs* tread moist dances ore the fields.

43.

Another.

Fishes now quarter where pavilions stood;
And the smooth Tench dies the sharp hook with blood.

44.

Another.

Finn'd Soldiers here in *Belgick* Quarters jar;
And the fierce Pike in troubled streams makes war.

45.

Another.

Dutchman! This Grove once hatcht the Warlick Speer,
Which angry Perches on their backs now wear.

46.

Another.

Gudgeons, where soldiers lay, ly trencht in Sand,
Fearing the bloudie Colours of the Land.

47.

A Dutch *Captain of Foot, having with his Soldiers entred a Breach, and there a while fought valiantly with a Two-handed Sword; In the very point of Victory, being mortally wounded, spake thus:*

I fighting die; How much more blest then they,
Whom a blind shot doth, standing idle, slay.

48.

Another.

We've conquer'd Boys; My wounds I highly rate,
When with such Honor they requite my fate.

49.

Another.

Thus conquering kild, my ashes triumphs gain,
And make me wish thus to be often slain.

50.

Another.

I die well paid, whilst my expiring breath,
Smiles ore the Tombs of foes made kin by death.

51.

Another.

Me the queld *Spaniard* to the next world sent
Not unreveng'd; his Troops before me went.

52.

His Will.

Let Heaven my soul, the foe my life, the grave
My corps, my fame let my sav'd Countrey have.

53.

To the Prince of Aurange, *on his famous Victory over the* Spaniards *in* Dukes-Wood.

Now Golden Fruit, Prince, hang on *Dukes-wood* Boughes;
Since it with Lawrell crown'd thy conquering Browes.

54.

Another.

Holland and *Aurange* may their Conquest boast
Of the quell'd *Spaniard*, but brave *Aurange* most.

55.

Another.

Spaniard, no more call *Golden Fleeces* thine,
Since the bright name of *Aurange* doth more shine.

56.

A Panegyrick *on the* Hollanders *being Lords of the Sea. Occasioned by the Authors being in their Army at* Dukes-wood.

Heathen! No more thy *Neptune* boast; Here see
A *Neptune* more Lord of the sea then Hee;
Whom fruitfull *Holland* feeds, *Holland* Sea-bred;
And neighbouring *Zealand* folds in watry bed.
Neptune's a *Dutch* God; Here his wandrings stay;
And his calm'd ragings conquering chains obey.
His standing Flood here to the Bridle yeilds,
And his fierce Torrent plaies through unknown *fields*.

Here the swoln sea views the inferiour ground,
And yet no green bush, even to wonder, drownd;
Whilst Billows, like huge mountains, do hang o're
The pleasing Vales which creep along the shore.
Banks hold waves captive, and through sluces free,
And *Glebes* from watry prisons snatcht we see.
Glebes, which were long of sun, and skie bereav'd,
Now the *Dutch Plowman* sees wel cornd & sheav'd.
Curbing the Ocean with stout Mounds and Bars,
And with the salt Gods of it waging VVars.
Making Art fetch from the deep's rav'nous womb
Pastures, lost towns, and houses; In which swomm
Shell'd Citizens, 'mongst pillars drencht in brine.
Should *Achelous* here joyn strengths with thine,
And wrestle for the conquest, *Holland*, here
Each *Drayner* would a *Hercules* appear;
And cosening Art with Art, in these dry'd Plains,
Would bind the oft shape-changing God in chains.
The oft tam'd *Maze* here the *Dutch* yoke endures,
And his fear'd Master to the VValls secures
Of the fam'd *Burse* now, *Dutchman*, fear no harms,
When against neighbouring Cities seas take arms.
The *Oceans* thine, with thee his waves have sworn
The *league* which *Philip* broke. By him th'art born
To the parcht Indians, and those lands of gold
Which the proud Tyrant doth in bondage hold:
Whose wealth transported from the plunder'd Mine
His Plate-Fleet calls his, But the Sea makes thine.
Each Duch-man is *Columbus*; Worlds unknown
To the discovering Spaniard, are his grown:
Nor can I here conceal, nor yet say well,
Where *Heynskirch*'s praise, or *Oliver*'s excell,
Or *Heyn*'s more bold adventure; whose bright Ore
Prest the Sea's back with wealth snatch from the shore
For whilst I do Dutch voyages rehearse,
And sail with thy victorious Ships in verse,
I, *Holland* in thy swimming Camp am roll'd
Into all Seas, and there both Poles behold.
The Africk sands to thee large tribute send,
And *Asia* glories to be stil'd thy friend;
America's rich Mines grow in thy lands,
And at thy conquests *Europe* wondring stands.

57.

To Sleep, stealling upon him as he stood upon the Guard in the corner of a running Trench, at the siege of Duke's-Wood.

Why dost besiege mine eyes, untimely Sleep?
And o'er my limbs with thy dull fetters creep?
Hence, hence, depart; To roofs well tyll'd repaire;
To beds of down, and mindes unvext with care.
Shut Virgins eyes, whilst Love tir'd with delay,
Unstrings his Bow, and lets his Arrows play.
Rock weary Ploughmen, and new strength beget
In those whose spirits were breath'd forth in sweat;
To men opprest with grief, who court thy charms.
And men unbusied lend thy Opium arms.
Be kinde to Men in bedlam, close the eyes
Of him who in a raging feaver lyes.
But let me watch; not as a spy, to mark,
With whom my wench steals meetings in the dark.
Here guards are kept, & from yond watchful *towres*,
The crafty Foe vyes broken sleeps with ours;
Seeking by slye plots, what pitcht fields deny;
Hence, hence, then *Morpheus*, from our quarters fly.
Our very standing still here business finde;
Duty imploys our bodies, cares our minde.
Duty which may the next hour double strike;
Whilst each man here stands grasping of a pike;
Waitings stoln onsets with our weary spears,
Examining even whispers with our ears.
Doubts of the coming Foe, with hopes are mixt,
And all eyes are one his approaches fixt.
All passengers we summon with our eyes,
Ask who they are, and question them for spies.
If well-known friends, they pass; if not, they stay
Till we their doubtful answers strictly weigh.
Wil not this serve, Sleep? wil not al this fright thee?
See, then, a night turn'd into day to light thee.
See a bright shine from coal-black powder spring,
And light from darkness once more issuing.
See flames like those belcht forth from *Ætna*'s Maw,
Such flames as no Fleece-stealing *Jason* saw.
Hecuba's child of fire in dreams begot,

Was not like that from murdring Canons shot.
If yet thou'lt stay, hear thunders mixt with flame,
Such as neer yet from *Cyclops* Anvil came.
Hark how the loud gun shakes the trembling sky,
Whilst threatning Bals in showres of murther fly.
Sicilian Bull did not so loudly roar;
Nor was the sword more dreadful which hung o're
Damocles neck from guilt roof. Then, away,
And to such dangers, Sleep, don't me betray.

58.

To his Fellow Sentinels.

ANd you, Comrades, with me this night endure:
Let our cause make us bold, Courage secure.
Lets with stout mindes our present dangers meet;
And let our stations from their toyls grow sweet.
Stations where souldiers are made brothers. Nights
In wine, and Revels spent make winged flights;
A coy whore is with patience watcht for, yet
No honor's gain'd; glory with dangers met
Here doth attend us; toyls are paid with praise.
Let's weave us Crowns, then, of immortal Bayes.
To Heaven our souls, to Earth let's flesh assign,
But in our mindes let loyal honor shine.

59.

In Comædam celeberrimam *Cinthiam* dictam ad instantiam alterius fecit.

SIc vaga formosas superabat Cinthia *Nymphas*
Ut tua nunc socias Cinthia *dicta tuas.*
Quæ tibi Majestas vultus, que gratia frontis!
Spiritus ut major quam muliebris inest?
Tam bene compositum suavis decet actio corpus
Ut posset credi singula membra loqui.
Cùm velis esse Venus, *vel cùm velis esse* Diana
Tam similis non est ipsa vel ipsa sibi,
Si velis esse Diana *hos ô non desere salius,*
Hæc nemus hæc fontem florida scena dabit.
O si te nudam semel hoc in fonte viderem
Cornua tunc essent pænaq; grata canes.

Si Luna esse velis fiat tibi sphæra theatrum,
Pascantur radiis Lumina nostra tuis.
Sed raro hinc abeas, & cùm discedere velles
O si te possent Lumina nostra sequi;
Aut tua cum desit fœlix præsentia nobis
Impressis liceat viribus usq; frui.

[60.]

Idem Anglicè *versum.*

AS wandring *Cinthia* all her Nymphs excells,
So dost thou all thy fellows; In thee dwells
Majesty mixt with loveliness, a spirit
That's more then womanish; thy graces merit,
And force a liking, as the lights above;
The Earths light vapours upwards force and move:
Thy action doth each passion so well fit,
As if each limb did help to utter it:
If thou wilt *Venus* or *Diana* be,
Neither will be so like her self as thee.
O wilt thou be *Diana*, haunt these fields,
This Theater both woods and fountains yeelds.
That I could see thee here but wash thy snow,
Acteon's fate Ide joy to undergo.
Wilt thou be th'Moon, then make thy sphere this stage;
But it were pitty thou shouldst change thy age;
And if from our *Horizon* thou shouldst go,
Still to view thee wee'd change *Horizon* too;
But that we may when thou art gone from hence,
Still be made happy by thy influence.

[61.]

On one particular passage of her action, when she was to be stript of her cloaths by Fulvio, *but not without much resistance.* Videns excogitavit.

AS *Fulvio Cinthia*'s glory would eclips,
And graced by her limbs, her robe off strips;
To see her how she strove, and pray'd, and cry'd,
But for the plays sake none could have deny'd.
And as she strove with him, so modesty
Did strive with anger for the mastery.

How was she pale with anger, red with shame!
Her colour chang'd, with choller went and came,
As when the winking moon strives with a cloude,
Whose glory darkness doth by fits enshroude:
was it nor envy, that we might not see
That which from th'smock could scarce discerned be;
Or wast for shamefastness: yes, yes, 'twas so,
That too much hiding of her face did show.
So look'd the Nymph which *Jupiter* beguil'd
I'th water with *Diana* got with child;
So *Salmacis* half ravish'd in the brook,
As she almost stript to her smock did look.
The Poet was too sparing, had she been
Like intrapt *Venus* nak'd to have been seen;
And with a net unhid been covered;
How on her limbs our hungry eyes had fed,
And dwelt on her seen members, whilst the rest
Had by proportion easily been guest:
But pitty 'twere that she enjoyn'd had been
So hard a penance, guilty of no sin.

Finis.

Appendix 2

Poems Associated with the Epigrams: Appropriations, Translations, Answers, and Attributions

Transcribed from manuscripts and early printed books, the poems presented below are associated in various ways with canonical epigrams. We have not attempted to present here every epigram ascribed to Donne in the manuscripts or attributed to him in prior editions; instead, we have selected certain noncanonical poems that Donne's contemporaries ascribed to him as they compiled their collections, poems that cast further light on the manuscript collections of epigrams discussed in the General Textual Introduction to the Epigrams above, and poems that illustrate the broader impact of Donne's epigrams in his time. We have also presented one recently discovered candidate for addition to the canon of Donne epigrams.

Translations, appropriations, and answer poems are grouped according to the Donne epigram with which they are associated, and these groups are ordered alphabetically according to the short forms of reference employed in this edition. The final category contains additional ascriptions and poems miscellaneously associated with the canonical epigrams in various artifacts.

1. *Antiq*

1.1 *An Herren K. der Antiquiteten Liebhabern*

Was alt vnd seltsam ist thust du mit müh vñ fleiss:
In dein Studier-stüblein auffhencken:
Darumb dein Weib (ist Sie ja weiss)
Mag ihr gewissen wol bedencken.

Printed in Weckherlin 1641, 187; repr. 1648, 808–09.

2. *Beggar*

2.1 An Epigram.

Dull: *sayes he is so weake he can not rise,*
Nor stand, nor goe: if that be true, he lyes.
True-lie: well sed, for so the case now standes,
He keepes his bed, yet lies i'the Surgions hands.

Printed in Deloney 1607 (siglum 2), sig. E6.

2.2 273. *On a Bed-rid man.*

A bed-rid man before the Judge was brought,
The Judge bids stand up sirrah as you ought;
Oh Sir, nor goe, nor sit, nor stand can I,
I am your friend, pray give me leave to lie:
Art thou my friend quoth he? then lie thy fill,
A Judge gives all his friends leave to lie still.

Printed in Mennes 1640 (siglum 27), sig. G2v.

2.3 *An die schöne Marina*

Ach! sprechet nicht / mein süsses hertz /
Wan ich euch sag / wie grosz mein schmertz /
Das ich pfleg ohn ein F zu Fliegen.
  Ich wolt (vnd schwör es ist kein scherz)
Mit euch stracks ohn ein E. gern liegen.

Printed in Weckherlin 1648, 829–30.

3. *Disinher*

3.1 Of one y^{t} vowed to disinhærit his Sonne.

A citizen y^{t} dwelt neare Temple barre
By happ one daye fell w:th his Sonne at iarre,
Whom for his evile life, & lewd demerritt,
He oft affirm'd, y^{t} he would disherritt.
Vowing his goods & lands all to ye Poore:
His Sonne what wth playe, what w:th his whore,
Was soe consum'd, at last, y^{t} he did lack
Bread to his bellye, cloathinge to his back.
  O craftye miserie, his ffather nowe
  Maye giue him all he hath, & keepe his vowe. |

Entered in LR2, p. 35, immediately above *Beggar* on that page. Also entered in the holograph of John Harington, British Library ms. Add. 12049, and printed in *The Most Elegant and Witty Epigrams of Sir Iohn Harrington, Knight* . . . . (London: Iohn Budge, 1618), sig. C8; repr. 1625 and 1633.

4. *Hero*

4.1 *Leander vnd Hero*

Wie vns die Lieb ein Liecht ein Lufft das leben gab
Vnd wie ein Fewr (vns beed verliebend) vns erleuchtet:
So hat ein Wasser auch erdrenckend vns befeuchtet
Vnd nu von einer Erd bedöcket Vns ein Grab.

Printed in Weckherlin 1641, 178; repr. 1648, 799.

4.2 *Hero & Leander.*

'Ηέρ' ἀποψύχονται ἰὴ ϗτι γαῖα καλύπτει,
Ευνὸν πῦρ κεῖε, ξυνὸν δὲ κατέκλυσε λαῖτμα.

Printed in Stubbs 1658 (siglum 46), 39.

5\. *Licent*

5.1 *An den Pfarrern Schandflecken*

Pfaff / die vergleichung deiner haaren
Mit deinen sünden must du sparen:
Dan jene nemen ab / die zu / mit deinen jahren.

Printed in Weckherlin 1641, 187; repr. 1648, 808.

5.2 *In Aſotum.*

Οὐκ ἴσαι σέθεν ἀμπλακίαι καὶ βόστρυχοι χαίτης,
Αὔξετ᾽ ἀτασθαλίη, ἡ δὲ κόμη μινύθει.

Printed in Stubbs 1658 (siglum 46), 41.

5.3 *The Authors Dreame*

My sinnes are like the haires vpon my head,
And raise their Audit to as high a score:
In this they differ: these doe daily shed;
But ah! my sinnes grow daily more and more.
If by my haires thou number out my sins,
Heauen make me bald before the day begins.

Printed in Quarles 1629, 162; numerous reprints. Repr. as no. "66," titled "*On Sinnes.*" in Francis Quarles, *Divine Fancies: Digested into Epigrammes, Meditations, and Observations:* (London: John Marriott, 1632), p. 97; three additional reprints. Also transcribed under the heading "Song" in B26, p. 9.

5.4 *An Answer to the same.*
Epig. 52.

YEs: If thy *Haires fall*, as thy *Sinnes increase*,
Both will ere long proue *æquall*, *Numberlesse*.

Printed in Fitzgeffrey 1617 (siglum 16), sig. D7v, as an answer to *Licent*; repr. in Henry Fitzgeffrey, *Certain Elegies, Done by Sundrie Excellent Wits. With Satyrs and Epigrames.* (London: Miles Partriche, 1618 [siglum 17a]), sig. D7v, and Fitzgeffrey, *Certain Elegies* 1620 (siglum 17b), sig. D7v.

5.5 Here lyes one whose scalpe is bare
Who in catching connyes, lost many a hare
Thy sinns and haire no man can equall call
For all thy sinns increase, thy haires doe fall.

As here, *Licent* entered with preceding extra couplet to form four-line poem in B23, f. 35.

6. *Niobe*

6.1 *Niobe.*

Gedrücknet durch die frewd vnd pein
Der Kinder / welche ich geboren /
Vnd wider durch den tod verloren /
Bin Ich selbs mein Grab vnd Grabstein.

Printed in Weckherlin 1641, 178; repr. 1648, 799.

7. *Phrine*

7.1 *An die Ross*

Ross / ewer Conterfeht ist Euch
(Zwar schöner dan jhr / jedoch) gleich
In dem / dass jhr beed hipsch gemahlet /
Vnd man auch für Euch beed bezahlet.

Printed in Weckherlin 1641, 190; repr. 1648, 825–26.

8. *Ralph*

8.1 Vppon an Vnthrifte. |

Spendall of late, hath often bouldley sed:
that noe disease, should make him keepe his bed:
his reasonn is (if you will haue me tell it)
hee wanteth mony, & hee needes must sell it. | .x.

Entered in CJ2, p. 43; also appears in LR1, f. 346, with subject named "Brabus" rather than "Spendall."

9. *Other Associated and Attributed Epigrams*

9.1 Two fallinge out in to a ditch they fell,
both fallinge out, theire fallinge in was well.

Entered in H5, p. 435, as part of the scribe's collection of epigrams; appears as last poem on page, where it follows *Beggar* immediately and precedes *Wall*, the first poem at the top of p. 436.

9.2 A silly John surpriz'd with ioy
For Joy hathe made the silly
Joy to enioy thy Sweetest Jone
Jone whiter then the Lillie. | J.D. |

Scribally entered as the fifth epigram in H3, p. 48, where it follows *Pyr* and precedes *Storm*.

9.3 Smugg the Smith for ale & spice
Sould all his tooles, but kept his vice.

Entered as the last of the scribe's epigrams in H8, f. 24v, where it follows *Klock* and precedes the non-canonical "On the blessed Virgin Mary"; printed from this source in Simeon 1856–57 (siglum 70), 31. Also printed in *Epigrams Both Pleasant and Seriovs, Written by that All-worthy Knight, Sir Iohn Harrington* . . . . (London: Iohn Budge, 1615), sig. C4v; repr. 1618, 1625, and 1633.

9.4 Art'not half mad, Thou askets? Nay, by my soule,
Hee's more half mad, That does not thinke thee whole

Entered in a seventeenth-century hand at the bottom of p. 43 in the *MH* copy of A, following the collection of canonical epigrams.

9.5 On a Ladyes window looking towards
the Thames

Shee that through glasse sees water runne, doth see
Her selfe, and through her selfe, They're one, not Three.

Labeled "Not Printed" in a second hand, the above is inscribed immediately above *Martial* in H6, p. 336, both poems having been inserted after the scribe had entered his primary collection of epigrams.

9.6 In Rabulam

Hinc te nec Satyræ nec sæua Epigramata mordent
Sublimes Satyræ sunt, Epigrama breue.

Labeled "Not Printed" in a second hand, the above appears between *Antiq* and *Disinher* in the scribe's primary collection of epigrams in H6, p. 337.

9.7 E. of Nottingham

I Earle of Nothing=am, am iustly soe
for I did nothing all the world doth know
when braue Count Essex landed on the shore
I landed too, but Cales was wonn before. |

Inscribed between *Break* and *Flea*, the above poem appears in a unique copy in TM1, p. 64. Gary A. Stringer attributes the epigram to Donne in *JDJ* 10:71–74.

Commentary

THE Epigrams

The Epigrams

Dates and Circumstances

Gosse (1899, 1:17, 51), while denying Donne's authorship of the epigrams purportedly translated by Jasper Mayne (see Appendix 1 in this volume), notes by contrast the existence of "juvenile English epigrams which are undoubtedly [Donne's]" dating "probably" from after 1591 (17). Speculating on the reliability of Izaak Walton's account (1640) of Donne's traveling in Italy and Spain after serving in Essex's Azores expedition of 1597, Gosse observes that of the twenty epigrams in the Westmoreland ms. (as opposed to sixteen in the early printed editions), several have Italian titles, but declines to conclude that they must therefore have been composed in Italy (51).

Grierson (1912, 2:59) maintains that *Ship*, *Wall*, *Beggar*, *Cales*, and *Wing* were composed during Donne's service under Essex in the Cadiz expedition of 1596.

Grierson subsequently (1929, xxviii) states, without further specificity, that "[o]ne or two [of the epigrams] were composed during the Cadiz expedition."

Hillyer (1941, xxvi), citing Ben Jonson's observations to Drummond to the effect that Donne's best work was written before he was twenty-five years old (see General Commentary below), identifies the epigrams and "some of the marriage songs" (not specified) as part of this group. "To a great extent," he maintains, "Jonson was anticipating the verdict of posterity. Most of the familiar poems of Donne are of early composition."

Milgate (1950, 229–31), commenting on the Davison manuscript miscellany of 1608 (see General Commentary below), notes that its various references to Donne are in somewhat different hands, suggesting entries at different times. He deduces from a reference to masques and entertainments that at least some of the manuscripts and papers to which Davison refers existed by 1606 and notes that the listing of a French book published in 1608 indicates that date as another such limit. On the whole, however, Milgate finds the evidence in Davison inconclusive for dating the reception and circulation of the epigrams.

On the basis of Jonson's observation to William Drummond (cited by Hillyer above), Ellrodt (1960b, 452–63) suggests that some of the epigrams were written before 1597 (if Jonson thought Donne was born in 1572) or 1598 (if Jonson supposed the birthday in 1573). Ellrodt dates *Ship*, *Cales*, *Wing*, and—tentatively—*Wall* from the Cadiz expedition of 1596, and from external evidence postulates the earliest possible dates of two others: *Merc*, because the journal to which the title alludes first appeared in 1598, and *Martial*, because the edition of Martial to which the poem refers appeared in

1602. He links *Antiq* to *Sat5* 87, because the antiquarian named in the epigram appears to be the same man named in the satire. Of the dates of the other epigrams nothing, he says, can be stated.

Shawcross (1967a, xvii–xxv) calls the chronology of Donne's poems uncertain, particularly that of the epigrams, the love elegies, and most of the songs and sonnets.

Subsequently, Shawcross (1986a, 120, 123, 142), analyzing the problems posed by the "arrangement and order" of Donne's poems, suggests that the epigrams may have been circulated in manuscript groups "prior to January 1615 when . . . [Donne] called in his poems for publication before his ordination" (120).

Shawcross (1988, 115–17) also notes the reprinting of six epigrams (*SelfAc*, *Phrine*, *Licent*, *Beggar*, *Antiq*, and *Disinher*) in William Oldys's *A Collection of Epigrams. To Which is Prefix'd, A Critical Dissertation on this Species of Poetry* (London, 1727).

Carey (1990, 425) notes that none of the epigrams is definitely datable after 1602.

General Commentary

The earliest allusion to the epigrams as a category occurs in Davison (c. 1608 [cited in Bullen 1890–91, 1:liii]), who lists under the heading "Manuscripts to get" the following: "Satyres, Elegies, Epigrams, etc. by John Don [sic]."

Drummond (c. 1612–16 [1711, 225–26]) observes, "I think if [Donne] would, he might easily be the best Epigrammatist we have found in English; of which I have not yet seen any come near the Ancients" (226), citing Ben Jonson as having affirmed "that *Donne* wrote all his best Pieces before he was Twenty five Years of Age" (225).

Jonson (1616, 797) characterized Donne as a master epigrammatist:

"To John Donne"
Who shall doubt, *Donne*, where I a *Poet* bee,
When I dare send my *Epigrammes* to thee?
That so alone canst judge, so'alone do'st make:
And, in thy censures, euenly, dost take
As free simplicitie, to dis-auow,
As thou hast best authoritie, t'allow.
Reade all I send: and, if I finde but one
Mark'd by thy hand, and with the better stone,
My title's seal'd. Those that for claps doe write,
Let pui'nees, porters, players praise delight,
And, till they burst, their backs, like asses load;
A man should seeke great glorie, and not broad.

Hayman (1628, 58) possibly alludes to Donne's epigrams in his *To the Reuerend and diuinely witty*, Iohn Dun, *Doctor in Diuinity*, *Deane of Saint Pauls*, *London*:

As my *Iohn Owen* Seneca* did praise,
So might I for you a like piller raise,
His Epigrams did nothing want but verse;

You can yours (if you list) that way rehearse:
His were neat, fine, diuine morality;
But yours, pure, faithfull, true Diuinity.

*Owen, *Lib.* 4. *Epig.* 40. [Hayman's note]

Bancroft (1639, sig. D3a) addressed his own epigram "To Doctor *Donne*:" "Thy Muses gallantry doth farre exceed / All ours; to whom thou art a *Don* indeed."

Weckherlin (1641, 178–90) published translations of *Niobe* (178), *Hero* (178), *Antiq* (187), and *Licent* (187), as well as an adaptation of *Phrine* (190), and in a 1648 reprint of his work added an adaptation of *Beggar* (829–30) (see Appendix 2). (Weckherlin's indebtness to Donne for these epigrams was first pointed out in Bohm [1893, 73–75], whose work is cited in the 1958 edition of Keynes's *Bibliography* [p. 259]. Following Keynes, Milgate [1967, 196] avers the presence of these epigrams in Weckherlin's 1648 edition—though not that of 1641—and states that Weckherlin wrote his poems "up to thirty-five years before their publication," an assertion repeated by Smith [1975, 50], who adds that although Weckherlin settled in England in 1626, he had been familiar with English writings long before that.)

Stubbs (1658, 38–39 [siglum 46]) prints *Hero* and *Licent* with facing translations into Greek (see Appendix 2).

Spence (1732–33? [1949, 247]) characterizes the greater part of Donne's poetry as no more than "a tissue of epigrams," an evaluation based on the supposed dominance in Donne's poetry of the allegedly decadent Italian element in English poetry of the period, characterized, according to Spence, by a rejection of natural simplicity in favor of rhetorical ornaments and by extensive use of word-play, clever ideas, improbable analogies, and bizarre figures of speech.

Cooper (1761, 37) imitates *Licent*, *Phrine*, and possibly *Klock* in a volume of original poems (his version of *Triple* is glossed as "Paraphrased from Dr. Donne," and he glosses the three epigrams as "Imitated from the same").

Characterizing Donne's poetry generally as "rugged and uncouth," Chalmers (1810, 5:124) partly excuses him on the grounds that he did not publish and so had little inducement to polish his work: "he was certainly not ignorant or unskilled in the higher attributes of style," Chalmers maintains, "for he wrote elegantly in Latin, and displays considerable taste in some of his smaller pieces and epigrams."

Sanford (1819, 153) prints *Hero*, *Pyr*, *Phrine*, *Philo*, and *Klock*, omitting the title for *Klock*, which is separated in his collection from *Philo* only by a space. (His arrangement almost certainly indicates that Sanford was following Chalmers [K] for his text, since that edition does the same—eds.)

Ward (1858 [1897, 324]) observes that "some of [Donne's] epigrams are very good."

Bond (1861, 90–91) declares his enthusiasm for Donne's satires but wishes he had written no epigrams. "The epigram," Bond asserts, "should have the flash of a sunstroke and strike its subject down at a blow. [Donne's] mind had not sufficient velocity for this species of composition" (90). He further characterizes the epigrams as "as bad as one might have expected them to be" (91), but cites *Beggar* as one of the better ones.

Grosart (1872–73, 2:266) notes the appearance of the epigrams in the edition of 1633 "and since in all the after-editions. One would very willingly have gone without them."

Furst (1896, 231) links the epigrams with the satires as having the "same characteristics of unusual thought and condensed expression," citing and quoting in full *Ship*, *Antiq*, and *Disinher*.

The anonymous reviewer of Gosse (1899) in *Ath* (1899, 646) cites Donne's elegies and epigrams generally in objecting to Gosse's alleged "assertion of Donne's practical independence of all the poetical influences in England when he began to write"; the review characterizes Gosse as suggesting that these categories of Donne's poetry are indebted to Marlowe's and Sir John Davies's publication of translations from Ovid's *Amores*.

Seccombe and Nicoll (1906, 1:155) describe the epigrams generally (as well as the verse letters, obsequies, elegies, and divine poems) as products of Donne's "later, more seraphic years," to be contrasted with his earlier, "most singular lyrics" (not identified), which they characterize as sensual, intellectual, realistic, and individualistic.

Citing Drummond (c. 1612–16) to the effect that Donne might have become England's best epigrammatist, Ramsay (1917, 8) nonetheless contrasts the praise she says was given his epigrams in his time with a modern perception of them as raw, brutal, and even obscene.

Hayward (1930, 58) finds Drummond's compliment, "though exaggerated," to be evidence of the epigrams' high reputation in Donne's day and says they "must be classed" with the early songs and sonnets.

Hillyer (1941, xxxi–xxxii) deprecates Drummond's evaluation, emphasizing Drummond's stated preference for classical examples of the genre; whereas, he argues, the Hellenistic and Roman epigram was an "independent form of art to which poets brought their best attention" and was characterized by "concentrated expression," the epigram as practiced by Donne and other "young poets of our tradition" was not a monument to a moment, but rather "a jotting down of a passing conceit, probably with some purpose of later expansion" (xxxii). He speculates that "many" were jottings made in notebooks, hastily composed during the Cadiz expedition. "Few of these poems have any distinction," he argues, citing lines 1–2 of *ElAut* as one of many instances of "far better epigrams" that occur "in the course of longer poems" (xxxii). Hillyer concedes some merit, however, to *Ship* (see Hillyer's comment on *Ship* below).

Milgate (1950, 246–47, 381–83) remarks on what he sees as the surprisingly early appreciation of the epigrams (as well as the verse letters, prose paradoxes, elegies, and satires) as opposed to the lyric poems. Early references to Donne's poems, he maintains, are to those written in fashionable rhetorical genres, especially the satire and the epigram; he suggests that Donne may have come to the pre-1600 lyric by way of the epigram and cites *Comp* as an example of the kind of lyric that would have "come easily under the heading of 'epigram' as Elizabethan England understood the term" (247). Donne's contemporaries, he argues, valued the "epigrammatic" quality in his verse; the epigrams, together with the satires, elegies, paradoxes, and verse letters, were probably the poems Donne preferred to circulate (247). He concludes that the poems "most widely known to the casual reader" before 1633 were those actually printed, the satires, and the epigrams (383).

Leishman (1951, 52) briefly comments upon the epigrams, which he compares to Jonson's. In particular, he finds Donne's to be much shorter and the impulse behind them to be, rather than moral, "purely intellectual and ingenious."

Reeves (1952, ix) explains in the introduction to his selection of Donne's poetry that poetic appeal rather than scholarly curiosity has guided his choices, which include *Ship*, *Beggar*, and *Antiq*, as well as *EpEliz*.

Simpson (1952, 121) identifies the epigrams and the paradoxes as richest in verbatim quotations from Martial, alleging that Donne quotes from him more than from any other Latin poet.

Ellrodt (1960a, 1, i:206; 2:24, 102–03, 303, 314, 315–17, 324) divides the sixteen epigrams of the edition of 1633 into three groups: (a) mythological epigrams based on Petrarchan conceits (*Hero*, *Pyr*, *Niobe*); (b) heroic epigrams (*Ship*, *Wall*); and (c) satirical epigrams (the remaining eleven), most of which strive for the effect of dramatic surprise found in the epigrams of Martial (2:324). Discussing paradox in Donne's poetry, Ellrodt cites the epigrams generally, and both *Pyr* and *Ship* specifically, as instances of "paradoxe objectif" or "paradoxe de circonstance" and, accordingly, relatively weak as poetry because of their dependence on external phenomena or, in scholastic terminology, "accidents" (he cites *Cor5* 11 as a parallel) (1, i:206). The vogue for epigrams, in Ellrodt's opinion, manifests the taste for subtlety and ingenuity at the root of the metaphysical style; Sidney in the *Arcadia* and *Astrophel and Stella* advanced this taste, he maintains, and Donne and his successors developed it principally in their exploitation of paradox (2:314). However, Ellrodt dismisses Donne's epigrams as negligible and Drummond's praise as that of a mediocre judge in such a matter (2:24). He suggests that Drummond's compliment is actually directed to Donne's elegies and lyric poems, arguing the slightness of Donne's production in the epigram form and the slight interest of the epigrams in comparison with Donne's other works (2:315). By citing evidence of such applications of the term in Donne's time, (e. g., Jonson's *Epigrammes*), Ellrodt extends the definition of "epigram" to include complimentary verses, panegyrics, and epitaphs (2:315–17). Donne's epigrammatic verse, understood by Ellrodt in this broad sense, appears to give generic and concrete expression to the atmosphere of the Inns of Court as Donne knew them in the 1590s, when, Ellrodt argues, the tone of conversation imbues literature with a sense of intimacy created by personal references and echoes of contemporary events (2:103).

Ellrodt further compares the extensive production of epigrams in English around the turn of the seventeenth century with the work of Martial, arguing that the English epigrams generally lack Martial's dramatic dialogue, tending rather to be third-person narratives or meditations characterized by plays on words. He says that Donne strove above all for conciseness and for the "conceit," to the loss of dramatic effect; the Donnean epigram, usually a distich, is too short to lend itself to dialogue, and is actually an apostrophe (by contrast, Jonson and others after 1600 are, in Ellrodt's view, truly "dramatic" epigrammatists). He cites *Antiq* and *Phrine*, however (and, as lesser examples, *Disinher*, *Philo*, and *Klock*), as instances of successful duplication of Martial's strategy of provoking surprise at the unexpected relationship that emerges between elements at the close of the poem (2:303).

Elsewhere, Ellrodt (1960b, 452) links the epigrams to Jonson's praise of Donne, as recorded by Drummond, as "the first poet in the world in some things," suggesting that what Jonson admired in Donne were passages of concrete and realistic description of a kind to be found in Donne's epigrams.

Bryan (1962, 170, 173), discussing "the number, kind, and frequency of appearance of Donne's poems in nineteen [seventeenth-century] poetical commonplace books located in private libraries throughout the United States" (170), explains that he has omitted from his discussion the dozen or so epigrams contained within the commonplace books because they are "so widely at variance with the established versions" that "it would be difficult to maintain that the book owners were always aware that Donne was the source of the epigrams they copied into their books" (173).

Poisson's selection (1962, 94–97) includes translations into French verse of *Hero*, *Niobe*, *Wall*, *SelfAc*, *Licent*, *Antiq*, *Disinher*, *Phrine*, and *Klock*.

Gardner (1965, xxvi, lv–lvi) uses the term "epigram" to characterize *Compu* and *Expir* and the expression "epigrammatic pieces" to characterize *Jet*, *Witch*, and *Para* (lv–lvi), further suggesting the possibility of characterizing *Prohib* as an epigram (lv). She defines the classical love-epigram as practiced by Martial as "one root of Donne's art," justifying her subgrouping of some of the songs and sonnets as "epigrammatic" on grounds that they are short and pointed; she describes "the development of Donne's art . . . in one way as his learning how to expand and enrich epigrammatic themes without losing the point and pungency that is characteristic of the epigram" (xxvi).

Gamberini (1967, 46–47) terms the epigrams facile as well as "conceited" ("*concettistiche*") exercises, appealing to an alleged contemporary fondness for paradox and sententiousness. Several, especially *Klock*, he argues, have more character than the others because of their "venomous wit" ("*battuta velenosa*"), and helped establish Donne's reputation in his youth (47).

Milgate (1967, xvii, xxiii) affirms the importance of classical models in Donne's pre-1600 poetry, including the epigrams, which he groups with the elegies as "perhaps . . . more basically experimental [than the satires] in extending the range of the genres." He finds that the epigrams achieve such extension by sometimes joining the musical and emotional qualities of song to the characteristic neatness and wit of the form (xvii). Noting in the satires "a constant tendency to aphorism and to epigram" (xxiii), Milgate characterizes them nonetheless as representing a lesser "confounding or extension of poetical 'kinds'" than do the epigrams (xvii).

Hughes (1968, 63–65) believes the epigrams (most of which, he argues, were written before 1600) were composed for Donne's own amusement and exhibit a "brief triumph of language" (63). He further describes them as "characterless, indistinguishable from any good instances of their kind" (63). Hughes finds that the effect of the epigram "depends on the protean quality of single words" (64), which he illustrates with examples from *Beggar*, *Antiq*, *Phrine*, *Klock*, and *Ralph*.

Castagna (1970, 198–99) includes French translations of *Licent* and *Klock* among the poems by Donne in the anthology section of his survey of Elizabethan England.

Summers (1970, 18–19) describes Donne's epigrams in general as "off-hand squibs, most of them only two-lines long and many of them very funny" (18). Further, he notes that the persona of the epigrams is a "witty, mercurial, 'interesting' young man" who is "more clearly defined in 'Paradoxes and Problems'" (19).

Noting the probable influence on Donne of Inns-of-Court epigrammatists Sir John Harrington and Sir John Davies, Bullough (1972, 60–61) briefly comments that "eleven out of Donne's nineteen epigrams, most attempting only a clever point, are a couplet long" (60) and then quotes *Pyr*, without commentary, as an example.

MacColl (1972, 30) questions how widely Donne was known as a poet in his youth, citing repeated misquotations of *Beggar* as "less than solid evidence of fame."

Menascè (1974, 37–39) contrasts Drummond's qualified praise of Donne the epigrammatist with what she characterizes as a small output of "*jeux d'esprit*," intended only to please or amuse, whose acuteness earned him applause at the time.

Warnke and Preminger (1974) cite the "brutal thrusts of Donne."

Smith (1975, 5, 9, 10) says that the epigrams were probably in circulation both singly and in groups early in their history (5), citing *Beggar* especially as one of the small number of Donne's poems quoted or cited fairly often in the second decade of the seventeenth century (10). Disputing Milgate (1950), Smith discounts the notion that Ben Jonson's preference for epigrammatic, satirical, rhetorical, and witty elements in Donne was representative of the taste of his age. He characterizes Jonson's epigram ("To John Donne") as "the seal of a small circle of associates," adding, "Jonson takes it for granted that the appeal of Donne's verse is esoteric" (9).

Hester (1979, 202–06) introduces his reading of *Wing* with general observations on "the complex mixing of genres and the ironic manipulation of generic expectations" (202) that he finds characteristic of Donne's epigrams, suggesting that attention to these techniques "can lead to a renewed appreciation of Donne's accomplishments in this genre." Hester maintains that the epigrams were probably among Donne's earliest works and that among them occur examples of all the major modes of epigrams as they were discussed by the leading genre critics of the period. Poems such as *SelfAc*, *Klock*, and *Antiq*, he says, show Donne's mastery of the Roman mode developed by Catullus and Martial, whereas *Ship*, *Hero*, and *Pyr* illustrate his skill with the epigram in the Greek manner. Hester concludes that "both groups evince the dialectical skill demanded by the form—the building of 'hyperdetermination' and verbal tension so as to set up a sharp reversal or 'sting' in the Roman form, or the satisfaction of the building tension by a sententious or proverbial truism in the Greek form" (203).

Marotti (1981, 212), in the context of an extended discussion of Donne's relationship to patrons, associates the epigrams of Donne and of others (Marston and Davies are specified), together with their satires and "iconoclastic Ovidian love poetry," as indicative of the preoccupations of Inns of Court men with "the major institutions of the society." These poems, Marotti asserts, affirm "the cultural centrality of the Court, reflecting not so much an antimaterialistic or socially rebellious withdrawal from the established social system as an intense interest in it, particularly when place, status, and patronage were concerned."

Roberts (1982b, 55–67) includes the epigrams and epithalamia in the group of poems (including *Metem*, the funeral elegies, and the lesser-known religious poems) that he considers most underrepresented in modern criticism (62).

Shawcross (1983c, 159–66) observes that Donne seems rarely to have assigned titles to his poems and that therefore biographical interpretations based on a title are suspect. In the epigrams, for example, a title may actually diminish the force of a poem; an example is *Hero and Leander*. Donne, Shawcross argues, was attracted, especially in the epigrams, to types rather than instances, and titles like "A Licentious Person" or "An Obscure Writer" more closely reinforce his verses than would more specific headings (160–61).

Claiming that "Donne's use of the riddle as genre needs to be more completely understood, especially in the *Songs and Sonets* and the *Epigrams*" (1), Rieke (1984, 1–20) states that "one recognizes a riddle epigram by its avoidance of naming the person or things described," citing *Niobe* as a poem that would be "enigmatic" without the answer furnished by the title. She further characterizes *Hero*, *Pyr*, *Beggar*, *Licent*, *Antiq*, and *Liar* as having "especially enigmatic qualities." She also states that "clearly" *Niobe* and *Hero* "are epitaphs in generic terms" (7).

Willmott (1985, 56–57) includes four of the epigrams with notes (*Hero*, *Pyr*, *Beggar*, and *Disinher*) and comments that in the epigrams, which were imitated from Martial, "we see in isolation the terse wit that [Donne] uses so effectively in his longer poems" (57).

Hester (1986, 80–91) claims that the epigrams as a whole "offer an instructive example of [Donne's] poetic achievement *in parvo*." Conceding that they lack the complexity of many of the lyrics, Hester nonetheless finds in them that "'sophistrie too subtile'" of Donne's major work, "exhibited here in the daring exploration of the limitations of deriving definitive conclusions from speech acts and of the traps that reside in tropes driven toward epigrammatic closure" (80). Hester concludes that Donne is "primarily concerned with the wondrous character of experience," although the epigrams and other poems "explore the inability as well as the ability of words to recreate those wonders. . . . Donne's manipulation of epigrammatic strategies and conventions serves to bring into question and open up the adequacy and creativity of human forms and signs" (91).

Shawcross (1986a, 123, 142) states that the manuscript groupings of Donne's poems seem to reflect genres and types. He summarizes:

> The epigrams appear as a group in many manuscripts, and one or more are copied incidentally into other manuscripts. Their order in 1633 is generally observable in the manuscripts except for "Mercurius Gallo-Belgicus," which, probably because it has eight lines rather than the more usual two, is given second to last in 1633 . . . . Five other epigrams, two of which have not always been accepted as Donne's ("The Juggler" or "Manliness" and "Faustus"), and two Latin epigrammatic book inscriptions complete this subgenre. Of the three epigrams accepted into the canon, "Cales and Guyana" and "Sir John Wingefield" (which occur only in *O'F* [H6] and *W* [NY3]) should be placed on the evidence of the manuscripts after "A Lame Beggar," and "The Liar" (which occurs in twelve manuscripts) should be placed after "Disinherited" (123).

Shawcross proposes that criticism of the epigrams consider their arrangement in three groups: "(1) three 'classical' subjects, (2) 'war' subjects ('A Burnt Ship' through 'Sir

John Wingefield'), and (3) satirized 'types' ('A Self-Accuser' through 'Ralphius'). Perhaps 'Mercurius Gallo-Belgicus' and 'Raderus' should be examined as specific satiric statements, but their potential as types—as this ordering suggests—should not be overlooked critically" (123). Shawcross further suggests that the arrangement of Donne's epigrams (as well as those of the satires and elegies) may have been produced with Donne's "cognizance and even, perhaps, original contribution" (142).

Asserting that there is no certainty that any of the titles for Donne's epigrams are his own, Hester (1990, 3–11) nonetheless finds it "useful to test the propriety of a title by using the poem's strategies or wit as a guide" (3). Although such an approach cannot indicate which manuscript titles belong to Donne, Hester argues, it can "suggest the most likely, the most perceptive, or the most instructive titles in the manuscripts for the epigrams, it can indicate how some Renaissance readers interpreted these poems, and it can provide data about the provenance and state of the many Donne manuscripts" (3). In particular, Hester divides the titles (here spelled as in Hester's article) into four categories. In the first (consisting of "Phryne," "Klockius," "Ralphius," and "Faustus") Hester perceives "a level of play on the name of the victim," but adds further that "none of these titles is essential to the display or enactment of the poet's wit" (3). The headings for the second category ("Raderus," "*Mercurius Gallo-Belgicus*," "Cales and Guyana," "Hero and Leander," "Pyramus and Thisbe," and "Niobe") "are essential, for omitting them modifies the reader's experience" (3). Hester explains that "without the headings these poems become riddles, forcing the reader to surmise the subject being described," yet with the headings "the wit of these poems confirms Donne's re-creative art, his ability to tell an old story in a new way" (3–4). The seven epigrams constituting the third category ("Antiquary," "A licentious person," "A selfe accuser," "Disinherited," "The Lier," "An obscure writer," and "The Jughler") "create more troublesome choices" (4). "Because of their interpretive or designatory character," Hester contends, these titles "often offer a succinct summary of the witty point of the poem or identify the satirical type which the poem addresses" (5). The final group of titles ("*Zoppo*" or "A lame begger," "*Caso d'un muro*" or "Fall of a wall," "*Naue arsa*" or "A burnt ship," and "*Il Caualliere Gio: Wingef.*" or "Sir John Wingefield"), according to Hester, "creates the most interesting problems, because of both their manuscript history and the possibility that they offer titles that Donne may have composed" (6). Focusing upon the Italian titles for these poems, Hester argues that "if these Italian titles are not Donne's, they yet show a keen perception of the wry satire embedded in these epigrams, especially in their evocation of the precise point or play on which the inventive admonitions of these satirical encomia depend" (6). Hester concludes with a brief list of the textual implications of his discussion (including the observation that "1633 took its titles and texts for the epigrams" apparently from the "later Group II tradition as seen in the Dolau Cothi MS" [9]) and then offers both the counsel that "it is probably wisest (and safest) to submit 'headings' for all of [the epigrams]" and the warning that "there is no need to invent new titles for the poems" (9–10). In fact, he says, many of the manuscript titles "bespeak an understanding of the wit and dexterity of the poems so succinctly that one is tempted to claim they are Donne's" (10).

Antiq

Commentary

Date and Circumstances

Chambers (1896, 2:247) argues that the central figure of the epigram "is evidently the person" named in *Sat5* 87 and that "the Epigram is therefore the earlier in date of the two poems."

Grierson (1912, 2:59–60) speculates that the variants "Hamon" or "Hammond" may refer to "John Hammond, LL.D., the civilist, the father of James I's physician and of Charles I's chaplain" (59). Grierson suggests that, despite the absence of evidence that this Hammond was an antiquarian, his profession and reputation as an authority on tithes recommend him, "and he belonged to the class which Donne satirizes with most of [sic] anger and feeling, the examiners and torturers of Catholic prisoners" (59–60).

Shawcross (1967a, 403), though printing the late text in his edition, acknowledges the reading of the earlier texts and cites Esth. chs. 5–7 as the source for the name "Hammon," glossing it thus: "Haman, a collector of great riches, who, through the advice of his wife, sought to have King Ahasuerus hang Mordecai, but he was hanged himself."

Hester (1986, 80–91) elaborates on the connection between the "Haman" of *Sat5* and the biblical figure, "who sold his treasures in order to pay off assassins but ended by being hanged on the gallows that his wife advised him to erect for the faithful Mordecai." Hester describes the antiquities that Haman sold as "God's people and the wisdom of their religion." He further speculates that the version of *Antiq* having "he" rather than the proper name may be Donne's rewriting, undertaken after John Hammond's son obtained his post as royal physician and prompted by Hammond's connection with Prince Henry (whose last illness he oversaw), or, alternatively, that Donne made the change at the time he was preparing his poems for publication before his ordination because the reference had become dated (83). Hester argues that the reference to "Hammond" is made more plausible by Donne's choice of words, especially *strange*, *old*, and *thing*. Citing *Sat4* for comparison, Hester characterizes these words as "nearly unanimous epithets for Catholics among establishment controversialists" (83–84).

Influences and Analogues

The Universal Spectator and Weekly Journal (15 September 1733, 2) published an anonymous apparent imitation of *Antiq*:

To Sir Gimcrack Noddy
Sir Gimcrack round his Hall *hangs* all Things *odd*,
An *embalm'd Pismire*, and a *Straw-stuff'd Cod*,

Alike to Things *antique* his Taste inclines,
Old *Roman Shields*, maim'd *Heads*, and rusty *Coins*;
But if the *oldest*, *oddest* Thing in Life
To these you'd *hang*, Sir *Gimcrack*—hang your *Wife*.

Clough (1920, 116) argues that *Antiq* inspired lines 83–84 of Dryden's *Upon the Death of Lord Hastings* ("Time's offals, only fit for the hospital! / Or to hang an antiquary's room withal").

General Commentary

Ellrodt (1960a, 2:324) finds the influence of Martial's strategy of "surprise" in the elliptical expression of the epigram, which requires the reader to be quick-witted.

Menascè (1974, 38) describes *Antiq* as a joke, even if not original with Donne, that is based on the danger that the aged spouses of antiquaries run of being put up for sale as if they were antiquities themselves.

Hester (1986, 80–91) argues that in *Antiq* the threat is to "Hammon's" *wife* rather than to his *life*: "the caustic variation on the traditional image of woman as vessel (*ware*) and the bitter level of topical satire combine with the fallacious ambiguity to create the sort of surprise-through-equivocation that is central to 'A Selfe-Accuser' and 'A Lame Beggar' also" (83). Even without the topical allusions (see Hester's remarks under Date and Circumstances above), the poem, Hester concludes, "retains its sting and its satirical typology in its unfolding tactical disclosure that Hammon's 'care' for his wife should make her 'wary'" (83–84).

Notes and Glosses

2 *To'hang* **PATRIDES** (1985): pronounced as one word (129).

AutHook

Commentary

The epigram appears in autograph in a copy of William Covell's *A Just and Temperate Defence of the Five Books of Ecclesiastical Policie: written by Mr. Richard Hooker* (London, 1603).

Gosse (1899, 1:270) attributes the couplet to Donne, adding, "we see Donne, like Dr. Johnson of Mrs. Montagu, inquiring of Covell whether he had estimated the value of his help before he proferred it."

Hayward (1930, xii, 324) calls *AutHook* "this small addition to the canon of Donne's writings, and the only known example of verse in his own hand" (324). (Hayward was of course writing before the subsequent discovery of other poetic materials in autograph, including *Carey*—eds.)

Gardner (1952, xxi) cites the epigram as evidence of Donne's admiration for Hooker, observing that the relationship between the two has been unjustly neglected. Hooker, she maintains, taught Donne and others of his caliber to apply certain philosophic principles to particular controversies: "Hooker did not tell them what to think, but how to think."

Field (1966, 307–09) affirms that Donne almost never gives "any indication of his knowledge of or dependence upon contemporary or near contemporary English spokesmen" (307). Within this context Field notes the existence of *AutHook* and provides the following translation: "Hooker does not need such great protection; but / he who attacks such great help would be safe." The judgment of the first line Field believes "would hardly seem possible were Donne not familiar with Hooker's *Laws*, as well as being in such substantial agreement as to be provoked into writing this epigrammatic comment—a unique action by Donne unparalleled in any of the other books known to be from his library" (309).

Shawcross (1967a, 167) offers the following translation:

> *To the author.*
> Hooker is not in need of so much defence;
> but he who attacks may be supported by so much assistance.

Shawcross further glosses the poem as alluding to the arguments of Hooker's antagonist, possibly Thomas Cartwright, author of *A Christian Letter of certain English Protestants to Master R. Hooker* (1599); Donne, in Shawcross's view, points out that by bothering to contest Cartwright's arguments, Covell's book lends them weight. Shawcross explains that Hooker's work, published in 1593 and 1597, was attacked by *A Christian Letter* on the grounds that it undermined the Anglican Church's Thirty-Nine Articles of Faith.

AutJos

Commentary

Keynes (1958, 108), announcing the identification of another volume from Donne's library (a copy of Joseph Scaliger's *Opus Novum de Emendatione Temporum in Octo Libros Tributum* [Paris, 1583]), notes his discovery of the epigram on the fly-leaf opposite the title page, and observes that it represents the longest extant verse writing in Donne's own hand (Keynes was of course writing before the subsequent discovery of *Carey*—eds.). In addition to the Latin text, Keynes supplies a translation by John Sparrow:

> Times, laws, rewards, and punishments, thou 'art fain
> To 'improve, friend Joseph; sure, thou'lt strive in vain;
> The zealot crew has found the task too tough;
> Leave them no worse than they are, and that's enough.

Sparrow (1958, 115) subsequently corrects the translation of the epigram he supplied for Keynes (1958). Sparrow comments upon a letter he received from Professor H. W. Garrod of Oxford, from which he quotes:

> I rendered the verses rather differently from you:—"Set to improve the times, Joseph, you will hardly succeed where laws, rewards, punishments and priesthood have failed. You must be satisfied if you don't make the times worse." The construe has obvious difficulty. But it does explain *conantur*; and it's easier to make Donne say that laws and rewards and punishments try to improve the times than to make him say (what isn't true) that Scaliger wishes to improve laws and rewards and punishments.

Sparrow states that he accepts the correction, which, he explains, "makes possible what is clearly the correct interpretation."

Shawcross (1967a, 166) explains that Scaliger's book (the title of which he gives as *A New Work Concerning the Correction of Chronology*) surveys methods of measuring time and attempts a scientific revision of ancient calendars and dates. He offers a translation:

> *To the author*
> You Joseph wish to improve chronology somehow; laws,
> rewards, punishment the pious throng
> undertake now in vain since you will in error presume;
> it is enough if on account of you the times are not worse.

3 *conantur* **KEYNES** (1958): although one might expect *conatur*, "there seems to be no doubt that the stroke above the fourth letter of *conatur*, as Donne has written it, is the usual contracted form of *n*" (108).

Beggar

Commentary

Date and Circumstances

Grierson (1912, 2:59) considers *Beggar* to be one of a series (including *Ship*, *Wall*, *Cales*, and *Wing*) apparently composed during the Cadiz expedition of 1596. *Beggar*, he argues, "records a common spectacle in a Spanish and Catholic town."

Influences and Analogues

For seventeenth-century adaptations of *Beggar* by Deloney (1607), Mennes (1640), and Weckherlin (1648), see Appendix 2.

Grierson (1912, 2:59) cites for comparison to *Beggar* the first couplet of the four-line epigram printed by Deloney (1607).

Milgate (1950, 229) observes that "in various mangled forms . . . [*Beggar*] became a hardy perennial in commonplace books of the 1620s and 1630s."

Milgate (1967, 198) subsequently characterizes Deloney's epigram (1607) as incorporating *Beggar* without acknowledgment and cites also "Drummond's copy" (see version 4 above). Milgate finds it "extraordinary both that nobody seems to have thought of this jest before, and that Donne's responsibility for it should have been so clearly recognized."

Granqvist (1975, 52) notes that *Beggar* is the only work by Donne that appears in Vicesimus Knox's *Poetical Epitome; or, Elegant Extracts . . . for the Improvement of Scholars at Classical and Other Schools*, and cites this fact as evidence of the epigram's continuous popularity throughout the eighteenth century. Granqvist cites the preface to the 1791 edition, which claims to offer only what was "'precisely known, and universally celebrated,'" with the proviso that it appeal to "'virtuous readers'." Granqvist notes subsequent appearances of *Beggar* in 1806, 1808, 1811, and 1824.

Smith (1975, 7, 10) states that *Beggar* appears fourteen times in all surviving manuscript poetical miscellanies (7) and that it is especially often cited or quoted (10) (the poem actually appears fifty-three times in seventeenth-century manuscripts—eds.).

Sorlien (1976, 219) notes the appearance of a version of the poem in the diary of John Manningham for 31 March 1603 (see version 5 above).

General Commentary

In the context of a discussion of the element of paradox in Donne's verse, Ellrodt (1960a, 1, i:203–04, 2:324) cites *Beggar* as an instance of the use of the pun, a form that (he argues) reveals with relative ease the difference between mere word-play and intellectual engagement in irony and ambiguity. Donne, he maintains, normally plays with ideas rather than with words, but puns rarely express a truth. The sort of ambiguity found in a pun, he asserts, is adulterated or debased ("de mauvais aloi") because one of the meanings offered by the pun is false or arbitrary (1:203). Ellrodt, who terms *Beggar* "médiocre" (2:324), finds Donne, in his use of the pun in the satires, elegies, and epigrams, unfortunately characteristic of the Elizabethan age (1:203). He illustrates his argument by an analysis of the last proposition of *Beggar*, which he says is true only in the first sense of "lie" (recline) but which is meaningless in the second sense (speak an untruth), although the apparent and merely verbal paradox derives from their identity (1:204).

Menascè (1974, 38) cites what she characterizes as the Renaissance-baroque love for the pun as abundant in *Beggar*.

Roston (1974, 89) cites *Beggar* as a type of "the contrived sophistry of the anti-classical mode" that appears throughout Donne's verse.

Hester (1986, 80–91) compares *Beggar* to the "mingled pleasures" of poems such as *Relic*: "the final equivoque, '*lies*,' turns the formal properties of the utterance into a paradox, showing or at least questioning the reliability of words themselves while wittily signaling their ability to suggest the wondrous mysteries of human motivation" (91).

Notes and Glosses

Title. **HESTER** (1990) (referring to the Italian title "*Zoppo*"): cripple or lame person"; however, "the word also identifies a weak, halting, or *defective speech*" (6–7).

2 *lyes*. **PLUMPTRE** (1811): the wit arises from the double meaning, "*lies down*" and "*tells an untruth*" (366).

Cales

Commentary

Date and Circumstances

Gosse (1899, 1:46), who first prints *Cales*, finds that it evokes a scene on board the Earl of Essex's ship at Cadiz in 1596: "It is not forbidden to us to be convinced that Donne was leaning over the side of the *Repulse* when [Sir Walter] Raleigh, flushed with hope and eagerness, returned from his visit of persuasion to [Lord Admiral] Howard, and as he passed under the great ship, shouted up to Essex, 'Intramus,' with so magnetic a thrill in his voice, that Essex flung his hat into the sea in an ecstasy of high spirits. Next morning broke the day of St. Barnabas the Bright (June 11, NS), with its magnificent victory by sea and land." Gosse dates the poem from the following day, and furthermore believes that it is addressed to Raleigh, who, "severely wounded in the leg by a splinter, had been unable to join Essex in his land-attack on the city of Cadiz." Gosse continues his reconstruction:

> On the morning of the 12th of June, hearing that a fleet of forty richly-laden carracks had fled down the Rio Puerto Real, with a view to escaping to the Indies, Raleigh communicated to Essex his desire promptly to pursue them even to the farther side of the world. This spirited proposal, before Essex could reply, had received its answer from the Duke of Medina Sidonia, who set the whole argosy on fire. But the matter must have been admiringly discussed on board the *Repulse*, and it must have been on the morning of the 12th of June 1596 that Donne addressed these lines to Raleigh.

Grierson (1912, 2:59) groups *Cales* with *Ship*, *Wall*, *Beggar*, and *Wing* as poems composed during the Cadiz expedition. He, also, argues that *Cales* "must clearly have been written when, after Cadiz had been taken and sacked, the leaders were debating their next step. Essex (and Donne is on Essex's side) urged that the fleet should sail west and intercept the silver fleet, but Howard, the Lord Admiral, insisted on an immediate return to England."

Milgate (1967, 198) endorses the same position, reading "th'old worlds farthest end" (l. 1) as a plausible allusion to Cadiz, which is west of Gibraltar and near the southern extremity of the Iberian peninsula, "kindled" (l. 2) as descriptive of Raleigh's and Essex's feelings in the flush of victory, and "spoyle" (l. 1) as alluding to the sack of Cadiz. Milgate supposes that some of the expedition may have considered sailing far to the west in pursuit of the Spanish silver fleet and notes the publication in 1596 of Raleigh's account of his own (1595) voyage to Guiana (*Discoverie of Guiana*).

Bald (1970, 88–89) contends that the epigram is addressed to Essex and Raleigh and reflects the hopes of the fleet to sail to the West Indies and attack the Spanish Main.

On the failure to attack Guiana, Patrides (1985, 132) cites *RWSlumb* 18 ("Guyanaes harvest is nip'd in the spring") for comparison.

General Commentary

Hester (1986, 80–91) finds that *Cales* "intimates some 'wise doubt'" about the valor of Elizabethan adventurers. Its form, he argues, is problematic—not conventionally closed but rather "mirroring the multiple and contradictory possibilities of human determination." Perceiving a symbiotic relationship between the form and the content, Hester finds that *Cales*, "like the aspirations of the adventurers, . . . 'bends' toward unexpected results, toward 'new ends' that are 'trewer' to human 'example.'" Citing the observation of Frank S. Caricato ("John Donne and the Epigram Tradition," PhD diss., Fordham University, 1973) that the last line alludes to Aristotle's theorem about the generation of matter, Hester urges that the puns on "a new" and "spoyle" suggest that "the poem may indicate Donne's own conflicting opinions about the wisdom of the English expeditionary adventures or his attempts to side with Essex in the continous struggle for royal favor" while still expressing the poet's desire to open up the genre of the epigram to expressions of irony beyond the customary sententiousness of the form (88–89).

Hester subsequently (1987, 53–54) characterizes *Cales* as "one record of Donne's critical response to Ralegh's clarion call . . . for the license to expand the Protestant empire to the New World [in] the rear-admiral's *Discoverie of Guiana*" and other petitions for funds (53).

Notes and Glosses

Title. SHAWCROSS (1967a): "Cadiz and Guiana" (162).

1 *old worlds* SULLENS (1964): "Under World, the *OED* gives the earliest ill[ustration] of Old World in this sense as 1888" (226).

1 *you* SHAWCROSS (1967a): "probably Sir Walter Ralegh" (163).

Disinher

Commentary

Milgate (1967, 200) notes resemblances to Martial, Epigrams 3.10 and 5.32. He remarks that Sir John Harington "absorbed Donne's epigram into one of his own, 'Of one that vow'd to dis-inherit his son and give his goods to the poor'" (see Appendix 2).

Hester (1985a, 135–37), reading the epigram as an example of Donne's practice as "a revisionist poet, an inventive artist who modifies whatever he borrows" (135), first notes some typical portrayals found in Martial of the disinherited son and then asserts that Donne's poem "inverts the usual treatment of this comic type." The reader's expectation that the son has been rendered poor, Hester argues, is overturned by "the surprising significance of a philanthropic father's final gesture," specifically by "the moral interpretation of the worth that should be 'all' to a loving son—the goodness of his father" (136). Further, Hester suggests that the poem may derive from "that popular medieval and Renaissance textbook of proverbial wisdom, the *Catonis Disticha*: *Quod tibi sors dederit tabulis suprema notato, / augendo serva, ne sis quem fama loquatur*. (III. 8) [A heritage bequeathed to you will / Keep and increase: so save your good name still]." "By accommodating this popular . . . adage to the context of a *disinherited* son," Hester concludes, "Donne increases the surprise of his poem" in so far as he thereby "illustrates an unforeseen applicability for [pseudo-]Cato's advice" (137).

Notes and Glosses

2 *good title* **SMITH** (1971): "a good legal claim to the legacy" (466). **HESTER** (1985a): "reverses the legal senses of 'title' and submits the unexpected observation that as the son of a generous and charitable father the disinherited son has gained the 'title' but has been given a 'title' metaphorically (or spiritually). Thus, the legal title of being his father's son, which the father could not donate to the poor, is 'still' 'good' both legally and morally" (136). **WILLMOTT** (1985): "an entitlement to claim his inheritance since, being disinherited, he is now poor" (57).

2 *still*. **HESTER** (1985a): "the son does have a title that is 'still' in the sense of being dead or worthless materially . . .; but finally he has 'good title' *yet*—his 'still' father has bequeathed him a heritage of honor and charity" (136).

Faust

Commentary

Date and Circumstances

Shawcross (1967b, 104–05) argues for the acceptance of this epigram, to which he gives the title "Faustus," into the canon, for four reasons: (1) it appears in the Hawthornden ms. on a page of poems all of which are attributed by the scribe (William Drummond) to "JD"; (2) it appears among authentic Donne poems elsewhere assigned to "JD"; (3) it accompanies an authentic epigram (*Beggar*) also assigned to "JD"; (4) "it is not unlike authentic epigrams in style" (104–05). "The use of the name Faustus in epigrams was commonplace," Shawcross observes, "as a glance at Sir John Harington's work will show" (105); he comments further that he has not found *Faust* elsewhere.

Beal (1980, 259) characterizes both *Faust* and *Jug* as "minor" and as admitted to the canon of Donne's poetry on the basis of arguments advanced by Shawcross (1967b) and of "some support from more recently discovered MSS."

Notes and Glosses

Title. **SHAWCROSS** (1967a) (reading "Faustus"): "common in epigrams of the period . . . and seems here not to refer to the necromancer of Wittenberg" (165).

Title. **HESTER** (1990): a multiple play "on the Latin meanings of *faustus* ('prosperous' and 'fortunate')" (3).

Hero

Commentary

Leishman (1951, 52) states that in *Hero* Donne has "ingeniously contrived to introduce the four elements."

In an extended discussion of *Hero*, Ellrodt (1960a, 2:323–24) cites the literary theorist Thomas Correa (author of a 1569 treatise on epigrams) to the effect that epigrammatic wit consists principally not in intellectual subtlety but in the element of surprise. Examining *Hero* in the light of this prescription, Ellrodt finds in it a paradoxical or antithetical treatment of a classical legend and thus a challenge not to fixed, preconceived ideas, but to the familiar process of thinking about the subject itself. *Hero*'s overriding interest in shortness constitutes, in Ellrodt's view, a development of the technique of the conceit inherited from earlier writers of sonnets. However, he continues, in *Hero* (as in *Pyr*) the poet offers the reader a set situation the elements of which are themselves surprising; the paradox lies in the given facts of the situation. Whatever surprise there is, Ellrodt argues, is not a consequence of dramatic manipulation of the elements (as in Martial's epigrams), but rather of their mere presentation. Ellrodt compares *Hero* unfavorably with Martial's epigrams, which, he argues, characteristically reveal themselves in stages, compelling the reader to supply the link in the chain of reasoning that will result in a complete and satisfying understanding.

Milgate (1967, 196–97) compares *Hero* with Sir Philip Sidney's *Arcadia*, Third Eclogue ("Man oft is plag'de with aire, is burnt with fire, / In water dround, in earth his buriall is").

Smith (1968, 204–06) prefaces her discussion of *Hero* with a definition of *hyperdetermination*, which, she maintains, occurs "not only when the conclusion of a poem is strongly determined by the entire structure that precedes it, but when it is also reinforced in that particular form by special closural devices" (204). Citing *Hero* as an impressive example of hyperdetermination, Smith centers her discussion upon the final three words, which are paradoxically "completely 'redundant,'" and yet "in a way surprising" (205). First, she configures the four clauses of the epigram in order to reveal their relation to one another as ratios: A:B::C:D, and its permutation, A:C::B:D. Stating that the mathematical symmetry allows the reader to solve D (water) once the values of A, B, and C (air, ground, and fire) are known, Smith concludes that what surprises the reader "is not the novelty of the material but the elegance and economy with which it was deployed." In other words, "while the inevitable completion of that series reflects the inexorable fate of the unlucky pair against whom all the elements of nature conspired, the formal patterns and symmetries suggest an ultimate justice in it" (206).

Shawcross (1983c, 159–66) finds death described in all four phrases of the poem and links the notion of death to sexual intercourse; he therefore reads the epigram "as a witty comment on love and lovemaking, which paradoxically leads to death, not to new life" (160).

Hester (1986, 80–91) finds that the "commemorative typology" present in *Wing* appears also in *Hero*, which he calls "an epigrammatic riddle." In *Hero*, he reasons, "the universality of the lovers' amatory conduct is figured forth in the Empedoclean circularity of their immersion in the four elements," adding that "the 'just circle' of their love has transformed the fragmented, elemental flux into a *concordia*." However, Hester notes, there is an element of irony "in the image of the two lovers as an emblem of the elemental unity of love." He maintains that "they have achieved an elemental 'perfection' only through their deaths, so the 'circle' of their love is 'just' only through their destruction." Hester finds that we are left not with "an image of eternality" but rather with "a sad completeness," arguing that the poem "suggests only a 'literary' immortality." He reasons that "the 'circle' of the lovers' action 'lies,' as the pun suggests—they are victims ('rob'd') as much as conquerors; their completeness is achieved only through their final immersion in death" (82).

Notes and Glosses

Title. Hero and Leander. **SHAWCROSS** (1967a): "the lovers who drowned in the Hellespont" (161). **SHAWCROSS** (1983c): the title diminishes the poem's scope by appearing to limit its reference to one story. However, it is not certain that Donne intended this title (160).

2 *one fyer* **MILGATE** (1967): the fire of mutual love (197). **WADDINGTON** (1974): "The flaming torch is necessary for a schematic treatment of the four elements" (155–56).

Jug

Commentary

Title and Status in the Canon

The epigram was first printed by Bennett (1942) with the title "Manliness" (see the Textual Introduction to *Jug*).

Milgate (1967, 200) accepts the manuscript ascription to Donne.

Shawcross (1967b, 104–05) reviews the manuscript history and verbal variants of *Jug*, arguing for accepting it as well as *Faust* into the canon.

General Commentary

Ellrodt (1960a, 2:49, 277), placing *Jug* within a context of supposed reaction to Elizabethan homosexuality, suggests that it condemns homosexual behavior; the poem, he argues, signals on the part of Donne and his generation an affirmation of virility and of Englishness.

Fowkes (1982, xvi), without identifying the objects of his criticism, decries the expenditure of critical effort on ingenious speculations about Donne's sexuality, ones that possibly reveal "more about . . . [the critics'] own proclivities and the fickleness of literary taste than about John Donne." He explains that "the dominant mother and early replacement of the father, together with an absurdly selective reading of some of the work, has led some latter-day Freudians to hint at homosexuality." Rejecting this interpretation, Fowkes cites the "nice epigram on 'manliness'" as evidence to the contrary.

Notes and Glosses

Title. **MILGATE** (1967): "The Jughler" is a "pointless" title; "Manliness," the title supplied by Bennett (1942), is preferable (200). **HESTER** (1990): "*to juggle* is Renaissance slang for 'to copulate' and derives from the Latin *joculare* which means 'to manipulate' and 'to jest'" (5).

1 *womens ioyes* **SHAWCROSS** (1967a): "both things enjoyed by women and the joys which women yield" (165).

2 *follow boyes*. **SHAWCROSS** (1967a): "both do as youngsters do and pursue boys for sexual purposes" (165).

Klock

Commentary

Title

For various headings given the poem in seventeenth-century sources and subsequent editions, see the Textual Introduction and Textual Apparatus for *Klock*.

Milgate (1967, 202), noting the reading "Rawlings" (for "Klockius") in LR1, says, "I doubt whether it is authentic."

Shawcross (1967a, 165) says that "Klockius" is "probably a 'sly person' from the Dutch *kloek*." He adds that "Rawlings" may point to John Rawlins, who was a witness against the Earl and Countess of Somerset (whose marriage Donne celebrates in *Eclog*) at their 1615 trial for the murder of Sir Thomas Overbury.

Subsequently, Shawcross (1983c, 159–66) compares the title to other title-names in Donne's poetry, arguing that its impression is indefinite, except insofar as the "sounds suggest some kind of meaning, or the form suggests some kind of status or characteristic, or the etymology suggests a kind of punning substruct" (159). The Latinate ending, he suggests, implies a fictional subject of possibly higher social status, and the name may alert us to register disapproval of some dishonest person of rank.

General Commentary

Gamberini (1967, 46–47) cites *Klock* as more successful than most of Donne's other epigrams because it is caustic and therefore comic.

Shawcross (1983c, 159–66) summarizes the poem as stating that Klockius's wife is in some sense a prostitute. He finds also the implication of a double standard towards the two sexes and suggests that the poem criticizes women who merely pretend to be respectable. Despite the possible allusion to Sir John Rawlins, Shawcross adds, the reader responds to the poem as a comment on categories of people.

Parfitt (1989, 19), though asserting that "Donne does not seem at home with the splintered pictures of epigram," prefaces his inclusion of *Klock* by noting that "Donne clearly has the wit and terseness required, and he can do viciousness."

Notes and Glosses

1 *come* **SHAWCROSS** (1967a): "both 'enter' and 'have seminal emission'" (165).

Liar

Commentary

Date and Circumstances: "Spanish dyeting"

Gosse (1899, 1:52) supposes that the epigram "reflects on the evil cuisine with which Elizabethan travellers in Spain were afflicted."

Inferring from Gosse (1899) that the poem is a "reminiscence" of Spanish fare, Grierson (1912, 2:60) proposes that *Liar* was written after the Cadiz expedition of 1596.

Ellrodt (1960b, 456) disputes the necessity of any personal experience of Spanish food as a condition of declaring it detestable and so discounts any dating linked to the Cadiz expedition.

General Commentary

Grierson (1912, 2:60) notes that *Liar* was first printed in Simeon (siglum 70), under the title *Supping Hours*, and argues from manuscript evidence for its place in the canon.

Lindsay (1931, 234) refers (without specifying them) to two allusions to *Liar* in William Browne's *Britannia's Pastorals* (Vol. I, 1613; Vol. II, 1616).

Granqvist (1975, 136) noting the date (1856–57) of Simeon's publication of the poem, cites its appearance in Simeon as evidence of the "broadened taste" of the period and of editorial decisions made on the basis of "individual preference."

Notes and Glosses

2 *And yet thou swearst thou hast supd like a king;* **BEAVER** (1976): the line is a single instance involving a contrastive stress on an auxiliary (115):

1 2 3 4 5 6 7 8 9 10
And yet thou swearst thou hast supd like a king
W S W S W S W S W S

3 *Like Nabuchadnezar* **GRIERSON** (1912): cf. *AWW* 4.5.20–21: "I am no great Nebuchadnezzar, sir; I have not much skill in grass" (2:60). **MILGATE** (1967): "King Nebuchadnezzar 'was driven from men, and did eat grass as oxen' (Daniel iv. 33)" (200).

4 *A Sallet, worse then Spanish dyeting.* **MILGATE** (1967): Thomas Nashe and James Howell testified to the reputation of Spanish food—that ordinary people sub-

sisted, like animals, on grass and water (200–01). **SHAWCROSS** (1967a): "refers to the preponderance of vegetables of the leek family in the Spanish diet" (163).

4 *then* **PATRIDES** (1985): "than" (132).

Licent

Commentary

Sources and Analogues

For various seventeenth-century answers (Fitzgeffrey, 1617), adaptations (Quarles, 1629; scribe of B23), and translations (Weckherlin, 1641; Stubbs, 1658) made in response to this popular epigram, see Appendix 2.

Grosart (1872–73, 2:268) cites Ps. 40.12 ("For innumerable evils have compassed me about: mine iniquities have taken hold upon me, so that I am not able to look up; they are more than the hairs of mine head: therefore my heart faileth me" [AV]) and 69.4 ("They that hate me without a cause are more than the hairs of mine head: they that would destroy me, being mine enemies wrongfully, are mighty: then I restored that which I took not away" [AV]).

General Commentary

Grosart (1872–73, 2:268) terms *Licent* "a justification" of the scriptural passages "by reference to the then commonest of jokes on baldness and French crowns."

Milgate (1967, 199) explains the baldness described in the epigram as the consequence of *morbus Gallicus*.

Smith (1971, 466) describes the subject's disease as syphilis.

Menascè (1974, 38), contrasts what she describes as the joke in the poem with the sorrowful biblical passage to which it alludes.

Hester (1986, 80–91) asserts that *Licent* not only conforms to the Planudean mode of the epigram, but also presents "an ironic literalization of the Psalmist's admission ... through an amusing amplification of the joke about the syphilitic's 'French crown'" (82). The poem's satirical force, he argues, results from the "pun on 'hairs'/'heirs' (which is prepared for by the synecdochic 'thy sinnes increase'). This pun not only intimates the extent of the satiric victim's contagion but also transforms the witty Roman epigram into a versification of both the Psalm adage and the biblical proverb about the visitation of the sins of the father on the son" (83).

Martial

Commentary

Date and Circumstances

Norton (1895, 1:248), explains that Matthew Rader (1561–1634), a "learned German Jesuit," published "an expurgated edition of Martial [M. *Valerii Martialis Epigrammaton Libri Omnes* . . .] in 1602."

Chambers (1896, 2:247) states that the date of composition of *Martial* "must be later than 1602."

Ellrodt (1960b, 456) suggests that although 1602 is the probable date of publication of Rader's edition, it may have appeared later.

Pafford (1965, 377) cites an early reference to the poem in a copy of Martial's *Epigrams* printed in Leyden in 1661. The volume in which the epigram appears apparently belonged to "Sir James Astry, of Harlington Woodend, Bedfordshire, 1653–1709, or [to] his son James, 1675–1716" (this copy is designated LU1 in this edition and has been collated; see the Textual Apparatus).

Milgate (1967, 202) cites Rader's own explanation (in Latin), that because the book was to be used in schools, only chaste, holy, and untainted material should be printed, so that a young person searching for knowledge would not lose his innocence. Rader further explains that he used asterisks to indicate places where he had censored material.

General Commentary

Grierson (1912, 2:60) cites Donne's *Ignatius* (1610), to the effect that "'Raderus and others of his order did use to geld Poets and other authors (and here I could not choose but wonder why they have not gelded their Vulgar Edition which in some places hath such obscene words, as the Hebrew tongue which is therefore called holy, doth so much abhorre that no obscene thing can be uttered in it). . . . [The explanation Donne gives is that the Jesuits] reserve to themselves the divers forms, and the secrets, and mysteries . . . which they find in the authors whom they gelde' [*Ignatius his Conclave*, pp. 94–96]." On the basis of these statements, Grierson concludes that "the epigram is therefore a coarse hit at the Jesuits."

Ellrodt (1960a, 2:274–75) cites *Martial* as an instance of the influence of Martial, whose sharp satire Ellrodt finds gaining influence about the year 1600. Martial's bitter flavor, he argues, is to the taste of the period; hence Donne's reproach to the Roman poet's emasculator.

Hester (1985b, 324–30) compares *Martial* to *Ralph* as "instructive examples" of Donne's poetic strategy: "the frustration or surprise of the reader's expectations" (324). Whether they appear as two isolated poems in Donne's canon or whether they appear consecutively as the last two poems in Donne's collected epigrams, Hester asserts, the "significance" of the two poems "is increased by their intertextual suggestiveness." He asserts further that "the attitude towards the reader of epigrams intimated in 'Raderus' raises certain interpretive questions about 'Ralphius.'" He maintains that "the major thrust of . . . [Donne's] jest [against Matthew Rader] is conveyed by the puns on 'use' (as sexual intercourse) and 'tricks' (as sexual stratagems), which are intensified by the description of the *priest* as 'this *man*.'" The indeterminacy of the name "Katherine" in the last line—whether it refers to one of Henry VIII's wives or Catherine de' Medici—is less important, Hester argues, than its comparison to the editor Rader himself: "identification of the specific queen is not essential to the satire here, for the Latin meaning of 'Katherine' ('pure') conveys the satirical thrust of the ironic simile—it accentuates the wry comparison between a 'pure' queen whose prohibitions may have been intended to serve her own sexual desires and a 'chaste' priest whose excisions may have been intended to further his own sexual knowledge" (325). Hester notes the Elizabethan slang senses of *queen* as both prostitute and homosexual, suggesting that the choice of a "queen" who prohibits prostitutes from serving their customers might have been meant as a facetious imputation of sodomy to Rader, who deleted Martial's poems on homosexual subjects from his edition. Hester adds that "the joke is complete" within lines 1–2, the simile of line 3 only reinforcing the sarcasm of what precedes (326).

Hester also points out two qualities of Martial's epigrams that he finds important for understanding *Martial*. First, Martial compared poems to husbands and readers to wives, whom husbands cannot please "*sine mentula*." Likewise, epigrams cannot please their readers unless they are wanton. Second, Martial compares the phallic-symbol god Priapus to the priests of Cybele, who castrated themselves at the conclusion of their rites. Hester suggests that Donne's reference to Raderus as a "man" implies that the Jesuit has "been less rigid about his priestly vows" even than the self-castrators, finding in line 2 the implication that Raderus is a type of Priapus. If Donne intended the reader to recall Martial's two comparisons, Hester reasons, then the reader, proceeding to *Ralph*, "seems to be invited to read . . . [*Ralph*] in the spirit of Martial's *iocosa carmina*" (327).

Notes and Glosses

Title. **HESTER** (1990) (reading "Raderus"): this title is preferable since, in the context of Matthew Rader's expurgated edition of Martial, it "plays on the Latin root of the editor's name (*rado*: 'to cut,' 'to lash') and raises questions about the Jesuit priest's commitment to the words of his vows as well as to the words of the Latin poet" (4).

1 *muse;* **GROSART** (1872–73): "make muse to myself" (2:269).

2 *Except himselfe alone his tricks would vse* **MILGATE** (1967): implies what Donne actually states in *Ignatius*, that the Jesuit Rader reserves for himself the information he censors for others (202). **SMITH** (1971): "unless Rader wanted to keep all Martial's licentious devices for his own exclusive use" (467).

3 *As Katherine . . . put downe Stews*. **MILGATE** (1967): Katherine suppressed brothels for the same reason Rader censored Martial (202).

3 *Katherine* **GROSART** (1872–73): "probably K. de Medici" (2:269). **MILGATE** (1967): Grosart offers no evidence for his reading. Henry VIII banned the brothels in Southwark (according to William Camden, *Britannia*, trans. Holland [1610], 434); Donne is probably "using some old joke connecting Henry's action with one of his three queens named Catherine" (202). **SHAWCROSS** (1967a): "a frequent name for cooks and servants, but perhaps punning on Catherine Parr, who managed the royal household both before and after Henry VIII's death, and who was married five times" (166). **SMITH** (1971): "Presumably the reference is to some Queen Catherine who suppressed the public brothels, but no one has identified her" (467).

3 *for the Coarts sake* **MILGATE** (1967): the phrase is ambiguous; however, "preaching to a congregation at Lincoln's Inn, some of whose members probably had this epigram copied in their commonplace books, Donne (with some courage) makes the same point: 'We may have heard of Princes that have put down Stewes, and executed severe Laws against Licentiousness; but that may have been to bring all the Licentiousness of the City into the Court'" (*Sermons* 1:256) (202). **SMITH** (1971): "(a) so as to benefit the morals of the Court; (b) so that the Court could have a monopoly of sexual licence" (467).

3 *Stews*. **SHAWCROSS** (1967a): "punning on the meaning 'brothels'" (166).

Merc

Commentary

Date and Circumstances

Grosart (1872–73, 2:269) identifies the wording of the title ("Mercurius Gallobelgicus") as a reference to "the well-known 'Gazette.'"

Norton (1895, 1:234) observes that the publication is often alluded to in literature of the first quarter of the seventeenth century, adding that it is thought to be the first journal of contemporary history; he dates the first issue in 1598 and says the journal published twice annually in the early seventeenth century.

Grierson (1912, 2:60) dates the journal from 1594, characterizing its Latin as sometimes flawed and its news sometimes untrustworthy (see also Shawcross [1967a, 164], who adds that the journal's news was not confined to France and Belgium).

Ellrodt (1960b, 456) dates the first publication of the journal in 1598, and concludes that *Merc* can be no earlier.

Milgate (1967, 157), in a note to *Sat4*, dates the first issue from 1588.

Patrides (1985, 131) terms the journal "an early representative of the yellow press, issued in Latin at Cologne."

Notes and Glosses

Title. **HESTER** (1990): "focuses the reader's attention on the poet's sardonic delight in the venereal and mendacious connotations of the name Mercury and the witty application of the adage *fide graeca* . . . in his attack on the wordy and inaccurate news-journal" (4).

1–3 *Like Æsops fellow slaues . . . which nothing;* **MILGATE** (1967): Aesop was sold as a slave along with two other men. The prospective purchaser asked each what he knew how to do. The others replied "everything," but Aesop replied "nothing," explaining that the others had already claimed all knowledge for themselves (201).

2 *fayth* **SMITH** (1971): "credulity" (467).

5 *Thy credit lost thy credit:* **MILGATE** (1967): "Your credulousness destroys my credulity ('faith,' power to believe)" (201). **SMITH** (1971): "Your credulousness cost you our trust" (467).

5–7 *tis Sinne . . . To beleeue all.* **MILGATE** (1967): "The Golden Rule (Matt. 7.12) does not apply here; it would be sinful to believe lies" (201).

7 *To beleeue all. Change thy Name; thou art like* **BEAVER** (1976): the line exhibits a "multiple cancellation of s.p. [stress prominence] in weak position":

1 2 3 4 5 6 7 8 9 10
To beleeve all: Change thy name: thou art like
W S W S W S W S W S

Because the only lexical stresses occur in weak positions (3, 5, and 7), "the reader's expectations are completely thwarted" (121).

8 *Mercury* **MILGATE** (1967): "patron of thieves" (Greek *Hermes*) (201). **SHAWCROSS** (1967a): "The name is, of course, in Latin. Mercury was the patron of thieves, and Sinon, who told the Trojans lies about the wooden horse, was proverbial" (164).

8 *stealing,* **SMITH** (1971): "filching scraps of news from all quarters without acknowledgement, as Mercury stole Apollo's cattle and denied it" (467).

8 *lyest like a Greeke*. **SMITH** (1971): "The ancient Greeks had a name for deviousness and lies in politics. Balancing a Roman title—Mercury—against Greek, the line suggests a combination of the vices of both ancient peoples" (467).

Niobe

Commentary

General Commentary

Fausset (1924, 216) comments that with the death of Donne's daughter Mary in May of 1614 and the illness of his wife from the birth of their son Francis in November of that same year, Donne found that this epigram "was becoming applicable to himself."

Shawcross (1967a, 161) summarizes the story of Niobe, who, "proud of her many children . . . compared herself to Leto, mother of Diana and Apollo, who for punishment slew her children. Weeping profusely, she was changed into a stone by Jove."

Smith (1971, 464) notes that there were twelve children, killed by Apollo and Artemis (i.e., Diana). "Wearied with shedding tears," Smith adds, "Niobe became a stone."

Shawcross (1983b, 7–8) compares the versions of *Niobe* in B7, H6, and A to illustrate his case that "close transcription from a manuscript will not necessarily give us a totally satisfactory text," adding that neither do the 1633 and later editions necessarily provide a text that can with certainty be called Donne's (7). After discussing the variants among the three versions, Shawcross focuses on the latter two to demonstrate how the differences affect interpretation. "Apparently," he argues, "because 'made' occurs in . . . [NY3] and 'sad' is omitted, Wesley Milgate prints that reading in his edition of the epigrams." Shawcross states that it is difficult to accept "made" as "artistically significant, let alone meaningful," because "made" implies "a maker rather than simply transformation." He suggests that "sad" may be "redundant with 'tomb' in many situations," but reads the word "as emphasizing her 'sadness' as well as indicating that 'tomb' is really metaphoric." Shawcross asserts that *Niobe* "does not seem to be alluding to the mythological explanation that the gods changed Niobe into a rock; the rock continued to weep." The epigram, he argues, "seems to be trying to get at the metaphoric importance of the tale: when one boasts, adversity may bring such sadness in the removal of that of which one boasted that he/she becomes an insensate thing." Shawcross further sees "a play between water imagery (generative) and stone (a part of earth but unregenerative), and between womb (generative) and tomb (unregenerative)" (8).

Patrides (1985, 128) numbers Niobe's children at seven sons and seven daughters and states that she "continued to weep even after she was changed into a stone."

Notes and Glosses

2 *dry*, **MILGATE** (1967): "The point seems to be that Niobe ('all tears,' cf. *Hamlet*,

I, ii, 149) by paradox claims to be 'dry.' The birth of her twelve children, their death, and her own death (by being changed into a stone) have left her dry. This contradicts the usual conception of Niobe as herself weeping the trickling waters of a stream or fountain, in sorrow for her children's death" (197). **SMITH** (1971): "(a) The dry humour in the body predominates, as happens with age or long suffering; (b) she has wept herself dry of tears" (464).

Philo

Commentary

General Commentary

Ellrodt (1960a, 2:143), in an extensive analysis of arguments advancing or refuting the proposition that Donne is an "obscure" writer, argues that Donne never declared himself in favor of obscurity and cites *Philo* as an instance of the ridicule of deliberate obscurity. Donne's goal, and that of his generation, Ellrodt maintains, is not obscurity but originality; Ellrodt discounts contemporary evidence that Donne was "obscure," arguing that Donne did not intend to be obscure and that readers have not actually found him so.

Notes and Glosses

1 *Philo*, **MILGATE** (1967): the name is found in Martial, Epigram 5.47; "no particular person is necessarily meant here" (201). **SHAWCROSS** (1967a): possibly a specific person, but probably used for its "pedantic connotation: it means 'love of' something" (164).

1–2 *griev'd / To be'vnderstood*, **SMITH** (1971): "it grieves him when people understand his writings, for he counts himself so learned as to be beyond the grasp of most readers" (466).

2 *To be'vnderstood*, **PATRIDES** (1985): "whenever he was understood" (130).

2 *To be* **PATRIDES** (1985) (reading "To'be"): pronounced as one word (130).

Phrine

Commentary

Influences and Analogues

An apparent imitation and expansion of *Phrine* appears in *The Universal Spectator and Weekly Journal* (1 December 1733, 1):

On Chloe's *Picture*
When *Chloe's* Picture was to *Chloe* shown,
Adorn'd with Charms and Beauty *not her own*;
Where *Hogarth, pitying Nature*, kindly made
Such *Lips*, such Eyes, as *Chloe* never had:
Ye Gods, she cries in Ecstacy of Heart,
How near can *Nature* be express'd by *Art*?
Well,—it is wondrous *like*!—Nay, let me die!
The very *pouting Lip*,—the killing *Eye*!
—Blunt and severe as *Manly* in the Play,
Downright replies,—*Like*, Madam, do you say?
The Picture bears *this Likeness*, it is true,
The *Canvas painted* is, and so are *You*.

Ousby (1974a, 89–90) suggests a possible imitation of *Phrine* by Everard Gilpin in *Skialetheia* (London, 1598): "O sir, she's painted, and you know the guise, / Pictures are curtained from the vulgar eyes" and "Painted *Nigrina* with the picture face." Ousby cites R. E. Bennett, "John Donne and Everard Gilpin," *RES* 15 (1939): 71–72, to make the case that Gilpin had seen a manuscript of *Sat1* and suggests a probable relationship, although she cannot fix an exact chronology. "*Skialetheia*," she observes, "appeared in 1598, and Donne could have composed 'Phryne' anytime between the early 1590s and 1619" (90).

General Commentary

Jonson (c. 1612–16 [1925, 1:150]) is reported by William Drummond to have "had this oft"; Drummond cites *Phrine* in full.

Chambers (1896, 2:247) glosses "had" (in the statement by Drummond) as "quoted."

Leishman (1951, 52) cites Drummond's comment that Jonson had memorized this epigram "as one more piece of evidence as to what Jonson especially admired in Donne."

Ellrodt (1960a, 2:324) cites *Phrine* as an instance of an epigram that successfully duplicates Martial's strategy of provoking "surprise" through dramatic handling of materials—specifically, the unexpected relationship that emerges between elements in line 2.

Hester (1986, 80–91) says that the "tenor" of *Phrine* "is clarified by the association of the 'painted' lady of the epigram with the Greek courtesan of the fourth century B. C. and by the mocking suggestion that, unlike the beautiful courtesan—who was said to have been the model for the Aphrodite of Apelles and for that of Praxiteles, and who was acquitted of impiety when Hyperides the Orator exposed her breast to the jury—the beauty of the Elizabethan Phryne is mere 'paint'" (86).

Notes and Glosses

Title and 1 *Phrine* **MILGATE** (1967): "might have been suggested by the famous courtesan of that name (cf. Burton, *Anatomy*, part. 3, sect. 2, memb. 2, subsect. 2)" (201). **SHAWCROSS** (1967a): "any courtesan" (164). **SHAWCROSS** (1983c): the title predisposes a reader to interpret the poem as a comment not only on cosmetics but also on sexual enticement, and on "the validity of the painting as presenting an outward and essentially real picture of the courtesan" (160). **PATRIDES** (1985): "any latter-day emulator of the famous courtesan of ancient Athens" (130).

2 *painted* **OUSBY** (1974a): the epigram plays on the double meaning of "painted" (89). **HESTER** (1986): "There was a gilded statue of Phryne at Delphi that Pausanias says she dedicated to herself" (86).

Pyr

Commentary

Sources and Analogues

Grierson (1912, 2:58) identifies Ovid, *Metamorphoses* 4.55–165, as the source of the story of Pyramus and Thisbe and finds that "every point in the epigram corresponds" to Ovid's narrative.

Shawcross (1967a, 161) describes the pair as "legendary lovers who made love through a chink in a wall. Keeping a tryst, Thisbe lost her cloak which a lioness smeared with blood. Pyramus, thinking her dead, killed himself, and Thisbe, returning, killed herself."

Smith (1971, 464) states that the lovers' parents sought to keep them apart, and in the end buried them.

Carey (1990, 425) refers the reader to *MND* 5.1.

General Commentary

Arguing that the punctuation of line 1 as found in the 1633 edition establishes "Love" and "Feare" as nouns rather than verbs, Grierson (1912, 2:58) terms *Pyr* "condensed but precise" and offers the following paraphrase: "These two, slain by themselves, by each other, by fear, and by love, are joined here in one tomb, by the friends whose cruel action in parting them brought them together here."

Milgate (1967, 197) adds that the punctuation of the 1633 edition "brings out the wit by which every detail of Ovid's account . . . is referred to in two short lines."

Smith (1971, 464) identifies "Slayne" and "haue ioynd" as the main verbs, offering the following paraphrase: "Cruel friends by parting them have joined two who were slain by themselves, each other, love, and fear."

Daniels (1978, 31) terms Grierson's paraphrase the "standard reading" but finds "a hint of doubt" present in what he terms the "echo" of Shawcross's (1967a, 161) gloss on line 2 (see below). Daniels challenges Grierson's (and Shawcross's) reading: "Though 'friends' is a word which may refer to parents, and though the parents of Pyramus and Thisbe may be characterized as cruel in having forbidden the lovers to meet, the wit of the first line of the epigram hinges upon the paradoxical cruelty of the lovers to themselves. That paradox is emphasized (and the unity of the epigram maintained) if, in the summation, the lovers may be said to have joined themselves as well as separated themselves, meriting the oxymoron 'cruell friends.'" Reading "Two" as the subject of "ioynd," and "cruell frinds" in apposition with "Two," Daniels proposes the following paraphrase: "Two lovers (cruel friends)—slain by themselves, by each other, and by love and fear—have in their parting come together here."

Hester (1986, 80–91) finds the situation in *Pyr* similar to that in *Hero*, both of which he terms "epigrammatic riddles," and links both poems with *Wing* as having the "same kind of commemorative typology." Of *Pyr*, he writes: "The oxymoronic exigencies of the lovers' situation—'by themselves'/'by each other,' 'by fear'/'by love,' 'friends'/'cruel,' 'parting'/'joyn'd'—are presented as having been overcome, or 'unmetaphorized,' by the essential love of this 'two-in-one'" (82).

Notes and Glosses

1 *other*, **GROSART** (1872–73): "I read 'other's,'" thus making "'love' and 'feare' nouns instead of verbs" (2:267).

1 *Love and Feare* **GROSART** (1872–73): "They loved while living apart and separated by a wall, and they feared for each other when separated by themselves at the trysting-place" (2:267).

2 *frinds . . . haue ioynd* **SHAWCROSS** (1967a): "Apparently 'frinds' is the subject of 'have joyn'd'" (161).

Ralph

Commentary

Influences and Analogues

Milgate (1950, 229–31) observes that Thomas Deloney's epigram (see the Commentary under *Beggar* and Appendix 2) is in part derived from *Ralph*.

Milgate later (1967, 202) notes that "an expanded and rewritten version" of *Ralph* appears in St. John's College, Cambridge ms. *James* 548 (CJ2) (see Appendix 2).

General Commentary

For a non-canonical couplet that follows *Ralph* in a copy of the 1633 edition at the Houghton Library, Harvard University, see entry 9.4 in Appendix 2.

Hester (1985b, 324–30) says that *Ralph* "initially impresses us as another of Donne's novel assimilations of a familiar Renaissance proverb: 'A crafty knave needs no broker.'" Hester argues that the lower-class associations of the name "Ralphius" suggest that he is "certainly a social 'knave,'" but that Donne "inverts the saucy adage so that his knave is not 'crafty' but has a knavish broker who is." Hester locates the satiric thrust of "this ironic inversion of the proverb" in the double meaning of "keeps": "the broker is sickened by the sickness of his client, whose death could bring about a loss of the money Ralphius owes him." Hester reasons that "the bedridden broker is not so 'compassionate,' of course, as to return Ralphius' pawned bed to him." Proposing, however, a reading of *Ralph* in terms of its manuscript position following *Martial* (see Hester's commentary on *Martial*), Hester raises the possibility that *Ralph*'s "suggestive language invites . . . a reading deriving from the provocative possibilities of 'Compassion . . . bred . . . sicke . . . the broker keeps his bed'" (327). The erotic undertones of *Martial* lead, Hester argues, to "a bawdy reading" of *Ralph*, "broker" in Donne's time being also slang for bawd, pimp, or pander (327–28). Hester suggests further that "'keeps his bed' means not only that the broker is bedridden or refuses to return the bed of Ralphius, but that he sexually possesses his client's wife or regulates those who enjoy her 'bed'." He argues that Ralphius' sickness might have at least two causes: venereal disease resulting from his wife's prostitution or grief at the broker's business arrangement with her (328). "In this sense," he adds, 'Compassion' is 'bred' 'in the world' for several reasons (as suggested by the rhyme of *bed/bred*)": (1) suffering together may stem from the spread of venereal disease "in the world"; (2) the "world" may pity Ralphius for being a cuckold; (3) the broker may be suffering the same disease as Ralphius, if the wife is being ridiculed in the poem. Also, Hester suggests, if the wife has been victimized by the broker, she may be an object of pity as well, "thus increasing the causes of Ralphius' suffering and thereby including her as another object of the world's 'Compassion'." Hester argues further that if the reader follows the suggestive rhyme and provocative hints in the poem, the general effect of *Ralph* is "broad—but indefinite at the same time, its bases not clarified by the sexual innuendoes." Hester suggests that Donne purposely creates this ambivalent perspective and that "the bawdy connotations encouraged by 'Raderus' and seemingly supported by the sexual hints of this poem are a barometer of the reader's habits of mind and interpretative proclivities" (328). Rather than provide the "maximal closure" characteristic of the epigram, Donne creates an "interpretive dilemma" that "raises questions about Ralphius and the broker, the poet and the reader" (329).

Notes and Glosses

Title. **SHAWCROSS** (1967a): "Ralph" was a common name among members of the lower class (165).

2 *the Broker keepes his bedd.* **MILGATE** (1967): "The broker's apparent act of sympathy is due to the shock induced by the prospect of losing, through Ralphius's possibly fatal illness, the sums of money Ralphius owes him; but Ralphius has pawned his bed also, and cannot lie on it, though ill" (203). **SMITH** (1971): depending on the sense of "keeps," either "(a) Ralphius is the broker, who now has to stay in bed and thus allows compassion to return to the world in his absence" or "(b) the broker is holding Ralphius' bed as security, so that when Ralphius is sick the broker 'keeps' his bed—stays by it as a solicitous attendant" (467).

2 *Broker* **SHAWCROSS** (1967a): "pawnbroker" (165).

SelfAc

Commentary

Ellrodt (1960a, 2:325) cites *SelfAc* as an example of an epigram that successfully duplicates Martial's strategy of surprise (see Ellrodt's commentary on *Phrine*). In *SelfAc*, Ellrodt argues, the procedure is elliptical and demands a quick-witted reader (he cites for comparison *Antiq*, *Disinher*, *Philo*, and *Klock*). Irony, Ellrodt maintains, is latent in the situation itself. He finds the woman's failure to realize that her reproaches will fall back upon herself comic. But, Ellrodt argues, the poem's sharpness derives from the malice of the poet's pretense that he understands her charge as an avowal. This, Ellrodt asserts, is the art of the epigrammatist, who surprises us first with the very expression of his surprise ("Tis strange") and then with the transformation of the reproach into an avowal ("confess"), before he lets us perceive, with the final peremptory affirmation, the ironic turnabout of the thought: the mistress herself is one of the whores whom she reproaches her lover for chasing. Ellrodt characterizes *SelfAc* as grasping a thought in the process of its birth, thereby producing what he describes as the dialectical effect also found in the songs and sonnets. He specifies a difference, however, in that in the lyrics the chain of reasoning is exposed, whereas in the epigram it is implicit. Thus, Ellrodt concludes, in the epigram the idea is spontaneously created in the mind of the reader who perceives the unexpressed relationships.

Notes and Glosses

Title. selfe accuser **SULLENS** (1964) (reading "self-accuser"): the *OED* "gives this title as the earliest occurrence of the word" (200).

2 *though'it* **PATRIDES** (1985): pronounced as one word (129).

Ship

Commentary

Date and Circumstances

Grierson (1912, 2:58–59) places *Ship* at the beginning of a sequence (including *Wall, Beggar, Cales*, and *Wing*) that, he argues, was composed during the Cadiz expedition of June 1596; he finds that *Ship* suggests, and was probably suggested by, the battle in the harbor when many Spanish ships were burned.

Milgate (1967, 197) discounts any linkage with events in Donne's life, saying *Ship* cannot be precisely dated.

Bald (1970, 82–83) assigns the circumstances of the epigram to the naval attack on Cadiz on 21 June 1596, and specifically to the attack upon the Spanish flagship *San Felipe*. After quoting Raleigh's account of the battle, Bald states that it can be assumed that Donne "was well within sight of this action" (83).

Dingley (1980, 318) contests Bald's argument (1970), proposing instead a literary source for the poem in the first chapter of Sidney's *Arcadia* (1590), which is itself modelled on the opening of Heliodorus' *Aethiopica*. Dingley points out the parallels between the epigram's description of a ship's burning and Musidorus's account at the opening of Sidney's work, noting further that Pyrocles, in *Arcadia*, later gives his own version of the same episode.

General Commentary

Furst (1896, 231) finds "the love of antithesis at its height" in *Ship*, which shares with *Antiq, Disinher*, and the satires the characteristics of "unusual thought and condensed expression."

Grierson (1912, 2:58–59) cites for comparison King James's letter of 1607 to the Earl of Salisbury on the Dutch demands for assistance against Spain: "'Should I ruin myself for maintaining them . . . I look that by a peace they should enrich themselves to pay me my debts, and if they be so weak as that they cannot subsist, either in peace or war, without I ruin myself for upholding them, in that case surely the nearest harm is to be eschewed: *a man will leap out of a burning ship and drown himself in the sea* . . .'" (emphasis in Grierson) (2:58).

Hillyer (1941, xxxii) calls *Ship* the only epigram that holds "more than a passing interest," quoting the last two lines as an instance of "tragic paradox."

Bewley (1966, xxvii) calls *Ship* Donne's "most graphic epigram."

Milgate (1967, 197) observes that "there is a play on 'rescued', 'lost', and 'found' as well as on 'burning' and 'drowning'."

Carey (1981, 95) compares *Ship* unfavorably to Raleigh's account of the sea battle at Cadiz, claiming that "we are inevitably struck by the superior humanity of Raleigh's."

Carey argues that "Donne treats the slaughter as a joke: the pretext for a smart paradox. There is no pity in his lines." He concludes, however, that a judgmental attitude is inappropriate, reasoning that "Donne was a young soldier, seeing action for the first time: he had to toughen himself, and could not afford to feel." He adds that "Donne's complicated, ingenious poetry was ill fitted to voice simple compassion."

Framing his discussion upon "the controlling paradox of *fire* and *water*," Hester (1990, 7–8) argues that "the absolute negation and cancellation of all alternatives (the essence of hell) are precisely epitomized by the diatyposis drawn by Donne's cumulative paradoxes" (7) and that, as a result, "all attempts to escape death are 'lost' in the scene, just as 'all' the words of the sentence are cancelled by opposites" (8).

Notes and Glosses

Title. **HESTER** (1990) (referring to the Italian title "*Naue arsa*"): "an anagram for *nausare* ('to sicken,' 'to nauseate')" (7). In addition, "the central *fire/water* paradox of the poem is intimated by the possible puns on *arsa/arca* (dry/fountain) and on *arca* as a 'sarcophagus'" (8).

4 *decay*. **SMITH** (1971): "die, wither away" (464).

6 *They in the Sea . . . drownd*. **MILGATE** (1967): an alexandrine (197).

Wall

Commentary

Date and Circumstances

Grierson (1912, 2:59) suggests that *Wall* is one of a group of epigrams composed during the Cadiz expedition of June 1596 and "may mark an incident in the attack of the landing party which forced its way into the city."

Bald (1937, 402–03) disputes Grierson's supposition, citing as Donne's source the 1589 expedition against Spain and Portugal (recorded in Hakluyt's *Principal Navigations, Voyages, etc.*) and the description of the death of a Captain Sydenham after a wall fell on him at La Coruña [i.e., "Corunna"] in that year. Bald speculates that *Wall* may be Donne's earliest poem. The event, Bald argues, was memorable because the city was saved from capture by the fall of this wall. Bald finds support for his identification of the event at Corunna as Donne's inspiration in the fact that in 1614 Sir George Buc commented on the 1589 incident, but that he commented on no such similar incident of the 1596 campaign—in which, Bald adds, Buc participated and about which he wrote an account printed in Stow's *Annals* (1615).

Milgate (1967, 197–98) observes that "Donne could have heard of the falling wall at Corunna at any time after the occurrence" (198).

Bald (1970, 51) reiterates his contention about the date and site of the event described in *Wall* and suggests "the possibility that Donne might have cut short his studies at Cambridge and was present at the occasion it commemorates."

Parker (1975, 14) cites the epigram as a clue that Donne's first experience of travel was as a soldier and that his poem refers to the 1589 siege of La Coruña.

Shawcross (1983a, 23–24) agrees with Bald that the 1589 incident at La Coruña is the incident to which the epigram refers, but he cites as the ultimate source *A True Coppie of a Discourse written by a Gentleman, employed in the late Voyage of Spaine and Portingale* (London, 1589), attributed to Anthony Wingfield. Shawcross cites pages 20–21 of this document, where the events apparently summarized in *Wall* are described, and argues that Hakluyt's account derives from it.

General Commentary

Hester (1986, 80–91) argues that in *Wall* "the epideictic prospect is drastically problematized. . . . [T]his poem wryly undercuts the subject's heroism by the application of the terms 'too-bold' and 'brave' to his actions, by the description of his death as 'perished by the fall,' and by the troubling conclusion that the collapse of the wall gave his 'corpse' (or 'bones') a place to 'hide.' These unflattering modifiers suggest that, in addition to exemplifying the fickle 'misfortune' of man, the death of the captain provides a witty reminder that 'pride goeth before a fall.'" Hester finds that line 1 not only intimates a pathetic fallacy that identifies the "fate of the wall/town with that of the captain," but also "exploits that most familiar of Renaissance motifs" of the relationship between the macrocosm and microcosm (body/town, soul/commander), as found also in *Ecst.* Nevertheless, Hester adds, Donne's treatment creates "surprising complications": "Like mortal man, the metonymic wall of the town is 'undermin'd' and 'bruis'd' [Hester cites Gen. 3.15]; and the proud captain is trapped by the mortality of the wall, just as the spirit is entombed within the body." In line 3, a "riddling oxymoron," Hester finds both these suggestions brought together in a rendering or literalization of "the paradox" of the human condition: "capable of courage ('brave') but doomed to sin ('misfortune'), man is capable of happiness but inclined to envy" (85). "Only the 'happiest' men," those "capable of a spiritual perspective," Hester continues, "can appreciate the captain's true liberation from the 'bruis'd' flesh; but, unhappily, they more often envy him for the wrong reasons, for the grandeur of his 'tomb,' thus extending their own entombment by the limited, the 'undermin'd,' the fallen. . . . [T]he panegyric of the lapidary epigram is problematized (or undermined) by a surprising play of metaphor that questions the wisdom of the 'brave example' the epigram ostensibly praises" (85–86). Affirming Donne's love of word-play with proper names, Hester suggests that the subject's name, Sydenham, is subtly embedded in the poem, "for *side* (or *syde*) is obsolete English for 'proud or boastful' ('too-bolde') and *ham* is Old English for 'town'" (86).

Notes and Glosses

Title. **HESTER** (1990) (referring to the Italian title "*Caso d'vn muro*"): "*caso* could refer to both the fall of the wall and the 'misfortune' of the captain; and the full Italian title, with the near homophones *caso/casa, muro/muorto*, sounds the play of metaphor that is central to the poem: the fall of the wall (*caso d'un muro*) = the house of death (*casa di muorto*)" (7).

1 *vnder-min'd,* **SULLENS** (1964): "Donne's use of the word antedates the examples given in the *OED* by more than two hundred years. The first quotation is dated 1844" (189).

1 *shott brusd* **SULLENS** (1964): a combination in Donne that the OED does not record (206).

2 *too bold* **SULLENS** (1964): a combination in Donne that the OED does not record (207).

3 *braue* **SMITH** (1971): "magnificent (in that he had such a splendid tomb)" (465).

4 *towne* **GROSART** (1872–73) (reading "tower"): "Towne" is an odd misprint in the 1633 edition (2:268).

4 *tombe* **SULLENS** (1964): predates the earliest use of the word with this meaning in the *OED*, sb. 1. b., 1812 (239).

4 *corps* **SHAWCROSS** (1983a) (reading "bones"): "Bones" is preferable to "corps," the reading given by Milgate (1967, 51), because the soldier's legs are recorded in *A True Coppie* . . . [see Shawcross 1983a in General Commentary above] as having been pinned down "and thus 'hidden'; 'corpse' might suggest that his full body had been covered by debris" (23–24).

Wing

Commentary

Date and Circumstances

Gosse (1899, 1:51–52) gives a brief account of the life and death of Sir John Wingfield, observing that he "doubtless was constantly brought into communication, up to the time of his death, with Donne" and observes that Wingfield's death, "probably under Donne's own eyes, at Cadiz in 1596, must have impressed the young poet, and produced, at a time when he was occupied with the Italian language, . . . [this] epigram" (52) (similarly Le Comte [1965, 31] and Bald [1970, 83–85]).

Grierson (1912, 2:59) places *Wing* at the end of a group, including *Ship*, *Wall*, *Beggar*, and *Cales*, that, he argues, was composed during the Cadiz expedition of 1596. *Wing*, Grierson observes, "chronicles the one death to which every account of the expedition refers."

Milgate (1967, 199) states that Wingfield was knighted in 1586 and served on the Cadiz expedition as quartermaster of the army, attached to Essex. "He was the only notable Englishman (there were two others) to be killed in the capture of the town," Milgate notes, "and all accounts mention him."

Marotti (1986, 102) interprets "our Earle" (l. 3) as evidence that Donne wrote *Wing* "to an audience of fellow Essex clients." Because the epigram is found only in two manuscripts, he argues that it was directed to a small audience.

General Commentary

Gosse (1899, 1:51–52) calls *Wing* "very characteristic of Donne in its style and versification" (51).

Hester (1979, 202–06) discusses "the complex mixing of genres and the ironic manipulation of generic expectations" (202) that he finds important to a "renewed appreciation" of Donne's epigrams generally and of *Wing* in particular. He states that *Wing* fulfills expectations of both the Planudean and the Roman form of epigrams, "combining the *mel* and *sal* of the mode equally so that the ultimate achievement of the poem is more than the sum of its generic parts" (203–04). He concludes that *Wing* transforms the death of its protagonist into an experience that "evokes universal norms of individual heroism, national pride and enduring human achievements under the aegis of eternity." He maintains that Donne also uses the colonel's death as the "occasion to fire one more volley at the aspirations and hopes of the dissolving Spanish Empire which he and his compatriots have so recently and boldly pillaged," and he further characterizes the poem, insofar as it is an "inscription," as a parody of the "inscription or *impresa* of the Spanish King, Philip II, which depicted Phoebus Apollo moving between the Pillars of Hercules from the 'cradle' to the 'bed' of the sun" (205).

Hester subsequently (1986, 80–91) discusses *Wing* as an instance of "commemorative typology" that presents Wingfield as "an embodiment of the Hercules emblem" (82). Focusing on the Hapsburg imperial motto *plus oultra*, he says that if we remember the imperial motto "that was transcribed across the Herculean Pillars and above an ever-rising sun in Spanish heraldic emblems—then Donne's epigrammatic 'pillering' of the Spanish is apparent." He argues that the "emblematic sun of Philip, which was supposed never to set on the Empire, the pillars that marked not the boundary but the start of the nation's empire, and the motto that expressed their expansionist achievements are all here rendered applicable to the daring colonel who pillaged their ports—'Farther then [*plus oultra*] Wingfield no man dares go.'" Hester argues further that the raid on Cadiz robbed the Spanish not only of their goods but also of their pride and that in this epigram Donne "defiantly waves their own banners in their faces." "By turning Philip's epigrammatic heraldic emblem against him," Hester maintains, Donne "shows the impossibility of (pre)determining the signification of public speech acts. Literally and generically anglicized by Donne (*plus oultra* = farther then), the elements of the Spaniard's emblem are compressed into the final line's epitaph for Wingfield and re-create the emblem/epigram, leading into vistas of signification beyond the boundaries of Philip's 'hyperdetermined' intentions" (84). Extrapolating from this example, Hester concludes that "Donne shows that no metaphor can be subjected to the imperialism of any single hermeneutic. The empire of metaphor is finally heuristic; its boundaries are not pillars of interpretive restrictions but imaginative traces of human 'travail.'" Terming *Wing* Donne's most "'Greek'" epigram, Hester argues that nevertheless the poet tends to "open up" the genre, "here by mixing modes of epigram in order both to fulfill and to surprise generic expectations" (84–85).

Notes and Glosses

Title. **HESTER** (1990) (referring to the Italian title "*Il Caualliere Gio: Wingefield*."): this title, "especially through the cognate *caballero/cauallero*, announces the satirical sting which Donne embeds in his epic praise of the English pill(ag)er" (9).

1–2 *Beyond th'old Pillers . . . and bed*. **HESTER** (1979): "Slain near the Pillars of Hercules, those promontories which mythologically marked the boundaries of the known world and which Emperor Charles V and his son Philip II designated as markers of the beginning of the supposedly endless Spanish Empire, Wingfield is associated in Donne's poem with this natural wonder in order to describe him as a Herculean figure whose heroism at Cadiz provides a model and a boundary beyond which human heroism on its own cannot unpresumptuously aspire." The diction, especially "travailled," "cradle," "bed," and "throne," resembles Donne's description of the "rectilinear, circumlocutious wanderings of the adventurers" in *Sat3* (204).

1 *th'old Pillers* **MILGATE** (1967): "the Pillars of Hercules, the two mountains (Gibraltar or Calpe on the north, Abyla on the south) opposite each other at the

western entrance of the Mediterranean, regarded as the limits of the old world, and supposed to have been parted by the arm of Hercules" (199).

1 *trauailed* **SMITH** (1971) (reading "travelled"): "pronounced as three syllables" (465). **PATRIDES** (1985): "travelled; also, laboured" (133).

2 *the Suns cradle*, **SMITH** (1971): "westward" (465).

2 *his throne*, **MILGATE** (1967): "the south, where he reigns in strength" (199).

2 *bed*. **HESTER** (1979): the earth's north (as the "throne" is its south) (204).

3 *A fitter Piller* **SHAWCROSS** (1967a): Wingfield himself. **SMITH** (1971): "a memorial or tombstone" (465). **HESTER** (1979): "Why his 'Piller' is fitter—that is, why both his monument and the actions (piller-ing) that brought about his death are more worthy of memory—is reinforced by the pathetic fallacy and puns in the last two lines of the epigram" (204).

3 *our Earle* **MILGATE** (1967): i.e., Essex, "who has given Wingfield to the soil of Cadiz, and made a new Pillar to mark the westward limit of human adventure" (199).

4 *late* **GRIERSON** (1912): "lately visited" or "where the sun sets late . . . a new Pillar of Hercules"; Donne characteristically treats words with such a "startlingly condensed force"; cf. "faire faith" (*BedfReas* 4) (2:59). **MILGATE** (1967): cf. Cadiz as "th'old worlds fardest end" (*Cales* 1) (199). **SMITH** (1971): both "lately in the news" and, possibly, deceased, "in that the town no longer existed after the English raid" (465).

4 *Iland;* **GRIERSON** (1912): Cadiz, situated on an island and connected to the mainland by a bridge (2:59). **SHAWCROSS** (1967a): Cadiz "is not an island, but is built on a narrow spit projecting five miles into the sea and lying northwest of the Isla de León" (163).

5 *then* **PATRIDES** (1985): "than" (133).

5 *Wingefield* **HESTER** (1979): a pun, i. e., "wing-field" (205).

THE EPITHALAMIONS

The Epithalamions

Dates and Circumstances

Smith (1971, 14–15) questions the generic grouping of the three epithalamions, calling attention to the probability that *EpLin* is an "early poem" and that the others date from shortly before Donne took holy orders, although we "perforce group them together and place them with the erotic writings of his early manhood" (14). "What matters much more than any harm to these particular poems," he argues, "is the possibility that a concern with genre may oversimplify the variegated texture of the poet's thought and work, and itself subvert our search for the coherence of Donne's poetic vision behind its apparent discontinuities" (14–15).

Shawcross (1983b, 11–12) argues that arrangement of the epithalamions would seem to pose no problem since there are only three, and they are datable. An obvious order, he says, is chronological, "if an editor decides to group the subgenres and casts . . . [*EpLin*] as a legitimate epithalamion." He contends, however, that *EpLin* is a "mock poem," a lampoon of Spenser's *Epithalamion* published earlier in 1595, and is therefore essentially a kind of satire. "The grouping of this particular poem," he maintains, "represents an editor's reading of it or editorial tradition, and subtly implies how the reader is to treat it" (11). Examining the arrangement of the epithalamions in the extant manuscripts and the edition of 1633, Shawcross finds it "reasonable to conclude that at one time 'Lincolnes Inne' was attached to the epigrams." He concludes: "If we relate 'Lincolnes Inne' to the epigrams and keep the epithalamions as a group, we might put them after the epigrams. If we emphasize the epithalamic tradition for the three poems as a group, we might put them after the songs and sonnets. In any case the order is not without its uncertainties" (12).

Influences and Analogues

Gosse (1893, 236–47) finds that the epithalamions are the only poems by Donne to show Spenser's influence. "These marriage songs are elegant and glowing," he observes, "though not without the harshness which Donne could not for any length of time forgo" (239).

In an argument for French influence on Donne, Lee (1910, 353–54) invokes Joshua Sylvester's 1592–99 translation of Du Bartas's *La Semaine* and alludes in passing to Donne's "eclogues" (354)—not further identified—as closely imitating its style.

Grierson (1912, 2:30) disputes the case made by Lee (1910) for Du Bartas's and Sylvester's influence, though without specifically mentioning the epithalamions.

Emperor (1928, 38–39) finds virtually no Catullian influence upon the epithalamions, despite what he takes to be the assumption that one would expect to find it there (he cites *EpLin* 43–45 and 48–49 as possibly showing such influence).

Atkinson (1951, 387–88) notes, without citation or explanation, that sixteen quotations from Donne's epithalamions appear in Samuel Johnson's *Dictionary*.

In a general discussion of the dislodging of rhetorical by conversational genres about the year 1600, Ellrodt (1960a, 2:105, 157, 173–74) characterizes occasional poetry ("*vers de circonstance*") as a type that arises from the exigencies of situations requiring unpremeditated responses and that therefore possesses a tone ("*ton*") harmonious with the general tendency of the period. Ellrodt distinguishes between poems born out of an occasion (e.g., the lyric or verse letter) and those fashioned for an occasion (e.g., the epithalamion, panegyric, or funeral elegy). Both categories, he argues, seek to express the reverberations of events, but the former is limited to the experience of the writer and his subject, partner, or addressee, whereas the latter universalizes the significance of the occasion (105). Ellrodt cites the epithalamions generally (and *Eclog* 215–16 specifically, q.v.) as evidence of Donne's lack of interest in mythology and classical legends, which he says occur in Donne's verse with the effect of intellectual engagement rather than esthetic pathos (157). In a discussion of the decline of the pastoral genre as practiced by Sidney and Spenser, Ellrodt argues that the epithalamion was less affected than the funeral elegy by the shift in taste to what he characterizes as metaphysical obscurity, comic hyperboles, and tormented conceits. He finds pastoral elements in both *EpEliz* and *Eclog*, noting especially the "Eclogue" in the latter; the genre, he maintains, encourages not personal meditation or metaphysical speculation but celebration, an obligatory element of sensuality, the evocation of ceremonies, and both public and private festive rites. He observes that epithalamions are generally, in his term, descriptive, a mode that he says is not usual with Donne: events, their sequence, and the feelings and even the imagery appropriate to each are to some extent prescribed. Ellrodt argues further that because Spenser's *Epithalamion* was his most personal and direct poem, it was less likely than his other works to provoke a reaction or revolt among younger poets. Yet Donne, Ellrodt maintains, makes the form his own: one finds Donne's characteristic obsession with the death or mystical union of lovers (173). The poems, Ellrodt asserts, are enamelled ("*émaillés*") with Donne's favorite theological or scientific conceits, and the strophes possess dramatic accent and, where appropriate, Donne's characteristic analytic turn. Ellrodt asserts that Donne's spirit repudiates not pastoralism itself but pastoral conventionality (174).

Raizis (1966, 3–14) examines Donne's epithalamions in the light of Greek and Latin models and of Spenser. He paraphrases Donne's three epithalamions, discussing them in their order of composition, according to Grierson's dating. Raizis's overviews of Donne's handling of the genre include the contention that *EpLin* "reveals Donne as a bolder poet" than Spenser, especially in the opening lines and in stanza 6, and that overall the work is "a deliberate satire on this genre of lyric poetry which, nonetheless, shows—though obliquely—Donne's familiarity with the special features of an epithalamion" (6). In his overview of *Eclog*, Raizis argues that of the three it is the "closest to tradition in terms of chronological organization . . . as well as allusions to classical mythology" (11), further arguing for Donne's influence upon Herrick's "An Epithalamie to Sir Thomas Southwell and his Ladie." Although Raizis finds in Herrick's adaptation of short stanzas the direct influence of Catullus, he contends not only that Herrick's "style and spirit are characteristically Donnean" (13), but also that had Donne lived to read Herrick's poem, "he would have been pleased with his triumph over Jonson" (14).

Observing the epithalamic tradition in English poetry from 1594 to 1635, Miller (1970, 405–16) traces the decline of the form, which he attributes to "the decline of the marriage myth that originally inspired the genre" (405). Miller attributes that decline to a loss of idealism about the ceremony and institution of marriage as reflections of divine and natural orders (406–07). Within this context he terms all Donne's epithalamions "distinguished" (405), and observes that both *EpEliz* 29–32 and *Eclog* 142–45 justify the fact that the wedding takes place in winter by claiming that the bride, the groom, or the union itself is somehow a greater phenomenon than the sun at its zenith could ever be.

General Commentary

In 1648 "G. O.," identified by Sampson (1921, 93) as the Royalist divine Giles Oldisworth (1619–1678), annotated a copy of the 1639 edition, entering rhymed couplets at the heads of several of the groupings of poems. Above the epithalamions, "G. O." wrote, "Learned [the word "Active" is crossed out] yet stupid all those Poetts are / Wch undresse Cupid, & paint Venus bare."

Scott (1808, 1:45–48) characterizes as "pedantic worship" (47) the attitude towards women at the pre-Civil War courts, citing an unspecified "Epithilamion" [sic] by Donne, as well as Abraham Cowley's "The Mistress," as works standing in contrast to a supposed sympathy for women's tastes shown by Restoration poets.

Hunt (1841 [1956, 497–98]) asserts that "next to Spenser's [*Epithalamion*] our best Epithalamions, and the only ones, we fear, worth much remembrance, are those of a great wit and intellect, who is supposed, by some, to be nothing but a bundle of conceits—Dr. Donne," and suggests that "in occasional passages, they are even superior in depth and feeling, though the very audacity of their truthfulness (honest in that depth) hinders them from being quotable to the 'general ear.'"

An anonymous commentator writing in *LEM* (1846, 230–32, 233 [the author is identified as "the late Dr. Samuel Brown of Edinburgh" in Grosart 1872–73, 2:xli–xlii and as Coventry Patmore in Milgate 1967, xxi]) associates the epithalamions with the songs and sonnets and the elegies and terms this entire category "greatly inferior" (231) to the satires, verse letters, and funeral elegies, which constitute another distinct group. The category that includes the epithalamions, the writer maintains, is "deformed by the intrusion of conceits" and lacks both spontaneous feelings and profound thought" (231). The epithalamions (and the elegies), however, "form a link" between the songs and sonnets and the poems of the second category (the third and last category consists of the divine poems) (233).

Arnold (1867 [1868?, 97–99]) characterizes the "youthful Epithalamia" as "tainted by a gross sensuality" (97).

Jackson (1894, 105–07) cites Donne's "Marriage Songs" along with the elegies and the satires as poems that will "repay attention" and says of the epithalamions that they are "far from reading as though they were perfunctory productions" (106).

Chambers (1896, 1:xli) argues a change from a younger, cynical, ethically lax Donne to an older man possessed of "intenser and more constant emotions, and . . . a growing spirituality of thought." Chambers suggests that the "Epithalamia, both in date and subject–matter, bridge the gulf" between the early compositions (the satires, songs and sonnets, and love elegies) and the divine poems.

Furst (1896, 235), characterizing the years 1611–14 as devoted by Donne to the study of theology and languages, observes that Donne nonetheless exploited the "lighter vein" of the epithalamions, which, "though quite conventional in thought, are thoroughly artistic and have a light and airy beauty which is quite striking."

Norton (1896, 18–19) cites the epithalamions as instances of Donne's "exercises of wit," characterizing them as vigorous and passionate poems that both impress by their convincing rendering of apparently sincere emotions and perplex by their dramatic and possibly fictitious circumstances; he suggests that what was for Donne a sincere feeling on one occasion might have been a feigned or dramatized one on another. Recognizing these distinctions constitutes "the main perplexity" in reading Donne (18).

Saintsbury (1896, 1:xxvi) evaluates the epithalamions as "good, but not consummate" and thinks them far inferior to Spenser's.

In the course of defending Donne's satires from accusations of "roughness," Saintsbury subsequently (1898, 366) invokes the epithalamions as instances of Donne's "intensity and fullness of thought."

Dick (1899, xi), introducing Walton's *Life of Dr. John Donne*, contrasts Walton's extensive coverage of Donne's ecclesiastical career, his marriage, and his "loyalty to the king" with his brief treatment "of the days when he was Jack Donne, when he wrote the *Satires*, the *Elegies*, and the *Epithalamiums*." Dick characterizes these three categories of Donne's poetry as "not more blameworthy in respect of coarseness than much of the literature of the time" and adds that they reveal "many of Donne's peculiar excellences as a poet."

Symons (1899, 734–45) characterizes the epithalamions and the funeral elegies as "written for friendship or for money" and remarks that they therefore somewhat alter the general impression given by Donne's poetry that the author was an "intellectual adventurer" who wrote "nothing lightly, or it would seem, easily; nothing for the song's sake" (735).

Richter (1902, 391–415) associates both *EpEliz* and *Eclog* with *FirAn* and *SecAn* as more regular in accent and as marked by a greater formality than Donne's lyrics; Richter further groups these two epithalamions with *FirAn*, *SecAn*, and *Henry* as public poems reflecting the receipt of patronage.

Grierson (1906, 155) contrasts the "courtly and adulatory *Epithalamia*," together with the verse letters, epicedes, and obsequies ("the product of [Donne's] later and more regular years"), with what he terms the sensuous, cynical, Platonic, and satirical earlier works.

Grierson (1912, 2:xlvi, 30) links the epithalamions with other categories of Donne's poetry: "Between his most sensual and his most spiritual love-songs there is no cleavage such as separates natural love from Dante's love of Beatrice, who is in the end Theology. The passion that burns in Donne's most outspoken elegies, and wantons in the *Epithalamia*, is not cast out in *The Anniversarie* or *The Canonization*, but absorbed" (xlvi).

Schelling (1913, 67) calls Donne a primarily "lyric" poet, citing the epithalamions, among other categories, as examples.

Sampson (1921, 82) terms the epithalamions, together with the "songs, elegies, and satires" as "the work of [Donne's] unregenerate youth."

Considering the epithalamions within the context of Donne's efforts to secure a position at Court, Payne (1926, 126–29) finds that "Donne was perhaps more consistently successful . . . [in this genre] than in any other kind" (129).

Fausset (1931, xix) finds that *EpLin* and *EpEliz* possess "a physical candour devoid of sensuality."

Watkins (1936, 80) notes Samuel Johnson's citations, in his *Life of Cowley*, of passages from *Eclog* and *EpEliz* as evidence of Johnson's extensive acquaintance with Donne's poetry.

Suggesting that Donne stands near the end of the major phase of the genre, McPeek (1939, 235) characterizes the epithalamion as "a form of writing which was chiefly resorted to as a means of flattering wealthy and noble patrons . . . [that] had in its own nature the dark spores of decay" and suggests that "even in the hands of so sturdy a figure as Donne it may become almost grossly adulatory."

In her chapter entitled "The Criterion of Sensuous Vividness," Tuve (1947, 98–99) comments that "Donne's epithalamia are full of descriptive circumstances," such as "the *cronographia* of dawn, of evening"; "the 'action' of the bride's dressing" in *EpLin*; "the time-worn prosopopoeia of Bishop Valentine's bird-filled diocese"; and "the lists of jewels that blaze upon the bride" of *EpEliz* (98). She further observes that "in so far as epithalamia are lyrical 'praises,' they find considerable room for ample sensuous figures" and adds that although epithalamions "are themselves *pragmatographia* of a sort, being studies in expectation they are bound to have less action than emotional intensity" (98–99).

Harding (1951, 427) notes in Donne's work an "attempted insurance" against the human failure to grasp the significance of the moment fully. "In one of its forms," says Harding, this attempt "shows as a prolonged effort of anticipation, as though to ensure full responsiveness to the event when it did come." The epithalamions in particular, observes Harding, provided Donne the natural generic context for "this process of leading up to the experience with an 'impatient' anticipation that allows him to dwell longer and more vividly on the idea of sexual union," and the genre "justified by the conventions of the occasion the onlooker's rather mental preoccupation with sexuality that goes with such anticipation."

Cox (1956, 112) notes briefly that Donne's epithalamions "have their rewarding moments" and that all three "show some approach to the melodious strophes of Spenser with a recurring refrain-line."

Kermode (1957, 25–26) states that the genre is not well suited to Donne (but cf. his observations on *EpEliz* 33–38 below).

Ellrodt (1960a, 1, i:252–53), in a discussion of Donne's use of white/black and white/red patterns of color contrast, cites the epithalamions as rare instances in which Donne uses color concretely. He concedes that Donne customarily presents antitheses in his poetry, but argues that they are usually antitheses of concepts rather than of perceptual images.

Bryan (1962, 170, 173), in a note that considers "the number, kind, and frequency of appearance of Donne's poems in nineteen poetical commonplace books [from the seventeenth century] located in private libraries throughout the United States" (170), concludes that the three appearances of the epithalamions "are so few in number that they seem not representative of any particular pattern of literary taste" (173).

Gamberini (1967, 78–79) compares what he calls the realism of Donne's epithalamions to the exaggerated idealism of Spenser's, finding in Donne an appreciation of the physical as well as of the spiritual excellencies of marriage. Donne's best work in the tradition of the epithalamion is, he asserts, *EpLin*; the two later epithalamions are, in his view, marred by inappropriate displays of scholastic learning.

M. Molho (1970, 20) characterizes the epithalamion as the "sensual apotheosis" of Donne's poetry, by contrast with related but more cerebral examinations of sexual love such as that in *Ecst.*

Tufte (1970, 207–8) compares and contrasts Donne's epithalamions with those of Jonson, finding both "marked by the verbal and structural ingenuity characteristic of the work of these two poets" (207).

McGowan (1972, 175–218) places *EpEliz* and *Eclog* "against the background of other poems, plays, and masques written to celebrate the same occasions" in order to convey "an idea of the spirit of James I's Court, and of the criteria of expectation assumed by poet and audience alike" (177). She argues that there was a change in mood at Court at the beginning of the reign of James, who leaves the impression of being not only "a much more dynamic personality" than Elizabeth, but also "the busy centre towards which all eyes turn and from which all activity begins" (178). In particular, McGowan comments, "King James and his Court *expected* a certain tone, in poems, plays and masques, reflecting not their aspirations to greatness but the glory they felt manifest in themselves every day" (182).

Menascè (1974, 12, 39–40) maintains that *EpEliz* and *Eclog*, written in the hope of gaining advancement, lack the freshness of the youthful *EpLin* (39).

Commenting that "genre does not hold a large place in . . . [Donne's] poetic strategy," Waddington (1974, 11) describes *EpEliz* and *Eclog* as "two insipid specimens" of the genre and then explains that "by burlesquing the form" in *EpLin* Donne was able to place "his usual stamp of identity upon it."

Granqvist (1975, 32–33) cites the statistics furnished without comment by Atkinson (1951) as evidence "that Johnson knew Donne's poetry thoroughly" (33).

Smith (1975, 214–15) addresses the question of Samuel Johnson's familiarity with Donne's poetry, disputing with Watkins (1936) and Atkinson (1951), who both take note of the presence of passages from the epithalamions in Johnson's *Dictionary*. Smith observes that Johnson never identifies the poems from which he cites passages, "merely ascribing the lines to Donne." The figures cited by Watkins and Atkinson, he maintains, "argue no more than that Johnson had used a copy of Donne's poems as a word quarry" (215).

Lewalski (1976, 196–97, 202) finds that Donne's epithalamions "yield three distinct *personae*: the city wit, the Spenserian Hymen-priest, and *Idios* the private man" (202). In particular, she maintains, the persona of *EpLin* possesses a sophisticated awareness of "the mercantile basis of city marriages" and, as a result, "ironically modifies his conventional Spenserian descriptions of the bride and the events of the day." In contrast, the persona of *EpEliz* "adopts the Spenserian high hymnic mode" in which he "presents himself as a kind of Hymen directing the events of the day, and as a priest celebrating those events in terms of the great cycle of nature and in the name of the entire natural and social order." She maintains that "rejecting the Spenserian priestly function and the Spenserian language," the "fully-dramatized *persona*" (196) of *Eclog* "offers his poem as evidence of his vicarious participation in the joys of the day" (197).

Milgate (1978, xv–xlv, liv–lv, 118), introducing his edition of the epithalamions, anniversaries, epicedes, epitaphs, and inscriptions, says that in "most" of them "the 'commerce' of earth and heaven is a central part of the theme" (xvi). Citing Donne's language in *InAA* 2–3 ("what is spoken of Christ may be said of each and every Christian"), Milgate affirms the centrality of the virtuous subjects of the poems as "mirrors," "glasses," or "exemplars" who are "represented as objects of the poet's (and our) 'study,' 'meditation,' 'consideration,' or 'contemplation,' as means of understanding spiritual truths and the nature of virtue" (xix). Milgate characterizes all the poems in his edition other than *EpLin* as "'public' poems, written to satisfy the demands of particular occasions and more or less by command, by inescapable request, or by social and political pressure." He points out that even *EpLin* repeats in its refrain the idea of "perfection," thus echoing the other poems' concern with ideal patterns of behavior. The inferior poems in this grouping will be better understood, Milgate suggests, through an appreciation of the serious intentions they share with the more successful ones (xxi). Milgate groups *Eclog* with *EpEliz* as "among the finest [epithalamions] in English," partly because both, despite the poet's successful transmutation of his sources into altogether original poems, are "based on a thoroughly professional and learned acquaintance with the tradition of the genre in classical and modern times" (xxv). Additionally, he asserts that the manuscript copies "offer no evidence" of Donne's having revised the epithalamions and states that it would have been "discourteous" (lv) for Donne to have reissued *EpEliz* and *Eclog* in any revised form, even had he wished to do so, because they were composed for patrons.

Partridge (1978, 121–26) describes Donne's epithalamions as "influenced by Spenser and the neo–Platonic tradition" (122), especially *EpLin*, which he takes to be the first despite its appearance as the last in the edition of 1633.

Zunder (1982, 2, 21, 26, 30–31, 36–42, 57, 79, 102) identifies the epithalamion, together with satire, elegy, lyric, and epistle, as a category of the "humanist" literature that he sees emerging at the end of the sixteenth century. Examining them within the context of Donne's other love poetry, Zunder finds that the epithalamions present the constant norm of a "transcendent union of two lovers in marriage" (42) while showing evolving responses to the social and political pressures of the time. Though Donne for the most part, according to Zunder, endorses traditional values, he does so with "decreasing conviction" in his later love poetry, emphasizing instead "the resolving significance of personal experience" (102). The "definite ideological sequence" (41–42) of the epithalamions culminates in the "arch-conservatism" of *Eclog* (102). Like the songs and sonnets and the elegies, the epithalamions, in Zunder's analysis, manifest a "comparative" structure by juxtaposing contrasting attitudes toward love within a poem (21). Unlike the other two genres, however, the epithalamions, he asserts, are not "dramatic," and they lack a spokesman for Donne himself (26). Claiming a resemblance between the Donne of the epithalamions and the Shakespeare of *TN*, Zunder finds that each writer views marriage as both hierarchical and equal. Both *EpEliz* and *Eclog*, he argues, though perpetuating a consciousness of instability characteristic of Donne's earlier love poetry, nonetheless express a late stage of the hierarchical structure of an essentially late medieval society (57). Zunder further discusses solar imagery in each epithalamion as expressive of hierarchy (37–41). Citing lines 9–17 of *SecAn* for their "morbidity," Zunder finds that passage expressive of the sensibility of the poet of *EpEliz* and *EpLin*, who, he suggests, has affinities with John Webster (79).

Marotti (1986, 269) characterizes both *EpEliz* and *Eclog* as "occasional works related directly or indirectly to . . . [Donne's] pursuit of patronage and preferment."

Ellrodt (1987b, 11), examining the relationship between "poetry" and "truth" in several of Donne's poems, rejects the notion (and notes his differences with Lewalski [1976]) that the epithalamions can be sharply distinguished according to their different *personae*. Donne's own circumstances, he argues, justify the differences in tone among the three poems.

Dubrow (1988, 197–219), in a detailed analysis of *Eclog*, compares it to *EpEliz* at several points. She finds *EpEliz* generally both more restrained and more playful, but *Eclog*, by contrast, more intent on complimenting the bride, the groom, and the King (201–02). She attributes the difference to Donne's increased anxiety, by the end of 1613, about his career and to his consequent different response to the demands of the patronage system (202–03). The use of the same generic conventions to opposite effects in either poem discloses, she argues, Donne's differing intentions; for example, in *EpEliz* he implies, conventionally, that the bride is impeded by her social duties from seeking the consummation of her marriage (*EpEliz* 71–72), whereas in the later poem, in an apparent strategy to dissociate Frances Howard from imputations of lustfulness, the bride herself seems reluctant (*Eclog* 193–95) (204). The religious ceremony is similarly contrasted (205), as are the roles of the guests and of the speaker himself (206–07). Noting that the fourteen-line stanza of *EpEliz* evokes the beneficence associated with Valentine's Day, Dubrow argues that a contrasting message of trespass and sin is associated with the eleven-line stanza of the main part of *Eclog* (209). A comparison of the two poems, she concludes, illuminates Donne's shifting status within the patronage system (214).

Dubrow (1990, 151–56) subsequently analyzes at length Donne's three wedding poems, which "illuminate both their genre and their author" (151). She argues that Donne's epithalamions "offer textbook examples of the tensions associated with their literary type and with marriage in Renaissance England" (152), providing "both an arena for conflicts and a storehouse of carefully crafted solutions to those conflicts" (153). Dubrow discusses several problems that this genre posed for Donne: his "predilection for seeing the community as a source of entrapment rather than support" (153), his "preference for addressing an individual or a coterie rather than the larger public audience to whom epithalamia are generally directed" (154), and his "problem of interpreting the nature—or natures—of women" (155). Detailed discussions of the individual epithalamions are linked by remarks on their comparative handling of similar situations, including what Dubrow finds to be the relative success of *EpEliz* in resolving the problems and tensions of *EpLin* and the subsequent difficulties in adapting the norms of *EpEliz* to the situation of *Eclog*.

COMMENTARY

Date and Circumstances

Chambers (1896, 1:235) comments that "Donne became a student at Lincoln's Inn on May 6, 1592, and the Epithalamion was probably written within the next two or three years." He adds, "it is less likely that it belongs to the period 1616–1622, when Dr. Donne was reader to the same learned society."

Gosse (1899, 1:76), in the course of a biographical reading of the songs and sonnets, dates *EpLin* as prior to Donne's marriage, adding, however, that "the occasion of this stately, sensuous ode is uncertain: all we know is that the bridegroom was one who was a member of the Inn, and not an assiduous one, for he combined 'study' with 'play' in it." Gosse characterizes *EpLin* as "so impersonal" and "so made to order" that "we know not whether to indulge a guess that the nuptials of Christopher Brooke form its theme." Gosse further argues that internal evidence does not prevent us from reading *EpLin* as a celebration of Donne's own secret marriage.

Richter (1902, 391) dates the poem at about 1601.

Grierson (1912, 2:91) cites its position in the Westmoreland manuscript (NY3) ("following the *Satires* and *Elegies* and preceding the *Letters*") as evidence for dating the poem from Donne's student years at Lincoln's Inn.

McPeek (1939, 209, 367) assigns it to the period of Donne's appointment at Lincoln's Inn in 1616–22 and considers it Donne's last effort in the genre.

Hillyer (1941, xxxiv) states that *EpLin* was written when Donne was nineteen.

Garrod (1946, 117), conceding that nothing is known of the occasion of the poem or the parties whose wedding it celebrates, suggests (citing ll. 29–31) that the bridegroom in the poem may be a student of the Inn. Garrod further argues that the rhythm of lines 25 and 66 "sorts well with an early date of composition," as "does the bad rhyme *cradle*, *able*" of lines 80–81.

Legouis (1955, 212) notes that Spenser's *Epithalamion* and *Prothalamion* were published in 1595 and 1596, respectively, and argues that *EpLin*, written (he believes) between 1592 and 1594, predates both. He cites M. Shapiro (*TLS*, 16 October 1930, p. 833) to the effect that Donne and an older fellow student had been elected "Masters of the Revels" of Lincoln's Inn on 6 February 1593 and that Donne had been fined for not having discharged his duties as "Steward of Christmas" in 1594.

Novarr (1956, 250–63) begins a four-part argument by noting in *EpLin* a "peculiarity of tone" and states that this poem differs from the other two epithalamions in that "its occasion is not known" and "its wit seems more crudely licentious, harsher, less neatly integrated." Novarr's initial discussion focuses upon "puzzling elements which disturb the conventional epithalamic attitude" (250). First, Novarr finds Donne's references to death in *EpLin* to be less conventional and "somewhat blunter than those in the other epithalamia" (251). The second puzzling element is that Donne refers to riches and money in ways that to Novarr "seem crude and tasteless" (252); he finds "something a little ungentlemanly, a little crass and vulgar," in the insistence upon riches as a particular virtue of the bride and bridesmaids. Novarr's third concern is the fact that the Lincoln's Inn bride is "conceitedly dressed, adorned with flowers and jewels." Fourth, Novarr is puzzled by the refrain, which "oddly concentrates attention on the occasion as it is important for the bride" so that "the groom seems slighted" (253).

In the second part of his essay, Novarr surmises that because "the wit is too close to insult," because it evidences "the heavy-handed raillery of his satires," and because "Donne is here crudely utilitarian in a genre which is customarily complimentary," Donne is probably not celebrating an actual wedding (254). Citing evidence from Grierson (1912) and Gardner (1952) concerning the Westmoreland manuscript, Novarr affirms that the poem was written between May 1592 and the middle of 1596, arguing further that there is no evidence that Donne left Lincoln's Inn or England until he joined the Cadiz expedition at the end of May, 1596 (255). Turning to further bibliographical considerations, Novarr concludes that the absence of *EpLin* from the Group I manuscripts indicates Donne's having considered it less worthy than the other poems in this genre. Further, Novarr states that "in about half of the manuscripts in which the poem appears it is entitled 'Epithalamion on a Citizen'" (255) and notes that the citizen is never named; Novarr therefore thinks it "likely that the use of 'Citizen' is generic" and speculates that Donne's contemporaries would have thought his intentions "not entirely serious." Novarr proposes that *EpLin* in fact celebrates a mock wedding, an occasion which is "in harmony with the long tradition of Inns of Court revelling"; he briefly lists a variety of masques performed for specific occasions, as well as several masques that were "entirely independent of occasion" (256), and discusses the extent to which masques and revels flavored life at the Inns of Court.

Part three of Novarr's article argues that "if we view Donne's epithalamia in the context of Inns of Court revelling, the strangeness of its tone and the oddness of its details disappear." What at first appears tasteless and crude in the poem would, in the context of masque and revel, Novarr contends, "convulse the young men of the Inn." In particular, since the part of the bride would be played by one of the men, "the refrain becomes a jocular device." When read as a mock epithalamion, the wit "becomes innocently salacious" (258) in that it emphasizes the confusion of sex caused by a man's playing the part of the bride. As such, Novarr believes the poem "a broadly satiric entertainment" (259) that is more closely akin to the satires and the love elegies than to the other epithalamions.

In the fourth and final part of his argument, Novarr proposes, "though more tentatively," that Donne "wrote his epithalamion for a performance at the Midsummer revels of Lincoln's Inn in 1595" (259). He bases this dating on three arguments: first, Donne's poem could only have been written after Spenser's *Epithalamion* made available a "blending of the epic narration of the bridal day with an essentially lyric intent"

(260); second, a Midsummer date of performance is consistent with evidence from within the poem and with the fact that "the most important revels at this time of year were held at Midsummer" (261); third, Donne was still at Lincoln's Inn in June 1595. Specifically, Novarr notes that on 26 November 1594 Donne was appointed Steward of Christmas at Lincoln's Inn, and although he was later fined for refusing to serve in this position, that does not to Novarr prove "that he was absent from London and from Lincoln's Inn during and after Christmas 1594" (263).

Gardner (1965, lvii) asserts that *EpLin* was "certainly written" by 1598.

Bald (1970, 77) notes the critical difficulties of "the forced and tasteless conceits" that occur in the poem before briefly discussing the argument by Novarr (1956), which, he argues, is "difficult to sustain, since there is no evidence that revels were ever held at Lincoln's Inn at any time other than the Christmas season."

Parker (1975, 20–21) maintains that the poem was written between 1592 and 1594 and then comments, "even if the poem was written as a joke, for a pretend-ceremony, and in it Donne was attacking the made marriages of the time, the joke is a grim one."

To Grierson's (1912) observations on the poem's location in the Westmoreland manuscript, Milgate (1978, 109–10) adds that no poem in the part of the manuscript in which *EpLin* is found, "with one explicable exception," dates from after 1598 (110).

Partridge (1978, 122) terms *EpLin* the first of the three epithalamions, despite its appearance as the last in the edition of 1633.

Marotti (1986, 29, 52) finds *EpLin* addressed to an audience of social familiars in the environment of "'study and play'" alluded to in line 30 of the poem (29). He characterizes *EpLin* as a comic celebration of the alliance of a Lincoln's Inn man with "a woman of the urban bourgeoisie," which Donne, a spokesman for his fellow students, treats (ll. 13–14) as a source of financial enrichment (52).

Shawcross (1986a, 121–22) calls *EpLin* a "mock poem." Because it may have been at one time attached to the epigrams, he suggests, it "perhaps should not be grouped with the other epithalamia." Placing it with the epigrams, Shawcross observes, would stress for the reader its "mock quality, its satirization." Grouping it with the other epithalamions, he says, "does not lead the reader to a contextual reading of parody." Shawcross argues that *EpLin* "was written for a midsummer revels in June, 1595, by all accounts, with an enactment of it by the men at the Inn."

General Commentary

Schipper (1888, 2:796) notes that the stanzaic form of the poem uses 12 lines with six rhymes.

Gosse (1899, 1:76) terms the place of *EpLin* in the canon "somewhat unique." He finds that Donne "drops his accustomed manner and closely imitates the imagery, the prosody, and the tone of Spenser," arguing that Donne's "own peculiar individuality lies below the rich Spenserian embroidery, and the result has a mellifluous glow which we could wish to see more frequent in Donne." He characterizes "this class of Elizabethan poem" as one in which "the best of men permitted themselves so fescennine a liberty, that it is difficult to give a specimen to modern readers." Gosse quotes lines 13–24 as "not unfairly" representative.

Fausset (1924, 109) contends that in spite of the "candour" and "disconcerting frankness" in the poem, it remains "entirely free from prurience." In particular, the poem is free of what he terms the "exotic licence" of Carew and the "exotic affectation" of Spenser.

Payne (1926, 129) describes *EpLin* as "energetic and tuneful."

McPeek (1939, 209–10, 367–68) finds that *EpLin* "exhibits what appears to be the mingled influence of Spenser, Jonson, and Catullus." He says the stanza form recalls Spenser's *Prothalamion* and *Epithalamion* (209), adding that "the immediate juxtaposition [in *EpLin* and Spenser's *Epithalamion*] of the stanzas on the slow declining sun and the appearance of the amorous evening star, through a natural conjunction, intimates that Donne remembered Spenser." He finds Spenser's influence perceptible in the resemblance of his *Epithalamion*, stanzas 15–16, and *EpLin*, stanzas 5–6 (i.e., ll. 49–72) (210).

Hillyer (1941, xxxiv) cites *EpLin* for its "Spenserian sweetness" and observes that "as time went on, Donne's style became smoother, more rhetorical"; Hillyer further argues that *EpLin* not only shows Donne's "grasp of the more literary style," but also "presages the tone of the later work, which conformed more clearly to the accepted idea of its intention."

Chase (1945, 114–19) contends that Donne is honored in part "for the dark mysteriousness with which he invests human life and for the kind of hieratic ritual his poems sometimes seem to perform." Chase believes that in *EpLin*, which he sees as a defense of the institution of marriage "against the wastage of apathy and artificiality," Donne "reasserts the vital *reality* of marriage as a custom and a ritual" (114). As a particular example of the ritualism at work in the poem, Chase cites the repetition of the refrain (114) and the mythical death and resurrection of the bride. Chase concludes that *EpLin* is "a hard-working poem, a poem that labors and gropes after the mythical" since there is "no prefabricated myth upon whose bosom the poem languishes" (116).

Gransden (1954, 115) describes *EpLin* as more Spenserian than *EpEliz*, except for line 5.

Legouis (1955, 212) explains that he chooses *EpLin*, alone among the epithalamions, for his anthology because it is both early and short.

Hunter (1965, 102–3) observes that in *EpLin* the genre "is freshened by Donne, in the directness and simplicity of the diction, without losing beauty or dignity" (102) and that Donne's love poetry exhibits "a reverence which avoids sanctimoniousness" (103).

Gamberini (1967, 78–79) finds in *EpLin* both adherence to traditional "rules" of the genre and a youthful sportive eroticism.

Shawcross (1967a, 403) argues that if Novarr (1956) is correct in maintaining that *EpLin* was written for a mock wedding, then "a man would have taken the part of the bride, adding another level of humor to such words as 'Hermaphrodits,'" in line 30. Shawcross further suggests a pun on "Temple" (l. 31) as a reference to the Inner or Middle Temple.

Hughes (1968, 20–23) believes *EpLin*, which is "quite possibly the earliest of Donne's poetry," exhibits "the green anger of the student rebel"; in the poem Donne can be seen "setting up distorting perspectives, creating a veritable *trompe-l'oeil*, where the apparent depth of the scene being portrayed is finally revealed as a sham" (20). For Hughes, the "grim tokens of death and debasement" that appear throughout the poem reveal it to be "a masquerade through and through." In addition, such images as "that warm balme-breathing thigh" (l. 7) and the "strange Hermaphrodits" (l. 30) create "the combination of scorn, sensuality, and immediacy" that for Hughes is "vintage Donne" (21). Finally, Hughes argues that *EpLin* is similar to the first two satires in its "basic pose" (22).

Bald (1970, 77) states that "the piece has real charm" and reflects "the all-pervasive influence of Spenser."

Miller (1970, 414–15) praises Donne, with respect to *EpLin*, as "the first and boldest of English epithalamists to raise questions concerning the marriage motives of the groom and the purity of his bride" (414).

Tufte (1970, 218–22) finds *EpLin* "puzzling, particularly if the reader assumes that it is or ought to be in the style of Spenser's *Epithalamion* and ignores other elements of the tradition" (218). She argues that by combining "sensual, fescennine, and ascetic elements" *EpLin* "becomes a paradoxical portrayal of earthly and heavenly aspects of marriage" (221–22).

Miller (1971, 140–53) states that even though its structure conforms to "the pattern of the conventional epithalamion almost perfectly," *EpLin* is "very unusual" in its pointing out of "flaws in the bride, the groom, the bride's maids and the groom's men, the ceremony, and finally in the consummation of the marriage, with the indelicate, masked, precision of a truly feminine malice" (143). Although Miller agrees with Novarr's (1956) arguments that the poem is broadly satiric, he disavows the use of historical evidence in favor of reading the poem "*sub specie aeternitatis*" (144). In particular, Miller contends that the satiric effect is "achieved by negative metaphors, but the tension of the poem is the result of contrasts between negative and positive possibilities," which must both be acknowledged "if the full quality of the poem is to be felt" (145). Miller concludes that "throughout the poem the reader has been asked to keep two readings in mind: a positive reading which mutes disparities and so is complimentary, and a negative reading which notes incongruities and so is satirical" (152). In Miller's opinion it is this ability of Donne's "to see unity in disparity without sacrificing the disparity" that readers find so attractive (153).

Lodi (1974, 86–99) finds *EpLin* unconventional "as it celebrates the less memorable wedding of a couple not belonging to the nobility" (96). Following Novarr (1956), Lodi justifies what some critics see as faults in the poem (primarily the references to death and riches), by seeing it within a context of court revels and lavish masques.

Throughout the opening section of her two-part essay, Ousby (1976a, 131–43) attacks the conclusions of Novarr (1956) and maintains that the poem need not be read as a parody of the genre in order to explain and account for the peculiarities in the imagery. After discussing a variety of the explanations Novarr offers for images that he finds puzzling, Ousby concludes that these problematic aspects of the poem fall into three categories: "the figures either hint at the reversal of the sexes during the revels, or criticize the wealthy middle classes, or crudely jest about sex and death." Because Donne, within this context, "apparently devotes comparatively little attention to mocking either the attitudes or the style of the epithalamic genre in general and Spenser's 'Epithalamion' in particular" (137), Ousby finds Novarr's reading unconvincing. In the second part of the essay Ousby offers her own reading of *EpLin*, which rests upon the assumption that the poem is an unsuccessful product of a poet whose early works reveal an interest "in exploring conventional genres in unconventional ways" (142). In particular, Ousby contends that "the Spenserian language, as well as the handful of direct echoes, indicate that Donne has studied the 'Epithalamion' and that he is practicing the lessons it has taught him" (140). Furthermore, she proposes that "the discordant images" of the poem "reflect the problems that can arise when one poet imitates another poet who is very different from himself; that is, Donne may be merging certain of the mannerisms he considered most characteristic of his own work with those of Spenser and discovering that the combination of these tones produces only discord" (140).

Milgate (1978, xxi–xxii, 110) discounts any connection between *EpLin* and an actual marriage, terming the poem, "like practically all Donne's other poetry" (other than the other two epithalamions, the anniversaries, the epitaphs, and the inscriptions), written to please Donne himself or his friends: "its primary motive seems to have been the fun of trying his hand at an epithalamion." *EpLin*, according to Milgate, conforms to the prescription that satire should stem from "any discrepancy between the actual behaviour of men and the ideal patterns which are supposed to regulate [that behavior]." The repetition in the refrain of the word "perfection," he asserts, links *EpLin* to Donne's other epithalamions and to the anniversaries and epicedes in their common concern for the rituals and symbols of ideal order and virtue (xxi). He further supposes it a response to Spenser's *Epithalamion*, in which Donne recognized "the ideal pattern of marriage, founded on true love, related intimately to the rhythms of nature and of the heavens, supported by both mythic apprehension and spiritual understanding, unfolded in poetry of joyful serenity and ritual stateliness." Milgate maintains that "to these qualities the poet in Donne could hardly fail to respond; his poem from time to time seems to assent to, and to express with some charm, the traditional motifs of the epithalamion, and it is not surprising that there is a sprinkling of verbal echoes of Spenser's poem." Asserting a discrepancy (which Donne "could not fail to notice") between marriage as presented in Spenser's poem and such occasions in the City, Milgate terms Spenser's poem a stimulus to Donne as satirist. He characterizes the presiding goddess of Donne's poem, Flora, as "highly equivocal"; "sun and moon," he continues, "pursue no ordered sequence but impinge on our consciousness in the poem as arbitrarily and fitfully as upon the notice of the city-dweller"; the physicality of Donne's poem, he suggests, inclines to the violent, the grotesque, and the bawdy. "Despite its verve and technical skill, which Donne apparently thought were sufficient to warrant his preserving the poem," Milgate concludes, "it is not a success as a whole." He finds it inconsistent both as satire and as celebration, between which "its wit and imaginative force are uneasily divided." Consequently, he adds, "the references to 'perfection' and to 'vertue' and 'truth' become rather empty gestures." Such would have to be the case, he continues, "when the 'praise and fame' due to the bride are based only on her wealth and beauty and an (apparently) equally adventitious virginity" (xxii). Disputing Novarr (1956), Milgate argues also that even if the poem was written (as his title has it) *at* Lincoln's Inn, it was not necessarily written *for* Lincoln's Inn (110).

Partridge (1978, 122) asserts that *EpLin* was, of the the three epithalamions, the most influenced "by Spenser and the neo-Platonic tradition."

In her study of androgyny in Donne's poetry, Mollenkott (1981, 23, 25) notes that Donne "described men at Lincoln's Inn who combined study (masculine) with play (feminine) to make 'strange Hermaphrodits' [l. 30]" (23).

Zunder (1982, 32–33, 35–36, 41) terms *EpLin* the most important of Donne's earlier poems to present a normative idea of "a hierarchically structured union in marriage," an idea that he claims "informs all the earlier poems" (35). In *EpLin*, however, Zunder finds that this idea is "something given and imagined, rather than something experienced" (35–36), with a consequent uncertainty in tone and imagery; he cites lines 89–90 as an instance. Citing lines 13–14 and 27, Zunder argues that *EpLin* reveals Donne's awareness of social changes, showing "that wealth was to be found in commercial London, the city—Donne's birthplace—rather than in the court" (32–33).

Craik and Craik (1986, 193–95, 253) summarize the perceived resemblances between *EpLin* and Spenser's *Epithalamion*, which they believe is the inspiration for Donne's poem (253), as lying in structure (the events of the wedding day in order), the refrain at the end of each stanza, and the archaism "nill" in line 57 of the Westmoreland manuscript (NY3). These resemblances, they assert, have led some to see Donne's poem as a parody of Spenser's, but the differences, they maintain, are profound, embracing the setting, the role of the poet as a character in the poem, and the poetic sensibility. Conceding a similarity in "composition," which they explain with an analogy to one painter's imitation of another, Craik and Craik nevertheless deny that *EpLin* is a parody. They find no "burlesque" or "derision" of an original model. "The differences-within-resemblance," they argue, "are less particular than parody in this sense would require" (193). They find the setting of *EpLin* evocative of the elegies and the satires (194) and cite the "worldly wit" in the descriptions of characters in the poem and in the comparison of the musicians and dancers at the end of the party to "toyl'd beasts" (l. 67). Yet Donne, Craik and Craik assert, "does not exercise his worldly wit at the expense of the bride and bridegroom, and he treats the wedding ceremony and the wedding night with seriousness and refinement," despite characteristic extravagances of style such as the comparison of the bride to a sacrificial lamb and of the groom to a priest (194). Craik and Craik discount the likelihood that *EpLin* "was written for any special occasion, either for a real wedding or for a mock one" (253), characterizing it generally as a "literary exercise" (195).

Shawcross (1986a, 121–22, 145), emphasizing the poem's mocking or parodic qualities, asserts that *EpLin* groups the patricians, the wealthy senators' sons, and the country men together as Inns of Court "Hermaphroditts," a name deriving from the fact that "they study (in this community of men) and 'play' (in sexual community with women)"; Shawcross also argues that "the 'bride' and the 'Daughters of London' in attendance were actually men in drag" (122). He further maintains that *EpLin* "travesties" Spenser's *Epithalamion* published earlier in the same year. Instances of the parody, he explains, include lines 14–15 of *EpLin*, which allude to Spenser's "Tell me ye merchants daughters did ye see / So fayre a creature in your towne before"; Shawcross calls

Donne's lines "parodic poetizing," adding that the "sexual double entendre is similar" to that in *LovAlch.* To Spenser's "seriously literal" lines "Open thy temples gates unto my love, / Open them wide that she may enter in," Shawcross compares line 37 of *EpLin*, claiming that it evokes "labia and vagina." Shawcross further seeks to establish the parodic status of *EpLin* by examining the way in which Spenser varies the closing line of the stanza in his poem—either "The woods shall to me answer, and my Echo ring" (in various permutations) or "Ne let the woods them answer, nor theyr echo ring" (in various permutations). The change occurs, he argues, "at the golden section (that is, at a position roughly .618 and .382 within the poem)," and we should remember the intralinear comma that breaks it at the golden section "as we read Donne's 'To day put on perfection, and a womans name,' which transcends into 'To night put on perfection, and a womans name' at mid-point in the poem although the comma of the line maintains a golden section." He adds that the phrase "put on" in Donne's later line "has an anatomical implication and stresses a male chauvinism." Shawcross concludes that "arranging the epithalamion as appendant to the epigrams is more meaningful for a reader than grouping it with the two others of that genre, which are almost consistently ordered by chronology" (122). He describes the "intent" of *EpLin* as satiric, raises the question of authorial intention as a factor in "genre definition," and labels *EpLin* generically as "a satire in verse, cast as an epithalamion" (145).

Hester (1987, 52), citing Novarr (1956), characterizes *EpLin* as a "wry critique" (with affinities to *ElBed*) of Spenser's *Epithalamion*, "or at least of that *type* of wedding hymn."

In a chapter discussing the anti-epithalamions of Donne, Crashaw, and Blake, Schenck (1988, 75–79) argues that the satiric treatment of the epithalamion is "as old as our association of love and death and issues from the chiasmus of epithalamium and elegy in the earliest of pastoral texts" (75). After briefly citing some examples of anti-epithalamions from classical poetry and prose, Schenck insists that in *EpLin* Donne responds directly to Spenser by using "the form of the epithalamium to announce its creator's very different sense of the poet's place in the world." In particular, Donne accomplishes what Schenck describes as a "desanctification of a rival poem" in two ways. First, Donne "apes the form of Spenser's poem, approximates its stanza form and mimics its refrain" (76). Second, he imputes "less than romantic motives to the groomsmen wanting to marry the wealthy Senators' daughters and to the fathers hastening to make rich matches for their girls" and therefore reminds his readers consistently that "these motives are mortal and materialistic" (77). Schenck notes two conceits that "account for much of the critical censure of the poem": "the likening of church architecture to the bride's genitals and womb" and "the superimposition of bridal rite and ritual disembowelling." Both of these conceits, Schenck asserts, not only "have antecedents in the erotic imagery with which Church mystics attempted to express the ineffable" (78), but also define *EpLin* in the genre of anti-epithalamions by collapsing the distinction between body and soul and marriage and death.

Examining the textual history of *EpLin*, Walby (1989, 17–35) asserts that the Westmoreland text of *EpLin* is "bibliographically superior to all other early copies of the work, including the 1633 first printing which Grierson, Milgate, and most other modern editors have used as their copy-text" (26). Walby argues for adopting a text based on the Westmoreland manuscript and provides a "Schema by Omission of Words" and a "Schema by Verbal Alterations" as support for his account of the transmission of the text (32–34). Walby argues further that "not only is the adoption of Westmoreland as copy-text justified by its textual authority, but its adoption also avoids the anachronism of eclecticism inherent in the creation of a 'critical text' and the dubious practice of imposing editorial interpretations in the guise of apparently objective principles" (26). In particular, Walby objects to the "common practice among modern editors" of emending the 1633 text of the poem with Westmoreland, and argues that "two such emended editions, Grierson's and Milgate's, adversely affect the interpretation of the poem" (18). Finally, by means of close readings of several key passages, and in the context of interpretations of the poem by Novarr (1956) and Ousby (1976a), Walby asserts that "restoration of the epithalamium to the Westmoreland state also clarifies several cruxes in the work, and supports the reading of the poem as parodic or satiric" (26).

Dubrow (1990, 156–64) takes issue with Novarr (1956). This earliest, and therefore least polished, of Donne's three epithalamions, "this curious lyric" (156), Dubrow argues, "is pulled between his primary aim, writing a 'straight' imitation of Spenser and his genre, and an impulse to undermine that imitation with parody, or, to put it another way, a characteristic impulse to view Spenser as not a model to emulate but a rival to challenge." As a result, "this lyric is so disturbing not merely or primarily because it mocks the conventions of its genre and the values it represents but because parody and imitation usurp and decenter each other" (160).

Notes and Glosses

Title. Epithalamium. **GARDNER** (1967): "The poem is not found in the Group I manuscripts and the editor of 1633 took it with its heading 'made at Lincolnes Inne' from his Group II manuscript. It is found in *W* [NY3], along with the *Elegies* and *Satires* and a collection of Verse-Letters written to the men friends of Donne's youth, headed simply 'Epithalamium'. The company it keeps in *W* suggests that the Group II manuscripts preserve a sound tradition in describing it as 'made at Lincolnes Inne', and that Donne may have added this distinguishing note to the bare title 'Epithalamium' after he had written the two court Epithalamiums. This suggests that in some cases titles in the Group II manuscripts may derive from Donne's papers. On the other hand, the title in the Group III manuscripts and elsewhere, 'Epithalamium on a Citizen', looks like a title intelligently supplied from the content of the poem, particularly its second stanza" (197). **MILGATE** (1978) (reading "Epithalamion"): "Possibly, the poem was first called 'Epithalamion' (as in *W*), and after the other two epithalamions were composed Donne added the words 'made at Lincolnes Inne' to distinguish it from them [Milgate is mistaken about the title in NY3, which reads "Epithalamium" as in this edition—eds.]" (109–10).

1 *The Sun-beames . . . are spred* For a pertinent comment by **GROSART** (1872–73), see the note to *Eclog* 131–32. **MILGATE** (1978): cf. Spenser, *Epithalamion* 20: "His golden beame upon the hils doth spred" (110).

4–5 *It nourseth sadnes . . . Downe doth dint.* **DOWDEN** (1895): love and death are frequently juxtaposed in Donne; even here, "when the bride rises on the wedding morning from her downy bed, the impression left by her body reminds him of the grave" (806).

4 *nourseth* **SHAWCROSS** (1967a): "fosters" (171).

5 *Like to a graue* **GRANSDEN** (1954): "un-Spenserian and truly Donnian" (115).

5 *Downe doth dint.* **MELTON** (1906): the line illustrates Donne's use of the "d" sound [see Melton's note to *EpEliz* 91–92] (162).

5 *dint.* **CLEMENTS** (1966): "indent" (56). **SHAWCROSS** (1967a): "dent, imprint" (171).

6 *other you* **MILGATE** (1978): "the bridegroom. Love makes two persons one (l. 39), and one person two"; cf. *BedfShe* 1–4 and Chapman's *Masque of the Middle Temple*, "Hymn to Hymen," ll. 3–6 (for Princess Elizabeth's marriage) (110).

6 *meete* **GROSART** (1872–73): "do meet"; "will meet" (1:278). **MILGATE** (1978): "are due to meet" (110).

7 *Put forth . . . balme-breathing thigh* **UL-HASAN** (1958): synesthesia is evidenced by "cutaneous sensitiveness to temperature and the nasal alertness on the part of the lover" (82). **GAMBERINI** (1967): the line expresses the bold and sensual young Donne (78). **BEAVER** (1976): "Here the misaligned 1–2 on the compounds is reversed to 2–1 in the presence of stress in Even position to the right" (98):

```
                                  1     2       1
Put forth, put forth that warm balme-breathing thigh.
 W   S    W    S    W     S    W    S       S
```

7 *balme-breathing* **CRAIK and CRAIK** (1986): "fragrantly scented" (253).

12 *To day put on . . . womans name.* **McPEEK** (1939): Jonson uses a similar theme in the epithalamion that concludes *The Hue and Cry after Cupid*, and Donne is here imitating Jonson, not the other way around (368). Grierson [(1912); see gloss to ll. 81–82 below] describes the metaphysical doctrine pertinent to this line, but is wrong to assume that Donne was its pre-eminent exponent (367–368). **UL-HASAN** (1958): the refrain shows Donne's interest in sex as both physical union and integration of identity between man and woman (a theme throughout Donne's poetry) (2–3). "Woman can achieve perfection only when she has enjoyed the love act and Donne considered this experience as the prerequisite of perfect womanhood" (11). **HALIO** (1964): this refrain reflects ideas derived from Aristotle's theory of conception and generation in *De Generatione Animalium* (179). "Aristotle relied upon teleological reasoning: since nature makes nothing in vain, where there are two sexes the male

must have some function in procreation," which is "to *perfect* the work of generation" by imparting "the sensitive soul, without which the embryo remains imperfect" (180). **RAIZIS** (1966): the passage is not just a refrain, for "in all civilizations and religions of mankind, a girl finds her rightful and honorable place in society with marriage and motherhood" (7). **SHAWCROSS** (1967a) (citing his note to *Prim* 25): ten "signifies the end of computation and is thus perfect; it is the whole and perfect number in Pythagorean thought" (141). "Man is ten in the symbol, and woman only half a man. According to Bonaventura, ten indicated the fallen angels who would be replaced as the tenth order by Man in the final perfection; and, according to Augustine and Methodius, five, because of the number of senses, was the symbol of flesh" (401–02). **MILGATE** (1978): cf. Gardner's [1965, 220–21] notes to *Prim*, on the idea that woman is imperfect and achieves full womanhood in sexual union (110). Cf. also *TN* 2.4.39–40 ("alas, that they are so; / To die, even when they to perfection grow") and *The Problemes of Aristotle* (Edinburgh, 1595, sig. H2): "the nature of women is imperfect" and "as the matter dooth covet a forme or perfection, so doth a woman the male." Jonson echoes the line in *Hymenaei*, ll. 473, 532, etc., and *The Haddington Masque*, ll. 379, 390, etc. (110).

13–36 (sts 2–3) *Daughters of London . . . and a womans name*. **LEGOUIS** (1955): these two stanzas, which allude to marriage between fortune-hunting young men of good family and bourgeois heiresses, are of a rare insolence, recalling the French nobility's famous "One must manure one's lands" ("*Il faut bien fumer ses terres*") (213).

13 *Daughters of London*, **LEGOUIS** (1955): daughters of wealthy citizens (212).

14–16 *golden Mines . . . mariage dayes* **MILLER** (1970): the emphasis on the dowries calls into question the groom's motives for the marriage (414–15).

14 *Our golden . . . Treasuree;* **SMITH** (1971): "They brought rich dowries with them" (453).

14 *Our* **LEGOUIS** (1955): refers to the fortune-hunting law students among whom Donne numbered himself (212).

14 *Mines* **SMITH** (1971): "has a sexual sense" (453). **MILGATE** (1978): "sources of wealth (cf. l. 16)." For the sexual innuendo, cf. *Oth.* 4.2.79–80 (111).

14 *furnish'd* **SMITH** (1971): "amply supplied" (453).

15–16 *You which are Angels . . . mariage dayes* **GOSSE** (1899): "The pun about 'angels'—the divine ministrants and the earthly coin—was a favourite one with Donne. [In *ElBrac*] he plays upon it until we lose all patience with so much self-satisfied ingenuity . . . . Yet it was precisely this dross and slag of his genius which endeared Donne as a poet to his immediate followers" (1:77). **MATSUURA** (1949): "Rich daughters of London, who are themselves likened to angels, are said to be accompanied by many angels at their marriage" (156) [see also Carey (1981, 265)].

16 *Angels* **BEWLEY** (1966): alludes to the dowries of rich citizens' daughters (165). **CRAIK and CRAIK** (1986): the gold coins were stamped with the figure of an angel on the reverse (253).

17 *Helpe with your presence and deuise to prayse* **GRIERSON** (1912): there ought to be no comma after "presence" because it would cause a modern, but not a seventeenth-century, reader to understand "devise" as a verb, when it is in fact the noun "device," meaning "fancy, invention." "'Devise to praise' would be a very awkward construction" (2:98).

17 *deuise* **MILGATE** (1978): "ingenuity" (111).

18 *grow due.* **MILGATE** (1978): "are becoming imminent (they too will soon marry)" (111).

19–22 *Conceitedly dres her . . . rich as Inde,* **GRIERSON** (1912): the "fancy and invention" suggested by "devise" (l. 17) "is to be shown in the attiring of the bride" (2:98).

19 *Conceitedly dres her,* **SMITH** (1971): "ingeniously adorn her with nuptial emblems" (454).

19 *Conceitedly* **MILGATE** (1978): "'fancifully, whimsically, in the manner of a conceit' (*O.E.D.*)" (111).

22 *Flora,* **SHAWCROSS** (1967a): "goddess of flowers" (171). **SMITH** (1971): her dedication day in late April "was celebrated with great sexual licence" (454). **MILGATE** (1978): her festival extended "for five days from 28 April" (111).

22 *Inde,* **SMITH** (1971): "India, which was proverbially opulent" (454). **MILGATE** (1978): "India, the land of gorgeous clothes and of gems" (111).

23 *lame* **SHAWCROSS** (1967a): "physically disabled, halting; perhaps with a sexual pun concerning her husband" (171). **SMITH** (1971): "deficient, imperfect" (454).

25–36 (st 3) *And you frolique Patricians . . . and a womans name.* **MILLER** (1970): "Donne sharpens . . . [his] satiric edge . . . by associating the groom with his attendants—dandified, would-be sons-in-law of wealthy senators" characterized unflatteringly in lines 27–28 (415).

25–31 *And you frolique Patricians . . . Here shine:* **MILGATE** (1978): "The subjects of the verb [shine] are arranged in anti-climax, and refer to City, Court, and Country, a familiar trio in Donne" (111). **LEPAGE** (1984): the language and content of these lines recall Sylvester's Du Bartas; Sylvester's "androgyny is directed solely at the greater referent of God," whereas "Donne's is in its own terms non-referential alteration" (633).

25–26 *And you frolique Patricians / Sonnes of these Senators, wealths deepe Oceans* **GRIERSON** (1912), referring to "the corruption of the text here [in his copy-text, the edition of 1633 (A)]," prints these lines as follows: "And you frolique Patricians, / Sonns of these Senators wealths deep oceans . . . ." In this rendition, Grierson modifies both the wording and the punctuation of A, printing a comma after "Patricians" (where A has nothing) and "Sonns of" for A's "Some of," which he explains as a scribal misreading (see the note on "Sonnes" below). Grierson follows A's punctuation of line 26, however, printing the line with no comma after "Senators"; and this punctuation, which turns the entirety of line 26 into an appositive for "frolique Patricians," supports his contention that confusion over "Donne's characteristic pun" on son/sun has led to the misidentification of the "Patricians." The "Patricians," Grierson avers, cannot be "the sons of 'these Senators' [i.e., wealthy citizens] by birth," as the sons of citizens, however rich, could not be so styled. Donne is rather thinking "of the young noblemen who are accompanying their friend on his wedding-day. They are, or are willing to be, the sons, by marriage not by blood, of 'these Senators', or rather of their money-bags" and are willing to "marry their daughters for money, as the hero of the *Epithalamion* is doing. . . . [T]hey are 'Sunnes' as well as 'Sonnes'—suns which drink up the deep oceans of these Senators' wealth . . ."(2:98). Grierson cites passages from the *Sermons* (1:208, e.g.) and the poetry (*Storm* 43–44, *MHPaper* 1–2, *HSDue* 5, and *Father* 15–16) to support these observations about Donne's vocabulary and habits of thought, adding that if read "correctly," line 26 "has a satiric quality which Donne's lines rarely want, and in which this stanza abounds" (2:99). **BELDEN** (1915) disputes Grierson's omission of the medial comma in line 26, arguing that "as sons of senators" the sons of wealthy citizens "could not well be styled anything else [but 'Patricians']" by "so good a Latinist as Donne." If Donne here intended the sun/son pun as a way of intimating that "the frolic patricians would dry up the senator's oceans of wealth," Belden continues, "he had ample warrant for it in the extravagance and social ambition of the sons of wealthy business men in London. But it is doubtful that he had here any such intention." "The preceding stanza," Belden says, "openly celebrates the bridesmaids in their quality of London heiresses; this stanza as clearly describes the groom's companions, under four heads: first, sons of wealthy citizens; second, courtiers; third, country gentlemen; fourth, students of Lincoln's Inn, of which the bridegroom himself is a member. No doubt the first three are included in the fourth . . . ." Donne himself belonged to the "first and fourth" groups and probably aspired to "the second," concludes Belden, "but it is no more reasonable to identify the 'patricians' with the 'courtiers' than it would be to identify the 'courtiers' with the 'country men'" (143–44). **GRIERSON** (1929), restoring the comma after "Senators" in line 26, accepts Belden's (1915) arguments about "Patricians" and the punctuation of the line (l). **LEGOUIS** (1955): Grierson's (1929) comma after "Senators" simplifies the syntax but sacrifices the characteristic subtlety of the passage (213). **SMITH** (1971): a simpler reading than that of Grierson (1912) is that the patricians "are the playboy sons of wealthy merchants, possibly with bought titles, who suck up their fathers' wealth and disburse it like rain. They are the suns/sons of the deep oceans of their fathers' wealth" (454). **WALBY** (1989): the placement of the comma after "senators" in the Westmoreland manuscript makes "'Sonnes of these Senators' and 'wealths deepe Oceans' appositives modifying 'frolique Patricians'" (22).

25 *frolique* **SMITH** (1971): "liberal, merry" (454).

26 *Sonnes* **GRIERSON** (1912) (reading "Sonns"): the "corruption" in the text arises from both copyists' and printers' confusion of "sonnes," "sonns," "sonne" (as written with a vestigial final "s"), and "some" and from "a misapprehension of Donne's characteristic pun" (2:98). "Sonns" is the most common reading of the manuscripts, and most manuscripts support the punctuation of the 1633 edition (2:98–99).

26 *these* **CRAIK and CRAIK** (1986): "indicates a whole class"; cf. *Ham.* 2.2.218: "These tedious old fools!" (253).

26 *Senators,* **GRIERSON** (1912): Donne so terms wealthy citizens of London in his *Sermon Preached at Pauls Cross . . . 26 Mart. 1616* (2:98).

26 *wealths deepe Oceans* **CRAIK and CRAIK** (1986): "deep oceans of wealth (applied to *senators*)" (253).

27 *painted* **SMITH** (1971): "ostentatious; artificial, and not what they seem" (454).

28 *Yee Cuntrymen . . . love none* **ELLRODT** (1960a): this, the only reference to the country in the poem, is sarcastic, and consistent with Donne's rejection of pastoral and mythological poetic rhetoric (2:174).

28 *Cuntrymen* **WALBY** (1989): in the Westmoreland manuscript spelling, "there is a certain contrary nature about 'cuntrymen' (a sexual oxymoron that itself suggests hermaphroditism) who love only their beasts" (23).

28 *Beasts,* **MILLER** (1970): the materialistic possessions of the "country bumpkins" (415).

29–30 *Yee of those fellowships . . . made strange Hermaphroditts* **G[ILES] O[LDISWORTH]** (1648), glossing a copy of the 1639 edition (siglum C10), notes that these lines refer to the Templars (120). Oldisworth is identified in Sampson (1921).

29 *those fellowships* **LEGOUIS** (1955): the Inns of Court (213). **SHAWCROSS** (1967a): "groups within Lincoln's Inn concerned with study or with frolicsome recreation" (171) [see note on "Hermaphroditts" below].

29 *he* **CRAIK and CRAIK** (1986): "the bridegroom" (253).

29 *one* **MILGATE** (1978): "a member of one" (111).

30 *Of study and play made strange Hermaphroditts* **GROSART** (1872–73): students

at the Inns of Court regularly presented masques and plays, especially before royalty, and at great expense (1:278). **MENASCÈ** (1974): Donne alludes to himself as a member of this group (12). The line marks Donne as a "metaphysical" poet, as it violently yokes together, as Samuel Johnson complained, "'the most heterogeneous ideas'" (40).

30 *Hermaphroditts* **GARDNER** (1952): "The word is used figuratively at this period for any striking conjunction of opposites" (102). **LEGOUIS** (1955): "Here Donne appears to describe himself at that age" (213). **SULLENS** (1964): predates the earliest use of the word with this meaning in the *OED*, 4. fig. 1659 (219). **SHAWCROSS** (1967a): "Since study (community with men) and play (community with women) are opposites, these fellows may be considered hermaphroditic" (171–72) [see note on "those fellowships" above].

31, 37 *Temple* **LEGOUIS** (1955): the church built by the Templars in this district (213). **SHAWCROSS** (1967a): a pun on the Inner or Middle Temple (403). **SMITH** (1971): "possibly the Temple Church in Fleet Street, which had close associations with the Inns of Court" (454). **MILGATE** (1978): "In the 'Roman' context (cf. 'Patricians', 'Senators', 'two-leav'd gates') the Temple . . . might be any fane; but it could, as the main or a punning meaning, refer to the chapel of the Inner and Middle Temples, a church closely associated with the Inns of Court" (111). **CRAIK and CRAIK** (1986): possibly a general allusion, as in Spenser's *Epithalamion* (254).

32–35 *Lo, in yon path . . . no griefe nor shame* **McPEEK** (1939): the influence of Catullus, though "more evasive" than that of Spenser or Jonson, is "not to be denied." It begins with these lines visualizing the bride going to the Temple; cf. Catullus, *Carmina* 61, lines 77, 83–86: "Virgo adest . . . / Tardet ingenuus pudor. / Quem tamen magis audiens, / Flet quod ire necesse est. / Flere desine." "Though the influence of Spenser and Jonson may be urged here and conceded," McPeek continues, "and though blushing and tears be admitted as conventions, the fact remains that these lines of Catullus afford a closer parallel for those of Donne than any which I have discovered elsewhere" (210).

32–34 *Lo, in yon path . . . t'is no other thing.* **MILLER** (1970): this, the most "devastating thrust" in the stanza, calls the virginity of the bride into question (415).

32 *strawd* **SULLENS** (1964): this use is not recorded in the *OED*, which "does not give the ppl. a. *strawed* for v.1" (266).

34 *Except my sight fayle . . . thing.* **TUFTE** (1970): "The commonplace idea that the beauty of the bride blinds the onlookers appears in King James's fragmentary wedding masque of 1588. A soldier speaks: 'I whome no bloodie battells coulde effraye / Am now become a simple womans praye, / Bot what? no woman bot a Goddesse bright / No shame to blinded be with such a light.' See *The Poems of James VI of Scotland*, ed. James Craigie (Edinburgh and London, 1958)" (312). **MILGATE** (1978): "If he can believe his eyes, there is a 'sober virgin' still to be found in the City, and the bridegroom is not improving his fortunes by marrying a rich widow" (111).

37–42 *Thy too-leaud gates . . . fatten thee.* **WILSON** (1980): the imagery of the lines depends on the root senses of "sarcophagus," from Greek words meaning "flesh-eating." "Poetically expressed, the sarcophagus—the 'flesh-eating' tomb—in the 'faire Temple' of the poem will hopefully remain a 'hunger-starved wombe' for a long time before it will have a chance to 'fatten' on the bodies of the betrothed." Such linguistic association, and subsequent tracing by the reader, is valid because by creating such a context, Donne "gives the reader a chance to surprise himself by making the connection between the stated connotative associations and the denotative meaning of an unstated synonym for the word 'tomb' in l. 36, a meaning which the reader discovers for himself by working back to the root words after considering the clues that Donne has provided" (72). The lines are "a witty way of satisfying the epithalamic convention of wishing the bride and groom a long life" (73). **CRAIK and CRAIK** (1986): there are no bawdy overtones, despite the assertion of Milgate (1978) [see Milgate's note to l. 40]; Milgate does not explain how "Temple" can have such a sense. Although "two-leav'd" may have a specifically sexual meaning, as in the rape episode in Nashe's *Unfortunate Traveller*, "yet the sequence 'two-leav'd gates . . . bosome . . . wombe' positively discourages any such innuendo." As Milgate notes, "two-leav'd" evokes the Latin *biforis*; thus its diction accords with "Senators" and "Patricians." Any "prurient" overtones may be a deliberate trap for the prurient-minded (194). **WALBY** (1989): "What Donne satirizes in this crucial stanza is a certain deathly aspect to the couple's temporal aspirations in marriage; and the church, by endorsing the marriage, participates in that death" (25).

37–39 *Thy too-leaud gates . . . one they bee:* **MENASCÈ** (1974): although *EpLin* is representative of the youthful, sensual poet of the elegies and the early songs and sonnets, the mature poet (found also in certain of the songs and sonnets that celebrate love as a mystical union) is also apparent (40).

37–38 *Thy too-leaud gates . . . bosome hold* **McPEEK** (1939): an apparent effort to improve on Spenser's *Epithalamion* 204–05 ("Open the temple gates unto my love, / Open them wide that she may enter in") (209–10).

37 *too-leaud* **MILGATE** (1978): "Latin *biforis*" (111). **CRAIK and CRAIK** (1986): "double door" (254).

39 *mistically* **MILGATE** (1978): "a reference to the analogy made in the marriage service, between marriage and the 'mystical union that is betwixt Christ and His Church'" (112).

40 *hunger sterved wombe* **MILGATE** (1978): "a phrase coarsely relevant to the bride (carrying on the bawdy sense of 'Temple' and 'two-leav'd'), though primarily referring to the vaults in, or crypts beneath, the church, which will swell with the buried bodies of the couple and their parents (l. 42)" (112).

40 *sterved* **SMITH** (1971): "pronounced as two syllables" (454).

40 *wombe* **LEGOUIS** (1955): appears to refer to a crypt, but it is not certain that one existed then (213).

41 *bodyes and ther tombe* **MILGATE** (1978): "Cf. ll. 4–5; the thought reaches an appropriate final development in ll. 79–80. Cf. Sidney, *Arcadia*, 'The Third Eclogues', i., ll. 31–2: 'Let one time (but long first) close up their daies, / One grave their bodies seaze' (*Poems*, ed. W. A. Ringler [1962], p. 92)" (112).

43–45 *All elder claymes . . . these two disseuer.* **EMPEROR** (1928): cf. Catullus, *Carmina* 61, ll. 146–48 (40): "Scimus haec tibi quae licent / Sola cognita: sed marito / Ista non eadem licent." **McPEEK** (1939): whether derived directly or through an imitator "[t]he conviction is almost inescapable that Donne is giving us here an English condensation of the advice to Manlius and Junia" in Catullus, *Carmina* 61, lines 101–05, 141–43, 146–48, 151–53 (210–11):

> Non tuus levis in mala
> Deditus vir adultera,
> Probra turpia persequens,
> A tuis teneris volet
> Secubare papillis,
> . . . .
> Diceris male te a tuis
> Unguentate glabris marite
> Abstinere, sed abstine.
> . . . .
> Scimus haec tibi quae licent
> Sola cognita, sed marito
> Ista non eadem licent.
> . . . .
> Nupta, tu quoque quae tuus
> Vir petet cave ne neges,
> Ne petitum aliunde eat.

Although Donne's lines are "a pale summary of the candid detail of Catullus," they present "a Catullan motif which had hitherto been ignored by English poets" (210–11).

43 *elder claymes* **SMITH** (1971): "previous claims on the affections of either" (454). **CRAIK and CRAIK** (1986): cf. "forsaking all others" in the marriage service (254).

46 *All wayes,* **MILGATE** (1978): "both 'all ways' (in every way) and 'always'" (112).

49–60 (st 5) O, *Winter dayes . . . and a Womans name.* **CASE** (1896): the stanza influences Robert Gould's "Mirtillo and Amynta: A Hymeneal Pindaric Poem" (*Works*, 1709) (178). **FOWLER** (1970): Donne "bisects" the poem into two four-stanza units by means of the change in the refrain from "To day" to "To night" and thereby highlights the temporal divisions typical of the genre (158).

49–50 O, *Winter dayes . . . soone bring night.* **EMPEROR** (1928): there is the possible influence of Catullus, *Carmina* 68, lines 81–83: "Coniugis ante coacta novi dimittere collum / Quam veniens una atque altera rursus hiems / Noctibus in longis avidum saturasset amorem" (41).

49 *Winter dayes* **SMITH** (1971): "evidently the wedding took place in summer" (455).

50 *for they* **MILGATE** (1978): "because they" (112).

51 *waight* **SULLENS** (1964): predates the earliest use of the word with this meaning in the *OED*, v.[1] I. 6. b. transf. 1745 (242).

51 *then* **PATRIDES** (1985): "than" (211).

52 *iolityes,* **MILGATE** (1978) (reading "jollities"): "This word, used by Spenser in *Epithalamion* 245, is found elsewhere in Donne's verse" only in *EpEliz* 32 (112).

54–58 *But that the Sun . . . downe the Westerne hill* **GARROD** (1946): "The sun still sweats, in our hemisphere (for it is the summer season). He moves swiftly in winter (taking, at the solstice, 7 3/4 hours for his whole journey). But at the moment he is stationary, though he shadows (throws a shadow indicating) his turning. (Cf. Epistle of St. James, i. 17, 'the Father of lights, with whom is no . . . shadow of turning'.) Helios reached noon (his turning-point); his steeds for the moment will go slow, but quicken ('gallop lively') as he descends to the west. When he has run the other half of his course, you shall put on perfection" (117). **PARISH** (1976): in these lines Donne "quotes directly" from the Old Testament story of the sun standing still (Josh. 10:12–14) (200). **MILGATE** (1978) (citing Hagopian 1957 [see below, l. 57]): "The midsummer sun is blazing in the eastern hemisphere and appears to be standing still. But shadows have moved from west to east, and the sun has passed its zenith (cf. 'A Lecture upon the Shadow'). Whereas in winter he hastens to the west, in summer he dallies, reining in his steeds; but once he has begun his descent into the western hemisphere he will go quickly" (112).

54 *But that the Sun . . . sweates.* **ELLRODT** (1960a): Donne treats the sun as casually here as in *SunRis*, evidence that he is urbane, colloquial, and contemptuous of sounding "poetical" (2:174).

54 *sweates.* **SULLENS** (1964): predates the earliest use of the word with this meaning in the *OED*, v. II. 5 (237).

55 *flyes* **PATRIDES** (1985): "hastens to the west" (211).

55 *stands still.* **PATRIDES** (1985): "appears to dally in the summer" (211).

56–57 *Yet shadows turne . . . nill be restrained* **LEGOUIS** (1955): Garrod's (1946) reading [see below] of "shadows" as a verb and of "turne" as a noun (i.e. the sun marks the turning of the day by the shadow it projects) allows the reading of all editions, "will" (l. 57), to be preserved; the "steeds" of the sun, at the onset of afternoon, begin slowly to descend (213).

56 *Yet shadows turne:* **SHAWCROSS** (1967a): "Past noon, shadows lie in an opposite direction" (172).

56 *shadows* **GARROD** (1946): "not a substantive, but a verb; the subject is the sun" (117).

57 *nill* **GRIERSON** (1912): "There can be no doubt" that "nill," found in the Westmoreland ms. [NY3], "is right." "The use of 'nill' for 'will' [sic; presumably Grierson means 'will not'] was one of Spenser's Chaucerisms, and Donne comes closer to Spenser in the *Epithalamia* than anywhere else"; further instances occur in Sylvester's translation of Du Bartas, in Davison's *Poetical Rhapsody*, and in *The Passionate Pilgrim* (2:99). **GARROD** (1946): Grierson's reading "is not more than a clever emendation" (117). **HAGOPIAN** (1957): Grierson was wrong to change *will* to *nill*; "if line 57 is read with a gradually rising pitch and a momentary pause at the end before beginning line 58, the passage will clearly signify that the sun stands still at noon before the shadows turn" (501). **SMITH** (1971): "will not" (455). **MILGATE** (1978) (reading "will"): "nill" is probably a "copyist's error, or a 'correction' anticipating Grierson's, who conjectured 'nill' before he found the reading in [NY3]" (112).

58 *But* **SHAWCROSS** (1967a): "Otherwise they will" (173).

61 *amorous euening Star* **SMITH** (1971): "Venus" (455).

62 *our amorous Star* **SMITH** (1971): "the bride" (455).

63 *release* **SULLENS** (1964): predates the earliest use of the word with this meaning in the *OED*, v.[1] II. 6. b. 1833 (229).

64 *Musitians;* **MILGATE** (1978): "four syllables" (112).

64 *truce* **SMITH** (1971): "respite" (455).

66 *As much wearines as perfection brings.* **MELTON** (1906): the line, with an accent on the middle syllable of "wearines," is an example of Donne's unconventional use of accent [see note to *EpEliz* 18]; cf. Shakespeare, Sonnet 142, l. 8: "Robb'd others' beds *revénues* of their rents" (100).

68 *dispenced*, **GROSART** (1872–73): dispensed with (1:278). **SMITH** (1971): "dispensed with, relinquished" (455).

68–69 *ther . . . ther* **LEGOUIS** (1955): the first "ther" refers to "beasts" (l. 67), the second to the wedded couple. This tactless juxtaposition could be avoided were "your" substituted for the first "ther"; in the writing of the time, "th" was often represented by "y," and so the two words were often confused; "your" would encompass both "Musicians" (l. 64) and "beasts" (213).

70 *Labors* **SHAWCROSS** (1967a): "punning also on child-bearing" (173).

70 *dainty feasts*. **SHAWCROSS** (1967a): "e.g., kisses, the food of the soul" (173). **MILGATE** (1978): cf. "sweetes" (l. 51) (112).

71 *turne* **SHAWCROSS** (1967a): "return, and with sexual meaning" (173).

73–84 (st. 7) *Thy Virgins girdle . . . and a Womans name*. **ELLRODT** (1960a): to the ample Spenserian stanza Donne gives both a dramatic accent and an analytic turn (2:174).

73–78 *Thy Virgins girdle . . . best in nakednes*. **MENASCÈ** (1974): where Spenser had been stately and serious, it was "inevitable" that Donne the student would be brisk and flippant, using overt and strongly realistic language (39).

74–75 *And in thy nuptiall bed, Loves Altar, ly / A pleasing Sacrifice:* **RUGOFF** (1939): this image, as well as that in lines 88–90, shows that "Donne finds parallels for all the rites of love and marriage, even to the most private, in church ceremony" (86).

74–75 *Altar . . . Sacrifice:* **MILGATE** (1978): "The metaphor is resumed in ll. 89–90" (112).

76 *Thee of these chaines and robes, which were put on* **BEAVER** (1976): "Stress was on the second member of the verb-participle combinations in the Elizabethan period, as it is now" (100):

> Thee of these chaines and robes which were *put on*.
> W S W S W S W S W S

79–84 *This bed . . . a Womans name*. **HUNTER** (1965) (citing these lines): *EpLin* is an example of "Donne's taste at its best" (102).

79–81 *This bed . . . thou wast but able* **LEGOUIS** (1955): "At first glance this passage would appear to prove that Donne was already a Protestant. In reality he believes, and always will believe, that virginity has a religious value only if it is consecrated to God, and he can cite St. Augustine and Saint Thomas Aquinas to buttress this thesis [see Grierson's note to ll. 81–82]"; cf. *SecAn* 353–55 (213).

79–80 *This bed . . . a Cradle* **UL-HASAN** (1958): Donne regards physical union as "creative" and "a holy affair"; conception is nobler for a woman than "virginitie" (15).

80 *A graue . . . a Cradle* **SOUTHALL** (1973), citing this line, comments that medieval schoolmen held the circle to be "the perfect shape." They saw the universe as "a system of nine concentric spheres," he notes, and measured time "as it was experienced" in terms of "the cycle of the seasons; the life of man, divided into its seven stages, began and ended in childhood" (88).

81–82 *Till now thou . . . what now thou art:* **GRIERSON** (1912): "She has realized her potentiality" and thus "puts on perfection"; see Aquinas, *Summa*, XXV, 1: "Praeterea secundum Philosophum . . . *qualibet potentiâ melior est eius actus*; nam forma est melior quam materia, et actio quam potentia activa: est enim finis eius." See also Aristotle, *Met.* 1050 *a* 2–16 (2:99) [similarly Milgate (1978, 112)]. Augustine (*De Sanct. Virg.* I. x, xi) and Aquinas (*Summa* II, 2, Quaest. cliii. 3) do not contradict this position, as their exaltation of virginity is not meant to devalue marriage (2:99–100).

85–90 *Euen like a faythfull Man . . . to'embowell her.* **McPEEK** (1939) finds this an instance of Donne's use of Jonson (see McPeek's note to l. 12): "Thus from Jonson's simple lines, 'Why stays the bridegroom to invade / Her that would be a matron made?' one can imagine Donne's fantastical mind conceiving his own unhappy image" (368). **CHASE** (1945): "The magical purpose of the metaphor is completed in the imaginative fusion of the lamb with the Bride and the elevation of the Bride to mythical status" (115). **DUBROW** (1990): the lines constitute "the nexus of the most disturbing elements in the poem, the core fantasy that shapes its darker vision" (162), evoking a religious ritual that is analogous to "the colonialized appropriation of the bride" implicit in the description of the "Daughters of London" (l. 13) as "Golden Mines" (l. 14) and of the bride herself as "rich as Inde" (l. 22); further, "the allusion to the priest mystifies and implicitly justifies the ways other men take possession of her." Psychological and cultural interpretations "coexist and interact," and "the consummation of the marriage is constructed as a disturbing interplay of sanctioned male aggression, willing female submission, holy violence, and unholy bawdiness" (163). The genre of the epithalamion "challenges Donne to resolve the problems inherent in his trope of the sacrificial lamb by untangling the knots between sexuality, violence, death, and religion" (164).

85–86 *Euen like a faythfull Man . . . should be spent* **CRAIK and CRAIK** (1986): "like a pious man ready to give up his life in this world for a better life in heaven" (254).

85 *faythfull* **SMITH** (1971): "full of faith" (455).

86 *That this life . . . should be spent* **SHAWCROSS** (1967a): "referring to the belief that sexual intercourse reduced one's life-span" (173).

86 *spent* **SMITH** (1971): "extinguished, and exchanged" (455).

87–90 *So She . . . to'embowell her.* **PARFITT** (1989): the bride wishes to be disembowelled; "her role is 'appointed' (by whom?)," although the sacrifice is performed gently. "Yet the 'rich style' of motherhood is only achieved through an image which makes a disembowelling knife of the penis and links the defloration of the virgin with the awful rituals of Elizabethan and Jacobean executions. The passage is disturbingly revealing, as the feast becomes gluttony and the alleged apotheosis of the woman becomes the violation of her guts" (82).

87 *So She a Mothers riche Stile doth prefer.* **BEAVER** (1976): "other incorrectly aligned back-to-back stresses will be corrected in the presence of a lexical stress in even (Strong) position to the right" (96):

2 1 1
So, shee a mothers rich stile doth preferre
W S W S W S W S W S

87 *Stile* **SHAWCROSS** (1967a): "'title, designation'" (173). **SMITH** (1971): "name and status" (455).

88–90 *And at the bridegroomes wish'd approch . . . to'embowell her.* **CAREY** (1981): the lines present a brutal image of sexual congress, and "round out" the idea of "priest and sacrifice touched on in 'The Comparison'" (143).

90 *to'embowell* **SHAWCROSS** (1967a): "punningly, 'to hide in the inward parts'" (173). **SMITH** (1971): "to disembowel, as for a paschal sacrifice" (455). **OUSBY** (1974b): "alluding to the contemporary use of 'bowel' as a synonym for 'offspring' (*OED*, s.v. 'bowel'), . . . [Donne] is implying that the bridegroom will engender an heir. This reading appears probable not only because Renaissance epithalamia often stress the birth of children but also because Donne himself refers to motherhood" in line 87 (item 49). **MILGATE** (1978): "'disembowell', as applied to the priest's role; as applied to the bridegroom's, the sense is that given in *O.E.D.* II. 3. which cites: 'all was embowelled, and enwombed in the waters'" (*Sermons* 9:99) (113). **CAREY** (1981): although "embowell" means, according to the dictionary, the same as "disembowel," Donne's line would have been much cruder had he used the latter; "embowell" sounds "as if something is going to be put into the bowels," thus fitting "the context of imminent insertion more naturally." Donne's choice of "embowell," however, only slightly obscures the "careful violence" implied by the analogy to the disemboweling of a lamb (143). **CRAIK and CRAIK** (1986): the figure of disembowelment, though shocking to many readers, stresses the bride's passivity (although she is not reluctant); Milgate's *OED* citation is, however, misleading, as the definition there given ("to put, convey into the bowels") is the opposite of the act described; "the phrase would have to be 'embowels himself in her'" (254).

90 *on his knees* **CAREY** (1981): "The detail of the priest crawling towards the lamb 'on his knees' has a curious lifelikeness when applied to the bedroom scene. We glimpse the bridegroom getting himself into position rather awkwardly. The whole

passage resembles the probe-and-wound simile in its conjunction of love with pain, and, of course, in the way it intensifies the body's vulnerability by bringing it up against something hard and instrumental" (143–44).

91–94 *and O Light . . . want her sight;* **ZUNDER** (1982): the solar imagery does not "compromise" the principle of hierarchy that operates in the poem, depending in fact for its effect "on the maintenance of hierarchical differences" (41).

91 *watche* **SMITH** (1971): "remain awake" (455).

93 *This Sun* **GROSART** (1872–73): "the bridegroom: a thought reversed from Psalm XIX. 4–5" (1:278). **SMITH** (1971): "the bride" (455). **MILGATE** (1978): cf. *EpEliz* 85 and *Eclog* 144–45 (113).

94 *want* **SHAWCROSS** (1967a): "lack" (173).

95–96 *Wonders are wrought,* **SMITH** (1971): "The wonder is a paradox, that what was previously without fault now becomes perfect" (455).

95 *which had no maime* **SMITH** (1971): "She was a virgin" (455). **MILGATE** (1978): cf. l. 33 (113).

95 *maime* **SHAWCROSS** (1967a): see note on "lame" (l. 23); "the word had the additional significance of 'privation of the use of a part of the body'" (173).

Epithalamion Vpon FREDERICK *Count Palatine and the Lady* ELIZABETH *marryed on* St VALENTINES *day.*

COMMENTARY

Date and Circumstances

In his *Annales* of 1625 the historian William Camden describes the events of 14 February 1613, the day of the events celebrated in this poem (translation given in Grierson, 1912, 2:92):

> . . . the Prince Palatine and that lovely Princess, the Lady Elizabeth, were married on Bishop Valentine's Day, in all the Pomp and Glory that so much grandeur could express. Her vestments were white, the Emblem of Innocency; her Hair dishevel'd hanging down her Back at length, an Ornament of Virginity; a Crown of pure Gold upon her Head, the Cognizance of Majesty, being all over beset with precious Gems, shining *like a Constellation*; her Train supported by Twelve young Ladies in White Garments, so adorned with Jewels, that her passage looked like a Milky-way. She was led to the Church by her Brother Prince Charles, and the Earl of Northampton; the young Batchelor on the Right Hand, and the old on the left.

Grierson cites further contemporary sources that comment on the splendor and expense of the wedding, observing that "the princess had been educated" by Lord and Lady Harington (the parents of Donne's patroness, the Countess of Bedford), who accompanied her to Heidelberg, although "Lord Harington died on his way home, Lady Harington shortly after her return." Donne thus had "links with the Princess, and these were renewed and strengthened later when with Lord Doncaster he visited Heidelberg in 1619, and preached before her and her husband . . . ."

Shawcross (1967a, 174) notes that in the year before the wedding Donne had accompanied Sir Robert Drury as his secretary on a trip to Germany to arrange the marriage settlement.

Hughes (1968, 59, 244) believes that, "more than a genuflection in the direction of Drury Lane," *EpEliz* is "an affirmation of life to counter the quiddities of Prince Henry's death" (244).

Bald (1970, 269) refers to *EpEliz* as "a charming epithalamion," noting that it is not known whether Donne hoped for or received a reward from the royal pair.

Smith (1971, 456) attributes the great pomp of the occasion to James's intention to strengthen his alliance with Protestant powers in Germany.

Parker (1975, 64–65) calls *EpEliz* "the last of . . . [Donne's] great erotic poems" and claims that it is "the best of the many poems written by various hands for the occasion" (64).

In the course of his argument for the public and patronage-orientated nature of Donne's work, Marotti (1981, 229) cites the observation of Bald (1959, 102–03) that Donne's patron Sir Robert Drury had "foolishly criticized the Elector Palatine" and supposes that "Donne may have tried to atone" for his mistake by composing *EpEliz*.

General Commentary

The death at Leicester House on 13 February 1661 of James I's daughter Elizabeth, Queen of Bohemia, the bride celebrated in *EpEliz*, prompted the following remarks from Robert Sidney, second Earl of Leicester, to Algernon Percy, Earl of Northumberland, in a letter dated 17 February 1661/62 (in Collins 1746 2:723): "It is pitty that she lived not a few Houres more to dye upon her Weddingday, and that there is not as good a Poet to make her Epitaph, as Doctor *Donne*, who wrote her *Epithalamium* upon that Day unto St *Valentine*."

Patmore (1857, 147) cites *EpEliz* as an example of the proposition that "poets of very high character have made the mistake of adopting an over-elaborate rhythmical form as a recurrent stanza, merely because its movement was inspired by, and suited to, the opening thought."

Schipper (1888, 2:796) describes the stanza's form as one of 3-, 4-, and 5-foot verses with a 6-foot refrain.

Gosse (1893, 239) terms *EpEliz* "perhaps the most popular of all Donne's writings."

Citing line 8 of the poem in particular, Case (1896, xxxv) applauds the generally "happy" quality of the "conceits" that, "tempered to a natural quaintness," give us "the most original of wedding-songs."

Following his comment of 1893 Gosse (1899, 2:12–14) thinks Donne in *EpEliz* "as happily inspired" as he had been "unfortunate" in *Henry* a few months earlier (12–13). It is, Gosse asserts, "one of his happiest productions, as fresh and gay as if a youth had written it, instead of a staid, melancholy paterfamilias of forty." Judging it "singularly little troubled by the prevailing faults of Donne's style," Gosse maintains that *EpEliz* "has all the characteristics required for an epithalamium." He states that "a certain levity or faint fescennine quality, which is disconcerting, perhaps, to the refined taste of to-day, detracted in no wise from its merits in the judgment of the gravest or the most exalted personages in the reign of James I" (13). Although he comments specifically on lines 1–14, 27–28, and 43–50 (see below), Gosse observes that "the cleverest and perhaps the most poetical things in this delightful epithalamium are removed too far from us by nearly three centuries to be conveniently quoted here" (14).

Stebbing (1907, 1:76) characterizes *EpEliz* as "audacious," but says that the age's admiration for novelty and tolerance for "unscrupulous coarseness" accounts for its not having been an impediment to the author's taking holy orders.

Sinclair (1909, 190) terms *EpEliz* "very musical and charming."

Fausset (1924, 206–08), who describes the poem as both "concentrated" and "garrulous," finds in *EpEliz* a "compelling rhythm" and a "gleeful naturalism" (207). Further, he believes that the poem is "so real" because Elizabeth awoke in Donne "the same homage as he felt for the Countess of Bedford, and with it all the extravagant worship of youth and innocence natural to a perplexed middle age, still troubled with romantic cravings" (208).

Payne (1926, 129–30) finds *EpEliz* "a much finer piece of work" (129) than *EpLin*, "really melodious and gay—the latter being an effect seldom found in Donne" (130).

Grierson (1929, xli) terms *EpEliz* "very pagan and sensuous."

Fausset (1931, xix) describes *EpEliz* as "very different" from the "laboured obscurity" of *Henry* and finds that the "gleeful naturalism" of *EpEliz* "is keyed up to a higher level, at once more recondite, more gracious, and more imaginative" than the "naturalism" of *EpLin*. He argues that "in affirming the generative joy of life, the marriage of its elements, of the earth spirit and the quickening flame of the sun," Donne could momentarily "forget both the ugly aspect of the physical, and his own morbid introspection." He adds that Donne's "homage, however, made no apparent impression upon the Court."

McPeek (1939, 207–08) finds Donne in *EpEliz* successfully imitating the melody and rhythm of Spenser's *Prothalamion* (208). *EpEliz*, he argues, "belongs in the great tradition" of Catullus' *Carmen* 61, although except for a few motives and images, among them the phoenix (which possibly derives from Claudian or from the *De Ave Phoenice*), "its immediate background is almost altogether English." The English sources themselves, McPeek argues further, are indebted to Catullus's ode (208). He concludes that, "despite the extravagant conceit of the Phoenix-bride," *EpEliz* "is the most beautiful poem of the kind in English after Spenser" (207–08).

Garrod (1946, 117) terms *EpEliz* "frank and pagan" and wonders whether Princess Elizabeth ever read it.

Gransden (1954, 112–13) states that in the early stanzas of *EpEliz* Donne combines "decoration" and "a tapestry-like use of visual imagery" (112) in the style of Spenser; however, in the final two stanzas "Donne 'abstracts' the consummation he is supposed to be glorifying, in a characteristic, purely intellectual conceit" (112–13).

Ellrodt (1960a, 2:174) cites as instances of "theological and scientific conceits" the passages on the phoenix (st 2), Noah's Ark (st 8), new stars (l. 39), infinity (l. 48), the mechanism of a clock (l. 74), the separation of soul and body (l. 78), and the heavenly spheres (ll. 81, 86).

Gros (1964, 52–53) terms *EpEliz* both a masterpiece of popular poetry (52–53) and an unprecedented work for Donne. He contrasts what he considers the obligatory (in an "official" poem) use of the phoenix imagery with the charm of the everyday birds otherwise evoked. By contrast with *Eclog*—which, he maintains, celebrates a scandalous criminal (52)—*EpEliz* is a true "valentine."

Raizis (1966, 8–9) calls *EpEliz* "a witty and cleverly composed poem" (9), its tone "joyful but rather restrained" (8).

Fowler (1970, 160) notes a numerological aspect of the poem in arguing that by employing a fourteen-line stanza, Donne achieves a "temporal decorum . . . through imitation of the date of the wedding."

Miller (1970, 413) mentions *EpEliz* as a variation of the more typical summer celebration of a wedding.

M. Molho (1970, 20) finds a resemblance between *EpEliz*, which he terms "admirable," and *Air*—both, he argues, turn upon a conceit of the mingling of rarified essences that, while uniting, remain distinct throughout eternity. Molho maintains that *EpEliz* nonetheless exhibits a "warm sensuality" in the disrobing of the bride, which suggests the liberation of the soul from the body.

Tufte (1970, 222) labels *EpEliz* "a more successful wedding song" than *EpLin* and argues that it "best demonstrates Donne's major contribution to the mode, the restoration of humor."

McGowan (1972, 175–218), noting that for the occasion of the marriage "epithalamia, congratulations, and paeans of praise poured in from every side" (182), details what she calls the "calendar of magnificence which stretched out over a fortnight" (184). Included among the formal celebrations were masques by Thomas Campion, George Chapman, and Francis Beaumont, which, McGowan affirms, implicitly express the conscious recognition by each of these poets both that "his success depends on recognising the specificity of the event, and on exploiting its general significance" and that "he is part of a ritual where strict adherence to its laws are essential" (194). Within this climate of awareness, she argues, Donne exercises an ingenuity in the poem that depends for recognition upon a reader knowledgeable of the generic rules of structure, tone, language, imagery, and chronology with which he plays throughout the poem before finally celebrating in a more conventional form "the revelling of two bodies made one" (210).

Smith (1971, 14), arguing the simultaneity of the supposedly "different" poetic sensibilities of Donne, observes that the "erotic" *EpEliz* was written at nearly the same time as "the pious meditation" *Goodf* and *Prim*.

Lodi (1974, 86–99) notes in the poem an emphasis upon the number two, which "contributes to the building up of the nuptial atmosphere being prepared for uniting young phoenixes whose love is not ephemeral" (88). In addition, Lodi draws attention to Donne's reversal of the traditional, Spenserian association of the sun with the man and the moon with the woman, a variation that may suggest "a veiled patriotic motive in exalting the English princess married to the German Count Palatine" (90). Donne's overall achievement, Lodi claims, is to add a new dimension to epithalamic poetry as he raises the consummation "to the level of abstraction" (91).

Granqvist (1975, 131, 136) cites reprintings of *EpEliz* to argue that "it retained its popularity throughout the [19th] century," citing Alford (1839), Shorter (1865), and Fields and Whipple (1878) (131). Granqvist argues further that "the popularity of various stanzas" throughout the 19th century "mark[s] a continuation of taste from the former period" (136).

Milgate (1978, xxii–xxiv) contrasts the certainty of purpose he finds in *EpEliz* with the "uncertainty of purpose" in *EpLin* (xxii), and credits *EpEliz* with qualities of "brilliance and *élan*" (xxiv) that would be maintained in the later *Eclog*. Milgate asserts that Donne shared in the universal approbation of both bride and bridegroom and that the event seemed to realize, "as fully as the world allowed, the ideal in the actual." The celebration was, in Milgate's view, both "joyous" and "relaxed," and the poem itself, bypassing "the trivial jocularities customary at weddings," is characteristically its author's in its respect for "the deeper joy of rituals engrained in the experience of mankind." By its "play of wit" as well as "the ordered movement of its intricate and skillfully wrought stanzas," the poem, Milgate maintains, mirrors both the "gaiety" and the dignity of the event. Milgate finds Donne outstripping his contemporaries in this genre of poetry in the "ease and originality" of his use of the conventions of praise and in his "coherent and harmonious ordering" of his materials. He attributes the linkage of St. Valentine's Day and the "Chaucerian gathering of birds" to Donne's "happy instinct"; from this "sparkling opening" there "flows effortlessly the sequence of images and emblems—the sparrow and the dove, the phoenix, the 'glorious flames', the gems, the stars and the spheres, and the complicated play with sun and moon, day and 'eve' and night." Cosmic imagery, Milgate argues, is balanced by an abundance of "homely, even domestic" details (xxiii) that "unobtrusively" set the scene for the depiction of the reconciliations and rejoicings that make a "perfect marriage" out of the conflicting principles of human nature and the conflicting claims of the two sexes (xxiv).

Partridge (1978, 122) describes *EpEliz* as "oft quoted."

Somura (1982, 133–45), after briefly describing classical and Renaissance epithalamic conventions, compares *EpEliz* to Spenser's *Epithalamion*, affirming Spenser's influence on Donne. Somura argues that, whereas Spenser balances pagan and Christian elements in his poem, Donne emphasizes the latter at the expense of the former. Except for the phoenix, he says, Donne minimizes references to classical mythology; instead of the traditional invocation to the classical muse, for instance, Donne calls on St. Valentine. Somura further maintains that Donne's emphasis on Christianity, together with his use of domestic imagery, makes the poem more nationalistic than Spenser's. Somura finds that Donne's principal themes are argumentation and wit, but that all the elements of the poem center on the topic of sex, couched, as Somura expresses it, in clever, courtly expressions. Somura claims that in the poem Donne secularizes the common Renaissance neo-Platonic theory of love, which he describes as the transcendental moment when two spirits make a complete union. Somura says that this is the situation of the hermaphrodite (see commentary on the phoenix below). Somura concludes that Donne employs the conventions of the epithalamion while adapting them to his own ends (i.e., wit and argumentation) and by so doing develops the tradition. Somura terms *EpEliz* therefore both public and personal, traditional and individualistic.

Dubrow (1986, 106–16) argues that in *EpEliz*, "as in so many of his mature poems, Donne discards that 'servile imitation' to which Carew's elegy [*An Elegie upon . . . Dr. Iohn Donne* 27] refers not in favor of total iconoclasm and deracination but rather for a type of creativity and originality that is rooted in the conventions of his genre" (116). Throughout the poem, she maintains, Donne "virtually ignores the political significance" of the marriage, implying rather that "what is most important about the wedding is the personal relationship between the two phoenixes" (111). She also argues that Donne transforms a prominent feature of the traditional epithalamion, references to buildings, most typically houses or churches. By minimizing the significance of the church in *EpEliz*, Dubrow concludes, Donne "once again plays down the community itself, the social codes that it embodies and transmits." Donne's brief references to the social and religious aspects of the ceremony, Dubrow further maintains, point both to his lack of interest in these elements and to his interest in the "diuers wayes" (l. 52) by which the couple will unite, "especially their emotional and sexual union." (113).

In the same vein, Dubrow says, Donne plays down "the celebrations of the masquers and the ministrations of the matrons." In the final stanza Donne "totally abandons the generic convention of the modest and reluctant bride. Instead, he characteristically portrays sex as a source of mutual and equal pleasure for both of his phoenixes." Dubrow also notes how Donne employs but transforms references to time (another conventional topic of epithalamions). Conventional epithalamions, she points out, generally play notions of linear time against perceptions of cyclical time. By opening and closing *EpEliz* with allusions to the rising and setting sun, Donne too, Dubrow reasons, is concerned with "a cyclical temporal movement." "But," she adds, citing lines 99–100, "unlike other authors of epithalamia, he suggests that it is the couple, not the children they will produce, who effect a cyclical pattern of rebirth and rejuvenation" (114). She suggests that throughout the poem, "the attitudes Donne's speaker advises the couple to assume toward the social codes of the wedding are not unlike the ones Donne himself assumes toward the literary codes of the wedding poem." Dubrow concludes her discussion by suggesting that Donne's attitude to the epithalamion is ambivalent. On the one hand, she argues, it provided him with an appropriate form with which to respond to the demands of the patronage system; but, on the other hand, Donne "appears to have relished the opportunity of adapting a genre some of whose norms were uncongenial to him, to have welcomed the challenge of playing the traditions of that genre against the demands of his individualistic talent" (115).

Marotti (1986, 271–72) suggests three reasons why Donne wrote *EpEliz*: (1) (citing Bald 1970) Donne "wished to atone for his patron Drury's indiscreet remarks" about the bridegroom; (2) he may have been influenced by Lady Bedford's connection with the Princess through her parents, who oversaw the Princess's earlier upbringing; (3) he may have wished to situate himself actively in the court milieu. Marotti finds that a "sophisticated comic perception built into the poem" marks Donne as a "social participant in the elaborate courtly ceremonies" rather than as one relegated to the margins (271–72), citing evidence in lines 103–04, where Donne "includes himself among the all-night revelers." Marotti concludes that "whatever the poem's function as a gift, it is clear that it assumes an audience of equals" (272).

Carey (1990, xxvii) remarks that Donne came to the notice of the Princess Elizabeth through Lucy, Countess of Bedford, and that *EpEliz* "belongs, in this respect, with the Bedford poems" (i.e., the verse-letters to the Countess and *Mark*, *BoulNar*, *BoulRec*, and *Har*).

Revisiting some of the points in her 1986 essay, Dubrow (1990, 164–77) contrasts the problems and tensions in *EpLin* and other Stuart epithalamions with their exceptionally skillful resolution in *EpEliz*. Noting the historical fact that this wedding was "widely viewed as an antidote to the grief occasioned by the recent death of the bride's brother" (165), Dubrow argues that Donne "connects the marriage in general and its consummation in particular with rebirth rather than death and destruction . . . by replacing the linear narrative structures that characterize many other works in this genre with a series of cycles." Donne expresses this structure, she reasons, not only by incorporating the natural cycles of day turning to night and then returning to day, but also "by invoking one of his favorite pets: he portrays the couple as a pair of phoenixes" (166). In addition, the connection of sexuality and spirituality, awkwardly handled in *EpLin* 89–90, is accomplished in *EpEliz* in part through the presiding figure of Bishop Valentine, who "is also germane to Donne's resolution of another generic problem" (170)—the inherent tension between public and private. Dubrow asserts that "composing this epithalamium invites Donne to resolve not only the couple's relationship to the public world but also his own," for it "challenges him to develop strategies for bestowing the praise that the occasion and the genre enjoin on him without descending to the cloying sycophancy that mars so many other wedding poems composed for the event"; in meeting this challenge,Dubrow avers, Donne is able to participate "in ritualistic compliments without surrendering his independence and self-respect" (173).

The Phoenix Image

McPeek (1939, 366, 373–74) cites lines 81–84 of Ben Jonson's *Epithalamion* on the marriage of Hierome Weston and Lady Frances Stewart (ca. 1633) as evidence of Jonson's disapproval of the phoenix imagery in stanzas 2, 3, and 8 of *EpEliz*, quoting Jonson as follows:

> Force from the Phoenix, then, no rarity
> Of sex, to rob the creature; but from man,
> The King of creatures, take his parity
> With angels, Muse, to speak these . . . . (366)

McPeek finds, however, that Robert Herrick's *Nuptiall Song . . . on Sir Clipseby Crew and his Lady* shows in its first three stanzas the influence of the phoenix imagery of stanza 3 of *EpEliz* (373) and that Herrick "approves of Donne's Phoenix-image" and apparently recognizes its origin and usage in *De Ave Phoenice*, lines 83–84, 93–98 (373–374); McPeek further suggests that "Donne . . . may have derived his use of the image from Claudian, *Carmina Minora*, xxvii (the probable source of the *De Ave Phoenice*)" (374).

Garrod (1946, 112, 117) cites Robert Chester's *Love's Martyr* (1601) as a precedent for figuring the bride and bridegroom as "two Phoenixes" (l. 18) (117), arguing that Donne's phoenix is not a classical but a "romantic creature" that figures in such other works as *Canon* and Shakespeare's *PhT* (112).

Allen (1947, 340–42) interprets lines 18–22 "in the light of 1640" and explains that in spite of the inclination of various Church Fathers to believe in the reality of the phoenix, the bird could not have been included in "Noah's aviary" (341) since according to a literal reading of the Genesis story the birds were admitted in pairs (similarly Shawcross [1967a, 174]—who notes that the phoenix contained both sexes, revived from its ashes on its pyre, and was immortal—and Milgate [1978, 115]).

Louthan (1951, 80) concludes that neither of the lovers is "satellite to the other, neither owes the other a marital debt" and that "through the act of love the two phoenixes become one, and nature's balance is restored."

Raizis (1966, 8–9) describes the Phoenix legend as "an artistically unifying device" (9) and "typically Donnean" (8).

McGowan (1972, 205) argues that Donne uses the phoenix image as a correlative of the "paradoxical nature" of the occasion, which demanded a recognition both of its specific and of its general significance.

Montgomery (1972, 269, 277–78), citing lines 20 and 22 in particular, argues that Donne conceives of the phoenix as altogether legendary. Alleging a similarity "in thought" to *Canon*, Montgomery terms *EpEliz* "almost as memorable" as *Canon* in its "ingenious use of the phoenix image," which is "a symbol of excellence in compliment to the bridal pair" (277). Because both bride and bridegroom are phoenixes, however, Donne has, in Montgomery's view, "willingly let himself be led into a problem" (277–78). The apparent contradiction of two identical yet unique creatures is resolved, she asserts, by the consummation in the marriage bed, where "each is both, and all" (l. 87) (278).

In a study of androgyny in Donne's poetry, Mollenkott (1981, 22–38) notes the consummation of the marriage in *EpEliz*, by which two phoenixes become one (ll. 99–102) (25).

Somura (1982, 133–45) finds that Donne's use of the phoenix is the most direct expression of the hermaphroditic condition of ideal spiritual union (see more under General Commentary to *EpEliz* above). Somura cites line 18 as an oxymoron that posits two birds rather than the traditional one, an apparent paradox resolved, Somura argues, in lines 25–26: "the phoenix lies by himself and is reborn from his own ashes in 500 to 600 years, and the expression 'such fires' [l. 25] refers to the fire of new life, but at the same time to the fire of sex, which will result in many descendants." Thus the couple, like the phoenix, represents the self and the other (142).

Lepage (1984, 634–41) traces Donne's use of the phoenix to Sylvester's translation (*Divine Weeks*) of Du Bartas's *Les Semaines*. Sylvester and Du Bartas, he maintains, develop the androgynous and Christlike properties of the phoenix into a symbol, or hieroglyph, of the highest kind of perfection (634–39). Donne uses it as such in *EpEliz* to represent the fusion otherwise figured in the poem in the language of politics and of alchemy. The phoenix is the primal bird, and precedes Sylvester's and Du Bartas's catalogue of more ordinary birds (639–40). Donne, by contrast, presents his everyday birds prior both to the phoenix and to the description of the "perfect love" of the royal couple (640).

Dubrow (1986, 109) argues that by comparing the couple to the phoenix, Donne "avoids the sycophancy into which . . . many other works on this wedding descend." Because the phoenix was a traditional symbol for Christ, she asserts, the compliment to the couple is high, but because the image is "so subterranean and so playful," even the most "sober of Donne's readers would hesitate to accuse him of blasphemy." Furthermore, "the phoenix image fulfills the epideictic functions of its genre by effecting a comparison between Princess Elizabeth and Queen Elizabeth, who was often associated with that mythical bird."

Dubrow subsequently (1990, 167) argues that the use of the phoenix allows Donne "to escape and reject the dichotomy of submissive female victim and respectful yet aggressive male attacker" that is "latent" in *EpLin*.

Notes and Glosses

1–14 (st 1) *Hayle Bishop Valentine . . . old Valentine*. **ALFORD** (1839): the "opening" of the poem shows that Donne "had and could turn to account a fine musical ear" (1:xxiv). **CHAMBERS** (1844): the stanza exemplifies "the merits of Donne, not his defects." The "merit" of Donne and his followers consists in their being "often direct, natural, and truly poetical—in spite, as it were, of themselves" (1:97). **ANONYMOUS** (1852): there is a place in Kent "where all day long, 'the lyric choristers,' as good Master Donne calls them—'the lyric lark, the grave whispering dove, and the household bird with the red stomacher' are blithe subscribers to Nature's great Sacred Harmonic Society" (312). **PATMORE** (1857): the rhythm of the stanza is excessively elaborate (147). **GOSSE** (1893): the stanza possesses "delicious vivacity" (239). **JESSOPP** (1897): "The beautiful opening stanza sounds like an echo of Chaucer" (84). **GOSSE** (1899): the stanza is "a melodious burst of garrulity" (2:13). **MORE** (1906): Donne is a rebel and innovator whose "asperities" and lack of "gentlemanly taste" are softened in the work of his disciples (74), in particular George Herbert. The opening lines of *EpEliz*, "a startling description of the morning," are "perhaps the most curious extravagance" in the "Museum of Wit" that is the poetry of Donne and his school (74–75), and Herbert, in *The Church-Porch*, lines 83–84, adapts lines 11–12, although "with no decrease in absurdity" (76). **SINCLAIR** (1909): the stanza is representative of the "Marriage Songs" in being "full of vivid observations of Nature" (197). **GRIERSON** (1912): cf. Chaucer's *Parlement of Foules*; "birds were supposed to choose their mates on St. Valentine's Day" (2:92). **KITCHIN** (1931): the stanza is a burlesque that "makes pretty use of the old play of the birds in the burlesque Court of Love" (71). **McPEEK** (1939): the "exquisite" stanza ensures that the poem will endure (207–08). **ELLRODT** (1960a): the stanza possesses a color and freshness that are uncharacteristic of the generic motif of the assembly of birds; the realism of the passage is Chaucerian even in its edge of malice (2:174). The fever of Donne's wit feeds upon such materials; the birds of the stanza are "the lyrical prelude to the conceit of the phoenix" of lines 17–18 (2:175). **GRANQVIST** (1975): the stanza "became a specimen highly cherished" in the "revival of Donne" after 1830 (174). **MILGATE** (1978): Ben Jonson borrowed "extensively" from the stanza for lines 1–7 of *A Tale of a Tub* (115). **LEPAGE** (1984): the catalogue of birds derives ultimately from Du Bartas's *Les Semaines* by way of Sylvester's translation, *Divine Weeks* (640–41). The birds do not precisely correspond, but Sylvester's influence is felt in the "lyric lark," evocative of Du Bartas's lark that sings with a "tire-lire." The parallel is important, though general, because Donne, like Sylvester, makes an encyclopedic inventory of birds "to exemplify the great chain of relationships perceived by Renaissance science, and as the source book for his hieroglyph of perfect love," i.e., the phoenix (641). **DUBROW** (1986): in the opening lines of the stanza Donne departs from epithalamic conventions in two ways: he replaces "pagan deities with a figure from the Christian calendar," and he lowers the tone of the initial invocation, ending the stanza on a "note of good-humored raillery." In the last line of the stanza Donne also employs one of the satiric patterns that recur in the love lyrics, mocking "a potentially imposing or threatening figure." Thus, while retaining the characteristic invocation, Donne avoids "the respectful subservience that invocation normally enjoins on the speaker" (108). Elsewhere in the stanza Donne incorporates descriptions of nature common to the genre, but "meets the challenge of responding to a potentially uncongenial norm neither by skirting it nor by mocking it, but rather by skillfully working within it." Donne "evokes a parliament of fowls" by referring to the folk custom that birds marry on St. Valentine's Day, introduces the marriage of the two phoenixes in the next stanza, and, by domesticating the birds he describes, "links these anthropomorphized creatures to a human milieu." For Donne, the natural world is "a source of neither awe nor fear"; "nature can be adapted to man's domain, tamed to man's needs" (109).

1–8, 13–14 *Hayle Bishop Valentine . . . the redd stomacher . . . This day more cheerefully . . . thy selfe old Valentine.* **RENTON** (1893) (printing the ten lines with no ellipsis as if they constituted the complete stanza): the lines exemplify the "better qualities" of the "school" of metaphysical poets, "its felicity, its sense of beauty, its tender and playful reflection" (116).

1–10 *Hayle Bishop Valentine . . . or the Halcyon,* **ANONYMOUS** (1846): the lines "are, perhaps, unsurpassed in descriptive poetry" (233).

1–8 *Hayle Bishop Valentine . . . redd stomacher.* **DUYCKINCK** (1841): the lines are a "happy passage" that "may counteract [Samuel] Johnson's catalogue of defects" (22) [see Johnson's remarks in the notes to ll. 85–88 below].

1 *Bishop Valentine* **SMITH** (1971): "one of the nebulous St. Valentines whose feast-day falls on 14 February was a martyred bishop" (456). **MILGATE** (1978): "a martyred Bishop of Terni" (114). **CRAIK and CRAIK** (1986): a bishop martyred in the reign of Claudius [A.D. 41–54] (255).

2 *All the Ayre is thy Diocesse* **SMITH** (1971): alludes to St. Valentine's supposed protection of flying creatures (because birds supposedly pair on 14 February) (456). **MILGATE** (1978): "The traditional belief that birds mate on St. Valentine's Day suggested that St. Valentine had charge of the air in which they fly" (114).

2 *Diocesse* **PATRIDES** (1985): "jurisdiction" (192).

3 *all the chirping Queristers* **McPEEK** (1939): this mention of these lucky birds (as opposed to the owl, vulture, raven, etc.) may have influenced Herrick's *An Epithalamie to Sir Thomas Southwell and his Ladie,* ll. 159–60 ("with all luckie Birds to side / With the Bride-Groom, and the Bride") (228).

4 *parishioners.* **SULLENS** (1964): this use is not recorded in the *OED* (264).

6–7 *The Lyrick Larke . . . his life for loue* **[PROCTOR]** (1824): the lines show Donne as a writer of "deep-felt things" (1:51–52).

6 *Lyrick* **SULLENS** (1964): predates the earliest use of the word with this meaning in the *OED*, a. and sb. A. 2. 1814, where the phrase given, "lyrick lark," is "exactly Donne's expression" (223).

7 *The Sparrow that neglects his life for loue* **CHAMBERS** (1896): cf. *Metem*, st 20 (1:234). **LOUTHAN** (1951): "No one has proved, I think, that animals were supposed exempt from post-intercourse emotional depression, any more than they are exempt from the life-attrition of intercourse" (155). **SMITH** (1971): "not out of faithful devotion, but because they kill themselves with lechery" (456). **MILGATE** (1978): see notes to *Metem* 193–211 (Milgate 1967, 180–81) on the sparrow's lechery and short life-span (114).

8 *The houshold bird . . . redd stomacher.* **GROSART** (1872–73): a "Wordsworthian touch" (2:xxxvii). **LOWELL** (1889 [1894]): "What is it Donne calls . . . [robins]? [quotes l. 8], or something prettier. I am doubtful about 'household'" (2:384). **BRADFORD** (1892): an unusual instance of "tenderness and grace," whereas Donne's poetry is generally characterized by "vigor and intensity" (361).

8 *redd* **ELLRODT** (1960a): an instance of Donne's characteristic use of color (in white/black or white/red patterns of contrast) (1, i:252–53).

8 *stomacher.* **SHAWCROSS** (1967a): "an ornamental covering worn by both men and women" (174). **PATRIDES** (1985): "waistcoat" (193).

9 *Thou makst the Blackbird speede as soone* **SMITH** (1971): "by St. Valentine's agency ugly ["black"] things get husbands as quickly as golden ones" (456).

9 *speede* **SMITH** (1971): "prosper" (456).

10 *Halcyon,* **SHAWCROSS** (1967a): the kingfisher, supposed to bring calm (174). **SMITH** (1971): the kingfisher calms the waves in order to breed in peace (456). **MILGATE** (1978): the kingfisher, "suggesting brightness because of its plumage" (114).

11 *spedd* **SMITH** (1971): "matched, satisfied" (456). **MILGATE** (1978): "successfully accommodated"; cf. "speed" (l. 9) (114).

12 *And meetes his wife which brings her feather bedd.* **GROSART** (1872–73): ms. variations include "and" for "which" and "his" for "her" (1:260); the present reading is preferable because there is evidence that it was customary for the bride to bring a bed as a wedding gift (1:260).

12 *feather bedd.* **SULLENS** (1964): predates the earliest use with this meaning in the *OED* (215).

13 *then ever shine* **GROSART** (1872–73): the reading "than [sic] ever shine" is

superior to the ms. reading "than others shine" because "the poet is speaking not of other days, but of past Valentines" (1:260).

14 *inflame* **SHAWCROSS** (1967a): "with the passion of these two. A bright red heart is an emblem of St. Valentine" (174). **SMITH** (1971): "stimulate sexually" (456).

15–28 (st 2) *Till now thou warmdst . . . ô Valentine*. **DUBROW** (1986): Donne manages the generic obligation to praise the bride and groom by means of the phoenix analogy and further addresses the generically central theme of the production of heirs, a matter in which he is "comparatively uninterested." Although he does not completely discount the social aspects of marriage (he refers briefly to children), Donne nevertheless subordinates those aspects "to what he considers more important, the sexual bond between the couple" (110).

18 *couplest* **MELTON** (1906): stress on the second syllable; it is an instance of irregular accentuation acceptable in seventeenth-century poetic practice (97). Such "harsh" accentuation is consistent with Shakespeare's and Jonson's usage (101).

18 *two Phænixes*. **PATRIDES** (1985): "in itself exceptional, since only one of the legendary birds could exist at any one time" (193).

19 *Taper* **CRAIK and CRAIK** (1986): "bedroom candle (compare l. 22, *one bed*)" (255).

21 *(Which was . . . cage and parke)* **GROSART** (1872–73): cf. *Metem*, st 3 (1:260).

25 *such fires* **SMITH** (1971): "Donne draws on the sexual sense implicit in the image of the phoenix"; see *Canon* 23–27 (456).

27–28 *Where Love and Courage . . . ô Valentine*. **GOSSE** (1899): "The bird-watching analogy is preserved by telling the Bishop that his duty to-day is to unite two phoenixes" (2:13)

27 *Courage* **LOUTHAN** (1951): "equivalent to the *corage* of Chaucer's *Merchant's Tale*; it is simply *sexual desire*" (78). **SMITH** (1971): "sexual vitality" (456).

29–42 (st 3) *Vp then fayre Phænix-Bride . . . thy Valentine*. **UNTERMEYER** (1959): the "intellectual and musical nuances" of the lines can be appreciated only after reading Spenser's *Epithalamion* (133). **DUBROW** (1986): Donne's imperatives in the latter part of this stanza "define the speaker at once as a respectful subject who must entreat the bride and as a knowledgeable guide who can and will command her" (112).

29 *frustrate the Sunne*. **DUBROW** (1986): "Reshaping the generic convention that the bride must get up because the sun has done so, Donne substitutes a combative bride who will rival and even surpass that celestial body" (111).

29 *frustrate* **MILGATE** (1978): "'render ineffectual' (*O.E.D.* v. I. 2); i.e. by anticipating and outshining the sun's rising (cf. l. 85)" (115).

31 *from thine eye* **MILGATE** (1978) quotes from Marsilio Ficino's commentary on Plato's *Symposium* on the analogy between the heart and the sun, both of which send forth their powers to the universe, or body, of which they are the center (115).

33–38 *Vp vp, fayre bird . . . falls but doth not dye.* **KERMODE** (1957): this passage contains "fine things." Donne "could not speak without wit; it is this naturalness that often redeems him" (26).

33–36 *Vp vp, fayre bird . . . a Constellacion of them all* **BROWNING** (1846 [1962]) (reading "faire Bride") in a letter to Elizabeth Barrett writes "of letters, this makes my 104th and, like Donne's Bride, '. . . I take / My jewels from my boxes; call / My Diamonds, Pearls, and Emeralds, and make / Myself a constellation of them all!'" (1:405)

34 *Thy Starrs* **REEVES** (1952): "The bride's hair and train, as well as those of her bridesmaids, were so ornamented with jewels that a contemporary compared her appearance to the Milky Way" (99).

35–38 *Thy Rubyes . . . but doth not dye.* **UL-HASAN** (1958): elsewhere Donne characteristically evokes softness and warmth, yet the imagery of jewels suggests the hardness and coldness of the constellation she will become (78–79). "The feeling of coldness introduced by mentioning the various precious stones culminates in the coldness of death—the image conjured by the words 'falls' and 'die'" (79).

36 *Constellacion* **SULLENS** (1964): the *OED* cites this as the earliest use (245).

37–38 *And by theyr blazing . . . but doth not dye.* **SMITH** (1971): "The appearance of a blazing comet was believed to portend the death of a prince" (456). **MILGATE** (1978): comets might presage not only the death of a prince, but some other disaster as well; cf. *JC* 2.2.30–31 (115). **CRAIK and CRAIK** (1986): "Comets and meteors were called *blazing* stars and thought to *signify* the death of princes. The princess Elizabeth, herself a star, *falls* (lies down in the marriage bed) but does not *die* (either literally or like a spent meteor)" (255).

37 *theyr blazing* **GROSART** (1872–73): "[the ms. reading] '*This* blazing' makes it an act of the princess"; "by context, 'their meteor portents' gives the better reading" (1:260).

38 *falls but doth not dye.* **SMITH** (1971): "'Falls' has its sexual sense and 'die' has its literal sense" (457).

39–40 *Bee thou a new Starre. . . And bee thou those ends.* **COFFIN** (1937): the lines are "the climax of a beautifully constructed stanza" (138) in which "the images of a new star are stripped of all unhappy connotations," and "in the face of popular fear and superstition the new stars with their glittering brilliance become symbols of beauty worthy of a princess and a presage" (139).

39 *Bee thou a new Starre . . . pretends* **DUBROW** (1986): the line relies on equivocations like those described above [see Dubrow's glosses on st 3 and on l. 29]. It is a compliment, but Donne delimits its force: "the line highlights the power of the poet who writes it almost as much as the power of the princess who figures in it" (112).

39 *new Starre* **MILGATE** (1978), referring to *FirAn* 259–60, notes the long-standing belief in the unalterability of the heavens and the shaking of that faith by the observation of new stars in the sixteenth and seventeenth centuries and by the observations of Galileo as reported in *Siderius Nuncius* (1610), which reported four moons of Jupiter and the apparently numberless stars of the Milky Way (115, 143–44).

40 *Ends of much wonder. . . those ends.* **MELTON** (1906): one of many instances in Donne of lines beginning and ending with the same word (148–49); nearly all such instances exhibit an arsis/thesis variation, evidence of Donne's purposeful innovation, consciousness of his art, and possession of "a metrical secret" (150).

40 *Ends* **SHAWCROSS** (1967a): "both 'conclusions' and 'purposes'" (175). **CRAIK and CRAIK** (1986): "consequences." The echoes in the sequence "portends / Ends ... ends" are "ingenious" (255).

42 *all men date Records* **MILGATE** (1978): "The most notable new star was that which led the Wise Men to Bethlehem at Christ's nativity, from which event, in the Christian world, records are dated (in years A.D.)" (115). **CRAIK and CRAIK** (1986): "It was usual to *date records* from the beginning of a reign" (255).

42 *this thy Valentine.* **GRIERSON** (1912): "This is the reading of all the editions except *1669* and of all the MSS. except two of no independent value. I think it is better than 'this day, Valentine', which Chambers adopts from *1669*. The bride is addressed throughout the stanza, and it would be a very abrupt change to refer 'thou' in l. 41 to Valentine. I take 'this, thy Valentine' to mean 'this which is thy day, *par excellence*', 'thy Saint Valentine's day', 'the day which saw you paired'. But 'a Valentine' is a true-love': 'to be your Valentine' (*Hamlet*, IV. v. 50), and the reference may be to Frederick,—Frederick's Day is to become an era" (2:92–93). **MILGATE** (1978): the phrase "seems to mean simply 'this thy Valentine's day, the day on which you married'" (115).

43–70 (sts 4–5) *Come forth, come forth . . . to thee ô Valentine?* **LINDSAY** (1931) (apparently alluding to these lines): William Browne's *Britannia's Pastorals*, II (1616), V, "show[s] alliance with Donne":

> Let thy chaste love to me (as shadows run
> In full extent into the setting sun)

Meet with my fall; and when that I am gone,
Back to thyself retire, and there grow one.
If to a second light thy shadow be,
Let him still have his rays of love from me;
And if, as I, that likewise do decline,
Be mine or his, or else be his and mine.

These lines form "an echo of the sun-and-moon tangle"; they may have actually been composed before 1613, and have influenced Donne (234). **JOHNSON** (1931) (replying to Lindsay [1931]): whereas Browne habitually borrowed, Donne did not; in cases of parallels one should assume Browne borrows from Donne (347). **MILGATE** (1950) notes that Lindsay (1931) compares these lines to verses from *Britannia's Pastorals*, but finds that "the parallels are by no means exact" (291).

43–56 (st 4) *Come forth, come forth . . . or Bishop Valentine*. **CASE** (1896): the stanza influences Robert Gould's *Mirtillo and Amynta: A Hymeneal Pindaric Poem* (*Works*, 1709, st 2) (xlii, 178). **DUBROW** (1986): in alluding to the marriage ceremony, Donne plays both on and with literary and social conventions (112).

43–50 *Come forth, come forth . . . Greate, and one*. **GOSSE** (1899): "In the address to the Bride, Donne rises to a great dignity and a rare music" (2:13). **GRIERSON** (1912), noting that the editions of 1633–1669 and Chambers punctuate this passage with a comma at the end of line 46 (where they read "goe" rather than "growe") and a period after "disunite" in line 49, states that this pointing attaches the clause "Since separation . . . can disunite" to "the *previous* verb," making the clause an explanation of "why they should 'go to an unseparable union'." By contrast, Grierson employs a full stop at the end of line 46 and a comma after "disunite" (l. 49), following "several good MSS." and making the clause "Since separation . . . can disunite" go with "what *follows*" as an explanation of "You are twice inseparable, great, and one." Grierson calls this punctuation "obviously right" (2:93).

43–46 *Come forth, come forth . . . an vnseperable vnion growe*. **TROST** (1904): the "as . . . so" construction is an instance of comparison in Donne's poetry; the passage as a whole is an instance of epizeuxis (45). **McPEEK** (1939): the lines are "more akin to the expression of Catullus than to any passage of Spenser"; cf. Catullus, *Carmen* 61, lines 96–100: "Prodeas, nova nupta, si / Iam videtur, et audias / Nostra verba. Vide ut faces / Aureas quatiunt comas. / Prodeas, nova nupta" (208).

46 *growe*. **GROSART** (1872–73) (reading "go;"): the manuscript reading "growe" is "equally good," yet "go," "might be defended, because he is speaking of before the marriage ceremony, and of 'going' to it" (1:261). **GRIERSON** (1912): the manuscript reading "growe" is preferable because it echoes "growes" in line 44 (just as "meet" in line 45 echoes "Meeting" in line 44) and because the phrase, which means "become inseparably incorporated with one another" is a "slightly violent but not unnatural application of the phrase 'grow to' so common in Elizabethan English" (2:93); cf.

AWW 2.1.36—"I grow to you, and our parting is a tortur'd body"—and *ElPart* 57–58—"First let our eyes be rivited quite through / Our turning brains, and both our lips grow to" (2:93–94). It is possible that the editor of the edition of 1633 did not understand the meaning of "growe to" and substituted "goe" by association with "goe" in line 51; it is unlikely that an original reading of "goe" would have been changed to "growe" (2:93).

47–50 *Since separation . . . and one.* **CRAIK and CRAIK** (1986): "Their greatness and their unity make them for both reasons inseparable" (255).

47–48 *separation . . . as ar infinite* **GAMBERINI** (1967): the learned tone is inappropriate (79).

48 *Falls not . . . ar infinite* **ELLRODT** (1960a): the passion for infinity, characteristic of Thomas Traherne, differs from that for totality, characteristic of Donne. This line is an instance of the purely conceptual and illustrative nature of Donne's use of the concept of infinity as a source for a conceit. The relationship between infinite and finite, on which this conceit is based, is clearly understood, however ineffable "infinity" itself may be (1, ii:335).

48 *infinite* **SMITH** (1971): "Their greatness has no limits" (457).

51–53 *Goe then Two . . . Must bee effected,* **DUBROW** (1986): the lines minimize the religious ceremony: except for this brief and vague reference, Donne virtually ignores the Church's role and the religious ritual (112–13).

51 *Goe* **DUBROW** (1986): "'Goe,'" in contrast to the numerous proximal deictics such as "here" and "this" that Donne consistently employs throughout the poem, "suggests [that] the speaker is physically—and by implication, emotionally—more distant from the rite in the church than from the other events he evokes" (112–13).

52 *his way,* **SHAWCROSS** (1967a): "through the marriage ceremony as contrasted with the way by which they themselves will make them one (sexually, emotionally)" (175) [so also **SMITH** (1971, 457) and **PATRIDES** (1985, 194)].

55–56 *You two haue one way . . . or Bishop Valentine.* **GRIERSON** (1912): the "O" of the edition of 1633 [for "or"] "does not make good sense"; "Chambers's ingenious emendation of 1669, by which he connects 'of Bishop Valentine' with 'one way left', lacks support. Bishop Valentine has paired them; the Bishop in church has united them; the consummation is their own act" (2:94).

55 *way* **SMITH** (1971): "sexual consummation" (457).

56 *knott* **PATRIDES** (1985): the marriage sacrament (194).

57–64 *But oh what ayles . . . Spectacle and talke?* **TUFTE** (1970): "The conventional complaint over the delay in the proceedings is voiced by the poet in . . . [this] series of questions which include fescennine teasing of the bridal couple" (224).

57–59 *But oh what ayles the Sunne . . . from these to get* **MELTON** (1906): "Day" and "dayes" (l. 58) are both stressed; cf. *Calm* 18 ("Feathers and dust, to day and yesterday"). "Even when 'day' is repeated [in l. 58], both times under the ictus, Donne contrives to bring in a thesis-variant with a similar sound: "But O, what *áils* the sun, that here *hĕ stáys*, / Longér *tŏ-dăy* than othér *dáys? / Stáys hé* new light from these to get?" (139)

57–58 *But oh . . . then other dayes!* **PARISH** (1976): Donne alludes obliquely to the Old Testament story of the sun's standing still (Josh. 10:12–14) as "the speaker voices impatience that the marriage ceremony, the feast, and the revels tediously postpone the more important business of bedding the royal newlyweds: though it is February, the day seems interminable" (199–200).

58 *then* **PATRIDES** (1985): "than" (195).

60 *starrs,* **SMITH** (1971) (reading "store"): "abundance" (457).

62 *Procession?* **MILGATE** (1978): "four syllables" (116).

65–68, 73–77 *The feast . . . into her bedd* **DUBROW** (1986): Donne's dismissal in these lines of the social rites and customs that precede the wedding night suggests his "customary emphasis on the privacy of love and lovers" (114).

67–68 *The Maskers come late . . . crow them away.* **RUGOFF** (1939): the image is unique in Donne's poetry, which exhibits a "virtual absence of images from fairy lore" (100). **NOVAK** (1955): "On the night of the wedding, Campion presented his *Lorde's Mask*, which reveals Orpheus," who sings at the end: "No longer wrong the night / Of her Hymenaean right; / A thousand Cupids call away, / Fearing the approaching day, / The cocks alreadie crow; / Dance then go" (471–72).

67 *Maskers* **SHAWCROSS** (1967a): "those who attend the festivities wearing masks; here, entertainers presenting a kind of play with dancing and music" (176).

67 *late,* **MILGATE** (1978) (reading "too late,"): the omission of "too" in some manuscripts "seems to have been due to independent sophistication for the sake of the metre" (116).

70 *ô Valentine?* **GROSART** (1872–73) (reading "old Valentine?"): the reading "old Valentine" "agrees better with context, 'Antiquity,' &c." (1:260).

71–77 *They did, and night is come . . . into her bedd* **ANONYMOUS** (1823): the passage is "exquisite in its way . . . . The simile of the clock is an example (not an offensive one) of Donne's peculiar mode of illustration. He scarcely writes a stanza without some ingenious simile of this kind" (49).

73 *these Ladyes*, **McPEEK** (1939): "The bride is put to bed by ladies, a fair equivalent for the matrons of Catullus [*Carmen* 61]" (208). Donne may be recalling Jonson's *Hymenaei*, the concluding epithalamium, st 7 (itself adapted from *Carmen* 61): "Good *Matrons*, that so well are knowne / To aged *husbands* of your owne, / Place you our *Bride* to night; / And snatch away the *light* . . ." (208).

74 *to take a Clock in peeces*, **SHAWCROSS** (1967a): "each talking to the bride a minute or two, followed by another lady, and so forth" (176).

75 *nicely* **SHAWCROSS** (1967a): "foolishly" (176). **SMITH** (1971): "delicately, meticulously" (457).

76–78 *A Bride . . . and are not spy'd.* **ELLRODT** (1960a), treating the subject of "Christian thought and double natures" while discussing the paradox (Matt. 16.25) of gaining to lose and losing to gain and the double (human and divine) nature of Christ, observes that Donne's conceits depend upon the Christian paradox of the Incarnation. This is true, says Ellrodt, even in profane verse: the concept of "double nature" is an intellectual category virtually inevitable in Christian thought of the period, and these lines are a somewhat "frivolous" example of this "preoccupation" (1, i:215). **COLLMER** (1961): "The parallels that could be drawn between going to bed and dying were legion: bed sheets became the winding sheet; yawning, the spirit's leaving through the mouth; stretching, the struggle of the body; the bed itself, the grave" (326).

77–78 *Should vanish . . . and are not spy'd.* **RUGOFF** (1939): the lines are "one of a surprising number of images wherein an aspect of death is used, usually grotesquely, to illustrate some phase of lovers' relations" (181).

79–81 *But now Shee's layd . . . Spheare after Spheare* **McPEEK** (1939): the same order is followed in Catullus, *Carmen* 61; cf. ll. 191, 199–201: "Iam licet venias, marite: / . . . Sed abit dies: / Perge, ne remorare" (208–09).

79 *But now Shee's layd* **TUFTE** (1970): "The traditional reference to the ceremonial placing of the bride on the *lectus genialis* becomes in Donne . . . [this] simple declaration" (225).

80–81 *Yet there are more delayes . . . Spheare after Spheare* **McFARLAND** (1977): "a conventional instance of anadiplosis" (397).

81 *Spheare after Spheare* **SMITH** (1971): "as a celestial body passes through the concentric zones or globes of the heavens to encounter another star" (457). **PATRIDES** (1985): refers to "the transparent, 'pure' spheres in which the planets were thought to be embedded" (195, 80).

81 *Spheare* **SULLENS** (1964): this meaning is not recorded in the *OED* (265).

84 *Eue* **MILGATE** (1978): "the time of preparation for a festival, usually the day before it" (116).

85–98 (st 7) *Heere lyes a Shee-Sunne . . . and Sparrows Valentine*. **HAZLITT** (1819): the stanza "has often been quoted against . . . [Donne], and is an almost irresistible illustration of the extravagances to which this kind of writing, which turns upon a pivot of words and possible allusions, is liable" (6:52–53). **McPEEK** (1939): Catullus, *Carmen* 61, is a source, and Jonson's epithalamion for Hierome Weston and Lady Frances Stuart, st 20, recalls the stanza: all encourage fertility (367). St 24 of Jonson's poem also recalls the stanza and suggests Jonson's admiration for Donne's poem (367). **TUFTE** (1970): "The use here of commercial imagery in describing the consummation is perhaps 'more remarkable for the invention' than any other such description in the English genre, but the reader may hear in it not only echoes of Chapman's earlier work but of some of the Italian epithalamia" (225–26). **SOMURA** (1982): like Spenser, Donne employs images of commerce, but Donne's "tenor" is the sexual act, and his "target is clearly wit" (140). **DUBROW** (1990) (reading the last word of line 85 as "here"): the stanza mirrors the restless motions of Donne's mind. "Thus his characteristic reliance on the tellingly named disjunctive conjunction 'or,' as well as his asyndeton [line 95], mime the rapid shifts in the argument and in so doing may even recall the sexual energies that the passage describes." These intellectual and syntactical shifts are only partially destabilizing, however; various rhetorical devices steady the passage, including epanalepsis in line 85 (Here . . . here), which "creates a sense of balance and stasis that literally and metaphorically encases the subversive ideas contained between the two words." The antitheses that structure the line "intensify its sense of balance" (168–69).

85–88 *Heere lyes a Shee-Sunne . . . vnto one another nothing owe*. **JOHNSON** (1779), citing these lines among a series of passages from Donne and other seventeenth-century poets that he claims suppose specialized knowledge on the reader's part or are "not easily understood," states: "On reading . . . [these] lines the reader may perhaps cry out, 'Confusion worse confounded'" (1:62). **EMERSON** (1815 [1939]) in a letter to his brother says he has been reading Samuel Johnson's *Lives of the Poets* and cites lines 85–88 and Johnson's comment, adding, "This is old fashioned Poetry—I should like to see the Poem it was taken from" (1:10). **HAZLITT** (1826), recalling a conversation about "old crabbed authors," reports that Donne was described as "uncomeatable." But, Hazlitt says, one "A-" (identified by the editor Howe as "Ayrton") exclaimed, "What have we here?" and read aloud lines 85–88 of *EpEliz*. "There was," says Hazlitt, "no resisting this" (17:124). **DUYCKINCK** (1841): "In spite of . . . [these lines], Donne, in many poems, deserves to be studied for his grace and ease" (22). **HUNT** (1848): the lines are "preposterous" (306). **TROST** (1904): the lines are an instance of the elaborate expression of a simple idea (32). **LINDSAY** (1931): cf. William Browne, *Britannia's Pastorals* [see Lindsay's note to lines 43–70 above]. Browne's lines may actually have preceded the composition of *EpEliz* and so have influenced these lines (rather than the other way around) (234). **JOHNSON** (1931): Lindsay's dating is incorrect, as the poem "was published before Browne started to write the second book of his pastorals." Consequently, if "a similarity between Donne's work and Browne's is discovered, one's *a priori* conclusion should surely be that Browne was the borrower" (347). **M. MOLHO** (1970): the "daring reversal" of a (conventionally masculine) sun that is here feminine results from Love's incarnation in the bride; from her emanates a "sacred fire" that "purifies matter." The bridegroom's soul is thereby exalted to the stars and united with Eros in a celestial embrace (20).

85–86 *Heere lyes a Shee-Sunne . . . to his Spheare* **DUYCKINCK** (1841): the lines are a "musical passage" that serves to "neutralize the celebrated metaphysical puzzle that occurs" in the poem (22). **GRIERSON** (1921): cf. the use of the "sun" in Sir Henry Wotton's "On his Mistris, the Queen of Bohemia": "You meaner *Beauties* of the *Night*, / That poorly satisfie our *Eies* / More by your *number*, then your light, / You *Common-people* of the *Skies*; / What are you when the *Sun* shall rise?" (24) "The bolder hyperbole [Donne's] is 'metaphysical'" (222).

85 *Heere lyes a Shee-Sunne, and a Hee-moone there* **HOOD** (1827) (describing a mock marriage-procession): "I beheld, not a brace of young lovers—a Romeo and Juliet, not a 'he-moon here, and a she-sun there'—not bride and bridegroom—but the happy *pear*, a solitary Bergamy, carried on a velvet cushion by a little foot-page" (128). **SHAWCROSS** (1967a): "Usually the sun was considered masculine, the moon feminine" (176). **SMITH** (1971): "Male and female exchange natures, and merge" (457). **MILGATE** (1978): cf. *Eclog* 120–25 (116). **MOLLENKOTT** (1981): by reversing the customary genders, Donne stresses the androgynous oneness of faithful lovers, each of whom is androgynous (25). **ZUNDER** (1982): the solar imagery expresses hierarchy (41). **PARFITT** (1989): "This is almost marriage as creator of hermaphrodites" (81).

86 *the best light to his Spheare* **SMITH** (1971): "She is now the sun who shares her light with the sphere of the moon" (457).

89–91 *And yet they doe . . . forbeare or stay* **CRAIK and CRAIK** (1986): "In paying their sexual debt to each other, both are so *just* that neither *would* (wishes to) for*bear*, and so *rich* that neither *needs* to *stay* (pause)" (255).

90–95 *So iust . . . they lend,* **PARFITT** (1989): "The idea of sex as debt and payment has a long history," and "it works here to anchor marriage in a sexual transaction figured as fundamentally economic, something which squares readily enough with the realities of Jacobean marriage and, specifically, with those of the socially and politically significant" (81).

90 *that coyne* **SMITH** (1971): "sexual pleasure, their own bodies" (457).

91–92 *That neyther would . . . nor to spare.* **MELTON** (1906): an instance of "â-sound" under the category of "arsis-thesis variation of repeated sounds and syllables in the interior of the line"; Donne herein differs from other poets in "'excess,' and very marvellous excess it is" (152).

93 *They quickly pay theyr debt, and then* **MAROTTI** (1986): Donne takes "the social liberty of writing teasingly about the sexual consummation of the marriage" (272).

94 *Acquittances*, **SHAWCROSS** (1967a): "receipts for debts paid" (177). **MILGATE** (1978): "'*Acquitance*, is a discharge in writing of a summe of money, or other duitie which ought to be payed or done' (J. Rastell, *The Exposition of . . . Termes of the Lawes*, 1609, f. 11[r])" (116).

95–96 *and so let fall . . . to bee liberall.* **SMITH** (1971): "They lose no opportunity to please each other" (457). **CRAIK and CRAIK** (1986): "lose no opportunity to be generous" (255). **HUNT** (1954): a pun on the sexual meaning of "liberally," which "carries its Renaissance ambiguity of 'lewdly'" (27).

96 *such* **GROSART** (1872–73): omitted in the 1669 edition either by mistake or because at some point Donne struck it out without deciding on another word (1:260).

97–98 *More Truth, more Courage, . . . Valentine.* **SHAWCROSS** (1967a): the turtle is the turtle-dove, symbolizing love (177) [so also **SMITH** (1971), who calls turtle-doves "types of true love" and sparrows "types of 'courage', or sexual vitality" (458)]. **MILGATE** (1978): the "turtle" stands for "truth" (116).

98 *Then* **PATRIDES** (1985): "than" (196).

99–102 *Now by this Act . . . as was before.* **CRAIK and CRAIK** (1986): cf. *Canon* 24 (255); "since the phoenix does not really exist in *nature* but is fabulous, the compliment is witty as well as graceful" (255–56).

100 *Nature agayne restored is* **REEVES** (1952): "According to legend there was only one Phoenix; their union would make the Prince and Princess one and so restore to these 'two phoenixes' their original uniqueness" (100). **SMITH** (1971): "The larger sense is that this miraculous union has put right the ruin caused by Adam and Eve" (458). **MILGATE** (1978): "It was 'natural' that there should be only one phoenix (that was its essential nature)" (117).

100 *restored* **SMITH** (1971): "pronounced as three syllables" (458).

103–05 *and wee . . . will stay / Wayting* **CHAMBERS** (1896): "It was a common Elizabethan custom to serenade a bride and bridegroom on the morning after a wedding. [Randle?] Cotgrave states that the song sung on such an occasion was called the *Hunt's up*" (1:234).

104 *Satyres* **SHAWCROSS** (1967a): "lecherous demigods, who would not be glad

to see the sunrise and thus end their pleasure-filled night" (177). **SMITH** (1971): "rustic spirits who loved wine and amorous sport. They were associated with Dionysus, whose marriage feast was celebrated in February or March" (458). **CRAIK and CRAIK** (1986): "mountain spirits with feet and horns like those of the goats they kept. They are here primitive sun-worshippers" (256).

104–06 *will stay . . . your face wee see.* **SHAWCROSS** (1967a): "The sense is: 'We will stay until your eyes are finally opened, letting day shine forth from them, for we wish the sun to rise only so that we may see your face'" (177).

105 *when your eyes opened let out day* **SMITH** (1971): "The day does not break until their eyes open and light the world" (458). **MILGATE** (1978): cf. line 29 and note to line 31 (117).

105 *your* **CRAIK and CRAIK** (1986): "The couple are one, so the sunrise will be made by either's opening eyes (compare ll. 108–10)" (256).

108 *at which side day will breake* **SMITH** (1971): "They are lying in a curtained four-poster bed" (458).

110 *That opens first a Curtayne, Hers, or His.* **GROSART** (1872–73): "A strange custom this of visiting the yesterday-married couple in their chamber at morn, and while yet asleep or not risen" (1:261). **CRAIK and CRAIK** (1986): the room will not have been full of people during the night; rather, they will be allowed in the next morning (256).

110 *Curtayne,* **SHAWCROSS** (1967a): "that around the bed" (177).

111 *try'd* **MILGATE** (1978): "tested, proved" (117).

111 *after Nyne* **MILGATE** (1978): "Ten o'clock was the usual hour for the first 'public' appearance of members of the fashionable world"; cf. *Sat4* 175 (117).

112 *enlarge* **SHAWCROSS** (1967a): "make longer than the normal twenty-four hours, the new day beginning only when a curtain is drawn" (177). **SMITH** (1971): "extend as far as that, by celebrating the marriage and keeping the vigil" (458).

Eclogue. 1613. December 26.

Commentary

Date and Circumstances

Hunt (c. 1837), in marginalia in an edition of Donne reported in Lewes (1838, 376), after general praise of the poem (described under General Commentary below), observes, "But what an ode when we think on the history of the parties! Donne's faith, however, was no doubt, good and true; and let us hope that there were more circumstances than we are aware of to extenuate, if possible, the crimes of Carr and his wife; one there certainly was—they were victims of their own beauty."

Hunt subsequently (1841 [1956, 498]) expands these remarks, describing the occasion of *Eclog* as "the marriage of poor wretched Car [sic], Earl of Somerset, with Lady Essex—singular personages for the feeling and thoughtful Donne to panegyrize. The faith expressed in their love, however, by this good and great child-like man, however startling to us when we know under what circumstances they were married, was, no doubt, as far as regards himself, good and true."

Jessopp (1855, xxxix) observes that in late 1612 Donne returned to England from abroad suffering from an eye affliction and that he was still complaining of weak eyes "even as late as January 1613": "Alas! it had been well, had they continued too weak to serve him in his next undertaking—it was an Epithalamion on the marriage of the Earl of Somerset to the Countess of Essex, in Dec. 1613. But the time was drawing near when Donne was to begin a life of more seriousness and more usefulness. The courtier and poet and wit, whose splendid powers had hitherto been comparatively trifled away, or turned to wholly unworthy purposes, was to be called on to dedicate them to a nobler end."

Grosart (1872–73, 1:271–72) finds it "fitting" that Ben Jonson should have written his "delicious Masque of 'Hymenæi' at the marriage of the Lady Frances Howard (in her fourteenth year) with the Earl of Essex (in his fifteenth year)," but thinks it "deplorable to read his verses 'To the most noble and above his titles, Robert, Earle of Somerset, sent to him on his Wedding-day, 1613' . . . and equally so to have Donne celebrating the same vilely adulterous second marriage of the divorced 'Countess' of Essex with the minion of James, Robert Carr, Viscount Rochester (created just before it Earl of Somerset)." Grosart further observes that this "infamous marriage led to the murder of Sir Thomas Overbury" and to "the trial and condemnation of the earl and countess—whose lives, reprieved by the king, were dragged out in mutual recrimination and loathing. Somerset died obliviously; his devilish wife the object of national horror." Grosart speculates that "as Bacon got Campion to write his Masque for the present occasion, he too over-persuaded Donne to prepare his Eclogue and Epithalamium" (271), concluding that "it is saddening to find the great names of Bacon and Jonson and Donne mixed-up with a marriage so disgraceful" (271–72).

Jessopp (1888, 15:223-34) asserts that Donne wrote a brief [Harleian ms. 39, fol. 416; *Eighth Report of the Royal Commission on Historical Manuscripts*, 1881, Appendix, part iii] supporting the case for the Countess of Essex in her divorce action, and characterizes Somerset as "that worthless nobleman" whose patronage "compromised" Donne (228).

Bradford (1892, 352–53) attributes Donne's connection with the "infamous" Robert Carr to Donne's "hope of secular preferment" (352) and characterizes *Eclog* as a failure insofar as that hope was concerned: "[Donne's] expectations, if he had any, were . . . disappointed by the exposure and condemnation of that well-matched pair" (353).

"One would gladly spare from Donne's works," states Norton (1895, 1:236–38), "this *Eclogue* and the *Epithalamion* which it prefaces, in celebration of the notorious marriage, in 1613, of the Earl of Somerset with the divorced Lady Essex. The adulation of the King and of his favorite is pushed to extravagance of servility." Terming Donne a "miserable . . . suppliant for the favors of those in power," Norton cites Donne's protestation, in a letter written to Carr "the year before" the marriage, that he had been "purchase[d]" by Carr "absolutely and intirely" (*Letters* 290) and calls it a "further illustration of the depth of flattery to which . . . [Donne] could descend." Norton finds it "painful" to see "a man of Donne's superiority thus degraded" (236) and adds that Donne nevertheless "descended to a still lower depth of baseness in offering his services to help in establishing the nullity of Lady Essex's marriage," citing the document described by Jessopp (1888) and *Letters* 168 and 180 (236–37). In regard to *Eclog* Norton specifically cites Donne's comment in *Letters* 180—"I deprehend in myself more than an alacrity, a vehemence to do service to that company"—and in light of "what that company was" judges that "these words are deplorable" (the letter is subscribed "Jan. 19" and was written in 1614; like Gosse after him, however, Norton seems to think it written a year earlier—ed.). Norton further cites a postscript to Donne's undated (1614?) letter to Sir Robert Drury: " 'I cannot tell you so much, as you tell me, of anything from my Lord of Som[erset] since the epithalamium, for I heard nothing' " (237). "The whole *Epithalamium*," Norton argues, "is a disgrace to [Donne], little palliated by his need, or by the fact that other men of great note united in doing honor to the occasion," but he nevertheless concludes that "disgust at the occasion and object of Donne's poem ought not to blind the reader to its extraordinary spirit, to the vivacity of fancy displayed in it, and to the beauty of many of its verses" (238).

Jessopp (1897, 85) terms *Eclog* "a poor performance, [that] does Donne little credit."

Gosse (1899, 2:25, 28, 31–33, 37) calls attention to the letter of 19 January 1614 (which he misdates 1613; cf. Norton [1895] above) that reads in part "My poor study having lain that way [i.e., in Gosse's view, towards arguing for the annulment of the Essex marriage], it may prove possible that my weak assistance may be of use in this matter in a more serious fashion than an epithalamium" (25). Accepting the thesis that Donne wrote the brief for annulment, Gosse observes:

> In judging men like Lancelot Andrewes [a member of the commission that tried the divorce case] and Donne, it is highly important to bear in mind that the cup of

> Frances Howard's wickedness was very far indeed from being full in 1613. Those who examined her case could hardly fail to see in her a callous, cruel, and indelicate woman; but the faults of her temper had not, as yet, publicly blossomed forth into crimes, and the worst charges brought against her before her marriage with Rochester were capable of being condoned or denied. But when every excuse has been made, it is difficult not to yield to Dean Church's objection that all the Jacobean churchmen were subjected to a sort of fate, which obliged them to become base at least once in their lives (28).

Supposing that Donne and Ben Jonson both presented their epithalamic verses to Somerset "[o]n the same winter morning" (32), Gosse thinks that Donne composed the pastoral setting of *Eclog* "just before the wedding" as a framework for "[t]he epithalamion proper, written to order several months before," and believes that "the fact of the nuptial song having been written before the event is curiously betrayed by a speech of Allophanes, who introduces it as a 'sacrifice' prepared beforehand, although, of course, 'not made / Either the Court or men's hearts to invade.'" Gosse reproaches Donne for styling the principals a "Blest pair of swans" (l. 171) and finds the "extremely disconcerting" poem dedicated to these "disgraceful" nuptials "very difficult to approach . . . without a strong feeling of repulsion," though he concedes that it "may be read with considerable pleasure" if we "forget the occasion for which it was composed" (31). After commending a number of specific passages in the poem (see Notes and Glosses below), Gosse concludes that Donne's attitude towards Somerset and Lady Essex shows a "strange blindness" (32). "What the feelings of these canorous [sic] persons [i.e., Donne and Jonson] must have been when the Overbury revelations so promptly followed," Gosse observes, "it is not easy to conceive" (33).

Reviewing Gosse (1899) in *Ath* (1899, 646), the anonymous author observes that "the Victorian is not the Jacobean conception of the social hierarchy; yet it goes against the grain to find Donne writing fine verse to countesses in the hope that they will pay his debts, and still more to find him doing dirty work for so poor a wretch as the Earl of Somerset." The reviewer notes that the brief in support of Lady Essex's case for divorce was apparently written by one Sir Daniel Donne and expresses the hope that John Donne was not a party to it.

Vincent (1899, 836), also in *Ath*, subsequently challenges the need for Gosse (1899) to defend Donne from reproach attending on his supposed composition of the divorce brief, pointing out that Harleian ms. 39, fol. 416, cited by Gosse, "is plainly headed 'A Discourse written by S[r] Daniell Dunn . . . ,' a well known and altogether different man."

Symons (1899, 738–39) suggests that to Donne's "speculative" and "abstract" brain (as exemplified in his defense of suicide in *Biathanatos*) "conduct must always have seemed of less importance than it does to most other people, and especially conduct which is argument, like the demonstrations on behalf of what seems, on the face of it, a somewhat iniquitous divorce and re-marriage, or like those unmeasured eulogies, both of this 'blest pair of swans,' and of the dead child of a rich father" (738). Donne is, Symons avers, "always the casuist, always mentally impartial in the face of a moral problem, reserving judgment on matters which, after all, seem to him remote from an unimpassioned contemplation of things" (738–39).

Lee (1904, 101) corrects Jessopp's mistake in the *DNB* about Donne's having authored a nullity brief defending the Countess of Essex's divorce.

Grierson (1912, 2:94) refers the reader to Samuel R. Gardiner, *History of England from the Accession of James I to the Outbreak of the Civil War, 1603–1642* (London: Longmans, 1883 and later editions), and affirms that "it is unnecessary to detail all the ugly history of this notorious marriage." Summarizing the circumstances of the relationship between Somerset, Lady Frances Howard, and the poet, Grierson agrees that Donne was not responsible for the divorce brief, while nonetheless arguing (on the evidence of his letters) Donne's willingness to help make the divorce possible. "Before the decree was granted," Grierson states, "[Donne] was already busy polishing his epithalamium."

Fausset (1924, 213–15) thinks the commission granted the Countess of Essex her nullity suit "largely" through Donne's "subtle advocacy" (213) and states that Donne sought to "strengthen his claims" on Carr's favors by presenting *Eclog*, "part of which he had already composed even before the divorce was assured," on the "flaunting celebration" of the marriage in December of 1613. In stating his desire to share in the "pageant of Court function" (214), concludes Fausset, Donne "could not be more explicit, and yet his efforts bore no fruit" (215).

Praz (1925, 59) denies, in the light of the customs of the age, that by calling the principals "Blest payre of Swanns" (l. 171) Donne is practicing brazen flattery ("sfacciata adulazione"). Praz further denounces the practice of evaluating poets according to modern conventions of decorum, citing both Ariosto's 1502 epithalamion for Alfonso d'Este and Lucrezia Borgia, the latter of whom Ariosto hails as most beautiful virgin ("pulcherrima Virgo"), and the same poet's epigram exalting the chastity of the newly appointed Bishop of Ferrara, Ippolito d'Este, who was, Praz states, outstandingly deficient in that virtue.

After recounting the circumstances surrounding the marriage, Payne (1926, 130–33) comments that the epithalamion "is much too good for the occasion" (132).

While restating the objection to any association of Donne with the divorce brief, Grierson (1929, xxxix) expands his prior disparagement (1912) of the poet's connection with the affair, stating that Gosse's characterization (1899) of this period in Donne's life is substantially convincing. "Donne nosed about the nullity case in a disagreeable manner," Grierson asserts, "willing to help, while he composed his adulatory *Epithalamion* for the adulterous marriage that was contemplated, 'honeying and making love over the nasty sty'."

"The poem is marred," argues McPeek (1939, 367), "by the author's attempt to justify the marriage by difficult conceits."

Legouis (1955, 17) terms the marriage "scandalous," but exonerates Donne to the extent of noting what he characterizes as Chapman's far more sycophantic celebration of the event.

Gros (1964, 52) pictures Donne as seeking Carr's patronage and offering him legal counsel in the matter of his desired marriage with the Countess of Essex. He describes *Eclog* as "poetically valid" other than in the objects of its dedication: Donne writes, asserts Gros, of the "debauched" Somerset as "*the great instrument of Divine Providence in this kingdom.*"

Le Comte (1965, 142–43) cites the letter to Carr in which Donne styles himself one of Carr's "purchases" (*Letters* 290) and calls *Eclog* "[o]ne fruit of the purchase." Summarizing the historical details of the divorce and remarriage, Le Comte notes that Donne, "who in the Eclogue calls himself Idios, i.e. the private man who holds no place at court, voiced approval of the divorce," although he did not (as Gosse mistakenly thought) aid in the proceedings. Le Comte finds in the poem "more nobility than [in] the alliance it celebrates" and concludes that Donne "gave some of the blithest verses of his latter years" to this "criminal marriage" (143).

Bewley (1966, 155) observes that, "as there had been much whispered scandal about the adulterous affair even before the divorce, the Epithalamion perhaps says more for Donne's ambition than for his sincerity."

Hughes (1968, 59, 244–45, 299), noting that Gosse "misrepresents" Donne's involvement in the nullity proceedings that dissolved Frances Howard's first marriage (299), discusses the poem in the light of Donne's attempt to enlist the aid of the Earl of Somerset in obtaining a post as clerk of the Privy Council. In this context, Hughes states that the poem sounds an "egregious begging note" (244) and that Donne, whose address to Somerset threatened to alienate the Countess of Bedford, risked "hazarding everything on one throw" (245).

Le Comte (1969, 131, 133) disparages the literary contributions of Bacon, Campion, Chapman, and Jonson to the marriage, arguing that "only John Donne came through with consistently good poetry, only he showed what fine flowers can spring from a fetid soil" (131) and adding that "Donne at the time of the wedding was suffering from eye trouble, blurred vision—symbolically enough" (133).

Bald (1970, 273–74, 278) reviews Donne's approach to, acceptance by, and consequent sense of indebtedness to Carr, citing *Letters* 180–81 (see entry for Norton [1895] above) to show that "a few weeks after the wedding Donne professed his ardour to write not merely an epithalamion but also a defence of the divorce . . . ." Though the "prose defence of the nullity was never needed," notes Bald, "[t]he epithalamion was written and presented, with a prefatory eclogue to excuse its not being proffered until some time after the occasion it celebrated" (274). Bald further suggests that the eye trouble Donne suffered during this time accounts for his not having produced his poem until some time after the occasion it celebrated.

Jackson (1970, 130–41), reviewing Donne's "supposed complicity in the obnoxious Rochester affair" (130) as presented by Gosse (1899) and Grierson (1912), finds *Eclog* to be "surely one of the most reluctant, ambiguous epithalamiums ever written" (131). Jackson focuses on two letters—one to Sir Robert Ker (*Letters* 270–71) and the other to G.K. (*Letters* 179–81)—both of which mention the possibility of Donne's writing an epithalamion. The first, Jackson believes, in which Donne responds to "a group of several poems which Sir Robert had sent him to comment upon" and proves himself "sensitive enough to the problems in the nullity action to wish to avoid . . . [negative] reflections" upon Frances Howard's former husband (the Earl of Essex), shows that Donne "specifically rejects the intention to write an epithalamium" at the time when "others are doing so" (132). The second, which Jackson contends was written on "Jan. 19" 1614 (and had been misdated 1613 by Gosse) and was actually addressed to G. B. (not G. K.), has Donne ambiguously declaring his "vehemency to do service to that company" as a possible "reason to make rhyme," but also shows him solicitous that "his correspondent 'shall escape the danger of approving'" any verses he might pen (132–34). Similarly finding the poem itself "ambiguous throughout," Jackson says it "ties together a whole series of dualities" (139) and cites several passages as proof (see Notes and Glosses). Jackson concludes by reversing Gosse's judgment of the poem—considered "in its circumstances," it was "a brilliant success." Representing neither "a slavish fawning upon a doubtful marriage in order to gain preferment" nor "a deliberate and foolhardy rejection of the possibility of that preferment," *Eclog* is a poem, Jackson contends, which "with its ambiguities wreathed around it, made possible Donne's aim: to have his suit for preferment presented to the king" (140–41).

Smith (1971, 458) terms the divorce proceedings "shabby," but observes that "Somerset's standing with King James made him a man worth pleasing; hence the present poem."

Parker (1975, 62) briefly recounts the historical context that occasioned the poem, which he describes as "sycophantic and not very good."

Milgate (1978, xx–xxi, xxiv–xxv, 118) cites the letter of 19 January 1614 (see Norton [1895], Gosse [1899], and Jackson [1970] above), which he suggests may have been written to Sir Henry Goodyer, as evidence of Donne's late composition of *Eclog*, the "Ecclogue" that prefaces the "Epithalamion" proper constituting "an apology for its not having been offered until some weeks after the wedding" (118). Although he links *Eclog* with *Henry* as an expression of Donne's readiness to accept the symbols and rituals of Court idealism (xx), Milgate calls attention to lines 99–100 and line 235 as "somewhat disingenuous" statements of Donne's hopes that the poem would benefit his career at Court (118). According to Milgate, Donne wrote *Eclog* "with an odd mixture of willingness and reluctance, for about the occasion clung doubts, disapproval, and even scandal, of at least some of which he must have appreciated the force." Milgate argues that in *Eclog* Donne deliberately alludes to the awkward circumstances of the marriage, possibly "to protect his integrity" and "certainly because he would not let a lively appreciation of the idealisms concerning royalty and marriage cloud his eyes to the actualities." Milgate elaborates on what he sees to be Donne's ambivalent strategy in *Eclog*: "The spiritual meanings of rituals are not . . . invalidated by unworthiness in those who perform them, and Donne could proceed to celebrate the nuptials, approved by Church and King, for all that they might ideally represent. Flattery the poem indeed contains; but if Somerset and his bride, and even the King and certain of his bishops and courtiers, did not entirely embody the ideal, at least it is the ideal and not the failure to embody it that Donne celebrates." The "essence" of the marriage, in Milgate's words, is thus celebrated with wit, charm, and intellectual ingenuity, both mirroring Court tastes and upholding the spiritual significance of the occasion (xxiv).

Carey (1981, 86–87) observes that Donne offered his legal and theological expertise to Rochester to defend the Countess' case in her divorce action, but that Rochester declined the offer and instead solicited the epithalamion. "Given the character of the bride," Carey adds, "even Donne seems to have found this ticklish, and the finished poem was not presented until some weeks after the marriage. He does not scruple, though, to allude to the scandal the affair had caused; he praises the bride for defying 'unjust opinion' (she went to the altar with her hair hanging untrimmed to her waist—the mark of a virgin)."

Marotti (1981, 230–31) characterizes Donne's service to Rochester as morally questionable and the epithalamion "shameless" in its depiction of the "degenerate" court as an ideal place (230). He cites the transformation of "the usual courtly vices of 'lust' and 'envy'" (l. 35) into "'zeale' and 'love'" (l. 37) (230–31), questioning the "'vertue'" (l. 84) that Donne attributes to that milieu. He finds in line 102 evidence that Donne is desperate for help from Somerset and the King. In Marotti's view, Allophanes's proposal (ll. 233–35) to carry the poem back to Court is a "bald appeal for favors" that got Donne nothing in return (231).

General Commentary

Hunt (c. 1837), in marginalia in an edition of Donne reported in Lewes (1838, 376), remarks that "the burden of this ode has a fine earnest sound of enthusiasm—a rushing fire."

An anonymous commentator in *LEM* (1846, 233), presumably discussing *Eclog*, characterizes "the longest and most famous" of Donne's "Epithalamions" as having "scarcely a quotable passage," but as deriving its "whole merit" from an "inexplicable, incommunicable *aura*—"aura" being the quality present in "true" poetry that reveals itself to the serious reader.

Grosart (1872–73, 1:271–72) suggests that several passages in the "Ecclogue" and the "Epithalamion" proper reflect popular opinions of the Countess of Essex; these are "ll. 25&c," stanzas 2, 4, 5 and others unspecified, and lines 122–24 (272).

Schipper (1888, 2:795) observes that the stanzaic pattern of the poem is one of many such derived from Spenser.

Gosse (1893, 239) finds the "Ecclogue" a "rather stiff setting" for the "Epithalamion," which he terms nonetheless "scarcely less felicitous" than *EpEliz*.

Gosse subsequently (1899, 2:32) terms the epithalamion "one of Donne's happiest efforts in this direction—rich, ingenious, and virile."

Ramsay (1917, 8) terms *Eclog* Donne's only epithalamion in the genre of Spenser, which she characterizes as an "artificial" kind of poetry that is almost of necessity "somewhat cold" and which could not have suited the youthful Donne's temperament.

Fausset (1924, 214) characterizes the marriage song itself (i.e., ll. 105–225) as "little more than a composite of flagrant flattery, ingenuous ornament and carnal convention," but states that the pastoral introduction has "real personal significance." He sees the dialogue between Idios and Allophanes on the opposed virtues of the "monastic life" and the "charms of the Court" as a debate "between the two sides of Donne's nature, the religious soul and the worldling," and finds "the latter . . . more convincing," even though Donne had in "earlier letters" assessed the "meretricious glitter" of court life "at its true value."

Fausset (1931, xx) reiterates his earlier condemnation of *Eclog*, adding the expression "bedizened diction," and reaffirms his earlier defense of the pastoral introduction.

McPeek (1939, 367) characterizes the epithalamion (i.e., ll. 105–225) as "carefully proportioned," and cites Ausonius's *Nuptial Cento* as precedent for the stanza headings.

Arguing that Donne never felt what Spenser's mind saw, Hunt (1954, 123) calls *Eclog* a "mechanically written piece," which is "bare of pastoral machinery and void of the pastoral mood."

Gamberini (1967, 78–79) maintains that *Eclog* carries to an extreme what he describes as the inappropriate displays of scholastic learning that mar *EpEliz*.

Bald (1970, 274) claims that the epithalamion proper "lacks the fervour of Donne's two earlier pieces in the same form" and finds the framing eclogue "an extravagant admission of the extremes to which court flattery obliged Donne to stoop."

As part of a general account of the decline of the epithalamic genre in England, Miller (1970, 405, 413–14) discusses the "flattering" *Eclog*, where "the decline of the form" of the epithalamion "is apparent" (405) in the subordination of the myth of marriage to the "flattery of the parents of the bridal pair, or certain distinguished wedding guests" (413). Although he calls *Eclog* "brilliant" (413), Miller feels that "the repeated, elaborate praises of King James . . . are excessive, and that they detract from the traditional mythic elements in the poem" (413–14).

Summers (1970, 32–33) describes *Eclog* as "a long and ambitious poem which is consistently interesting and entertaining and which . . . contains not a single lapse, social or literary."

Tufte (1970, 226) asserts that *Eclog* is "chiefly interesting for its form, a few brilliant passages, and its hint of the same melancholy we have seen in the final epithalamia of Spenser and Jonson."

McGowan (1972, 175–218) amplifies her general comments about *EpEliz* and *Eclog* with a specific discussion of the latter, addressing the problems for the different poets who eulogized the Somerset/Howard wedding. In the masques presented by Thomas Campion, Ben Jonson, and Thomas Middleton, McGowan maintains, "the King remains the principal focus of interest" (199), and "any references to the circumstances leading up to the marriage are, on the whole, studiously avoided" (201). McGowan finds that within the context of these masques *Eclog* "strikes a strange and contentious note" since its thematic structure "is founded on a complex set of contraries: the block 'East, Sun, Warmth, Light, King, and Heaven' opposes a second block 'Winter, West, North, Cold, Night, and Hell'" (210). Nevertheless, she explains, the apparently contrary arguments of Idios and Allophanes are used "not to prove opposite cases, but to reinforce their shared view that the King is the source of all power and good" (211). Further, McGowan contends that the nuptial song that follows the opening eclogue is "extremely formal" (212) in its stanzaic structure, its chronological sequence, and its thematic use of metaphor; and she expresses reservations about how successful this epithalamion is, particularly with regard to Donne's "presentation and evocation of the Bride," which she finds "especially laboured" (215). McGowan concludes that when the social context determines the form, "participation and celebration are key concepts for a proper understanding of any poetic work of this period" (217).

Lodi (1974, 86–99) finds *Eclog* "composed on the pattern of Theocritus and Virgil" (91) and "traditionally Spenserian" in structure. Further, Lodi believes that the pastoral aspect of the opening dialogue and the protestation of love, which is too humble for the occasion, invest the poem "with an air of tenderness" (92).

Ousby (1976b, 33) states that even though *Eclog* is written in the pastoral mode, "it reflects little sympathy for the values of pastoral."

Partridge (1978, 121–26) finds that the poem "emulates the language of current Court masques, while retaining Spenser's blend of Platonism and Christian belief" (124). Partridge maintains that the necessity of pleasing a patron is a disadvantage to poetry and that Donne seeks to avoid insincerity "by making the subject of his tribute a symbolic figure, and his eulogy a form of Christian reverence," a practice that to the modern reader is not satisfying. "Donne is a poet of ideas and paradoxes," Partridge maintains, adding that "when the hermeneut does not convince, the *raison d'être* of his meditation falls away, except where saved by the poet's verbal skill" (126).

Zunder (1982, 61–63) examines what he terms the "political and social inadequacy" (61) of *Eclog* within the context of Donne's alleged failure to confront the social implications of realities he nevertheless recognized. As instances of that alleged inadequacy, Zunder cites lines 15–24, 33–38, and 73–90. Zunder summarizes the scandals preceding, surrounding, and following the marriage, as well as the supposed shortcomings of Somerset's successor at Court (Buckingham) as evidence of Donne's failure to criticize what he idealizes.

Comparing *Eclog* to Velazquez's painting *Las Meninas*, Hurley (1986, 357–69) proposes that just as the speaker of *Eclog*, who imagines himself present at a ceremony he did not attend, "dislocates" the reader, so the figure of the painter in *Las Meninas* dislocates the viewer, the result being that "his true role as artist is no longer possible and thus is present yet not present." By developing this perspective, Hurley claims, both Donne and Velazquez reveal the limitations and the power of their "specifically human instruments." By developing witty violations of its logical property, she says, Donne questions the "expository clarity" of language (357). Hurley argues that Donne's poem questions the possibility "or even the desirability, of representation as a valid act," adding that Donne "not only calls into question the issue of representation but also appears to actively supplant it as a mode of insight with a kind of visionary stance which is for him superior to that sense perception upon which our notations of representation are based" (363).

More specifically, Hurley asserts that a direct representation of the marriage would have been embarrassing and inaccurate. In order to overcome these difficulties, she claims, Donne dislodges his readers from "their familiar and comfortable assumptions about language, specifically its logical efficacy." Donne's speaker dissociates himself from the event by asserting his absence; in this way, Hurley says, "the poem as *projected* epithalamion resists any direct link between speaker and reader" (364). Hurley then illustrates how Donne dislocates logic by employing various metaphors, especially of sight; "interestingly," she states of the introductory pastoral eclogue, "there is not one instance of direct sight in this part of the poem. Perhaps fittingly (given the sins of the wedded pair and the future vocation of the celebrating poet), the dominant image of the Somerset epithalamion is fire," as in lines 219–21 (365). She concludes that "there is not one instance of clear vision in the epithalamion . . . ; its admissions and insights are achieved, rather, through indirection and distortion." Thus, Hurley says, "the fictive epithalamion is transmuted from private plea to public tribute in the very act of acknowledging its own failure" (366). The supplanting of logic by metaphors and of sensuous by visionary experience does not, however, Hurley argues, resolve the issues raised in the poem; rather, such displacements are a point of departure for the poem's development because "the destruction of the literal releases those fictive powers which for the poet or painter briefly transform him into a maker or creator."

For Donne, then, Hurley says, logic, though "fallacious from a sensory and referential point of view," is "efficacious from the transcendent perspective. In short, representation as a valid intentional act is found wanting, but as an *in*-valid intentional act it is essential" (367). Donne's fictive problem in the epithalamion, Hurley claims, is to reconcile temporal, imperfect individuals with a perception of them as exemplary figures in a hierarchical world. She contends that Donne "miraculously solves that discordancy by wittily manipulating tactile metaphors of sight into transcendent metaphors of vision." Hurley summarizes her argument thus: "It is not only that the 'truth' of art requires that the relation between language and vision be kept open; such a void is essential to the potency of genuine literature and art, for the experience conveyed to the reader or spectator cannot in fact be conditioned by the object, but by language (whether in words or paint) itself, and while the reality thus re-created may act as an essential reality, it can never be identical with it" (369).

Marotti (1986, 272–73) characterizes *Eclog* as an interlocking matrix of poetic, social, and biographical concerns. The poem's purpose, he says, is to advertise "Donne's social connections both to his friend Sir Robert Ker and to that man's more powerful namesake and cousin, the Earl of Somerset." The poem's structure, Marotti argues, aptly expresses this social and personal function: "the poem-within-a-poem format . . . served Donne's purpose as a way of belatedly presenting a marriage poem to Somerset, whose wedding festivities he had missed." Elaborating on the personal, social, and historical elements of the poem, Marotti argues that it is "unusually preoccupied" (272) with the Court as a *locus* of patronage and favor. "In portraying the Jacobean court as a place of 'zeal and love' [l. 37]," says Marotti, "Donne went as far as he ever allowed himself to go in verse toward flattering idealization of the courtly establishment—desperate as he was" for Somerset's help in obtaining a post at Court. Although *Eclog* praises Somerset and Howard, Marotti observes, it nevertheless contains a suppressed undercurrent of criticism of them—visible, for instance, in the words "diuorce" (l. 127) and "fall'ne" (l. 207). Despite this element of criticism, Marotti concludes, Donne "did not allow his satirically analytical intelligence to operate freely" in the poem (273).

In an extensive review of commentary on *Eclog*, McClung and Simard (1987, 95–106) argue that criticism has usually reflected the critics' prejudices about the sexual behavior of its subjects, Somerset, Lady Frances Howard, and King James. They maintain that "the suppression of direct reference to the central role of homoerotic behavior in Somerset's career" and "the displacement of homophobic feelings into overwrought accounts of the supposed adulteries and homicides of the famous pair" constitute the "bad faith" characteristic of the bulk of commentary on *Eclog* (95). McClung and Simard characterize major historical treatments of the events surrounding the marriage as sensationalist, dishonest, and evasive, citing especially the accounts of Arthur Wilson, *The History of Great Britain, Being the Life and Reign of King James the First . . .* (London, 1653) and Samuel R. Gardiner, *History of England from the Accession of James I to the Disgrace of Chief-Justice Coke. 1603–1622* (London: Hurst & Blackett, 1863; rev. & expanded eds. London: Longmans, 1883 & later). They find in the diction, emphases, and omissions of these texts a shaping of the evidence (itself challenged at several points by McClung and Simard) to produce a desired moral lesson about the threat of sexuality to the State, and argue further that this pattern of historical commentary has passed into the literary criticism of *Eclog*.

Examining the comments of nineteenth-century editors and biographers of Donne, McClung and Simard argue further that the combination of veiled references to Somerset's relations with James and vehement denunciations of Somerset's and Lady Frances's alleged activities constitute an evaluation of the poem on the grounds of its sexual correctness. They survey the history of the (now discredited) accusation that Donne wrote a legal brief supporting the Countess in her divorce suit, finding in the perpetuation of this charge a desire on the part of critics to challenge the poem's integrity. They especially call attention to critical terminology that, they maintain, transfers the supposed vice, corruption, or decadence of the principals' behavior to both Donne and *Eclog*, noting a "countermovement" in the comments of such critics as Praz (1925) and Dubrow (1988, read by McClung and Simard in manuscript). Citing Louis Crompton's *Byron and Greek Love: Homophobia in 19th Century England* (Berkeley: University of California Press, 1985), McClung and Simard argue that in the absence of an accepted language of discourse on homosexuality, criticism of *Eclog* has been crippled by the displacement of homophobic feelings into attacks on the alleged adultery and associated crimes in the background of the poem. "How much blame attaches to the couple is debatable," they conclude, "but the loathing attached to their names and by extension to Donne's unremarkable role in the affair suggests the problem of Hamlet in T. S. Eliot's famous formula, unable to find an objective correlative for disgust and thus trapped in the repetition of a complaint that, though not without merit, exceeds the facts of the case" (103).

Shami (1987, 9–23) cites *Eclog* together with verse letters to noblewomen, the Anniversaries, *Pseudo-Martyr*, and Donne's sermon in defense of the King's *Directions to Preachers* as works that "have all been invoked to prove that in awkward situations Donne consistently sacrificed conscience to political expediency" (9), but argues that his sermons seek to "channel and guide" power in church and state (21).

Dubrow (1988, 197–219) rejects readings either that see the poem as "the outward and visible sign" of Donne's subjection to the patronage system or that read it as a successful subversion of that system, arguing that *Eclog* embodies the tensions between Donne's desire for advancement under the patronage of Somerset and his disapproval of the marriage. Attributing the "fulsome" praise of Somerset in part to the fact that he was in an exceptionally good position to help Donne obtain a court appointment, Dubrow also suggests that Donne was conscious of the "fragility" of such power as the favorite possessed (198) and that "such perceptions . . . help to explain certain characteristics" of *Eclog* (198). Although she acknowledges Donne's use in other poems of the "symbolic praise" defined by Lewalski (1973) as a component of the Anniversaries, Dubrow nevertheless discounts it here, on the grounds of the subjects' bad reputations; she further discounts "the technique [Donne] had used in certain verse letters to sidestep flattery: composing a philosophical essay only marginally related to the recipient." Epithalamic conventions, Dubrow argues, allowed no evasion of "extensive praise" for the couple (199).

Reviewing those conventions, Dubrow stresses the genre's "subterranean motifs," especially that of the reconciliation of opposing forces. To have deployed certain overt conventions, such as the prayer for children (a perceptible insult to Lady Frances' former husband), might have wrought the opposite effect to a reconciliation. Yet by invoking those very conventions, she asserts, Donne solves his problem by using the poem to comment on both "the peculiarities of this particular wedding" and "the more general problems of complimenting a patron" (200). Dubrow characterizes Donne's approach as a "spectrum" ranging from "uncritical adulation" to "uncompromising criticism" (201). Making several comparisons to *EpEliz* (see General Commentary on the Epithalamions), she finds *Eclog* more flattering to the persons of the bride and groom, possibly as a compensation for the author's distaste for them (202). She especially notes that praise is often expressed through references to fire, light, and the sun, imagery that, she argues, is "typically negative" in other poems dealing with the court (201). *Eclog*'s elaborate compliments to the King, she argues, are both appeals to the highest of patrons and a way of holding him accountable for the marriage. She argues that the poem also "responds to the pressures of patronage" by "implicitly defending" the principals from the charges leveled against them: for example, by reducing Cupid (l. 87) to an unthreatening force (203–04), by pretending to rebuke the bride (ll. 71–72, 193–95) for not leaving her guests and hastening to bed, by converting the customary prayer for children (ll. 177–78) into a homily on courtly service, and by using religious terminology (ll. 103–04, 234–35) while stressing the cooperation of the Church in the proceedings.

Many passages, Dubrow argues, "slip back and forth between compliment and criticism" (205)—for example, the repetition of the phrase "inflaming eyes," connoting both the strength and the illicitness of the couple's passion (205–157 06), or the solar imagery of line 150, which has the effect of neutralizing or containing a blinding, and therefore dangerous, power. By these and other "subdued, ambiguous" suggestions, Donne presents sensitive issues for the reader's consideration (206). He also, she maintains, blends praise and blame by distancing speaker, community, and reader from the wedding: the speaker is generally distant; customary attendants and participants in the event are either absent or vaguely defined; and the titles to the stanzas frame and isolate the episodes, as if the event were a court masque (206–07). Donne levels uncompromising criticism at the principals, Dubrow argues, in language that carries unmistakeable warnings (207–08). "Hair often represents sexuality," Dubrow asserts, and therefore praise of the bride's hair by an allusion to Phaëton implies danger. In praising her hair, Dubrow continues, Donne also alludes to the virginity, problematic in Frances Howard's case, symbolized by a bride's wearing her hair loose at the marriage ceremony; "hence the lines comment . . . on her deceptive semiotics, suggesting that predilection for falsehood represented by her hair needs to be controlled, chastened" (208). Donne conveys further censure numerologically by manipulation of the quantity "eleven," a number declared by St. Augustine to represent sin (209–10).

Dubrow then examines the framing pastoral for evidence of Donne's comments on the patronage system, finding in the pastoral dialogue no mere apology for the poet's absence at the wedding, but rather a representation of Donne's ambivalent feelings about the event; the two speakers of the eclogue embody the two halves of Donne's ego (211–12). Because the epithalamion is "a fundamentally dialogic medium" (212), she argues, Donne is able to deploy generic conventions to dramatize "the moral necessity to condemn the wedding and the financial necessity to praise it" (212–13). Her conclusions extend to an appeal for including formalist and New Critical strategies in the analyses of this poem—strategies which, she argues, are designed to measure the "generic conventions" and "verbal ingenuity" that Donne himself uses to explore the "social and political tensions that interest so many critics today" (213). Collaterally, she warns against synchronic readings of Renaissance texts, calls for a revaluation of patronage relationships as more complex and more often marked by a "licensed license" for poets than is generally acknowledged (214–15), and invites discussion about the "role of criticism and dissent within poetry addressed to a patron" (215).

Zunder (1988, 78–95) contrasts *Eclog*, "a classic utterance of absolutist sentiment" (93), with the "radicalism" he finds in earlier Donne works (especially *Sat3* and *SunRis*). He finds "abject self-degradation" even more evident in *Eclog* than in Donne's verse letters to female patrons (92). The pastoral dialogue form is a way, Zunder suggests, by which Donne apologizes to Somerset for failing to attend the wedding. Solar imagery in this poem, he argues, is used to defend royal authority, unmitigated by the claims of any other institution or tradition. The poem's "recondite reference[s] and involuted syntax," Zunder maintains, are "typical of the public poems Donne wrote in the years preceding his entry into holy orders" (93).

Parfitt (1989, 44–46) discusses the poem in the context of Donne's aspiration to secure a position at court, noting that Donne's flattery of Frances Howard and Somerset constitutes flattery of the king as well. He argues that even though such flattery is an expected consequence of the use of the conventions of the epithalamion, Donne is nevertheless able to use the pastoral eclogue within the poem for satirical purposes.

Dubrow (1990, 178–200), expanding her earlier (1988) argument, finds that Donne had "triumphantly" resolved in *EpEliz* the generic problems first confronted in *EpLin* and states that the challenge he confronted in *Eclog*—that of "adapting generic norms to celebrate the union of Somerset and Frances Howard"—was "a perilous undertaking" (178). Dubrow argues that "Donne responds to the clash between his reluctance to celebrate the wedding and the pressures to do so in two principal ways"—by "once again . . . [transforming] linear patterns into cyclical ones" and by devising "a whole range of strategies to distance his speaker and his audience from the events being described" (180). The cyclical pattern, Dubrow contends, reveals itself primarily in the connection between marriage and death, as Donne resolves some of the tensions implicit in the circumstances of the poem "by transforming death into one stage in a cyclical process of renewal." *Eclog* thereby achieves "Donne's own aim of rescuing the couple themselves from the death of their reputations" (182).

Dubrow then suggests that Donne accomplishes his strategy of distancing, first, by a blatant and extensive use of flattery that shows Donne to be "even more desperate about patronage than he had been a year earlier and hence more eager to scatter compliments as widely as possible" (183–84). Next, she maintains, Donne creates a more subtle kind of distancing by presenting a "tamed, controlled, and rechanneled" sexuality (184). Finally, Donne's strategy of distancing involves "playing up the church ceremony" and thereby "stressing that the church blesses this marriage and hence sanctions it" (186). In spite of Donne's attempts "to contain the fires ignited by this wedding, to turn a conflagration into a hearthside glow" (188), Dubrow states, he nevertheless "at several points in the poem . . . offers uncompromising criticisms of the couple" (189) and, in particular, uses numerology to censure the wedding (191).

Believing it no accident "that eleven stanzas, each consisting of eleven lines, comprise the poem" (191), Dubrow explains that "just as the number goes beyond the decalogue and hence represents sin, so the couple have gone beyond the decalogue, especially its seventh commandment, in committing their own sins" (192). Further, she argues that the numerology here "also involves an autobiographical reference: Donne is violating his own moral dictates in praising bride and groom" (192). In this context, Donne is "working out—which entails acting out—his relationship to the event" (194) in a way showing that "the main function of the eclogue is to express and embody the problems of courting a patron" (195). Dubrow asserts finally that the ambiguities and tensions found in *Eclog* "reflect the fact that Donne was pulled between the moral necessity to condemn the wedding and the financial necessity to praise it—and also, perhaps, between his desire to absent himself from the court and his urge to participate in courtly rituals, even morally dubious ones" (199–200).

Norbrook (1990, 18–19) describes *Eclog* as a decidedly "ambivalent" poem (18) and then compares Donne's relationship with Somerset to that of Samuel Daniel, who makes it clear in a letter that he thought Somerset's character worth defending. This comparison "brings out the complexity of the questions of agency and courtly discourse," says Norbrook, who concludes that "to speak of the discourse of power as something one had either to accept or to subvert *en bloc* is to overlook the degree to which that discourse could be refashioned by individual choices" (19).

Patterson (1990, 52–53, 59–60) discusses at length the so-called Addled Parliament, which she describes as an example of "that aspect of Jacobean culture that we have so far been unable to recuperate with adequate sensitivity, when the rules of public and private behavior were under major strain, and everyone had to make, as it were, a separate treaty with circumstances" (60). Reading *Eclog* within this larger context, she contends that the poem "provides the most sharply delineated version in Donne's work of that formally divided self to which he apparently had recourse when attempting to deal with ambivalence, here personified as Idios ('one's own,' 'pertaining to one's self') and Allophanes ('appearing otherwise,' or, perhaps, 'the face of the Other')" (52).

Headnote *Allophanes* **GRIERSON** (1912): probably Sir Robert Ker, later Earl of Ancrum, to whom Donne wrote concerning the Essex divorce and who was, like Donne, a protégé of Somerset. The word suggests "seeming like another" or "having another's name," the "other" being Somerset himself (who was also named Robert Ker or Carr) (2:94). **SHAWCROSS** (1967a): the name means "having another sound" or "sounding like another" (178). **SMITH** (1971): having the appearance of another (458). **MILGATE** (1978): Ker was also kin to Somerset (118). **DUBROW** (1988): "an alternative side of Idios, an alter ego [who] stands for the attraction to the court that motivated so many of Donne's actions" (211).

Headnote *Idios* **GRIERSON** (1912): Donne himself, "the private man, who holds no place at Court" (2:94). **SHAWCROSS** (1967a): the word means "proper" or "peculiar" and thus "a private or ignorant person" (cf. l. 91) (178).

Headnote his Absence from Court **MILGATE** (1978): on Donne's illness, cf. l. 39 (118).

1–104 *Vnseasonable man . . . some sacrifice*. **GRIERSON** (1912): "The *Eclogue* introducing the Somerset *Epithalamion* is Donne's only experiment in this favourite convention" (2:lvii). **GRANSDEN** (1954) finds these lines and the concluding dialogue of Idios and Allophanes (ll. 226–35) inherently ironic because of Donne's attempt to procure a position at Court (113–15). **ELLRODT** (1960a): in 1613 the pastoral mode was at its highest popularity at Court since 1603. Though Donne was a leader rather than a follower, he here is surprisingly in accord with Court taste. The extreme flattery is directed both at Somerset and at the Court, but, fortunately, the poet is more honest than the man in that this eclogue constitutes both a critique of pastoral illusionism and a personal confession of Donne's sense of exile from the center of life and honor and his uncertainty about the relative claims of the active and the contemplative lives (2:175).

1 *Vnseasonable* **SULLENS** (1964): predates the earliest use of the word with this meaning in the *OED*, I. transf. 1722 (241).

5 *Courage* **SHAWCROSS** (1967a): "sexual desire" (178). **MILGATE** (1978): "'Natures instinct'" (118).

6 *numerous* **SULLENS** (1964): predates the earliest use of the word with this meaning in the *OED*, I. b. 1647 (225).

6 *fleets* **GROSART** (1872–73): cf. Marvell's usage in *The Unfortunate Lover* (1:272). **GROSART** (1872): a "fleet" is "a nautical phrase applied to a flock of sea and sea-swimming birds" (135).

7–12 *What delicacy . . . sweete murmure lost?* **GOSSE** (1899): "an ingenious description of a winter landscape" (2:31).

8 *Flora* **SHAWCROSS** (1967a): "goddess of flowers" (178).

8 *buff* **SMITH** (1971) (reading "freeze"): both "a bare coarse cloth" and "frozen" (459).

8 *Ierkin* **SULLENS** (1964) (reading "jerkin"): not recorded in the *OED* (261).

8 *weare* **SULLENS** (1964): predates the earliest use of the word with this meaning in the *OED*, v.[1] I, 1 fig. 1697 (243).

9 *stripp* **SULLENS** (1964) (reading "strip"): predates the earliest use of the word with this meaning in the *OED*, v.[1] I. 6. 1697 (236).

12 *Haue taken* **GROSART** (1872–73) accepts this reading (from the edition of 1633) as preferable to the "colloquial and irregular" construction "having taken" found in his copy-text, the edition of 1699 (1:272).

14 *in Lent.* **MILGATE** (1978): "not in this Christmas season" (118).

15–19 *At Court the Spring . . . like heauens two great lights* **MILGATE** (1978), referring to his own punctuation of the lines (which follows the edition of 1635), says this pointing clarifies the sense that "it is not the sun that brings spring to the Court, but Somerset's loyal zeal and his love for his bride, both springing from the 'light' of the Prince's favour" (118).

16 *The Sunne* **SMITH** (1971): "the king" (459).

21–22 *And then that early light . . . created were)* **SMITH** (1971): "God ordained light on the first day of the creation, but set the sun and moon in place on the fourth day. The light that precedes sun and moon here is the king himself, or his favour" (459). **MILGATE** (1978) (citing his own [1978] note to *FirAn* 202): biblical commentators had difficulty in rationalizing the apparent discrepancy between Genesis 1.3 and 1.14–19 (118).

23–32 *The Princes fauour . . . and good desire.* **JOHNSON** (1779) enters these lines directly beneath his subheading "The poetical propagation of light," but perhaps intends them further to illustrate the proposition stated just previously in his essay that the metaphysical poets' "thoughts and expressions were sometimes grossly absurd, and such as no figures or license can reconcile to the understanding" (1:62).

24 *From which all fortunes names and natures fall.* **SMITH** (1971): "The king's favour creates a world as God created the world at first, giving things their fortunes, titles and distinctive characters" (459). **MILGATE** (1978): by creating noblemen,

the King creates "more elevated 'natures', as well as names (in the peerage) and wealth. 'God made light first, that his other works might appear' (*Sermons* 2:240)" (118–19).

25–29 *Then from those wombes . . . other Ladyes eyes* **RUGOFF** (1939): "This is one of the figures which Samuel Johnson used in his life of Cowley to illustrate the so-called 'metaphysical' conceit. Considering the ornate artificiality of the figure, it is not hard to understand why Johnson could introduce it with the words, 'Their thoughts and expressions were sometimes grossly absurd, and such as no figures or licence can reconcile to the understanding,' but it is very significant concerning his entire approach to Donne that he chose to deal with one of the most affected of the poet's images as if it were typical" (197). **MILGATE** (1978) cites his own note to *EpEliz* 31 (119).

26–32 *At every Glaunce . . . and good desire*. **GOSSE** (1899): "Donne's ideas at this time were greatly set upon court functions, and he expatiates in graceful conceits about the charms of a life among the smiling faces of the great [quotes these lines]" (2:31–32).

27 *sowes* **SULLENS** (1964) (reading "sows"): the *OED* cites this as the earliest use (254).

27 *prevent* **SHAWCROSS** (1967a): "precede" (179). **SMITH** (1971): "outstrip, exceed" (459). **MILGATE** (1978): "exceed (*OED* v. 3. b). The bride's eyes assume some of the Creator's power in producing the firmament of fixed stars" (119). **BEWLEY** (1966): "anticipate" (156).

28 *the all-eyd firmament*. **COLERIDGE** (1800 [1957]) enters "'The all-ey'd Firmament' Donne—" in his notebook for February/March 1800 (1:1, entry no. 698).

28 *firmament*. **PATRIDES** (1985) (citing his note to *Fever* 24): "According to the Ptolemaic astronomy—increasingly obsolescent in Donne's time—the regions above the moon were regarded as *unchangeable* because incorruptible" (198, 65).

29–32 *First her eyes kindle . . . and good desire*. **DUBROW** (1988): the images of heat, light, and fire, which in his other court poetry connote disease and disorder, here testify to Donne's yielding to the pressures of patronage (201).

32 *good desire*. **HUNT** (1954): "Note the moralistic distinction implied by "*good* desire" (225).

34 *plotts*, **GRIERSON** (1912): a piece of ground; "here its meaning is only a little extended." Cf. *Metem*, l. 129: "a darke and foggie Plot" (2:94). **SMITH** (1971): both "places, corners," and "conspiracies" (459).

34 *fire without light* **GRIERSON** (1912): cf. *Sermons* 2:239: "Fool, saies Christ, this night they will fetch away thy soul; but he neither tells him, who they be that shall

fetch it, nor whither they shall carry it; he hath no light but lightnings; a sodain flash of horror first, and then he goes into fire without light"; cf. also *Sermons* 2:240: "This dark fire, which was not prepared for us" (2:94). **MILGATE** (1978): cf. *Paradise Lost* 1.63: "No light, but rather darkness visible" (119).

36 *artificiall)* **MILGATE** (1978): "by contrast to the warmth of loyal gratitude engendered by the natural 'light' of the King's favour" (119).

36 *heate.)* **MILGATE** (1978): cf. *Har*, l. 125 (119).

37–91 *Heere Zeale and Loue . . . ô Ignorant man?* **PARTRIDGE** (1978): the lines constitute a pastoral dialogue of "more substance" than what is suggested by Spenser's definition of eclogues in his Argument to *The Shepheardes Calender*—"extraordinary discourses of unnecessary matter." The dialogue between Idios and Allophanes "emulates the language of current Court masques, while retaining Spenser's blend of Platonism and Christian belief" (122). "The *Ecclogue* is not . . . a debate, but consonant poetry of praise, in which both speakers extravagantly extol divine right" (125).

37 *digest* **GROSART** (1872–73) (reading "disgest"): "separate in a reflective sense, tend to dissolve as things digested in a retort or in the stomach" (1:272). **SHAWCROSS** (1967a) (reading "disgest"): "discharge, send forth" (179). **SMITH** (1971): "disperse" (459). **PARTRIDGE** (1978) (reading "disgest"): this word, "with the opposite sense to *congest*, does not appear in the OED" (124).

39 *from thence?* **GROSART** (1872–73): "This reduplication is now a forbidden colloquialism" (1:272).

40–49 *As Heauen to men disposd . . . then a worldling can.* **PARTRIDGE** (1978): "Kings are the vicarious pattern of God; it behoves them to be generous, of their means and their capacity to make the narrow-minded more liberal, especially in feeling and comprehension. Kings, ideally, are religious hermits, who often know more of heaven's glory than wordlings" (124).

40 *to men disposd* **SMITH** (1971): "to men who are fitly disposed for heaven, or capable of apprehending it" (459).

40 *disposd* **GROSART** (1872–73): here and in line 62 used as in *LLL*, act 2, scene 1, to mean "disposed to be merry." Cf. Ben Jonson's A *Tale of a Tub*, act 4, scene 5, "where out of three uses, the second," like the example in *LLL*, "seems to show" this meaning (1:272). **MILGATE** (1978): "open, or receptive in attitude, to spiritual truth" (119); cf. *SecAn* 154 and *Sermons* 7:340: "'the Joy, and the sense of Salvation, which the pure in heart have here, is not a joy severed from the Joy of Heaven, but a Joy that begins in us here, and continues, and accompanies us thither'." Cf. *Sermons* 6:235–36; 7:71; 8:108 (160).

43 *full* **SMITH** (1971): "having all they want" (459). **PARTRIDGE** (1978): "abundantly supplied with means" (124).

44–49 *Kings (as theyr patterne God) . . . then a worldling can.* **MILGATE** (1978): "The 'correspondence' between the King in the State and God in the universe emerges in l. 22, and is further developed from l. 40. The argument is that God can enlarge the capacities of men to understand their blessings and know more of His glory as their blessings increase. Idios is able to share in festivities at Court, though absent from it, because the King has a similar power to enlarge his understanding of what it is like to be there" (119).

44 *patterne* **SMITH** (1971): "the origin of their authority and the model for the exercise of it" (459). **MILGATE** (1978): "God provides a 'paradigm' or analogy of the King's status, and a 'model' for the exercise of kingly power." Cf. *Sermons* 4:240–41; 8:115–17 (119).

46 *narrow* **SULLENS** (1964): predates the earliest use of the word with this meaning in the *OED*, a. and. sb. A. 4. b. and c. 1664 and 1657 (225).

47 *they* **SMITH** (1971): "the kings" (459).

48–52 *So reclus'd Hermits . . . neede no farther looke:* **COLERIDGE** (1809), in Essay XVI of *The Friend*, adapts these lines to illustrate his argument that "the first step to knowledge, or rather the previous condition of all insight into truth, is to dare commune with our very and permanent self" (1:115). **EMERSON** (1834 [1960–82]) (citing with variations Coleridge's adaptation): "a few wise instincts" (4:291).

48–49 *So reclus'd Hermits . . . then a worldling can.* **UL-HASAN** (1958): these lines exemplify enlightening, as opposed to neurotic, moods of withdrawal and seclusion in Donne's poetry, ones that bring "serenity and wisdom." Nevertheless the simile discloses that the poet "felt out of tune with his times." The repetition of the image of the hermit "bespeaks Donne's psychological aloofness from his age." Donne "felt lonely and was forced into seclusion by circumstance" (38).

48 *reclus'd* **MILGATE** (1978): although the *OED* cites this as the earliest example of this usage of the word, it had already been so used in *BedfRef* 17 (119).

49 *then* **PATRIDES** (1985): "than" (199).

50–55 *As man is of the world . . . am I then from Court?* **KAWASAKI** (1971): Idios "tries to justify his own unsociableness (and, at the same time, Donne's absence from his patron's wedding) by an overserious exposition of the microcosm philosophy" (39).

50–54 *As man is of the world . . . giue life to both* **PARTRIDGE** (1978): viewing the world emblematically, Donne is able to pretend that the country resembles the Court because "both are animated by the soul of peace" (124–25).

50–52 *As man is of the world . . . Of Creatures*, **ELLRODT** (1960a): in orthodox Christian theology, the concept of the "Book of Creatures" as a manifestation of divinity (by contrast with Scripture) is inadequate, and Donne is especially aware of this inadequacy—despite the apparent import of this passage. Donne's theology on this point, propounded in his essays and sermons, is clear and Calvinistic (1, ii:56). **SMITH** (1971): "As man is an epitome of the world, so man's heart is an epitome of God's book of creatures" (459). **MILGATE** (1978): "Man, the microcosm, is an epitome of the universe (the macrocosm); his heart is an epitome of God's book of creatures" (119); cf. *Essays* 30 and *Har* 110. See also W. Schleiner, *The Imagery of John Donne's Sermons* (1970), pp. 94–103 (119). **PARTRIDGE** (1978): the lines describe "the allegory of Creation, looking back to Plato's *Timaeus* and to the works of Philo Judaeus, the Platonist of Alexandria" (124).

53 *the Country of Courts*, **SMITH** (1971): "The country is an epitome of Courts" (459) [on the background of country/court debates, see Milgate (1967, 225–26)].

53 *sweete peace* **MILGATE** (1978): "A reference to James I's peace-making foreign policy"; cf. *Henry* 32–38 (120).

54 *owne common Soule*, **MILGATE** (1978) (reading "one common soule"): "Peace is in the soul of the King which 'animates' all his 'State' (ll. 41–2), country and Court alike" (120).

55–58 *Dreamer thou art. . . . in thy tast?* **MELTON** (1906): despite the omission of " East" (l. 57) from the early editions, the metrics of the entire passage demand the manuscript reading ("East-Indian") (178–79).

56–60 *Thinkst thou, fantastique . . . because thou seest no harme?* **PARTRIDGE** (1978): the images in Allophanes's three rhetorical questions recall the imagery found in emblem books of the period and Marcelline's *Triumphs of King James the First* (1610) (125).

57 *East India* **GRIERSON** (1912) (reading "East-Indian"): "It was the East-Indian fleet which brought spices, the West-Indian brought 'plate' i.e. gold or (more properly) silver, to which there is no reference here" (2:95).

57 *fleete*, **SULLENS** (1964): predates the earliest use of the word with this meaning in the *OED* (216).

58 *Amber* **GRIERSON** (1912): "'Ambergris' . . . was much used in old cookery, in which considerable importance was attached to scent as well as flavour" (2:95); cf. Milton, *Paradise Regained* 2.344 and Beaumont and Fletcher, *The Custom of the Country* 3.2 (2:95). Cf. also *Sermons* 3:359 (2:272). **PARTRIDGE** (1978): "derived, through Italian or Provençal, from M. Latin *ambar*, the ultimate source being Arabic *anbar*, meaning 'ambergris' ('grey amber'), a product of the sperm whale" (125).

59–60 *Because thou art not frozen . . . thou seest no harme?* **MELTON** (1906) cites these lines in the category "When Arsis-Thesis variations do not occur," subsection "Inverted Phrases" (202).

61–68 *The Earth doth in her inward Bowells . . . the vse of kings.* **GROSART** (1872–73) (citing ll. 62–63): "If this be a piece of mediaeval natural science, it is unknown to me" (1:272). **DUNCAN** (1942): Allophanes here argues the advantages of closer contact with the Court, using a figure that depends on "an alchemical doctrine regarding the natural generation of gold. . . . The alchemical practice of associating each metal with a particular planet" is the basis for the figure, which illustrates the influence of majesty (i.e., the sun) on "stuffe well dispos'd" (266). Both Paracelsus and "The Glory of the World"—an anonymous treatise found in the *Musaeum Hermeticum*—expound the theory, followed here by Donne, that metals are generated "in accordance with the Aristotelian theory of the condensation of sulphur and mercury vapors among the stones within the mountains of the earth." According to *The Hermetic Museum Restored and Enlarged* (London, 1893, 1:195–96), the excellence of a particular ore depends upon the quality of the stones and earth of its mountain, the consequent fineness of the vapor that condenses into sulphur and mercury, and the planets influencing that mountain; " 'mountains that are turned toward the sun have subtle stones and earth, and produce nothing but gold'." The sun thus "quite literally 'plays the alchemist.' As Donne applies the figure, the king becomes the alchemist-playing sun. The country, in which Idios is living in retirement, is like unto those less-favorably placed mountains in which only the baser metals may be procreated; while the denizens of the Court feel the full transmuting force of the 'tinctures' of 'wisdom, and honour from the use of kings'." This alchemical figure is characteristic of Donne's use of "the theoretical rather than the experimental or practical side of the science" (267) [similarly, though more simply, Mazzeo (1957, 108) and Carey (1981, 185)]. **ZUNDER** (1982): the solar imagery affirms the divine right of kings, like the Stuart masque or Louis XIV's use of the sun as his emblem (39–40). **ZUNDER** (1988): no limit is placed on royal authority, nor is any other source of authority acknowledged (93).

61–64 *The Earth . . . with his eye.* **SMITH** (1971): "In the qualitative physics all minerals aspired to the pure harmony of gold, but might attain it only if they were inherently well disposed and encountered some subliming power" (460). **MILGATE** (1978) (citing for comparison his note to *Mark* 23–25 on page 179 and *Paradise Lost* 3.583–86, 606–12; 6.478–81): the minerals should be "sufficiently near the surface of the earth to feel the influence of the sun" (120). **ZUNDER** (1988): "Just as, in contemporary chemistry, base metals underground need the sun's rays to be turned into gold, so the people need the practice of kingship in order to be truly civilised" (93).

62 *Stuff well disposd,* **PATRIDES** (1985): i.e., "certain minerals" (200).

64 *that heauen guild it with his eye.* **SHAWCROSS** (1967a): "Alchemy believed that the sun's rays changed elements in the earth to precious metals or jewels" (180). **SMITH** (1971): "(a) that the sun's rays transmute it to gold; (b) that God refines

earthy flesh to pure spirit; (c) that the king's favour elevates ordinary mortals to nobility" (460).

64 *heauen* **PATRIDES** (1985): i.e., "the sun" (200).

65–68 *As for diuine things . . . the vse of kings.* **PARTRIDGE** (1978): "As gold is produced in the bowels of the earth by the sun's rays, so divine things are argued to be tinctures of faith from higher powers, and so kings are the source of wisdom and honour" (125). **ZUNDER** (1988): "The people are passive, waiting for wisdom and honour in the way that, according to Protestant theology, they wait for the gift of faith from God" (93).

66 *tinctures* **BEWLEY** (1966): "principles causing modifications in things or persons" (157). **SHAWCROSS** (1967a): "active principles of any substance; roseate hues which alchemically symbolized resurrection or immortality"(180). **SMITH** (1971): "the pure quintessences of things" (460). **MILGATE** (1978): "purifying and ennobling forces. The 'tincture' was a spiritual quality in a substance, specifically in gold; through mortification and regeneration, or 'ripening,' gold could be refined into a tincture, which had the power to change other metals to itself" (120). **PARTRIDGE** (1978): "enigmatic principles that might be infused into material things, giving them a 'spirit' or soul" (125).

68 *the vse* **SMITH** (1971): "the nature, functions, customary practice" (460).

69 *vnbeguile* **MILGATE** (1978): "undeceive" (120).

70–72 *That Angels . . . to honest Actions come.* **THOREAU** (1840s [1964]) entered these lines in his Notebook (320). **MATSUURA** (1949): angels, "enfranchised of time and space . . . are essentially free from our human limits" (161).

70 *employd* **PATRIDES** (1985): i.e., "primarily as guardian angels" (200).

72 *abrode to honest Actions come.* **SMITH** (1971): "(a) acts honestly away from his home; (b) takes part in the honourable ceremonies of the world of public affairs" (460). **MILGATE** (1978): "rise to a place of honour in the performance of state duties" (120).

73–90 *Chide thy selfe . . . his Secrets rest.* **ZUNDER** (1982): although parallel statements in such passages as *BedfWrit* 27 and *Sal* 31–34 are poetically unconvincing, these lines have "animation" (though it is "somewhat forced") because Donne's assumptions about hierarchy are still vigorous (62). Nevertheless, Donne fails here to give voice to the conflicting impulses and obligations felt under such circumstances; cf. Kent's reprimand to Lear (*Lr.* 1.1.138–50), which is relevant to Somerset's ascendancy and therefore to *Eclog* (63–64).

74 *then* **PATRIDES** (1985): "than" (200).

74 *bewray*. **SHAWCROSS** (1967a): "reveal" (180). **SMITH** (1971): "disclose" (460).

75–84 *Hast thou a History . . . vnto which they all pretend?* **PARTRIDGE** (1978): the lines contain three more rhetorical questions. Sir Robert Ker (i.e., Allophanes) explains that the Court "has a history of unrivalled loyalty and unanimity on the concept of royal justice; . . . scandal is therefore a supererogation" (125).

75 *History* **BEWLEY** (1966): "a book of history" (157).

76–84 *where all . . . all pretend?* **NORBROOK** (1990): "The convoluted syntax in this passage, and the 'bend' and 'pretend,' seem almost to undermine the overt praise of the court's plain-dealing and openness" (18).

76–77 A *Court . . . that the kings are iust?* **UL-HASAN** (1958): the lines show that Donne despised the Court and considered courtiers deficient in character and the capacity for moral judgment (52).

76 *Affections* **SMITH** (1971): "motives, sentiments, wills" (460).

77 *and that the kings are iust?* **SMITH** (1971) (reading "and that, that King's are just?): "and in which that king's affections are just (as his choice of confidant is—see lines 89–90)" (460).

72–77 *that* **SHAWCROSS** (1967a) (reading "and that, that Kings are just?"): "a Court" (180).

78 *no Leuity to trust* **MILGATE** (1978): "neither frivolous nor foolish to trust others" (120).

78 *no Leuity* **PATRIDES** (1985): "not frivolous" (200).

83 *To them in him,* **GROSART** (1872–73): "the particular one favoured, the bridegroom" (1:272). **SMITH** (1971): "In favouring one he favours all, because he prospers what they all aspire to and seek to share in" (460).

83 *in him,* **MILGATE** (1978): "in anyone he favours; for example, Somerset. All share in the favour shown to any particular person, since the favours that he, in his turn, can then bestow are directed to virtue to which they all aspire" (120).

84 *Vertue* **PARTRIDGE** (1978): the glorification of "vertue" here is "specious" (125).

84 *pretend?* **SMITH** (1971): "aspire to" (460). **MILGATE** (1978): "lay claim, make pretension" (121).

85–90 *Thou hast no Such . . . his Secrets rest.* **GRIERSON** (1912): "What Donne says is: 'Here *was* all this,—a court such as I have described, and more—an earnest lover (viz. the Earl of Somerset), wise in love (when most men are foolish), and wise before, as is approved by the King's confidence. In being admitted to that breast Cupid has ceased to be a child, has attained his majority, and the right to administer his own affairs" (2:95). Cf. "*I love them that love me, &c* . . . . The Person that professes love in this place is Wisdom herself . . . so that *sapere et amare*, to be wise and to love, which perchance never met before nor since, are met in this text" (*Sermons* 1:238) and Herrick, *To Silvia to Wed*, lines 5–8: "Then, sweetest Silvia, let's no longer stay; / True love we know, precipitates delay. / Away with doubts, all scruples hence remove; / No man at one time can be wise and love" (2:95–96).

85–86 *Thou hast no Such: yet heere was this and more / An earnest Louer, wise, then, and before.* **GRIERSON** (1912), who follows the punctuation of the 1633 edition, placing a comma after "more" and a period after "before," points out that the later seventeenth-century editions confusingly place a period after "more," so that each line "concludes a sentence." He notes that Chambers (1896) connects line 86 with line 87 by placing a comma after "before," but argues that although this solution "looks ingenious," it leaves the passage without a clear meaning, as one cannot tell when Cupid was "wise," when he had been so before, or on what grounds Cupid is termed "an earnest lover" (2:95).

85 *Thou hast no Such:* **SMITH** (1971): "You cannot point to any such history, since there have been no other courts like this" (460).

86 *An earnest Louer, wise, then, and before* **GROSART** (1872–73): "The allusion is to the saying that one cannot love and be wise" (1:273). **BEWLEY** (1966): "the Earl of Somerset, wise both before he lost his heart, and after he had fallen in love with Frances Howard" (158). **SMITH** (1971): "The bridegroom is not an infatuated boy who is no more wise in marrying than he was in wooing" (460). **MILGATE** (1978): this "true lover" is "wise in love (where many men are foolish), and before he became a lover. The wisdom that earned him the king's confidence is shown equally in his love and marriage. . . . Cf. Erasmus, *Adagia* 476 E: 'Amare et sapere vix Deo conceditur'" (121). **PARTRIDGE** (1978) reads the wisdom of the "earnest lover" as "specious," and asserts that this "constitutes a defect in Donne's poetry of praise" (125).

87–90 *Our little Cupid . . . his Secrets rest.* **JOHNSON** (1928): "The traditional figure of Cupid is accepted by Donne, but his allusions invariably have an individual note" that differs from "the conventional treatment of the God of Love by the Court poets" (1100). **BEWLEY** (1966): "Cupid, dwelling in Somerset's breast, learns new wisdom from the proximity, ceases to be a child," and demands his inheritance (158). **MILGATE** (1978): "Cupid is no longer a minor but a grown man, and can now enter and take possession of the heart of a statesman. Love claims its rightful and lasting place in Somerset's breast, which had hitherto held only the confidences of the King"

(121). **PARTRIDGE** (1978): these lines constitute "unsavoury flattery of the King and his favorite" (125).

87 *Our little Cupid* **DUBROW** (1988): the epithet may suggest "fondness or condescension or both." The passage "effectively tames" Cupid; "sexuality becomes not an enemy of the court and its values but rather its pet" (203).

87 *su'd Lyvery* **GROSART** (1872–73): "Livery" means "release from wardship" (1:273). **CHAMBERS** (1896): "Land held by feudal tenure lapsed to the lord at the death of a tenant, until it was ascertained if the heir was of age; if so he took possession at once, on payment of a year's profits, known as *primer seisin*; if not, the estate remained in the lord's hands, as his guardian, until he became so, when he could claim *livery*, or *delivery*, *of wardship*, by suing for a writ of *ouster le main* and paying half a year's profits" (1:235). **SHAWCROSS** (1967a): "*sued*: pleaded for. Cupid, as a small boy, was usually depicted naked; livery indicates that he now is in the service of another (Somerset)" (180). **SMITH** (1971): "has sought service with a great man" (460). **MILGATE** (1978): in Donne's day the law cited by Chambers "applied specifically to tenants of the King (see J. Cowell, *The Interpreter*, 1607, s.v. 'Liverie', SS 3[r])" (121). **DUBROW** (1988): the readings proposed by Shawcross (1967a) and Milgate (1978) are both plausible because both "make Venus's son seem less menacing than readers . . . might otherwise assume. If Cupid is petitioning the legal system, he is not an opponent of society but rather a participant in it" (203). "Alternatively," if Cupid is clothed, then "the image is a literalized version of one way Donne defends the couple throughout the poem: here and elsewhere he suggests that the raw forces of sexuality choose to wear the vestments of society" (204).

88 *is no more in his Minority* **DUBROW** (1988): "He has traded the childish fecklessness and recklessness normally associated with him for adulthood . . . of legal rights and political responsibilities" (203–04).

89–90 *Hee is admitted now . . . his Secrets rest.* **SHAWCROSS** (1967a): "into the breast of Somerset, the King's confidant" (180).

90 *Where the Kings Counsells and his Secrets rest.* **MELTON** (1906): the stress on "the" is an instance in which an "insignificant" word is "stressed to meet the exigencies of rhythm and meaning," a practice Donne shares with Shakespeare, Jonson (who therefore had no right to tax Donne for failure to "keep accent"), Pope, Coleridge, Shelley, Poe, and Tennyson (65–66).

91 *lost,* **MILGATE** (1978): "by being absent from such a Court" (121).

91–95 *—I Knewe . . . Of his owne thoughts.* **DUBROW** (1988): "As this passage suggests, the pastoral world in this poem exemplifies the pathetic fallacy; its deathlike coldness and barrenness mime the mental landscape of Idios" (210).

92 *onely therefore* **SMITH** (1971): "for this reason only" (460).

93–96 *To knowe and feele . . . hauing no grace to say* **TUVE** (1947) finds that in these lines Donne achieves an effect of "*catachresis*" bordering on "*abusio*" (131–32).

93–95 *To knowe and feele . . . Of his owne thoughts*. **ELLRODT** (1987a): the lines bear witness to a characteristic preoccupation of Donne's esthetics, the preeminence of matter or "idea" over form or poetic expression (54).

95 *therefore* **SMITH** (1971): "for this following reason" (461).

96 *no grace to say* **MILGATE** (1978): "no thanks to utter" (121).

97 *I scap't not* **MILGATE** (1978): cf. "I think I shall not scape" in Donne's letter of 19 January 1614 (*Letters* 180–81) (121). **DUBROW** (1988): given the "ambiguities and tensions" of Donne's position, this is "one of the most revealing lines of the poem" (213).

98 *Full of the common Ioye* **JACKSON** (1970): "can be interpreted to mean the joy common to all who went to that feast" or "the joy common to all weddings regardless of special persons and circmstances" (139).

99–100 *was not made . . . mens harts to inuade* **JACKSON** (1970): may mean that the poem "was not designed for flattery but was rather sincere and genuine praise" or, "since what is written is so obviously equivocal and halfhearted, that anyone can see that the poet would gain no entrance to the court by having written it" (139).

101 *since* **SHAWCROSS** (1967a): "until" (181).

101 *dead and buryed*, **SMITH** (1971): "the state of men in the country, away from the Court" (461).

102 *might aduance my fame* **JACKSON** (1970): "it might—or might not" (139).

103–04 *So much as this poore song . . . some sacrifice*. **DUBROW** (1988): here as in lines 234–35 and elsewhere "the act of writing the poem is repeatedly described as sacerdotal" (205).

105–15 (st 1) *Thou art repriu'd Old yeare . . . or of this louing hart*. **DUBROW** (1988): the compliments to the couple, less playful but more fulsome than in the first stanza of *EpEliz*, may reflect both Donne's "increasing desperation" over obtaining a court appointment and his "distaste" for the wedding (202).

105 *repriu'd* **SULLENS** (1964): predates the earliest use of the word with this meaning in the *OED*, v. 4. fig. 1648 (230).

107 *fiue dayes* **MILGATE** (1978): "referring to the date of the marriage, 26 December" (121).

109 *Then* **PATRIDES** (1985): "than" (202).

110 *When hee doth . . . largest Circle runn.* **SMITH** (1971): "In northern skies the sun reaches the highest point of his largest circle, his summer solstice, in late June" (461).

111–12 *The passage of the West . . . theyr easy liquid Iaw* **CAREY** (1981): in connection with the concept of "melting," the lines "conjecture that if Frances Howard's 'enflaming eyes' or Somerset's 'loving heart' were transported to the frozen North, they would unstop the trans-Arctic trade routes." The image of a "gargantuan dripping mouth" was inspired not by Howard's eyes or Somerset's desire, but by Donne's need for a "pretext for writing about melting on a global scale" (176).

111 *The passage of the West or East* **MILGATE** (1978): "the North-West passage for ships round the north of the American continent, and the presumed passage to the north of Russia to the East Indies" (121).

113–15 *could a Promethean Art . . . of these inflaming eyes,* **JOHNSON** (1928): these lines illustrate both Donne's "analysis of the meaning of the myth" and his ability to arrive at "a synthetic conclusion as to its significance," to apply it "to the particular matter in hand" (1107).

113 *Promethean* **SHAWCROSS** (1967a): "referring to Prometheus, who stole fire from heaven and gave it to man" (181).

115 *The fire of these inflaming eyes, or of this louing hart.* **DUBROW** (1988): the refrains that close each stanza pay tribute to the couple's charms, but contain "a subterranean rebuke" of their illicit passion; however, the rhythm of the lines, which are fourteeners, subdues the effect of the rebuke (205). Thus, "on the prosodic level" the poem "attempts to contain the fires ignited by this wedding, to turn a conflagration into a hearthside glow" (206).

St 2, Heading Equality of Persons. **MILGATE** (1978): "Rochester was raised to the Earldom of Somerset just before the marriage, so that he would be equal in rank to his bride" (122).

116–26 (st 2) *But vndiscerning Muse . . . and both the Loving hart.* **McPEEK** (1939): a possible source is Catullus, *Carmen* 61, ll. 196–99 and 176–78. "Here Donne insists on the comparable beauty of both bride and groom, and on their mutual ardor, motifs reminiscent of . . . [*Carmen* 61] not hitherto expressed in English verse" (209).

116 *vndiscerning Muse,* **JOHNSON** (1928): "Donne adopts toward his Muse the critical attitude of the familiar friend" (1102).

120–24 *Bee tryd by beauty . . . Becomes a man;* **SHAWCROSS** (1967a): "The lines denote that Somerset is handsome and Frances courageous" (182).

120 *Bee tryd* **SHAWCROSS** (1967a): "if these hearts or eyes are tested (or compared)" (182).

120 *than* **PATRIDES** (1985): "then" (202).

121 *The Bridegrome is a Mayd and not a man.* **GROSART** (1872–73) (citing also ll. 142 and 222): these lines "remind us that the plea of divorce being that she forcedly remained a virgin, she was married as a virgin-bride, with 'untrimmed locks,' that is with loose and flowing hair" (1:272).

121 *Mayd* **MILGATE** (1978): "i.e. if judged for his beauty" (122).

122–24 *If by that manly Courage . . . chance or enuyes Art* **NORTON** (1895): the lines allude to popular attitudes towards the marriage (1:238).

122 *Courage* **SHAWCROSS** (1967a): "sexual desire" (178).

123–24 *Which scornes vniust opinion . . . chance or enuyes Art* **SMITH** (1971): "The circumstances of this marriage gave ample scope to scandalmongers" (461). **MILGATE** (1978): Donne blames the scandal on envious persons (122).

126 *Since both haue both th'enflaming eyes,* **GRIERSON** (1912): the second "both" is "the reading of all the MSS." and its omission in the seventeenth-century editions ruins the meter; expansion of the contracted "th'enflaming" in the editions of 1635–1669 is an effort to compensate for this damage. "Both th'enflaming eyes," moreover, is "a Donnean device for emphasis. He has spoken of *her* flaming eyes, and now that he identifies the lovers, that identity must be complete. Both the eyes of both are lit with the same flame, both their hearts kindled at the same fire." Cf. the mention in line 225 of "foure enflaming eyes" (2:96).

127 *diuorce* **MILGATE** (1978): "In the circumstances, a rather daring use of the word" (122).

129 *Yet let* **GRIERSON** (1912): although the seventeenth-century editions read only "Let," "Yet let" appears in manuscripts and it "improves both the sense and the metre." "Yet" was probably mistaken as a duplication of "let" and dropped from the editions (2:96).

129 *contemplate* **SMITH** (1971): "stress falls on the second syllable" (461).

131–32 *How thou prevent'st . . . horses dost outrunn* **GROSART** (1872–73): cf. lines 160 and 172 and "the opening of" *EpLin*; all "have greater point and appropriateness when we remember the customs of the period. In more than one old play the people rise before sunrise to be ready for a bridal; and in one the father is surprised" that the girls are not up; but "not surprised when from their absence he supposes that they rose before him, and slipped off to church" (1:273). **ELLRODT** (1960a): the lines show how Donne, when he uses classical imagery, infuses it with the vigor and color of a completely new metaphor (2:174–75). **MILGATE** (1978): cf. *EpEliz* 29 (122).

131 *preven'tst* **SHAWCROSS** (1967a): "surpass" (182). **SMITH** (1971): "anticipate" (461).

133 *How (hauing layd downe in thy Soueraignes brest* **MILGATE** (1978): i.e., "having confided to the care of the King" (122).

133 *brest* **SMITH** (1971): "confidential care" (461).

134–35 *reinvest / Them,* **SMITH** (1971): "take them up again" (461). **MILGATE** (1978): "reclothe yourself in them (as in clothes 'laid downe'); i.e. take up your responsibilities again" (122).

135 *forward* **MILGATE** (1978): "eager" (122).

136 *doth the like empart* **SMITH** (1971): "kindles a like fire in you" (461).

138–48 (st 4) *But now to thee (fayre Bride) . . . to him thy louing hart.* **McPEEK** (1939): the stanza influences stanza 1 of Herrick's *Nuptiall Song, or Epithalamie on, Sir Clipseby Crew and his Lady* (229, 373).

141 *allow* **SULLENS** (1964): predates the earliest use of the word with this meaning in the *OED*, v. 16, 1663 (208).

142–45 *Powder thy radiant hayre . . . wouldst bee Phaeton.* **DUBROW** (1988): "It is surely no accident that ashes are traditionally associated with penitence. This passage subtly but unmistakably warns the bride that only repentance will preserve her from danger: she must control her passions (and also, perhaps, beware of her desire to be too close to powerful members of the court) lest she be destroyed as tragically as that arrogant young astronaut Phaëton" (208).

142 *Powder thy radiant hayre* See **GROSART** (1872–73) above on line 121. **SMITH** (1971): "Brides commonly powdered their hair for the wedding day"; cf. Webster, *The White Devil* 5.3.117–18 (461). **MILGATE** (1978): "Powdering the hair had only recently become fashionable" (122).

144–45 *Thou . . . wouldst bee Phaeton.* **GROSART** (1872–73) (glossing "bee Phaeton"): "and scorch them" (1:273). **NORTON** (1895): she would scorch those who looked on her (1:237). **BEWLEY** (1966): "The sunlike radiance of Frances Howard's hair, unless dimmed by powder, will scorch her admirers. The ensuing images follow this line" (160).

144, 188 *to all that come to looke vpon . . . For every part to dance and revells goes* **DUBROW** (1988): the lines present members of the community in terms so vague as to "play down the presence of the personages they ostensibly evoke" (207).

145 *Phæbus*, **SHAWCROSS** (1967a): "the son [sic] (Somerset)" (182). **SMITH** (1971): "Apollo the giver of light" (461). **PATRIDES** (1985): Helios, the father of Phaeton (204).

145 *Phaeton*. **BEWLEY** (1966): "Apollo's son, who being unable to manage his father's horses, scorched the earth by driving the sun-chariot too near" (160).

146–50 *For our ease giue thine eyes . . . the sunn in water see;* **DUBROW** (1988): the bride is "radiant . . . like the Idea that cave dwellers [in Plato's *Republic* 7.515–16] would find it difficult to look upon," but also capable of blinding the gazer. The passage implies that it is dangerous to be near Frances Howard (206).

147 *So quenchd* **MILGATE** (1978): "the fire in your eyes thus quenched" (123).

149–50 *Thus thou discendst. . . the sunn in water see;* **SHARP** (1940): the conceit found in Dryden's *Astrea Redux*, ll. 61–62—"That Sun, which we beheld with couz'ned eyes / Within the Water, mov'd along the Skies"—"probably" echoes these lines (181).

149 *Thus* **MILGATE** (1978): "by the powder in her hair (l. 142) and more especially by the tear of joy" (123).

149 *our Infirmity,* **SMITH** (1971): "We cannot look upon the sun directly" (462).

150 *Who can the sunn in water see;* **GROSART** (1872–73): the manuscript reading "winter" is preferable: "line 152 'cloud'st' shows Winter to be the true reading, because the thought [sic]. It is no question of non-viewing the direct splendour of the sun" (1:273). **GRIERSON** (1912), noting that Lowell (1895) employs a semicolon after "see" (as here) and that Chambers (1896) cites the manuscript reading "winter" (for "water"), thinks that both have misapprehended the reference of the line. "Water," he says, continues the sense of "Teare" (l. 147) from the previous stanza, and "the opening of a stanza with two lines which in thought belong to the previous one is not unprecedented in Donne's poems." Grierson cites *ValName* st 6 and his note to it, further finding that Dryden—in *Eleonora*, ll. 134–39—has borrowed Donne's image (2:96). **MILGATE** (1978): cf. Plato, *Republic* 7.514 ff., where one who had emerged from a cave would progressively become accustomed to looking at reflections in water and then the sun itself (123).

150 *see;* **SHAWCROSS** (1967a): i.e., "reflected, for we cannot look directly without being blinded" (183).

154 *fruites of wormes and dust.* **SHAWCROSS** (1967a): "silk and gold" (183).

156 *Yet Starrs ar not so pure as theyr Spheares ar* **GRIERSON** (1912): the spheres are crystalline; each planet is fixed in one (2:97). **SMITH** (1971): both stars and the

spheres in which they were thought to rotate were sometimes thought of as being composed of grosser and purer quantities of the same substance (462). **MILGATE** (1978): "Though usually thought to be of the same substance, the spheres in which the stars were fixed, and in which they rotated, were purer (less 'mixed') in composition, the crystalline sphere especially so. 'We take a Star to be the thickest, and so the impurest, and ignoblest part of that sphear; and yet, by the illustration of the Sun, it becomes a glorious star' (*Sermons* 4:83)" (123).

157–59 *And though thou stoope . . . within his louing hart*. **MILGATE** (1978): "Though she deigns to show herself to us in a way accommodated to our limited perceptions, her full glory is conveyed through her eyes to form the image of her imprinted on Somerset's heart"; cf. *ElPict* 2 (123).

157 *stoope* **SMITH** (1971): "condescend to the level of our senses and understanding" (462). **MILGATE** (1978): "might condescend" (123).

157 *in part,* **SMITH** (1971): "as much as we are capable of gazing on, and understanding" (462).

158–59 *Still in that picture . . . within his louing hart*. **GILMAN** (1986): here, as elsewhere in Donne, the reflection of the lovers in each other's eyes and the safekeeping of those pictures in their hearts are "virtually sacred emblems of fidelity" (86).

158 *entirely* **SMITH** (1971): "the whole, her qualities at full" (462).

160–70 (st 6) *Now from your Easts . . . by Angels eye or heart*. **GOSSE** (1899): the stanza is an example of the qualities for which the poem as a whole is admirable (2:32) [see General Commentary above]. **FOWLER** (1970): the lovers' "triumphant renewal of the old sun's life after the last 5 days of the year is mimed formally in the sixth and central stanza-day, when it is the new sun of the lovers that rises" (71–72). Furthermore, "each of the first 5 stanzas has a refrain mentioning the 'inflaming eyes' of the lovers, whereas none of the second 5 has" so that "out of 2 groups of 5 stanzas comes the higher unity of the last, which is concerned with the one flesh . . . . This 10 + 1 pattern of stanzas is replicated microcosmically by the metrical pattern of individual stanzas" (72). An additional instance of complex symmetry occurs in the stanza titles (107).

160–65 *Now from your Easts . . . thenceforth one*. **ELLRODT** (1960a): the lines instance the precise observation of nature that (in this poem) becomes a mental trait. The illusion of two suns as seen through a cypress, the illusion that the bride and bridegroom are two, is destroyed when the two are resolved into one (2:175).

160–62 *Now from your Easts . . . do thinke it two)* **MILGATE** (1978): "I have not found any reference to this optical illusion in writers on optics or elsewhere. In *Biathanatos* [pp. 109–10], Donne refers to Pliny's account (*Nat. Hist.* II. 31) of the sighting of several suns at an angle to the real sun 'either at sunrise or sunset'" (123).

160 *Now from your Easts* **BEWLEY** (1966): "Since Somerset and his new countess are both compared to the sun, each one rises from his respective East to meet at the church" (161).

160 *Easts* **SULLENS** (1964): this use not recorded in the *OED* (258).

161 *Cypresse* **GROSART** (1872–73): "crape" (1:273). **CHAMBERS** (1896): "a crape veil" (1:235). **BEWLEY** (1966): "Donne apparently means that the sun, veiled behind the foliage of a tree, appears to be larger because the leaves disperse its light" (161). **MILGATE** (1978): "can mean crepe cloth; or the tree, whose foliage can also be thought of as a veil (l. 164)" (123). **CAREY** (1990): "fine, semi-transparent cloth" (469).

164 *that vayle* **SMITH** (1971): "the impediment of our sight, by which we see them as two distinct beings" (462).

166–67 *The Church Triumphant . . . the Militant doth striue no more*. **CAREY** (1981): the lines imply "that the Archbishop of Canterbury, the Bishop of London, and the three doctors of law among the commissioners who had voted, with them, against the divorce, were vainly attempting to circumvent the will of heaven" (87).

166 *The Church Triumphant* **MILGATE** (1978): it is invoked "because marriages are 'made by God in Heaven'" (*Sermons* 3:249) (124).

166 *Triumphant* **PATRIDES** (1985): "celestial" (205).

167 *And now . . . striue no more*. **GROSART** (1872–73): "refers to the differences of opinion among those who tried the case of divorce" (1:272). **SMITH** (1971): "The Church Militant, champion of the faith and moral law, now has no office here since these two people are made one by a sacrament of the Church" (462). **MILGATE** (1978): "In the special Court of Delegates commissioned by the King to consider [the Countess of Essex's] petition for divorce, Archbishop Abbot and John King, Bishop of London, with three out of five doctors of law, gave judgement against the divorce, but they were outvoted seven against five by other Bishops and two doctors of law who judged in favour" (124).

167 *Militant* **PATRIDES** (1985): "earthly" (205).

169 *Dictates* **SULLENS** (1964): the *OED* cites this as the earliest use (245). **SHAWCROSS** (1967a): "authoritative powers as clergyman" (183).

171 *Blest payre of Swanns*, **McPEEK** (1939): "an image taken from [Spenser's] *Prothalamion*" (367). **TUFTE** (1970): the phrase "calls to mind death, and wisdom grown 'stale'" (229). **SMITH** (1971): "emblems of purity and nobility" (462).

171 *enter-bring* **MILGATE** (1978) (reading "interbring"): "bring to each other. This use of the verb is the only example recorded in *O.E.D.*, s.v. 'inter-'; the word is possibly a coinage of Donne's own." (124). **CAREY** (1981) (reading "interbring"): the word illuminates Donne's fondness for neologisms that use the prefix "inter-": "The mutual action, given and received, is like the balm which passes between the lovers' clasped hands, or like their threaded eyebeams [in *Ecst*]. It bonds by interchange; and in that respect it resembles the returned love which Donne keeps seeking in the poems as a match for his own—'So thy love may be my loves spheare.' The imaginative habit, regulating Donne's choice of prefix and type of coinage, is determined ultimately by emotional need. The subtle embrace of action and passivity within a single verb satisfies him, because it helps to order his world, rescuing it from 'fragmentary rubbidge' (as he called it in *The Second Anniversarie*) and suffusing it with unity and mutuality" (270).

172 *never sing.* **GROSART** (1872–73): "and therefore never die; the allusion being to the myth that swans sing [only] before they die" (1:273). **MILGATE** (1978): cf. *FirAn* 407–08 (124).

173 *grounds of* **SHAWCROSS** (1967a): "foundations, bases (for)" (184). **MILGATE** (1978): "reasons for; until all their wishes are fulfilled" (124).

177–79 *Rayse heyres . . . and nothing Art.* **GRIERSON** (1912)—noting that his copy-text, the edition of 1633 (A), has a comma at the end of each of the last five lines of the stanza and that the editions of 1635–1669 introduce a period after "give" in line 178—alters the punctuation of A by inserting a period after "Art" at the end of line 179 (as here). This pointing, he argues, clarifies the "force" and "connexion" of line 179: "It seems to me that this line must go with what precedes. The force of 'may' is carried on to 'do all': '. . . may here, to the worlds end, live / Heires from this King, to take thanks, you, to give, / Nature and grace doe all and nothing Art.'" Grierson then paraphrases: "May there always be heirs of James to receive thanks, of you two to give; and may this mutual relation owe everything to nature and grace, the goodness of your descendants, the grace of the king, nothing to art, to policy and flattery" (2:97). **SHAWCROSS** (1967a): "Nature (the raising of children) and grace (virtues such as of a king) accomplish all things; art (artifice and craft) achieves nothing" (184). **SMITH** (1971): "And in this continuing interchange of benefits and courtesies may everything be the natural and gracious outcome of the relationship itself, and may nothing be due to crafty self-interest and policy" (462).

177–78 *Rayse heyres . . . yours, to giue.* **DUBROW** (1988): "The syntax is knotty, but the main point seems to be that the heirs of the couple will serve those of the king" (204); the passage deflects attention from the delicate question of the bride's sexuality (204–05).

178 *yours, to giue.* **PATRIDES** (1985) (reading "you, to give"): "which you are to give" (205).

179 *Art.* **CAREY** (1990): "shady dealing; artfulness" (470).

180–81 *May never Age . . . this hart.* **LEWES** (1838) (reading "May never age nor error overthwart / *With any West those radiant eyes—with any North this heart,*") calls this "a fine Shaksperian conceit" (376).

180 *ouerthwart* **SMITH** (1971): "place counter to" (462). **MILGATE** (1978): "obstruct" (124).

181 *West . . . North* **SHAWCROSS** (1967a): "The West symbolized decline; the North, coldness" (184) [so also **SMITH** (1971), who adds that they also suggest, respectively, "fading" and "barrenness" (463)]. **MILGATE** (1978): cf. *GoodM* 18 (124).

181 *radiant* **SULLENS** (1964): predates the earliest use of the word with this meaning in the *OED*, 1. c. 1794 (228).

182–92 (st 8) *But you are overblest . . . a Center to this hart.* **McPEEK** (1939): the stanza recalls Chapman's *Epithalamion Teratos*, ll. 37–46 (367).

182–85 *plenty this day . . . destroy all fowle and beast* **DUBROW** (1988): "These lines may be playful, but they also hint at a negative judgment on the lavishly expensive festivities." The excesses of gluttony recall the couple's other excesses, "and perhaps, too, those of the poet when he bestows hyperbolic praise" (209).

182 *overblest,* **SULLENS** (1964) (reading "over–blest"): a combination in Donne which the *OED* does not record (205). **MILGATE** (1978): "The festivities are too lavish, delaying the consummation of the marriage"; cf. *EpEliz* st 5 (124).

184 *grone,* **SULLENS** (1964): predates the earliest use of the word with this meaning in the *OED*, v. 4. b. 1697. "Donne's exact expression, 'The tables groan,' is found in a quotation dated 1764" (218).

185 *floud,* **PATRIDES** (1985): i.e., Noah's flood (206).

186–89 *And, were the doctrine new . . . and fall not where they rose.* **JOHNSON** (1928): the allusion here indicates that Donne "has investigated and is familiar with the Copernican theory of the universe" (1103) [similarly, **SMITH** (1971, 463)]. **COFFIN** (1937): these lines show "the levity of the poet playing with one of the common arguments against the motion of the earth and the familiarity with the matter which makes this levity possible" (113). **MILGATE** (1978): "The idea that the earth rotated was first proposed by Aristarchus of Samos (and was therefore hardly 'new') . . . . The popular objection to the notion was that if the earth 'moved', one would not be able to jump up, and land in the same place—an objection to which Copernicus made a careful reply" (124). **CAREY** (1981): although elsewhere (e.g., in his 1609 letter to Goodyer [see *Letters* 61–64]) Donne seems to accept the Copernican theory of the cosmos, in these lines he apparently subscribes to the Ptolemaic view (249). Donne here presents a "Du Bartasian picture" of what would happen as a result of the earth's rotation—people jumping up but landing in a place other than where they started—"for the sake of its liveliness." Whether Donne seriously supported one theory or the other is immaterial; "as with other scientific ideas, he could accommodate them or not as the fancy took him" (250).

188–92 *For every part to dance . . . a Center to this hart.* **LEWES** (1838), following his characterization of ll. 180–81 (see above), cites these lines (with slight variations in the wording) without comment, except a note to l. 190 (see below) (376).

189 *fall not where they rose.* **SMITH** (1971): "as the sun or other cosmic bodies, whose dance of joy these revellers reproduce" (463). **PATRIDES** (1985): "i.e., because of the earth's rotation!" (206).

190 *Though sixe howers since the Sun to bedd did part* **LEWES** (1838): "Their notion of *late* hours is rather different from ours" (376).

190 *part* **MILGATE** (1978): "depart" (125).

191 *Masques* **SHAWCROSS** (1967a): "both masks for the eyes and entertainments" (184).

192 *Center* **MATSUURA** (1949): " 'the earth,' i.e. the bride, around which the bridegroom, compared to the sun, is to turn, i.e. in embrace" (131). **SMITH** (1971): "a single focus, the centre of a planet's orbit"; cf. *SunRis* 30 (463). **MILGATE** (1978): "the centre of the planetary system" (125).

192 *hart.* **MILGATE** (1978): "the unified heart of the couple" (125).

193–95 *What means't thou, Bride . . . when th'art layd, doe so.* **DUBROW** (1988): "On a very subterranean level the passage acknowledges one tension associated with this wedding: it posits a clash between the demands of society, of 'companie,' on the one hand and the demands of sexuality on the other. But of course Donne is reversing the way that tension actually functioned in the events behind that marriage: he suggests that Frances Howard is prone to fulfill her social duties at the expense of her sexual drives, and not vice versa. Thus the passage serves to obfuscate and even deny her actual behavior" (204).

200–01 *Rise in one point . . . fayre Bride, depart* **GRIERSON** (1912): a semicolon is preferable to a period at the end of line 200 because the thought of line 201 "is an immediate inference" from what precedes. The sense is "You rose at the same hour this morning, but you (the bride) must go first to bed" (2:97).

200 *Rise in one point . . . not sett so too* **SHAWCROSS** (1967a): "If you both rise to leave, you will not leave the banquet hall together; you, the moon, must precede him, the sun" (184).

200 *point*, **PATRIDES** (1985): "i.e., of time" (207).

202–03 *Th'art not gon . . . thy louing hart.* **LEWES** (1838): "His idea of absence being love-peopled . . . is eminently poetical" (376). **EMERSON** (1841) in his essay "Love" quotes these lines (144) and in a subsequent anthology (1875) includes them as an extract under the heading "Love" (62). **FIELDS and WHIPPLE** (1878) include these lines under the heading "Conjugal Affection" (142).

204–07 *As hee that sees a Starr fall . . . and finds her such.* **McPEEK** (1939) cites these lines as an instance of how "the poem is marred by the author's attempt to justify the marriage and by difficult conceits" (367). **JACKSON** (1970): "How could this fallen star fail to suggest to anyone at court not only its coarse erotic meaning but also the unsavory character of the bride, her previous marriage, and the scandalous nullity suit just over?" (139–40). **CAREY** (1981): here Donne takes "furthest" the "device of substituting an inanimate object for part of the living situation in a love scene" (144). **PARFITT** (1989): the associations of the fall are complex. Conventional ideas of sex oblige a woman, "in Jonson's inelegant phrase, to 'fall upon her back'," possibly evoking associations with Eve, "and there is the suggestive decline of the sharp-edged autonomous star into the soft, amorphous, relatively undefined ('feminine') 'jelly'." This fall has in fact been anticipated, because in the previous stanza "the bride had become a feast for the groom—'Thyself must to him a new banquet grow'—this providing an elegant version of the brutal appetitiveness of the lyric 'Community'" (81). **PATTERSON** (1990) notes that the figure of a star become jelly appears in the Journal of the House of Commons for 14 May 1614: "'divers [are] taxed. as Stars of the last Parliament, now Jelly,'" and says that the lines reflect "an aspect of the Addled Parliament's semantics, an image of disintegration and the collapse of political integrity" (59).

204–05 *As hee that sees . . . a gelly in the place* **GROSART** (1872–73): "'gelly'=jelly. One of those popular beliefs which in all probability arose from a coincidence, some gelatinous matter having been found where an aerolite had buried itself and been lost, or where a star had seemingly fallen" (1:273). **GRIERSON** (1912) cites an analagous passage in Dryden's *The Spanish Friar* and asserts that Dryden probably borrowed the image from Donne for "more poetic or at least ambitious" use in the Dryden-Nathaniel Lee *Oedipus* (cites lines from act 2, scene 1) (2:97–98). **MILGATE** (1978): "The word 'jelly' was 'applied to the alga *Nostoc*, which appears as a jelly–like mass on dry soil after rain, and was popularly supposed to be the remains of a fallen "star" or meteor' (*O.E.D.*, 'jelly', 2. b)" (125). **CAREY** (1981): by "turning his bride into jelly" Donne conveys not only "her shivering apprehension," but also an "element of perplexity and disappointment" in the "bridegroom's feelings." The simile mingles "shock" with "a sense that this is not what he had anticipated, and that the girl, seen naked for the first time, is not the person he thought he knew," an "alienation effect comparable . . . to that of meeting friends in new clothes or unfamiliar fashions. The explanation is itself cleverly deadening. Since seeing a girl naked is like seeing someone in odd clothes, nakedness becomes as inert and separate as a garment. Further, by converting his bride into something as lifeless as jelly Donne conveys the bridegroom's fleeting impression that she is, in her nakedness, more wholly composed of flesh than he had quite taken into account" (144).

204 *As hee that sees a Starr fall, runns apace* **CHAMBERS** (1896): cf. *SG0* (1:235).

205–07 *a gelly . . . and finds her such.* **SMITH** (1971): "He finds something which has quite changed its appearance, having lost its brilliant external glitter and fire; also, perhaps, something chaste (gelid) or fear-struck, yet soft and yielding" (463).

205 *gelly* **SULLENS** (1964) (reading "jelly"): the *OED* cites this as the earliest use (249).

207 *such* **SHAWCROSS** (1967a): "that is, gone from the room" (185).

210–11 *Theyr Soules, though . . . never yet had seene.* **LE COMTE** (1965): "ignoring all rumors, outfacing them, indeed, . . . [Donne] carefully adheres to the Epithalamion tradition that the bride and groom's confrontation on their wedding night was their first" (144). **DUBROW** (1988): "the most outrageous lie of the poem" (204).

211 *These Clothes,* **GROSART** (1872–73): equivalent to "their bodies" (1:273). **SULLENS** (1964): this predates the earliest use of *clothes* with this meaning in the *OED*, sb. pl. 1 fig., 1655 (210). **MILGATE** (1978): i.e. "of the soul; 'this muddy vesture of decay' (*The Merchant of Venice*, V. i. 64)" (125).

215–25 (st. 11) *Now as in Tullias Tombe . . . and of 2 louing harts.* **McPEEK** (1939): "a poetic development of Jonson's lights that burn all night" (in the epithalamion concluding *The Hue and Cry after Cupid*) (367). **LE COMTE** (1969): "It would have been hard for any couple to deserve such poetry" (132).

215–16 *Now as in Tullias Tombe . . . for fifteene hundred yeere* **GROSART** (1872–73): cf. Browne, *Pseudodoxia Epidemica* I, iii, c. 21: "'Why some lamps included in close bodies have burned many hundred years, as that discovered in the sepulchre of Tullia, the sister of Cicero, and that of Olibius, many years after, near Padua?' The belief is supposed to have arisen from the taking fire of pent-up gases at the moment of opening" (1:273). **NORTON** (1895): the tomb was opened during the papacy of Paul III (1534–49); "it was said that an inscription in the tomb bore the words *Tulliolae filiae meae*, and it was supposed that the body was that of Tullia, often affectionately called Tulliola, the daughter (not the sister, as Sir Thomas Browne says) of Cicero. All that is known of the discovery of the tomb may be found in the *De Lucernis Antiquorum reconditis* of Licetus, 1653, and in the *De Lucernis sepulchralibus veterum* of Ottaviano Ferrari, 1670. Licetus was a believer in the perpetual fire of the lamp; but Ferrari sufficiently exposed the absurdity of the notion, and put a stop to the arguments of learned ignoramuses. The matter is discussed with good sense by Sir Kenelm Digby in his treatise *Of Bodies*, 1645, ch. VII [section 9]" (1:238–39). **GRIERSON** (1912) reiterates some of the information found in Norton (1895) and further cites John Lempriere, *Biblioteca Classica; or, A Classical Dictionary* (London, 1788, and many later eds.): "'The body of a woman was found [in the tomb], which was reduced to ashes as soon as touched; there was also a lamp burning, which was extinguished as soon as the air gained admission there, and which was supposed to have been lighted above 1500 years.'" (2:98). **ELLRODT** (1960a) (see General Commentary on the Epithalamions) cites the allusion to Tullia's tomb as an instance in which a classical figure is used to illustrate a concept rather than to move the reader esthetically (1, ii:157). **MILGATE** (1978) summarizes the glosses of previous annotators and adds: "The story was well known, but Donne would have found it in the work by Guido Panciroli which he certainly read [Milgate cites his notes to *Mark*], *Rerum Memorabilium* . . . , 1599, in the chapter 'De Oleo Combustibili'; see note to 'The Undertaking' in Gardner, *Elegies etc.* [1965], p. 180" (125). Cf. *Sermons* 3:357: "They had a precious composition for *lamps*, amongst the *ancients*, reserved especially for *Tombes*, which kept light for many hundreds of yeares; we have had *in our age* experience, in some casuall openings of ancient vaults, of finding such lights, as were kindled, (as appeared by their inscriptions) *fifteen* or *sixteen* hundred yeares before; but, as soon as that light comes to our light, it vanishes" (126).

219–20 *Fyre . . . turnes all to fyre* **MILGATE** (1978): "This common idea was attacked by J. C. Scaliger (*Exercitationes* . . ., p. 69)" (126).

219 *aspire* **SMITH** (1971): "seek to rise upwards" (463).

222 *none of them is fewell but fyre too*. See **GROSART** (1872–73) above on line 121. **SMITH** (1971): "Neither of them is merely fuel to the other's fire; both are themselves fire. Hence neither can reduce the other to ashes" (463).

223 *bonfire*, **MILGATE** (1978): "a fire lit in celebration of a festive occasion (e.g. a marriage)" (126).

225 *harts*. **LE COMTE** (1969): every preceding stanza ends with "heart," but the final stanza ends appropriately with "hearts," expressing the couple's union (132).

226–35 *As I haue brought . . . your deuotion*. See **GRANSDEN** (1954) above on ll. 1–104.

230 *of all*. **SMITH** (1971): "It belongs to all" (463). **MILGATE** (1978): "shared by all" (126).

234–35 *Back to the Court . . . prize your deuotion*. See **DUBROW** (1988) above on ll. 103–04.

235 *Such Altars* **SMITH** (1971): "Probably he proposes to lay the poem before the bridegroom, or the king himself" (463). **MILGATE** (1978): Donne's friend Robert Ker had access to Somerset (126).

Epitaphs and Inscriptions

Epitaphs and Inscriptions

General Commentary

An unsigned poem in the 1632 edition of Donne's sermon *Deaths Duell* (siglum 22a), differing only slightly (in l. 6) from the one signed "Edward Hyde" in the 1633 edition of Donne's poems, observes (ll. 5–8):

> The Epitaphs thou writt'st, have so bereft
> Our pens of wit, there's not one fancy left
> Enough to weepe thee, what henceforth we see
> Of Art and Nature, must result from thee.

Granqvist (1975, 131) alleges that although Alford (1839) claims to omit poems from his edition on the grounds that Donne's fondness for compression resulted in many disagreeable verses, Alford's real objection is to frank eroticism; Granqvist cites Alford's inclusion of epitaphs as evidence that he does not object to compression as such.

Milgate (1978, v–viii)—referring to the epitaphs for Elizabeth Drury, Robert Drury, Ann Donne, and the poet himself, as well as to the inscriptions in the Lincoln's Inn Bible and the *Album Amicorum*—says "these compositions occupy a position mid-way between prose and verse, and have relationships at some points with the poems" (v). (See also Milgate's comments recorded on p. 339 above.)

Ray (1986, 465) states that in two satiric poems in *Death in a New Dress: Or Sportive Funeral Elegies* the author (known only as S. F.) "evokes the memorial and commendatory poems, as well as the epitaphs, of Donne and Jonson."

Authorship and Circumstances of the Drury Epitaphs

Cullum (1784, 52–55) prints both Drury epitaphs for the first time, attributing them to Donne: "his connection with the family makes the supposition probable; and the singularity of the expression, 'Anno sui Jesu,' in both of these, and in his own written by himself, seems to confirm it" (55).

Sparrow (1949, 208), terming the epitaphs "interesting enough to deserve reprinting," endorses Cullum's (1784) attribution and presents the two epitaphs, along with the epitaphs on Donne's wife and on himself, as examples "of Donne's performance as a Latin epigraphist." However, Sparrow evaluates the possibility that Joseph Hall was the author, a possibility arising from the fact that Hall, like Donne, was a Drury protégé, having held the living of Hawstead, where the Drurys are interred in the parish church. Sparrow cites Jonson's *Conversations with Drummond* to the effect that Hall contributed verses on Elizabeth Drury that were included in the publication of *FirAn* (1611) and considers Hall's possible authorship of at least the Hawstead epitaph for her. He concludes that by 1615 Hall's connection with the Drurys had probably ceased, whereas Donne remained under Drury patronage until at least 1617 (the London site of Ann Donne's burial, he argues, points to the Donnes' having lived until that time in Drury House in the parish of St. Clement Danes). "Both epitaphs are from the same pen," Sparrow asserts; "therefore Donne is the more likely candidate for their authorship." Sparrow argues from internal evidence as well, terming the "epigrammatic style" of the Drury epitaphs, "with its strained antitheses ('sine remis, sine remoris') and conceits ('angelos aemulata,' &c) . . . strongly reminiscent of Donne. . . . [T]he phrase 'anno aetatis . . . et sui Jesu . . . ,' which occurs in both" and is not found in other epitaphs of the period, is "tantamount to a signature; for it is to be found in each of the three inscriptions known to be composed by him." "The case for Donne's authorship," Sparrow concludes, "is clinched by the following further indications: (1) the unusual 'secessit' occurring both in the epitaph of Elizabeth Drury and in that of Mrs. Donne; and (2) the collocation 'V ANTE FEBREM QUA CORREPTUS, ANNIS (IDQUE PERENNITER) EROGATA' in Sir Robert Drury's epitaph, which oddly resembles 'VII POST XII PARTUM (QUORUM VII SUPERSTANT) DIE IMMANI FEBRE CORREPTAE" in Mrs. Donne's."

Epitaph for Elizabeth Drury.

Commentary

Date and Circumstances

For discussion of the dates of Elizabeth Drury's death and burial, see the Textual Introduction to *EtED* and Notes and Glosses on line 20 below.

Cullum (1784, 53–54), prior to presenting the text of *EtED*, notes that the epitaph is inscribed "on a tablet of black marble" on a monument "in the south east corner of the chancel" at Hawstead Church and describes the monument in detail:

> It consists of a basement about 3 feet high, on which, under an ornamented arch, lies the figure of a young female large as life, her head reclining on her left hand; her mantle is drawn close about her neck, and edged with a small ruff; her hair is in many small and short curls, without any cap or covering; above is an emblematical female personage, surrounded with a glory, and scattering flowers on the figure below: on each side of the basement sits a greyhound, the cognizance of the family. This is a very pleasing monument, of painted alabaster, and well executed; only disgraced by an ugly death's head . . . , [which seems] not consistent with the spirit of Christianity . . . .

As noted above (p. 409), Cullum adduces both biographical and stylistic reasons for attributing the epitaph to Donne. Similarly Ford (1818, 273), who cites Cullum as his source of information, and Bald (1959, 68), who finds that in "design and execution the monument does not lack distinction"—its "worst feature," the "work of a provincial carver," is "the alabaster statue of Elizabeth herself"—and thinks the epitaph "almost certainly" composed by Donne.

Sparrow (1949, 208) suggests that the monument "is evidently based on the portrait preserved in the Cullum family" (the portrait is reproduced in Cullum [1784, facing p. 146] and in Bald [1959, facing p. 68]).

Milgate (1978, xxix–xxx, 212–13) speculates that Donne was invited to compose the epitaph in response to his having written *FunEl* (xxix–xxx); Milgate offers the following translation (212–13):

> Thou knowest not, wayfarer, whither thou goest. Thou hast come to the Cadiz of all men, even to thine own. Thou liest here thyself, if thou art virtuous; for indeed here lies Virtue herself, Elizabeth,—in that, as in beauty and innocence she had eagerly vied with the angels, she strove besides to excel them, nay even in this, that she lived sexlessly and wished on that account to restore to God an undefiled body, unimpaired as it was fashioned (an Eden without the serpent), not so much allured by

the splendours of that palace that she was banished from her true self, nor so much made a cloister for herself that she denied herself to company, nor for all her endowments of body or fortune less endowed in intellect, nor for all her skill in tongues the less able to hold her peace; neither weary of, nor pursuing, life or death she followed God her guide without straining oars or hindering delays, and reached this haven after almost 15 years—by erecting this monument to whom Robert Drury, Knight, and Anne his wife, stripped of their only daughter and thus of the very name of parents, vainly palliate their most grievous bereavement with the presence of some small fragment of their daughter (alas, utterly lost); she withdrew from the world in the tenth month of her fifteenth year, and in that of her Saviour 1610.

General Commentary

Ford (1818, 272–73) introduces his printing of the text of *EtED* (which is itself printed as a introduction to *FunEl*) by briefly identifying Elizabeth Drury, repeating the traditional stories that she "died from a box on the ear" given her by her father and that she was "destined to be the wife of Prince Henry," and noting that she was "immortalised by the muse of Donne" in the two Anniversaries (272). Ford quotes *FirAn* 447–51 and *SecAn* 244–46, noting that the latter lines have been "erroneously" presented as "a description of Donne's mistress" in the forty-first number of the *Spectator* (273).

Tymms (1854, 7) cites *SecAn* 244–46 as a parallel celebration of Elizabeth Drury's memory.

Notes and Glosses

2 *GADES* **CULLUM** (1784): "The word is plain enough. In the Monumenta Anglicana it is *Cades*, with *Clades* q." (52). **MILGATE** (1978): "Cadiz, as bourne or goal (the ultimate West)" (213).

6 *CVI*, **CULLUM** (1784): "QUÆ q." (52). **SPARROW** (1949) suggests that "cvi" may be a mistake for "quae" and quotes Professor Heathcote Garrod thus: "'Is it conceivable that *cui* is governed by the distant *extruendo* in l. 23, despite the long relative clauses of ll. 13–20 and the punctuation?'" (208). **MILGATE** (1978): *Cui* is governed by *extruendo* (213).

8 *ID* **SPARROW** (1949): the word is "obscure: should it be, or can it be the equivalent of, *sic*?" (208).

9 *SINE SEXV* **MILGATE** (1978): "She could excel the angels because she voluntarily abandoned what the Angels, being sexless, could not enjoy" (213).

13 *AVLÆ* **MILGATE** (1978): refers to her body: "She did not allow her bodily perfections to distract her from attending to her soul's welfare" (213).

20 *POST XV FERE ANNOS* **CULLUM** (1784), in an extract from the Hawstead Church

register of 1610, notes that Elizabeth "was buried 17 Dec." (69). **BALD** (1959) cites in the parish register at Redgrave the record of Elizabeth's "baptism on 8 February 1595/96" (29) [so also Milgate (1978), who puts these birth and death dates together in a gloss on this line (213)].

21 *ROB: DRVRI EQ: AVR:* ET *ANNA VXOR*, **MILGATE** (1978): Drury was knighted in 1591 and married in 1592 (213).

22 *VNICÂ FILIÂ, ITÂQVE ET IPSO PARENTVM NOMINE SPOLIATI*, **BALD** (1970): "Sir Robert and Lady Drury had had two daughters. Dorothy, the elder, died at the age of four in 1597" (238).

27 *AN^I: ÆTAT: XV^I MENSE X°, ET SVI IESV CIϽIϽCX.* **BALD** (1959): when the younger daughter Elizabeth died, "she was within two months of her fifteenth birthday; and her death left her parents childless" (68).

Epitaph for Robert *and* Anne Drury.

Commentary

Date and Circumstances

For discussion of the dates of Robert Drury's death and burial, see the Textual Introduction to *EtRD* and Notes and Glosses on line 15 below.

Cullum (1784, 54) prefaces his printing of the text of *EtRD* with a description of the monument upon which it is incised:

> Opposite . . . [the monument to Elizabeth Drury] is a noble mural monument, consisting of a basement, on which is a sarcophagus of black marble, beneath a double arch supported by Corinthian pillars. Over the arch, in an oval frame, is a most spirited bust in armour, large as life. The warlike implements on the arch, and the rest of the ornaments are all in a good taste. This is a performance of Nicholas Stone, who received for it £140.

As noted above (p. 427), Cullum adduces both biographical and stylistic reasons for attributing the epitaph to Donne.

Sparrow (1949, 208) also notes that the monument containing the epitaph was made in 1617 by Nicholas Stone and adds that Stone made Ann Donne's monument the same year and Donne's own in 1631.

Bald (1959, 135–36) reiterates Stone's authorship and the date of the monument, but observes that the epitaph "must be slightly later, since in describing Lady Drury's lineage it refers to Francis Bacon as Lord Chancellor, an appointment which he did not receive until January 1618" (136).

Milgate (1978, 213–14) offers the following translation:

> Anne, the wife of Robert Drury—than whom scarcely any other of his rank sprang from more noble forefathers; distinguished with the honor of knighthood in the year 1591 (and that not at home, but at the siege of Rouen) when he had neither come to man's estate nor left off the mourning garments for his father's death; whom military expeditions, travels abroad, and posts at Court had sufficiently trained (as envy itself, by which he was often touched but never broken, bears witness) whether for commanding troops, conducting embassies, or handling civil affairs; at last in his fortieth year, and in the year of his Saviour 1615, having given his soul to God with utmost and Christian constancy, having disbursed a goodly portion of his wealth to

the poor five years before the fever by which he was carried off (and that for eternity)—made it her task in this spot to return to the earth (its rightful condition) the body, once the temple of the Holy Ghost, which must be restored to the soul as its rightful home.

[She was] neither barren nor yet a mother, having been bereaved of her daughters Dorothy and Elizabeth; a descendant of the illustrious family of Bacon, to which lineage God gave this unparalleled honour, that father and son should discharge the same office, and that the most eminent, Nicholas the father that of Keeper of the Seal, Francis the son that of Chancellor as well; so, having faithfully discharged her duty to him who faithfully discharged his, she leaves this space on the stone tablet, to be filled in with those things which should be said of her (as God wills, and as they will) by those who come after.

Notes and Glosses

3–5 *Cvm nec Ephæbos . . . honore*, **CULLUM** (1784), in an extract from the Hawstead Church register of 1589, notes that "the funerall of the right worshipfull Sir William Drury, knight, was executed 10 March" (69). **BALD** (1970): Sir William Drury, "a courtier and soldier," was "killed in France early in 1590, not on the field of battle but in a duel with a fellow officer. Sir William was succeeded by his eldest son Robert," who was dubbed a knight in the fields outside Rouen "while still only sixteen" (237).

5 (*nec id Domi*, **SPARROW** (1949): the parenthesis "clearly" should extend to *Rhotomagensi* in l. 6 (208).

8–14 *Et Bellicæ Expeditiones . . . Avt Res Civiles pertractandas*, **BALD** (1959) quotes a letter to Lady Drury from the physician Thomas Short that "reveals . . . disappointments which Sir Robert had endured [in his efforts to receive employment in the King's service]" (135) and finds that the "same note of disappointment with its hint of bitterness creeps even into the epitaph which Donne composed at Lady Drury's behest, and which was carved upon Sir Robert's monument in 1618 or later." Bald quotes these lines and observes that Sir Robert "achieved none of those things for which he had been so ambitious" (136). Subsequently **BALD** (1970) summarizes Sir Robert's military experience, placing him in 1596 at Cadiz, in 1596–97 at Ostend, and in 1599 with Essex in Ireland; he further cites Drury's travels, including his return to the Low Countries in 1600, a tour of Italy two years after that, a visit to Spain in 1605 (237–38), and in 1611–12 a tour of Europe on which he "invited Donne to accompany him" (241). Again observes that although he became Gentleman of the Chamber and was a member of the first two Parliaments of James, Robert Drury "never obtained the appointments which he sought, or succeeded in achieving the recognition to which he felt he was entitled" (238).

15 *Iam A° svo 40: Et svi IESV 1615* **CULLUM** (1784) (quoting an extract from the Hawstead Church register of 1615): "The funeralls of the right worshipfull Sir

Robert Drury, of Hawstead, knight, were celebrated, and his corpse buried in Hawstead church chancell, 1 June" (69). **BALD** (1959): Drury died on 2 April [the assertion of Milgate (1978) that "Sir Robert died late in May 1615" (214) is in error—eds.].

17–18 *BONORVM* . . . *EROGATA* **BALD** (1959): "Almost certainly one of the consequences of Elizabeth's death was the establishment by Sir Robert (in part, perhaps, at his wife's instigation) of a charitable foundation. On 18 March 1610/11 trustees were enfeoffed of 'all those lands and tenements called Hardwick or Hardwick Wood' and an annuity out of the manor of Hawstead Hall to provide almshouses and make other provision for six poor women out of the villages which lay within the Drury estates" (142).

23–24 **MILGATE** (1978) prints the epitaph with a gap between lines 23 and 24 (as here) and, following Bald (1959, 156), states that "the gap between these lines was left for the date of Lady Drury's death (5 June 1624)," adding that although she was buried "in the chancel of Hawstead church, the inscription was never completed" (214). See the Textual Introduction to *EtRD* for further information on Milgate's formatting of this epitaph on the page.

29–31 *NICOLAO PATRE* . . . *ETIAM* **MILGATE** (1978): "Lady Drury was the granddaughter of Sir Nicholas Bacon (1509–79), Lord Keeper of the Great Seal, and the daughter of Sir Nicholas his son (d. 1624), premier baronet, Sir Robert Drury's guardian. The younger Sir Nicholas was half-brother to Francis Bacon, who became Lord Keeper in March 1617 and Lord Chancellor on 7 January1617/18 (D.N.B.)" (214).

31 *ETIAM* **CULLUM** (1784, 1813): "*et jam* q." (55).

33–36 *HOC QVOD RESTAT* . . . *POSTERIS RELIQVIT*. **CULLUM** (1784): "The space continues uninscribed, no friendly hand having been found to fill up the void" (56). The parish register for 1624 records Lady Drury's death on 5 June in Hardwick House and her burial "in Hawstead church chancel" on 6 June (70) [similarly, Sparrow (1949, 208)].

Epitaph for Ann Donne.

Commentary

Date and Circumstances

Stone (1617 [1918–19, 50]) describes the monument on which *EtAD* was originally incised as "a letell tombe in a wall" for which he had "15 peces."

Stow (1633, 889) prints *EtAD* and describes its situation in St. Clement Danes, London: "A faire Monument in the Chancell, on the North side, at the upper end."

Gosse (1899, 2:93) records Stone's authorship of the monument and the payment he received, envisaging "an elaborate composition of . . . [Stone's] characteristic class, with coloured figures of the lady, her husband, and her children in a vanishing perspective." Gosse further observes that Ann Donne's tomb "fell to pieces or was destroyed" when the church was rebuilt, but quotes the epitaph from the holograph copy "at Loseley" (siglum F1), averring that Donne composed the inscription for the monument and submitted it "to the criticism of Sir George More."

Grierson (1912, 2:235), glossing *HSShe* 1, a line that he says dates the Holy Sonnets, notes the date and circumstances of Ann Donne's death, points out the disappearance of her monument from St. Clement Danes, and quotes the epitaph.

Clive (1966, 139–40) describes the circumstances of Ann Donne's death and the details of the memorial and then notes that the Latin epitaph Donne wrote "enumerated Ann's kindred, lineage, her virtues, her children and the sorrow of her bereaved husband" (140).

Bald (1970, 324–26) explains the events surrounding the death of Ann Donne and describes the monument that Donne erected to her memory, quoting the above-noted details recorded in Stone and Stow. Bald further cites the holograph copy of *EtAD* (in F1) that Donne "apparently sent to Sir George More for his approval" (325) and quotes the inscription. Disputing Gosse's imagination of an "elaborate composition," Bald believes that the monument was "likely to have been similar to the wall monument which Stone executed about the same time in Enfield Church to the memory of Martha Garrard, which cost £16 and consisted of a panel to contain the inscription surrounded by a cartouche" (326).

General Commentary

Gardner (1965, xxix) briefly compares *EtAD* to lines 1–2 of Crashaw's "Epitaph upon a Young Married Couple Dead and Buryed Together" ("To these, whom Death again did wed, / This Grave's their second Marriage-bed") and to Henry King's "The Exequy," all three having the common theme of the burial together of husband and wife.

Milgate (1978, 215) offers the following translation:

> John Donne, D.D., formerly (most sadly that can be said) her dear husband, to his dear Ann—daughter of George More, sister of Robert More, grand-daughter of William More, great-grand-daughter of Christopher More, Knights of Loseley; a lady most rare, most beloved; a wife most dear, most pure; a mother most dutiful, most tender; who, having completed 15 years of wedded life, seven days after bearing the twelfth of her children (of whom seven are living) was seized by a dire fever (at which he himself, speechless when confronted with the sorrow, commanded this stone tablet to speak)—commits her dust to be united with dust in a new marriage (may God bless it) in this place. She withdrew from the world in the 33rd year of her age and in the year of her Saviour 1617, on the 15th of August.

Ann Donne's Age at Her Death

Noble (1821 [1968, 1–32]) provides a manuscript transcription of *EtAD* and gives the Roman numerals of line 20 as "xliii." Noble comments that "in Seymour's Survey of London &c the age is given: xxiii. which could [not (*editor Shawcross's emendation*)] be true. She had been mother of twelve children & she was the same age as Dr. Donne, who is said to have been born in 1573 but by this it would appear that he was born in 1574. Lee Neve in his Mon. Anglicana has the age xxiii: it is evidently wrong. The mistake [may (*editor Shawcross's emendation*)] have been the sculptor's" (16–17).

Shawcross (1968, 1-32) then notes that Noble's source does indeed erroneously give Ann Donne's age at her death as twenty-three and the "death date [l. 21], which Noble exactly copies, as 'CICDCXVII'" (32). Shawcross further identifies "Lee Neve" as John Le Neve (1679–1741), antiquarian and author of *Monumenta Anglicana* (London, 1717), who gives the age correctly (as it is in fact in the inscription) as 33 (32); Shawcross notes several other errors in Noble's transcription (24).

Notes and Glosses

1–5 *Annæ . . . Pronept:* **MILGATE** (1978): "Ann More, Donne's wife, was the daughter of Sir George More (1553–1632) of Loseley Park, near Guildford, Surrey. His son Sir Robert (1581–1626) was the only one of Ann's brothers to survive to marry and have children. Ann's grandfather was Sir William More (1520–1600), son of Sir Christopher, the purchaser of Loseley Park, who died in 1549 (see A. J. Kempe's introduction to *The Loseley Manuscripts*, 1835)" (215).

9 *Xv annis in coniugio transactis*, **MILGATE** (1978): Donne's statements (as recorded in Gosse [1899, 1:101]) indicate that his marriage took place in early December, 1601; as Ann Donne died on 15 August 1617, the marriage in fact lasted fifteen full years (215).

10 *Vii post xii^{m} partum (quorum vii superstant) dies* **BALD** (1970): on 10 August Donne's wife "gave birth to a still-born child, and her prolonged labours left her utterly exhausted" (324). The Parish Register shows that five days later she was buried

in the Church of St. Clement Danes and that "evidently mother and child were buried in the same grave" (325). Ann was survived by seven of her twelve children (Constance, John, George, Lucy, Bridget, Margaret, and Elizabeth) (326).

12–13 *(Quod hoc saxum . . . Infans)* **MILGATE** (1978): cf. *BedfCab* 8: "When we are speechlesse grown, to make stones speak" (215).

14–15 *Maritus . . . spondet suos* **GARDNER** (1965): cf. the lovers of *Anniv*, who cannot expect to be buried together. Donne's desire to be buried with his wife suggests the discrepancies between the songs and sonnets and Donne's own life (xxix).

18 *Sacr: Theolog: Profess:* **MILGATE** (1978): "Donne was made an honorary Doctor of Divinity by the University of Cambridge . . . by royal mandate in March 1615" (215).

John Donne's *Epitaph for Himself in St. Paul's Cathedral.*

Commentary

Date and Circumstances

Stow (1633, 776) describes the epitaph's location: "In the South side of the Quire of Saint *Pauls* Church stands a white Marble Statue on an Vrne, with this Inscription over it" [the epitaph follows, omitting line 8].

EtSP is printed in Donne's *LXXX Sermons* (1640) between Walton's *Life of Donne* and the "Table" of sermons and texts; Walton subsequently (1658, 111–14), in a description added to this edition of his *Life of Donne*, gives the following account:

> Dr. *Donne* sent for a Carver to make for him in wood the figure of an *Urn*, giving him directions for the compass and height of it, and to bring with it a board of the height of his body. These being got, and without delay a choice Painter was in a readiness to draw his picture, which was taken as followeth.—Severall Charcole-fires being first made in his large study, he brought with him into that place his winding-sheet in his hand, and having put off all his clothes, had this sheet put on him, and so tied with knots at his head and feet, and his hands so placed as dead bodies are usually fitted for the grave. Upon this Urn he thus stood with his eyes shut, and so much of the sheet turned aside as might shew his lean, pale, and death-like face, which was purposely turned toward the East, from whence he expected the second coming of our Saviour. Thus he was drawn at his just height; and when the picture was fully finished, he caused it to be set by his bed-side, where it continued, and became his hourly object till his death, and was then given to his dearest friend and Executor Dr *King*, who caused him to be thus carved in one entire piece of white Marble, as it now stands in the Cathedrall Church of S. Pauls; and by Dr. *Donn*'s [sic] own appointment these words were to be affixed to it as his epitaph. (111–13)

Walton then quotes the epitaph, with many divergences from the text given in *LXXX Sermons*.

Dugdale (1658, 62–63) reproduces an engraving of the monument with the inscribed tablet (62) and transcribes, with various inconsistencies, the epitaph (63).

Fisher (1684, 55–56) also describes the monument, observing that the "Epitaph, made by Himself [i.e., Donne] (as 'tis said) thus modestly represents the Merits of that Incomparable Person, both the Wonder and Envy of that Age" (55). Fisher prints an inaccurate Latin transcription (among other errors, the phrase *ORDINES SACROS AMPLEXUS* in l. 8 is omitted, MDCXX replaces "1621" in l. 12 [although Fisher's

English translation reads "1621"], and MDCXXXV replaces "1631" in l. 14). He offers the following translation (56):

JOHN DONNE a Professor and Doctor of Divinity,
After several Studies from his Child-hood,
Which He pursued with no less industry, than good Success,
By the instinct, and impulsive motion of the Holy Ghost;
And by the Counsail, and perswasion of King *James*,
Was in the year of Grace 1614. and of his Age 42.
Dignified with the Deanry of St. *Pauls*,
The Seven and twentieth of *November*, 1621.
And was at length devested of that Dignity
The last of *March* 1635.
Who though now Benighted, and setting in the *West*,
Yet doth He stedfastly behold
The Sun of Righteousness Gloriously arising out of the *East*.

The following translation, attributed to Archdeacon Francis Wrangham (1769–1843), appears in Gosse (1899, 2:282):

JOHN DONNE,
Doctor of Divinity,
after various studies, pursued by him from his earliest years
with assiduity and not without success,
entered into Holy Orders,
under the influence and impulse of the Divine Spirit
and by the advice and exhortation of King James,
in the year of his Saviour 1614, and of his own age 42.
Having been invested with the Deanery of this Church,
November 27, 1621,
he was stripped of it by Death on the last day of March 1631:
and here, though set in dust, he beholdeth Him
Whose name is the Rising.

Grierson (1912, 2:248–49, 271) argues that despite Walton's (1658) account of Donne's standing on an urn for the execution of the portrait on which the effigy was to be based, three circumstances point to Donne's having lain down for the portrait: (a) Walton's description of the board brought by the painter, which was said to be the length of Donne's body; (b) the argument of Hamo Thornycroft (in Gosse [1899, 2:288]) that the folds of the drapery are consistent with a recumbent rather than an upright figure; and (c) the state of Donne's health (249, 271). Grierson asserts, however, that "the monument, as designed by himself [i.e. Donne], and executed by Nicholas Stone, was intended to represent him rising at the Last Day from the urn, habited as he had lain down" (271).

Gransden (1954, 1–3) cites Walton's account of the origins of the monument and then provides the Latin text of the epitaph with the following translation (3):

John Donne, theologian. After various studies to which from his earliest years he had applied himself faithfully and not unsuccessfully, he took holy orders, through

> the power and inspiration of the Holy Ghost and on the advice and persuasion of King James, in the year 1614 and the 42nd year of his life. On 27 November 1621 he assumed the office of Dean of this church; death took it from him on the last day of March 1631. Here although in dust that passes away, he looks upon Him whose name is Rising.

Milgate (1978, 218–19) notes that there is little punctuation in the actual inscription in St. Paul's Cathedral and that "the mason made no attempt at an intelligent distribution of the words (breaking 'moni/tu', 'Iac/obi', and 'amplex/us' at the ends of lines)" (218).

Donne's Authorship

Noble (1821 [1968, 1–32]) attributes the epitaph to Henry King, Donne's executor (11).

Jessopp (1855, lxviii) contends, "He wrote his own epitaph; he would not let his tombstone lie."

Grierson (1912, 2:248–49, 271) affirms the epitaph as Donne's composition (248).

Milgate (1978, 218–19), while allowing the possibility of doubts about Walton's (1658) account, nevertheless admits no doubt of Donne's authorship (apart from the actual date of death) (218).

After quoting Walton's description of the events surrounding the establishment of Donne's monument in St. Paul's, Gardner (1979, 33–34) concludes that one of the two unquestionable facts of the account is that "Donne composed the epitaph." In particular, she cites the conceit in the final line, the wording of the statement of his taking orders in lines 6–7 (which, she argues, "recalls the 'agente Spiritu S[to], suadente Rege,' in the inscription in the Bible at Lincoln's Inn"), and the "idiosyncratic method" of dating his ordination as "unmistakable signs of Donne's authorship" (34).

General Commentary

Grierson (1912, 2:248–49, 271) describes the epitaph as "the natural supplement" to *Sickness* (248).

Keeble (1927, 232) describes *EtSP* as "a very curious and characteristic epitaph, matching the monument."

Legouis (1955, 22) says that in *EtSP* Donne recalls with pride his successes in studies pursued from earliest youth.

Potter and Simpson (1962, 10:38) comment that Donne's last message to the world "was one of hope and trust in Christ, the East, the Sun of Righteousness who rises with healing in his wings."

Bald (1970, 534–36) states that *EtSP* "must have been of Donne's own composition" and finds it "characteristic of his thought and expression" (534).

Foxell (1978, 1–22) analyzes the poem in the context of the effigy, which he sees as a figuration of death and resurrection that constitutes Donne's last sermon (1–2). Arguing that the effigy originally faced east (5–6), Foxell maintains that the antithesis of west vs. east as a metaphor for death and resurrection is frequent in Donne's writings (e.g., in *Goodf* and throughout the sermons). He further describes the epitaph as "characteristic" of Donne in "thought and expression" (6). Foxell emphasizes the importance of the final word of the epitaph, "*oriens*," and discusses at length both its Latin meanings; its sources and analogues in Hebrew, Greek, and English; and its significance in relationship to the effigy (7–12). These etymologies and associations point to an identification of Christ with the sun, a familiar pun (son/sun) that Donne nevertheless uses to express the catholicity, or universality, of the Anglican Church (8–9). The literal "orientation" of the monument, Foxell asserts, distinguishes the Anglican "geographical" and "liturgical" positions from those both of Roman Catholics (who worship at altars on the north and south sides of the nave) and of Puritans (who reject all orientations as "superstitious") (9–10).

Foxell further argues that the epitaph plays upon the contrast between "*occiduo*" and "*oriens*" as symbolic of "death and sin" on the one hand and "life and innocence" on the other. "*Occiduo cinere*," he suggests, alludes also to the Court at Westminster, to the west of the effigy, and even to the structure of St. Paul's itself, "which was divided between God and Mammon, the choir alone functioning as a place of worship, while the nave was a scurry and hubbub of trade and job-seeking." Because the choir of the cathedral is physically higher than the nave, Foxell concludes, "*oriens*" implies not only "East" but "Ascent."

Foxell finds Donne's entrance into the Church, briefly described in lines 6–8, the turning-point of his life and maintains that the conceptual framework of the epitaph (a duality of falling and rising, East and West, life and death, and secular and religious experience) is structured around this turning point. The opening and closing lines of the epitaph, Foxell asserts, sum up the movement of Donne's life, which Foxell characterizes (arguing that the three words are synonomous) as a "turnabout," a "conversion," and a "resurrection." In fact, Foxell asserts, the last sentence of the epitaph itself expresses the falling and rising motions characteristic of the poem as a whole in "*occiduo*," which he says means "descending" as well as "western," and "*oriens*," which he says means "rising" as well as "east" (10). The effigy itself, Foxell argues, expresses these meanings because "the statue of Donne's body celestial is above the urn that represents his death," whereas "the actual corpse is to the West of the statue, which *rises* to Christ although He is in fact not *above* him but to the *East*" (10–11). Foxell sums up this part of his argument by asserting that both the monument and the epitaph express a double resurrection: "a resurrection from sin, and a resurrection of the body on the Last Day," and "the first is a *sine qua non* of the second."

After discussing evidence in the *Sermons* for Donne's exposition of the concept of a dual resurrection, Foxell focuses upon what he calls the "tensions" (11) in the epitaph. Conceding that such tensions are only weakly present in the poem's pairing of "*fideliter*" with "*infeliciter*" and of the Holy Ghost with King James, Foxell nevertheless stresses the last sentence, whose oppositions of west to east and of ashes to the sun he terms forceful. He then tentatively suggests that, despite his earlier disclaimer (which he himself deprecates as possibly too "bland"), we read King James, the Holy Ghost, and "*oriens*" as parallel within the poem, with the result that the King becomes "on one hand a reflection of the celestial, and on the other a terrestrial contrast to it." Thus there may exist another tension or duality of the kind Foxell has been proposing as the underpinning structure of the poem.

The final sentence of the poem, Foxell argues, "holds the whole tension within itself." This tension, he observes, is expressed in further pairings of words: *cinere/aspicit* ("his body in dust and his soul in Heaven") and *Hic/Eum* ("here" and "that," i.e., "himself and Christ") (12). The body's claims, Foxell explains, are not so self-evident as are the soul's, and Donne's emphasis on its resurrection in the epitaph is consistent with the arguments of many of his sermons (12–16). Foxell regards the monument generally as both an expression of Donne's character, itself a "violent yoking" of heterogeneous elements, and a symbol of Donne's entire work (17). The monument, Foxell argues further, represents not only Donne but also the Church Militant, "not yet able to see *Oriens* face to face, but dimly in the mirror provided by the pulpit and the altar at the East End of the church" (17–18). "Aspicit," he reasons, signifies the taking of the sacrament, by which the earthly church comes into contact with God (18). The tensions of the poem, Foxell adds, call to mind both *SecAn* 113–14 and *EgDD* (20–21).

Commenting on the epitaph in relationship to the effigy, Smith (1982, 36–37) asserts that it "succinctly points the conjunction of meanings which make up one truth" (37).

Notes and Glosses

2 *SAC: THEOL: PROFESS* **MILGATE** (1978): cf. *EtAD* 18; "Donne was made an honorary Doctor of Divinity by the University of Cambridge" in 1615 (219, 215).

5–9 *INSTINCTV . . . AMPLEX-/-VS* **GARDNER** (1952): these lines express Donne's final acceptance of the "advice of others," particularly that of the King, and his assent to his vocation (131).

5–8 *INSTINCTV . . . REGIS IAC-/-OBI* **FOXELL** (1978): Donne understood his movement from a secular to an ecclesiastical life in terms of the conceptual framework established in the epitaph, that is, from West (sin and death) to East (innocence and life) (10).

6–8 *MONI-/-TV ET HORTATV REGIS IAC-/-OBI* **MILGATE** (1978): cf. *InLI* 6–9 and note to line 2 above (219, 215, 216). Donne "frequently and gratefully" alludes to the King's persuasions that he enter the Church (216).

9 *1614* **MILGATE** (1978): i.e., 1614/15; cf. *InLI* 15 (*Ad Ordines Sacros Evectus*); Donne was ordained deacon and priest in 1615 (219, 216). **BALD** (1970): "It has been shown, after a close examination of the sometimes conflicting evidence, that John must have been born between 24 January and 19 June 1572" (35).

11–12 *27° / NOVEMB:* **BALD** (1970): "Donne's epitaph states that he became Dean on 27 Nov., but the copy of the notary's certificate in Register Donne at St. Paul's quite clearly gives 'die Jovis vicesimo secundo die mensis Novembris' as the day on which he took his oath and was installed" (381).

14–16 *HIC LICET . . . ORIENS* **NOBLE** (1821 [1968]): "Is the latter part of the epitaph in reference to his not being buried at St. Clement's in the grave of his beloved Ann? It is it only one ye of [i.e., "It is one of the" (*editor Shawcross's note*)] quaint ideas of the age" (11). "I did not recollect St. Dunstan's in the East—the idea is not very wise, there was no reason for burying him there but there was the greatest to have interred him in St. Clement's Church with his beloved and lamented WIFE" (17). **LIGHTFOOT** (1877 [1895]) translates the lines "'The man whose effigy stands beneath, though his ashes are mingled with western dust, looks towards Him whose name is the Orient'" and says that they allude to the Vulgate's rendering of Zechariah 6.12, a verse translated "The man whose name is The Branch" in the Authorized Version. "This text," Lightfoot asserts, "is quoted several times in Donne's *Sermons* and appears to have been a favourite with him" (222). **GRIERSON** (1912): these lines express the faith bodied forth symbolically by the monument, which represents Donne rising as he had lain down (2:271). **HUNT** (1954): "The general connotations of this West-East imagery to Donne appear from the concluding lines of the epitaph," in which Donne puns on "two meanings of *occiduo*—(a) falling, and (b) western—so that the ambiguity of this word parallels the ambiguity of *Oriens* = (a) rising, and (b) east" (242). **SHAWCROSS** (1968): Donne had the vicarage of St. Dunstan in the West; Noble's error [1821], supposing that Donne held the vicarage of St. Dunstan in the East, is "curious since Walton gives . . . [Donne's parish] correctly; in fact, this was Walton's own parish" (25). There is therefore no pun on "Oriens" and St. Dunstan's in the East; "instead there is the antithesis of *Occiduo* and *Oriens* (a name for Christ) such as underlies" *Goodf* (26). **FOXELL** (1978) says that the lines could be translated either "Here, though in western dust, he looks towards Him whose name is the East" or ("without any real change in meaning") "Here, though in descending dust, he looks towards Him whose name is Ascent" (6). Wrangham's translation (cited in Gosse [1899, 2:282] and above), says Foxell, is faulty: there is no justification for translating *occiduo* as if it were *occiduus*, and his "beholdeth" (for *aspicit*) is inconsistent with the idea that the body awaits its resurrection (and so its view of Christ). If *aspicit* meant "beholdeth," Foxell maintains, it would properly have been in the future tense. Because *aspicit* governs *evm cvivs nomen est oriens*, Foxell further argues, "it suggests *aspicit lumen*, meaning 'he sees the light,' hence 'he lives,' thus emphasizing the antithesis of life and death: the essence of the sentence is 'Though his body is dead, it is (*in potentia*) alive.'" The primary meaning of *aspicit*, however, Foxell asserts, is "looks towards" and therefore "awaits." Foxell thinks that Gosse was wrong to reproduce Wrangham's translation and (see note on l. 16) wrong to cite St. Hilary as the justification for equating *Oriens* with Christ—Donne rebukes St. Hilary for giving Christ names not found in the Bible or learned from the Holy Spirit (7). Zech. 6.12 refers to Zerubbabel, rebuilder of the Temple, avers Foxell; *oriens*, in the Vulgate, translates the Hebrew *ẓemaḥ* ("shoot," i.e., a plant), and is the antithesis of *occiduo cinere*: "a living shoot (or sprout) rising from the dead earth." Foxell connects *ẓemaḥ*, by way of what he says is its figurative sense of "dawn," to "*Oriens*" and observes that "the East is the direction of the Holy Land" and the direction also of the altar and the pulpit, where Christ is symbolically present (8). **SHAW** (1981): the lines witness to Donne's acquisition by the end of his life of the faith necessary not only to turn from sin but also to turn towards God; the latter motion, not realized in *Goodf*, is evident both in the epitaph and in the positioning of the effigy facing east (53–54). **FOXELL** (1983): the French translation should be either "Celui-ci, quoique gisant dans la poussière à l'Occident, regarde vers Celui-là, Dont le nom est Orient" ["He, though lying in the Western dust, looks towards Him Whose name is the East"] or, with no substantial difference in meaning, "Celui-ci, bien que dans une descente poussiéreuse, regarde vers celui-là, Dont le nom est Ascension" ["He, although descended into dust, looks towards him, Whose name is Ascension"]. Although the body remains in earth, the soul already gazes upon Christ in Heaven; this duality is lost in Wrangham's translation (202).

14 *HIC* **FOXELL** (1983): Wrangham's reading this as the adverb "here" (instead of as a demonstrative pronoun) is wrong because it suggests that the remains (dust and shroud) are what will see Christ (202).

15 *ASPICIT* **FOXELL** (1983): the Latin does not signify only "je regarde" ["I look"] but also "je regarde vers" ["I look toward"], and therefore "j'attends" ["I await"], thus reinforcing the sense that it is the soul that gazes upon Christ while the body expects to do so (203).

15–16 *CVIVS NOMEN / EST ORIENS* **GOSSE** (1899): the phrase indicates that Donne intended to be buried facing east. Donne was fond of the expression *Oriens nomen ejus*, which he uses elsewhere (e.g., "*Oriens nomen ejus*, the East is one of Christ's names" [Gosse cites a letter of 1624 to Sir Robert Ker, which he prints (2:191) from the "Tobie Matthew Collection"]). "Oriens is used by St. Hilary as a name for Christ" (2:282). **GRIERSON** (1912) compares this passage to the figure of the map in stanzas 2 and 3 of *Sickness*, citing for comparison to both poems a passage in Donne's sermon on Ps. 6.8–10 (*Sermons* 6:59) that discourses in part on the identity of Christ as "*Oriens, The East*" and that of Lucifer as "*Filius Orientis, The Son of the East*" (2:248–49). Donne's marginal note to this sermon cites the Vulgate Zech. 6.12: "Et loqueris ad eum dicens: Haec ait Dominus exercituum, dicens: ECCE VIR ORIENS NOMEN EJUS; et subter eum orietur, et aedificabit templum Domino"; this, and not the Geneva Bible or the Authorized Version, where the phrase is translated "whose name is the Branch" (the Hebrew for "rising" and for "branch" being easily confounded), is Donne's source (2:249). **GARDNER** (1952): the line expresses the faith ("not vision . . . not lit by any flashes of ecstasy") that characterizes the Divine Poems (xxxiv–xxxv). **MILGATE** (1978): the Vulgate Jer. 23.5, *regem, orientem, justum*, was understood by St. Hilary to refer to Christ. Zech. 6.12 [cited above] was understood in the same way by St. Gregory the Great. The root meaning of *oriens* ("rising") points to the symbolism of resurrection in and through Christ; hence the meeting of east and west in the flat maps of *Sickness* and in the sermon and letter to Sir Robert Ker [see Gosse's (1899) note on these lines] (219).

16 *ORIENS* **FOXELL** (1978): the word points to the statue's having originally faced east (10). Referring to the sun, *oriens* sums up Donne's "three main interests": "it

is fiery, symbolizing the passions of the body; it is splendid and powerful, symbolizing glory; it is the chief source of light, symbolizing knowledge" (17). **FOXELL** (1983): the word promises that the body will rejoin the soul: "Quoique la poussière, étant poussière, ne puisse voir, on peut lui prêter son désir de voir, par licence poétique . . . c'est l'âme qui voit, tandis que le corps verra" ["although dust, being dust, cannot see, it can, by poetic license, borrow the desire to see . . . it is the soul that sees, while the body will see"] (203).

Epigraph in DEATHS DVELL.

Commentary

Gardner (1952, 112–13), the first to comment on this epigraph as poetry, maintains that this line of hexameter verse poses problems both of scansion and of translation. The line must be scanned, she argues, either to end with two spondees—"Sȳndōn Jēsū"—or with "a false quantity in the second 'Syndon' and the 'J' of 'Jesu' . . . vocalized: 'Sȳndŏn J̆ēsū.'" She rejects the first scansion as "highly improbable" because it "gives a line ending with four successive spondees," preferring instead the second on grounds that it involves elements found elsewhere in Donne's poetry: the "false quantity in 'Syndon' would be a parallel to that in 'Catechismus'" in line 18 of *GHerb*. Gardner offers the following scansion of the entire line—"Cōrpŏrĭs hāec Ănĭmāe sīt Sȳndōn, Sȳndŏn J̆ēsū"—further noting that both "Catechismus" and "Syndon" are Greek words that have been "borrowed into Latin and then into English," that references in the *OED* show "'sindon', from Matt. xxvii.59" to have been "in current use," and that Donne uses "sindon" in *Pseudo-Martyr* (112).

The translation problem that Gardner identifies centers upon the word *Jesu*, which can be read either as a vocative ("O Jesus") or as a genitive (the shroud "of Jesus"). Accepting the second reading, Gardner provides a literal translation—"May this shroud of the body be (i.e., typify) the shroud of the soul: the shroud of Jesus"—and a paraphrase—"As the body is shrouded in white linen, may the soul be shrouded in a white garment also, which is not its own but is the white garment of Jesus." Gardner describes the line as "a rather tortured rendering" of lines 113–14 of *SecAn*: "Thinke that they shroud thee up, and think from thence / They reinvest thee in white innocence." Gardner also finds a parallel to the image of someone's being wrapped in the garment of another in line 26 of *Sickness*: "So, in his purple wrapp'd receive mee Lord." Finally, Gardner contends that no one but Donne could have written this line, which she believes he composed during his last illness explicitly for the purpose of appearing beneath the picture of himself in his shroud that he intended as a frontispiece to "DEATHS DVELL": "He wished that being dead, he might yet speak" (113).

Sparrow (1953, 169) accepts Gardner's explanation of the sense of the line, but contends that this reading involves metrical difficulties. Suggesting that "a puzzled copyist" might have inserted "the unfamiliar words *Syndon, Syndon*" in the wrong place, Sparrow offers the following transposition: "*Corporis haec Syndon, Syndon animae sit Jesu*" ("This is my body's shroud, may my soul's shroud be that of Jesus"). Sparrow confirms Donne's interest in the "Sindon" by citing his reference in *Ignatius* to *Paleotus de Sindone* (*Iesu Christ Crucifixi Stigmata Sindoni impressa*), a treatise on the Shroud of Turin published at Venice in 1606, and suggests that the epigraph contains a "play on words—*John Donne: sin done*." This pun, he suggests, "has something approaching an echo" in *Father* 2—"Which is my *sin*, though it were *done* before"—but he concludes that recognition of the wordplay does not help in interpreting the epigraph.

Kermode (1957, 41) notes parenthetically, and without elaboration, that the epigraph contains a pun upon Donne's own name.

Keynes (1973, iv, 43–44), as frontispiece to his edition of *Death's Duel*, reproduces the Droeshout engraving containing the epigraph and summarizes the comments of Gardner and Sparrow on its meaning.

Foxell (1978, 20–21) believes the epigraph is Donne's prayer for the Second Coming when his body and soul will both "be one with Jesus, who is also body and soul; indeed Donne, like all the saved, will *be* Jesus" (21).

Lewalski (1979, 201) paraphrases the epigraph—"a prayer that his own white shroud might typify the white shroud (Christ's shroud) covering his sinful soul"—and then comments, "Donne's last action was thus to make of himself in his burial weeds an emblem for his own and others' contemplation."

Novarr (1980, 205) characterizes the epigraph as "a single Latin hexameter, perfect for the occasion, stamped with his idiosyncratic marks, cryptic, conceited, conclusive."

Reading the inscription in terms of Donne's monument in St. Paul's, Norbrook (1990, 26–27) comments that "even now that at last he has achieved a secure niche, he is already embarked on a journey in which there is no middle way, only an end and a beginning, and he has but a precarious foothold on his well-wrought urn."

Inscription in a Bible Presented to Lincoln's Inn.

Commentary

Tomlins (1852, 79–80), the first to print *InLI*, introduces the inscription by explaining that on resigning his appointment as lecturer in divinity at Lincoln's Inn after assuming the Deanship of St. Paul's, Donne presented to the Society "in enduring testimony of his affection, a fine copy of the latin version of the Holy Scriptures, printed at Douay, in 1617, in six volumes folio, with the Gloss of Walafrid Strabo, and the Commentary of Nicholas de Lyra" (79). This Bible, Tomlins continues, "was inscribed by the donor on the fly leaf of the first volume, with the following interesting record of the occasion, his connexion with the Society, and of his transitory studies and pursuits, until summoned by the divine will, and by his sovereign's persuasion, to the sacred calling of the ministry". (79–80).

Jessopp (1897, 132), though he does not print the inscription, notes the circumstances of its composition and bequeathal to Lincoln's Inn library and states that it "may still be read by those who are not above confessing to a sentimental interest in such relics."

LIBB (1898, 229–30, 445), in the Council minutes for 11 February 1622, records the circumstances of Donne's resignation from his Lincoln's Inn office and his gift of the Bible to the Society. In acknowledging "this and many other the kind and loving respectes of the said M[r] Doctor Donne" towards the Society, the minutes record the members' unanimous assent that Donne should retain his chamber and privileges in the House. A footnote cites the appearance "in the first volume . . . [of a] Latin inscription which states that Donne laid the first stones of the new Chapel with his own hands" (230), and *InLI* is printed on page 445.

Gosse (1899, 2:113–14) prints the inscription and comments that the Bible in which it is inscribed "seems to have supplied Donne with his references [in sermons preached at Lincoln's Inn]" (113) and for that reason was a suitable farewell gift.

Sparrow (1949, 208) states without elaboration that Gosse (1899) prints the inscription "not quite accurately."

Milgate (1978, 216) offers the following translation:

> That these six volumes of the entire Scriptures should be placed in the Library of Lincoln's Inn, London—most renowned in the City, in the whole World, a Society of those professing the Civil Law—is the wish (nay rather, the request) of John Donne, D.D., chaplain to the most serene and most generous King James; who, sent here in

early youth to master the Laws, turning aside to other things—equally to other studies, to employments and travels, in the midst of which notwithstanding he never neglected the study of Theology—after many years impelled by the Holy Ghost and at the urging of the King being brought into Holy Orders, having fulfilled his duty of preaching often and earnestly in this place for five years, having set with his own hands the first stones of the new Chapel and well-nigh prepared the last, was bidden to transfer to the Deanship of the Cathedral Church of St. Paul, London, by the King (whom may God bless), in the 50th year of his age, and in the year of his Saviour 1621.

Notes and Glosses

6–9 *Sacræ . . . A Sacris* **MILGATE** (1978): Donne "frequently and gratefully" alludes to the King's persuasions that he enter the Church (216).

11–12 *Qui huc . . . deflectens*, **SHAPIRO** (1930) says that Izaak Walton properly dated Donne's travels after his entry into Lincoln's Inn and cites these lines as evidence. Shapiro thinks there would be "little point in the inscription unless Donne's 'peregrinationes' followed fairly closely on his residence at Lincoln's Inn." Donne may have carried out his travels between July 1593 and February 1594, Shapiro speculates, although they possibly occurred as late as spring 1598 (861).

11 *Qui huc, in prima iuuentute, ad perdiscendas leges, missus* **BALD** (1970): "The admission register of Lincoln's Inn shows that . . . [Donne] was admitted from Thavies Inn on 6 May 1592" (54) [similarly **MILGATE** (1978), who adds that Donne "is not mentioned as a student of the Inn in the surviving records after the end of 1594, and he did not formally qualify as a barrister" (216)].

15 *Ad Ordines Sacros euectus*, **BALD** (1970): Donne was ordained deacon and priest by Bishop John King on 23 January 1615 (302).

16–19 *Munere suo . . . fere paratis*, **BALD** (1970) notes that on 24 October 1616 Donne was chosen Reader at Lincoln's Inn, a post which "involved the preaching of about fifty sermons a year" (319), and continues that "in all, twenty-one of Donne's sermons preached at Lincoln's Inn have survived" (320). **MILGATE** (1978), citing the above-noted facts from Bald and explaining that "Reader" means "preacher and spiritual director," adds: "In 1617 the building of a new Chapel was actively undertaken by the Benchers, and Inigo Jones was commissioned to design the building (which still stands). In (?May) 1618 Donne preached a sermon at the Inn 'preparing them to build their Chappell' (*Sermons* 2, no. 10). He was installed as Dean of St. Paul's on 22 November 1621, almost exactly five years (l. 17) after his appointment as Reader at the Inn, though there is no mention of his resignation, or of his gift of the Bible, in the Inn records until 11 February 1622. The Chapel was consecrated on Ascension Day (22 May), 1623, when Donne, who preached the sermon (*Encaenia*

. . . . [*Sermons* 4, no. 15]), spoke of being 'a poore assistant in laying the first stone' (cf. l. 18; and see *Sermons* 2:1–8); he went on to say that he was 'a poore assistant again in this laying of this first formall Stone, the Word and Sacrament' (*Sermons* 4:371)" (216–17).

21–22 *A Rege . . . iussus est* **BALD** (1970): acting as temporal head of the Church, King James appointed Donne Dean of St. Paul's (374–79).

23 *A° L° Ætat: Suæ, et sui IESV* **BALD** (1970): "It has been shown, after a close examination of the sometimes conflicting evidence, that John must have been born between 24 January and 19 June 1572" (35).

Inscription in the Album Amicorum *of* Michael Corvinus.

Commentary

Milgate (1978, 217–18) explains that *InAA* appears in a leaf of Michael Corvinus's autograph album in the library of Geoffrey Keynes (and now in Cambridge University Library—eds.), who reproduces it in facsimile in his *Bibliotheca Bibliographici* (1964, 191). Milgate speculates that Corvinus may be the Hungarian student of that name who was at Wittenberg between 1619 and 1622 (217), adducing further data about Corvinus's travels and religious opinions that seem to fit the character of the man in the inscription, who, Milgate suggests, appears to be an outcast from his own people. Donne, says Milgate, "expresses the wish that wherever he goes and in the church of Christ to which all Christians belong (*apud omnes*) he will be accepted into Christian communion, as Donne had welcomed him both in the Cathedral (as a communicant) and in his own house" (217–18). Milgate offers the following translation :

> "He came unto his own, and his own received him not". John i. 11
>
> for what is spoken of Christ may be said of each and every Christian "for all things are yours". 1 Cor. iii. 22.
>
> May God, most good, most great, grant that that most distinguished and most learned Hungarian, Michael Corvinus, may meet among all men with this Communion of Saints which is offered and pledged to him in St. Paul's and in his own house by John Donne, Dean thereof. September 27 1623 [Milgate has misread "17" as "27"—eds.]. (218)

Notes and Glosses

2–3 *qd enim . . . dicere licet;* **MILGATE** (1978): in his verse letters to the Countess of Bedford and other great women, in the epicedes, and in the Anniversaries, Donne develops the thesis stated in these lines: "what is spoken of Christ may be said of each and every Christian" (xviii–xix, 218).

4 *Omnia enim uestra sunt. 1. Cor: 3. 22.* **MILGATE** (1978): "The context is: 'There-fore let no man glory in men: for all things are yours; Whether Paul, or Apollos, or Cephas, or the world, or life, or death, or things present, or things to come; all are yours; And ye are Christ's; and Christ is God's' (1 Cor. iii. 21–3)" (218).

Miscellaneous Poems

Amicissimo, et meritissimo BEN: IONSON.

COMMENTARY

Grosart (1872–73, 2:iv, 99–100) classifies *Amic* as a verse letter (iv); he offers what he claims (iv) is the first English translation (99–100):

TO MY MOST FRIENDLY AND DESERVING Benj. Jonson.
On his 'Volpone,' or The Fox.

What thou hast dared with thy poetic pen,
If ancient teachers of the laws of men
And God had dared to follow out like thee,
Wise to salvation all of us would be.
Those ancients, with what cobwebs they abound!
Nor is such follower of those ancients found
As thou, who, following, darest break new ground.
Go on and prosper, then; and let thy books
Put on from their first moment reverend looks:
No literary effort childhood brooks.
Old at their very birth books needs must be
To which thou givest immortality.
Genius and toil thee on a level place
With ancients: them excel, that the new race
Rise from our wickedness, in which, alas,
Both past and future ages we surpass.

Chambers (1896, 2:227) remarks that, although the poem appeared in the 1607 quarto of *Volpone*, it was not included in editions of Donne's poems until 1650.

In a discussion of evidence of Donne's youthful interest in the theater, Ellrodt (1960a, 2:189) notes that, although Donne rarely refers to contemporary writers, he praises Jonson by name as the author of *Volpone* and the object of his public admiration.

Shawcross (1967a, 218) offers the following translation:

To the most friendly and deserving
Ben Jonson. On his "Volpone."

If, what here you have dared with your skill, O Poet,
the deliberators of the law of men and God

had dared to follow and to emulate the ancients,
O might we all taste of salvation.
But to these men the ancients are full of cobwebs;
no one is such a follower of the ancients as you
because you, restorer of the old, follow those you approve.
Follow still what you pursue; and may your books
be adorned with old age from their first hour:
for assuredly youth is to be denied to literary works,
and it is necessary that these books are born aged things,
by which let your power be given immortality.
Genius and toil render you equal
to the ancients; outlive them so that
you may ransom future men from our corruption,
in which we surpass the past and future ages.

Vizioli (1967, 4) suggests that had Donne dedicated himself to writing Latin rather than English verse, he would have been the major English exponent of baroque Latin poetry. But as things now stand, he argues, Donne's Latin poetry "appears in the complete editions of his work as a curious exoticism," constituting "a little abandoned province within his poetry," and Vizioli remarks in particular on the absence of references to Donne's Latin verse in Leishman (1951). Explaining his search for either historical or intrinsic significance in the Latin verses, Vizioli says that he first considered them as analogous to Milton's Latin poetry (that is, as preparatory stages for the English works), but that he ultimately came to study the influence of the English upon the Latin poetry. Vizioli focuses his discussion on the satires and their connection with Donne's Latin verse letters to George Herbert and D. D. Andrews—"occasional verses" to which Vizioli thinks Donne attached little importance. Vizioli specifically cites *Amic* in the course of an argument for the resemblance of Donne's Latin to his English poems, both of which, he asserts, develop arguments in dramatic, urgent, conversational language that uses conceits, paradoxes, puns, and unusual sound effects. Mentioning the witty paradox of lines 6–7 and 14–16 as analogous to effects in the English verse, Vizioli calls these techniques "baroque" and further cites this poem as indicative of the influence of Catullus on Latin poetry of the period generally.

Bald (1970, 195) comments that in 1607, "in pointed hendecasyllabics," Donne wrote for Jonson "such things as his friend most wanted to hear." Bald further notes Jonson's return of the favor in several of his epigrams.

Notes and Glosses

Title **GARDNER** (1952), noting the "curious" absence of a Latin heading to *GHerb*, says that this poem to Jonson is "briefly but properly addressed in Latin" (142) (see the Textual Introduction for further discussion of the title).

3 Consulti, veteres sequi æmularierque, **MILGATE** (1967) (reading "Consulti,

sequi aemularierque,") explains that he is following the suggestion of Professor P. Maas (in Jonson [1925–52, 11:318]) in deleting "veteres," an "interpolation from l. 5 which destroys both sense and metre." Milgate finds, however, "authority for the hiatus after 'sequĭ' in Catullus, lxii, l. 7, 'uno in lectulŏ, eruditi'" (278).

3 Consulti, **SHAWCROSS** (1967a): "(*deliberators*): referring to those who argue the 'true' religion, those who follow their own interpretation rather than the words of the Great Fathers (like Augustine). Donne emphasizes Jonson's adherence to classical form and classical comic aims of satire and reform" (218).

6 sequutor, **MILGATE** (1967): "*secutor*, 'champion', or perhaps 'follower'" (278).

Verse from *Conclaue Ignati* and *Ignatius His Conclave*.

Commentary

Chambers (1896, 2:312–14), noting that the "scraps of Latin verse" that appear in *Conclaue Ignati* are translated in *Ignatius*, pairs the Latin and English versions of each verse item and prints all seven pairs seriatim. Chambers says that he has been "unable to identify any of the Latin passages" except those attributed to the Emperor Hadrian (i.e., *Animula, vagula, blandula, / Comes hospesque corporis*,—of which *IgSport* is a translation) and speculates that "the rest, which do not always scan, are of Donne's own writing" (314).

IgAver/IgResemb

For Healy (1969, 102) "the point of the allusion is that, like the two faces of Janus, the papacy and the French Church will never see eye to eye."

Flynn (1987, 172) says that "Donne's stationing a Janus at the beginning of his book sets its tone of ambiguity" and asserts that such an indication of hidden meaning in the front matter was "a common signal in texts of the period written in defiance of authority."

IgSport

Simpson (1924, 195–97), quoting these lines, explains that *Ignatius* "begins with an interesting reference to the astronomical discoveries of Galileo and Kepler, which helps us to date the composition of the book." Further, she believes that "this must be the earliest English rendering of Hadrian's famous lines" (196).

Coffin (1937, 204), in citing these lines, observes that although most of the events in *Ignatius* occur in Hell, "the author takes advantage of the 'extasie' into which . . . [he] has fallen, before descending to the lower regions."

Nicolson (1940, 273–74) finds that the sentence of which these words are a part provides "a complete outline of a cosmic voyage," although "the device [of the cosmic voyage] is entirely neglected in the work itself" and the "theme of the ecstatic trance, too, completely disappears." Speculating that Kepler's *Somnium* appeared and was circulated in manuscript in 1610, Nicolson explains these structural inconsistencies in *Ignatius* by suggesting that Donne originally wrote his work (which was entered in the Stationers' Register in January of 1611) "merely as a series of dialogues in Hell, a satire on the Jesuits," but that he received a copy of the *Somnium* after his own work was ready for the press and, rather than recasting the whole piece, "contented himself with the mere addition of a new introduction and conclusion in which he deliberately adopted the double device of dream and cosmic voyage used by Kepler" (274).

Weidhorn (1970, 79–81) observes of these lines that it is not important whether or not Donne borrowed the idea of the dream from Kepler's *Somnium*; what matters is that the dream Donne utilized "accords with the Stoic and Neoplatonic notion that in sleep the soul undertakes farflung voyages to obtain knowledge" (81).

IgOper/IgLark

Raspa (1965, 488–89), arguing that "the *Conclave* is structured on three parodies of the type of Jesuit profane poem depicting stages in the *Exercises*, one each at the beginning, middle, and end" (488–89), identifies these lines as the first of the poems and notes that they present the lark as "the symbol of the soul in flight early in the meditation" (489).

Healy (1969, 103) states that in these lines Donne puts into verse the description of the lark by Albertus Magnus in his *De Animalibus*, xxiii. 5: "Alauda . . . cantat ascendendo per circulum volans, et cum descendit, primo quidem paulatim descendit, et tandem alas ad se convertens in modum lapidis subito decidit et in illo casu cantum dimittit."

Flynn (1987, 182) disputes Healy's association of these poems with Albertus Magnus, asserting that "comparison of Donne's twenty-seven Latin words in five lines of verse to Albert's thirty words of Latin prose shows that they have only one word in common (i.e. 'subito')," a fact suggesting that "Donne was not merely versifying Albert the Great."

IgTanto/IgNoise

Flynn (1987, 172–76) argues that this poem appears "at the climax of the book's narration" (172) and that the significance of this verse passage resides in the friendship and the political objectives shared by Donne and Henry Percy, ninth Earl of Northumberland. Flynn notes that by February 1611 a copy of the Latin *Conclave Ignati* was owned by the Earl (see the Textual Introduction) and expresses his belief that "Donne also used Northumberland's library in writing the book" (173). Flynn then explains that even before James came to the English throne, Robert Cecil had attempted in secret letters "to alienate the King from Northumberland, whose own secret letters before 1603 were urging James to offer religious toleration to English Catholics." Flynn further asserts that although Cecil's actions against Northumberland did not at first succeed, "he finally prevailed after the Gunpowder Plot in raising the King's suspicions about the Earl, who was imprisoned and had proceedings brought against him by the Star Chamber" (175). With this historical context in mind, Flynn concludes that "for Northumberland, reading his copy of *Conclave Ignati* in the Tower, the climax of the book had a special significance" in that "Donne likens the roaring of Ignatius to the importunate outcry and flood of propaganda that helped bring down

Northumberland and forever ruled out one of his longstanding political objectives: that the King should grant toleration to English Catholics" (173–74).

IgPiece

Flynn (1987, 182) notes that "*Parsque minor tantum tota valet / integra quantum.*" and *IgPiece* are "a quotation and translation from a book Donne cites in the margin at the place [i.e., Quaranta's *Summa Bullarii*—see the Textual Introduction]."

IgPlum/IgFeath

Healy (1969, 137) states, "as far as I can determine, these verses are Donne's own" and then notes further that these lines are reminiscent of passages from two other poems by Donne: *ElServe* 15–17 ("So, carelesse flowers strow'd on the waters face, / The curled whirlepooles suck, smack, and embrace, / Yet drowne them") and *Sat3* 103–08 ("As streames are, Power is; those blest flowers that dwell / At the rough streames calme head, thrive and do well, / But having left their roots, and themselves given / To the streames tyrannous rage, alas are driven / Through mills, and rockes, and woods, and at last, almost / Consum'd in going, in the sea are lost").

IgQual/IgFlow

Healy (1969, 153) states, "as far as I can determine, these verses are Donne's own."

Flynn (1987, 182), crediting the identification to a "marginal annotation" preserved in a Houghton Library copy of the 1652 *Ignatius* and written in a hand identified by Dayton Haskin as that of Charles Eliot Norton, asserts that these verses constitute "a translation into Latin and English" of Dante's *Inferno* 2.127–30.

Translated out of *Gazæus*, *Vota Amico facta. fol.* 160.

Commentary

Category and Sources

Angelin Gazet (Gazæus) (1619, 160) published a second edition of the Latin verses of which Donne's poem is a translation, the initial edition having appeared in 1618. The following transcription is taken from the 1619 edition that Donne used:

Vota Amico facta.

TIbi quod optas & quod opto, dent Diui,
(Sol optimorum in optimis Amicorum)
Vt anima semper læta nesciat curas,
Vt vita semper viua nesciat canos,
Vt dextra semper larga nesciat sordes,
Vt bursa semper plena nesciat rugas,
Vt lingua semper vera nesciat lapsum,
Ut verba semper blanda nesciant rixas,
Ut facta semper æqua nesciant fucum,
Ut fama semper pura nesciat probrum,
Ut vota semper alta nesciant terras,
Tibi quod optas & quod opto, dent Diui.

Lowell[?] (1855, 328) in his edition places *Gaz* at the end of the category of epigrams.

Grosart (1872–73, 2:321–22) classifies *Gaz* as a "Divine Poem."

Norton (1895, 1:186, 248), classifying *Gaz* as an epigram (186), further explains that "there were three learned brothers of this name who wrote much in the sixteenth and seventeenth centuries," but admits ignorance of their works and of the original of which Donne's lines are a translation (248).

Chambers (1896, 1:252) identifies the first printing of *Gaz* in the edition of 1650, adding, "Enée de Gaza, at the end of the fifth century, wrote a dialogue on Immortality and Resurrection, called *Theophrastus*. An edition was published at Zurich in 1559–60."

Grierson (1912, 2:262–63) locates and publishes the original Latin verses in *Pia Hilaria Variaque Carmina Angelini Gazæi* (Dillingen, 1623), but notes that "the folios of this edition do not correspond to those of that which Donne seems to have used" (263).

Milgate (1967, 279–80) notes that *Gaz* was among the material added by the younger John Donne to the 1650 edition (279); he observes further that "in one of his letters to Goodyer (*Letters* 207–8) Donne mentions a translation (of which he seemed rather proud) that he thinks the Countess of Bedford might like to see; there is no evidence, however, that it was this one." Milgate adds that Angelinus Gazaeus was a Belgian Jesuit and that although the 1650 edition identifies the location of the original as "fol. 160," it does not in fact appear on that leaf in either the 1623 or the revised 1629 edition of *Pia Hilaria Variaque Carmina*. However, Milgate notes, the text of the lines in both editions is identical, and so the question of which Donne used is unimportant (280).

Shawcross (1967a, 383–84) states that the 1623 edition of Gazaeus was "not the one used by Donne" (383); he offers a literal translation of the Latin:

> May God grant you what you desire and what I wish
> ([May] the sun of fruitful friends [shine] on the best friends),
> that your soul, ever cheerful, know no cares,
> that your life, ever lively, know no gray hairs,
> that your right hand, ever abounding, know no base men,
> that your purse, ever full, know no wrinkles,
> that your tongue, ever true, know no lapse,
> that your word, ever mild, know no quarrels,
> that your deeds, ever equal, know no deceit,
> that your fame, ever pure, know no reproach,
> that your prayers, ever lofty, know no earthly things,
> may God grant you what you desire and what I wish. (384)

General Commentary

Gosse (1899, 2:118) terms the verses "eminently characteristic of Donne" and "instinct with grace and sincerity."

Notes and Glosses

Title **SHAWCROSS** (1967a) explains "out of *Gazaeus*": from "'Prayers composed by a friend'" in Gazaeus's *Poems and Songs to Saint Hilary* (383).

4 *Nor thy life, ever lively, know gray haires*. **MELTON** (1906): cf. the metrics of *EpEliz* 91–92 (159).

6 *pleits*, **SHAWCROSS** (1967a): "folds; that is, be so empty that its cloth will lie in folds" (383).

9 *equall*, **SHAWCROSS** (1967a): "just" (383).

9 *disguise*, **SHAWCROSS** (1967a): "falsity" (383).

Stationes, from *Devotions upon Emergent Occasions*

Commentary

Chambers (1896, 2:315–18) prints both the Latin and an English version of *Stat*, deriving the latter from a copy of the 1627 edition of the *Devotions* "in Dr. Grosart's possession." It is unclear whether Chambers regards the Latin version as poetry, but he calls the English rendition "another poem, to which Donne seems to have some claim" (315) and notes that Grosart believes it to be in Donne's handwriting. The English version reads as follows (317–18):

THE STATIONS OR PERIODS IN THE DISEASE TO
WHICH ARE REFERRED THE MEDITATIONS
FOLLOWING.

1. Sickness' first grudge: 2. Senses
 and action fall:
3. We take our bed: 4. And the
 physician call:
5. He comes alone: 6. Fears:
 7. Craves more may unite:
8. The King himself sends his:
 9. They medicines write:
10. They strive my grief as
 slowly to oppose,
 As, slowly and insensibly,
 it grows.
11. Still'd juices, and consorted
 pearls; what Art,
 Or Nature can, are used,
 to keep the heart
 From quick infection: 12.
 By a dying dove
 The vapours downward to
 the feet remove—
13. Th' ingenuous sickness on
 my spotted breast
 His kind and his malignity
 confess'd;

14. This too, the set days
Critical discover;
15. Meanwhile I sleepless
nights and days pass over;
16. And, from the adjoining tower,
the noise of bells
For others' funerals
Mine own foretells:
17. Soft gentle tolling, now, says
Thou must die;
18. Thou'rt dead, proclaims
the ringing out, by and bye.
19. At length the earth out of the
sea doth rise,
And the physicians, from
just grounds, surmise
They may with drugs fight
the weak enemy;
20. They purge. 21. He prospers
who by them dost cry,
Now Lazarus, leave thy bed:
22. Wisely take care.
Of thy disease's fuel;
23. Relapse fear.

Keeble (1927, 223) states that the *Devotions* are divided into twenty-three stages or *Stationes*, which he describes as "detailed" and "often amusing" and which for him constitute "if not a professional diagnosis of [Donne's] disease, at least the pathology or natural history of it."

Leishman (1951, 249) identifies *Stat* as prefixed to the *Devotions* proper and refers to them as "Latin verses describing the various stages of [Donne's] sickness and recovery."

Gransden (1954, 165–80) notes that Donne lists at the beginning of the *Devotions* "a series of twenty-two Latin hexameters which have all the fascination of a seventeenth-century medical case" (166).

Webber (1968, 19–20, 31–32) describes *Stat* as a Latin poem in dactylic hexameters "disguised as a table of contents" (19). Webber contends that rather than simply mirroring the Latin poem, the *Devotions* become an "*explication de texte*," Donne's "sermon upon his own text, to and upon his own soul" (20). Webber further argues that "the word 'station,' in another sense which Donne could hardly have escaped, refers to the Catholic service of the Stations of the Cross, in which a series of prayers is uttered before each of fourteen representations of Christ in his progress toward Calvary." This association, Weber concludes, "thus underlines the public context in which . . . [Donne] hoped to justify and immortalize his private experience" (32).

Lander (1971, 94) maintains that the Latin heading of each Devotion "recalls the form and language of the *historia morbi*, as patients' histories (generally recorded in Latin) were then called." Lander states that "the Latin hexameters employed in the first edition of *Devotions* were later discarded, possibly as appearing too contrived." (Lander is in error, since the Latin appears in every known seventeenth-century edition and issue of the *Devotions*; see the textual introduction and apparatus to *Stat*—eds.)

Printing *Stat* as an editorially formatted poem of 30 lines, Raspa (1975, xxiii, liii–liv, 144, 155, 164, 170) identifies several errata in *Stat* in the early editions of the *Devotions*: the second edition (1626) prints "*stignate* for *stigmate*, and II for 18" (liii); and the third edition (1626) repeats these errors and introduces four new ones—*incubitus* for *insultus* (l. 1), *iungitur* for *iungier* (l. 6), *obstrepera* for *obstreperae* (l. 29), and *sonita* for *sonitu* (l. 33) (liv).

Savage (1975, xvi, cxvii–cxviii), in her edition of the *Devotions*, prints *Stat* with line numbers and identifies the Latin headings as "Donne's own poetic description of his illness" (xvi). Savage further describes printings and interpretations of *Stat* in editions from Alford (1839) through William Draper, introduction to *Devotions upon Emergent Occasions together with Death's Duel*... (London: Simpkin, Marshall, Hamilton, Kent & Co., 1926) (cxviii).

Novarr (1980, 161–70) states that although *Stat* appears to be a Latin table of contents, these lines constitute a poem made up of twenty-two hexameters. Despite this assertion, Novarr argues that certain features make the lines seem "hardly to be a poem at all." In particular, he contends that, even though the poem has "a metrical design" and its words have "some sonority," it nevertheless lacks "Donne's customary wit, drama, and imagination." "We get emphasis," Novarr explains, "but not coherence; 'Stationes' strikes us as a group of tags, some very short, some longer" (165). Questioning the poetic intention that lies behind "these tags, these spots of time" (166), Novarr concludes that "for the purpose of his own devotion" Donne creates in *Stat* "pictures of his own sufferings" (167) that imitate the Stations of the Cross, which function for the worshiper as a vivid pictorial representation of the sufferings of Jesus. In other words, *Stat* contains "the spots or letters written by God and by himself," the "literal scriptural text" (169) that Donne then fully interprets in the prose Meditations, Expostulations, and Prayers that follow. Furthermore, Novarr avers, in recreating himself in the words of the Latin poem ("his own child") Donne "imitated his own Maker." Novarr concludes that within the "ingenious sterility" of the *Stat* Donne shows his willingness "to attempt a mode new to him, to fashion a bold conceit in the manner of God, stripped of correspondences" (170).

Frost (1990, xi, 18, 68, 93, 109–10, 125) describes *Stat* as "the story of the illness in twenty-two lines of Latin hexameter" (xi), a story in which Donne presents a type of the thanksgiving hymn of Hezekiah in "his own rather idiosyncratic version" (68). She adds that a consideration of the formal elements of the *Devotions*—which comprise not only Meditations, Expostulations, and Prayers, but also *Stat* and the "Epistle Dedicatory"—reveals a structure "patterned both autobiographically and temporally by the use of number symbolism" (93). Arguing that "a twenty-two-line metrical preface was not unique," Frost notes in particular that "the number was often used for structural composition because of its association with the books of the Bible and the letters of the Hebrew alphabet, a structure reflected in Psalm 118, the Book of Lamentations, and in Jerome's manipulation of the books of the Old Testament to achieve the total number of letters in the Greek alphabet" (109). Frost further avers that "the number 22" is "associated with the soul," for "in the *Timaeus*, twenty-two terms compose the 'double interval' series involved in the formation of the soul" (110). Finally, Frost identifies 359 metrical feet in *Stat* and argues that these, spread over the twenty-three sections of the *Devotions*, constitute a numerological arrangement that both reflects the imperfect circularity of time in this life and associates the poem with Spenser's *Epithalamion* (125).

Notes and Glosses

7 *his owne Phisician*. **RASPA** (1975): "James sent the Swiss-born French-educated Sir Theodore de Mayerne, who was appointed his physician in 1611, to examine Donne" (144).

12 *venim* **RASPA** (1975): "Venom was not a specific illness, but a word grouping all illnesses afflicting the body from the outside ('Venom is a thing, which being taken at the mouth, or applied outwardly, doeth overcome our bodies, by making them sicke, or by corrupting of them, or by killing them,' Monardes, 1580, Fol. 115)" (155).

23–24 *the criticall dayes*. **RASPA** (1975): "The arrival of this crisis is indicated in the previous meditation by the 'accidents' of the red spots on his body. Donne's description of his crisis is largely metaphoric rather than literal, serving as the occasion for a meditation on the role of time in human happiness" (164).

28–29 *From the bels of the church adioyning*, **RASPA** (1975): "The sixteenth devotion is the first of three devotions on bells. Each devotion deals with one of the three bells recommended to be rung by the minister for his ill or deceased parishioners in the section on 'Ministers to Visit the Sick' in *Constitutions and Canons* of the Church of England . . . . However, Donne does not deal with the bells in their logical canonical order, which is the passing bell, the death knell and the funeral bell, but begins with the third and then returns to the first and second. The section in the canons reads: 'When any man is dangerously sicke in any Parish, the Minister or Curate (having knowledge thereof) shall resort unto him or her, (if the disease be not knowen or probably suspected to be infectious) to instruct and comfort them in their distress, according to the order of the Communion booke, if hee be no Preacher: or if he be a Preacher, then as he shal thinke most needefull and convenient. And when any is passing out of this life, a Bell shalbe tolled, and the Minister shall not then slacke to doe his last duetie. And after the parties death (if it so fall out) there shall bee rung no more but one short peale, and one other before buriall, and one other after the buriall'" (170).

Apotheosis Ignatij Loyolae.

Commentary

Stanwood (1967, 984) first notes *Apoth*—a previously unrecorded Latin poem attributed to "D[r] Dun. Deane of Paules"—in volume 27 of the Hunter manuscript collection in the Cathedral Library of Durham and observes that the poem "evidently refers to the canonization (the 'apotheosis') of St. Ignatius of Loyola," whose Feast was fixed on July 31 in 1622. Following a comment that the "playfully satirizing" manner of the poem is typical of Donne, Stanwood offers a prose translation:

> Loyola, who was already venerable, now begins to be holy, and, being numbered among the saints, he triumphs. But he complains that the Calendar is full, margins and back alike, and that there is no place left for him to stand in red. But see, he has found one: the most audacious Copyist, blotting out Germanus, has had the temerity to substitute an interloper. From this arises a hot contention, for the new arrival will not go away, the first comer will not budge, and they will not agree to share. What says the Holy Father to this? He who binds and looses everything, looses this knot too with original cleverness. "Stand together," he says, "and be quiet in your stable, like Simon and Jude who share a day [i.e. October 28]. If not, then let Ignatius wait for February 15 in every fourth year and have as his own the conflated day."

Stanwood adds that although the poem does not actually echo *Ignatius*, "the satiric tone is the same in both . . . with an irreverence and wittiness that suit well with Donne's." The last half of the article discusses the identity and history of Thomas Carre (or Carr), the scribe of this copy of the poem. Stanwood concludes that there is no reason to doubt the authenticity of the poem.

Dionisotti (1967, 1037) challenges Stanwood's translation at several points (see glosses below), arguing that his own readings will lead to a "slightly different" and "more cogent interpretation" of *Apoth*.

Shawcross (1967a, 505–06), citing Stanwood's discovery, categorizes *Apoth* as an epigram and prints it in his edition. He glosses the word "Apotheosis" as a reference to the canonization of Ignatius in 1622 and offers the following translation (506):

The Apotheosis of Ignatius of Loyola

> Loyola, who previously was venerable, now begins to be holy,
> and, numbered among the divine, he rejoices.
> But he complains that the calendar is filled on the back and margin
> in red, and a place does not remain [for him] to be present.

He finds one: the most audacious copyist blots out
Germanus, by no means afraid to substitute a counterfeit.

A fierce dispute arises from this, for the new arrival will not go away,
the first will not budge, and they will not share.

What says the Holy Father to this? He who binds and looses all things
unloosens this knot with singular cleverness.

"Stand together," he says, "and be quiet in your stable,
like Simon and Jude who share one day.

If not, let Ignatius wait for the fifteenth of February
in every fourth year and take possession of the conflated day."

Healy (1969, 174–75), citing Stanwood as his authority, prints the poem and states that Carre had connections with some of Donne's friends, although it is uncertain whether he knew Donne personally. Following Stanwood, Healy observes that the handwriting appears to date from the early 1630s, although attribution of the copy to Carre cannot be verified. "There are, however," Healy argues, "certain internal reasons for saying that these verses could well be by Donne. The dramatic (and outrageous) situation, the technical accuracy and the good-humored wit are all reminiscent of *Ignatius His Conclave*" (175).

Haley (1971, 133–34) concludes his discussion of Donne's satirization of the Jesuits with brief comments upon *Apoth*, which he characterizes as "no more than a 'conceit' that does little beyond showing what a clever fellow its author was." In addition, Haley provides the following translation (134):

You (long accursed) begin now to be holy,
Loyola, and stand numbered with the saints.
Complaint? Yes, that the Calendar is full,
Margins and back alike. There is no place
For anyone to show in red, but see!
You've found a spot: th'Audacious Copyist
Rubs out Germanus, and temerariously
Has substituted you, an illegitimate, there.

Wherefore sharp strife has come, and (new arrival)
You yield not to the old nor he to you,
And neither will consent to co-exist.
What says the Holy Father who binds and looses?
This knot he looses with new dexterity:
"Stand ye together, be quiet in your stall
Like Simon and Judas who share so a day.
If not, then you, Ignatius, must wait
The twenty-ninth of February and shine
One year in four on your Conflated Day."

Kaplan (1971, 27–28) cites *Apoth* to account for a similar piece of apparent mockery in the Induction to Thomas Middleton's A *Game at Chesse*. He cites Stanwood (1967) and Shawcross (1967a) (see note on l. 14 below) to explain Middleton's reference to leap-year, suggesting that Donne's "fuller version" of the story of Ignatius's supposed indignation complements that in Middleton's verses (28).

In addition to the copy in Durham Cathedral, Beal (1980, 259, 380) notes another manuscript transcription "in a scribal hand" that contains variations in the wording of the title and of line 1 and appears "without attribution, but subscribed 'Th.', on a single leaf in a composite volume of papers of William Camden [1622–23]," Bodleian ms. Smith 17, p. 192 (380). Beal characterizes *Apoth* as "a somewhat questionable addition to Grierson's version of the canon . . . in uninspired Latin" and advances the possibility that the ascription to Donne in the Durham manuscript reflects only an association of the lines with Donne's prose tract *Ignatius His Conclave* of 1611 (259).

Also contesting Donne's authorship, Novarr (1980, 159–61) points to the pressure of Donne's duties as a new Dean as a factor making his authorship of such a work at such a time improbable, but concedes that internal evidence is suggestive of Donne's hand: both the content and the style of *Apoth* recall his early writings, and the poem's position toward the saint resembles the one taken in *Ignatius*. However, Novarr argues, the external evidence is unconvincing—although the poem is attributed to Donne by Thomas Carre, "there is no evidence that . . . [Carre] knew Donne," and "it is difficult to imagine how Carre might have got a copy of a poem by Donne otherwise unknown" (160). Novarr reasons that "any man faced with an anonymous satiric poem on the subject of Loyola's apotheosis might have guessed that the poem was Donne's," especially in the 1630s, because of the recent publication of Donne's poems, which, despite the absence of the author's full name in the edition, were widely known to be Donne's. Furthermore, Novarr argues, Donne had not written a satire since 1611 (i.e., *Coryat*), nor any Latin poems before 1622 other than three markedly different from *Apoth* in "motive and purpose"—*Amic*, *Libro*, and *GHerb* (161).

Beal and Kelliher (1982, 162) argue that *Apoth* was in fact written by Raphael Thorius (d. 1625) "and has no connection with Donne." Besides the text found in Carre's miscellany (discovered by Stanwood), Beal and Kelliher describe three other texts of the epigram: the one subscribed "Th." (described above) in the papers of William Camden, whom Beal and Kelliher identify as a friend of Thorius, and two others in British Library manuscripts, both identified by Beal and Kelliher as in Thorius's hand. They describe Carre's version as late and corrupt and restate Beal's (1980) suggestion that Carre's ascription of the poem to Donne reflects an understandable but erroneous association with Donne's 1611 tract against Loyola.

Notes and Glosses

1 *sacer . . . sanctus* **STANWOOD** (1967): these words "refer respectively to Loyola's beatification and canonization" (984). **DIONISOTTI** (1967): *sacer* and *sanctus* are "obviously opposed to each other: they cannot 'refer respectively to Loyola's beatifi-

cation and canonization.'" *Sacer* means "cursed" (cf. Vergil, *auri sacra fames*); "cursed" properly describes the attitude of non-Catholics to Loyola (1037).

1 *sacer* **SHAWCROSS** (1967a): "venerable," with a possible pun on "accursed" (505).

1 *ante fuit*, **DIONISOTTI** (1967): Stanwood's "already" does not "rightly translate *ante*" (1037).

1 *nunc* **SHAWCROSS** (1967a): "now"; "Ignatius had been beatified earlier in 1609" (505).

3 *Sed queritur plenis a tergo & margine fastis* **STANWOOD** (1967): the line "contains a reminiscence of Juvenal, I 5–6, appropriate for setting satirical tone" (984).

4 *in minio*, **SHAWCROSS** (1967a): "in red"; i.e., "in rubrics; that is, in red letters" (505). **STANWOOD** (1967): "the technical liturgical word for what was to be set out in the rubrics, that is, in red letters" (984).

6 *Germano*, **SHAWCROSS** (1967a): St. Germanus of Auxerre, who was dropped from the calendar when his feast day (July 31) was assigned to St. Ignatius (505).

6 *nothum*. **DIONISOTTI** (1967): not "interloper" as in Stanwood's translation, but "illegitimate" or "bastard" (1037).

9–10 *qui vincit . . . hunc nodum* **SHAWCROSS** (1967a) finds here a reference to Matt. 16.19: "and whatsoever thou shalt bind on earth shall be bound in heaven; and whatsoever thou shalt loose on earth shall be loosed in heaven" (505–06); "the text was used by the Roman Catholic Church to prove the powers of the Papacy" (506).

11 *stabuloque* **STANWOOD** (1967): "*Stabulum* might mean any kind of humble dwelling or inn" (984). **DIONISOTTI** (1967): the alternatives Stanwood suggests are possible in other contexts, but in *Apoth* his translation "stable" is the only possible one (1037).

12 *Ut Simon & Judas, quos tenet una dies;* **DIONISOTTI** (1967): "The sinister *cleverness* of the Holy Father is underlined by his coupling of Germanus of Auxerre and Ignatius of Loyola in the Calendar 'ut Simon et Judas . . . .' No contemporary reader of the poem would have failed to think of another *Judas*" (1037). **SHAWCROSS** (1967a): "The feast day of both St. Simon and St. Jude is October 28" (506).

13–14 *Sin minus expectet . . . possideatque diem*. **STANWOOD** (1967): Donne refers here to Leap Year, "but according to the Old Style, or Julian Calendar, which added the extra day after the 24th. Donne lets us reckon with the Gregorian Calendar too, for we must add ten days according to the New Style in order to arrive at the

25th, or *dies bissextus*, the Leap Year day. This reading naturally assumes that Donne is using the classical Latin sense of *februa*, or the purificatory offerings made on the festival which fell on February 15. He could, however, be using *februa* loosely as a convenient metrical equivalent for February; then the right sense for *februa* would be February, a reading justified as a rhetorical figure, synecdoche. One might now translate, 'let [him] wait for the February of every fourth year and appropriate the 29th as his own day'" (984). **HALEY** (1971): these lines refer to "the fact that Donne disliked as an innovation the Gregorian calendar of 1582" (133).

13–14 *quartani . . . anni / Februa*, **DIONISOTTI** (1967): a possible pun on *quartana febris* (1037).

14 *Februa*, **DIONISOTTI** (1967): "The original meaning of *februa* may have been partly preserved" in *Apoth*, with implications of "a much needed purification," but the author cannot have meant 15 February ("the actual date of the classical feast"), which was not "a *conflatus dies*, i.e., a fictitious day." Rather the intended date is 29 February, "which did not figure in the traditional calendar but which was included in the new popish calendar" (1037). **SHAWCROSS** (1967a): i.e., February 15th. "This was the feast of purification and expiation. But the lines involve 'conflated' dates. The fifteenth under the Julian Calendar would be the twenty-fifth under the Gregorian Calendar (since there was a ten-day difference between them in the seventeenth century). But the twenty-fifth in the Julian Calendar was Leap Year, and thus the poet is assigning only the one day of Leap Year to Ignatius" (506).

A sheaf of Miscellany EPIGRAMS. Written in *Latin* by *J. D.* *Translated by* J. Main *D. D.*

Commentary

Sixty poems in English appear under the title *A Sheaf of Miscellany EPIGRAMS. Written in Latin by J. D. Translated by* J. Main *D. D.* within *Paradoxes, Problemes, Essayes, Characters* (1652), a volume of Donne's prose works edited by his son John Donne, Jr. The fifty-ninth poem appears in Latin as well. The dedicatory epistle by the younger Donne characterizes the volume as containing both "entainment [sic] of the Author's Youth" and weighty, mature examples of his father's work.

Wood (1691, 1:col. 474), in his biographical essay on Donne, cites "Jasp. Mayne" among the "Wits and Virtuosi of his time" who "celebrated" Donne and had his memory "in great veneration."

Brydges (1814, 225–26) calls these poems Mayne's only "poetical publication" other than two plays. Observing that "these trifles hardly afford a specimen worth selecting," he quotes *Sheaf50* and *Sheaf52* in full (226).

Noble (1821 [1968, 13]), in a brief catalogue of Donne's works, lists "2 Epigrams written in Latin, translated into English by J. Maine D. D. his Friend."

Jessopp (1855, xiii, lxx), calling these poems "some youthful efforts at verse, which were discovered after [Donne's] death, and published by his son" (xiii), characterizes them thus: "The epigrams and poems were written in Donne's boyhood. The wretched man [i.e., John Donne, Jr.], who would not even leave them in their Latin dress, could not see that there was anything disgraceful in putting forth this obscene trash in the meretricious garb of a English rhyme, and attaching to the unworthy rubbish his father's revered name. —On the son, not the father, the scandal of their publicity must rest" (lxx). On the basis of internal evidence understanding the poems to be connected with the siege of Bois-le-Duc (s'Hertogenbosch) by Prince Maurice of Nassau in 1587, Jessopp, although noting that boys were commonly introduced early to soldiering, finds it "vain to attempt any explanation of the probable circumstances under which . . . [Donne] joined the forces of Prince Maurice." Jessopp further observes that the epigrams demonstrate strong sympathy for the side on which the author served and questions the likelihood of Donne's having fought for the Protestant cause in this conflict (xiii).

Grosart (1870a, 504) appeals for information on *Sheaf* for his forthcoming edition of Donne.

Grosart is answered by "Cpl." (T. R. O'Flaherty) (1870, 565), who characterizes *Sheaf* as "in great part a collection of filth, which the reverend translator had not the decency to leave under the veil of its original language. . . . The only interest in the Epigrams is in those that refer to Donne's adventures in early life, when he was 'at the siege of Duke's Wood,' or Bois-le-Duc, under the Earl of Leicester."

Grosart (1870b, 587) responds to "Cpl." by querying "Is not *filth* rather too strong a word?" and by conceding that Mayne ought to have left "*a few*" in Latin only. Grosart appeals for help in locating the Latin originals of which the poems are purported to be translations.

Grosart (1872–73, 2:xviii–xxv, 266) subsequently rejects the ascription to Donne of the poems contained in *Sheaf*, terming such exclusion "a satisfaction" based on "multiplied external and internal proofs of the imposture perpetrated by probably the impecunious younger Donne" (266). Against Donne's authorship Grosart presents a detailed argument (xviii–xxv) grounded in the discrepancies between the events purportedly described in some of the poems and their chronology. Citing *Sheaf*53, Grosart states that "most of the Epigrams and Poems in this Collection" refer to Duke's Wood, and that the phrase "Golden Fruit" in *Sheaf*53, as well as other references to "Aurange" (in, among others, *Sheaf*55), allude to the Prince of Orange as commander throughout the siege and the fighting and as the victor. However, Grosart argues, between 1584 and 1618 there was no Prince of Orange in Holland; Philip William, the eldest son of William Prince of Orange, was, Grosart maintains, detained in Spain, while his younger brother, Prince Maurice of Nassau, captain-general of the Dutch armies after 1587, did not assume the title of Prince of Orange until his brother's death in 1618. An attempt on Bois-le-Duc was made in 1587, Grosart notes, but Prince Maurice would not have been "Prince of Orange" then. Grosart characterizes the 1587 engagement as merely "the "skirmish of a detachment," although the epigrams "distinctly speak of a leaguer and a siege" (xix–xx). Grosart questions the likelihood of Donne's having been sent to this war at all, because of his age (which Grosart, assuming a birthdate in 1573, calculates as 14) and because of his early dedication to his studies, which, Grosart maintains, his family intended him to pursue thoroughly. Also, Grosart argues, the epigrams themselves "are the sole foundation for this supposed incident, at whatever age it occurred."

Grosart further argues that evidence for Donne's having been in Flanders in 1590 as furnished in the 1852 reprint of Walton's *Life* by Henry Kent Causton (with notes by Thomas Edlyne Tomlins) is inaccurate. Tomlins places the Earl of Essex in Flanders fighting the Spanish in that year, when in fact, Grosart argues, he was then in France fighting the French. Grosart observes that Walton places Donne at the Inns of Court in 1590 (xx). Prince Maurice, he adds, unsuccessfully besieged Bois-le-Duc in 1600 and 1603, when Donne was successively secretary to the Lord Keeper, in love with his future wife, a married man, and a prisoner. Grosart concludes that the Causton edition's citation of evidence is misapplied, misunderstood, "preposterous and incorrect."

Grosart's arguments also involve the character "Heyn" named in *Sheaf*56 41, a man, Grosart states, born only in 1570 and well known for his martial actions from 1624 onward and especially (according to Grosart) for an exploit in 1628, when Donne was a preacher (xxi). Grosart concludes that the references to Bois-le-Duc, the Prince of Orange, the latter's victory, and Heyn and his exploits "all concur in pointing to the successful siege of Bois-le-Duc by Frederick William Prince of Orange in 1628, while difficulties and improbabilities concur in making one disbelieve that Donne engaged in any of the operations in Holland before 1596, much less in any siege of Bois-le-Duc." Grosart concedes that Donne might have served as a volunteer in Holland in the interval between the Cadiz expedition of 1596 and the Islands Voyage and Expedition of 1597, "but at that time," he continues, "there was no siege of Bois-le-Duc, and so no authority for Donne's authorship of the Epigrams." Moreover, he continues, "the theory that Donne went abroad previous to 1596 is wholly contrary to two passages in Walton's Life" to the effect that Donne went directly from the university to London for study (xxii), "and when . . . [Walton] mentions . . . [Donne's] going abroad, he says so in words which imply that he had not gone abroad before." Moreover, according to Grosart, although Donne often spoke of his travels, Walton does not record any that correspond to the episodes apparently recorded in these epigrams.

Grosart also raises the issue of Donne's religion, questioning why Donne, still a Catholic, would enlist on the Protestant side in another country's war. Grosart further notes that the younger Donne's epistle dedicatory to the 1652 edition does not refer to *Sheaf*, nor do any of these epigrams appear "in his editions of his Father's Poems," although in the edition of 1633 and afterwards other epigrams appear (xxiii). Referring to Mayne as the "alleged" translator, Grosart surmises that the bookseller may have used Mayne's name as "a trick to pass the publication." Expressing regret at the loss to the canon of numbers 56, 57, and 58, Grosart nevertheless says that "it is a relief to be able to take from him" the "pieces to an Actress [*Sheaf*59 and *Sheaf*60?], and the run of the Epigrams." Responding to Jessopp (1855), Grosart terms the poems "not 'rubbish,' although faulty in many ways" (xxiv).

A prolonged exchange in *Ath* begins with Jessopp's (1873a, 81–82) laying blame on Donne, Jr., for allegedly selling his father's work for ready cash "whenever the fit took him." Jessopp argues that Donne, Jr., published *Paradoxes, Problemes, Essayes, Characters* in 1652 only for profit, having "suppressed" it twenty years previously. As the *Paradoxes*, however, "were not nasty enough for . . . such profligates as he appealed to, he threw in the 'Sheaf of Epigrams,' which it seems that his father had scribbled as a boy in that prurient stage of a lad's development when he deals in uncleanness and profanity." Deploring this publication, Jessopp explains that the presumed difficulty of Donne's original Latin necessitated the translations. Jessopp characterizes Mayne as "notorious" for his "impure comedies" and "gross humour," and further defends his characterization of Donne, Jr., citing a "filthy and obscene" letter of the younger Donne's to Lord Newport (the dedicatee of the 1652 edition) in his own possession, but arguing that Donne, Jr., was nevertheless "not a fool, and . . . had nothing to gain by pretending that his father wrote the Epigrams" and that he undoubtedly believed that his father "did so write them." Conceding on the subject of dating only that the date of the engagement at Bois-le-Duc was 13 July (not 13 June) 1587 (81), Jessopp furnishes an account of the Prince of Parma's siege of Sluys, which, he argues (citing John Lothrop Motley, *History of the United Netherlands* [London, 1860 and later eds.]), entailed the effort of Prince Maurice of Nassau to relieve Sluys in part by a siege of Bois-le-Duc, "a post of extreme importance." Jessopp cites three published references to the siege, offers to provide more, and concludes that there definitely was a major engagement at Bois-le-Duc on that date. Concurrently Jessopp dismisses any objection to the lack of a so-called "Prince of Orange" at that time, arguing that Prince Maurice was then regarded as representative of the House of Orange and is referred to in many accounts as "Mauricius Auriacus." Of the Heyn mentioned by Grosart Jessopp disclaims any knowledge, while demanding proof that the Heyn named in *Sheaf56* is in fact the man celebrated for his exploits in 1624 (82).

Responding to the previous correspondence, "R. D." (1873, 148) identifies the "Heynskirch" of *Sheaf56* 40 as the Dutch navigator Hemskerk, who sought a northeast passage to China in 1596 and the "Oliver" of the same line as Oliver Van Noort, Admiral of a Dutch squadron that circumnavigated the globe between 1598 and 1601, fighting the Spanish along the way. "R. D." further identifies the "Heyn" of line 41 as Peter Peterson Heyn or "Piet Heyn," a valiant Dutch admiral killed in action at sea in 1629. "R. D." argues that this Heyn was quite famous as of 1624 and that the passage in question refers to Heyn's capture of the Spanish silver fleet in 1628.

Grosart (1873, 179–80) rejects Jessopp's arguments (1873a) as "hysterics," claims that Jessopp is "carping at one or two points—which he does not understand— . . . [while leaving] the crucial ones untouched." Grosart finds Jessopp's account of the younger Donne's character and actions in regard to the epigrams unsupported by evidence, arguing that the presence of one Latin poem in the group implies that Donne, Jr., did not possess the others. Grosart also states that Jessopp's condemnation of Mayne's character is unsupported by evidence. As for the evidence of lewdness in the poems themselves, Grosart maintains, from number 27 onward (all treating of Bois-le-Duc) "there is nothing beyond a young soldier's casual reference to the loose women of the camp, and a young man's somewhat loose admiration of an actress. The others, which seem separated from them, are coarse and stupid, but not coarser than may be published. . . . There are, too, good bits" (179). Grosart further advances the following arguments in defense of his former position: (a) even if the epigrams are conceded to refer to the 1587 campaign, Jessopp has not answered Grosart's prior arguments about the improbability of Donne's having been there; (b) the identity of Heyn demands a date no earlier than 1624.

Jessopp (1873b, 211) accepts the arguments of "R.D." (1873), commenting, "I can but rejoice that Mr. Grosart has cleared the good Dean's reputation from the scandal of having written such discreditable rubbish." Jessopp attributes his change of mind altogether to "R.D."'s evidence about Heyn, but observes that "Heynskirch," identified by "R.D." as a major explorer, "would be difficult to put into Latin."

On the subject of Heyn, Nicholson (1873, 210–11) argues that the evidence supports a date in the 1620's rather than 1587, and finds that the references in *Sheaf56* are clearly to Dutch naval events and men of the 1620's. Nicholson further supports a 1629 date for the siege at Bois-le-Duc, also observing that numbers 1–26 "have no marks of place or date, and rather appear to belong to a different period" (211). But the language of *Sheaf*53, he argues, presenting an image of the Prince of Orange crowned with laurel, must refer to the significant capitulation of Bois-le-Duc in 1629. Further, he maintains, in *Sheaf*54 "Holland" is distinguished from and subordinated to "Aurange" in praise of the victors over the Spanish because the States-General of Holland had initially resisted the Prince of Orange in his project for the siege of Bois-le-Duc. Nicholson, citing historians, claims that there was no such siege in 1587.

Bullen (1884, 90) terms the epigrams "possibly spurious."

Jessopp (1888, 15:233), appends to a bibliographic entry (*Fasciculus Poematum & Epigrammatum Miscellaneorum. Translated into English by Jasp. Mayne, D. D. . . . London, 8vo, 1652*) the comment, "This collection is almost wholly spurious."

Chambers (1896, 2:308–11) terms the poems in *Sheaf* "in all probability spurious," observing that internal evidence makes it clear that the author "was or had been serving in the Netherlands." Despite the absence of references in Walton's *Life* to travels before 1596, Chambers notes, the 1591 Marshall portrait shows Donne with his hand on a sword-hilt, "and therefore he may, rather than must have been at some time a soldier" (309). Chambers observes, however, that Grosart's arguments of 1873 have carried the day, summarizing thus: "It goes without saying that Donne did not write these Epigrams, many of which are not particularly refined, in 1628; and if, therefore, some of them are clearly of that date, the whole must be rejected as inauthentic." Conceding that the evidence is not sufficient to justify much speculation on the epigrams' origin, Chambers allows the possibility that the younger Donne might have written them, that there were never any Latin originals, or that they are by "John Done" (another man altogether). He calls attention, however, to Donne's letter in Latin to Sir Henry Goodyere (printed in the edition of 1633, 351–52, but not referred to by Jessopp or Grosart) that contains a reference to "epigrammata mea Latina," a passage "which proves, certainly not that these Epigrams are Donne's, but that he did write a set of Latin Epigrams" (310). Chambers further notes that the "Catalogus librorum satyricus" also mentioned in the letter "was printed in the Appendix to the *Poems* of 1650," although it was not "accompanied by any Latin epigrams" (311).

In his copy of the 1652 *Paradoxes* (in the Houghton Library, Harvard University), Charles Eliot Norton (1897) wrote on a blank page "The Epigrams are certainly (?) [sic] not Donne's" and refers the reader to Grosart (1873). Norton comments that though Grosart is "generally little to be trusted," he seems to have won this point.

Gosse (1899, 1:16–17; 2:321–23) calls the case of the Latin epigrams a "mare's nest," most of them being "merely gross." Gosse accepts the arguments of Grosart (1873) and Nicholson (1873) and characterizes the 1652 *Sheaf* as a "fraud" (1:16), further describing Mayne as a celebrated practical joker, driven by poverty either to connive in misrepresenting his own verses as translations of Donne's or to deceive the younger Donne into so believing. Gosse also suggests that the alleged fraud might date from 1633, a year in which an edition of Donne's *Juvenilia* became the object of a Star Chamber inquiry. In its original form, before censorship, the book might have contained the *Sheaf*, Gosse speculates, for extant copies of *Juvenilia* show evidence of mutilation. Gosse further notes that in 1651 the younger Donne brought out the *Essays in Divinity*, at the close of which is an advertisement of the forthcoming publication of the *Fasciculus*. Gosse describes this as "the fraudulent collection of spurious pieces in Latin, of which repeated mention has been made. Had these verses been genuine, they would now have been at least sixty years old" (2:322–23). Noting that all that eventually appeared were the translations included in the 1652 *Sheaf*, Gosse concludes that the facts about "this exasperating and not very important piece of mystification" will probably never be known and that probably no Latin originals ever existed (2:323).

Simpson (1924, 134–35) notes the entry in the Stationers' Register on 15 March 1650 of a license to the publisher Humphrey Moseley for a work entitled *Fasciculus Poematum et Epigrammatum Miscellaneorum Authore Johanne Dome* [sic] *D. D. Englished by Jasper Maine, Doctor in Divinity*. She concludes that this entry indicates an intention to issue the epigrams as a separate volume and characterizes the poems as "mostly coarse and trivial in the usual style of seventeenth-century epigrams, but which include also a small group of verses referring to wars in the Low Countries" (134). Citing the prior arguments of Jessopp, Grosart, Chambers, and Gosse (see above) about the figure of Heyn and the date and circumstances allegedly referred to in the *Sheaf*, she discounts the idea of identifying any of these poems with the Latin epigrams Donne mentions in his letter to Goodyere.

Simpson (1930, 3–4) subsequently alludes to the Latin epigrams referred to in the Goodyere letter and suggests 1611 as the date of the letter, basing the suggestion on Donne's mention there of a projected trip to the continent, "probably the visit to France with Sir Robert and Lady Drury, which occupied part of 1611 and 1612" (Simpson cites Chambers 1896, 2:310, for the information on the trip with the Drurys) (4).

Milgate (1950, 383) notes that William London's *Catalogue of the most vendible Books in England* (1657) lists both the 1652 *Paradoxes* and—under "Hebrew, Greek, and Latin Books"—the following: "D. *Donn Fasciculus Poematum et Epigrammatum Miscellaneorum*." Milgate cites this entry as evidence that "this volume of Latin poems, falsely attributed to Donne" might have been printed as a single book.

Keynes (1958, 73) also cites the listing of the *Fasciculus* in London's *Catalogue* with the date 1658.

Whitlock (1962, 15–19) dismisses as "dishonest" Gosse's advancement (1899) of the argument that the allusions to "Duke's Wood" refer to events of 1628. He objects to Gosse's dating of the supposed earlier engagement in 1585 (when "Donne was only twelve") rather than 1587 and labels "fallacious" Chambers's thinking (1896) that if any of the epigrams should date from 1628, then all should necessarily be dismissed. Whitlock argues that such logic, if applied to "almost every collection of Donne's poetry" (15), would entail wholesale dismissals from the canon, inasmuch as spurious poems (he maintains) appear in all of them. Noting that the Latin epigrams mentioned by Donne in his letter to Goodyere have generally been thought to be lost, Whitlock suggests that they might be the Latin originals putatively translated by Mayne. He further questions Gosse's supposition that the 1632 *Juvenilia* was suppressed on account of the epigrams' possibly forming a portion of the volume, arguing that "if this is so, someone did a hurried job of putting epigrams from 1628 into the Donne poems." He also maintains that no one has adequately explained Mayne's reasons for passing off his own work as that of Donne, whom, Whitlock asserts, Mayne admired.

Whitlock divides the poems into five categories: (1) poems on bawds; (2) poems on an old, scolding wife; (3) poems on tobacco; (4) poems on the Bois-le-Duc engagement; (5) poems "on a piece of stage business" (*Sheaf*59). He terms the first two groups "purposely 'outrageous'," citing number 4 in full and comparing it to *ElProg* 91–96 and *ElAnag* 35–50. "We must remember," Whitlock continues, "that Donne had been reading Ovid, Martial, Ruiz, and even his grandfather's work (from which the figure of the old woman could easily derive). The section on tobacco seems to denote a trial of something quite new" (16). Whitlock cites numbers 20, 21, 24, and 25, noting the apparent connection to William Camden's 1585 account of the evils of tobacco, and concludes that Donne's epigrams "have the sound of a new discovery rather than an experience which by the late 1620's was anything but extraordinary." Conceding that some of the "Duke's Wood" poems probably date from 1628, Whitlock nevertheless argues that *Sheaf*41 and *Sheaf*47 show characteristics of Donne's epigrammatic style. Whitlock disclaims any intention of arguing "for the inclusion of the 'Duke's Wood' epigrams among Donne's poems," but states that he is "not completely convinced that all are not his."

Whitlock then takes up the question of the younger Donne's intentions and motives, arguing that although Donne, Jr., "may have altered letter headings, or misread manuscripts, or taken illegal possession of documents," he "never misrepresented his father's work nor sought to hurt his reputation." Citing Donne, Jr.'s, dedication to Lord Newport, Whitlock argues that the younger Donne must have intended the epigrams in *Sheaf* to be recognized as examples of his father's lighter, younger work, and would not have expected them to enhance the poet's reputation, though he nevertheless "printed them as genuine" (17). If he knew that his father had not been on the continent fighting in 1587, Whitlock maintains, then he could not have been deceived by Mayne; on the other hand, if the younger Donne—who, Whitlock asserts, was neither stupid nor crassly dishonest—knew that his father had fought on he continent during his youth, then he might have been misled into accepting the poems as genuine. Such reasoning by Donne, Jr., would not prove that Donne was at "Duke's Wood," but it might "give some evidence of Donne's activities after Oxford and . . . supply the reason for the Will Marshall engraving of Donne in soldier garb in 1591" (18). In view of his belief that the *Sheaf* is genuine, Whitlock denounces the "editorial suppression" of the epigrams of 1652 (which are not included in any subsequent editions). "Students of Donne," he maintains, have thereby "been robbed of much potentially important material." He calculates that approximately half of them may be of Donne's authorship "and may represent his earliest literary endeavors." "Neither their form nor their bawdy content," Whitlock argues, "is surprising when considered against his own family tradition of epigrammatic expression and his unusually early and precocious reading of highly-sexed literature." He links the editorial treatment of these poems to what he terms the "prim, Victorian" attitude of editors towards Donne's poetry generally, citing Grierson (1912, 2:86–88) on *ElFatal* as an instance (19).

Flynn (1984, 121–30) attempts to establish the authenticity of *Sheaf*, arguing that it consists, for the most part, of translations of lost Latin epigrams by Donne. He characterizes the internal evidence for denying Donne's authorship as "scant" (121) and examines the anachronisms on the basis of which Grosart and others refuse to attribute the epigrams to Donne. Flynn argues that the poems in *Sheaf* refer to two quite different sieges, separated by several decades. He argues that the references to s'Hertogenbosch (i.e., Bois-le-Duc or Duke's Wood), though prominent in the titles of numbers 53–57, have nothing to do with the subject-matter of most of the thirty-two poems (numbers 27–58) that describe military events in the Netherlands. Twenty of these poems (*Sheaf*27–*Sheaf*46), he argues, record "in a detailed and precise way" (122) episodes of the Spanish siege of Antwerp of 1584–85. Poems 27–31, Flynn argues, describe the construction of siege headquarters in the village of Calloo by the Prince of Parma (the Spanish commander-in-chief); s'Hertogenbosch, Flynn argues, underwent no such transformation, but Calloo did. Flynn identifies the subjects of numbers 32–36 as the twelve-mile canal dug by Parma's pioneers and argues the inappropriateness of an association with s'Hertogenbosch, where rivers were not created, but dammed up. It was at Antwerp in 1584, Flynn maintains, that the besieged Dutch caused the surrounding plain to be flooded, and numbers 39–41 describe the consequences; by contrast, he notes, at s'Hertogenbosch there was no flooding. A fourth group of five epigrams (numbers 42–46), Flynn maintains, describes how the former site of the Spanish camp appeared as a result of the flooding; by contrast, he argues, the Dutch besiegers of s'Hertogenbosch pitched their tents on marshes that were being drained.

Terming "incongruous" the two references to "Dukes-Wood" (in the title of *Sheaf*27 and *Sheaf*41 1) in these four sets, Flynn insists that these twenty poems exhibit a "clear emphasis on events of 1584–85" and that the anachronistic references do not constitute evidence that the poems are not Donne's. Noting that the anachronisms, especially the references to s'Hertogenbosch in numbers 53–57, "cannot have been translated from Donne's Latin" (125), he further points out that seven epigrams on the Low Countries fighting contain no datable references and that a further twenty-eight of the entire group of sixty have nothing to do with the Netherlands at all. In view of these details, he concludes, the case against the authenticity of the Mayne translations is weak. Flynn suggests that Mayne "for some reason may have inserted anachronisms into his translations of poems originally written about a unique combination of events that occurred half a century earlier," asking "What more likely explanation can there be for the bizarre and superficial appearance of references to the siege of s'Hertogenbosch in poems primarily about the siege of Antwerp?" (128).

Flynn attributes what he regards as the defects of existing criticism on the epigrams to a preoccupation with internal evidence and to a lack of acquaintance with important pieces of external evidence. Observing that "conclusions about authenticity based on purely external evidence have generally come down to judgments about the moral character of Jasper Mayne or of Donne's son" (126), he terms such judgments a matter of opinion. He surveys and draws conclusions from external evidence, citing the evidence of Donne's letter to Goodyere, which apparently refers to Latin epigrams by Donne; of the entry in the Stationers' Register showing that the *Fasciculus* was licensed to Humphrey Moseley on 15 March 1650; of Moseley's 1652 publication of *Paradoxes* (including the Mayne translations); of the younger Donne's epistle dedicatory to *Paradoxes*; and of Ben Jonson's poem (in the same volume) praising Donne as an epigrammatist. These pieces of evidence, he argues, point "to the existence of a copy of Donne's Latin Epigrams in the hands of Humphrey Moseley, and to the belief by Moseley and John Donne, Jr., that the Mayne translations published in 1652 did substantially represent Donne's originals" (126).

Flynn then advances bibliographical evidence suggesting that the *Fasciculus* did at one time exist. He cites the listing in Moseley's advertising catalogs of 1653, 1654, and 1656 of *Paradoxes*, the *Fasciculus* (projected for publication) and the *Fasciculus* (in print). Although, Flynn notes, no copy of the *Fasciculus* appears to be extant, William London's preface (see Milgate [1950] and Keynes [1958] above) states that for the Latin books included in the catalog only those London has actually seen and knows to be widely available are listed. Whether actually printed or not, Flynn concludes, the Latin epigrams would therefore appear to have existed. Furthermore, Flynn continues, in 1660 Moseley added to his catalogue an entry apparently describing a volume of the Latin poems combined with Mayne's translations, no copy of which is known to survive, and Wood (1691, 1:col. 474) lists such a volume of Donne's works with a publication date of 1632. Although no copy of this 1632 *Fasciculus* is known to be extant, references to events of 1628 and 1629 would, Flynn argues, have been topical in 1632, and it is probable, he maintains, that Mayne was making use of such recent events in his translations of Donne's Latin originals. In 1632, Flynn notes, both the younger Donne and Mayne were students at Christ Church, Oxford, and 1632 is a much likelier date than 1652 (by which time he was writing pamphlets and sermons) for Mayne to have been translating poetry. Flynn concludes that Mayne, "for some reason," may have inserted anachronistic references to events of 1628–29 into his translations of poems describing the much earlier events at the siege of Antwerp (128). Finally, he asserts, nothing in most of the translations contradicts their claim to be based on Donne's Latin epigrams.

Within the context of his argument that Donne had close and complex relationships with the English Catholic nobility, Flynn (1989b, 305–23) subsequently presents evidence that Donne, to avoid taking the Oath of Supremacy, went to France in 1585 as a waiting-gentleman to the Earl of Derby. Summarizing his argument of 1984 as evidence that Donne remained on the Continent to participate in the siege apparently described in some of these epigrams, Flynn further maintains that the thirty-two epigrams that he believes pertain to Parma's siege of Antwerp reflect Donne's association with Catholic fugitives preparing for an invasion of England. He cites *To Sleep, stealling upon him* (*Sheaf*57) as a record of the situation and events of the siege (317–18) and *To his Fellow Sentinels* (*Sheaf*58), which in alluding to Queen Elizabeth through a reference to a whore, he argues, expresses English Catholic attitudes. The poem, Flynn argues, pictures Donne as a member of the fugitive Catholics, who are united by devotion to honor.

Works Cited

Alford, Henry, ed. 1839. *The Works of John Donne, D. D., Dean of Saint Pauls 1621–1631, With a Memoir of His Life*. 6 vols. London: John W. Parker.

Allen, Don Cameron. 1947. "Donne's Phoenix." *MLN* 62:340–42.

Anonymous. 1633? Marginalia to "Ralphius." In *Poems, by J. D. With Elegies on the Authors Death*. London: John Marriott. [The Houghton Library, Harvard University.]

——. 1733. "To Sir Gimcrack Noddy." *US* 15 September:2.

——. 1733. "On Chloe's Picture." *US* 1 December:1.

——. 1823. Rev. of *Poems, &c by John Donne . . .* (1669). *RR* 8.1:31–55.

——. 1846. "Gallery of Poets: Specimen No. 1. The Poetry of Donne." *LEM* 1:228–36.

——. 1852. "Dumbledowndeary." *HW* 5:312–17.

——. 1899. Rev. of Edmund Gosse, *The Life and Letters of John Donne, Dean of St. Paul's*. *Ath* 11 November: 645–46.

Armitage, C. M. 1966. "Donne's Poems in Huntington Manuscript 198: New Light on 'The Funerall'." *SP* 63:697–707.

Arnold, Thomas, [Jr.]. 1867. *A Manual of English Literature: Historical and Critical*. Rev. as *Chaucer to Wordsworth. A Short History of English Literature from the Earliest Times to the Present Day*. London: Thomas Murby, n.d. (1868?).

"A. S." and T[homas] E[dlyne] Tomlins. 1906. [Untitled note]. *NQ*, 10th s., 6:228–29.

Atkinson, A. D. 1951. "Donne Quotations in Johnson's Dictionary." *NQ* 196: 387–88.

Bald, R. C. 1937. "Three Metaphysical Epigrams." *PQ* 16:402–05.

——. 1959. *Donne and the Drurys*. Cambridge: Cambridge University Press.

——. 1970. *John Donne: A Life*. Wesley Milgate, ed. New York and Oxford: Oxford University Press.

Bancroft, Thomas. 1639. *Two Bookes of Epigrammes, and Epitaphes*. London: Matthew Walbancke.

Beal, Peter. 1980. *Index of English Literary Manuscripts*, Vol. 1, Part 1. London: Mansell; New York: R. R. Bowker.

——, and Hilton Kelliher. 1982. "John Donne" [correspondence]. *TLS* 12 February: 162.

Beaver, Joseph C. 1976. *The Prosody of John Donne*. Chicago: n.p.

Belden, Henry M. 1915. Rev. of *The Poems of John Donne*, ed. Herbert J. C. Grierson. *JEGP* 14:135–47.

Bennett, Roger E., ed. 1942. *The Complete Poems of John Donne*. Chicago: Packard.

Berry, Lloyd E., comp. 1964. *A Bibliography of Studies in Metaphysical Poetry, 1939–1960*. Madison: University of Wisconsin Press.

Bewley, Marius, ed. 1966. *The Selected Poetry of Donne*. New York: New American Library. Rpt. 1979.

Bohm, Wilhelm. 1893. *Englands Einfluss auf Georg Rudolf Weckherlin*. Diss. Georg-Augusts-Universität. Göttingen: Univ.-Buchdruckerei.

B[ond], R[ichard] W. 1861. "Donne the Metaphysician." *TB* 3:78–91.
Bowers, Fredson. 1972. "Multiple Authority: New Problems and Concepts of Copy-Text." *Library*, 5th s., 27:81–115.
Bradford, Gamaliel. 1892. "The Poetry of Donne." *AR* 18:350–67.
British Museum. Addl. MS. 10309, f98v.
[Browning, Robert.] 1962. *The Letters of Robert Browning and Elizabeth Barrett Barrett, 1845–1846*. Ed. Elvan Kintner. 2 vols. Cambridge: Belknap Press of Harvard University Press.
Bryan, Robert A. 1962. "John Donne's Poems in Seventeenth-Century Commonplace Books." *ES* 43:170–74.
Brydges, Samuel Egerton. 1814. *Restituta; or, Titles, Extracts, and Characters of Old Books in English Literature, Revived*. Vol. I. London: Longman, Hurst, Rees, Orme, and Brown.
Bullen, A. H., ed. 1884. *Walton's Lives of Dr. John Donne, Sir Henry Wotton, Mr. Richard Hooker, Mr. George Herbert, and Dr. Robert Sanderson*. London: George Bell.
——, ed. 1890–91. *Davison's Poetical Rhapsody*. 2 vols. London: George Bell & Sons.
Bullough, Geoffrey. 1972. "Donne the Man of Law." In *Just So Much Honor: Essays Commemorating the Four-Hundredth Anniversary of the Birth of John Donne*, edited by Peter Amadeus Fiore, 57–94. University Park and London: The Pennsylvania State University Press.
Carey, John. 1981. *John Donne: Life, Mind and Art*. New York: Oxford University Press.
——. 1990. *John Donne*. The Oxford Authors. Oxford and New York: Oxford University Press.
Case, R. H. 1896. *English Epithalamies*. The Bodley Anthologies. London: John Lane; Chicago: A. C. McClurg.
Castagna, André. 1970. *Le Siècle Elisabéthain*. Collection «Panoramas Illustrés». Paris: Seghers.
Chalmers, Alexander, ed. 1810. *The Works of the English Poets, from Chaucer to Cowper*. 21 vols. London: J. Johnson.
Chambers, E. K., ed. 1896. *The Poems of John Donne*. With an Introduction by George Saintsbury. 2 vols. The Muses' Library. London: Lawrence and Bullen.
Chambers, Robert, ed. 1844. *Cyclopaedia of English Literature: A History, Critical and Biographical, of British Authors, from the Earliest to the Present Times*. 2 vols. Edinburgh: W. & R. Chambers.
Chase, Richard. 1945. *Quest for Myth*. Baton Rouge: Louisiana State University Press.
Clements, A. L., ed. 1966. *John Donne's Poetry*. Norton Critical Edition. New York: Norton.
Clive, Mary. 1966. *Jack and the Doctor*. London: Macmillan; New York: St. Martin's Press.
Clough, Benjamin C. 1920. "Notes on the Metaphysical Poets." *MLN* 35:115–17.
Coffin, Charles Monroe. 1937. *John Donne and the New Philosophy*. New York: Columbia University Press.
Coleridge, Samuel Taylor. 1809. *The Friend*. Ed. Barbara Rooke. 2 vols. *The Collected Works of Samuel Taylor Coleridge*, 4. Bollingen Series, 75. Cambridge: Belknap Press of Harvard University Press, 1969.
——. 1957. *The Notebooks of Samuel Taylor Coleridge*. Ed. Kathleen Coburn. Vol. I: 1794–1804. Bollingen Series, 50. New York: Pantheon.
Collins, Arthur, ed. 1746. *Letters and Memorials of State, in the Reigns of Queen Mary, Queen Elizabeth, King James, King Charles the First, Part of the Reign of King Charles the Second, and Oliver's Usurpation*. 2 vols. London: T. Osborne.
Collmer, Robert G. 1961. "The Meditation on Death and Its Appearance in Metaphysical Poetry." *Neophil* 45:323–33.
Cooper, Myles. 1761. *Poems on Several Occasions*. Oxford: W. Jackson.
Cox, R. G. 1956. "The Poems of John Donne." In *The Pelican Guide to English Literature, III: From Donne to Marvell*, edited by Boris Ford, 98–115. Hammondsworth, England, and Baltimore: Penguin. Rpt. with revisions, 1960, 1962.
"Cpl." [T. R. O'Flaherty]. 1870. "Dr. Donne." *NQ* 4th ser. 5 (11 June):565.

Craik, T. W., and R. J. Craik, eds. 1986. *Donne: Selected Poetry and Prose*. London and New York: Methuen.
Cullum, John. 1784. *The History and Antiquities of Hawsted in the County of Suffolk*. London: J. Nichols. 2d ed., 1813.
Daniels, Edgar F. 1978. "Donne's 'Pyramus and Thisbe'." *Expl* 36.2:31.
Deloney, Thomas. 1607. *Strange Histories, or Songes and Sonets, of Kings, Princes, Dukes, Lordes, Ladyes, Knights, and Gentlemen* . . .. London: W. Barley.
Dick, Charles Hill, ed. and intro. 1899. *The Lives of Dr. John Donne, Sir Henry Wotton, Mr. Richard Hooker, Mr. George Herbert, and Dr. Robert Sanderson. By Izaak Walton*. London: Walter Scott.
Dingley, R. J. 1980. "Donne's 'A Burnt Ship'." *NQ* ns 27:318.
Dionisotti, Carlo. 1967. "A Donne Discovery" [correspondence]. *TLS* 2 November: 1037.
Donne, John. 1640. *LXXX Sermons Preached by that Learned and Reverend Divine, Iohn Donne, Dr in Divinity, Late Deane of the Cathedrall Church of S. Pauls* London. London: Richard Royston and Richard Marriot [includes first edition of Izaak Walton's *Life* and Donne's epitaph].
——. 1652. *Paradoxes, Problemes, Essayes, Characters, written by Dr Donne Dean of Pauls: To which is added a Book of Epigrams: Written in Latin by the same Author; Translated into English by J: Maine, D.D.* . . . London: Humphrey Moseley.
Dowden, Edward. 1890. "The Poetry of John Donne." *FR* ns 47:791–808.
[Drummond, William]. 1711. *The Works of William Drummond of Hawthornden*. Ed. John Sage and Thomas Ruddiman. Edinburgh: James Watson.
Dubrow, Heather. 1986. "Tradition and the Individualistic Talent: Donne's 'An Epithalamion, Or mariage Song on the Lady Elizabeth . . .'." In *The Eagle and the Dove: Reassessing John Donne*. Claude J. Summers and Ted-Larry Pebworth, eds. Pp. 106–16. Columbia: University of Missouri Press.
——. 1988. "'The Sun in Water': Donne's Somerset Epithalamium and the Politics of Patronage." In *The Historical Renaissance: New Essays on Tudor and Stuart Culture*, edited by Heather Dubrow and Richard Strier, 197–205. Chicago: University of Chicago Press.
——. 1990. *A Happier Eden: The Politics of Marriage in the Stuart Epithalamion*. Ithaca: Cornell University Press.
[Dubrow] Ousby, Heather. *See* Ousby, Heather Dubrow.
Dugdale, William. 1658. *The History of St Pauls Cathedral in London, From its Foundation untill these Times*. London: Thomas Warren.
Duncan, Edgar Hill. 1942. "Donne's Alchemical Figures." *ELH* 9:257–85. Rpt. in Kermode, 1962. 73–98.
Duyckinck, Evert Augustus. 1841. "Dr. Donne." *Arc* 2:19–26.
Ellrodt, Robert. 1960a. *L'Inspiration personelle et l'esprit du temps chez les poètes métaphysiques anglais*. 2 vols. in 3. Paris: José Corti.
——. 1960b. "Chronologie des poèmes de Donne." *EA* 13:452–63.
——. 1987a. "L'Esthétique de John Donne." In *Le Continent européen et le monde anglo-américain aux XVIIe et XVIIIe siècles: actes du colloque tenu à Paris les 24 et 25 octobre 1986*. Société d'Études Anglo-Américaines des XVIIe et XVIIIe Siècles. Publications du Département d'études anglaises de la Faculté des lettres et sciences humaines de Reims. Pp. 50–61. Reims: Presses Universitaires de Reims, Université de Reims Champagne-Ardennes.
——. 1987b. "Poésie et vérité chez John Donne." *EA* 40:1–14.
Emerson, Ralph Waldo. 1841. "Love." *Essays*. Boston: J. Munroe.
——, ed. 1875. *Parnassus*. Boston: James R. Osgood.
[——]. 1939. *The Letters of Ralph Waldo Emerson*. Ed. Ralph Leslie Rusk. 6 vols. New York: Columbia University Press.

[——]. 1960–82. *The Journals and Miscellaneous Notebooks of Ralph Waldo Emerson*. Ed. William H. Gilman et al., 16 vols. Cambridge: Belknap Press of Harvard University Press.

Emperor, John Bernard. 1928. *The Catullian Influence in English Lyric Poetry, Circa 1600–1650*. University of Missouri Studies 3, no. 3. Columbia: University of Missouri Press.

Fausset, Hugh I'Anson. 1924. *John Donne: A Study in Discord*. London: Jonathan Cape.

——, ed. 1931. *The Poems of John Donne*. Everyman's Library. London and Toronto: Dent.

Field, George C. 1966. "Donne and Hooker." *ATR* 48:307–09.

Fields, James T[homas], and Edwin P[ercy] Whipple, eds. 1878. *The Family Library of British Poetry from Chaucer to the Present Time (1350–1878)*. Boston: Houghton, Osgood.

Fisher, Payne. 1684. *The Tombs, Monuments, And Sepulchral Inscriptions, Lately Visible in St Pauls Cathedral . . . Compleatley Rendred in Latin and English*. London: The Author.

Fitzgeffrey, Henry. 1617. *Satyres: and Satyricall Epigram's: with Certain Observations at Black-Fryers?* London: Miles Patrick.

Flynn, Dennis. 1984. "Jasper Mayne's Translations of Donne's Latin Epigrams." *JDJ* 3:122–30.

——. 1987. "Donne's *Ignatius His Conclave* and Other Libels on Robert Cecil." *JDJ* 6:163–83.

____. 1989a. "Donne and a Female Coterie." *LIT* 1:127–36.

——. 1989b. "Donne and the Ancient Catholic Nobility." *ELR* 19:305–23.

Ford, James, ed. 1818. "A Funerall Elegy on the Death of Mrs. Elizabeth Drury: By John Donne, D. D. and Dean of St. Paul's." In *The Suffolk Garland: Or, A Collection of Poems, Songs, Tales, Ballads, Sonnets, and Elegies, Legendary and Romantic, Historical and Descriptive, Relative to that County . . .*, 272–77. Ipswich: J. Raw.

Fowkes, Charles, ed. 1982. *The Love Poems of John Donne*. New York: St. Martin's Press.

Fowler, Alastair. 1970. *Triumphal Forms: Structural Patterns in Elizabethan Poetry*. Cambridge: Cambridge University Press.

Foxell, Nigel. 1978. *A Sermon in Stone: John Donne and His Monument in St. Paul's Cathedral*. London: Menard Press.

——. 1983. "Un Sermon de Pierre." In *John Donne: Les Dossiers H*, edited by Jacqueline de Roux and François Denoël, 199–211. Evreux: L'Age d'homme-Herissey.

Frost, Kate Gartner. 1990. *Holy Delight: Typology, Numerology, and Autobiography in Donne's* Devotions Upon Emergent Occasions. Princeton: Princeton University Press.

Furst, Clyde Bowman. 1896. "The Life and Poetry of Dr. John Donne, Dean of St. Paul's." *Ci* 2:229–37.

Gamberini, Spartaco. 1967. *Saggio su John Donne*. Genoa: Università degli studi di Genova: Facultà di lettere e filosofia. Pubblicazioni dell'istituto di lingua e letteratura inglese e anglo-americana.

Gardner, Helen, ed. 1952. *John Donne: The Divine Poems*. Oxford: Clarendon Press.

——, ed. 1965. *John Donne: The Elegies and the Songs and Sonnets*. Oxford: Clarendon Press.

——. 1967. "The Titles of Donne's Poems." In *Friendship's Garland: Essays Presented to Mario Praz on His Seventieth Birthday*, vol. 1, edited by Vittorio Gabrielli, 189–207. Rome: Edizioni di storia e letteratura.

——. 1979. "Dean Donne's Monument in St. Paul's." In *Evidence in Literary Scholarship: Essays in Memory of James Marshall Osborn*, edited by René Wellek and Alvaro Ribeiro, 29–44. Oxford: Clarendon Press.

Garrod, H. W., ed. 1946. *John Donne: Poetry and Prose, with Izaac Walton's Life. Appreciations by Ben Jonson, Dryden, Coleridge and others*. Oxford: Clarendon Press.

Gazet, Angelin. 1619. *Pia Hilaria Variaque Carmina*. Douai: B. Belleri.

Gilman, Ernest B. 1986. "'To adore, or scorne an image': Donne and the Iconoclastic Controversy." *JDJ* 5: 62–100. Reprinted and slightly revised in *Iconoclasm and Poetry in the English Reformation: Down Went Dagon*. Chicago and London: University of Chicago Press, 1986.

Gosse, Edmund W. 1893. "The Poetry of Donne." *NewR* 9:236–47. Revised for *The Jacobean Poets*.
——. 1894. *The Jacobean Poets*. London: John Murray.
——. 1899. *The Life and Letters of John Donne, Dean of St. Paul's*. 2 vols. London: William Heinemann.
Granqvist, Raoul. 1975. *The Reputation of John Donne 1779–1873*. Acta Universitatis Upsaliensis. Studia Anglistica Upsaliensia, 24. Stockholm: Almqvist and Wiksell.
Gransden, K. W. 1954. *John Donne*. Men and Books Series. London: Longmans, Green. Rev. ed. Hamden, CT: Archon Books, 1969.
Greg, W. W. 1950. "The Rationale of Copy-Text." *SB* 3:19–36.
Grierson, Herbert J. C. 1906. *The First Half of the Seventeenth Century*. Periods of European Literature, 7. Edinburgh and London: William Blackwood and Sons.
——, ed. 1912. *The Poems of John Donne*. 2 vols. Oxford: Clarendon Press.
——, ed. 1921. *Metaphysical Lyrics & Poems of The Seventeenth Century: Donne to Butler*. Oxford: Clarendon Press.
——, ed. 1929. *The Poems of John Donne*. London: Oxford University Press.
Gros, Léon-Gabriel. 1964. *John Donne*. Ecrivains d'hier et d'aujourd'hui, 15. Paris: Seghers.
Grosart, Alexander B. 1870a. "Dr. Donne." *NQ*, 4th s., 5 (28 May):504.
——. 1870b. "Dr. Donne." *NQ* 4th ser. 5 (18 June):587.
——, ed. 1872. *The Complete Works in Verse and Prose of Andrew Marvell, M. P.*. Vol. I. The Fuller Worthies' Library. London: n.p.
——, ed. 1872–73. *The Complete Poems of John Donne, D. D.* 2 vols. The Fuller Worthies' Library. London: Robson and Sons.
——. 1873. "Epigrams Misassigned to Dr. Donne." *Ath* 9 August:179–80.
Hackett, John. 1757. *Select and Remarkable Epitaphs on Illustrious and Other Persons, in Several Parts of Europe, with Translations of such as are in Latin and Foreign Languages, and Compendious Accounts of the Deceased, Their Lives and Works*. 2 vols. London: T. Osborne and J. Shipton.
Hagspian [Hagopian], John V. 1957. "Some Cruxes in Donne's Poetry." *NQ* ns 4:500–02.
Haley, Martin. 1971. "Donne and the Jesuits: A Satirist Goes Through His Paces." *TCA* 26:124–34.
Halio, Jay L. 1964. "*Perfection* and Elizabethan Ideas of Conception." *ELN* 1:179–82.
Harding, D. W. 1951. "Coherence of Theme in Donne's Poetry." *KR* 13:427–44. Rpt. in expanded version in *Experience into Words*. London: Chatto & Windus, 1963. 11–30.
ul-Hasan, Masood. 1958. *Donne's Imagery*. Aligarh, India: Faculty of Arts, Muslim University.
Hayman, Robert. 1628. *Quodlibets, Lately Come Over from New Britaniola, Old Newfoundland* . . . . London: Elizabeth Allde for Robert Michell.
Hayward, John, ed. 1929. *John Donne: Complete Poetry and Selected Prose*. London: Nonesuch; New York: Random House. Rpt. with corrections and additions, 1930.
Hazlitt, William. 1819. *Lectures on the English Comic Writers. Delivered at the Surry Institution*. In *The Complete Works of William Hazlitt*, edited by Percival Presland Howe. 21 vols. London: Dent, 1930–34.
——. 1826. "Persons One Would Wish to Have Seen." In *The Complete Works of William Hazlitt*, edited by Percival Presland Howe. 21 vols. London: Dent, 1930–34.
Healy, T. S., ed. 1969. *John Donne: Ignatius His Conclave. An Edition of the Latin and English texts with introduction and commentary*. Oxford: Clarendon Press. Appendix D: "A Donne Discovery."
Hester, M. Thomas. 1979. "*Genera Mixta* in Donne's 'Sir John Wingfield.'" *ELN* 16:202–06.
——. 1985a. "The Heritage of Donne's 'Disinherited.'" *ANQ* 23:135–37.
——. 1985b. "Reading Donne's Epigrams: 'Raderus/Ralphius.'" *PLL* 21:324–30.

——. 1986. "Donne's Epigrams: A Little World Made Cunningly." In *The Eagle and the Dove: Reassessing John Donne*, edited by Claude J. Summers and Ted-Larry Pebworth, 80–91. Columbia: University of Missouri Press.

——. 1987. "Donne's (Re)Annunciation of the Virgin(ia Colony) in *Elegy XIX*." *SCRev* 4:49–64.

——. 1990. "The Titles/Headings of Donne's English Epigrams." *ANQ* ns 3.1:3–11.

Hillyer, Robert S., 1941. Introduction to *The Complete Poetry and Selected Prose of John Donne and the Complete Poetry of William Blake*. New York: Random House.

Hood, Thomas. 1827. *Whims and Oddities, In Prose and Verse; with Forty Original Designs*. 2nd Series. London: Charles Tilt.

Hughes, Richard E. 1968. *The Progress of the Soul: The Interior Career of John Donne*. New York: William Morrow; Toronto: George J. McLeod.

Hunt, Clay. 1954. *Donne's Poetry: Essays in Literary Analysis*. New Haven: Yale University Press; London: Geoffrey Cumberlege, Oxford University Press.

Hunt, Leigh. c. 1837. Marginal notes in an edition of Donne's poetry. Reported in [George Henry Lewes], "Restrospective Reviews.—No. VII . . . Donne's Poetical Works." *NMag* 9 (1838):373–78.

——. 1841. "Epithalamiums. Wedding-Days. Vivia Perpetua." In *Leigh Hunt's Literary Criticism*, edited by Lawrence Huston Houtchens and Carolyn Washburn Houtchens, 497–98. New York: Columbia University Press, 1956.

——. 1848. *The Town: Its Memorable Characters and Events*. Austin Dobson, ed. London: Oxford University Press, 1907.

Hunter, Jim. 1965. *The Metaphysical Poets*. Literature in Perspective. London: Evans Brothers.

Huntington Library MS. EL6893.

Hurley, Ann. 1986. "The Elided Self: Witty Dis-Locations in Velasquez and Donne." *JAAC* 44:357–69.

[Hyde, Edward]. 1632. "An Epitaph on Dr. Donne." In John Donne, *Deaths Duell, or, A Consolation to the Soule, against the dying Life, and living Death, of the Body*. London: T. Harper for R. Redmer and B. Fisher.

Jackson, Charles K. 1894. "John Donne: An Appreciation." *Art* 15:105–107.

Jackson, Robert S. 1970. *John Donne's Christian Vocation*. Evanston: Northwestern University Press.

Jessopp, Augustus, ed. 1855. *Essays in Divinity by John Donne D. D.*. London: J. Tupling.

——. 1873a. "Donne's Epigrams." *Ath* 19 July:81–82.

——. 1873b. [Untitled]. *Ath* 16 August:211.

[——]. 1888. "Donne, John." *DNB* 15:223–24.

——. 1897. *John Donne, Sometime Dean of St. Paul's, A. D. 1621–1631*. Leaders of Religion Series. London: Methuen.

Johnson, Beatrice. 1928. "Classical Allusions in the Poetry of Donne." *PMLA* 43:1098–1109.

Johnson, Samuel. 1779. *Prefaces Biographical and Critical to the Works of the English Poets*. Vol. I. London: C. Bathurst et al.

Johnson, Stanley. 1931. "Donne's 'Autumnal Elegy'" [correspondence]. *TLS* 30 April:347.

[Jonson, Ben]. 1616. *The Workes of Beniamin Jonson*. London: William Stansby.

[——]. 1925–52. *Ben Jonson*. Ed. C. H. Herford, Percy Simpson and E. M. Simpson. 11 vols. Oxford: Clarendon Press.

Kaplan, Joel H. "The Feast Day of Middleton's Loyola." *N&Q* 18:27–28.

Kawasaki, Toshihiko. 1971. "Donne's Microcosm." In *Seventeenth-Century Imagery: Essays on Uses of Figurative Language from Donne to Farquhar*, edited by Earl Miner, 25–43. Berkeley, Los Angeles, London: University of California Press.

Keeble, Samuel E. 1927. "The Musings of a Memorable Dean." *LQR* 147:221–32.

Kelly, T. J. 1973. "A Burial for John Donne." *CR* 16:91–104.
Kermode, Frank. 1957. *John Donne*. Writers and Their Works, 86. London: Longmans, Green. Rpt. in *Shakespeare, Spenser, Donne: Renaissance Essays*. London: Routledge and Kegan Paul, 1971. 116–48.
——. 1962. *Discussions of John Donne*. Discussions of Literature. Boston: Heath.
Keynes, Geoffrey. 1914; rev. 1932 (2nd ed.), 1958 (3rd ed.), 1973 (4th ed.). *Bibliography of the Works of Dr. John Donne. Dean of Saint Paul's*. Cambridge: Baskerville Club.
——. 1958. "Dr. Donne and Scaliger." *TLS* 21 February:93, 108.
——. 1964. *Bibliotheca Bibliographici*. London: Trianon.
——, ed. 1973. *Deaths Duell: a sermon delivered before King Charles I in the beginning of Lent 1630/31 by Dr. John Donne, late Dean of St. Paul's*. London: Bodley Head; Boston: David R. Godine.
Kitchin, George. 1931. "Jacobean and Later Seventeenth-Century Parody and Burlesque." In *A Survey of Burlesque and Parody in English*, 68–98. Edinburgh and London: Oliver and Boyd.
Lander, Clara. 1971. "A Dangerous Sickness Which Turned to a Spotted Fever." *SEL* 11:89–108.
Le Comte, Edward. 1965. *Grace to a Witty Sinner: A Life of Donne*. New York: Walker & Co.
——. 1969. *The Notorious Lady Essex*. New York: Dial.
Lee, Sidney. 1904. *Dictionary of National Biography. Errata*. New York: Macmillan.
——. 1910. *The French Renaissance in England*. New York: Scribner's.
Legouis, Pierre, ed. 1955. *Donne: Poèmes choisis*. Collection Bilingue des Classiques Etrangers. Paris: Aubier.
Leishman, J. B. 1951. *The Monarch of Wit: An Analytical and Comparative Study of the Poetry of John Donne*. London: Hutchinson University Library.
Lepage, John Louis. 1984. "Sylvester's Du Bartas and the Metaphysical Androgyny of Opposites." *ELH* 51:621–44.
Lewalski, Barbara Kiefer. 1973. *Donne's "Anniversaries" and the Poetry of Praise: The Creation of a Symbolic Mode*. Princeton: Princeton University Press.
——. 1976. "Donne's Epideictic *Personae*." *SoQ* 14:195–202.
——. 1979. *Protestant Poetics and the Seventeenth-Century Religious Lyric*. Princeton: Princeton University Press.
[Lewes, George Henry]. 1838. "Retrospective Reviews.—No. VII . . . Donne's Poetical Works." *NMag* 9:373–78.
[*LIBB*]. 1898. *The Records of the Honorable Society of Lincoln's Inn. The Black Books*. Vol. 2. From A. D. 1586 to A. D. 1660. London: Lincoln's Inn.
Lightfoot, Joseph B. 1877. "Donne: The Poet-Preacher." In *The Classic Preachers of the English Church*, edited with Introduction by John Edward Kempe, 1–26. Rpt. in J. B. Lightfoot, *Historical Essays*. London: Macmillan, 1895. 221–45.
Lindsay, Jack. 1931. "The Date of Donne's 'Autumnal' Elegy" [correspondence]. *TLS* 19 March:234.
Lodi, M. K. 1974. "Donne's Epithalamic Verse." In *Essays on John Donne: A Quater Centenary Tribute*, edited by Asloob Ahmad Ansari, 86–99. Aligarh, India: Aligarh Muslim University.
Louthan, Doniphan. 1951. *The Poetry of John Donne: A Study in Explication*. New York: Bookman Associates.
[Lowell, James Russell, ed.?]. 1855. *The Poetical Works of John Donne, with a Memoir*. Boston: Little, Brown.
[——]. 1894. *The Letters of James Russell Lowell*. Ed. Charles Eliot Norton. 2 vols. New York: Harper & Bros.

MacColl, Alan. 1972. "The Circulation of Donne's Poems in Manuscript." In *John Donne: Essays in Celebration*, edited by A. J. Smith, 28–46. London: Methuen.

Marotti, Arthur F. 1981. "John Donne and the Rewards of Patronage." In *Patronage in the Renaissance*, edited by Guy Fitch Lytle and Stephen Orgel, 207–34. Folger Institute Essays. Princeton: Princeton University Press.

——. 1986. *John Donne, Coterie Poet*. Madison: University of Wisconsin Press.

Matsuura, Kaichi. 1949. "A Study of Donne's Imagery." *SELit* 26 (1949): 125–84. Revised as part of *A Study of Donne's Imagery*. Tokyo: Kenkyusha, 1953.

Mazzeo, Joseph A. 1957. "Notes on John Donne's Alchemical Imagery." *Isis* 48:103–23. Rpt. in *Renaissance and Seventeenth-Century Studies*, 12. New York: Columbia University Press; London: Routledge and Kegan Paul, 1964. 60–89.

McClung, William A., and Rodney J. Simard. 1987. "Donne's Somerset Epithalamion and the Erotics of Criticism." *HLQ* 50:95–106.

McFarland, Ronald E. 1977. "Figures of Repetition in John Donne's Poetry." *Style* 11:391–406.

McGowan, Margaret M. 1972. "'As Through a Looking-glass': Donne's Epithalamia and their Courtly Context." In *John Donne: Essays in Celebration*, edited by A. J. Smith, 175–218. London: Methuen.

McPeek, James A. S. 1939. *Catullus in Strange and Distant Britain*. Harvard Studies in Comparative Literature, 15. Cambridge: Harvard University Press.

Melton, Wightman Fletcher. 1906. *The Rhetoric of John Donne's Verse*. Baltimore: J. H. Furst.

Menascè, Esther. 1974. *"A naked thinking heart": Introduzione alla poesia di John Donne*. 2nd. ed. Milano: Cisalpino-Goliardica.

M[ennes], J[ohn]. 1640. *Wit's Recreations. Containg,* [sic] 630. *Epigrams.* 160; *Epitaphs, Variety of Fancies and Fantasticks, Good for melancholly humours*. London: Humphry Blunden.

Milgate, Wesley. 1950. "The Early References to John Donne." *NQ* ns 195: 229–31, 246–47, 290–92, 381–83.

——, ed. 1967. *John Donne: The Satires, Epigrams, and Verse Letters*. Oxford: Clarendon Press.

——, ed. 1978. *John Donne: The Epithalamions, Anniversaries, and Epicedes*. Oxford: Clarendon Press.

Miller, David M. 1971. *The Net of Hephaestus: A Study of Modern Criticism and Metaphysical Metaphor*. The Hague and Paris: Mouton.

Miller, Paul W. 1970. "The Decline of the English Epithalamion." *TSLL* 12: 405–16.

Molho, Blanca, and Maurice Molho, eds. 1970. *Poetas ingleses metafísicos del siglo XVII*. Trans. María Gomis. Barcelona: Barral.

Mollenkott, Virginia Ramey. 1981. "John Donne and the Limitations of Androgyny." *JEGP* 80:22–38.

Montgomery, Lyna Lee. 1972. "The Phoenix: Its Use as a Literary Device in English from the Seventeenth to the Twentieth Century." *DHLR* 5: 268–323.

Moorman, Charles. 1989. "One Hundred Years of Editing the *Canterbury Tales*." *ChauR* 24:99–114.

More, Paul Elmer. 1906. "George Herbert." *Shelburne Essays* 4th ser. Boston and New York: Houghton Mifflin.

Nichols, John. 1790. *Antiquities in Cambridgeshire, Suffolk, Scotland, and Wales*. Vol. 5 of *Bibliotheca Topographica Britannica*. London: J. Nichols.

Nicholson, Brinsley. 1873. "The So-Called Donne Epigrams." *Ath* 16 August:210–11.

Nicolson, Marjorie. 1940. "Kepler, the *Somnium*, and John Donne." *JHI* 1:259–80. Rpt. in part in *Voyages to the Moon*. New York: Macmillan, 1948. 49ff. Rpt. with slight revision in *Science and Imagination*. Ithaca: Cornell University Press; London: Oxford University Press, 1956. 58–79.

Noble, Mark. 1821. "Some Curious Particulars of the very learned and reverend John Donne." Rutgers University Library ms., Acquisition No. 700. Edited by John T. Shawcross, "An Early-Nineteenth Century Life of John Donne: An Edition with Notes and Commentary." *JRUL* 32 (1968):1–32.

Norbrook, David. 1990. "The Monarchy of Wit and the Republic of Letters." In *Soliciting Interpretation: Literary Theory and Seventeenth-Century English Poetry*, edited by Elizabeth D. Harvey and Katharine Eisaman Maus, 3–36. Chicago: University of Chicago Press.

Norton, Charles Eliot. 1895. Preface, Introduction, and Notes. *The Poems of John Donne*, from the Text of the Edition of 1633. Revised by James Russell Lowell. 2 vols. New York: Grolier Club.

——. 1896. "The Text of Donne's Poems." *SN* 5:1–22.

——. 1897. Marginalia in *Paradoxes, Problemes, Essayes, Characters, written by Dr Donne Dean of Pauls: To which is added a Book of Epigrams: Written in Latin by the same Author; Translated into English by J: Maine, D.D.* . . . London: Humphrey Moseley, 1652. [The Houghton Library, Harvard University.]

——. Undated. Marginalia in *Poems, By J. D. With Elegies on the Authors Death*. London: John Marriott, 1633. [The Houghton Library, Harvard University.]

Novak, Max. 1955. "An Unrecorded Reference in a Poem by Donne." *NQ* ns 2:471–72.

Novarr, David. 1956. "Donne's 'Epithalamion Made at Lincoln's Inn': Context and Date." *RES* ns 7:250–63. Rpt. as chapter 3 of Novarr (1980).

——. 1980. *The Disinterred Muse: Donne's Texts and Contexts*. Ithaca: Cornell University Press.

Osborn, James M. 1949. "The First History of English Poetry." In *Pope and His Contemporaries: Essays Presented to George Sherburn*, edited by James L. Clifford and Louis A. Landa, 230–50. Oxford: Clarendon Press.

Ousby, Heather Dubrow. 1974a. "Donne and Gilpin: Another Conjecture." *NQ* ns 21:89–90.

——. 1974b. "Donne's 'Epithalamion Made at Lincolnes Inne,' 90." *Expl* 32: Item 49.

——. 1976a. "Donne's 'Epithalamion made at Lincolnes Inne': An Alternative Interpretation." *SEL* 16:131–43.

——. 1976b. "John Donne's Versions of Pastoral." *DUJ* 69:33–37.

Pafford, J. H. P. 1966. "An Early Donne Reference." *NQ* ns 13:377.

Parfitt, George. 1989. *John Donne: A Literary Life*. New York: St. Martin's.

Parish, John E. 1976. "'Sun, Stand Still!' Secular Parody of Sacred Wonders." *EMisc* 25:191–209.

Parker, Derek. 1975. *John Donne and His World*. London: Thames and Hudson.

Partridge, A. C. 1978. *John Donne: Language and Style*. The Language Library, edited by Eric Partridge and David Crystal. London: André Deutsch.

[Patmore, D. K. D.]. 1857. "English Metrical Critics." *NBR* 27:127–61.

Patrides, C. A., ed. 1985. *The Complete English Poems of John Donne*. Everyman's Library. London and Melbourne: Dent.

Patterson, Annabel. 1990. "All Donne." In *Soliciting Interpretation: Literary Theory and Seventeenth-Century English Poetry*, edited by Elizabeth D. Harvey and Katharine Eisaman Maus, 37–67. Chicago: University of Chicago Press.

Payne, Frank Walter. 1926. *John Donne and His Poetry*. Poetry and Life Series, 35. London: George G. Harrap.

Plumptre, James. 1811. *Letters to John Aikin, M. D., on His Volume of Vocal Poetry: and on his "Essays on Song-Writing . . ."*. Cambridge: F. Hodson.

Poisson, Jean-Roger. 1962. "Introduction" to *Poèmes de John Donne*, translated by Jean Fuzier and Yves Denis. Paris: Éditions Gallimard.

Potter, George R., and Evelyn M. Simpson, eds. 1953–62. *The Sermons of John Donne*. 10 vols. Berkeley: University of California Press.

Praz, Mario. 1925. *Secentismo e marinismo in Inghilterra: John Donne-Richard Crashaw*. Firenze: Casa Editrice "La Voce."

[Proctor, Bryan Waller]. 1824. *Effigies Poeticae: or, The Portraits of the British Poets Illustrated by Notes Biographical, Critical, and Poetical*. 2 vols. London: James Carpenter.

Quarles, Francis. 1629. *Argalus and Parthenia: the Argument of yᵉ History*. London: John Marriott.

"R. D." 1873. "Donne's Epigrams." *Ath* 2 August:148.

Raizis, M. Byron. 1966. "The Epithalamion Tradition and John Donne." *WSUB* 62.4:3–15.

Ramsay, Mary Paton. 1917. *Les Doctrines médiévales chez Donne, le poète métaphysicien de l'Angleterre (1573–1631)*. London: Oxford University Press.

Raspa, Anthony. 1965. "Theology and Poetry in Donne's *Conclave*." *ELH* 32:478–89.

——, ed. 1975. *John Donne: Devotions upon Emergent Occasions*. Montreal and London: McGill-Queen's University Press. Reissued by Oxford University Press, 1987.

Ray, Robert H. 1986. "Unrecorded Seventeenth-century Allusions to Donne." *NQ* ns 33:464–65.

Reeves, James, ed. 1952. *John Donne: Selected Poems*. The Poetry Bookshelf. Melbourne, London, and Toronto: William Heinemann.

Renton, William. 1893. *Outlines of English Literature*. University Extension Manuals, edited by Professor Knight. New York: Scribner's.

Richter, Rudolf. 1902. "Über den Vers bei Dr. John Donne." In *Beiträge zur Neueren Philologie, Jakob Schipper zum 19. Juli 1902 Dargebracht*, 391–415. Wien und Leipzig: Wilhelm Braumüller.

Rieke, Alison R. 1984. "Donne's Riddles." *JEGP* 83.1:1–20.

Roberts, John R. 1973. *John Donne: An Annotated Bibliography of Modern Criticism, 1912–1967*. Columbia: University of Missouri Press.

——. 1982a. *John Donne: An Annotated Bibliography of Modern Criticism, 1968–1978*. Columbia and London: University of Missouri Press.

——. 1982b. "John Donne's Poetry: An Assessment of Modern Criticism." *JDJ* 1:55–67.

Roston, Murray. 1974. *The Soul of Wit: A Study of John Donne*. Oxford: Clarendon Press.

Rugoff, Milton Allan. 1939. *Donne's Imagery: A Study in Creative Sources*. New York: Corporate.

Saintsbury, George. 1896. "Introduction. John Donne." In *Poems of John Donne*, edited by E. K. Chambers, 1:xi–xxxiii. London: Lawrence and Bullen.

——. 1898. *A Critical History of English Literature*. New York and London: Macmillan. Rpt. as *A Short History of English Literature*, 1919.

Sampson, John. 1921. "A Contemporary Light upon John Donne." *E&S* 7:82–107.

Sanford, Ezekiel, ed. 1819. *The Works of the British Poets. With Lives of the Authors*. Vol. IV. Philadelphia: Mitchell, Ames, and White.

Savage, Elizabeth, ed. 1975. *John Donne's Devotions upon Emergent Occasions: A Critical Edition with Introduction and Commentary*. Salzburg Studies in English Literature, Elizabethan & Renaissance Studies, 21. 2 vols. Salzburg: Institut für Englische Sprache und Literatur, Universität Salzburg.

Schelling, Felix E. 1913. *The English Lyric*. Boston and New York: Houghton Mifflin.

Schenck, Celeste Marguerite. 1988. *Mourning and Panegyric: The Poetics of Pastoral Ceremony*. University Park and London: Pennsylvania State University Press.

Schipper, Jakob. 1888. *Neuenglische Metrik*. Vol. 2 of *Englische Metrik in historischer und systematischer Entwickelung dargestellt*. 2 vols. Bonn: Emil Strauss.

Scott, Sir Walter, ed. 1808. *The Works of John Dryden, Now First Collected . . . Illustrated with*

Notes Historical, Critical, and Explanatory, and a Life of the Author .... Vol. I. London: W. Mille.
Seccombe, Thomas, and W. Robertson Nicoll. 1906. *The Bookman Illustrated History of English Literature*. 2 vols. London: Hodder and Stoughton.
Sellin, Paul. 1988. *So Doth, So Is Religion: John Donne and Diplomatic Contexts in the Reformed Netherlands, 1619–1620*. Columbia: University of Missouri Press.
Shami, Jeanne. 1987. "Kings and Desperate Men: John Donne Preaches at Court." *JDJ* 6:9–23.
Shapiro, I. A. 1930. "John Donne and Lincoln's Inn, 1591–1594—II." *TLS* 23 October:861.
——. 1953. "Publication Dates Before 1640." *TLS* 6 February:96.
Sharp, Robert Lathrop. 1940. *From Donne to Dryden: The Revolt Against Metaphysical Poetry*. Chapel Hill: University of North Carolina Press.
Shaw, Robert B. 1981. *The Call of God: The Theme of Vocation in the Poetry of Donne and Herbert*. Cambridge: Cowley Publications.
Shawcross, John T., ed. 1967a. *The Complete Poetry of John Donne*. Anchor Seventeenth-Century Series. Garden City, NY: Doubleday.
——. 1967b. "John Donne and Drummond's Manuscripts." *ANQ* 5:104–05.
——. 1968. "An Early-Nineteenth Century Life of John Donne: An Edition with Notes and Commentary." *JRUL* 32:1–32 (transcribes Mark Noble, "Some Curious Particulars of the very learned and reverend John Donne . . . ," 1821. Rutgers University Library ms., Acquistition No. 700).
——. 1980. "The Book Index: Plutarch's *Moralia* and John Donne." *JRMMRA* 1:53–62.
——. 1983a. "The Source of an Epigram by John Donne." *ELN* 21:23–24.
——. 1983b. "A Text of John Donne's Poems: Unsatisfactory Compromise." *JDJ* 2:1–19.
——. 1983c. "A Consideration of Title-Names in the Poetry of Donne and Yeats." *Names* 31:159–66.
——. 1986a. "The Arrangement and Order of John Donne's Poems." In *Poems in Their Place: The Intertextuality and Order of Poetic Collections*, edited by Neil Fraistat, 119–63. Chapel Hill: University of North Carolina Press.
——. 1986b. "Poetry, Personal and Impersonal." In *The Eagle and the Dove: Reassessing John Donne*, edited by Claude J. Summers and Ted-Larry Pebworth, 53–66. Columbia: University of Missouri Press.
——. 1988. "On Some Early References to John Donne." *JDJ* 7:115–17.
Shorter, Thomas. 1865. *Love: A Selection from the Best Poets*. London: Frederick Pitman.
Simeon, John. 1856–57. "Unpublished Poems of Donne." *Miscellanies of the Philobiblon Society*. Vol. 3. London: Charles Whittingham.
Simpson, Evelyn. 1924. *A Study of the Prose Works of John Donne*. Oxford: Clarendon Press.
——, ed. 1930. *The Courtier's Library, or, Catalogus librorum aulicorum incomparabilium et non vendibilium, by J— D—*. London: Nonesuch.
——, ed. 1952. *Essays in Divinity by John Donne*. Oxford: Clarendon Press.
Sinclair, William MacDonald. 1909. "John Donne, Poet and Preacher." *Transactions of the Royal Society of Literature of the United Kingdom* ns 2.29:179–202.
Smith, A[lbert] J[ames], ed. 1971. *John Donne: The Complete English Poems*. Harmondsworth: Penguin.
——, ed. 1975. *John Donne: The Critical Heritage*. Critical Heritage Series. London and Boston: Routledge and Kegan Paul.
——. 1982. "No Man Is a Contradiction." *JDJ* 1:21–38.
Smith, Barbara Herrnstein. 1968. *Poetic Closure: A Study of How Poems End*. Chicago and London: University of Chicago Press.
Somura, Mitsutoshi. 1982. "Donne Kōki no Shukukonka: Sono Dentōshūkan tono Kanren

[Donne's Later 'Epithalamion'—in Relation to its Tradition and Convention]." In *Eigakuronsō: Ishii Shōnosuke Sensei Kokikinen Ronbunshū* [*Collected Papers in Celebration of Professor Shonosuke Ishii's Seventieth Birthday*], edited by Osamu Fukushima et al., 133–45. Tokyo: Kinseido.

Sorlien, Robert P., ed. 1976. *The Diary of John Manningham of the Middle Temple, 1602–1603*. Published for the University of Rhode Island. Hanover, NH: University Press of New England.

Southall, Raymond. 1973. "The Little World of John Donne." In *Literature and the Rise of Capitalism: Critical Essays Mainly on the Sixteenth and Seventeenth Centuries*, 86–95. London: Lawrence & Wishart.

Sparrow, John. 1949. "Two Epitaphs by John Donne." *TLS* 26 March:208.

——. 1953. "More Donne." *TLS* 13 March:169.

——. 1958. "Dr. Donne and Scaliger." *TLS* 28 February:115.

Spence, Joseph. [1732–33?]. "Quelques Remarques Hist: sur les Poëts Anglois." In J. M. Osborn, "The First History of English Poetry." *Pope and His Contemporaries: Essays Presented to George Sherburn*, edited by James L. Clifford and Louis A. Landa, 230–50. Oxford: Clarendon Press, 1949.

Spencer, Theodore, and Mark Van Doren. 1939. *Studies in Metaphysical Poetry: Two Essays and a Bibliography*. New York: Columbia University Press.

Stanwood, P. G. 1967. "A Donne Discovery." *TLS* 19 October:984.

Stebbing, W. 1907. *The Poets: Chaucer to Tennyson, 1340–1892. Impressions*. 2 vols. London: Oxford University Press.

Stone, Nicholas. 1617. *The Notebook and Account Book of Nicholas Stone*. Ed. Walter Lewis Spiers. The Seventh Volume of the Walpole Society, 1918–19. Oxford: Walpole Society.

Stow, John [et al.]. 1633. *The Survey of London: Contayning The Originall, Increase, Moderne Estate, and Government of that City* . . . . London: E. Purslow for N. Bourne.

Stringer, Gary A. 1991. "Donne's Epigram on the Earl of Nottingham." *JDJ* 10:71–74.

Strype, John. 1720. *A Survey of the Cities of London and Westminster . . . Written at first in the year MDXCVIII by John Stow . . . Now lastly, cor., improved and very much enl.* . . . . 2 vols. London: A. Churchill.

Stubbs, Henry. 1658. *Deliciae Poetarum Anglicanorum in Graecum Versae. Quibus accedunt Elogia Romae & Venetiarum*. Oxford: H. Hall.

Sullens, Zay Rusk. 1964. "Neologisms in Donne's English Poems." *AION-SG* 7: 175–271.

Summers, Joseph. 1970. *The Heirs of Donne and Jonson*. London: Chatto and Windus; New York: Oxford University Press.

Symons, Arthur. 1899. "John Donne." *FR* ns 66:734–45.

[Thoreau, Henry David]. 1964. *Thoreau's Literary Notebook in the Library of Congress*. Ed. Kenneth W. Cameron. Facsimile text. Hartford: Transcendental Books.

Tomlins, Thomas Edlyne, ed. 1852. *The Life of John Donne, D. D., Late Dean of St. Paul's Church, London*. By Izaak Walton. With Some Original Notes by an Antiquary [Tomlins]. London: Henry Kent Causton.

Trost, Wilhelm. 1904. *Beiträge zur Kenntniss des Stils von John Donne in seinen "Poetical Works."* Marburg: The University.

Tufte, Virginia. 1970. "Jonson and Donne." In *The Poetry of Marriage: The Epithalamium in Europe and Its Development in England*, 207–29. University of Southern California Studies in Comparative Literature, 2. Los Angeles: Tinnon-Brown.

Tuve, Rosemond. 1947. *Elizabethan and Metaphysical Imagery: Renaissance Poetic and Twentieth-Century Critics*. Chicago: University of Chicago Press.

Tymms, Samuel. 1854. "Hawsted Church." *Proceedings of the Suffolk Institute of Archaeology and Natural History* 2.1:1–9.

Untermeyer, Louis. 1959. "The Metaphysical Man: John Donne." In *Lives of the Poets: The Story of One Thousand Years of English and American Poetry*, 122–36. New York: Simon & Schuster.

Vincent, Arthur. 1899. "The Life of Donne." *Ath* 16 December:836.

Vizioli, Paulo. 1967. "A poesia latina de Donne." *O Estado do São Paulo, Suplemento Literário* 4 February:4.

Waddington, Raymond B. 1974. *The Mind's Empire: Myth and Form in George Chapman's Narrative Poems*. Baltimore and London: Johns Hopkins University Press.

Walby, Celestin J. 1989. "The Westmoreland Text of Donne's First Epithalamium." *JDJ* 8:17–35.

Walton, Izaak. 1658. *The Life of John Donne, Dr. in Divinity, and Late Dean of Saint Pauls Church London*. 2nd ed. London: Richard Marriot.

Ward, Adolphus William, ed. 1858. *The Poetical Works of Alexander Pope*. London: Macmillan. Reissued 1897.

Warnke, Frank J., and Alex Preminger. 1965. "Epigram." In *Encyclopedia of Poetry and Poetics*, edited by Alex Preminger, Frank J. Warnke, and O. B. Hardison, Jr. Princeton: Princeton University Press.

Watkins, W. B. C. 1936. "Spenser to the Restoration (1579–1660)." In *Johnson and English Poetry Before 1660*, 58–84. Princeton: Princeton University Press.

Webber, Joan. 1968. *The Eloquent "I": Style and Self in Seventeenth-Century Prose*. Madison, Milwaukee, and London: University of Wisconsin Press.

Weckherlin, Georg Rudolf. 1641. *Gaistliche und Weltliche Gedichte*. Amsterdam: Iohan Iansson. Repr. 1648.

Weidhorn, Manfred. 1970. *Dreams in Seventeenth-Century English Literature*. The Hague and Paris: Mouton.

Whitlock, Baird W. 1962. "Donne's University Years." *ES* 43:1–20.

Wilson, Gayle Edward. 1980. "Donne's Sarcophagal Imagery in 'Epithalamion Made at Lincolnes Inne,' VV. 37–42." *ANQ* 18:72–73.

Willmott, Richard, ed. 1985. *Four Metaphysical Poets: An Anthology of Poetry by Donne, Herbert, Marvell, and Vaughan*. Cambridge: Cambridge University Press.

Wood, Anthony à. 1691. *Athenae Oxonienses*. 2 vols. London: Thomas Bennet.

Zunder, William. 1982. *The Poetry of John Donne: Literature and Culture in the Elizabethan and Jacobean Period*. Brighton: Harvester Press; Totowa, NJ: Barnes and Noble.

——. 1988. "The Poetry of John Donne: Literature, History, and Ideology." In *Jacobean Poetry and Prose: Rhetoric, Representation, and the Popular Imagination*, edited by Clive Bloom, 78–95. London: Macmillan.

Index of Authors Cited in the Commentary

(Pages in boldface contain primary entries.)

Index of Titles

(Entries for epigrams appearing in more than one sequence and poems lacking titles are alphabetized here according to the short forms of reference listed on pages xx–xxvi of this volume. Specific titles for epigrams presented in variant versions are listed under these main entries.)

Index of First Lines

(For ease of reference and alphabeticization, the spelling here has been lightly modernized. For epigrams presented in multiple versions, the line listed is that of the poem's first appearance, and the multiple page numbers refer to the poem's various appearances. The first lines of two epigrams printed in Greek appear directly below rather than in the alphabetical list.)

About the Editors

Jeffrey Johnson is Associate Professor of English at College Misericordia, where he teaches a variety of writing and literature courses. He has published articles on Donne, Herbert, and Vaughan, as well as several poems.

William A. McClung is Professor of English at Mississippi State University, where he teaches seventeenth-century English literature and architectural rhetoric. His books include *The Country House in English Renaissance Poetry* and *The Architecture of Paradise: Survivals of Eden and Jerusalem.* He has published on seventeenth-century literature in *Milton Quarterly* and *The Huntington Library Quarterly* and on literary/architectural relationships in many architectural journals, including *The Journal of the Society of Architectural Historians.* His essays have also been published by the Canadian Centre for Architecture and the National Gallery of Art. He has recently completed articles on *Utopia* for *Moreana* and on a long-lost plan for an ideal city, *Napoléonville*, for *Via* (University of Pennsylvania).

Ted-Larry Pebworth is William E. Stirton Professor in the Humanities and Professor of English at the University of Michigan-Dearborn. He is author of *Owen Felltham;* co-author of *Ben Jonson;* and co-editor of *The Poems of Owen Felltham* and of collections of essays on Herbert, on Jonson and the Sons of Ben, on Donne, on the seventeenth-century religious lyric, on poetry and politics in the seventeenth century, on Marvell, and on Renaissance discourses of desire. He has served as President of the John Donne Society of America.

John R. Roberts is Professor of English at the University of Missouri-Columbia. He is author or editor of ten books, including *John Donne: An Annotated Bibliography of Modern Criticism, 1912–1967; John Donne: An Annotated Bibliography of Modern Criticism, 1968–1978;* and *Essential Articles for the Study of John Donne's Poetry.* In addition, he has published annotated bibliographies of modern criticism of the poetry of Richard Crashaw and George Herbert as well as essays on Donne, Southwell, Crashaw, Herbert, the English Recusants, and bibliography. Roberts is past president of the John Donne Society.

Gary A. Stringer is Professor of English at the University of Southern Mississippi. Editor of volumes 4–9 of *Explorations in Renaissance Culture*, he has published essays on Donne, Milton, Dryden, and others, and has edited *New Essays on Donne* and co-edited a special issue of the *South Central Review* on John Donne. He is Chair of the Committee on Scholarly Editions of the Modern Language Association and a past president of the South Central Modern Language Association.

Ernest W. Sullivan, II, is Edward S. Diggs Professor of English at Virginia Tech. He is editor of *Biathanatos by John Donne*, *The First and Second Dalhousie Manuscripts: Poems and Prose by John Donne and Others*, and *The Harmony of the Muses*, as well as author of *The Influence of John Donne: His Uncollected Seventeenth-Century Printed Verse*. Sullivan is also the General Textual Editor of the Collected Works of Abraham Cowley. He is past President of the John Donne Society.

DESIGNER: Sharon L. Sklar
TYPESETTER: J. Syd Conner
PRINTER AND BINDER: Maple-Vail Book Manufacturing Group
TYPEFACE: Goudy Old Style